More
Memorable Americans
1750-1950

MORE
MEMORABLE AMERICANS
1750-1950

By

ROBERT B. DOWNS
JOHN T. FLANAGAN
HAROLD W. SCOTT

LIBRARIES UNLIMITED, INC.
Littleton, Colorado
1985

LIBRARIES UNLIMITED, INC.
P.O. Box 263
Littleton, Colorado 80160-0263

Biographies of William Beaumont, Oliver Wendell Holmes, Edward Bellamy,
Abraham Flexner, and Benjamin Cardozo have been reprinted from *Books That
Changed America* by Robert B. Downs (New York: Macmillan, 1970) with the
permission of the publisher, Macmillan Publishing Co., Inc. Copyright © 1970 by
Robert B. Downs.

Biographies of Fannie Farmer, Edward Bok, Emily Post, Wendell Willkie, and
Alfred Kinsey have been reprinted from *Famous American Books* by Robert B.
Downs (New York: McGraw-Hill, 1971) with the permission of the publisher,
McGraw-Hill Book Company. Copyright © 1971 by McGraw-Hill.

Library of Congress Cataloging in Publication Data

Downs, Robert Bingham, 1903-
    More memorable Americans, 1750-1950.

    Includes index.
    1. United States--Biography--Dictionaries.
I. Flanagan, John Theodore, 1906-   .
II. Scott, Harold W. (Harold William), 1906-
III. Title.
CT214.D69   1985   920'.073 [B]   84-27780
ISBN 0-87287-421-4

Libraries Unlimited books are bound with Type II nonwoven material that meets
and exceeds National Association of State Textbook Administrators' Type II
nonwoven material specifications Class A through E.

For

JANE
JOANN
and
VIRGINIA

Table of Contents

Introduction

When *Memorable Americans* was published (Littleton, Colorado: Libraries Unlimited, 1983), the authors recognized that many important and significant names had not been included. Further research and recommendations from experts in various fields convinced them that a second volume was required to do justice to the many noteworthy men and women omitted in the first book. In the present work, the individuals dealt with are generally somewhat less prominent historically speaking, but in a majority of cases their lives are equally meritorious and of comparable interest.

The selection criteria for *More Memorable Americans* were essentially the same as those applied in the first effort: entries were limited to persons whose contributions occurred within the two-hundred year period, 1750-1950; living persons were not included; people from all fields were considered for inclusion, except ephemerally popular figures.

A high degree of selectivity is needed in an undertaking of this kind as a look at such standard reference sources as the *Dictionary of American Biography*, *Who Was Who*, and the *National Cyclopedia of American Biography* will reveal. Thousands of individuals over the course of American history, have been "memorable." For practical reasons, however, the authors limited their choices to men and women whose careers were likely to be of greatest interest to the general reader and useful to the researcher.

The December 1983 issue of the *Journal of American History* reported its findings from a poll of 840 historians who were asked to rate American presidents from Washington to Carter. The results were grouped in six classes from "Great" to "Failures." The authors of the present work were not influenced by this report, which was published after their selections had been completed. However, either in *Memorable Americans* or *More Memorable Americans*, all names are included from the "Great" category (Abraham Lincoln, George Washington, Thomas Jefferson, and Franklin D. Roosevelt), all "Near Great" (Theodore Roosevelt, Woodrow Wilson, Andrew Jackson, and Harry Truman), all "Above Average"(John Adams, Dwight D. Eisenhower, James K. Polk, James Madison, James Monroe, John Quincy Adams, and Grover Cleveland, excluding John F. Kennedy and Lyndon Johnson, who do not fit into the time frame), and one name from the "Average" group (Herbert Hoover, included for reasons other than his record as president). The remainder of the "Average" and all "Below Average" and "Failures" are omitted. Thus of the total of 36 presidents rated, half, 18, are included.

Also of interest is the distribution among careers of the approximately 300 names included in *Memorable Americans* and *More Memorable Americans*. The largest single category is literary figures — 41 of the total — followed by statesmen, numbering 36. Artists (painters, sculptors, architects and musicians) total almost as many, 35. Other well-represented groups are social critics (23), business leaders (21), educators (16), military leaders (16), scientists (15), inventors (13), explorers (12), and journalists (12). Smaller categories are religious leaders (8), medical scientists (9), historians (7), legal lights (7), folk heroes (7), and showmen (6). The proportion of women leaders increased with the passage of time, especially in the last fifty years of the two centuries covered, as women became more active in fields previously less open to them. Twenty-four women are included in the two volumes.

In a few cases, individuals have been included whose life spans extended beyond 1950, but only if their main achievements occurred prior to this date. Several persons discussed were born abroad but later became prominent as American citizens. Birth and death dates are listed for all entries, and biographies and selected references are appended for the information of readers who may wish to read more about the lives of particular individuals.

The sketches are arranged alphabetically by the names of the subjects and there are two appendixes: the first, a chronological list by birth dates, and the second, a classified list by the principal careers of these memorable Americans.

R. B. Downs
J. T. Flanagan
H. W. Scott

Abigail Adams

(November 11, 1744—October 28, 1818)

If Abigail Adams were alive today, she would undoubtedly be in the fore-front of the women's liberation movement. As the wife of Vice-President and President John Adams, she established a reputation as a prolific letter-writer, with a terse and vigorous style, and exerted considerable influence on the social and political life of her time. From her marriage in 1764 to Adams until her death in 1818, she proved herself an ideal wife and companion. Intelligent, well-read, and resourceful, Abigail's wise counsel aided John Adams throughout his long public career.

Abigail was a descendant of several generations of New England clergymen, herself the daughter of a congregational church minister. In one of her letters, she writes, "My early education did not partake of the abundant opportunities which the present days offer, and which even the country schools now afford. I never was sent to any school. I was always sick." Female education at the time was generally limited to writing and arithmetic, and occasionally music and dancing. Later, Abigail educated herself by becoming well versed in English literature.

It was a stormy period, though the first ten years of the Adamses' married life were relatively calm. John, a lawyer, was frequently absent following court on circuit. Abigail shared his deep interest in the growing disputes that culminated in the Revolution. Her letters often referred to the progress of revolutionary events. In 1772, she wrote that she and John had been separated for thirteen years of their married life. From 1774 to 1784, John was absent attending Congress and serving on diplomatic missions to Europe. During these years, however, Abigail raised three daughters and a son, John Quincy Adams, who later became sixth president of the United States.

In 1784 came Abigail's opportunity for travel abroad. She went to Paris to join her husband, who had been several years overseas as one of the commissioners to France and had just been appointed first minister to England from the United States. Although their nine months spent in Paris were colorful and exciting and John and Abigail enjoyed the brilliant French court and high society, they were distressed by its superficiality and the degraded life of the peasants and urban poor of France. The infidelity, deception, degeneracy, foppery, waste, and indolence characteristic of the French aristocracy aroused Abigail's horror and scorn. French refinements and grace by no means compensated for governmental oppression, poverty, and moral decay.

During the stay in Paris, the Adamses and Thomas Jefferson, (then serving as minister to France), became intimate friends. The two families frequently exchanged dinners, and Abigail and Jefferson came to deeply admire each other, a relationship which later soured, during political controversies in the early years of the Republic.

Moving on to England, Abigail and John liked the elegant, disciplined feeling of life in London, in contrast to the disorder and impoverishment of much of France. Also appealing to them were the more prosperous and better regulated lives of the English common people. Yet Abigail's reactions to English polite society were mixed. Judging from the acerbic tone of a number of her letters, she resented some of the social discourtesies she experienced. That began to change with time, as she came to know the English better. Long afterward, she wrote to her son, "England, you know, is the country of my greatest partiality." In London, her simplicity and refinement of manners gained her many friends.

The Adamses returned to America in 1787. John was elected vice-president the following year, served during George Washington's two administrations, 1789-1797, and succeeded Washington as president in the 1798 election. These twelve years in Washington are said to have been the happiest period in Abigail's life. She was the center of a remarkable society, and is reported to have exercised great political influence over her husband. Naturally, she was caught up in the violent social and political feelings of the Federalist party, as it contended with Jefferson's Republican party. Her prominent position aroused a certain amount of jealousy. For example, Albert Gallatin, later Jefferson's secretary of the treasury, referred to Abigail as "Her Majesty."

Because of ill health, Abigail was forced more and more to withdraw from the gaieties of the capital and much of her time was spent in the old Adams home at Quincy. Even there, according to her grandson, her cheerful nature "enlivened the small social circle around her." She died of typhoid fever in her seventy-fourth year.

A perceptive commentator, Ralph Ketcham, characterized Abigail Adams as "the quintessential puritan — purposeful, pietistic, passionate, prudish, frugal, courageous, well-educated, and self-righteous." She was certainly the leading woman of the American Revolution, and it has been observed that the Adams family, which had been in the New World since the 1630s, never amounted to anything important until John married Abigail Smith in 1764.

Abigail's place as a defender of women's rights is worthy of note. She resented the inferior status of women and the neglect of their education, typified by the remark of a Boston chauvinist who thought "girls knew quite enough if they could make a skirt and a pudding." She went far toward converting her husband to the idea that there should be no difference in the education of the two sexes, and he shared her opinion that women should not be considered as empty-headed adornments. There is evidence, too, that Thomas Jefferson, who had not previously given serious thought to female education, became convinced of Abigail's views. Thus, in the late eighteenth century, Abigail helped to plant the seeds of the twentieth century women's rights movement.

RBD

References: Dorothie Bobbé, *Abigail Adams* (New York: Minton, 1929); Laura Richards, *Abigail Adams and Her Times* (New York: Appleton, 1917); Janet Whitney, *Abigail Adams* (Westport, Conn.: Greenwood Press, 1970).

John Adams

(October 19, 1735 — July 4, 1826)

Of all the American Revolutionary War heroes, John Adams, second president of the United States, probably possessed the least charm of personality. His opponents derisively referred to him as "His Rotundity," because of his stoutness, short stature (five feet seven inches), and his aristocratic manner. He was charged with being antidemocratic, a vain, stiff, stubborn man who often offended friends as well as enemies.

In Adams' defense, it has been pointed out that he was a brilliant writer with a deep insight into human motivations, a tireless reader and independent thinker, an able Revolutionary leader, statesman, political philosopher, orator, and scholar. Therefore, though never personally popular, Adams was widely respected for his abilities.

John Adams was a native of Massachusetts, whose American ancestors dated back to the early seventeenth century. After graduation from Harvard and several years of school teaching, he was admitted in 1758 to the Boston bar. What proved a major event in his career was his marriage in 1764 to Abigail (Smith) Adams. The eldest of their children, John Quincy Adams, became sixth president of the United States.

Adams first became involved in the long struggle for colonial rights and independence in 1765 when he wrote a statement of arguments against the Stamp Act. He was also the author of a series of articles on taxation and other controversial matters. In one of the articles he wrote, "Liberty cannot be preserved without a general knowledge among the people." His formal entry into politics came with election to the Massachusetts General Court in 1770. Soon thereafter, along with his cousin Samuel Adams, he became one of the political leaders of the colony. He disapproved of mob action, but supported the Boston Tea Party in 1773 and denounced the Boston Port Act.

On a wider scale, Adams was a delegate to both the First and Second Continental Congresses in 1774 and 1775. After returning to Boston, he served on the Revolutionary Provincial Congress in 1774-1775. A series of newspaper articles presented his views on the dispute with Britain. His most important actions during that critical period were to support the naming of George Washington as commander in chief and to serve on the committee drafting a declaration of independence. Jefferson was the actual author of the declaration, but Jefferson called Adams "the pillar of its support on the floor of Congress" and "its ablest advocate and defender."

Adams' diplomatic service extended from 1777, when he left Congress, until 1788. His several missions to Paris, the Netherlands, and London met with varying success. While still in Congress, he was appointed as minister to negotiate a treaty of peace and commerce with Great Britain. Soon thereafter he went to the United Provinces of the Netherlands, where he obtained a loan of $2 million and negotiated a treaty of commerce and friendship. The next assignment was in Paris in 1782 with Franklin and Jay to take part in the final negotiations with the British commissioners, a meeting that concluded with the Treaty of 1783. That action brought the Revolution to a close and established the independence of the United States.

Adams' final diplomatic post was his appointment in 1785 as the first American minister to the Court of St. James's. Relations between the United States and Britain were so strained that Adams' efforts to work out favorable trade agreements with the British failed. He resigned in 1788 to return home. While in London, Adams wrote a three-volume work, *Defense of the Constitutions of Government of the United States of America*, the most extensive treatise on political science written by any American up to his time.

While still busy with diplomatic affairs, Adams drafted the Massachusetts Constitution of 1780, still the organic law of that commonwealth.

Adams had hardly returned to Massachusetts when the new government under the Constitution was being formed. Washington was unanimously elected president. Votes for the vice-presidency were divided, but in the end Adams was chosen. It appears that he found the job thoroughly boring. As he wrote to his wife, "My country has in its wisdom contrived for me the most insignificant office that ever the invention of man contrived or his imagination conceived." He could only exert his influence by casting the decisive vote in breaking ties—a situation not uncommon in a closely divided Senate. He was constantly in George Washington's shadow. Whenever there was an opportunity, Adams sided with the Federalist party. Thus his vote decided the president's power of removal from office, the issue of commercial reprisals against Great Britain and the policy of neutrality, support for Washington's administration, and aid for Hamilton's financial measures.

In the 1796 election, Adams succeeded Washington as president, defeating Thomas Jefferson by the narrow margin of three electoral votes. Under the prevailing rules, Jefferson, his Republican party rival, became vice-president— the only such instance in United States history with the president and vice-president belonging to opposing parties. Another handicap for Adams was the division within the Federalist party caused by Alexander Hamilton's enmity.

Adams' four years as president were beset by a succession of intrigues which embittered him as long as he lived. The Federalist party was discredited by such events as passage of the Alien and Sedition Acts. A disloyal cabinet looked to Hamilton instead of Adams for leadership. A crisis was faced with France over the role of the United States in the European wars of the French Revolution. The Hamilton faction of the Federalist party, pro-British and pro-war, wanted a declaration of war against France, with which an undeclared naval war between French and American ships had gone on from 1798 to 1800. Adams was determined to maintain peace. A special commission appointed by him in 1800 met Napoleon Bonaparte, as a result of which the Treaty of Morfontaine was signed.

The government was moved to Washington in 1800 and Adams became the first occupant of the White House. In the same year, he was renominated for the presidency, but the bitter factional disputes in the Federalist party, the popular disapproval of the Alien and Sedition Acts, and the popularity of his opponent, Thomas Jefferson, caused his defeat. He retired to his home in Braintree, Massachusetts, feeling that he had been unjustly rejected by a people whom he had served so long and loyally. His last twenty-five years were spent happily on his beloved farm. During that period his once warm friendship with Thomas Jefferson was resumed, marked by a memorable exchange of letters. Both Adams and Jefferson died on the same day, July 4, 1826, fifty years after the passage of the Declaration of Independence.

Historians have generally united in their praise of Adams' abilities, integrity, high intentions, and unquestioned patriotism. His administration showed statesmanship and independence. Through his prolific writings, he left an extraordinarily complete record of his thoughts and experiences, which he hoped would be of benefit to succeeding generations.

RBD

References: L. H. Butterfield, ed., *The Diary and Autobiography of John Adams*, 4 vols. (Cambridge, Mass.: Harvard University Press, 1961); J. B. Peabody, ed., *John Adams: A Biography in His Own Words* (New York: Harper, 1973); Page Smith, *John Adams*, 2 vols. (Garden City, N.Y.: Doubleday, 1962).

Samuel Adams

(September 27, 1722—October 2, 1803)

Samuel Adams, Revolutionary War leader, second cousin of President John Adams, was a failure in his every undertaking except as a political agitator, an activity in which he was preeminently successful.

It required a period of years for Adams to find his niche in life. After graduation from Harvard College in 1740, "he studied law to please his father, but gave it up to please his mother," according to one commentator. He showed a complete ineptitude for business, his next venture. Another failure came as tax collector of Boston, when Sam fell behind in his collections and was sued because of his tax methods. In fact, he fell so far in arrears in his collections that he owed Boston £8,000 for back taxes. Thus, at age forty-two Sam Adams was in debt, he lived in a rundown house, and his family often depended on friends and neighbors for food and clothing.

At that dismal stage, Adams discovered his true forte—local politics and agitating against Britain's colonial policies. His effective career began in 1764, though he had been active in several political clubs earlier. The disputes with Great Britain gave him a perfect opportunity to exercise his talents as a radical speaker and writer. He was appointed to draw up instructions for Boston's representatives to the Massachusetts General Court. These influential directions proposed cooperation among the colonies and attacked the Stamp Act on the basis of illegal taxation without representation.

From then on, Adams was the leader of the opposition in Boston to arbitrary measures of the British government and to the exclusive, wealthy, conservative class typified by Governor Thomas Hutchinson. Indeed, Adams, more than any other man, prepared the way for the American Revolution. Before the outbreak of the war, he stirred up the colonists against Great Britain through writings, speeches, and influence with key individuals. His enemies called him the "Chief Incendiary," as he exploited differences with Britain in promoting his own radical views. But to his supporters he was the "Firebrand of Independence," dedicated to the cause of American liberty.

Adams took a prominent part in protests against the Sugar Act of 1764 and the Stamp Act of 1765. In the latter year, he helped form the Sons of Liberty, a secret revolutionary society. While serving in the Massachusetts legislature, 1765-1774, and as Clerk of the House, 1766-1774, he led the radicals in stirring up opposition to the 1767 Townshend Acts (taxing glass, lead, paint, paper, and tea imported into the colonies), and was an organizer of the Non-Importation Association in 1768, a group of merchants and planters who refused to buy any of the taxed items. Tensions created by the Townshend duties led to the Boston Massacre in 1770. All import duties were repealed by the British Parliament that year, except on tea. Objections to the tea tax eventually ended in the Boston Tea Party in 1773.

Adams was unsurpassed as a polemical writer. He kept discontent alive by writing numerous inflammatory newspaper articles. As Clerk of the House, he drafted most of the official papers of that body. He also wrote many letters to prominent persons in England and America, aiming to gain their support. Some forty articles were contributed by him to the Boston newspapers in which he elaborated on the colonists' grievances. He was instrumental after the Boston Massacre in having two British regiments quartered in Boston withdrawn, and in the appointment of the Boston Committee of Correspondence, an effective means for intercolonial union and cooperation. As one biographer, Carl L. Becker, commented, Adams "wrote with concentrated bitterness, in the manner of a Jeremiah denouncing the sinister aims and wicked conduct of those in high places, warning the people of the concealed conspiracy intended to deprive them of their liberty."

Adams drafted the Boston Declaration of Rights in 1772. This document, which stressed natural rights and asserted America's legislative independence of Parliament, aroused the wrath of Governor Hutchinson, who attempted to respond to it himself in a series of newspaper articles. Naturally, Adams inspired the bitter enmity of the royal authorities in Massachusetts, who regarded him as the chief source of trouble. It was partly to capture him that the 1775 expedition which ended in the battle of Lexington was sent out from Boston. Adams and John Hancock were specifically excluded in the Proclamation of Pardon issued by Governor Gage later that year.

A major crisis was precipitated in 1773 by Parliament's enactment of Lord North's Tea Act. A Boston town meeting, called to protest the unloading of the tea, was overruled by Governor Hutchinson. The outcome was the dumping of three cargoes of tea in Massachusetts Bay on December 16, 1773. A party of Bostonians disguised as Indians, calling themselves "Mohawks," boarded three British ships and threw 342 chests of tea, valued at £18,000, into the harbor. No British tea was landed in Boston.

Inspired by the Boston Tea Party and other events, Adams concluded that a congress representing all the colonies was an "absolute necessity." He was chosen by the Massachusetts General Court as one of five delegates to attend the First Continental Congress meeting in Philadelphia in 1774, and later chosen to attend the Second Continental Congress in 1775. At Philadelphia, Adams exercised a powerful influence in the debates, favored immediate independence, proposed a confederation of the colonies, supported the resolution for the formation of state governments, and voted for and signed the Declaration of Independence.

During the Revolutionary War, Adams served as Massachusetts secretary of state, took an important part in drafting the first state constitution, 1779-1780, and in 1781 was president of the state senate. He served in Congress until 1781 and was a member of the committee to draft the Articles of Confederation. John Adams' speech nominating George Washington as commander in chief of the army was seconded by him. At first opposed to the U.S. Constitution, fearing too much power concentrated in a central government, Adams eventually supported its ratification.

Samuel Adams was essentially a revolutionary agitator, with little talent for constructive statesmanship. After the Revolution, his influence and popularity declined. His greatest services were rendered immediately before and during the Revolutionary War. Though not a great orator, he was always an effective speaker, and probably the most prolific American political writer of his time.

Samuel Adams received belated recognition from Massachusetts voters when he was elected lieutenant governor, 1789-1794, and governor from 1794 to 1797. After parties were formed, he joined the Democratic-Republicans rather than John Adams' Federalists.

RBD

References: Stewart Beach, *Samuel Adams* (New York: Dodd, 1965); Noel B. Gerson, *The Grand Incendiary: A Biography of Samuel Adams* (New York: Dodd, 1973); Elizabeth Lawson, ed., *Samuel Adams from His Writings* (New York: International Publishers, 1946); J. C. Miller, *Sam Adams* (Boston: Little, Brown, 1936).

Jean Louis Rodolphe Agassiz
(May 28, 1807 — December 14, 1873)

Science in America in the mid-1850s was still in a primitive stage. For the most part, scientists were known as naturalists. Their interests spanned several disciplines, including biology, chemistry, physics and geology. They were generalists instead of specialists. Few universities had separate departments of science and were ill-prepared to train young people in specific subject matter. Many Americans went to European universities for training, particularly those in Edinburgh, London, Paris and Germany. American education was still in its early stages of development.

The science of geology was especially neglected. The first courses taught in a university had been offered by John Walker, a professor of natural history at Edinburgh University in 1782. The science had made little progress in America prior to 1850. Biology was taught in the broadest terms, without emphasis on special fields.

This was the prevailing situation when Louis Agassiz, well-known European naturalist, arrived in Boston in 1846 to give a series of lectures at the Lowell Institute. These lectures were popular and Agassiz was soon invited to become professor of zoology at Harvard University. America's scientific community had found one of its leaders.

Agassiz' life had two distinct phases: the first was his life in Europe as an outstanding young researcher, and the second involved his life in America as a leader in teaching methods and research. Agassiz was born in French Switzerland, near Motier-en-Vuly, the son of Rodolphe Agassiz, a Protestant minister. Louis grew up in a home which stressed religion. His parents were middle-class professional people, intelligent and respected in the community, who played an active role in the social and economic affairs of Switzerland. His religious background would in later life lead Agassiz to one of his most unfortunate scientific conclusions. His youth was spent in comfort but not affluence. While training for a career in medicine, he showed great interest in nature and was a keen observer of the natural environment. His medical training began at the age of seventeen at the University of Zurich. Two years later he entered Heidelberg University where he quickly showed an aptitude for research in natural history. After a year of study at Heidelberg he found a more intellectually stimulating environment at the University of Munich, where his training in science under Ignaz von Döllinger, an embryologist, laid the foundation for his future work.

Agassiz had a knack for making friends among important scientists of the day. These included Baron Georges Cuvier, the great French anatomist; Sir Charles Lyell, the foremost English geologist; and Alexander von Humboldt, the explorer. These associations enlarged his perceptions of the plant and animal kingdoms, as well as of the physical world. While a student at Munich, he met Cécile Braun, an accomplished artist, and married her in 1833. Cécile illustrated some of his early works.

Agassiz had shown an interest in fishes as a youngster. While still a student at Munich, he completed a study of Brazilian fishes in 1829 and dedicated the publication to Cuvier. *The Fishes of Brazil* established Agassiz as an outstanding researcher. In the same year, he received his Ph.D. degree from Erlangen and began his work on *Recherches sur les Poissons Fossiles*. Full attention could not be given to research on fishes because after receiving his medical degree from Munich in 1830, he spent part of his time practicing medicine. Fortunately, within a year he had an opportunity to go to Paris and work at the Museum of Natural History of the Jardin des Plantes, where he soon attracted the attention of the world's best known comparative anatomist, Cuvier. He adopted Cuvier's system of classification and began the study which resulted in his monumental treatise on fossil fishes in which he described almost 340 new genera illustrated on 1,290 plates in five quarto volumes. It was published in parts between 1833 and 1843 and became the most definitive study of fossils up to that time.

While in Paris Agassiz lived in the world which he enjoyed most, the world of research, science and intellectualism. Among his new friends was Alexander Humboldt, who developed a liking for the young paleontologist and advanced him a thousand francs to support his work. In addition, Humboldt made it possible for Agassiz to get an appointment as professor of natural history at Neuchâtel in 1832. Though the professorship at Neuchâtel paid only a modest salary, Agassiz was delighted with this new position because it gave him time to pursue research. At age twenty-five his training was behind him. He had earned two degrees, had influential friends, and was now ready to initiate new studies in the field of natural history.

At Neuchâtel, Agassiz began his studies on the glaciers of Switzerland in 1836. For the next ten years he compiled data concerning the movement of glaciers, their composition, and the characteristics of their deposits. These studies resulted in one of the remarkable discoveries of science, namely, recognition of the Ice Age. Agassiz had observed that mountain glaciers moved down the valleys of the Alps and as they progressed, produced various recognizable traits in rocks. Among the most striking features were striae, or grooves, left on rock surfaces. These grooves were found on bedrock surfaces over which the ice moved, as well as upon the surfaces of loose cobbles held in the ice. The most important observation he made was that the cobbles and boulder found on the plains far from the mountains were also striated and polished. Therefore, since only ice could produce such features, he concluded that the flat plains of northern Europe had once been covered with a vast sheet of ice.

In the process of unfolding the glacial story from his headquarters at Neuchâtel he published *Études sur les Glaciers* (1840), *Système Glaciaire* (1846), and *Nouvelles études et expériences sur les Glaciers actuels* (1847). As early as 1840 he made a trip to Great Britain for the purpose of studying the soils, rocks and drift of that country. His observations confirmed his belief that a glacier had deposited these materials, and substantiated his concept of a widespread ice sheet during an Ice Age. Later, he would find evidence of extensive glaciation in North America. Agassiz had solved one of the riddles of science and earth history. Foremost naturalists of the day, especially Lyell and Darwin, accepted his conclusion.

The discovery of the Ice Age attracted the attention of the scientific world. On his first visit to America in 1846 his lectures were so well received in Boston that he gave some in other cities, including Charleston and South Carolina. The popularity of the lecture series and his demonstrated ability in research resulted in an offer from Harvard University of a professorship in zoology in 1847. Agassiz accepted the Harvard appointment and the second stage of his career began. His arrival on the Harvard campus was an event for all American science. He would become one of the leaders of the new American scientific community. Though the early years were exciting, sadness came into his life with the death of his first wife. In 1850 he married Elizabeth Cabot Cary, a well-known leader for women's education.

Agassiz deeply involved himself in the educational affairs of Harvard. He became absorbed with the education of his students, the establishment of a museum for zoological research, and fund raising for various ventures and administration. Not the least of his efforts was spent on popularizing the subject of natural history. He revolutionized the methods of teaching it in America by presenting the student with specimens for study. As a result, Agassiz became the best known teacher of science in the middle nineteenth century. His students became leaders and his methods and concepts were made known to a whole generation of young people.

Ground was broken for the Museum of Comparative Zoology in 1859, fulfilling one of Agassiz' dreams. Also, in the same year, he received a complimentary book from Darwin called *Origin of Species* with a letter that said in part: "I have ventured to send you a copy of my Book ... I hope that you will at least give me credit, however erroneous you may think my conclusions, for having carefully endeavored to arrive at the truth." Agassiz' life had been spent describing animal life and he was familiar with the embryology and morphology of much of the animal kingdom. But he saw life in the light of pre-Darwinian biology, each form specially created by a Divine Being who acted with a purpose.

Agassiz had defended the thesis of separate and special creation throughout his career, both in the classroom and in public. He was not mentally prepared to accept Darwin's concept of gradual evolution. Agassiz' lectures to the public on special creation by a thinking deity might have impressed the layman, but they alienated the scientific community, including such men as Asa Gray, James Dwight Dana, Joseph D. Hooker, Joseph Leidy and even Charles Lyell.

Hooker wrote, "I have long been aware of Agassiz's heresies." Lyell commented after hearing one of Agassiz' lectures, "it was so delightful, that he could not help all the time wishing it was true." The most bitter condemnation was in a letter from Gray to Hooker in 1863: "This man ... has been for years a delusion, a snare, and a humbug." Agassiz had lost his influence in the scientific community though he was still a bright star with the public. Such friends as Henry Wadsworth Longfellow and James Russell Lowell wrote glowingly of his accomplishments.

Agassiz' influence waned so rapidly in his later years not only because of his anti-Darwinist beliefs, but also because he was unable to evaluate his own data in an objective, scientific manner. He was a disciple of Cuvier and believed that an infinite number of catastrophes had wiped out life and that each new species had been created by a thinking creator. In 1848 he wrote, "The link by which they (faunas) are connected ... is to be sought in the view of the Creator himself ... In the beginning the Creator's plan was formed, and from it He has never swerved." This blind spot in his logic carried him to ridiculous conclusions, such as finding evidence of glaciation near the mouth of the Amazon. This false conclusion could be used to support a theory of vast glaciation that wiped out life and therefore required a god to recreate it.

Agassiz could not accept Darwinism and continued to believe in special creation until his death on December 14, 1873. His last article, begun shortly before he died, was titled "Evolution and Permanence of Type." In other words, he never accepted the progressive evolution of life but believed in the permanency of all types. Although the last of the pre-Darwinian biologists, he had an important influence on American science. His many students supported Darwin but carried on the research methods of Agassiz. He helped both the American Association for the Advancement of Science and the National Academy of Science, and his beloved Museum of Comparative Zoology would continue to function.

HWS

References: Edward Lurie, *Dictionary of Scientific Biography*, 1, 1970, pp. 72-74; Edward Lurie, *Louis Agassiz: A Life of Science* (Chicago: University of Chicago Press, 1960).

Louisa May Alcott

(November 29, 1832—March 6, 1888)

The author of *Little Women*, one of the best known American children's books, was educated at home, grew up in an intellectual atmosphere but in genteel poverty, chose to contribute materially to a family of six which was headed by a brilliant but improvident father, never married, and suffered much of her life from ill health. Louisa May Alcott was born in Germantown, Pennsylvania, but spent most of her youth in Concord and Boston. Her mother was Abigail May, sister of a well-known abolitionist, who provided much needed stamina and wisdom for her four daughters. Her father, Bronson Alcott, was a thoroughgoing transcendentalist, a persuasive conversationalist, a school teacher and superintendent of schools in Concord, and an associate of Henry Thoreau, Theodore Parker, and Ralph Waldo Emerson.

Louisa was taught chiefly by Bronson Alcott, who himself ran the Temple School in Boston from 1834 to 1839 and tried to modify the rigid curriculum of the day by introducing singing, dancing, reading aloud, and even physiology. Alcott was admired for his idealism and his educational experiments but his family did not thrive on a sparse vegetarian diet, and Fruitlands, the cooperative community which he founded in 1842, did not long survive. Eventually Louisa would tell the story of Fruitlands in the fictional sketch "Transcendental Wild Oats."

Louisa demonstrated her interest in writing at an early age and even showed some desire to be an actress. Her poems and short stories began to appear in the *Atlantic Monthly* in 1860. Subsequently, in an effort to help the Alcott family financially, she tried sewing, teaching, and even domestic service. After the outbreak of the Civil War she worked as a nurse at the Union Hospital in Georgetown but had to give up this work because of deteriorating health. A collection of letters written to her family was published by Frank B. Sanborn in the magazine *Commonwealth* in 1863 and in the same year appeared as a book. This work was followed by a novel, *Moods*, published in 1864. She made a trip to Europe in 1865 and two years later edited a juvenile magazine, *Merry's Museum*. The following year saw the appearance of *Little Women*, an instant and phenomenal success. Frank Luther Mott estimates that it sold at least three hundred thousand copies before the end of the decade and that its sales eventually passed 2 million. Royalties from the book helped the family finances considerably.

Little Women is obviously autobiographical with a few significant changes. The main characters are the four sisters, Meg, Jo, Beth, and Amy March, Jo being the alter ego of the author. The father becomes an improvident army chaplain and the mother is cheerful and indubitably busy. The story deals with the growing up of the four daughters, their domestic adventures in a small New England community, their efforts to increase the family income, and eventually their maturity. Louisa Alcott's knowledge of family life and her sympathy and emotional concern do much to explain the success of this American children's classic.

Similar books continued to come from the author's pen. *Little Men* in 1871 was less successful than its predecessor. But *An Old-Fashioned Girl*, a novel entitled *Work*, and *Jack and Jill* found readers, and as late as 1886 *Jo's Boys* became a best seller for the year.

Miss Alcott spent her remaining years in Boston and after her death she was buried in Sleepy Hollow Cemetery in Concord. She was a striking figure during her time of celebrity but she became ill and increasingly neurotic as she aged, often turning futilely to such remedies as Christian Science, homeopathy, and the milk cure. Inheriting some of her father's idealism, she supported women's suffrage and the temperance cause. Literature meant morality to her rather than aesthetic pleasure, but she wrote without sophistication and made no attempt to inflict religious piety on her readers. Her simple style, command of detail, and sense of humor as well as her understanding of children account for the remarkable success of her juvenile books.

JTF

References: Caroline Ticknor, *DAB*, I, 1928, pp. 141-42; Katherine Anthony, *Louisa May Alcott* (New York and London: Knopf, 1938); David E. Smith, in *Notable American Women*, 1607-1950, I, pp. 27-31 (Cambridge, Mass.: Belknap Press of Harvard, 1971); Sarah Elbert, *A Hunger for Home: Louisa May Alcott and 'Little Women'* (Philadelphia: Temple University Press, 1984).

Roy Chapman Andrews

(January 26, 1884 — March 11, 1960)

Man's curiosity has led him to explore every nook of the earth. Explorers' reasons for undertaking expeditions have ranged from a personal desire for fame to the more prosaic search for knowledge. But most explorers have been impelled by their love of adventure and have had the great drive and stamina needed to reach their goals. Whether we consider Robert E. Peary struggling across the ice to the North Pole, Robert E. Byrd sitting alone at Little America, or Meriwether Lewis wading through the snow fields of the Bitter Root Mountains on his famous trip with William Clark and Sacajawea to the Pacific Ocean, the pattern is the same: courage, boldness, high intelligence, dedication, and perseverance are the marks of these leaders. Many expeditions involve one or more of the sciences, such as Darwin's famous voyage of the *Beagle*, and achieve spectacular results.

The expeditions of Roy Chapman Andrews were carried out to gather scientific evidence, primarily in the fields of biology, paleontology and geology. Though the expeditions didn't produce new theories of evolution, they found abundant support for Darwin's concepts and provided more details about the history of life, especially the development of dinosaurs and mammals. Andrews' most famous discovery was nests of dinosaur eggs in the Gobi Desert. He did not win fame as a scientist, rather as a leader of expeditions that found scientific materials.

Andrews' energy and drive toward fulfillment of difficult tasks attracted attention, and he was assigned to study, collect and prepare whales for museum display. As a result of this project, he planned expeditions to collect data. In the process of completing one exploration venture he was already planning the next step in a long series of adventures. The five major trips to Central Asia between 1922 and 1930 were the most significant of his numerous expeditions. Many of these exploratory excursions were dangerous, including confrontations with Mongolian brigands, civil war in China, and mutiny of his native attendants. But he always felt that the danger was minor, less in fact than he might find on the street of an American city. Andrews' seeming indifference to danger was only one factor contributing to his success as an explorer. The success of Andrews' expeditions was due to three other factors as well: his ability to raise adequate money to properly finance the entourage, his adeptness in handling public relations, and his leadership in the field.

Andrews was born in Beloit, Wisconsin, the son of Charles and Cora Andrews. He graduated from Beloit College in 1906 *cum laude* and was honored by election to Phi Beta Kappa. Though he was a superior student, he felt that he was born to be an explorer and was more interested in hunting and nature lore than an academic career. At an early age he learned the art of taxidermy and became so proficient that he was able to earn the cost of his education at Beloit. There appeared to be no future in Beloit for an ambitious young man who wanted to be an explorer. During his senior year Dr. Edmund O. Hovey, Curator of Geology at the American Museum of Natural History of New York, appeared in Beloit to lecture on the eruption of Mt. Pelée. Andrews showed him some of his taxidermy mountings and asked to recommend him for work in the museum. A trip to New York and a conference with the director of the museum resulted in a job after Andrews commented that he would even scrub the museum floors, because they "are different. I'll clean them and love it."

Andrews' first major assignment came shortly after he arrived at the museum. He was asked to help construct and assemble a model whale. He knew nothing about whales, but he learned fast and soon was involved in the recovery of a whale off the coast of Long Island at Amagansett. This was so successful that in the spring of 1908 he was allowed to begin his first expedition on whaling vessels out of Vancouver Island. He had equipped himself with camera, field glasses and notebooks, but was unprepared for the seasickness caused by the violent tossing of the small whaling vessel. Watching the slaughter of whales was a gruesome job, but Andrews was there to collect information on their habits and was not about to stop his studies. His knowledge of whales led to his appointment as museum representative on the U.S.S. *Albatross* during its voyage in 1909-1910 to Borneo, Celebes, and the Dutch East Indies. He continued the study of whales in 1911-1912 by going to the waters between Korea and Japan where he discovered the grey whale, a mammal that had been considered extinct. Finding and capturing a whale was one thing, but getting its bones back to the museum was quite another thing. In spite of the problems of shipment Andrews succeeded in supplying the museum with enough material to overflow their storage rooms. By age twenty-nine he had become a leading expert on whales.

The First World War years were an interlude for Andrews, but he was planning for the future. He began raising funds in New York to finance future expeditions into the Gobi. His primary backers were J. P. Morgan and John D. Rockefeller, Jr. To prepare for the Gobi expedition, Andrews had made reconnaissance trips to northern Korea, Tibet and Burma. He was assisted in his plans by Dr. Henry Fairfield Osborn, America's foremost vertebrate paleontologist and

Director of the Museum of Natural History. Osborn had predicted that Central Asia was the place of origin of many mammals and reptiles which he had studied in America, especially those arising in Cretaceous and Tertiary geological times. Andrews became obsessed with the theory and dedicated himself to organizing and leading the American Asiatic Expeditions that would collect the material; even ancient man's heritage might be involved. Later discoveries would prove that Africa, not Asia, held the key to earliest man, even though the expedition found twenty thousand year old man-made relics.

Financing for large expeditions was obtained and the first was undertaken in 1922. Similar groups were organized in 1923, 1925, 1928 and the last in 1930. The groups were supported by specialists from the various scientific disciplines. Andrews' wife, Yvette, whom he had married in 1914, served as photographer. Transportation in 1922 was by camel and motorcar with a retinue of forty people. These expeditions were at times threatened by brigands, local revolutions and man-eating dogs, but all succeeded in obtaining a wealth of new scientific data. Although expedition scientists studied the general geology, paleontology, ancient climatology and botany of the Gobi region, they also made two spectacular discoveries: they found three nests of dinosaur eggs and a species of giant rhinoceros known as *Baluchitherium*, a 30 million-year-old mammal. These two discoveries, especially the dinosaur eggs, received tremendous publicity. The fossil eggs, found in 1928, were nine inches long and belonged to a small dinosaur known as a duck-billed iguanodon. Paleontologists had always assumed that dinosaurs laid eggs but not until Andrews found them did they have evidence that at least some dinosaurs reproduced by this method. Finding dinosaur eggs which had been laid 100 million years ago and were perfectly preserved was a remarkable discovery.

Andrews acted as vice-director of the American Museum of Natural History between 1931-1934 and director between 1935-1942. Throughout his life he shared his experiences with the public by writing many books. Most were successful and included *Camp and Trails in China* (1918), *The New Conquest of Central Asia* (1932), *Under a Lucky Star* (1943), and *Heart of Asia* (1951).

Andrews belonged to several scientific societies including the American Association for the Advancement of Science, the American Geographical Society, the American Philosophical Society of Philadelphia, the New York Zoological Society, the California Academy of Science, and the Washington Biological Society. He received many honors, including a Doctor of Science Degree from Brown University (1926) and Beloit College (1928). He received the Explorers' Club Medal (1932) and acted as president of that organization from 1931-1935. He was awarded numerous other medals including the Vage Gold Medal of the Royal Swedish Geographical Society (1937).

Andrews lived a zestful life and experienced what most people only dream about in his expeditions to faraway places. His greatest contribution was his ability to attract international attention to research and to gain support for the exploration necessary to obtain scientific knowledge. After a divorce from his first wife in 1931 he married Wilhelmina Christmas in 1935. He died in Carmel, California.

HWS

References: Roy Chapman Andrews, *Under a Lucky Star* (New York: Viking Press, 1943); John Whiteclay Chambers II, *DAB*, Supplement 6, 1980, pp. 17-19.

George Bancroft

(October 3, 1800 — January 17, 1891)

The early nineteenth century produced a remarkable group of American historians, men who had a strong academic background and went on to assemble relevant documents and to do historical research in private and public foreign libraries. John L. Motley, Francis Parkman, and William H. Prescott were fortunate in their choice of subject matter, since telling the story of the Dutch republic, of the struggle between France and Great Britain in North America, and of Spanish colonialism in the New World ensured the inclusion of dramatic events and exciting personalities.

George Bancroft, on the other hand, chose an equally important but somewhat duller subject, the constitutional history of the United States. As a consequence, Parkman and Prescott still have many readers and their books are still available, but Bancroft's work has been virtually ignored in the twentieth century. Bancroft, however, like Motley and Prescott, accepted political appointments and served with distinction as American minister to Great Britain and Prussia. Van Wyck Brooks has characterized Bancroft well: "He was a conscientious student, laborious, open-minded, enquiring, zealous, with the strong will of an old Puritan settler."

George Bancroft was born in Worcester, Massachusetts, in 1800 and graduated from Harvard in 1817. He was one of the first New England intellectuals to study in Germany and took a doctoral degree at the University of Göttingen in 1820. At home, he founded with Joseph Cogswell the Round Hill School in Northampton and was associated with it from 1823 to 1830. About this time he severed his connection with the Boston Whigs and joined the newly formed Democratic party. For much of his life he was a partisan nationalist. An 1831 magazine article which attacked the Bank of the United States as well as subsequent speeches and writings won Democratic support for him, and in 1837 he was appointed collector of the port of Boston by Martin Van Buren. President James K. Polk named him Secretary of the Navy in 1845, and in that capacity and later as acting secretary of war, he issued the orders which empowered Captain John Sloat of the Pacific squadron to seize various California ports and General Zachary Taylor to invade Mexico. It was also during Bancroft's tenure in Polk's cabinet that the United States Naval Academy was established in Annapolis.

From 1846 to 1849 Bancroft served as American minister in London and spent some of his time abroad collecting important material for his history from British and French archives. Bancroft had been allied with the antislavery Democrats, but became a staunch supporter of Lincoln during the Civil War and delivered the official eulogy for the martyred president before Congress on February 12, 1866. In 1867 Andrew Johnson appointed him minister to Prussia, a post he retained until 1874. Much of Bancroft's remaining life was spent in reworking and completing his historical study. The monumental *A History of the United States*, which originally appeared in ten volumes from 1834 to 1875, was reduced to six volumes in the final edition, 1883-1885. It has never been reprinted. Bancroft died in Washington, D.C.

Despite the considerable time Bancroft devoted during his life to education, politics, and diplomacy, he published steadily. A volume simply called *Poems* appeared in 1823; *Literary and Historical Miscellanies* in 1855; and *The American Revolution*, 1860-1875. Much of his correspondence was edited by Mark A. De Wolfe Howe in two volumes in 1908, *The Life and Letters of George Bancroft*.

Bancroft was the first important American historian to be influenced by German historiography. His foreign training and his personal diligence in assembling material and searching archives served him well. During his lifetime his voluminous history was highly praised and respected. But later critics have found his style florid and needlessly rhetorical even though the revised edition of his chief work benefited from his vigorous pruning and rewriting. Bancroft also evinced a strong anti-British bias and a kind of chauvinism which weakened his claim to be an objective historian. It is unfortunate that the man who is often called the father of American history is little read by his twentieth century descendants.

JTF

References: M. A. De Wolfe Howe, *DAB*, I, 1928, pp. 564-70; Van Wyck Brooks, *The Flowering of New England* (New York: Dutton, 1940); Russel B. Nye, *George Bancroft: Brahmin Rebel* (New York: Knopf, 1944); David Levin, *History as Romantic Art: Bancroft, Prescott, Motley, and Parkman* (Stanford: Stanford University Press, 1959).

John S. Barrymore
(February 15, 1882 — May 29, 1942)

One of the many interesting aspects of the history of the American theater is the way in which family groups of actors have dominated the stage. In some cases the sons became better actors than their fathers. Thus Joseph Jefferson, Jr. was far better known than Joseph Jefferson, Sr., and Edwin Booth, the greatest American tragedian of the nineteenth century, surpassed Junius Brutus Booth, although the father enjoyed a celebrity of his own. In other cases a family of actors played together, although there was only one star. George M. Cohan, admired as a comedian and a song and dance man, excelled but the rest of the Four Cohans were relegated to supporting roles. But in the twentieth century no American group had a greater impact than the Barrymores, beginning with Maurice Barrymore, an Englishman who changed his name from Herbert Blythe and emigrated to the United States in 1875. He was father to three thespian personalities, all brilliant and unique, Lionel, Ethel, and John Barrymore. In a sense they drifted on to the stage. Even though acting was a family tradition they were not infant prodigies like the violinist or pianist who becomes famous before his age has reached double digits, but they found the theater an institution that would provide them a living and they worked hard to gain prosperity and celebrity. When Edna Ferber and George Kaufman brought a satirical play entitled *The Royal Family* to Broadway in 1927 it was generally assumed that the

Barrymores were the models. Ethel Barrymore never quite forgave the authors for their affrontery.

John Barrymore was born in Philadelphia and like his older brother and sister was reared in the home of his grandmother, Mrs. John Drew. His parents were both actors and were generally on Broadway or touring during the season. Mrs. Drew, herself an actress, also managed the Arch Street theater in Philadelphia but proved to be both a loving and a domineering mentor. In 1893 the family fortunes suddenly collapsed and John's schooling became somewhat irregular. He attended the school attached to the Academy of Notre Dame in Rittenhouse Square and later the Georgetown, D.C. academy and Seton Hall Academy, where his brother Lionel had preceded him. After Mrs. Drew's death he enrolled at Kings College in Wimbledon, where he was a rugby star more than a student. For a short time he attended the Slade School of Art in London showing more interest in painting and cartooning there than in a theatrical career. After leaving London, he shared a bachelor apartment with a New York newspaperman, Herbert Bayard Swope, and contributed a weekly drawing to the Hearst press. But he needed to find a more dependable way of supporting himself, and the atmosphere of the theater was both familiar and congenial. Although he had little training for his new role, when he had an opportunity to try acting he seized it. On October 31, 1903, he made his debut playing Max in Herman Sudermann's drama *Magda* and appeared on December 28 in New York in Clyde Fitch's drama *Glad of It*.

When Ethel Barrymore produced Ibsen's *A Doll's House* in 1905 she invited her brother to take the part of Dr. Rank. Ethel thought that his performance was satisfactory but made the perceptive remark that John needed discipline, a criticism that proved valid much of his life. William Collier engaged him to join a company which would tour California and Australia, but Barrymore was back in New York in 1909 starring as Nathaniel Duncan in Winchell Smith's play *The Fortune Hunter*. By this time, as Brooks Atkinson remarked, Barrymore was "a popular matinee idol because of his personal beauty and magnetism, his lean profile, his quick mind, and his gift of gaiety." In 1910 he was cast as Anatol in Arthur Schnitzler's play *The Affairs of Anatol*. And in the same year he made the first of four marriages (to Katherine Corri Harris), all of which ended in divorce.

Most of these early roles were superficial and didn't demand much from Barrymore. But in 1916 he was chosen to play the defaulting bank clerk Falder in John Galsworthy's *Justice* and proved that he could do something beyond light comedy. Somewhat earlier he had made the acquaintance of the playwright Edward Sheldon, who constantly urged him to try more dramatic roles. In 1917 he starred in *Peter Ibbetson*, a dramatization of a novel by George du Maurier. Lionel Barrymore also appeared in the production. Next came *Redemption*, a play based on Tolstoy's *The Living Corpse* and produced by Arthur Hopkins. It was admirably performed and spread Barrymore's reputation further. The playwright Edward Sheldon, a personal friend, was responsible for Barrymore's appearance in another foreign play, Sem Benelli's *The Jest*, which again had a part for brother Lionel. Arthur Hopkins was once more the producer and Robert Edmond Jones designed the play's bold and colorful set. It was a spectacular success.

Up to this point Barrymore had avoided Shakespearian roles. But in 1920 he tried *Richard III* and triumphed in his interpretation of the malevolent monarch who was by turns cruel, sardonic, and fiery. The production might have had a long run but it was exhausting, and Barrymore was also courting his second wife to be (she used the pseudonym Michael Strange). Barrymore had a nervous breakdown and went to a health farm for a cure. Two years later, however, he was back on the stage in what was undoubtedly his greatest role, Hamlet. He had sedulously paved the way for his triumph. At forty-three he was ideal for the part, and the play was heavily cut. As Brooks Atkinson wrote, "Lean, handsome, moody, sensitive, cultivated, passionate, and manly, he acted a vibrant Hamlet that elated just about everybody." Edwin Booth had played Hamlet one hundred consecutive times: Barrymore eclipsed his record by one performance.

After his long run he again performed in *Hamlet* for several weeks in New York in the fall of 1923 and took the production on tour. In February, 1925, he rented the Haymarket Theater in London and acted there for twelve weeks. But at the end of his engagement in England Barrymore practically left the stage, deserting Broadway for Hollywood. To be sure, he returned once some fourteen years later, then fifty-seven and virtually bankrupt, to play in a mediocre vehicle called *My Dear Children*. This play, which burlesqued his own life and in which he could ad lib and even appear half sober at will, held the boards for four months in 1939. But when it closed he entered a hospital and less than two years later he died in Hollywood.

In his lifetime Barrymore had courted the motion picture industry, earned enormous sums of money, married and divorced twice more, spent and lived recklessly. His earliest film role came in *The Dictator* in 1912. Subsequently he made fourteen pictures in nine years, most of them for the Famous Players organization. One of his more substantial parts was the dual role in *Dr. Jekyll and Mr. Hyde* in 1920. Five years later he signed a contract with Warner Brothers for three photoplays, netting him $76,250 plus ten percent for overtime for each production. He made two pictures in 1926, *The Sea Beast* (a version of *Moby-Dick*) and *Don Juan*. Talking pictures, which proved to be the nemesis for Douglas Fairbanks, were no obstacle for Barrymore. In 1932 he joined the Metro-Goldwyn-Mayer studio, signing for $150,000 a picture. In the same year he joined Ethel and Lionel in *Rasputin and the Empress*, the only time the three Barrymores appeared together in a film. During his cinema career he appeared in such pictures as *Reunion in Vienna*, *Dinner at Eight*, and *Twentieth Century*, and in bizarre roles in *Svengali* and *Topaze*.

His third marriage, to the film star Dolores Costello in 1928, produced two children but ended in divorce seven years later. This was a period of uncurbed extravagance. He bought a three-and-a-half acre estate in Beverly Hills which included a fifty-five room house, six swimming pools, a rathskeller, a bowling green, and a skeet range. He began to collect rare birds and first editions, and he acquired a monkey. Barrymore also began to show signs of mental and physical deterioration. He had fits of jealousy and insane rage, suffered loss of memory, and had bouts of alcoholism, which eventually affected his liver. His fourth marriage to Elaine Barrie, a young actress who interviewed him while he was hospitalized in New York, ended in divorce in 1940.

Both Lionel and Ethel Barrymore survived their famous, erratic brother and all three wrote autobiographies. But John Barrymore's life story did not continue beyond 1926. He was fortunate in not being obliged to chronicle his own debacle.

JTF

References: H. L. Kleinfield, *DAB*, Supplement 3, 1973, pp. 34-36; Gene Fowler, *Good Night, Sweet Prince* (New York: Viking, 1944); Brooks Atkinson, *Broadway* (New York: Macmillan, 1970).

Charles Austin Beard

(November 27, 1874 — September 1, 1946)

Certainly the most controversial and probably the most influential American historian of the twentieth century, Charles A. Beard had a long career as a professor of political science and history and as a commentator on political and economic trends. He was the author of constitutional histories and of widely used textbooks. With his wife Mary Beard, also a professional historian, he wrote *The Rise of American Civilization*, which gave a broad view of American culture and attracted a large audience in part because of its graceful and fluent style. It was followed by two sequels.

Beard was associated with Columbia University for much of his professional career. His reputation in related fields was confirmed by his election as president of the American Political Science Association in 1926 and president of the American Historical Association in 1933.

Beard was born near Knightstown, Indiana, in 1874, to a family known for its independence. He attended a Quaker school, worked on a newspaper in Knightstown with his brother Clarence from 1891 to 1895, and enrolled at De Pauw University from which he graduated with a Ph.B. degree in 1898. During a year spent at Oxford University he became interested in English local government and in 1899 helped to establish Labour (later Ruskin) College. He also campaigned briefly for the Labour party. Back in the United States he taught at Cornell for a short time and then spent two more years in England. Beard was a graduate student at Columbia, which awarded him the degree of M.A. in 1902 and the Ph.D. two years later. His doctoral dissertation in political science was entitled "The Office of Justice of the Peace in England," a study which was reprinted in 1962.

In 1907 Beard was appointed an adjunct professor of politics at Columbia, an associate professor in 1910, and a professor of politics in 1915. Two years later he became involved in protesting the entrance of the United States into World War I. As a result of the faculty protest, two of Beard's colleagues were dismissed and he subsequently resigned his academic post. In 1939 Beard was named a visiting professor at Columbia and the next year accepted a professorship of history at Johns Hopkins University in Baltimore. But in the meantime he had devoted himself to writing on political and historical subjects. He contributed articles to *Harper's Magazine*, the *New Republic*, and *Scribner's Magazine*. He was also one of the founders of the New School for Social Research and for five years, 1917 to 1922, was director of the Training School for Public Service in New York City.

While still at Columbia Beard joined with Professor James Harvey Robinson in the writing of a well-known textbook, the two-volume *Development of*

Modern Europe, 1907-1908, but thereafter limited his professional writing to the American scene. In 1913 he published a book which excited much discussion, *An Economic Interpretation of the Constitution*. This and a subsequent volume, *Economic Origins of Jeffersonian Democracy*, 1915, argued persuasively that the founders of the republic were not motivated exclusively by personal idealism but had vital economic interests in establishing a strong central government and a durable constitution. Beard's point of view alienated the traditional historians and even today it is still debated, but the books established his role as a liberal historian. He continued to produce other volumes, theoretical studies, historical works, and textbooks, until he became, in the words of Cushing Strout, author of the sketch of Beard's life in the *Dictionary of American Biography*, "the most widely read of American scholars."

But none of Charles Beard's books achieved the success of *The Rise of American Civilization*, coauthored by Mary Beard, published in two volumes in 1927, and reprinted as one volume with over sixteen hundred pages in 1930. It even had two sequels, *America in Midpassage* (1939), and *The American Spirit* (1943), both somewhat less successful.

Many volumes have been devoted to the American story but few have equalled the achievement of the Beards in their breadth of coverage, wealth of reference, and vitality of style. The thirty chapters proceed chronologically from the colonial age to the machine age, from John Smith and William Penn to William James and Eugene O'Neill, from clipper ships and whalers to tractors, telephones, and radios, from tobacco to corn and wheat. Political parties rise and fall, wars are fought and won as the nation expands, administrations succeed in erratic sequence, the United States grows in affluence and might as Americans populate the continent and build cities on the shores of the Pacific. But no single theme seems to dominate the story that the Beards tell in amazing detail. They have room for the story of agriculture and the development of industrialism. Public education enters in as it should as well as the rise of the labor movement, the surges of immigration from almost every foreign land, and both the formalism and evangelism of religion. Jacksonian democracy, the triumph of business enterprise, and the Gilded Age are all given their due. Nor are the arts neglected. Literature in all its forms, painting, music, and architecture are touched upon until a reader is almost overwhelmed with these facts of American culture.

It is true that many of the discussions are superficial. Herman Melville and *Moby-Dick* are alluded to only once while Eugene Field because of his irreverent youthful satire gets triple the space. William James and Henry James are together cited eight times but no book by either man is named by title. The index refers more often to Samuel Gompers than to U. S. Grant, and Henry Adams is mentioned several times but John Quincy Adams not at all. Nevertheless, the reader who is not a trained historian will appreciate a history that can evaluate political leaders and at the same time can deem painters like Gilbert Stuart and John Trumbull or writers like Emerson, Hawthorne, and Whitman significant enough to mention. The Beards do not weave a historical tapestry as rich as Francis Parkman's; in describing an age remarkable for its multiplicity they do a remarkable job.

Charles Beard's early radicalism was considerably modified in later years. Although generally he supported Franklin D. Roosevelt's New Deal he disagreed with some of the president's domestic policies such as the desirability of peacetime conscription and he believed that overseas economic expansion was needed to prevent domestic collapse. He also was opposed to Roosevelt's attempt to pack the Supreme Court with justices more sympathetic to his point of view than the men currently on the bench. Thus at the end of his life Beard was criticized for his isolationism and conservatism by liberals who had previously been aligned with him.

Charles Beard was a highly successful lecturer and public speaker and for a long time an outspoken defender of civil rights. But he will be remembered best for his attempts to revise early American constitutional history and for his success in broadening and brightening the writing in his chosen field.

JTF

References: Cushing Strout, *DAB*, Supplement 4, 1974, pp. 61-64; Staughton Lynd, *Encyclopedia of American Biography*, pp. 66-68 (New York: Harper & Row, 1974); Lee Benson, *Turner and Beard, American Historical Writing Reconsidered* (Glencoe, Ill.: Glencoe Free Press, 1960); Richard Hofstadter, *The Progressive Historians: Turner, Beard, Parrington* (New York: Knopf, 1968).

William Beaumont

(November 21, 1785 — April 25, 1853)

It remained for an army surgeon on the American frontier, early in the nineteenth century, to resolve one of the great mysteries of medical science: the physiology of digestion.

William Beaumont's preparation for the practice of medicine was typical of his era, before the advent of university medical schools, research hospitals, and well-equipped laboratories. He began as an apprentice to a Vermont country doctor, learned to fill prescriptions, studied the symptoms of diseases, assisted in surgical operations, made autopsies, and read available medical literature. After completing his apprenticeship he was licensed in 1812 as a physician.

Beaumont found private practice to be neither lucrative nor stimulating, and in 1820 he enlisted in the army, was given the rank of post surgeon, and ordered to Fort Mackinac in the Michigan territory. There he was presented with an opportunity to make medical history.

Erroneous theories of digestion are traceable to such ancients as Hippocrates and Galen. Early medical theories, rarely based on facts, existed by the hundreds. Beaumont was the first man of medicine to learn what actually happens in the stomach during the digestion of food and to present a detailed and comprehensive picture of the whole cycle of gastric digestion. A medical historian, Harvey Cushing, a century later, called Beaumont's work "the most notable and original classic of American medicine."

Beaumont's chance to win medical fame came about by a freak accident. The primitive frontier community of Mackinac had become a center for John Jacob Astor's American Fur Company. Early each summer, there was an influx of Indians, half-breeds, trappers, and Canadian voyageurs, bringing in their winter's collection of pelts to sell or barter at the company's retail trading post. It was in this crowded store, on the morning of June 6, 1822, that a gun went off accidentally and a young French Canadian, Alexis St. Martin, fell with a huge wound in his side. His shirt caught fire and burned until it was quenched by the flow of blood. Dr. Beaumont was sent for and arrived within a few minutes.

As described by Beaumont, the charge, consisting of powder and buckshot, was received in the left side of the nineteen-year-old youth, who had been standing not more than a yard from the muzzle of the gun. A portion of the lungs as large as a turkey's egg protruded through the external wound, lacerated and burned; below this was another protrusion resembling a portion of the stomach, "which at first sight I could not believe possible to be that organ in that situation with the subject surviving," wrote Beaumont, "but on closer examination I found it to be actually the stomach with a puncture in the protruding portion large enough to receive my forefinger." The frightful wound had torn open the chest wall, leaving a hole as large as the palm of a hand, and ribs were fractured. A mixture of food, blood, and splinters of bone escaped from the wounded stomach. Further, "The whole mass of materials forced from the musket, together with fragments of clothing and pieces of fractured ribs, were driven into the muscles and cavity of the chest."

Beaumont proceeded to render first aid, cleansing the wound and applying a superficial dressing, though he was convinced that it was impossible for the patient to survive twenty minutes. The surgeon underestimated the tenacity and toughness of the dark, wiry half-breed youth. About an hour later, the wound was dressed more thoroughly—Beaumont still "not supposing it possible or probable for him to survive the operation of extracting the fractured fragments of bones and other extraneous substances, but to the utter amazement of everyone he bore it without a struggle or without sinking." Before the protruding lung could be returned into the cavity of the thorax, Beaumont was forced to cut off with a penknife the point of a fractured rib on which it was caught, and thereafter the lung had to be held in place by pressure to avoid its being forced out by coughing.

The patient was removed to the primitive base hospital, and there under Beaumont's expert care he rallied slowly, though his body was still full of shot, wadding, and splintered bone. After four months, St. Martin's tissues miraculously began to expel all foreign matter. For the better part of a year, day after day, and month after month, Beaumont continued to treat the youth, dressing the terrible wound at frequent intervals, opening successive abscesses, removing fragments of indriven cartilage or bone, as the damaged area began gradually to form healthy scar tissue.

A new kind of crisis developed some ten months following the accident. The town officials refused further assistance to the destitute patient, now a pauper without funds, relatives, or friends. Beaumont was confronted with a dilemma: he had the alternative of packing the youth off in an open bateau to his native place fifteen hundred miles away—a voyage which he could scarcely have survived—or of taking him into his own home. Impelled by motives of charity and kindness, Beaumont chose the latter course—a decision he could ill afford, since he was supporting a family on an Army surgeon's salary of forty dollars per month. Nonetheless, Beaumont moved the patient into his household, where he nursed, fed, clothed, and lodged him, while continuing with the daily dressing of the slowly healing wound. By the end of another year, Alexis had recovered his health and strength sufficiently to do household chores for the Beaumonts, but was still incapable of earning his own living. Thus began a long relationship between the military surgeon and the young French Canadian who was destined to go through life with a hole in his stomach.

After the first year, the skin tissue around the opening had healed. St. Martin, however, stubbornly refused to submit to an operation to suture the lips together. A most fortunate circumstance was that, instead of dropping back into the abdominal cavity, the rim of the stomach puncture adhered to the rim of the external wound. As a result of the union of the lacerated edges of the stomach and the intercostal muscles, a phenomenon known to physicians as a gastric fistula developed. Eventually an inner coat of St. Martin's stomach folded across the opening, forming a leakproof valve. A round hole, large enough to admit the doctor's forefinger directly into the stomach, remained permanently. The valve held the food in "but was easily depressed with the finger," Beaumont reported.

Quite early in his treatment of young Alexis, Beaumont realized that he had been given a unique opportunity to explore the great mystery of human digestion. In May 1825, about three years after the gunshot episode, Beaumont began his first series of gastric experiments on the patient, who by now was fully recovered. In the daily routine of dressing the wound, Beaumont had made a momentous discovery. When Alexis lay on his right side, causing the stomach to fall away from its attachment to the margins of the healing wound, "I can look directly into the cavity of the stomach," Beaumont wrote, "observe its motion, and almost see the process of digestion. I can pour in water with a funnel and put in food with a spoon, and draw them out again with a siphon.... The case affords an excellent opportunity for experiment upon the gastric juices and the process of digestion. It would give no pain or cause the least uneasiness to extract a gill of fluid every two or three days, for it frequently flows out spontaneously in considerable quantities; and I might introduce various digestible substances into the stomach and easily examine them during the whole process of digestion."

The walls of the fistula could be pushed apart with a thermometer, giving Beaumont a chance to peer five or six inches into the interior of the cavity. He found that the stomach walls were pale pink in color, soft and velvety-looking, and lined with a mucous coat. When a few bread crumbs were inserted, the stomach brightened in color, hundreds of tiny droplets began to rise through the mucous film and trickle down the walls — the "gastric juice," as Spallanzani had called it, tasting of hydrochloric acid. Here was the first step in the digestive process.

Over a period of years Beaumont tried a variety of experiments, using all the foods found in a frontier community. The surgeon passed into the stomach through the fistula pieces of raw beef, cooked beef, fat pork, stale bread, raw sliced cabbage, and other vegetables. In all, he tested hundreds of foodstuffs to determine the length of time required for their digestion in the stomach. The items were tied to a long piece of silk string at spaced intervals and pushed individually through the opening, which was about two and one half inches in circumference. An hour later, Beaumont withdrew the food particles and found the cabbage and bread about half-digested. At the end of a second hour, they had vanished completely along with the pork and boiled beef. Hourly examinations throughout the day showed the other foods being digested at a slower rate. The raw meat turned out to be almost wholly indigestible.

Beaumont was the first person in history to isolate pure human gastric juice but lacking chemical training, he was unable to analyze it. He observed, however, that the liquid is "a clear, transparent fluid; inodorous, a little saltish; and very perceptibly acid." It was concluded, too, that the gastric juice is "powerfully antiseptic," and is "the most general solvent in nature, of alimentary matter — even the hardest bone cannot withstand its action." From its behavior, Beaumont had no doubt that the fluid was a chemical agent. The gastric juice, he found, does not accumulate in the stomach during a period of fasting — thus a starving person would produce no gastric fluid — but only appears in response to ingesting food or to artificial stimulus. Beaumont suggested the possible presence of another agent in digestion, though he could not identify it. Research by Theodor Schwann, German botanist and physiologist, a few years later isolated the substance; he gave it the name of pepsin.

Beaumont's investigations did not proceed smoothly and without incident in other respects. Feeling the need for a laboratory and medical library, he asked for a transfer eastward, and received an assignment to Niagara Falls, taking his patient with him. Two such different personalities, however, were incompatible, and there was constant friction between them. Alexis St. Martin resented being treated as a human guinea pig and hated the discomfort of having interminable tubes, strings, and bags moving in and out of his stomach, and being required to go on diets and fasts. He frequently ate his meals lying down, while Beaumont watched the food pass through the gullet; he was ordered to carry small bottles under his armpits — Beaumont's method of demonstrating that animal heat is not different from ordinary heat — and many of the experiments made him ill. He was illiterate, addicted to drunken binges, homesick for his old life in the forest, and longed for the girl he had left behind him in Canada.

It is scarcely surprising, therefore, that in the new post, so temptingly near his native land, St. Martin tied his belongings in a bundle one night and vanished. Beaumont was deeply distressed to have his promising experiments interrupted so suddenly and apparently permanently. While he searched without avail for his missing patient, Alexis had gone off to marry Marie Jolly, father two children, and to resume his career as a voyageur, in the Indian country, for the Hudson Bay Company. Four years passed before the truant was found, living in a village near Montreal. Reluctantly he agreed to return, and to submit to a new series of experiments, but only on condition that his family accompany him and he be generously compensated. To ensure Alexis' loyalty, a detailed legal contract was drawn up, to which the young Canadian affixed his mark. The financial burden on Beaumont was removed by enrolling St. Martin in the Army and assigning him to the medical service.

At the conclusion of 238 experiments, Beaumont published his findings in 1833 in a definitive work: *Experiments and Observations on the Gastric Juice and the Physiology of Digestion*. The diverse discoveries he reported have entered into general knowledge. A six-month stay in Washington, D.C., enabled him to read widely in the available medical literature on digestion, most of which he found filled with errors. The reception of Beaumont's book at home and abroad was gratifying. His revelations were even more fully appreciated in Europe during the early years after publication than they were in his native country. Because of his precise observations and careful recording of the experiments, there was little inclination anywhere to question Beaumont's conclusions. Sir William Osler called him "the first great American physiologist."

In 1834, presumably for a visit, Alexis St. Martin was given leave to return to Canada. At approximately the same time, Beaumont was transferred by the military authorities to St. Louis, where he resided for the remainder of his career. Efforts over a period of twenty years to persuade St. Martin to return, for a continuation of the experiments, were fruitless. Thus ended the strange alliance so inadvertently begun. Alexis St. Martin outlived his partner in medical research by twenty-seven years and sired seventeen children in all; at the time of his death in 1880, he was chopping cordwood for a living, having lived for fifty-eight years with a hole in his vitals. After his death, his family adamantly refused to permit an autopsy, and to ensure that he would not be dug up, buried him secretly in an unmarked grave eight feet deep.

RBD

References: James S. Myer, *Life and Letters of Dr. William Beaumont* (St. Louis: Mosby, 1912); George Rosen, *The Reception of William Beaumont's Discovery in Europe* (New York: Schuman's, 1942).

David Belasco
(July 25, 1853—May 14, 1931)

In the half century between 1880 and 1930 no figure in the American theater had a greater impact than David Belasco. He was well known in two cities, San Francisco where he grew up and New York where he won his greatest fame. He had wide experience as an actor, playwright, adapter of plays, stage manager, and director. He was fascinated by the physical possibilities of the stage and he experimented ingeniously with lighting and properties. The historian of American drama, Arthur Hobson Quinn, wrote, "With every instinct tingling with the love of romance, he has sought to make that necessary compound tangible by lavishing upon his productions every known device by which stage realism is secured." Belasco also successfully opposed the Theatrical Syndicate that controlled the booking of plays, and had the satisfaction of building his own theater in New York in 1906, first called the Stuyvesant and later rebaptized the Belasco.

Born in San Francisco in 1853, Belasco was the son of English Jews. Five years later the family moved to Victoria, British Columbia, where the boy received some guidance from a Catholic priest, an experience which left a deep influence on him since he later affected an almost clerical garb and was nicknamed the "Bishop of Broadway." Belasco's father had had some theatrical connection in London and probably encouraged his son to try stage roles even as a child. After the family returned to San Francisco about 1865 Belasco entered the Lincoln Grammar School. He frequently was given bit roles in local theaters and at a young age began to write plays himself.

In the 1870s he formed an acquaintance with the actor and playwright, James A. Herne, who would eventually become his major collaborator. The two combined to rewrite an earlier melodrama which they called *Marriage by*

Moonlight and which was soon forgotten. More successful was a play originally called *Chums*, eventually retitled *Hearts of Oak*, in which Herne and his wife acted for many years. Belasco appeared in minor roles at Maguire's New Theater in San Francisco and later was employed by the Baldwin Theater as both actor and dramatist. He directed Joaquin Miller's play *The Danites* and toured with it on the west coast. But a meeting with the eastern theatrical producer Gustave Frohman produced an attractive job offer, and in 1882 Belasco became the stage manager at the Madison Square Theater in New York, succeeding Steele MacKaye. His first offering there, *May Blossom*, had at least a thousand productions and was one of the first Belasco plays to be printed. In 1886 Belasco returned briefly to San Francisco to direct a stock company but in the same year accepted the position of stage manager at the Lyceum Theater under the direction of Daniel Frohman.

This position led to an association with Henry C. DeMille. The two men collaborated on four plays between 1887 and 1890: *The Wife*, *Lord Chumley*, *The Charity Ball*, and *Men and Women*. These were popular successes in part due to the presence of notable stage figures like E. H. Sothern and Maude Adams but they have not proved of lasting interest. In 1890 Belasco withdrew from the Lyceum Theater to become an independent producer and director. Three years later he and Franklyn Fyles, a dramatic critic of the period, collaborated on *The Girl I Left Behind Me*, a play of Indian and army life which had a long run and even lasted through a second company.

One of Belasco's greatest successes originated in a short story by John Luther Long entitled "Madame Butterfly." Belasco had a strong feeling for the romantic in his makeup and Long complemented this with an equally strong taste for the exotic. The result became the memorable story of Cho-Cho-San and Lieutenant Pinkerton. Blanche Bates starred in the first production at the Herald Square Theater in New York in 1900. Six years later Giacomo Puccini's opera was produced in English and the following year Geraldine Farrar and Enrico Caruso sang the roles in Italian at the Metropolitan Opera House.

The Belasco-Long collaboration produced two more dramas. Long argued that a great play should have such themes as heroism, patriotism, and love; he also suggested that the Japanese setting be used once more. The result was *The Darling of the Gods*. The play ran for two years and had productions in both London and Berlin but is hardly known today. A romantic tragedy called "Adrea," which was a third Belasco-Long collaboration, had a long run in 1905 and was extravagantly praised by Arthur Hobson Quinn but it too has dropped from sight.

Toward the end of his life Belasco was more concerned with revision of other plays and problems of direction than with original playwriting. He also aided the careers of two favored performers, Mrs. Leslie Carter and David Warfield. The role of the courtesan Mme. DuBarry was one of Mrs. Carter's triumphs, and Warfield excelled as Shylock in Belasco's production of *The Merchant of Venice*. Two other spectacles based on the history of the American west should be mentioned. *The Girl of the Golden West* made use of improbabilities in the manner of Bret Harte but ran for three years after its initial production in 1905. It too became an opera under the hand of Puccini, once again starring Enrico Caruso. *The Rose of the Rancho*, 1906, was a revision of an earlier play by another playwright. Both productions were sumptuous.

Belasco was involved in so many collaborations and adaptations that it is difficult to compile a list of his original work. In addition many of his plays were never published and manuscript versions of others are mutilated or incomplete. Quinn provided a list of early plays, most of them one-act, produced in California before 1872, and appended a chronological list of later plays with initial production dates. A volume published in Boston in 1928 includes six plays: *Madame Butterfly, DuBarry, The Darling of the Gods, Adrea, The Girl of the Golden West*, and *The Return of Peter Grimm*.

Belasco's long stage experience and his deep interest in more efficient and exciting production brought him fame for his theatrical spectacles. He used color and illumination brilliantly and employed what Montrose J. Moses called "the psychology of the switchboard" to emphasize changes in mood and tone. He also sought scenic effects, and if the action of his plays was often improbable and romantic their detailed stage realism impressed audiences. Dinners given to him in 1921 by the Society of American Dramatists and Composers and the Society of Arts and Sciences testify to his reputation as the best theatrical director of his time in the United States.

Unfortunately for his status as a playwright, however, his plays no longer hold the stage. A revival of a Belasco play today is rare indeed. Even at the height of his popularity his plays were obviously different from the work of dramatists like Shaw, Ibsen, Chekhov, and Hauptmann, who dealt seriously with social and economic problems. At a time when a wave of naturalism was sweeping both drama and fiction Belasco's romantic plots were old-fashioned and conventional. Even his expert stagecraft and direction could not compensate for artificial situations and characters far removed from actual life. Belasco probably made an intelligent decision in not insisting on the printing of his plays during his lifetime. Readers deprived of scenery and illumination might not have found the texts as exciting as the staged works.

JTF

References: William Winter, *The Life of David Belasco*, 2 vols. (New York: Moffat, Yard, 1918); Arthur Hobson Quinn, *A History of the American Drama from the Civil War to the Present Day* (New York: Crofts, 1945); Craig Timberlake, *The Bishop of Broadway: The Life and Work of David Belasco* (New York: Library Publishers, 1954).

Edward Bellamy

(March 26, 1850 — May 22, 1898)

Descriptions of an ideal social state, providing happiness for all and bringing mankind into a new golden age, appeared at least as early as Plato's *Republic*, and the concept has inspired such works as Campanella's *City of the Sun*, Francis Bacon's *New Atlantis*, Sir Thomas More's *Utopia*, and William Morris' *News from Nowhere*. Of the many American writers who have tried their hand at utopian themes, only Edward Bellamy caught the public fancy to any appreciable degree.

Bellamy, a native of Massachusetts, born in 1850, was a descendant of a long line of ministers. His thinking on social problems was undoubtedly influenced, at age eighteen, by a trip to Germany. "It was in the great cities of Europe," he wrote, "that my eyes were fully opened to the extent and consequences of man's inhumanity to man." Similar conditions were equally evident in the Massachusetts mill towns a few miles from Chicopee Falls, where Bellamy was reared.

When Bellamy sat down to write his masterpiece, *Looking Backward*, he had in view "a literary fantasy, a fairy tale of social felicity," but as it progressed, he said later, the novel "became the vehicle of a definite scheme of industrial reorganization."

Looking Backward, 2000-1887, tells the story of a fashionable young Bostonian, Julian West, who, after calling on his fiancee, Edith Bartlett, goes home to bed. A chronic sufferer from insomnia, he has had an underground chamber specially constructed in order to be able to sleep without being disturbed by the noises of the town. On this night of May 30, 1887, his doctor sends him into a deep sleep by mesmerism. While he remains in that comatose state, his house burns down, and West lies hidden in his hypnotic trance until the year 2000, when he is found in the course of some excavations. He is awakened by a Dr. Leete, who becomes his host. From here on, the tale is concerned with Julian West's reactions to the amazing world of the year 2000 and his romance with Dr. Leete's young and beautiful daughter, Edith, who happily turns out to be a great-granddaughter of West's nineteenth-century love.

West discovers that during the period of 113 years in which he has slept America has become a cooperative commonwealth, where all work and share alike. Private enterprise has been completely abolished; everything is run by the state. The economic situation is strikingly unlike that of 1887, for labor troubles are unknown, as are private monopolies, wasteful, competitive, and profit-seeking production, the concentration of wealth, and the accompanying social inequalities characteristic of Bellamy's nineteenth-century America. All resources are nationally owned, and agencies of production and distribution include even food preparation and house-cleaning service. Until age twenty-one, every citizen is in the process of education. From twenty-one to forty-five, citizens are members of an industrial army, paid not in money (which has been abolished), but in vouchers accepted at state warehouses. Each person has an allotted trade or profession, assigned as far as possible on the basis of individual choice and aptitude. At forty-five, because of immense advantages of the cooperative system, all except a few leaders retire and spend the rest of their lives occupying themselves as they wish.

In the model world of the year 2000, society is classless, all social inequalities have disappeared, men and women have identical status, crime is virtually unknown, peace reigns everywhere, armies and navies are no longer needed, the race has been improved eugenically, and individual security is complete.

To dramatize the virtues of his ideal republic, Bellamy used a parable depicting the absurdity of the economic system prevailing in 1887:

> By way of attempting to give the reader some general impression of the way people lived ... I cannot do better than compare society ... to a prodigious coach which the masses of humanity were harnessed to and dragged toilsomely along a very hilly and sandy road. The driver was

hungry, and permitted no lagging.... Despite the difficulty of drawing the coach at all along so hard a road, the top was covered with passengers who never got down, even at the steepest ascents. These seats on top were very breezy and comfortable. Well up out of the dust, their occupants could enjoy the scenery at their leisure, or critically discuss the merits of the straining team. Naturally such places were in great demand and the competition for them was keen, every one seeking as the first end in life to secure a seat on the coach for himself and to leave it to his child after him.

A significant feature of *Looking Backward* is Bellamy's wholehearted acceptance of scientific and technological progress. Unlike some other utopian writers, he assumed that the machine is not the enemy but the potential servant of mankind. The mechanical conquest of Nature, with the immense savings in the use of human energy it brings about, has, through social control, finally placed mankind by the year 2000 in a secure world, surrounded by plenty. Bellamy's exposition of the benefits of science and invention, a belief almost universally shared by the American people, helped to make real his visualization of a utopia based on efficiency.

From the beginning *Looking Backward* was a best seller. Since its first appearance, over a million copies have been sold. As evidence of its continuing appeal, an edition of one hundred thousand copies was issued as recently as 1945. The work has been translated into every important language, and it has inspired innumerable other utopian writings. By 1890 the enthusiasm for Bellamy's socialistic theories resulted in the creation, in the United States and abroad, of scores of Nationalist Clubs and Bellamy Societies, some of which are still flourishing. Among Bellamy's contemporary admirers were Mark Twain, William Dean Howells, Edward Everett Hale, Frances E. Willard, Thomas Wentworth Higginson, and Thorstein Veblen.

Bellamy's theories, as set forth in *Looking Backward*, have been called "socialism without Marx, the class struggle, or the dictatorship of the proletariat." Though perhaps influenced by European socialism, Bellamy's dream was basically American, highly simplified, and appealing to the imaginations of millions who would regard Marxist dogma with abhorrence. His voice was authentically that of the American middle class protesting against plutocracy.

The validity of Bellamy's views is still widely debated. Since his day, collectivist forms of society and the role of government have vastly expanded throughout the world, but for the most part in forms of which Bellamy would have thoroughly disapproved. Still, his writings have indicated the nature and possible extent of future governmental social controls. The central theme of *Looking Backward* — the full social use of our resources and productive powers — remains one of the great unresolved problems of modern civilization.

After publication of *Looking Backward*, Bellamy Clubs were organized to discuss the social implications of the romance, which became a kind of Bible to many people. William Dean Howells later wrote, "The solution of the riddle of the painful earth through the dreams of Henry George, through the dreams of Edward Bellamy, through the dreams of all the generous visionaries of the past, seemed not impossibly far off."

RBD

References: Francis Bellamy, "Edward Bellamy," *National Magazine*, October 1898 (an obituary); Caroline Tichnor, *Glimpses of Authors* (Boston: Houghton Mifflin, 1922); Sylvia E. Bowman, *The Year 2000* (New York: Bookman Associates, 1958).

Thomas Hart Benton

(April 15, 1889 — January 17, 1975)

Many American painters near the turn of the century had some training abroad before they reached artistic maturity and then frequently rebelled against the traditional discipline they had tried so hard to master. This was the course of events Thomas Hart Benton followed. He drew pictures on the walls of his home as a child, worked briefly as a newspaper cartoonist, attended art schools in Chicago and Paris, turned his attention to mural painting, and eventually became known as an aggressive regional artist who concentrated on midwestern scenes and figures. In the 1930s and early 1940s he was the preeminent muralist in the nation and his work still adorns many state and federal buildings. His friendship with Harry S. Truman resulted in his commission to paint a mural depicting a pioneer scene in the library at Independence, Missouri, which houses the former president's papers.

Benton, born in Neosho, Missouri, in 1889, belonged to a political family long established in his native state. Senator Thomas Hart Benton, who served thirty years in the Senate, was his granduncle; Maecenas Benton, for a time a congressman from southwest Missouri, was his father. The boy spent some of his youth in Washington until his father lost his bid for reelection, went to school in Neosho, and lived briefly in Joplin where he was employed as an artist by the local newspaper. When he accompanied his father during political campaigns, he saw much of rural and small town life. In Joplin he visited pool halls and bars where he observed the idlers, Negroes, and Indians who appeared in many of his later canvases. A visit to the St. Louis World's Fair in 1904 where for the cost of a quarter he could see Geronimo face-to-face destroyed any illusions he might have had about the noble red man.

Young Benton was not happy in school and begged to be allowed to study art. After less than a year in a military school he went to live in Chicago and attended the Chicago Art Institute in 1906 and 1907. From 1908 to 1911 he studied painting in Paris and enrolled at the Académie Julien. Until the United States entered World War I his life was centered in New York City, where he did commercial art, experimented with symbolist and cubist painting and often depended on a family subsidy for his wherewithal. In his autobiography, *An Artist in America*, Benton explained in detail his New York days, which had done little to advance his art, and his decision to enlist in the navy. He was sent to Norfolk, Virginia, and his experience there had a crucial effect on his later painting. He was forced to mix with men from the hinterland who were neither intellectuals nor aesthetes, and he realized for the first time the significance for the artist of machinery, of engines and dredges and airplanes. As a boy he had always drawn trains; suddenly he became aware of ships and construction activities. When he left the navy Benton was ready to introduce into the murals which would make him famous the human figures and the physical objects which had captured his attention. He was also influenced by the Mexican muralist school which was enjoying a vogue at about that time. But the cowboys, gamblers, squatters, and Indians who appear in typical Benton pictures were largely the result of personal observation and his conviction that they were appropriate subjects for pictorial art.

In 1930 Benton received the first of many commissions to do a large scale mural. He was asked to create a picture for a specific place, the dimensions of a room on the fifth floor of the New School for Social Research in New York City. For fifty-two years it remained in place. But in 1982 the school sold the mural, which consisted of ten panels of varying width, most of them seven feet and seven inches tall, to a private dealer, Christopher F. Janet. In the spring of 1984 the mural was acquired by the Equitable Life Assurance Society for its new headquarters in midtown Manhattan. The cost was more than $3 million.

Benton also painted murals for the Whitney Museum Library in 1932, for the Indiana Building at the Chicago World's Fair in 1933, for the Missouri state-house in Jefferson City, Missouri, in 1936. This last work brought him a fee of sixteen thousand dollars and accolades as well as some adverse comment. A few critics felt that the artist did no service to his native state to include such unsavory figures in his pictorial history of Missouri as the James boys and T. J. Pender-gast, the unscrupulous Democratic boss of Kansas City.

By this time Benton was again a resident of the Midwest, widely known as a provocative lecturer as well as a painter and an articulate defender of regionalism in art. From 1935 to 1940 he served as the director of painting at the Kansas City Art Institute. After Pearl Harbor he did ten large paintings collectively called *The Year of Peril*, which were used by the government as propaganda for the war effort and were widely distributed as posters. A typical painting in this series is *Negro Soldiers* of 1942. Among his better known paintings are *Cotton Pickers*, *Lonesome Road*, *Meal*, *Homestead*, and *Susanna and the Elders*. His *July Hay* is owned by the Metropolitan Museum. Shortly before his death he completed a mural for the Country Music Foundation in Nashville.

Benton's book, *An Artist in America*, published in 1937 and revised in 1968, includes sixty-four illustrations in two colors and is a lively volume both pictori-ally and textually. It is highly anecdotal and not always coherent but it gives an animated account of his apprenticeship in art and of his travels in the Midwest and Southwest seeking local color. Benton remarked in a speech in 1932 that "no American art can come to those who do not live an American life." Benton visited a Holy Roller gathering, stopped at camp meetings and miners's cabins, listened to fiddlers in the hills, heard the blues on Beale Street in Memphis, took a trip on a Mississippi tugboat, traversed the Ozarks and the Texas Panhandle, always talking to and sketching people, and sometimes catching their idioms as well as their expressions. Thrown in for ballast are sage remarks on tenant farming, southern violence, fluvial life, and the debts owed by the South to the Negro race. After years in New York City Benton came back full circle to Missouri, his roots still intact.

Summarizing Benton's achievement, Oliver Larkin pointed out that Benton's Americans — racketeers, crooners, shantyboat fishermen, strippers, cowboys, Negro preachers — shared energy and color, and they appeared both on walls and on easels. If they sometimes seem to be made of the same fabric, it is because they all share vitality and realism.

JTF

References: Patricia Failing, in *Encyclopedia of American Biography*, pp. 85-86 (New York: Harper & Row, 1974); Thomas Hart Benton, *An Artist in America* (New York: Halcyon House, 1939, rev. ed. 1968).

Greene Vardiman Black

(August 3, 1836 — August 31, 1915)

Greene V. Black, familiarly known as "the father of modern dentistry," was born on a farm near Virginia, Illinois, and spent virtually his entire career in that state. He began the study of dentistry at age twenty, when he entered the office of a practicing dentist at Mt. Sterling, Illinois. A year later he opened his own office in Winchester, Illinois. During the Civil War, Black served in the Illinois Volunteer Infantry, until disabled by a knee injury.

Black had a variety of experience as an educator and practicing dentist. He maintained a dental office in Jacksonville, Illinois; lectured at the Missouri Dental College on pathology, histology, and operative dentistry from 1870 to 1880; served as professor of dental pathology in Chicago College of Dental Surgery, 1883-1889; introduced the teaching of dental techniques in 1887. He was professor of dental pathology and bacteriology in the University of Iowa, 1890-1891; and professor of dental pathology and bacteriology in Northwestern University Dental School from 1891 until his death. Beginning in 1897, Black served also as dean of the Northwestern University school and professor of operative dentistry.

In the history of dentistry, Black is famous for his inventiveness and development of new techniques. One important investigation, reported in 1891, was concerned with an idea called "extension for prevention," that is extension of the cavity in order to prevent further decay, which is now the accepted method of preparing cavities for filling. In a paper published in 1895, Black destroyed two myths previously accepted as true. The first was that some teeth are soft and easily become susceptible to cavities, while others are hard and practically immune. It was shown that neither state has anything to do with liability to decay. The second popular belief, also disproved, was that the teeth of women during pregnancy are leached of their lime-salts, thereby making them liable to cavities.

Another of Black's major contributions was a method of making silver alloys for amalgam that assured their stability; as a consequence, nearly all dental amalgam alloys today are made by the Black method and amalgam is valued second only to gold as a filling for tooth cavities.

Black was a prolific writer. One published record lists more than five hundred books, reports, and papers by him. His first book, *The Formation of Poisons by Microorganisms* (1884) is still regarded as an authoritative work on the subject. Another landmark book, *Dental Anatomy* (1891), a detailed investigation of the macroscopic structure of the human teeth, continues to be a standard textbook in dental colleges. Another contribution, undertaken as chairman of a committee, for the Columbian Dental Congress, was a comprehensive report laying the foundation for a scientific dental nomenclature. Black's most monumental work was a three-volume treatise, the last volume of which was published the year of his death, with an overall title of *Operative Dentistry* (1908-1915).

Black was also a skillful and imaginative inventor. Early in his career, he designed one of the first cord dental engines. In 1904, he provided the patterns for 102 "cutting instruments" for the proper excavation of cavities. As an artist of some talent, he prepared the illustrations for many of his books and papers.

Numerous honors came to Black during his lifetime, including the presidency of the National Dental Association, the first Miller Prize in 1910, given by the International Dental Federation, and honorary degrees from five institutions.

One of Black's biographers summed up his career as follows: "he was great in achievements, great also in his simplicity and sincerity. He climbed the heights, but he took his fellows with him every step of the way." The last sentence was in reference to Black's generous habit of sharing freely with the dental profession his expert knowledge, the results of his research, and his inventions.

RBD

References: *DAB*, II, 1929, pp. 308-10; A. W. Harris, *Science*, N.S.V. 42, Oct. 8, 1915, pp. 496-97.

Franz Boas
(July 9, 1858 — December 21, 1942)

The cradle of the human race is in Africa: at least as long as three and one-half million years ago the hominid called "Lucy," scientifically known as *Australopithecus afarensis*, roamed the savannah country of Ethiopia. The hominids continued to evolve until true man, *Homo*, appeared. Like all forms of life, early *Homo sapiens* expanded their range into all possible environmental areas. In due course of time some became isolated in China, others in Europe and still others on islands. Geographic separation resulted in the development of certain genetic traits that produced different physical types of humans. Also, different cultures and subcultures developed, including languages and methods of survival.

Investigators had recognized these differences in the human species at an early date, but scientists had not developed procedures and methods of study to unravel the story until Franz Boas set the standards for research in the field of anthropology. Anthropology, the study of man, was a late addition to the curriculum of American education. Though the science had made a little progress in Europe, the culture of ancient and primitive societies was not a general subject for classroom discussion in American universities prior to 1900. Boas became responsible for setting the standards of research and education in a neglected field. Though his primary research interest was in the study of the language and culture of North American Indians, his greatest impact came from establishing a new kind of anthropology based on a culture-centered, nonracist concept. He was influential in the education of the first students of anthropology and developed the standards for scientific research in the areas of linguistics, ethnology, folklore and ancient art. His 600 articles, mostly short, cover a wide range of subject matter that today form the base of anthropological research. Most, if not all, modern American students of anthropology can trace their professional family tree back to Boas.

Franz Boas was born in Minden, Westphalia, in 1858. His early interest was in mathematics and physics. After studying at Heidelberg and Bonn and Kiel, he received a doctoral degree in physics at Kiel (1881). His research was on *Contributions to the Understanding of the Color of Water*. His interest in geography and his friendship with Theobald Fisher turned his attention to ethnology. This resulted in his first exploration trip into the polar area in 1883 to study the Eskimo culture of Baffin Island. The Baffin Island study was the turning point in Boas' life. His primary observation at that time was that human behavior was not determined by the physical environment. Boas returned to Germany and published several accounts, including his first scientific contribution, in the *Journal of the American Geographical Society* for 1884.

He began a study of the Indians on Vancouver Island in 1886 and, after a visit to *Science* magazine in January, 1887, was offered a position as assistant editor. He accepted and felt affluent enough to marry Marie Krackowizer. A steady stream of articles and reviews appeared under his name. He found that freedom in America was more to his style of thinking than the regimentation of German society; he became an American citizen. His first teaching job was for a four-year term at Clark University where he supervised the work of the first Ph.D. in anthropology in America in 1892.

Boas left Clark University in 1892 to become Chief Assistant of the Department of Anthropology at the World's Columbian Fair at Chicago. This led to a position at the new Field Museum, but dissension among the staff brought about his resignation. He was then appointed to the American Museum in New York as Curator of Ethnology and Somatology in January 1896. This was a fortunate association because it led to his appointment as professor of anthropology at Columbia University in 1899.

In 1897 Morris K. Jesup, president of the American Museum of Natural History, gave financial support to a field program directed by Boas to investigate the Indian tribes of northwestern America and their relationship to the Asian mainland.

By 1901 Boas was involved in a heavy schedule of research, teaching and administration, but his relations with the museum had improved to the point where he was appointed Curator. In addition, the Bureau of Ethnology, formed by John Wesley Powell in 1879, made him honorary philologist. Boas was now in a position to exert a major influence on American anthropology. He wanted to raise anthropology to a professional level to bring about cooperation between universities, government and private initiative on major research projects. He expected to lead these forces, and at the turn of the century he was on the threshold of a fabulous career.

One famous result of his research on American Indians was the publication of the *Handbook of American Indian Languages*, the first two volumes printed by the Bureau of Ethnology in 1911 and 1912 and a third by Columbia University Press in 1933-1938. Additional articles on the subject were published in other journals until nineteen languages had been analyzed. Most of these were by Boas and his students. They covered such diverse groups as Chinook, Keresan, Iroquois, Nathuatl and Kathlamet, to mention only a few. The recording and evaluation of such primitive languages was difficult work, requiring sustained intellectual effort.

By 1905 Boas' relationship with the American Museum had deteriorated and his formal connection was terminated, though he retained some control over the Jesup Expedition. This break did not affect his research or teaching efforts at Columbia. He continued to publish about one article or report a month, and by 1910 had organized a new cooperative research organization, the International School of American Archaeology and Ethnology, in Mexico. Several agencies, both American and foreign, were involved. In less than a decade, however, the School dissolved because of international tensions and the beginning of the first World War.

Ethnology is the study of the origin and distribution of the various races of mankind. It seeks to discover through researching the distinctive characteristics of any group the origin of specific customs, institutions and culture. Boas wanted to apply the rigorous analytical approach of a physical scientist to the objective data compiled in the study of primitive cultures. In the process he deviated from the historical approach in interpreting the origin of ancient cultures. As a trained physicist he was capable of dealing with abstract form and could interpret data. Consequently, he believed that he could apply his talents to the study of linguistics and anthropometry to solve the problems in anthropology. He wanted to study culture through objective data and thereby understand the subjective.

The key to ethnological studies was the methodology of the investigation. Prior to Boas, accounts were piecemeal, collected by travelers and missionaries. One of his contributions to anthropology was the establishment of data collection procedures. He stated that: "We must understand the process by which the individual culture grew before we can undertake to lay down the laws by which the culture of all mankind grew." He was interested in "cultural dynamics, [the] integration of culture and ... the interaction between individuals and society." In addition to his own research, he was able to promote anthropological studies by others through his editorship of the *Journal of American Folk-Lore* from 1908 to 1925 and the *Publications of the American Ethnological Society* from 1906 until his death. He assisted with the publication of the *Columbia University Contributions to Anthropology* and the *International Journal of American Linguistics*.

One of Boas' greatest achievements came in the field of linguistics. He believed that "a command of the language is an indispensable means of obtaining thorough knowledge." His students followed his precepts. To understand a tribal language allowed him to hear and probe in depth the folklore of a given group. He was one of the founders of the *American Folk-Lore Society* in 1888 and actively participated in the publications of the *Journal of American Folk-Lore*.

Boas' interest in archeology was not in objects but in what problems the object could help solve. Though he had an interest in the archeology of the Bering Sea area and its relation to the migration of Asian people to North America, he was a more active worker in anthropology. His interests in the physical form of the human species, their mental development, classes and racial characteristics were more relevant subjects for research. These interests are illustrated by the titles of some of his articles: *Changes in Bodily Form of Descendants of Immigrants* (1910), *Studies in Growth* (1932), *Evidence on the Nature of Intelligence* (1940), *Class Consciousness and Racial Prejudice* (1943), and a collection of papers in *Race, Language and Culture* (1940).

Boas was not without critics. During his lifetime he was pro-German during the first World War and anti-Nazi during the second World War. At times he was severely condemned for his actions, but respected for his professional attainments. After his death in 1942, anthropologists turned more and more to the study of culture through the evolutionary process. Some even considered his contributions in a negative light. However, his influence upon the American social sciences was fundamental to the thinking of the post-1950 period. The social changes which permeated American society in reference to race may be, at least in part, due to the brilliant émigré from Westphalia.

HWS

References: A. L. Kroeber, et al., "Franz Boas," *American Anthropologist*, new series, 45:3, pt. 2 (1943): 1-119; Fred W. Voget, *Dictionary of Scientific Biography*, 2, 1970, pp. 207-13.

Edward William Bok

(October 9, 1863 — January 9, 1930)

The individual contributions of millions of foreign-born citizens to American culture and civilization are largely unchronicled.

An eminent representative of the group was brought to the United States at the age of six. Edward Bok was born in 1863 in the Dutch seaport, den Helder, a descendant of a distinguished line of public officials. Severe financial reverses persuaded his parents to emigrate to New York in 1870 in hopes of bettering their condition. Edward entered public school in Brooklyn without knowing a word of English. From here on out, Bok's career was another Horatio Alger epic.

Bok's genius as an entrepreneur was exhibited at a tender age, beginning with window cleaning for a baker at fifty cents a week, delivering papers, and working at odd jobs. His first journalistic venture was reporting children's parties (being certain that the name of every person present was included) for the Brooklyn *Daily Eagle*. At thirteen, Edward quit school to become an office boy for the Western Union Telegraph Company, where his father was employed as a translator. He continued to develop more money-making schemes on the side, including a profitable one writing or editing one-hundred-word biographical sketches of well-known actors and actresses and famous Americans to be printed on the backs of pictures enclosed in cigarette packages.

Now thoroughly bitten by the journalistic bug, young Bok proceeded to report public speeches for the local paper, edit a church paper entitled the

Brooklyn Magazine, write theater news for the *Daily Eagle*, publish theater programs (which he designed), and to serve successively as stenographer in two publishing firms, Henry Holt and Charles Scribner.

Bok soon observed that few women read newspapers and the concomitant fact that the papers of the time paid slight attention to women's interests. Thus was born an embryo idea which was to lead to the young journalist's greatest success. He began to gather material designed to appeal to women and to influence their reading habits. Ella Wheeler Wilcox and others were engaged to write on women's topics, and shortly, through his syndicate, Bok was supplying newspapers with a full page of women's features.

Another void to be filled, in Bok's view, was news about books and authors. This feature, known as "Bok's Literary Leaves," soon had a following of readers in more than forty newspapers. In 1887 Bok was placed in charge of advertising for the newly established *Scribner's Magazine*, and in that capacity a year later helped to make famous Edward Bellamy's utopian novel, *Looking Backward*.

The foregoing accomplishments were all crowded into the first two decades after Bok came to America. In April 1889 Cyrus H. K. Curtis, who had been impressed by Bok's book reviews in the Philadelphia *Times*, invited him, at the age of twenty-six, to become editor of the *Ladies' Home Journal*, then a six-year-old magazine. After considerable hesitation and against the advice of his friends and relatives, Bok accepted the post. Thus began the career which was to make him an internationally known figure. Under his guidance, the *Ladies' Home Journal* became a national institution to a degree which no other magazine had ever achieved. By the time Bok retired, after thirty years in the editorship, two records had been set: the magazine's circulation had reached 22 million, and each issue carried advertising in excess of a million dollars.

The story of Bok's amazing life, from his earliest recollections until he left the *Ladies' Home Journal*, is recounted in *The Americanization of Edward Bok* (1920), an autobiography told in the third person.

An important element in Bok's success was his self-confidence and complete lack of false modesty, as demonstrated by the ease with which he dealt with celebrities. Apparently, even as a youth, he never stood in awe of famous personages. At the age of about thirteen, Bok started to assemble an autograph collection, beginning with a letter from James A. Garfield. In pursuit of this hobby, and later through his editorial activities, he became personally acquainted—in some cases on intimate terms—with every president from U. S. Grant to Woodrow Wilson, and he met Mrs. Abraham Lincoln. In addition, he developed close and friendly relations with most of the prominent American and English authors of the time: Dr. Oliver Wendell Holmes, Emerson, Longfellow, Robert Louis Stevenson, Rudyard Kipling, Mark Twain, Harriet Beecher Stowe, Eugene Field, William Dean Howells, James Whitcomb Riley, and others. Quite legitimately, therefore, *The Americanization of Edward Bok* is a record of name-dropping par excellence.

For a mere man, furthermore an unmarried one, to undertake editorship of a woman's magazine exposed Bok to a great deal of jocular comment and even ridicule. As a first step, to compensate for his own want of intimate knowledge of the gentler sex, Bok offered prizes for the best suggestions for improving the contents of the magazine. Thousands of answers poured in, and combining them with his own ideas Bok proceeded to establish departments to advise girls on their personal problems, young mothers on infant and child care, and mature women on their spiritual needs. As Bok saw his function, he should not only "give the people what they want," but "give the people what they ought to have and don't know they want." He was unwilling to stop with trivia.

Guided by such principles in editing a magazine for women, Bok inaugurated a series of crusades, using the *Ladies' Home Journal* as a forum. Some campaigns ended in splendid victories, others in ignominious defeats.

Bok soon learned that the average American girl was quite unprepared for motherhood, and a department was set up to distribute information about prenatal and postnatal care. After several years of successfully raising babies by mail, the editorial decision was made to deal with a less popular subject. At the turn of the century even the mention of venereal disease was banned in polite society and in every decent periodical and newspaper. With considerable courage, in 1906 Bok broke the conspiracy of silence in his magazine. Seventy-five thousand readers of the *Ladies' Home Journal* canceled their subscriptions when the first articles on the subject appeared. Gradually, as understanding and education grew, the matter became accepted as suitable for public debate and discussion.

Theodore Roosevelt once declared that Bok was the only man who ever changed the architecture of an entire nation. The editor had a keen desire to improve the architecture of the small American home. To that end, for years he published small-house plans by the country's foremost architects, and the plans were extensively used throughout the United States. All of them eliminated the useless parlor, previously a proud feature of the American home.

A similarly successful attempt was made to upgrade the interior appearance of homes. The *Ladies' Home Journal* carried pictorial representations of what were considered the best and most tastefully furnished rooms, as a result of which the physical appearance of domestic furniture completely changed within a few years. The next problem was to improve the pictures on the walls of the American home. After the invention of four-color presses, Bok obtained permission to reproduce art masterpieces from the greatest American private collections. More than 70 million copies were distributed through the magazine.

Beautiful homes were out of place in ugly cities, and Bok's next target was to get rid of the unsightly spots disgracing residential and business areas. A photographic campaign stirred the municipalities represented to initiate cleanup measures. A parallel drive to abolish offensive billboards was fought by vested interests and ended largely in failure — in the same manner that the industry has resisted reform ever since.

One of Bok's most notable journalistic triumphs followed an announcement in the *Ladies' Home Journal* that no more patent medicine advertisements would be accepted — at the time a chief source of revenue for magazines and newspapers. The profits of the patent medicine business in the United States, almost totally unregulated, ran into hundreds of millions of dollars annually. The *Ladies' Home Journal* showed the actual contents of the most popular medicines, to demonstrate their worthlessness. Some contained as high as 40 percent alcohol. Next to an advertisement representing Lydia Pinkham in her laboratory, Bok placed a photograph of Mrs. Pinkham's tombstone showing that she had been dead twenty-two years. Mark Sullivan, later to achieve distinction as a journalist, was assigned to write a series of muckraking articles on the unethical practices prevailing in the business. The ensuing fights with the nostrum makers, several lawsuits, and general public outcry finally led to the Food and Drugs Act of 1906.

Among Bok's "failures," to use his own word, was an attack on Parisian couturiers, protesting their lack of taste and questionable morals, their "deceit and misrepresentation." American women of refinement and position were actually dressing like Parisian streetwalkers. Bok employed the most expert designers in women's wear to create American designs, but the American woman ignored them. She continued to be a slave to Parisian styles, with absolutely no patriotic instincts. After a year, Bok abandoned any hope of reform and dropped the matter.

In another area involving women's fashions, Bok first lost and then won a campaign. A national mania for egret feathers used for decoration was threatening the extinction of the beautiful birds. An article with photographs and text exposing the cruelty of the craze made no impact on the readers of the *Ladies' Home Journal*. Instead, the demand for the feathers more than quadrupled. Having failed to enlist feminine support, Bok carried his case to the state legislatures and persuaded them to pass laws banning the butchery of the birds and making it a misdemeanor to import, sell, purchase, or wear egret feathers. Later a federal law came into existence, prohibiting the importation of bird feathers into the country.

Bok deliberately stirred up a hornet's nest in a series of attacks against women's clubs—in particular against the puerility and superficiality of their programs. He saw the clubs as a potential power for good in the civic life of the nation; instead, he felt that their energies were being wasted on pseudoculture. The clubs were urged by Bok to place less emphasis on cultural subjects and to pay attention to numerous questions dealing with the life of their communities. Again there were widespread protests against Bok's criticisms and cancellations of subscriptions, but the end results appear to have been wholesome, for under the prodding many clubs began to broaden their interests.

During the period of Bok's editorship, the question of women's suffrage became a burning issue. Bok interviewed such leaders in the movement as Susan B. Anthony, Julia Ward Howe, Anna Howard Shaw, and Jane Addams. The editor claimed that "he was ready to have the magazine, for whose editorial policy he was responsible, advocate that side of the issue which seemed for the best interests of the American woman." But when Bok made up his mind, he came down on the unpopular side: "He felt that American women were not ready to exercise the privilege intelligently and that their mental attitude was against it."

Publication of an editorial stating Bok's position stirred up the greatest storm of all. As he wrote, "The denunciation brought down upon him by his attitude toward woman's clubs was as nothing compared to what was now let loose." President Cleveland, President Eliot of Harvard, Lyman Abbott, and a few women rallied to Bok's defense, but the final outcome was inevitable. The year after Bok retired from the editorship of the *Ladies' Home Journal*, the Nineteenth Amendment extended the franchise to women in all states of the Union.

Despite the preeminent position which he had attained in his field and the great material success which came to him, Bok was unhappy when he reached the end of his thirty years of editorial service. In short, he was disillusioned with women, and to some extent with his adopted homeland. In a chapter of *The Americanization of Edward Bok*, "Where America Fell Short with Me," the author condemned American wastefulness and failure to provide for the future; the emphasis on quantity rather than quality, with a resulting sloppiness in work produced and a general lack of thoroughness; the inadequacy of public school education, characterized by incompetent methods of teaching; lack of respect for and the poor enforcement of laws; and the meager preparation which Americans receive for exercising the privileges of citizenship.

On the other hand, in discussing "What I Owe to America," Bok concluded that no other nation in the world offered the foreign-born the opportunities they had in the United States; he commended the "wonderful idealism" of the American people, a trait in the American character not generally realized abroad; and he found that the true American plays fair and is generally honest, despite the fact that some men succeed by unscrupulous behavior.

Bok's will provided $2 million for charities and he established the Woodrow Wilson Chair of Government at Williams College. His son Curtis became a federal judge noted for his liberal opinions in intellectual freedom cases. His grandson Derek Curtis Bok became President of Harvard University.

RBD

References: Edward Bok, *The Americanization of Edward Bok* (New York: Scribner, 1920); Edward Bok, *A Dutch Boy Fifty Years After* (New York: Scribner, 1921).

Edwin Thomas Booth

(November 13, 1833 — June 7, 1893)

The nineteenth century American theater was fortunate enough to have two great tragedians, Forrest and Booth, each of whom held a prominent place on the stage for many years. Edwin Forrest reached stardom before the Civil War and excelled in Shakespearian roles and in popular plays which he commissioned contemporary playwrights to create for him. He was the more flamboyant of the two, physically impressive, given to posing and fond of bombastic rhetoric, but an audience favorite. Edwin Booth, rather short in stature and not gifted with an extraordinary voice, served his apprenticeship in California and Australia but made triumphant appearances in New York and Boston in the late 1850s. In 1864-1865 he consolidated his fame by appearing in *Hamlet* in New York for one hundred nights. He operated his own theater for four years, a period which became an epoch in the history of the American stage.

Booth belonged to a famous theatrical family. He was born on a farm near Bel Air, Maryland, in 1833, the second son of Junius Brutus Booth, an English actor who came to America in 1821 and quickly won thespian celebrity. The boy had irregular local schooling and gained a different kind of education when he accompanied his father on tours. Junius Brutus Booth was known for his erratic behavior, for his addiction to alcohol and occasional fits of insanity. The father died in California where Edwin had early acting experience and where his older brother managed a theater in San Francisco.

Booth was by temperament serious and intellectual, and had a melancholy streak that was probably exaggerated by the ordeal of his early years. He was somewhat reluctant to enter the acting profession but made his debut in Boston in 1849 playing the minor role of Tressel in *Richard III*. Other juvenile parts followed, such as the role of Titus in John Howard Payne's tragedy *Brutus*. In 1851 his father, temporarily incapacitated, plunged him into the role of Richard III. Booth was later engaged by a Baltimore theater but was not a success. He appeared in the Jenny Lind theater in San Francisco and was a member of a stock company in Sacramento. In Australia in the middle 1850s he attempted various Shakespearian roles and consistently played Shylock as a malicious villain. Back in California he appeared in a number of cities, often barely avoiding starvation, but in 1856 he enjoyed a successful role in *King Lear* in Sacramento. Booth incidentally was not a star in comedy. His forte was something quite different, and he soon became a greater tragedian than his father.

After his return to the East Booth played in Baltimore, in Boston, and at Burton's Metropolitan Theater in New York City. He excelled in such roles as Sir Giles Overreach in Massinger's *A New Way to Pay Old Debts* and the French cardinal in Bulwer-Lytton's blank verse tragedy *Richelieu*, sometimes deemed his greatest achievement. Many American cities saw Booth perform and he acted at the Haymarket Theater in London as well as at Liverpool and Manchester. In New York he was featured at Niblo's Theater and at the Winter Garden, the scene of his remarkable interpretation of *Hamlet*. Booth chose to act the parts of many Shakespearian characters, including Romeo, Othello, Iago, Richard III, Benedick, Brutus, Marc Antony, and Macbeth. Some of these performances must have been in the memory of the poet Thomas Bailey Aldrich when he wrote his tribute in "The Grave of Edwin Booth":

> In narrow space, with Booth, lie housed in death
> Iago, Hamlet, Shylock, Lear, Macbeth.
> If still they seem to walk the painted scene
> 'Tis but the ghosts of those that once have been.

But if Booth's professional life was a series of triumphs, his personal and domestic life was less fortunate. His marriage to Mary Devlin in 1860 ended with her death three years later. His second wife, Mary McVicker, became insane and died in 1881. Most tragic of all, of course, was the assassination of Abraham Lincoln by Booth's brother, John Wilkes Booth, in 1865. Immediately thereafter Booth left the stage and remained aloof for some months. But his audiences, convinced that he had no connection with his brother's fanatical deed and aware of the fact that he had consistently supported the Union in the Civil War, encouraged him to return to acting on January 3, 1866.

Booth had to endure other calamities. In 1867 a fire at the Winter Garden Theater destroyed his properties, his costumes, and his theatrical library. He immediately began the construction of another playhouse and the Booth Theater opened February 3, 1869. For a time this endeavor prospered. Some of the best known actors and actresses of the time worked with Booth and the theater became known for spectacular productions. Booth, however, lacked a strong business sense and when the panic of 1873-1874 hit the country he was forced to declare bankruptcy.

Showing the resiliency of Sir Walter Scott or Mark Twain in similar circumstances, Booth gave up a permanent theatrical home and reverted to his life as a traveling actor. He again visited various American cities and performed abroad. In 1880-1881 he acted at the Princess's Theater in London for 119 nights, and at the Lyceum Theater he and Henry Irving alternated the characters of Othello and Iago. In 1882 he toured Europe. With the exception of one year when he performed with Mme. Modjeska he played with Lawrence Barrett from 1887 to 1891.

But almost twenty years of this peripatetic life took its toll and his voice, never too strong, was probably weakened further by an excessive indulgence in alcohol in his early years and his continuous smoking. After departing from the stage following his final performance of *Hamlet* in Brooklyn in 1891, he retired to his home at Sixteen Gramercy Park, New York City, the building occupied by the Players' Club. Booth had given the building to the club and was both its founder and its first president. He died in 1893.

To several generations of American playgoers Edwin Booth was Hamlet. In assessing Booth's interpretation of the role Lawrence Hutton wrote as follows: "Mr. Booth's Hamlet is original in many respects; it is intellectual, intelligent, carefully studied, complete to the smallest details, and greatly to be admired. Nature has given him the melancholy, romantic face, the magnetic eye, the graceful person, the stately carriage, the poetic temperament, which are in so marked a degree characteristic of Hamlet." Edwin Booth had the physique, the temperament, and the ability required by his profession. He remains one of the greatest of American actors.

JTF

References: Ernest Sutherland Bates, *DAB*, II, 1929, pp. 444-47; William Winter, *Life and Art of Edwin Booth* (New York and London: Macmillan, 1893; reprinted 1968); Eleanor Ruggles, *Prince of Players: Edwin Booth* (New York: Norton, 1953).

Louis Dembitz Brandeis

(November 13, 1856—October 5, 1941)

Following the collapse of the revolutionary liberal movements in central Europe in the 1840s, there was an exodus to America of some of the oldest and most cultivated Jewish families. Among them were the parents of Louis Brandeis, who was destined to become one of the most brilliant members of the U.S. Supreme Court. Louis was born in Louisville, Kentucky, where his father established a grain and produce business.

From the outset, Louis was a precocious student, graduating from high school at fifteen as a gold medalist. During an extended tour of Europe with his parents, he spent the years 1873-1875 at the Annen Realschule in Dresden, where his intellectual development continued. Shortly after his return, he entered the Harvard Law School and received his law degree in 1877 after achieving an academic record said to have been unsurpassed since in the history of the school.

Brandeis began the practice of law in St. Louis, but was unhappy there and after a few months returned to Boston to form a law partnership with a Harvard classmate Samuel D. Warren, Jr. In Boston, he became well acquainted with Oliver Wendell Holmes, Jr., later a Supreme Court Justice, and served as a part-time clerk to Chief Justice Horace Gray of the Supreme Judicial Court of Massachusetts, who also became a U.S. Supreme Court Justice. Gray rated Brandeis as "the most ingenious and most original lawyer I ever met." Brandeis' own legal practice flourished and his earnings soon amounted to fifty thousand dollars a year. At the same time, he organized a national association of Harvard Law School alumni and served as the first treasurer of the recently formed *Harvard Law Review*.

Early in his career, Brandeis became active in public causes, often without compensation. The first major case developed from the steel plants at Homestead, Pennsylvania, where Brandeis said "organized capital hired a private army to shoot at organized labor for resisting an arbitrary cut in wages." As one biographer noted, "Brandeis found his greatest satisfaction in trying to find remedies for social ills."

Among the causes to which Brandeis devoted himself as a young lawyer were the right to privacy, monopolies in public utilities, the problem of rates and services in the gas industry, and devising a plan of savings—bank insurance for workingmen—the last of which he regarded as his most significant achievement. His views, presented in a series of magazine articles, later collected in book form as *Other People's Money and How the Bankers Use It*, inspired early New Deal legislation for the protection of investors and consumers, requiring full disclosure in the sale of securities, separation of investment from commercial banking, and simplification of public utility holding company systems.

A controversy reminiscent of those that erupted during James Watt's administration of the Department of the Interior in the 1980s brought Brandeis into conflict with the Taft administration. The affair was concerned with the conservation of mineral lands in Alaska. Interior department officials were charged with colluding with Guggenheim interests to open those lands for sale. Brandeis was appointed to represent the "informer." A good deal of skullduggery, highly embarrassing to the Taft administration, was revealed. For Brandeis, conservation of natural resources was of major significance. The Alaska case ended with the resignation of the Interior Secretary and the appointment of a successor who established policies for the conservation of Alaskan resources in accord with Brandeis' recommendations.

In time, Brandeis became known as the "people's counsel," because of his activities in the public interest. As counsel for the states concerned, he proved the constitutionality of the women's ten-hour law in Oregon, and Illinois, the California eight-hour law, the Ohio nine-hour law, and the Oregon minimum-wage law. Brandeis was also associated with many other cases involving social legislation. He became known for the "Brandeis brief," incorporating not only legal arguments but also masses of facts from the social sciences and statements of standard legal precedents. For example, in defending the Oregon law setting a maximum of ten hours of labor a day for women, Brandeis' brief for the Supreme Court devoted only three pages to the legal principles while taking more than a hundred pages to describe the effects of longer hours on health, the experience of other countries, and the opinions of experts on the subject.

In the field of labor relations, Brandeis was a firm believer in industrial democracy. He opposed the closed shop. Typical of his views was an argument worked out by him as mediator to settle a strike in the New York garment industry in 1910. A preferential union shop was agreed upon, giving preference to union members in hiring, but without dictation by the union in final selection.

Not until about middle age did Brandeis begin to take a profound interest in his Jewish origin and become actively dedicated to Zionism. He believed that the Zionist movement stood for many of the ideals that he had long cherished. At the beginning of World War I, the World Zionist Organization headquarters were moved to the United States and Brandeis was chosen as chairman of the operating committee. His friendship and influence with President Wilson were instrumental in obtaining approval for the Balfour Declaration in 1917, pledging the creation of a national homeland for the Jewish people in Palestine and later for a British mandate.

Brandeis was a political independent, voting at various times for Cleveland, Taft, and the Progressive Party. Later, Wilson's stand on economic power won his support. Brandeis was an influential adviser in the early years of the Wilson administration, especially in such matters as the structure and control of the Federal Reserve banking system. He collaborated in drafting a bill which led to creation of the Federal Trade Commission in 1914.

A vacancy on the Supreme Court bench in 1916 led to Wilson's nomination of Brandeis as an associate justice. A bitter controversy over the nomination went on for months in Congress and the country at large. The opposition appears to have been based on the fact that he was a Jew (the first to be named for the Supreme Court), his lack of judicial experience, and the charge that he was a radical. Wilson stood firm, despite the powerful forces arrayed against his nominee. Brandeis finally won confirmation in the Senate on June 1, 1916, by a vote of 47 to 22.

As a Supreme Court justice, Brandeis was usually in accord with Justice Holmes, though both of them were frequently in dissent, in support of federal and state social and economic legislation. Brandeis believed that government should not be restricted by judges in experimentation, even though undesirable legislation might result. In the cases that came before him, he did not attempt to be a sentimental reformer nor a dangerous radical. His belief was that judges, like other men, could be mistaken. He mistrusted too much concentration of power in the federal government, and endorsed the sharing of power and responsibility with the states.

An area of primary concern to Brandeis was liberty of speech, press, and assembly. He was constantly alert, therefore, to reject and strike down state or federal controls, unless it could be demonstrated that they were justified by a clear and present danger of serious public harm.

Brandeis won the esteem of his colleagues in the Court, even those who differed sharply from his constitutional views. Chief Justice Taft, after serving two years with him, said, "I have come to like Brandeis very much indeed," and another chief justice, Charles Evans Hughes, wrote that he was "the master of both microscope and telescope. Nothing of importance, however minute, escapes him, microscopic examination of every problem, and, through his powerful telescopic lens, his mental vision embraces distant scenes ranging far beyond the familiar worlds of conventional thinking."

For the most part, Brandeis was an admirer and supporter of Franklin D. Roosevelt, though he held strong reservations about the New Deal's emphasis on centralized planning. He joined in the decision declaring the National Industrial Recovery Act unconstitutional, and also opposed Roosevelt's "court-packing" proposal in 1937. On the other hand, Brandeis concurred in the New Deal legislative program to establish minimum wages and unemployment insurance, guaranteeing collective bargaining, regulating securities issues and the stock exchange, requiring the reorganization of holding companies, and setting up the Tennessee Valley Authority.

A Brandeis biographer, Paul A. Freund, concluded that "Brandeis's distinctive eminence in the history of American law rests on an extraordinary fusion of prophetic vision, moral intensity, and grasp of practical affairs."

Brandeis University was founded at Waltham, Massachusetts, in 1948, endowed by American Jewry as a contribution to higher education, and was named in honor of Justice Louis D. Brandeis.

RBD

References: Alpheus T. Mason, *Brandeis, A Free Man's Life* (New York: Viking, 1946); Iris Noble, *Louis D. Brandeis* (Philadelphia: Westminster Press, 1969); Samuel J. Konofsky, *The Legacy of Holmes and Brandeis* (New York: Macmillan, 1956); Catherine O. Pearce, *The Louis D. Brandeis Story* (New York: Crowell, 1970).

Van Wyck Brooks

(February 16, 1886—May 2, 1963)

After a short career in teaching and journalism Van Wyck Brooks turned to literary criticism and became one of the best known critics in the first half of the twentieth century. His earliest work was an attack on Puritan tradition in American culture and a reappraisal of such figures as Emerson, Twain, and James. His often acerbic analyses seemed to ally him with militant critics like James G. Huneker and H. L. Mencken. But conscientious study of what he called the "usable past" and certainly the mellowing influence of time produced a great change in Brooks's focus, and he eventually became a prolific literary historian whose erudition and graceful style brought him a 1937 Pulitzer Prize in history for his book *The Flowering of New England, 1815-1865*. If Brooks began by being a scornful critic of American letters, he ended by being a consistent cultural nativist.

Brooks was born in Plainfield, New Jersey, in 1886 and was educated in the local schools. He entered Harvard in 1903 and two years later combined with John Hall Wheelock to produce the privately printed *Verses by Two Undergraduates*. Following graduation in 1907 Brooks went to England for a time working as a free-lance journalist. *The Wine of the Puritans*, 1908, was his first book to criticize the Puritan heritage, which in his view emphasized material values and discounted aesthetic qualities. Brooks condemned the shallowness and timidity of American writing and identified Whitman as the first great organic personality to appear on the American scene. The book brought him an invitation to teach English at Stanford University, where he remained from 1911 to 1913.

After another trip to England and the publication of *America's Coming-of-Age* in 1915, Brooks relinquished academic life for magazine work in New York City. He was on the staff of *Collier's Encyclopedia* and the Century Company, and from 1917 to 1919 served as associate editor of the *Seven Arts Magazine*. Essays contributed to that periodical were collected in *Letters and Leadership* in 1918. From 1920 to 1924 he was a contributor to and literary editor of the *Freeman*, a weekly magazine devoted to political and aesthetic criticism. Ill health from 1925 to 1931 precluded further editorial work and he was also beset by financial worries. From this time on he devoted himself to his own writing. He had already published books on John Addington Symonds and H. G. Wells, and his life of Emerson would appear in 1932. More important were *The Ordeal of Mark Twain* in 1920 and *The Pilgrimage of Henry James* in 1925.

In the first of these studies Brooks argued that Twain would have been a greater writer than he was save for the domestic censure of his wife and the stultifying criticism of William Dean Howells. Moreover, Twain did not picture the America which he knew intimately. After Bernard De Voto in *Mark Twain's America* published a fiery rebuttal, Brooks issued a revised edition of his book in 1933 in which he modified his position considerably. In his study of James Brooks condemned the novelist for withdrawing from America and concentrating on the European scenes. Brooks retained his dislike for materialism and industrialism and remained an Emersonian idealist.

As he scrutinized the American record and examined various strands of American culture, he found previously overlooked virtues which led him to shift his literary focus. As a result he decided to write a series of books devoted to a hundred years of American literary history. The five volumes which were collectively entitled *Makers and Finders: A History of the Writer in America, 1800-1915* are his most memorable achievement.

Brooks was at his best in describing and evaluating the painters, scholars, historians, essayists, poets, and novelists of New England. *The Flowering of New England: 1815-1865* extends from the Boston of Gilbert Stuart to the Boston of Lowell and Holmes. Brooks skillfully intertwined painting and history, poetry and journalism, anecdotes and portraits, always drawing liberally on diaries, travel sketches, essays, and biography. He compared and interpolated with equal facility and produced a broad canvas alive with vibrant figures. The second volume, *New England: Indian Summer, 1865-1915*, extending from Howells and James to Frost and Robinson, uses the same method. But somehow the book lacks the elevation, to use one of Brooks's favorite terms, of its predecessor and a chapter entitled "The Epigoni" suggests that the author was adjusting in large part to discussing second rate figures.

In later volumes, notably *The World of Washington Irving*, 1944, and *The Times of Melville and Whitman*, 1947, Brooks seemed to lack the intimate touch and familiarity with subject which characterized the New England volumes. But the generally elegiac tone continues and the author's erudition and his amazing ability to search out relationships and spot interesting coincidences remains. In the final volume, *The Confident Years: 1885-1915*, published in 1952, Brooks's basic method does not change but he reveals less sympathy with the writers he treats. Moreover, as James D. Hart has pointed out, he becomes more concerned with the personalities and quirks of the authors and slights the actual books they have written.

Brooks continued his literary activity in his later years. He translated several volumes from the French. He edited both the journals and the correspondence of Gamaliel Bradford, once well known for his psychological biographies. He wrote studies of Helen Keller, William Dean Howells, and the painter John Sloan. And he produced several autobiographical and reminiscent volumes, such as *Days of the Phoenix: The Nineteen-Twenties I Remember*, 1957. These last books were combined in *An Autobiography*, posthumously published in 1965.

In one earlier volume, *Opinions of Oliver Allston*, 1941, Brooks used his obvious alter ego to combine fragments of personal life, bits of miscellaneous reading, and critical insights. The second to last page of this mélange states his belief that literature properly has three dimensions: breadth, depth, and elevation. Although great writers have all three, no modern seems to claim more than two. He doesn't cite texts to confirm his points, but his examples are revealing: Dreiser and O'Neill have breadth and depth but no elevation, Sinclair Lewis has breadth but little else, Frost and Robinson have depth and elevation but little breadth.

Brooks died at Bridgewater, Connecticut, at the age of seventy-seven. He was identified in one obituary as the literary voice of New England and branded as a liberal turned conservative. But like Edmund Wilson, another genuine man of letters, Brooks helped to make literary criticism more readable at a time when many practitioners were making it esoteric and involute.

JTF

References: William Wasserstrom, *DAB*, Supplement 7, 1981, pp. 79-81; Fred B. Millett, *Contemporary American Authors* (New York: Harcourt, Brace, 1940); William Wasserstrom, *The Legacy of Van Wyck Brooks: A Legacy of Maladies and Motives* (Carbondale, Ill.: Southern Illinois University Press, 1971).

William Jennings Bryan
(March 19, 1860—July 26, 1925)

In the course of his long and active political career, William Jennings Bryan won such sobriquets as "Boy Orator of the Platte," "Great Commoner," and "Peerless Leader"—all indicative of his powerful hold on the Democratic Party from about 1896 to 1916.

Bryan's early training was for the legal profession. From 1883 to 1887 he practiced law in Jacksonville, Illinois, and afterward moved to Lincoln, Nebraska, where he was admitted to the Nebraska bar. Bryan never achieved more than moderate success as a lawyer, however, and soon abandoned the profession for politics. He won two terms, 1890-1894, as the Democratic nominee for Congress in a normally Republican district, but was defeated in a race for the U.S. Senate in 1894. To make a living thereafter, Bryan served as editor in chief of the *Omaha World-Herald* and was popular as a lecturer for Chautauquas.

When monetary policy became a prime political issue, he was in much demand as an advocate of the free coinage of silver. In Congress, he had allied himself with the silver men, voted against the repeal of the silver purchase law of 1890, and violently denounced President Cleveland for demanding repeal of the law.

Bryan burst upon the national scene in spectacular fashion at the 1896 Democratic convention in Chicago. In a remarkable performance, while discussing the platform, Bryan delivered his "Cross of Gold" speech. He maintained that the producing masses of the world, the laboring class, and toilers everywhere were opposed to the gold standard. He concluded with a stirring battle cry, "You shall not press down upon the brow of labor this crown of thorns, you shall not crucify mankind upon a cross of gold." The speech swept the ranks of the delegates and on the fifth ballot Bryan won the presidential nomination, at age thirty-six.

Bryan waged an extraordinarily energetic campaign. He traveled over 18,000 miles, making 600 speeches in 27 different states. To no avail, however, for his opponent William McKinley, campaigning mainly from his front porch and uttering platitudinous speeches, won a narrow popular majority in the November election and 271 to Bryan's 176 electoral votes.

Shortly thereafter the Spanish-American War began. Bryan was made a colonel by the governor of Nebraska and raised the Third Nebraska Volunteer Infantry Regiment, but did not serve outside the United States. He resigned the day the treaty with Spain was signed.

In 1900, Bryan was again the Democrats' presidential nominee. He ran on an anti-imperialism and free silver platform. McKinley, again the Republican candidate, defeated him by a larger margin than in 1896.

In 1901, Bryan established in Lincoln, Nebraska, a weekly political journal *The Commoner*, which he edited to 1913. The journal attained a wide circulation.

By 1904, conservative elements in the Democratic party had gained control and nominated their candidate, Judge Alton B. Parker of New York, for the presidency. The party platform was largely shaped by Bryan. Parker's support of a gold standard was offensive to Bryan's wing of the party. Thus the divided Democrats were soundly defeated by Theodore Roosevelt in the ensuing election. Shortly thereafter, 1905-1906, Bryan made a trip around the world.

Bryan quickly regained control of the party organization and in the 1908 convention he was named presidential candidate on the first ballot. Roosevelt's support of William Howard Taft was influential, and so for the third and last time Bryan lost his bid for the White House.

The break between Roosevelt and Taft left the Republicans hopelessly split in 1912, opening the way for a Democratic victory. Bryan announced that he was not a candidate for the nomination, but he attended the Baltimore convention and dictated the platform. It was mainly due to his influence that the nomination went to Woodrow Wilson instead of to Champ Clark. In recognition of his support, Wilson appointed Bryan secretary of state in 1913.

As secretary of state, Bryan's principal responsibility was negotiating peace treaties with foreign nations. All disputes that could possibly lead to war were to be submitted to impartial inquiry and there would be a full year's delay before going to war. Although the principle was agreed to by thirty-one nations, the peace movement was upset by the outbreak of World War I. Bryan also used his position as secretary to promote U.S. recognition of China and to oppose "dollar diplomacy" in Latin America.

After World War I began, Bryan was deeply involved in attempts to restore peace. His advocacy of neutrality and opposition to American intervention of any kind in the war soon led to his resignation as secretary of state. After the sinking of the *Lusitania* in May 1915, he signed a strong note of protest to Germany. As the president prepared to send a second note on the matter, Bryan felt that Wilson's policy toward Germany would lead to war and on June 9, 1915, he presented his formal resignation. When war was actually declared, in April 1917, however, he urged strong support of the president's war measures.

Bryan was a consistent and influential advocate of important causes favored by progressive forces, most of which were subsequently adopted, including the popular election of senators, a graduated income tax, creation of a department of labor, women's suffrage, and national prohibition. As a member of Wilson's cabinet, his large political influence was successfully used to carry administration measures through Congress. A notable instance was his aid in forming and passing the bill for the Federal Reserve System.

Bryan's "last hurrah" in politics was anticlimactic. He attended, but had little impact on the final three Democratic national conventions held during his lifetime, 1916, 1920, and 1924.

As he grew older, Bryan had a childlike faith in a literal interpretation of the Bible and became increasingly hostile to the teachings of biological science, especially theories of evolution. He drafted a bill passed by the Florida legislature to ban the teaching of Darwinism in public schools. A similar bill was enacted by the Tennessee legislature, to prohibit the teaching in public schools of any theories that denied the divine creation of man as taught in the Bible. When John T. Scopes, a biology teacher in Dayton, Tennessee, was indicted for violation of this statute, Bryan was invited to join the prosecuting attorneys. In the course of the trial Bryan was called as a witness by Clarence Darrow, one of the attorneys for the defense, and subjected by Darrow to relentless cross examination. The trial and his testimony revealed the naiveté of Bryan's religious faith and his lack of knowledge of biological science. The ordeal was evidently too much for Bryan. Five days after the trial ended he was found dead in his bed from a heart attack.

RBD

References: Paul W. Glad, *William Jennings Bryan* (New York: Hill, 1968); Louis W. Koenig, *Bryan, A Political Biography* (New York: Putnam, 1971); Charles M. Wilson, *The Commoner, William Jennings Bryan* (Garden City, N.Y.: Doubleday, 1970).

Pearl S. Buck

(June 26, 1892 — March 6, 1973)

The third American writer to win the Nobel Prize for literature, Pearl Buck is one of the most prolific authors of the twentieth century. She wrote eighty-five books, mostly fiction but including biography, autobiography, and essays, in addition to scripts and speeches. Her works were translated into some thirty foreign languages, including French, German, Russian, Chinese, and the Scandinavian tongues. Her long residence in China enabled her to write novels about Chinese rural life during a critical time, and for a considerable period she was looked upon as a reliable interpreter of the Orient for the West. In her later years she was honored for her support of humanitarian causes, notably for her labors to benefit handicapped or orphaned children.

Pearl Sydenstricker Buck was the daughter of Presbyterian missionaries whose ancestors had emigrated from Holland and Germany to seek religious freedom. Although she was born in 1892 in Hillsboro, West Virginia, where her parents were temporarily on furlough, she was taken to China as an infant and spent many years there. It is said that she learned to speak and write Mandarin Chinese before she became competent in English. As a child she heard Chinese legends told her by her nurse and she was taught history by her mother. When she learned to read she began to admire the Victorian novelists, especially Charles Dickens. The Sydenstricker family managed to flee China during the Boxer Rebellion of 1900 but returned later, and the girl was privately tutored and also sent to missionary and boarding schools. Back in the United States a little later, she enrolled at Randolph-Macon Women's College, from which she graduated in 1914 and where she held briefly an assistantship in psychology. About this time she was recalled to China because of her mother's illness and for a time she ran the household, taught in a boys' school, and read Chinese literature.

In 1917 she married John Lossing Buck, an American agricultural specialist in China. One of their daughters was mentally retarded, and this tragic experience developed in Buck a strong compulsion to do what she could to aid defective children.

For a time the Bucks lived in northern China where both were exposed to peasant life. Later they moved to the University of Nanking where John taught agriculture and Pearl English literature. During this period Pearl Buck began to write for various magazines, the beginning of a long career.

While she was in the United States on leave in 1924-1925 Buck took a master's degree in English at Cornell University. But she once again returned to China and retained her association with the University of Nanking from 1921 to 1931. Temporarily she also taught at Southeastern University, 1925-1927, and at Chung Yang University, 1928-1931. Magazine editors soon began to accept her articles but she found that such journalism was not very remunerative. Consequently she turned to fiction and produced her first novel, *East Wind: West Wind*, which was published in 1930 by the John Day Company. The novel received little notice.

But the next year the same company, headed by Richard J. Walsh, brought out *The Good Earth*. It was a phenomenal success, won a Pulitzer Prize in 1932, was made into a Broadway play, and sold over two million copies in a short time. This story of the illiterate and impoverished Wang Lung, whose hard work and love of the earth made him a wealthy landowner, attracted readers throughout the world. Eventually he became the father of three sons, whose stories were narrated in two sequels, *Sons* in 1932 and *A House Divided* in 1935. Eventually the three volumes were combined into a trilogy and published together as *The House of Earth*.

After the Bucks separated and were divorced, Pearl Buck married her publisher, Richard J. Walsh, in 1935. Subsequently she became involved in business interests and in humanitarian enterprises. She managed a New York state farm and owned property in Vermont and an apartment in New York City. She and her husband adopted six children and supported two foster children of various races. She inaugurated Welcome House, an adoption agency for Asian-American children, in 1949, and the Pearl S. Buck Foundation of Philadelphia in 1964 to assist fatherless and often stateless children. She consigned most of her royalties to the latter organization.

Despite many humanitarian activities Buck continued to write fiction and for some time China remained her preferred setting. In *The Mother*, 1934, she dealt with childbirth and abortion. Other examples of novels set in China are *Dragon Seed* (1941), *Pavilion of Women* (1946), and *Peony* (1948). Earlier she had published a two-volume translation of a well-known Chinese saga, *Shui Hu Chan* (1933). In biographies of her parents, *The Exile* and *The Fighting Angel*, both 1936, she again used the background familiar since her childhood. She was awarded the Nobel Prize in 1938.

In her later years Buck was frequently admonished to write less about a China now receding into memory and more about her own country. Nettled by such criticism she ventured to write historical novels of American life and even employed a masculine pseudonym to assure readers that they had met a new novelist. The most successful of these books was *The Townsman*, published in 1945, a story of Kansas and supposedly the work of "John Sedges." An omnibus volume including *The Townsman* and two other novels appeared as *American Triptych* in 1958.

Pearl Buck lived a long and active life. Her early years in China, roughly half her life span, gave her an intimate knowledge of a vast country and resulted in a consistently sympathetic and understanding treatment of Chinese themes. But the China she knew as a girl and young woman has faded away, and her stories about a land which she obviously admired eventually lost their immediacy. Moreover, she wrote largely about domestic and rural life and about woman's role in Sinitic society. As a result her fiction began to appeal chiefly to women and largely to the American middle-class woman who reads novels.

Her books are informative, readable, facile in plot, sometimes almost biblical in style, qualities which explain their relative success in foreign translations. But despite her winning of the Nobel Prize she has never been accepted as a significant literary figure and critics today do not rank her highly. The bibliographical volume of the *Literary History of the United States*, fourth edition, 1974, has only a single reference to Pearl Buck and cites only one title, *The Good Earth*. Considering the limitations of her work it seems unlikely that time, notwithstanding her past popularity, will reverse this judgment.

JTF

References: Jane R. Cohen, in *Notable American Women: The Modern Period*, IV, pp. 116-19 (Cambridge, Mass.: Belknap Press of Harvard, 1980); Paul A. Doyle, *Pearl S. Buck* (New York: Twayne, 1965); Theodore F. Harris, *Pearl S. Buck: A Biography*, 2 vols. (New York: John Day, 1969-1971).

Luther Burbank

(March 7, 1849 — April 11, 1926)

Genius permeated American society in the late 1800s. Every field of human endeavor seemed to produce an individual who made great contributions to the welfare of man. Rockefeller and Morgan in business, Edison and Bell in inventions, Gray and Powell in science, and a host of others in all disciplines had an outstanding impact upon society. Joining this group of men touched with genius was Luther Burbank, plant breeder and developer of new varieties of food for man.

In 1850 little was known about the laws of the biological world. Darwin's *Origin of Species* (1859) was in the process of preparation and Mendel's principles of genetics would not be published until 1901. In spite of his lack of scientific training Luther Burbank became a successful plant breeder, creating more than eight hundred new varieties of plants including twenty kinds of plums and prunes of commercial importance, the Burbank potato, ten new varieties of berries, at least fifty kinds of lilies, and a host of ornamental plants. He was not the first or the only plant breeder of the period, but he was by far the most versatile and possessed a special sense of touch, sight, and smell that enabled him to produce commercial varieties of new plants.

Burbank was born in Lancaster, Massachusetts, the thirteenth child of Samuel Burbank and Olive Ross, Samuel's third wife. Luther did not have the advantage of a rigorous formal education. He grew up on a farm and though he attended Lancaster Academy he received no more than a high school education. Perhaps the most important aspect of his education was his life on a farm where he felt a kinship with nature. Young Luther's early life certainly was not devoid of intellectual stimulation, because his parents were acquainted with Ralph Waldo Emerson, Daniel Webster, and Henry Ward Beecher. His cousin, Levi Sumner Burbank, was involved in educational affairs. Levi Burbank had held several positions, including curator of geology of the Boston Society of Natural History, president of Paducah College, principal of Lancaster Academy, and was an early member of the American Association for the Advancement of Science. Levi, a follower of Louis Agassiz, inspired Luther to learn from observing nature.

The real turning point in Burbank's life came at age nineteen when he read Darwin's *Variation of Animals and Plants under Domestication*, as well as his paper on *Cross and Self-Fertilization in the Vegetable Kingdom*. These were the most impressive scientific works that Burbank had ever seen. In 1870 he purchased a small tract of land for the purpose of supplying superior vegetables to the market. In this garden, at the age of twenty-four, he produced his first new variety, the Burbank potato, and initiated his lifework. The new potato had been developed from a rare seed pod. The pod contained twenty-three seeds, and after planting them Burbank selected two seedlings from which a new variety of potato was grown. It was extremely successful and became the dominant potato in the commercial market. Burbank profited very little from the new potato, selling his rights for $150, which financed his trip, in part, to Santa Rosa, California, in 1875. He took ten of the new potatoes with him for seed.

Burbank was delighted with California. He considered it a paradise and wrote glowing letters extolling the virtues of his new home. He called it "the chosen spot of all this earth," even though to survive he worked as a laborer and slept in a greenhouse. By 1877, after his mother arrived, he rented some land and started a garden. He spent a modest $15.20 on supplies the first year. Three years later he earned more than one thousand dollars and published his first catalogue of twelve pages. In the spring of 1881 a customer offered to purchase twenty thousand plum trees. This was a colossal order, but Burbank decided he could accomplish such a project. In December he delivered more than nineteen thousand of the new trees. This order went far toward establishing his reputation as a "wizard" in the propagation of plants.

Burbank's first marriage was a disaster. While returning from a trip to Massachusetts in 1888 he met Helen Coleman on a train. After a two-year acquaintance he married her. Trouble soon developed and the last two years before their divorce in 1896 Burbank slept in a workroom above the stable. He was forty-one when he married Helen. His second marriage in 1916 at age sixty-seven was to Elizabeth Jane Waters; Elizabeth was about forty years his junior but their relationship was a good one. It was Elizabeth, a year before her marriage, who acted as hostess for the famous visit of Henry Ford and Thomas Edison. The three sat on the steps of Burbank's home and posed for a picture. At the time of the meeting they were among America's best known men, each a leader in his chosen field, and each what Burbank might have designated a *special creation*.

The nursery business took much of his time and taxed his energies. He sold his interest to his partner, R. W. Bell, in 1888 but retained his operating name of Santa Rosa Nurseries so that he could devote his time to "new creations." His goal was to create "better fruits and fairer flowers." He was not interested in scientific data or proving scientific theories. He kept records only long enough to succeed in the propagation of a new variety. Once a better plum or a more beautiful lily was produced the records were destroyed. His goal was to introduce to commerce a better product, to sell the product he advertised and hope to make a profit. An attempt was made by the Carnegie Institution of Washington to preserve some of Burbank's records. The institution paid ten thousand dollars a year for the privilege of sending Dr. George H. Shull to Santa Rosa in 1906 to collate Burbank's records. This agreement was dissolved after five years, but Shull came to appreciate the unique abilities of Burbank. Burbank had a talent for selection of unusual characteristics in plants. Regardless of the faintness of the feature, he had an uncanny knack for choosing the variation which would yield the desired color, shape, taste, texture, or scent. It was this heightened ability to recognize plant variations that permitted him to produce "new creations" for the market. His energies were directed toward producing a new plant that the public would buy, not to prove Mendel or Darwin right or wrong.

Most of Burbank's methods involved selection of desired features and cross-fertilization. These were standard practices and not original with Burbank. His ability to choose desirable characteristics and his persistence in pursuing his goals set him apart. He had turned plant breeding into an art; like an artist he was patient, and from thousands of experiments his senses told him which variation would produce the most desirable taste, color, or smell.

Burbank considered experimentation with plants as "the sole ... purpose of my life." He was not a scientist, and did not try to prove any Mendelian principle or work out any genetic code for plants. He was to plant breeding what Edison was to invention or Ford to automobiles. His lack of records, his fame with the public, his reputation as the "wizard of Santa Rosa," his advertising of "new creations" all combined to develop hostility among most of the scientific community, even though he was one of the most admired Americans of the time. His aim was to apply scientific principles to benefit people. Since he was creating new kinds of plants, he came into direct conflict with religious fundamentalists who believed that only God could create new forms of life.

Burbank had a wide correspondence throughout the world. He obtained many seedlings from foreign sources and crossed them with closely related American varieties. Some were of economic importance, others were not. He acquired from Japan varieties of plums and ultimately produced more than twenty new kinds. Many of Burbank's plums became the most successfully grown and still dominate the market. In addition to plums and prunes, he experimented with berries over a period of thirty-five years. He was able to hybridize blackberries, raspberries and dewberries, producing among others an exotic white blackberry. In his *New Creations* catalogue of 1894 he mentions that he retained only twenty-four berry bushes out of sixty-five thousand for further experimentation. This indicates the scope of his experiments in the process of cross-breeding. Though he specialized in developing new varieties of lilies, he worked with many kinds of flowers including roses and daisies.

Among the best known of Burbank's creations are the Burbank potato, the Shasta daisy, a spineless cactus, Blood plum, Paradox and Royal walnuts and a host of fruits and vegetables, including the commercially grown Admiral pea. The complete list of creations is far too long to include here, but the good he did for mankind lives today in the form of new varieties of edible fruits, nuts and vegetables which he developed at Santa Rosa. In addition, the esthetic joys of smelling and viewing the flowers which evolved from his selective processes of cross-breeding still remain. Although Burbank left no heritage of scientific discovery, no profound contributions to genetics, he left a world with a richer and more abundant food supply, and fields and gardens with more daisies and roses. It was appropriate that this famous American, who was honored by his country with his picture on a three-cent postage stamp, should be buried near his home under a cedar of Lebanon as his only monument.

HWS

References: Vernon L. Kellogg, *DAB*, III, 1929, pp. 265-70; Peter Dreyer, *A Gardener Touched with Genius* (New York: Coward, McCann & Geoghegan, 1975).

Nicholas Murray Butler

(April 2, 1862 — December 7, 1947)

Ralph Waldo Emerson's dictum that "An institution is the lengthened shadow of one man" is nowhere better exemplified than in the case of Columbia University and Nicholas Murray Butler. Butler's association with Columbia extended over nearly seventy years, from the time Butler entered as a student in

1878 until his death late in 1947. He found a college and through dynamic leadership transformed it into one of the world's major universities.

Butler's career was extraordinarily versatile—educator, administrator, politician, internationalist, and advocate of peace. As an undergraduate at Columbia, he was a leader in student activities, particularly journalism, largely supported himself by teaching and newspaper writing, and won honors in a wide variety of subjects. Following graduation, Butler went on to complete M.A. and Ph.D. degrees. His original intention to concentrate on law and politics was changed by President A. P. Barnard who persuaded him that special opportunities in the field of education awaited him.

After a year of study and travel in Europe, Butler returned to Columbia in 1885 as an assistant in philosophy. His rise in the teaching ranks thereafter was rapid. By 1890, he had become professor of philosophy, ethics, and psychology, and lecturer in education, and in 1895 professor of philosophy and education. His colleagues in the new faculty of philosophy elected him dean. Butler helped to choose Morningside Heights for Columbia's site, and he was responsible for establishing a highly successful summer school, starting in 1890.

The next step up for Butler came in 1901, when he succeeded Seth Low as president of Columbia University, a position in which he remained for forty-four years, until age eighty-three.

Even before this important event, Butler had been gaining widespread recognition as an educational leader. In 1887, he was elected president of the Industrial Education Association, an organization dedicated to training public school children in domestic and manual arts. In 1889, he became president of a new institute, the New York College for the Training of Teachers, which subsequently became Teachers College, affiliated with Columbia. During the year 1894/95, Butler served as president of the National Education Association. He led in founding the College Entrance Examination Board (1900) and served as its chairman.

In various related activities, Butler took part in reorganizing the New Jersey public library system, advised in reorganization of the Library of Congress and later the Vatican Library, founded and for thirty years edited *The Educational Review*, an influential educational journal, served as a member of the New Jersey state board of education, and, on the local level, served as president of the Paterson (N.J.) board of education.

Butler held strong views on education at all levels. For the public schools, he fought for nonpolitical appointment of teachers, centralization of control (such as a city superintendent of schools for New York and a powerful commission of education for New York State), removal of teacher certification from local authorities, and the introduction of manual training courses. He argued that the old educational system was hopelessly hampered by dull routines, though he had little sympathy for the child-centered theories of progressive education, then coming into vogue.

Early on, Butler was a strong proponent of advanced and graduate study. Before becoming president, he had been in the forefront of the movement to make Columbia a university in opposition to "college-minded" faculty members and trustees. As president, he was able to reinforce these ideas. In his first years in the office, advanced work in the arts and sciences was actively promoted, an outstanding faculty was further strengthened by the addition of such notable scholars as John Dewey in philosophy and Thomas Hart Morgan in zoology.

Soon Columbia became the foremost American university in its emphasis on graduate work. By 1911, Columbia with seventy-five hundred students was the largest university in the world and had the largest endowment of any American university. There was marked de-emphasis of undergraduate education, which Butler felt was badly in need of reform. Like Robert Maynard Hutchins some years later at the University of Chicago, he repeatedly urged shortening the length of the college course, and for some years Columbia abolished football as a college sport.

A black mark on Butler's reputation resulted from his flagrant violations of academic freedom. A series of dismissals and resignations occurred before World War I, but some of the most publicized cases grew out of wartime controversies, such as those of Henry W. L. Dana in comparative literature for speaking against the Conscription Act, and J. McKeen Cattell, professor of psychology, who urged that draftees not be sent overseas against their will. Both were summarily dismissed. Several other faculty members resigned in protest, including Charles A. Beard, one of America's most distinguished historians, who maintained that "A small group of trustees (unhindered, if not aided, by Dr. Butler) sought to take advantage of the state of war to drive out or humiliate every one who held progressive, liberal, or unconventional views on political matters." Such attacks on academic freedom at Columbia ceased after the termination of the war. In fact, as one commentator observed, "the wide variety of styles and political views at the university made it one of the most stimulating academic communities in America."

Nevertheless, Butler appears to have been an autocratic administrator. He was an uncompromising nationalist in wartime. Deans at Columbia were appointed by the president, not elected by their faculties. Butler was basically a conservative, who opposed direct democracy, wanted government by a trained, enlightened elite class, and spoke out against the direct primary, direct election of senators, and initiative, recall, and referendum. He also condemned the income tax, the Child Labor Amendment, and the Adamson Eight-Hour Act. He did, however, support women's suffrage.

Throughout most of his long career, Butler was actively involved in politics. A life-long Republican, he was on intimate terms with Theodore Roosevelt during the early years of the latter's term as president. This relationship gradually cooled, because of Roosevelt's trust-busting campaign and advocacy of tariff reductions. Butler supported Taft in the 1912 election against Roosevelt and was rewarded with the Republican vice-presidential nomination after the death of the regular nominee James S. Sherman. Both Taft and Roosevelt were defeated, of course, by Woodrow Wilson. It was during this campaign that Roosevelt pinned on Butler the nickname "Nicholas Miraculous."

As early as 1888, Butler was a delegate to the Republican national convention and again from 1904 to 1932. He helped to draft platforms, campaigned for the party's nominees, and tried to influence the policies of those elected. He declined to run for mayor of New York City or governor of New York State, but served as advisor to state constitutional conventions. In 1920 and again in 1928, Butler campaigned actively for the Republican presidential nomination for himself, without success. He became increasingly unhappy with his party, especially because of its support of the prohibition law. The Eighteenth Amendment he considered a radical departure from the federal government's proper role and an ineffective method of controlling the liquor problem.

One of the areas in which Butler was most active was his work for international relations and peace. In 1907 and 1909-1913 he was chairman of the Lake Mohonk conference on international arbitration. He influenced Andrew Carnegie to establish the Carnegie Endowment for International Peace with a $10 million dollar gift, and followed Elihu Root as president of the foundation. In 1905, Butler held a meeting with Kaiser Wilhelm II and attempted to mediate the differences between Britain and Germany. During the struggle over American entry into the League of Nations, he favored ratification of the treaty with mild reservations. Later, Butler was actively involved in the creation of the Kellogg-Briand Pact for the renunciation of war. His efforts for international understanding were recognized by his receiving the Nobel Peace Prize in 1931.

Butler became an international figure of considerable consequence. He was made an officer in the French Légion d'Honneur in 1921 and received decorations from eight other European nations. He also lectured on American history, literature and institutions at eight British universities. The Carnegie Endowment under his leadership rebuilt war-damaged libraries, sponsored exchanges of professors, students, and journalists, and financed courses on international relations in American universities.

Although a prolific author who produced some twenty books, Butler's writings are not rated as important in educational literature. Most of the books consisted of his addresses on various occasions.

Butler was gregarious and a great joiner. He belonged to more than fifty scholarly societies and many social clubs. Dinner parties, where he was usually the center of attention and dominated the conversation, were his favorite diversion. Throughout his career he was much in demand as a consultant, speaker, and editor in the field of education. He had a considerable rhetorical gift, though his thought generally lacked originality. The general opinion among his colleagues at Columbia was that he remained in the presidency there too long and should have retired before age eighty-three. The trustees' election of Dwight D. Eisenhower as his successor met with his full approval.

RBD

References: Nicholas Murray Butler, *Across the Busy Years*, 2 vols. (New York: Scribner, 1939-1940); Richard Whittemore, *Nicholas Murray Butler and Public Education* (New York: Teachers College Press, 1970).

Alexander Campbell
(September 12, 1788 — March 4, 1866)

Thomas Campbell, Seceder Presbyterian minister of Scotch ancestry, emigrated from County Antrim, Ireland, to Washington County, Pennsylvania in 1807. He was a graduate of the University of Glasgow though his ancestors had settled in Ireland a century before his birth in 1763. Thomas became minister of the Seceder branch of the Presbyterian Church at Ahorey, County Antrim, where his son Alexander was born. Thomas left his family in Ireland and they were delayed two years before they could make their way to America. In the meantime, Alexander spent one very happy year at Glasgow University.

Upon arrival in America, Thomas was assigned by the Associate Synod in Philadelphia as an itinerant pastor in southwestern Pennsylvania. After discovering that his concepts were unorthodox, he was rebuked and finally deposed from the Holy Ministry. His strongest heresy was to state that Christ had died for all men, not just the elite. In September of 1809 Thomas drew up a "Declaration and Address" citing thirteen propositions in which he deplored the division among Christians and argued for Christian unity. The "Declaration" became the foundation of the Restoration Movement and resulted in The Christian Church, The Churches of Christ and The Disciples of Christ. Also, it was the basis of one of the great religious movements indigenous to America, though it was a split from the Presbyterian and Baptist churches. It is ironic that though the basic tenet of the Campbells was union of denominations his "Declaration" ultimately resulted in division. As the new Christian Association of Washington County got under way, Thomas asked his family, including his wife and six children, to emigrate from Ireland and join him in Pennsylvania.

The Campbell family, including twenty-one-year-old Alexander, arrived in Philadelphia and made their way by wagon westward across Pennsylvania. Thomas met them on a lonely stretch of the road and that night, in an inn, he showed Alexander a copy of the "Declaration." Alexander became an immediate convert to the principles expounded. After three more days of travel, they arrived at their home in the village of Washington and settled down to start on the road of destiny that would lead eventually from the Christian Association with thirty members to congregations totalling more than one million in The Disciples of Christ Church in 1982. On June 16, 1811, the Brush Run Church was established, and Alexander became the leader at age twenty-two. At this time division among churches was considered an evil by the Campbells. They were thinking in terms of union of all faiths into a common church for all Christians.

Religious leaders periodically arise in different parts of the world. They gather about them a group of disciples who fervently work toward advancing an espoused cause. The new denomination is often a branch or offshoot of a large and well-known group. The new movement may arise from a variation in interpreting some aspect of the Bible. On the other hand, a vision or divine revelation may play a part. Mohammed communicated with an angel to prepare the Koran, the foundation of Islam. Pioneer America, during the first half of the nineteenth century, was filled with religious fervor. Evangelical meetings were popular as social gatherings and forms of entertainment on the frontier. Each evangelist carried the message of divine truth and believed that his interpretation of the gospel was the only road that led to salvation. Numerous denominations appeared and met with varying degrees of success. The democratic mood on the frontier challenged the old Calvinism. The pioneer was looking toward freedom of the individual and a break with the past. He was not concerned with damnation while living, but was searching for a good life on earth. He believed in the free enterprise system and was as receptive to changes in religion as he was to changes in economics. Alexander Campbell was part of the frontier and became the leader of the Reformation. His reform movement was designed to unite all Christians under an umbrella of complete freedom in religious opinion. But what is freedom for one may be considered coercion for another, and Campbell met with opposition in his attempts to unite Christians. Campbell was well suited by temperament to lead a religious reform. He was convinced that his father's "Declaration" embodied the principles which should be followed. He was a thorough student of the Bible and possessed the public presence and oratorical ability to be accepted as a leader.

Campbell's Brush Run Church affiliated with the Redstone Baptist Association in November 1813. It was an uncomfortable association for all parties. Campbell was looked upon by the Baptists as something of a rebel. He questioned the Baptist's reliance on Moses as the authority. In forms of worship and discipline why was not Christ the ultimate authority? "Christ is the end of the Law for righteousness, and to everyone that believeth."

Campbell accepted invitations to preach or debate at any time or place. His most famous debate was with Richard Owen, the founder of New Harmony, Indiana. Owen, the English utopian, had established a socialistic community based upon the principles of communism long before Marx and Engels, and was energetically promoting his ideas. Owen believed that "all religions of the world have been founded on the ignorance of mankind," and challenged the clergy to debate him. Campbell accepted the challenge, and the initial meeting was arranged for the second Monday in April 1829. It was held in a large Methodist Church in Cincinnati. After eight days of debate, Campbell closed his argument by asking all in the audience of twelve hundred who believed "in the Christian religion" to rise. All but three arose, and Campbell was projected into the national limelight, whereas Owen's star faded away. In time New Harmony failed, but Campbell's Christians continued marching forward.

Campbell understood the power of the written word and established the religious periodical *Christian Baptist* in 1823. The very name aroused the antipathy of the Baptists. His assistant editor, Walter Scott, was one of the most noted frontier preachers of the day and had distinguished himself in the Western Reserve area of Ohio. Scott had the gift of expressing himself both as an orator and with the pen. The words of the *Christian Baptist* reverberated throughout the Midwestern area. The periodical denounced creeds and supported the union of Christian churches. It decried the pompous trappings of the clergy and called for a return to a belief in Christ. Such thoughts successfully penetrated the log meetinghouses on the frontier. Small voluntary groups were breaking away from both the Baptists and Presbyterians, especially in Ohio and Kentucky, and calling themselves Christians.

Campbell had become a student of the English Bible and published a new translation in 1827. His publishing business was so large that the federal government established a post office in Bethany, West Virginia, and made him postmaster. While the iconoclastic *Christian Baptist* delighted many, it outraged others. The opposition grew in intensity and Campbell's followers, though becoming more numerous, were left without formal church affiliation. The *Christian Baptist* was circulated for almost seven years and became the means by which Campbell reached thousands of readers. But it had served its purpose, and the time had come to bring his followers together under one banner. The *Christian Baptist* was discontinued in late 1829 and replaced with the *Millennia Harbinger*. The name had been suggested, in part, by Campbell's faithful follower, Walter Scott, as a harbinger of glad tidings.

Campbell travelled through most of the Ohio Valley states and became one of the best-known pioneer preachers. He carried the word of the Disciples of Christ into the sparsely settled areas. He was responsible for the building of many small country churches that served the religious and social needs of rural communities. As an example, Campbell visited Centerton, Indiana, on June 9, 1844, and officiated at the wedding of the writer's great-grandparents, John Scott and Mary Robb. After Campbell's visit, the community erected a new church and six years later, when John emigrated to Appanoose County, Iowa, while raising his log cabin he began construction of a new Campbellite church. Campbell's Reformation had a pronounced influence on pioneer society with a rapidly growing membership that reached three hundred thousand during his lifetime.

Campbell was aware that he needed trained disciples who could awaken the youth to the principles of the movement. After his debate in Cincinnati in 1837 with Catholic bishop John B. Purcell, he gave serious thought to establishing a school on his farm. For the next few years the school became the chief subject of conversation. A charter was granted to Bethany College in 1840, and the first class graduated in 1843. The Bible was one of the required textbooks. Campbell acted as president and taught classes in the Bible, moral philosophy and political economy.

Politically, Campbell was a reformer. He favored elimination of the poll tax, elimination of the property qualification for voting, and popular election of governors and county court justices, and he was antislavery. At the Virginia Constitutional Convention of 1829-1930, James Madison was asked to name the greatest man at the convention. Madison said, "the greatest man was Alexander Campbell.... His mastery of the great questions which came before us, his skill in debate, was a constant surprise." Though Campbell, in general, favored democracy he was, on the other hand, opposed to women's suffrage and believed that the owner of slaves was not a sinner. He supported free public schools, defended capital punishment and believed in the separation of church and state. He was an ardent supporter of the free enterprise system and had expanded a three-hundred-acre farm to one of fifteen hundred acres and had a net worth of two hundred thousand dollars at death. There were similarities between Jacksonian democracy and Campbell's practices and policies, but he objected to what he considered some of Jackson's excesses.

Campbell's success did not come quickly. The tempo of the movement was in general slow, but collectively was like an epidemic that refused to go away, infiltrating every hamlet on the frontier. He was the leader of a long campaign that ultimately formed the movement into the strongest indigenous American Christian Reformation. His stature has grown over time, and if he were still living he would be accorded a seat of preference in ecumenical councils.

HWS

References: Robert Richardson, *Memoirs of Alexander Campbell* (Cincinnati, Ohio: Standard, 1913); Perry E. Gresham et al., *The Sage of Bethany* (St. Louis, Mo.: Bethany Press, 1960); Louis Cochran and Bess White Cochran, *Captives of the World* (Garden City, N.Y.: Doubleday, 1969).

Benjamin Nathan Cardozo

(May 24, 1870—July 9, 1938)

Benjamin Cardozo was rated by Roscoe Pound, an eminent legal scholar himself, as one of the ten greatest judges produced by the American bench. The names included in the illustrious line, beginning with John Marshall, shared certain common characteristics, according to Pound: "First of all, they were great lawyers, masters of their craft, masters of the authoritative materials in which judges in the English-speaking world are expected, as a duty of their office, to find the grounds of decision, and masters of the technique of applying those materials to the decision of cases."

Cardozo's American ancestry antedates by well over a century the beginnings of the nation. Forebears on his mother's side came from Portugal to America in 1654. His paternal ancestors left the Spanish peninsula during the expulsion of the Jews in the sixteenth century, migrating first to Holland and then to England. The founder of the American line came to the Colonies about 1752. For the next two centuries the family produced a succession of distinguished patriots and cultural leaders.

The first of the Cardozos to gain prominence—though not honor—in judicial circles was Benjamin's father, who cast an unfortunate blight on the family name. Judge Albert Cardozo was a member of the infamous Tweed Ring in New York, where his conduct finally led to charges of malfeasance and corruption being filed against him; in order to escape impeachment he resigned. It has been remarked that much of Benjamin Cardozo's life was devoted to the atonement of his father's sins.

As a child Benjamin was taught by a tutor, Horatio Alger, who later became famous as the author of the most popular books for boys of the period, in all of which the hero triumphed over poverty and adversity by courage and hard work. Benjamin was a voracious reader of the Alger thrillers, and he credited his admittance to Columbia University at the early age of fifteen to the preparation for college received from Alger.

Cardozo's rise in the legal profession was rapid and brilliant. He served successively as a justice of the Supreme Court of New York, associate judge of the Court of Appeals, and finally as associate justice of the United States Supreme Court. Throughout his career his opinions, numbering some 470 in written form, were monuments of legal scholarship. Further, they are famous for literary style—in Santayana's words "clothed in a language that lends the message an intrinsic value, and makes it delightful to apprehend, apart from its importance in ultimate theory or practice."

Aside from the opinions, scattered through the *New York Reports* and *United States Reports* from 1914 to 1938, Cardozo's writings were not voluminous. Most widely known are four small books: *The Nature of the Judicial Process, The Growth of the Law, The Paradoxes of Legal Science*, and *Law and Literature*. It is generally agreed that the most original and significant of these works, the one exerting greatest influence on the legal profession and giving laymen the clearest insight into the workings of the law, is the first, *The Nature of the Judicial Process* (1921).

The extraordinary success of *The Nature of the Judicial Process* was due in part to the charm of the author's style, but more importantly to Cardozo's careful analysis of the factors, conscious and unconscious, which guide a judge in reaching his decisions.

As viewed by Cardozo, law is a living body of principles capable of growth and change. The assumption is erroneous, he declares, that law is unchangeable and everlasting. Nothing is stable or absolute, even principles. Decade by decade and century by century, law is being modified, with the result that "hardly a rule of today but may be matched by its opposite of yesterday." Most of the changes have been wrought by judges. Still, the search must go on for "the essential and the permanent" in the field of justice.

Four primary approaches, as applied to the judicial process, are analyzed in detail by Cardozo: (1) the method of philosophy or the rule of analogy; (2) the method of evolution or historical development; (3) the method of tradition or the customs of the community; and (4) the method of sociology or of justice, morals, and social welfare.

The position of property under the law is clarified by Cardozo. He points out that "property, like liberty, though immune under the Constitution from destruction, is not immune from regulation essential for the common good. What that regulation shall be, every generation must work out for itself." Property has a social function to perform and legislation toward that end is an appropriate exercise of governmental power.

Altogether in the field of law, Cardozo observes, "the tendency today is in the direction of a growing liberalism. The new spirit has made its way gradually; and its progress, unnoticed step by step, is visible in retrospect as we look back upon the distance traversed. The old forms remain, but they are filled with a new content."

In a separate chapter, Cardozo deals with "the judge as a legislator." Therein he finds that "in countless litigations, the law is so clear that judges have no discretion." Their right to legislate becomes evident when there are gaps in the law, and rules and precedents must be established. Certain general precepts, however, must be adhered to, Cardozo observes.

A majority of the cases which come before the courts can reasonably be decided only one way, in Cardozo's opinion. A small percentage, however, are less clear-cut, and "these are the cases where the creative element in the judicial process finds its opportunity and power ... where a decision one way or the other, will count for the future." It is in such instances that the judge assumes the role of a lawgiver. Looking back upon his own career, Cardozo recalls, "I was much troubled in spirit, in my first years upon the bench, to find how trackless was the ocean on which I had embarked. I sought for certainty. I was oppressed and disheartened when I found that the quest for it was futile.... I have become reconciled to the uncertainty, because I have grown to see it as inevitable."

Cardozo concedes that the power placed in the hands of judges is great and subject to possible abuse. He quotes Ehrlich to the effect that "there is no guaranty of justice except the personality of the judge." Below the more or less tangible factors which influence judgments are subconscious forces far more difficult to appraise. As expressed by Cardozo, "Deep below consciousness are other forces, the likes and the dislikes, the predilections and the prejudices, the complex of instincts and emotions and habits and convictions, which make the man, whether he be litigant or judge."

In conclusion, Cardozo cites with approval a statement by Theodore Roosevelt, "whose intuitions and perceptions were deep and brilliant," in the author's eyes: "The chief lawmakers in our country may be, and often are, the judges, because they are the final seat of authority. Every time they interpret contract, vested right, due process of law, liberty, they necessarily enact into law parts of a system of social philosophy; and as such interpretation is fundamental, they give direction to all law-making."

Benjamin Cardozo is most frequently described, with Oliver Wendell Holmes, as one of the two preeminent American judges of the past fifty years. Cardozo's enduring reputation will doubtless be as an interpreter of the common law. In reviewing *Selected Writings of Benjamin Nathan Cardozo*, published posthumously, Newman Levy concluded that "no judge in our history, with the possible exception of Holmes, offered such a rare combination of legal erudition, judicial poise, and broad, humanistic culture." These qualities are demonstrated on every page of *The Nature of the Judicial Process*.

RBD

References: George S. Hellman, *Benjamin N. Cardozo* (New York: McGraw, 1940); James P. Polland, *Mr. Justice Cardozo* (New York: Yorktown Press, 1935).

Christopher (Kit) Carson
(December 24, 1809 — May 22, 1868)

With the possible exception of Daniel Boone, no American scout, guide, or Indian fighter is better known than Christopher "Kit" Carson. From early youth until he was appointed a brevet brigadier general and commandant at Fort Garland, Colorado, in 1866, he was a trapper, frontiersman, and army guide. Myths have arisen about him as they did about Boone, but in most cases the stories concerning Carson have a strong basis in reality. His home in Taos, New Mexico, still attracts visitors.

Carson was born in Madison County, Kentucky, December 24, 1809, the birth year of Lincoln. The Carson family, with ten children, moved to the Boone's Lick district of Missouri in 1811. The boy, who never had any schooling, was apprenticed to a saddler but in 1826 he ran away from home and joined a trading caravan bound for Santa Fe. Subsequently he moved to Taos, which remained his headquarters for most of his life. In 1829 he joined a party of trappers and entered the fur trade; before he returned to his home he had crossed the Mojave Desert and got his first glimpse of California. In 1831 a larger trapping group recruited him and he joined a party led by Thomas Fitzpatrick of the Rocky Mountain Fur Company. It was during this period that he was involved in a battle with the Blackfeet in which he was severely wounded. For the next ten years he was active in the fur trade in the region which now includes the states of Utah, Wyoming, Idaho, and Montana. About 1836 he contracted an Indian marriage with an Arapaho girl, who bore him a daughter, and after the mother's death he married a New Mexican woman named Maria Jaramillo who owned some land.

By chance he was a passenger on a steamboat on the Missouri River in 1842 and a fellow traveler was John C. Frémont, the explorer and politician. This meeting changed the course of his life. Frémont, bound for a survey of the Oregon Trail, recruited Carson as his guide and the party followed the Platte River Valley, traversed South Pass, and explored the Wind River Range. Subsequently Carson accompanied Frémont in 1843 in an expedition which took him to Utah and California. On Frémont's third expedition in 1845 Carson again served as guide and participated in the conquest of California. Thereafter he carried dispatches to Washington and met with President James K. Polk.

When the United States Senate refused to confirm a commission for Carson in the regular army, he settled down on a profitable sheep ranch near Taos. One of his exploits during this somewhat sedentary period in his life was to escort a herd of sixty-five hundred sheep to California where they were sold. For some seven years he acted as a federal Indian agent for the Ute tribes and won the esteem of all who dealt with him for his honesty and responsibility. At the outbreak of the Civil War Carson resigned his position and organized and led the First New Mexican Volunteer Infantry. He participated in the battle of Valverde and also campaigned against the hostile Mescalero Apaches, the Navajos, and the Comanches. Shortly after the federal government finally gave him a regular army appointment, Carson's health began to fail. He died in Boggsville, Colorado, May 23, 1868.

Although he loomed large on the western horizon, Carson was a small man with light brown hair and blue eyes. Bernard De Voto, in recounting a fur trade rendezvous in which Carson killed a bully, called him "five-feet-four but cougar all the way." Although Carson was slight in stature De Voto's description is probably an exaggeration. He was certainly unlike the familiar image of the mountain man, who was generally known as energetic and competent but coarse, rough-spoken, and contumacious. Carson on the other hand was modest, given to few words, and respected for his integrity. He was illiterate for most of his life but at the very end he had learned to read a little and write his name. This limitation undoubtedly accounted for his failure to achieve early promotion in the army.

In 1858 he dictated his autobiography to a friendly army surgeon, Lieutenant Colonel De Witt C. Peters, who published a much amplified version of the manuscript. The amanuensis or editor who inflated the original manuscript and prettified the style is still not identified. But the volume carefully edited by M. M. Quaife for the Lakeside Classics in 1935 is readable and fully annotated. This autobiography is still the main source for the facts of Carson's life, although later biographers have filled in the gaps and corrected some of the chronology.

JTF

References: W. J. Ghent, *DAB*, III, 1929, pp. 530-32; Edwin L. Sabin, *Kit Carson Days* (Chicago: McClurg, 1914; reissued 1935); Stanley Vestal, *Kit Carson: The Happy Warrior of the Old West* (Boston and New York: Houghton Mifflin, 1928)

Mary Cassatt

(May 22, 1844 — June 14, 1926)

Generally identified as the foremost American woman painter, Mary Cassatt lived an unusual professional and artistic life. A member of a prominent Philadelphia family, she spent most of her adult years abroad and was associated with the French impressionist school of painting more than with any American movement. A modest inheritance allowed her to study art and even to buy some paintings. She never married and she lived with her parents in Paris. Her mother's semi-invalidism for many years produced domestic problems. Although she joined the French impressionist group, chiefly through her friendship with Edgar Degas, and contributed her work to several of their exhibitions, she frequently refused to enter competitions and rejected honors offered to her. She was adept in creating etchings and pastels but probably is best known now for her numerous paintings of mothers and infant children. Major museums today exhibit her work.

Mary Cassatt was born in Allegheny City, Pennsylvania, to a family which claimed descent from a seventeenth century French émigré to the United States, but the family had a mixture of Dutch and Scotch-Irish blood strains. Her father, Robert Cassatt, was a moderately successful Philadelphia businessman who was involved in various real estate transactions and eventually decided to live as a gentleman abroad. Her brother Alexander Cassatt, trained as a civil engineer, became president of the Pennsylvania Railroad, enjoyed affluence, and through the aid of Mary became both a connoisseur and a collector of paintings. Brother and sister remained very close and the Alexander Cassatt family frequently visited Mary in France.

In 1851 Mary was taken to Europe by her parents and first saw Paris, eventually her permanent home, at the age of seven. Before returning to Philadelphia in 1855 the family spent time in Heidelberg and Darmstadt. When Mary evinced a strong interest in art she was sent to the only art school in Philadelphia, the Pennsylvania Academy of the Fine Arts. After some years of study there, 1861-1866, much of it limited to copying plaster casts and old masters, she pleaded to be allowed to continue her training in Europe. Robert Cassatt finally consented and his daughter spent time in both Italy and Spain, including some eight months in Parma where she concentrated on Correggio and visits to the Prado in Madrid and to Antwerp so that she could follow the career of Rubens. To escape the turmoil of the Franco-Prussian War she returned to the United States and visited Philadelphia and Chicago, where she lost several early pictures in the great fire of 1871. But by 1874 she had settled permanently in Paris with her family. Much later when her own paintings began to sell she was able to buy with her own funds a seventeenth-century manor house, the Chateau de Beaufresne, at Mesnil-Théribus, which became her country residence and where she died in 1926.

Cassatt was less interested in the old masters than she was in contemporary work and through Degas she made a kind of commitment to impressionism, eventually advising American collectors to purchase paintings by the group. Painters like Manet, Monet, Pissarro, Courbet, and Puvis de Chavannes were among her friends, and she owned works by Degas, Monet, and Pissarro. She also knew the American artist, James McNeill Whistler, in Paris. The Fourth Impressionistic Exhibition, held in Paris in 1879, included the canvas by Cassatt called *La Loge*. The subject was a girl with orange-red hair, wearing a pink evening dress, and sitting in an opera box. Behind her, partly obscured by her figure, can be seen the sweep of the seats. The girl, radiant and obviously pleased, seems to be more American than French. The painting is probably Cassatt's best impressionistic canvas. But she did send later pictures to four other impressionist exhibitions.

There were other exhibits too. The first major American impressionist show held in New York in 1886 included two Cassatt paintings, both owned by her brother. The artist exhibited canvases in Philadelphia, New York, and Boston. In 1891 she was invited to contribute a mural to the Woman's Building at the Columbian Exposition, initiated two years later, and she was paid three thousand dollars including her fee and expenses. The Parisian art dealer, Durand-Ruel, mounted an important exhibition of her work in 1893 which included ninety-eight items with seventeen paintings, fourteen pastels, and miscellaneous prints. Among the pictures were two now in the Boston Museum of Fine Arts (*A Cup of Tea* and *At the Opera*), one in the Metropolitan Museum (*The Cup of Tea*), and one at the Chicago Art Institute (*The Bath*). One honor which she received with gratification came in 1904 when she was named a chevalier of the Légion d'Honneur by her adopted country. And in 1914 the Pennsylvania Academy of the Fine Arts awarded her its Gold Medal of Honor for eminent services to the institution.

Cassatt returned to the United States twice in the latter part of her life for brief visits, once in 1898 and again in 1908. But she had domestic and personal afflictions. Her mother died in 1895 freeing the daughter from what had become an onerous duty. And in 1906 her brother Alexander, who had meant so much to her, also died. She herself did not enjoy good health. When she was invited to join a yacht cruise on the Mediterranean she had to terminate the trip because she became violently seasick. In her youth she had liked horseback riding and in France she had maintained a riding horse, but in 1888 she suffered a severe fall which dislocated her shoulder and broke the tibia of her right leg so that she had to forego one of her chief pleasures. She was also afflicted with eye trouble, was burdened by cataracts, and became virtually blind so that reading as well as painting eventually became impossible. In her final years at Mesnil-Théribus she became querulous and vindictive.

Cassatt's services to the world of art were multiple. She advised American collectors like her close friends the Henry Osborne Havemeyers. She urged the Chicago Art Institute to purchase one of its famous canvases, the El Greco *Assumption*. She became interested in Japanese art, publicized it as much as she could, and bought prints for her own walls by Utamaro and Hokusai. Her contacts with the French impressionists resulted in the purchase by American museums of many of these paintings. She also produced color prints, aquatints, and about a hundred dry points.

Some Cassatt canvases are remarkably colorful, notably the early Spanish painting *Toreador* and the 1893 *The Boating Party* (now in the National Gallery at Washington). But her name is generally associated with domestic pictures, paintings of mothers and babies, in soft colors and romanticized if not sentimentalized. Samuel Isham pointed out that although Cassatt drew well and showed a true feeling for arrangement, her color was often "made up of subdued whites and grays and pale, sad tones." Moreover, she gave "stubby toes and pudgy noses" to the babies which she painted so frequently. Many of her subjects were infants just before or after the bath and held in the arms of doting mothers who glanced down at their offspring. Even the charming *Woman and Child Driving* of 1880 shows the proud mother on display. She did not paint men well, the stiff portrait of her brother and nephew being a good example, and she generally refrained from trying. Although she painted what she wished, her subject matter might explain the fact that she never achieved the artistic recognition that her training, her devotion to her profession, and her innate ability merited.

In 1927, a year after her death, the Pennsylvania Museum held a memorial exhibition of the work of Mary Cassatt. It included forty oils and pastels, fifteen water colors and drawings, and over one hundred prints. But her declining reputation seems partly confirmed by the failure of Oliver W. Larkin even to mention her in his study *Art and Life in America* of 1949.

JTF

References: Helen Wright, *DAB*, III, 1929, pp. 567-68; Frederick A. Sweet, *Miss Mary Cassatt, Impressionist from Pennsylvania* (Norman: University of Oklahoma Press, 1966).

Willa Sibert Cather

(December 7, 1873 — April 24, 1947)

One of the major American novelists of the twentieth century, Willa Cather became celebrated for her treatment of rural and small town life in pioneer Nebraska and for her sensitive characterizations of feminine protagonists. She wrote with sympathy and understanding and she was frugal in her descriptions. A well-known essay, "The Novel Démeublé," published in *Not Under Forty* in 1936, expressed her distaste for the excessive documentation of the naturalistic school and her rejection of the piling up of facts which she deemed redundant and even irrelevant. Her own short stories and novels were generally concise and carefully wrought.

Willa Sibert Cather was born in Virginia, December 7, 1873. Her middle name, which was not conferred on her at birth, she chose in middle life to honor her grandmother. Her father, Charles Cather, had studied law but was a sheep farmer in Virginia and later for a brief period in Nebraska. When he settled his family in Red Cloud, Nebraska, he became a real estate and insurance agent. Willa was only nine when the Cathers moved west, and although she did not forget her Virginia heritage she became more familiar and more intimate with the Nebraska prairies. The town of Red Cloud, on the Burlington Railroad and in the Republican River Valley, was her home for many years, and projected imaginatively it served as the model for several of the writer's fictional communities. Readers of her stories will recognize it whether it is called Black Hawk, Sweet Water, or Haverford. In Red Cloud she attended public schools and benefited from perceptive teachers and extensive reading. Her family was bookish and the young girl read nineteenth century and earlier literature without leaving the house. One of her favorite novels, published in the year she left Virginia, was *Huckleberry Finn*.

For a small provincial town Red Cloud was culturally unusual. It even had an opera house where road companies performed. But the first great change in Willa Cather's life occurred in 1890 when she moved to the state capital, Lincoln, to attend the University of Nebraska. Because her high school training had been limited she was compelled to spend another year in preparation before admission to the university was granted; she did not graduate until 1895. But she profited from the extra time in Lincoln. She attended the local theaters, continued to read widely, and began to express herself in essays. Originally she had been attracted to science and once thought seriously of studying medicine, but when her teachers encouraged her to write for publication she changed her goal. She contributed to the undergraduate magazine and in time she wrote dramatic criticism for the *Lincoln Journal*. Success in journalism won her a minor reputation, and in 1896 she had the good luck to get an editorial position with a small magazine in Pittsburgh. The steel city remained her home for some ten years, during which time she free-lanced, served as copy editor and drama and music critic for the *Pittsburgh Daily Leader* from 1897 to 1901, taught Latin and English at the Pittsburgh Central High School and the Allegheny High School, and began to contribute to national magazines. Although Willa Cather was never widely known as a poet she did publish verse in various periodicals and in 1903 a collection of her poems became her first published book, *April Twilights*. More important is the fact that national magazines like *Cosmopolitan*, the *Overland Monthly*, the *Library*, and the *Saturday Evening Post* had begun to accept her stories.

Another crucial event in her life occurred in 1903, a meeting with the publisher S. S. McClure. He offered to publish her stories in book form and to accept her future work. *The Troll Garden*, appearing in 1905, included some of her best writing, for example, "The Sculptor's Funeral," "Paul's Case," and "A Wagner Matinee." But McClure also offered to Cather a staff position, which she accepted promptly, and from 1906 to 1912 she was managing editor of *McClure's Magazine*. Thus at thirty-three she finally had a stable position, an adequate salary, and some literary fame. But as James Woodress points out, this success had its cost since in her editorial years she wrote very little fiction. But she also in these years emerged from the influence of Henry James, and eventually found her true metier when she began to use the Nebraska material.

With the publication of her first novel, *Alexander's Bridge*, in 1912, Willa Cather decided to give up journalism and devote herself to creative writing. Eleven novels were to follow as well as several volumes of short fiction and criticism. Some of her strongest work dealt with the Nebraska background and especially the immigrant groups who sometimes had trouble adapting to the life of pioneer farmers. Later in her career she turned to historical themes and achieved her greatest success with *Death Comes for the Archbishop*, 1927, the story of two French missionary priests who built a diocese in New Mexico.

O Pioneers, 1913, chronicles the life of Alexandra Bergson, daughter of a Swedish immigrant, who assumes the management of the family farm and through determination and hard work succeeds. Her optimism is rewarded and at the end of the novel she is not only prosperous but reunited with a male admirer.

The heroine of *My Ántonia*, 1918, is of Bohemian parentage and also has a rural background. But Antonia Shimerda works as a domestic in the neighboring town where she has an unfortunate relationship with a railroad conductor who deserts her and her child. Twenty years later when the narrator of the story, Jim Burden, returns to Nebraska, he finds Ántonia happily married to a Czech farmer and the mother of a large family. Ántonia, like Alexandra Bergson, has strength and courage as well as the ability to laugh in times of despair. *Song of the Lark*, 1915, also has a female protagonist who overcomes early adversity. But Thea Kronborg, daughter of a Swedish minister, has musical ability and soon escapes the small Colorado town where she grew up. Her career takes her to Chicago and to Europe and she ends her life as a Wagnerian soprano in the Metropolitan Opera. All three novels are largely success stories with the heroines emerging from obscure beginnings because of determination, strength, and faith.

A Lost Lady, 1923, tells a somewhat different story. Marian Forrester is young and charming but married to a retired railroad builder and wealthy pioneer. He is devoted to her but accustomed to a different life. Both find life in Sweet Water dull and Mrs. Forrester acquires a lover. When her husband dies after a paralytic stroke she finds herself in financial straits and must sell her beautiful home. Little is heard of her thereafter; she is lost physically and morally, much to the distress of a young neighbor lad through whom the story unfolds.

Two other novels deserve mention before those in which she turned to history. *One of Ours*, 1922, about a young Nebraskan who served in World War I, won a Pulitzer Prize for the author but was generally not well received. Her subject in this case was beyond her experience. Much more interesting, though a flawed novel, is *The Professor's House*, 1925, the story of Professor St. Peter and a brilliant student Tom Outland. The professor is curiously like Willa Cather herself in family background and indulges in certain romantic dreams which were the author's own. But the interpolated tale of Tom Outland's discovery of a remote Indian pueblo in New Mexico is never well integrated with the novel and occupies seventy-four pages of a short book.

Willa Cather's decision in middle age to choose topics from nineteenth century New Mexico and late seventeenth century Quebec suggests that she had exhausted her rich memory of the Nebraska prairies and that she was deliberately turning her back on contemporary life. About this time she made the well-known remark that the world had broken in two for her about 1922; she obviously preferred the first part. She also had fallen in love with the American Southwest and to some extent with French Canada; these were both romantic spots colored by time and distance. She had only to populate them and fill in the background. Both *Death Comes for the Archbishop* and *Shadows on the Rock*, 1931, were popular successes, and the first, based on the career of the historical Archbishop Lamy, is probably her masterpiece. Certainly it remains her most distinguished stylistic achievement.

In the closing years of her life Willa Cather became less productive and late novels like *Lucy Gayheart*, 1935, and *Sapphira and the Slave Girl*, 1940, added little to her reputation. She lived in an apartment on Park Avenue in New York City and saw a good deal of old friends like Edith Lewis and Dorothy Canfield Fisher. Summers she spent in Jaffrey, New Hampshire, and there she died on April 24, 1947. Her will stipulated that no collection of her letters could be published and she herself burned most of her correspondence. In 1970 William M. Curtin edited in two volumes *The World and the Parish: Willa Cather's Articles and Reviews*, so that much of her early journalistic writing is available to biographers who were deprived of more personal material.

JTF

References: E. K. Brown, *Willa Cather: A Critical Biography* (New York: Knopf, 1953), completed by Leon Edel; James Woodress, *Willa Cather, Her Life and Work* (New York: Pegasus, 1970); Leon Edel, in *Notable American Women, 1607-1950*, vol. I, pp. 305-8 (Cambridge, Mass.: Belknap Press of Harvard, 1971).

Carrie Chapman Catt

(January 9, 1859—March 9, 1947)

Carrie Chapman Catt belonged to the small group of indomitable American women—Susan B. Anthony, Elizabeth Cady Stanton, Julia Ward Howe, Lucy Stone, and others—who agitated, demonstrated and propagandized until the Nineteenth Amendment, extending voting rights to women, was added to the U.S. Constitution in 1920.

Carrie was born in Ripon, Wisconsin, and early showed herself to be a high-spirited, ambitious, and intellectually precocious girl. In the process of earning a bachelor of science degree at Iowa State College, she followed a curriculum emphasizing science courses. As she became thoroughly acquainted with the theories of Darwin and Spencer, Carrie developed a belief in evolutionary progress through social change, which remained her lifelong philosophy. Her original ambition was to prepare for a legal career, but she was diverted from that idea, first by serving as principal of the Mason City high school, followed by the superintendency of the Mason City schools, and then marriage to Leo Chapman, owner and editor of the *Mason City Republican*.

As assistant editor of her husband's newspaper, Carrie attended the 1885 meeting of the Iowa Suffrage Association and quickly became converted to the suffrage cause. The following year, on a visit to California, her husband contracted and died of typhoid fever. Carrie found work on a San Francisco trade paper and witnessed firsthand the exploitation of working women. She resolved to devote the rest of her life to the emancipation of her sex. On returning to Iowa, she became recording secretary of the Iowa Suffrage Association. Four years after her first husband's death, she married George W. Catt, a civil engineer who strongly supported his wife's activities in the suffrage reform movement.

Carrie Chapman Catt began to extend her work to the national scene when she was sent to Washington, D.C., in 1890 as an Iowa delegate to the historic convention which led to the organization of the National American Woman Suffrage Association. There she met Susan B. Anthony, who recognized in her a valuable recruit and arranged for her to campaign in South Dakota for an approaching suffrage referendum. After 1892, the Catts lived in New York City.

His death in 1905 left her financially independent and free to devote the rest of her life to the suffrage movement.

From 1890 to 1895 Carrie Chapman Catt participated in a series of state suffrage referenda and congressional hearings on the federal suffrage amendment, working closely with Susan Anthony. A national organization committee was set up in 1895 to intensify support for woman suffrage. Mrs. Catt showed her genius for organization by directing operations, training and sending out organizers to establish new branches, raising funds, and related activities. When Susan Anthony, in her eightieth year, retired from the presidency in 1900, she chose Carrie Chapman Catt as her successor.

As president of the National American Woman Suffrage Association, Carrie Chapman Catt emphasized political action in such matters as the direct primary, the initiative and referendum, and civil service reform. She influenced outstanding women like Florence Kelley and Jane Addams to become active in suffrage work. A highly disciplined organization succeeded in enfranchising the women of New York state in 1917.

During this period, Mrs. Catt began to turn her attention to international feminism. As president of the International Woman Suffrage Alliance, established at Berlin in 1904, she presided over congresses in Copenhagen (1906), London (1908), Amsterdam (1909), Stockholm (1911), and Budapest (1913). In company with the Dutch feminist Dr. Aletta Jacobs, she toured the world in 1911-1913, organizing feminists in several Asian and African countries. Her global travels were rounded out in 1922-1923 by an organizing trip to South American countries, where women were not yet enfranchised.

The coming of World War I in 1914 was a major setback for international feminism. It diverted attention by Mrs. Catt and such other leaders as Jane Addams to working for world peace.

By popular demand, Carrie Chapman Catt returned to the presidency of the National American Woman Suffrage Association in 1915. The strategy decided upon was to intensify pressure on Congress to pass the federal amendment, pressure on state legislatures to grant women the right to vote for presidential electors, and pressure to vote in primaries. Both parties included suffrage planks in their platforms in the 1916 election. An important convert to the course was Woodrow Wilson, who by 1918 was giving woman suffrage his unqualified support. With funds provided by a million dollar bequest, a nationwide educational and publicity campaign was launched. On January 10, 1918, the federal amendment passed the House of Representatives and was endorsed by the Senate on June 4, 1919. Fourteen additional months were required before ratification was obtained from two-thirds of the states. The amendment became part of the Constitution on August 26, 1920.

At the 1919 convention of the National American Woman Suffrage Association, Mrs. Catt proposed to organize a league to provide the final push for the equal rights amendment and to prepare women to play a political role. A year later the National League of Women Voters was established under her leadership.

Following the successful outcome of the long, drawn-out fight for women's suffrage, Mrs. Catt turned her attention to writing and speaking on behalf of the League of Nations. In 1921, she urged the League of Women Voters to organize the sentiment for peace existing among women and to increase public understanding of the need for international cooperation to prevent war. Under her inspiration, leaders of nine organizations signed a call for a conference on the Cause and

Cure of War, which met in Washington in 1925 and annually thereafter until 1939. Mrs. Catt remained chairman of the conference committee until 1933.

Carrie Chapman Catt's last major project was the Women's Centennial Exposition, held in New York in 1940, honoring distinguished women in a hundred professions that had not been open to women a century earlier. Eight years later, at age eighty-eight, she died of a heart attack in her home near Ossining, New York.

Mrs. Catt was one of the most admired women of her time. By general consent, she and Susan B. Anthony stand together as having made the greatest contributions to the emancipation of women.

RBD

Reference: Mary Gray Peck, *Carrie Chapman Catt* (New York: H. W. Wilson, 1944).

John Chapman

(September 26, 1774 — March 18, 1845)

American history has spawned a number of folk heroes, most of whom have benefited from a sparseness of fact and a plethora of myth or legend. There is no better example than Johnny Appleseed, the famous alias of John Chapman, who has been credited with planting apple trees from Pennsylvania to Indiana and has become the patron saint of pomology. In the words of Benjamin Botkin, Chapman "occupies a unique place in the pantheon of folk heroes—the poetic symbol of spiritual pioneering, of self-abnegation combined with service." Although Chapman's wanderings have never been completely mapped and he has been credited with establishing orchards which he never began, his personality has become a permanent part of the memory of the American people. Poems, plays, and stories have been written about him, and the spirit of the man whom Vachel Lindsay described ("And he ran with the rabbit and slept with the stream") survives.

Chapman was born in Leominster, Massachusetts, September 26, 1774. His father, a carpenter and farmer, was a Minute Man in the Revolution and later a soldier in the Continental Army. After the mother died while Chapman was still a youth, his father remarried and raised another family. Little is known about the boy's adolescence but he began his wanderings early and by 1797 he turned up in northwestern Pennsylvania, already accustomed to life in the wilderness. He early claimed land but as in later years neglected to obtain a deed for it. He was never the pauper that legend sometimes makes him, but he was careless about purchasing or leasing land and it was only in late maturity that he could claim ownership of some twelve hundred acres. As a young bachelor in the Allegheny country he was voluble and active but he did not talk about apples. It was somewhat later that he began to collect apple seeds from the Pennsylvania cider mills and proceeded westward to plant them.

An early article by W. D. Haley in *Harper's New Monthly Magazine* for November 1871 brought together many of the facts about Chapman's career and also provided details about his appearance and exploits that have surfaced in later accounts. At least once he roped two canoes together, filled them with apple seeds, and drifted down the Ohio River as far as Marietta, then turned north on the Muskingum River and headed into north central Ohio. This 1806 voyage was unique since subsequently he filled leather saddlebags with a similar cargo and employed a horse or he carried the burden himself. Appleseed's appearance generally created an impression. His clothes were ragged but usually clean. He sometimes wore a coffee sack with holes for the neck and arms to which he would add cast-off clothing secured in a trade for apple seedlings. He frequently walked barefoot, even in winter, and although for a time he used a tin mush pot for a hat he finally devised a pasteboard contrivance with a large peak in front which shaded his eyes from the sun. Personal descriptions are contradictory and inaccurate. He apparently was a slight, rather small man, with either blue or black eyes, and a scraggly black beard.

Chapman had another motive in his peregrinations through Ohio and Indiana. He was a convert to the mystical theology of Emanuel Swedenborg, and he would stop at various cabins and read excerpts to his surprised audience or sometimes tear sections out of his books and leave them for later collection. He was also known for his gentleness and unwillingness to hurt man or beast. He would avoid killing even snakes or mosquitoes and once apparently slept on the ground so that he would not disturb a bear ensconced in a nearby hollow log. His tastes were as simple as his garb. He lived off the country and was always welcome as a visitor. Tradition has it that in the troublesome Indian wars of the first decade of the nineteenth century, he more than once warned frontiersmen of imminent raids by savage war parties. On the other hand, he experienced no difficulty with the Indians. They looked upon him calmly and did not interfere with his wanderings or with his planting of apple trees.

Robert Price in his biography of Johnny Appleseed has attempted to map his subject's journeyings and has incorporated substantial evidence about routes and places. Long after Appleseed's death settlers in Illinois, Iowa, and Michigan were claiming that the primitive horticulturist had visited their states and had planted seeds that eventually proved productive. It is extremely doubtful that Chapman ever ventured across the Ohio or the Wabash rivers. But he knew central and northern Ohio intimately and frequently went into northeastern Indiana. He acquired land in Richland County, near Mount Vernon, Ohio, and he used the towns of Perrysville and Mansfield as his basis of operation from 1810 to 1830. In 1836 he purchased land in Allen and Jay counties, Indiana, not far from Fort Wayne. Indeed he died near Fort Wayne on March 18, 1845.

Most American folk heroes, real or mythical, tend to be blustering, aggressive figures, swashbuckling and domineering. One thinks of Mike Fink, Paul Bunyan, Davy Crockett, and John Henry. In contrast Johnny Appleseed was a mild, kindly, benevolent figure whose greatest error was his inadvertent scattering of fennel in the farmyards of the Middle West on the supposition that it might help cure malaria. Although his favorite apple was the Rambo, he never grafted a tree and he had nothing to do with the establishment of particular kinds of apples. But even if he did not always succeed in planting orchards which survived, he certainly made pioneer farmers aware at a critical time of the need to plant for the future.

JTF

References: Donald C. Peattie, *DAB*, IV, 1930, pp. 17-18; Benjamin A. Botkin, *A Treasury of American Folklore*, Botkin includes the W. H. Haley essay, pp. 261-70 (Garden City, N.Y.: Garden City Books, 1951); Robert Price, *Johnny Appleseed, Man and Myth* (Bloomington, Ind.: Indiana University Press, 1954).

Frederic Edwin Church

(May 4, 1826 — April 7, 1900)

A painter usually identified with the Hudson River School and an artist admired for his monumental landscapes, Frederic Edwin Church came to prominence after the Civil War. Although like Winslow Homer he was not trained in Europe, he traveled extensively in both North and South America as well as in the Near East and chose boreal as well as tropical landscapes to paint. Long after his death his painting *Icebergs*, which had remained unidentified in a reformatory in Manchester, England, was sold at auction at the Sotheby Parke-Bernet galleries in New York City for the sum of $2.5 million. This sale in October, 1979, marked the highest price ever paid for an American painting up to that time.

Church was born in Hartford, Connecticut, in 1826. He early showed skill in drawing, and after being taught by local artists he was sent for further instruction to Thomas Cole in 1844 and actually lived in Cole's home in Catskill, New York. At the age of nineteen Church exhibited some of his work at the National Academy of Design, and in 1846 with the financial aid of his father he opened a studio in the Art Union Building of New York City. Full membership in the National Academy of Design was accorded him in 1847. Reading Alexander von Humboldt's account of travels in South America interested him in that continent, and he consequently spent some time in Ecuador, actually living in the house that Humboldt had occupied in Quito. In 1859 a journey along the coasts of Labrador and Newfoundland permitted him to study the formation of icebergs at close hand and provided material that some years later he employed in some of his most successful paintings. His large oblong canvas measuring seven feet by three feet entitled *Niagara* was exhibited at the Paris International Exhibition in 1867 and won him a medal. The picture, which has been called the most satisfactory painting of the great cataract, was afterwards sold for $12,500. The next year Church made his only trip to Europe and the eastern Mediterranean; he actually preferred the second half of his journey.

In June of 1869 Church married Isabel Carnes and shortly thereafter he began to build a villa for his family which he called Olana and which was located directly across the Hudson River from Cole's home at Catskill. It was an eclectic structure which incorporated elements from Church's recent travels in Syria, Palestine, and Greece. Olana included turrets which resembled minarets, while a large square tower provided a fine view of the river and mountains. The architecture revealed other oriental aspects, and the rooms held inlaid tables, wrought-metal hanging lamps, and tiled fireplaces which exhibited Church's interest in collecting Near Eastern objets d'art.

When the painter came to memorialize the exotic scenes he had visited, especially those in South America, he produced enormous canvases, for example, *The Mountains of Ecuador, View of Cotopaxi*, and *The Heart of the Andes*. Two paintings, *Chimborazo*, Church's delineation of the twenty thousand foot Ecuadorian peak, and *The Parthenon* were exhibited at the Philadelphia Centennial Exposition in 1876. When Mark Twain, a friend of Church, saw *The Heart of the Andes* in St. Louis, he was struck by the extraordinary details, including ferns and leaves on tropical plants, and he could only gasp while striving to take in the wonder of the whole.

Church had a wide group of friends, including Theodore Winthrop, a minor novelist who was his frequent fishing companion, William J. Stillman, a landscape artist, and Louis Moreau Gottschalk, the Creole composer of New Orleans. Church was also a member of a group of artists and businessmen who organized the Metropolitan Museum of Art in New York City in 1870. It was certainly appropriate that after Church's death in 1900 the Metropolitan organized a memorial exhibition of his work.

In his late years Church was unable to continue his work. Inflammatory rheumatism afflicted his right arm and hand and made further painting impossible. He spent part of his time in Mexico. Church was an accomplished draftsman with a gift for incorporating details into a unified composition. But the enormous size of some of his paintings seemed less impressive as tastes changed; moreover, he was inclined to fill up superfluous space with plumes of smoke, rainbows, and reflected sunsets. On the other hand, the huge bulk of the icebergs he depicted and their frozen white horror, much like Melville's hideous white whale, won attention well into the twentieth century.

JTF

References: Robert J. Wickenden, *DAB*, IV, 1930, p. 101; David C. Huntington, *The Landscapes of Frederic E. Church: Visions of an American Era* (New York: Braziller, 1966).

George Rogers Clark

(November 19, 1752 — February 13, 1818)

One of the important aspects of the Revolutionary War was the campaign in the West led by George Rogers Clark. The area that became Ohio, Kentucky, Indiana, Michigan, Wisconsin and Illinois was occupied by Indian tribes supported by the British. The remainder of the continent was claimed by foreign nations, primarily Britain, France and Spain. Washington's army had all it could do east of the Allegheny Mountains and could not defend the western frontier. At the beginning of the war the British recognized the importance of establishing control of the area lying between the Appalachian Mountains and the Mississippi River. Their natural allies were the Indian tribes. Lieutenant Governor Henry Hamilton was appointed by the British to organize an aggressive campaign from the Detroit headquarters. Clark was commissioned to carry out the defense of the vast area, but had only a handful of men under his command. The region was sparsely settled by white people and difficult to defend. Kentuckians were concentrated at Boonesborough, Harrodsburg and Logan's Fort, but English or French occupied Vincennes, Cahokia, Kaskaskia, and Detroit. The Continental Congress was engrossed with the problems of a new government as well as the need to support Washington by raising money and supplying him with soldiers. The Congress had little to offer in the way of military support for the Northwest Territory, and it was due to Clark's initiative that Patrick Henry, governor of Virginia, gave him the authority to act against the British. His conquest of a large area with only a few men aided in solidifying the American claim to the Northwest Territory.

Clark was the descendent of sturdy Virginia pioneers. Though born near Charlottesville, he grew up on a farm in Caroline County. His formal education was very limited, and whatever he learned was acquired mostly through individual effort. His grandfather taught him how to make land surveys, one of the income-producing vocations in a pioneer society. A strong six-foot youth with red hair, his courage and love for adventure were soon recognized, and at age twenty he first went down the Ohio River to the mouth of the Kanawha to locate desirable land for settlement. The following year he explored the Ohio River area as far as three hundred miles below Pittsburgh, spending the winter with a companion at the mouth of Fish Creek. Later, as farmers moved into the area, he acted as surveyor. His leadership was acknowledged in 1774 when he was appointed captain of militia serving in Lord Dunmore's War with the Indians.

Subsequently Clark made his way in 1775 to the interior of Kentucky as a surveyor for the Ohio Company and was immediately accepted by Kentuckians as one of their leaders. He corresponded with Patrick Henry and encouraged him to include Kentucky under the protection of Virginia. He supported the development of law and order through the development of government and opposed Judge Richard Henderson's attempt to establish the claims of the Transylvania Company over a vast portion of Kentucky. The squabble over land claims caused Clark to return to Virginia in the spring of 1776 in an attempt to convince the Virginia Council to support Kentucky. He told the Council "if a Cuntrey was not worth protecting it was not worth Claiming." The veiled threat had the desired effect, and the Council awarded him 500 pounds of powder to be delivered to Fort Pitt. The powder allotment was a timely gift, because the Indians were stepping up their attacks on white settlements at the instigation of the British from their Detroit headquarters. Clark, now at Harrodsburg, decided that the only way to protect the new settlements was to go on the offense. It was suicidal to wait for the Indians to attack at their leisure. Therefore, he established a spy system that furnished him information concerning the defenses of Cahokia, Kaskaskia and Vincennes.

In October of 1777 Clark returned to Virginia for supplies and to convince Patrick Henry of the necessity of a campaign in the West. It was a propitious time because General Burgoyne had recently surrendered to General Gates at Saratoga and Thomas Jefferson and Henry were optimistic. Clark was made a lieutenant colonel and guaranteed generous land grants to men who might enlist under his command. The Assembly approved the new force designed to defend Kentucky but, in fact, was organized to invade territory and carry the war in the West to the enemy. The public order read in part, "proceed to Kentucky & there to obey such orders & Directions as you shall give them." The secret order read, "attack the British post at Kaskasky."

By June 24, 1778, after rounding up some deserters, Clark was ready to start his expedition from the Louisville area down the Ohio on his way to Kaskaskia. He took his little band of 178 men as far as old Fort Massac where he started overland to Kaskaskia. Surprise was an essential element of his plans and no enemy scouts would observe a cross-country trek. The "army" trudged across the hills and swamps of southern Illinois for six days, unobserved in the primeval trackless forests. Kaskaskia was surprised and captured on July 4, 1778, and Clark, in a short time, proceeded to capture Cahokia. The capture of French Kaskaskia was accomplished without gunfire, and after a few days of stern control Clark was able to get the French inhabitants on his side as Americans. They were happy to be anti-British and anti-Indian, and were quickly reconciled to Clark's control. The inhabitants of Kaskaskia persuaded the French in Cahokia that the Americans were their friends and within a few days all had sworn allegiance to the new United States. A new chapter had been written in American history.

Cahokia fell on July 6, and Father Pierre Gibault convinced the residents of Vincennes to yield on the fourteenth. In the days following Clark held numerous conferences with the local Indian tribes, especially the Winnebagos, and convinced them that they should not make war against the Americans. He received the aid of the French in alienating the Indians from the British and was successful in preventing Indian attacks upon his small army.

Hamilton, in charge of the British fort at Detroit, heard about the capture of his Illinois bases as soon as a courier could reach him. Hamilton was the most feared and hated man in the Northwest Territory. The settlers referred to him as the "hair-buyer," a reference to his habit of paying Indians for scalps. As soon as he heard of Clark's successes he organized 175 white troops and 60 Indians and set out to recapture the forts. They headed for the Wabash River and thence to Vincennes, adding to the size of the Indian force as they progressed. On reaching Vincennes, Clark's representative with a single soldier surrendered. Hamilton reoccupied Vincennes on December 17, 1778, but because of the lateness in the season decided against moving across Illinois to attack Clark. When Clark learned of the recapture of Vincennes from the report of Francis Vigo, a merchant, near the last day of January, his reaction was quite different. He resolved to take the offensive and attempt to capture Hamilton.

Clark quickly organized his little army of 130 to 170 men and by February 5 was on his way across Illinois, the march that has become famous in literature and history. The speed of his preparation is indicated by the arming of a Mississippi river boat, the *Willing*, with two four pounders and four swivels. He purchased the *Willing* on February 1 and started it out on February 4 to make its way to the Wabash River and meet with Clark's overland party. The 140 mile trek was across trackless country in February when the swamps and creeks were near overflowing with the snowmelt water. The Wabash Valley was in flood stage and the party crossed the river with great difficulty. Hamilton rested in the false security of Fort Sackville at Vincennes. He never dreamed that an enemy could approach the fort from the west. He felt secure with the raging river protecting his westward flank. Clark's men occupied the village and were fed by the French inhabitants before Hamilton became aware of their presence.

Hamilton attempted to negotiate for favorable terms, but Clark exaggerated the size of his army and dictated the terms of surrender. Prior to the surrender a group of Indians with a few white leaders were captured as they returned from a raiding foray with scalps. Clark's men were so incensed that some of the Indians were brought to the gate of Fort Sackville, within sight of Hamilton, and tomahawked. Hamilton made much of the fact in later reports, forgetting that his orders to the Indian raiders had cost the lives of many white settlers and their families in the same manner over the years. On March 8, 1779, Hamilton and twenty-six additional prisoners were sent to a Virginia prison. At age twenty-seven Clark had reached the pinnacle of his career.

The surrender of Cornwallis at Yorktown on October 19, 1781, brought the Revolutionary War to a close, but it did not end the strife west of the Alleghenies. The following two years were among the most bloody in the history of the Ohio-Kentucky area. Indian raids led by the British kept the region in a constant turmoil. Clark organized a small army to attack the Shawnees in their stronghold at Chillicothe, Ohio. The Shawnees were the Kentuckian's worst enemy and after they defeated the settlers at Blue Lick, Clark found it necessary to go on the offense. Clark had not taken part in the Blue Lick defeat. His expedition against the Shawnees in 1782 at Piqua and Chillicothe, Ohio was successful, thus ensuring the safety of Kentucky settlements.

George Rogers Clark saved the Northwest Territory while still in his twenties and won the admiration of his countrymen. His life had opened splendidly and he was the outstanding hero of the new West. But the hero's life faded rapidly, and in his early thirties tragedy struck and led to unhappy and disastrous consequences.

In 1783 Clark was investigated by a board of commissioners from Richmond. During the various campaigns, Clark had often signed for supplies for his men. Considering the environment of warfare on the frontier, it was only natural that many documents were lost. The commission found many irregularities in the record of purchases but no evidence of fraud. When the commission refused to pay all the bills, many of which were not found until 1913, Clark was harassed by creditors. The refusal of government to acknowledge the indebtedness may have been due in part to the fact that Kentucky, after December, 1776, was considered to be a county of Virginia.

The commission's decision was a severe blow to Clark's economic and physical well-being. Added to his woes from government sources, his troubles were magnified by General James Wilkinson who led a campaign of character assassination against him in 1786. Wilkinson was in the employ of Spain and later was involved in the Aaron Burr conspiracy. Wilkinson wanted to be appointed Indian Commissioner. He succeeded in destroying Clark and getting the appointment. Clark was only thirty-four years old but his professional career was over.

Clark was broken in spirit, disappointed, saddened, and despondent. His remaining years were spent in the Louisville area, in part in the home of his brother William, co-explorer with Meriwether Lewis. He spent some time in his cabin on the Indiana side of the river, but after 1808, when one leg was amputated, he was forced to live with his sister, Lucy Croghan, at Locust Grove. His despondency led to excess drinking, and his health continued to decline. His former companions in arms buried him in a simple but moving ceremony. Judge John Rowan gave the oration at the grave and said, "The mighty oak of the forest has fallen & now the scrubby oaks may sprout all around." In 1928 the United

States Government erected a $1 million memorial to him at Vincennes, Indiana, the site of his greatest feat. The monument probably cost more than all the unpaid debts of his aggressive campaigns in behalf of the Northwest Territory.

HWS

References: John Bakeless, *Background to Glory: The Life of George Rogers Clark* (Philadelphia and New York: J. B. Lippincott, 1957); James Alton James, *The Life of George Rogers Clark* (Chicago: University of Chicago Press, 1928); Frederick Palmer, *Clark of the Ohio: A Life of George Rogers Clark* (New York: Dodd, Mead, 1929).

Stephen Grover Cleveland

(March 18, 1837 — June 24, 1908)

Grover Cleveland (he dropped the Stephen in his christened name early) was born in New Jersey, the son of a Presbyterian minister, the fifth of nine children. His father's death when Grover was sixteen forced him to give up plans for a college education, and to earn his own living and to help support his mother and sisters. In 1855 he went to Buffalo, New York, where an uncle persuaded him to settle down and study law.

After admission to the bar in 1859, Cleveland became assistant district attorney for Erie County in 1863, but was defeated for district attorney two years later. He was elected sheriff without campaigning for the office, and then returned to private law practice. In 1881 Cleveland was elected mayor of Buffalo on a reform ticket. The city had become notorious for corruption, extravagance, and maladministration. The new mayor proceeded to reform it. He gained wide attention for his independence and businesslike methods and before his term as mayor ended the various departments of the city government were thoroughly reorganized.

The next step up the political ladder for Cleveland came in 1882 when he was elected governor of New York State. His followers had expected to be rewarded according to the usual system of political spoils and patronage, but he refused to play the game. He and Theodore Roosevelt worked for municipal reform legislation for New York City, thereby incurring the enmity of the Tammany organization. Cleveland also promoted the passage of a good civil service law.

In 1884, the Democrats had been out of power in national affairs for twenty-three years. A split in the Republican party that year opened the way for the Democrats to make a comeback. Despite the opposition of the Tammany delegation, Cleveland was nominated to run against James G. Blaine of Maine for president, on a platform calling for radical reforms in the administrative departments, the civil service, and national finances. The campaign was one of the bitterest in American history. An insurgent group in his own party, tagged as "mugwumps," opposed Blaine, and viciously attacked him for corruption. As a counter attack, Blaine's supporters gave wide publicity to a report that eight years earlier Cleveland had become the father of an illegitimate child, whom he had since supported. Any harm done to the Cleveland candidacy by the scandal was probably offset by a speech in which the Democrats were condemned as the party of "rum, Romanism, and rebellion." Cleveland was elected by a narrow margin, though Congress was divided, the Senate going to the Republicans and the House to the Democrats. Cleveland was said to have "made up in bulk what he lacked in height, and weighed over 250 pounds when inaugurated" — still substantially less than William Howard Taft's huge figure some years later.

Immediately after his election as president, Cleveland was besieged by Democratic job hunters who demanded that Republicans be thrown out to make room for them. The president gave limited support to partisan demands, but steadily supported the work of the Civil Service Commission. He persuaded Congress to repeal the Tenure-of-Office Act that had handicapped presidents since 1867.

Even more controversial and difficult to fend off were massive raids on the federal treasury staged by war veterans and their organizations. A flood of private pension bills, many fraudulent, were approved by Congress. Cleveland vetoed those he considered without merit. His courage created innumerable opponents, who denounced him as an enemy to old soldiers.

The principal achievements of the Cleveland administration during its first term, 1885-1889, included the Interstate Commerce Act, placing railways under control of a federal commission; the Anti-Polygamy Act, dissolving the Mormon Church as a corporation; Chinese Exclusion Act, forbidding further immigration of Chinese; establishment of the federal Department of Agriculture; and the admission as states of North Dakota, South Dakota, Montana, and Washington.

A major issue in the 1888 election was tariff rates, which Cleveland thought were too high but were vigorously supported by protected domestic industries. Cleveland was renominated for a second term and gained a plurality of the popular vote, but lost in the electoral college to Benjamin Harrison.

By 1890 there was strong revulsion against high tariffs, especially in the South and West. Cleveland was urged to take the lead in the anti-tariff movement, and to become again candidate for president. An attempt was made by the New York delegation to sabotage his nomination. The Cleveland movement overrode the opposition, and he was nominated on the first ballot at the Chicago convention. The vice-presidential nomination went to Adlai E. Stevenson of Illinois. The ticket proceeded to defeat Benjamin Harrison and Whitelaw Reid.

Cleveland's second term in the White House was far stormier and perhaps less productive than the first. One of the worst depressions in U.S. history struck in 1893, following a financial panic. Cleveland was adamantly opposed to inflation. He called Congress into special session to repeal the Sherman Silver Purchase Act of 1890. That act, which required the purchase of 8.5 million ounces of silver monthly, was reducing the government's gold reserve to the danger point. Repeal of the legislation was obtained with support by many Republican votes. It left Cleveland's new party badly split, however, and gained for him the permanent hostility of the inflationist wing, later dominated by William Jennings Bryan.

One of the consequences of the business depression was a series of labor disputes. Most controversial was the Pullman strike of 1894 in Chicago, which led Cleveland to obtain a federal court injunction restraining the strikers and to send troops to Chicago to protect the mails. Governor John Altgeld of Illinois protested that he had not asked for troops and the president had no right to send them without the governor's request. The strike, which had caused riots and bloodshed, was over in about a week's time, but Cleveland's action lost him the support of labor.

Foreign affairs occupied Cleveland's time and attention on various occasions. When Great Britain quarreled with Venezuela over the British Guiana-Venezuela boundary, the U.S. government urged that the dispute be arbitrated. The British replied that the Monroe Doctrine did not apply and the matter did not concern the United States. Cleveland warned that if the British refused to arbitrate, the United States would consider war necessary to enforce the Monroe Doctrine. After days of intense negotiations, the British agreed to arbitrate.

In another area, there was much sympathy for Cuban patriots and pressure for American intervention during the period of Cuban insurrections, 1895-1897. Cleveland insisted upon enforcing the neutrality law and refused to be driven into a war with Spain, though he warned Spain against molesting U.S. citizens or property in Cuba.

Before the end of his second term, Cleveland had essentially lost control of his party. Western and Southern demands were driving the Democrats into a campaign for free silver. Cleveland was denounced before and during the 1896 convention, which went on to nominate Bryan for the presidency. William McKinley, an Ohio congressman who had sponsored a high protective tariff, succeeded Cleveland as president.

Following his retirement, there was a general change of sentiment toward Cleveland. The animosities died out and he became widely respected as one of the few independent and disinterested public citizens in America. In his last years he made valuable contributions in helping to restore confidence in insurance companies, arbitrating labor disputes, and serving as a trustee of Princeton University.

RBD

References: Grover Cleveland, *Letters* (Boston: Houghton, 1933); Edwin P. Hoyt, *Grover Cleveland* (Chicago: Reilly, 1962); R. E. McElroy, *Grover Cleveland*, 2 vols. (New York: Harper, 1923); Allan Nevins, ed., *Grover Cleveland: A Study in Courage* (New York: Dodd, 1932).

William Frederick Cody
(February 26, 1846—January 10, 1917)

To many people no man captured better the spirit or myth of the American West than William Frederick Cody, better known as "Buffalo Bill." He spent many years of his life on the great plains as scout, messenger, and professional hunter, and as a showman he performed throughout the world with his own troupe. After retiring from public life he lived on a ranch in the Big Horn basin of Wyoming.

Cody was born in Scott County, Iowa, near Davenport, February 26, 1846, the fourth of eight children. His father Isaac Cody was an unsuccessful farmer who moved his family to Kansas in 1854. Living there on the edge of the prairies the boy was exposed to the pageant of western migration, to wild animals which could be trapped or shot, and to various Indian tribes. Schooling was desultory, and when Isaac Cody died suddenly in 1857 it was necessary for the son to find work of some sort. He was employed first, as a kind of office boy on horseback, by the freighting company of Russell, Majors & Waddell. Other tasks followed. He was for a short time a pony express rider, who once made a continuous ride of 320 miles, a gold seeker in the vicinity of Denver, a temporary prisoner of the Mormons. In 1864 he enlisted in the army at Fort Leavenworth and was enrolled in the Seventh Kansas regiment; actually he saw little service in the Civil War and served as an orderly in a Missouri hospital before he was released in 1865. The next year he married Louisa Frederici in St. Louis and he turned for his livelihood to hotel keeping and freighting. The construction of the Kansas Pacific Railroad required the employment of many laborers, who had to be fed. Cody became a meat hunter for the construction crew and by his own count killed 4,280 buffalo in seventeen months.

By this time Cody had become known for his ability as a scout and his knowledge of the terrain. General Philip Sheridan employed him for service around Fort Hays. In later years Cody became famous as an Indian fighter and scout and was attached to the Fifth Cavalry. But he had no official army position and remained a civilian engaged by the military. In 1872 he was awarded the Congressional Medal of Honor for bravery.

Cody's meeting in 1869 with Ned Buntline, the pseudonym of the playwright and dime novelist E. Z. C. Judson, changed his life and led to his becoming an actor and showman. Buntline later wrote sensational tales in which Cody was a character and these together with other stories by Prentiss Ingraham were published by the firm of Beadle and Adams in New York. A typical Ingraham title was *Buffalo Bill's Death-Deal; or, The Wandering Jew of the West.* Buntline, however, induced Cody to go on the stage and provided the vehicle for the neophyte actor. A play called *The Scouts of the Prairies* opened in Chicago in 1872 and was later staged in New York; it attracted audiences but scant critical approval. Cody remained an actor until gold fever in the Black Hills and rumors of Indian unrest lured him westward; General E. A. Carr appointed him chief of scouts for the Fifth Cavalry. Cody had only a small role in the Sioux uprising of 1876 but one of the most spectacular events of his life occurred in that year.

While confronting a small party of Cheyennes Cody rescued two army couriers. Yellow Hand, son of a Cheyenne chief, challenged him individually. Cody, dressed with odd inappropriateness in a stage costume of Mexican velvet which was slashed with scarlet and ornamented with silver buttons and lace, accepted the challenge. The two horsemen approached each other at a gallop; Cody killed the Indian's horse but his own animal fell into a gopher hole. On foot the two men fired at each other. Yellow Hand missed but Cody's bullet was accurate. He then plunged his knife into the Indian's heart and immediately scalped him. Then he struck a pose, according to an onlooker, and holding his trophy aloft shouted, "The first scalp for Custer."

For the next few years Cody was the partner of Major Frank North in a ranch near North Platte, Nebraska. But in 1883 he organized his Wild West Show, a flamboyant exhibition which opened in an Omaha arena on May 17 and subsequently appeared throughout the United States and in many foreign countries. This potpourri of western life included cowboys, Indians, broncos, an old Deadwood mail coach, buffalo, Texas steers, feats of marksmanship, and eventually the girl sharpshooter, Annie Oakley, and for awhile even Sitting Bull. The show was especially successful in London where a parade of royal figures saw it. By 1886 it took a train of twenty-six cars to transport the company's personnel.

Much of the meretricious fame of Cody was due to the dime novels of Buntline and Ingraham, but he was also indebted to the indefatigable efforts of his press agent John Burke. On the other hand, Cody was hardly a modest man. Both on and off stage he relished attention, which the known events of his life and his personal showmanship excited. Cody was not illiterate like his hero Kit Carson (he named his only son, who died at six, Kit Carson Cody) but he certainly was not the author of various books which he signed. Yet his autobiography, which appeared first in 1879 and was dedicated to General Sheridan, is substantially his own work, and despite its chronological errors and inflated events it remains an indispensable personal record. The reprint, published in 1978 by the University of Nebraska Press with an introduction by Don Russell, is extremely useful.

Cody died in Denver, January 10, 1917. The annual stampede in the Wyoming town which was named after him commemorates Buffalo Bill's fame and memory.

JTF

References: W. J. Ghent, *DAB*, IV, 1930, pp. 260-61; Richard J. Walsh, *The Making of Buffalo Bill: A Study in Heroics* (Indianapolis, Ind.: Bobbs-Merrill, 1928); Donald B. Russell, *The Lives and Legends of Buffalo Bill* (Norman: University of Oklahoma Press, 1960).

Samuel Colt

(July 19, 1814 — January 10, 1862)

The exact date and place of the development of gunpowder are unknown, but the Western world was made aware of it by Roger Bacon in 1242. The earliest weapon using gunpowder was probably one made by Berthold Schwartz, a German monk, in 1313. Cannon were certainly used by King Edward III during the siege of Calais in 1347, but small arms were not developed until about 1400. During the next four hundred years a great variety of cannon and small arms were designed. The development of guns changed the life of man for better or worse. Firearms played an ever increasing part in warfare, from siege cannon destroying medieval forts to cannon on ships and small arms in the hands of individuals. Nevertheless, improvements in armaments were relatively slow. The repeating revolver, a pistol capable of shooting more than one bullet without being reloaded, was not recognized in the United States until February 25, 1836, when Samuel Colt received his first American patent.

Samuel Colt was born in Hartford, Connecticut, the son of Christopher and Sarah Colt. By the time he was six years old his father had failed in business and his mother had died. Samuel was not interested in school and avoided studying at every opportunity. Samuel's early youth was spent working in his father's factory, laboring on farms and sometimes going to school. He seemed more interested in explosives and inventing things than in the normal pursuits of a youth. At age fifteen he had discovered that electricity would fire power. On July 4, 1829, he advertised that "Sam'l Colt will blow a raft sky-high on Ware Pond." He had a big audience and the experiment worked so well that it covered the spectators with mud.

After Samuel's very short and unhappy experience at Amherst Academy, his father arranged for him to be apprenticed to a sea captain sailing from Boston to Calcutta. Sea life bored him, and it was on this trip that Samuel first conceived the idea of a revolver. He began making a wooden model of a pistol with a revolving magazine. At the time he was only sixteen years old but took precautions to hide his model until he returned home. He refused to serve on shipboard after returning to Ware and shortly thereafter left home to paddle his own canoe.

Immediately, Colt began looking for a mechanic who could make a working model. Two pistols were constructed in 1831 and the following year he applied for a patent. In 1833 he constructed an improved pistol and a repeating rifle, for both of which he acquired patents in France and England in 1835. By age twenty-two he had received patents in three countries on the first firearm that was based on the principle of a revolving cylinder controlled by the cocking mechanism.

To make his way he began to give lectures on chemistry and laughing gas under the name "Dr. Coult." Even though Colt was a youth he had a flare for showmanship. He advertised himself as "Dr. Coult of London, New York, Calcutta! Tickets 25 cents." While earning a living with his laughing gas he kept his mind on the perfection of his revolving pistol and, after obtaining the American patent, formed the Patent Arms Manufacturing Company to manufacture the new revolver at Paterson, New Jersey. He was unable to get either the army or navy to adopt the new pistol and the company failed in 1842. For the next few years Colt turned his attention to the development of an underwater bomb to destroy vessels approaching a harbor. Between 1842 and 1844, under the supervision of the navy, he destroyed four ships. However, the navy remained skeptical and did not adopt his submarine mine.

Colt designated his six-shooter the "Peacemaker." In post-Civil War times, as the West was rapidly becoming settled, the terms "Colt," "Equalizer," "Six-shooter" and "Peacemaker" became synonymous. Every law enforcement officer in every frontier town carried a brace of "Colts." At the same time the adventures and outlaws carried their own six-shooters and lgends grew concerning many famous figures. From Wyatt Earp, the sheriff who always got his man, to Buffalo Bill Cody and Annie Oakley, the sharpshooters, to Wild Bill Hickock, the West produced a series of characters who have been immortalized in one way or another. The gun-fighter of the West with his Colt revolver on his hip has become a legend in American lore. As the West settled down, the demand for Colt's product declined, but police still depend on the six-shooter for law enforcement.

The Mexican War (1846-1848) presented Colt with a new opportunity. The government ordered a thousand revolvers and desired quick delivery. Colt's old factory was gone so he commissioned Eli Whitney to manufacture certain parts. The guns were delivered on time, and though they played a small part in the victory Colt used the event to glorify the value of the "Colt Revolver." It was this publicity that created an aura around the six-shooter. By 1848 Colt had built a new factory at Hartford. He adopted mass production as an economical method of operation. This concept was not new to Colt; Whitney had used it much earlier. War clouds began appearing in various parts of the world. Colt became the arms supplier for many governments, including Russia, the United States, England, Brazil, China, Chile, Egypt, France, Turkey, Austria, and Prussia. But the most important aspect of the new business was the fact that every pioneer settling the West considered the possession of a Colt a necessity. Sales skyrocketed and Colt became a wealthy supplier of arms.

One of Colt's outstanding business concepts concerned his attitude toward his employees. He believed that he had a responsibility for their welfare and that this included a pension for life. If workers knew they had security, Colt believed that they would do better work and thus serve Samuel Colt better. To Colt this meant good business practice.

Colt postponed a family until June 5, 1856, when he married Elizabeth H. Jarvis. For their wedding trip he arranged to attend the coronation of Czar Alexander of Russia. He had fulfilled the American dream, rising from the poor "Dr. Coult" who supported himself by showmanship to arms-maker for the world. He died in Hartford, Connecticut.

HWS

References: Carl W. Mitman, *DAB*, IV, 1930, pp. 318-19; Jack Rohan, *Yankee Arms Maker* (New York and London: Harper, 1935).

John Singleton Copley
(1738—September 9, 1815)

America in the colonial period was hardly the most desirable place for an ambitious and aspring artist to learn the rudiments of his trade, but among the cities of the New World Boston was probably the richest in opportunities. Although art schools did not exist and most successful artists were self-taught, engravers and portrait painters could make a living there. But even before the Revolution trade had flourished, and the merchant class had become affluent enough to commission family portraits from established journeymen. John Singleton Copley, who was to become one of the greatest eighteenth century painters, was fortunate in being able to spend his formative years in Boston before sailing to England on the eve of the Revolution, never to return to his native soil.

Copley was born in Boston in 1738, the son of Irish parents who had emigrated two years earlier. His father came from Limerick, his mother from County Clare. The senior Copley died in 1748 and the mother remarried in the same year. Copley's stepfather, Peter Pelham, at times a mezzotint engraver, a portrait painter, and a schoolteacher, strongly influenced the boy, who early showed some facility in drawing and coloring. Despite the lack of adequate training Copley studied anatomy on his own and at the age of fifteen began to paint professionally. He did portraits and used both oils and pastels, even producing miniatures on ivory and copper. In 1766 he sent his picture of his half-brother Henry Pelham playing with a pet squirrel to Benjamin West in London with the hope that it would attract attention abroad. West was impressed. He replied by letter that both he and the famous Joshua Reynolds agreed the painting showed great promise, and he encouraged Copley to come to England for further training and exposure.

During the next few years Copley was extremely busy and successful. He spent six months in New York where he had a temporary studio, he visited Philadelphia, and some of the best known Bostonians came to sit for him. Among his subjects were John Hancock, Paul Revere, and Samuel Adams. His portraits were carefully observed and realistic, notable for precise features, meticulous costumes, and pertinent background. Many of these pictures, including the superb double portrait of Mr. and Mrs. Isaac Winslow, are now in the Boston Museum of Fine Arts. Increasing prosperity enabled Copley to buy land on Beacon Hill in Boston, and he informed West in a letter that he had an annual income of three hundred guineas and doubted that he could do better in England. But Copley's family connections were Loyalist, he had no strongly partisan feeling in politics, and he was upset by the growing social and economic turbulence in the colonies. He was also extremely ambitious to excel in his chosen field. He sailed to England in June 1774, leaving his wife (he had married Sussannah Farnum Clarke in 1769) in Boston.

Copley spent some time on the continent, visiting France and Italy especially. In 1775 his wife and family joined him in London, which was his home for the rest of his life. He was extremely energetic. From 1776 to his death he exhibited some forty-three paintings at the Royal Academy, of which he became a full member in 1783. He continued his work as a portraitist, painting celebrated Americans like John Adams and John Quincy Adams when they came to London, but he also diverged into historical painting, accomplishing memorable work. Examples are *Death of Major Pierson* in the Tate Gallery and the reportorial *Watson and the Shark* in the National Gallery of Art.

In Copley's later years his expensive London household and his own ill health drained his finances somewhat. His pictures did not always sell and he felt, perhaps unrealistically, that the sale of his Beacon Hill property in Boston did not bring the profit he had expected. But he could depend on his father-in-law for financial assistance. He was the merchant to whom the tea made famous by the Boston Tea Party was consigned. His father-in-law appears in Copley's domestic picture which also includes Copley himself, his beautiful wife, and the four children: *The Copley Family* in the National Gallery of Art. In later years the artist's son became celebrated in his own right. As Lord Lynhurst he was three times lord chancellor of England in the reign of Queen Victoria, the first American to play such a role.

Copley's position as one of the major American painters seems secure today. His portraits of Colonial and Revolutionary figures are a national treasure. His command of color remains unquestioned and the verisimilitude of his historical canvases is still admired. He has had a strong influence on French historical painting from David to Meissonier.

JTF

References: Frederick W. Coburn, *DAB*, IV, 1930, pp. 423-30; Jules David Prown, *John Singleton Copley*, 2 vols. (Cambridge, Mass.: Harvard University Press, 1966); Jules David Prown, in *Encyclopedia of American Biography*, pp. 227-28 (New York: Harper & Row, 1974).

Ezra Cornell

(January 11, 1807 — December 9, 1874)

Ezra Cornell was born at Westchester Landing in New York, where his father, Elijah, was an unsuccessful farmer and potter. Elijah moved his family in 1819 to De Ruyter where Ezra attended the local school and helped his father with the manufacture of earthenware. In the spring of 1828 Ezra, twenty-one years old, left his Quaker home in De Ruyter, New York and trudged forty miles to Ithaca looking for work. Ithaca was connected to the Erie Canal by way of Lake Cayuga, and the possibility of employment was good. Ezra already had eight years of experience as a carpenter, having built his family residence in De Ruyter at age sixteen. After a short time working as a carpenter in Ithaca, he became manager of a mill and remained in this work for twelve years. During this period he married Mary Ann Wood in 1831, and because she was not a Quaker, Ezra was excommunicated from the faith. This event had a pronounced effect upon his actions in later years when he established Cornell University.

While still a millwright, he gained a reputation as an innovative mechanic and a public-spirited citizen with Yankee shrewdness. When Fall Creek needed a school, he supported it; when the mill needed a new and better power source, he built a tunnel through solid rock; and when the Whigs needed campaign help in 1840, he supplied it. While promoting a patented plow in Maine in 1841 he met F. O. J. Smith, congressman and editor of the *Maine Farmer*. Smith, as congressman, was aware of Samuel Morse's new invention, the telegraph. Cornell set out from Ithaca in 1843 to visit Smith. He walked the first 160 miles to Albany in four days, took a train to Boston, and then walked the last 100 miles in two-and-a-half days. He found that Smith had accepted a contract to lay Morse's telegraph line from Washington to Baltimore for one hundred dollars a mile and was trying to devise a machine to do the job. Cornell's inventive mind soon produced a design for a machine that could dig the ditch, lay the pipe, and cover it all in one operation. He took over the job of laying the new experimental line, but before it was completed he had convinced Morse that a line strung on poles was more serviceable. To suspend the line on poles he had to invent a new type of insulation, and when this succeeded the first message, "What has God wrought?" was delivered on May 1, 1844. Cornell's mechanical genius is clearly illustrated in the sequence of events that led to Morse's final success.

The public was slow to realize the importance of the telegraph. The owners of the patent were unable to raise capital. They offered it to the government for $100 thousand, but the offer was declined because the government saw no economic value in the new contraption. Cornell, however, visualized it as a great aid to commerce and with foresight, drive and enthusiasm involved himself in promoting the construction of new lines. Capital was very difficult to raise; those with money would not invest. Cornell turned in desperation to poor people for small sums. With such funds he build many short lines in numerous small towns of the East, and slowly Morse's Age of the Telegraph came into existence. Cornell tried Chicago, but could not raise a single dollar in that young city. He persevered and under extreme hardship, obligating himself for more than he owned, built a line connecting Cleveland, Detroit, Chicago and Milwaukee. Later, a line reached Pittsburgh. Competition among the short lines was bitter, and many competing lines faced bankruptcy. The only solution was combination of the many small units into one large operating company.

In this merger Cornell led the way in consolidation, and Western Union Telegraph Company came into existence in 1855, Morse joining in 1866. Cornell was the largest stockholder and remained a director for twenty years. As Western Union grew, Cornell's income reached $100 thousand per year and his son, former governor Alonzo B. Cornell of New York, reported that his father earned more than $2 million from the company. This was enormous wealth for the day. Though Morse was the inventor of the telegraph, Cornell became its builder.

As a youth Cornell had to borrow a book if he wished to read. He felt the deprivation of education that reading would have brought him. In 1857, after attaining wealth, he turned his attention to the welfare of his community at Ithaca. In 1863 he decided to establish a library as the most important gift he could bestow upon the public. This was certainly one of the first such gifts made to any American community. One of the unusual features of the library was Cornell's choices for the board of trustees. He chose his political opponents and ministers of different churches, and thus acquired the cooperation of all for the benefit of the public. This was a reflection of his personal experience with prejudice.

Cornell never lost his love for the land and purchased a farm at the edge of Ithaca in 1857. He called it Forest Park and turned it into a model farm. He became president of the New York State Agricultural Society and thereby *ex officio* trustee of the New Agricultural College located in Seneca County. He recognized that the college was inefficient and offered to endow it with three hundred thousand dollars provided that it were removed to Ithaca and that one-half of the College Land Grant be given to it. This was the beginning of the chain of events that led to the formation of Cornell University.

In 1861 his community elected him to the state legislature where he served two years in the Assembly and four in the Senate. Here he became a close friend of Andrew D. White, who opposed Cornell's suggestion of dividing the land grant. White proposed that it be held as a unit for the creation of a single university of note. Cornell agreed with White and increased his proposed endowment to five hundred thousand dollars. Shortly thereafter a vicious campaign was begun, attacking Cornell's motives as well as his character. Sectarian colleges sent delegates to Albany to protest. Lawyers were hired to address the legislative committee on education. It was implied that Cornell was in some way a swindler, a man who was trying to rob the state. Through all the bitter testimony Cornell merely sat in silence. Although it is surprising that a bill to create a new university was introduced in the New York State Legislature during the Civil War, with the attention of the assembly undoubtedly on matters of national interest, it is to the credit of the Cornell-White team that any progress was made. The bill was passed on September 5, 1865. Cornell turned over the half million dollars to the new institution and added his farm free of cost.

Cornell said that he had established "an institution where any person can find instruction in any study." This was a break with the tradition that required students to follow a set curriculum. Also, it was a departure from the classical education in Greek and Latin. The charter of the new university provided that no appointment, staff or administrative, should be based upon religious or political views. This raised the charge of a "godless university," but Cornell's idea was that all sects were welcome and free to pursue an education, unhampered by denominational or political pressures. He broke again with tradition when he favored the enrollment of women and made it possible for them to compete with men for free four-year scholarships from each assembly district. Finally, he encouraged graduates of the university to participate in its government. On Inauguration Day at Cornell University, Cornell read his address. He believed that he was laying the foundation of "an institution which shall combine practical with liberal education, which shall fit the youth of our country for the professions, the farms, the mines, the manufactories ... which will prove highly beneficial to the poor young men and the poor young women ... which shall furnish better means for the culture of all men ... preparing them to serve society better ... [and] without dwarfing or paring them down to fit the narrow gauge of any sect." Cornell had created a modern university providing equal education for all, men and women, poor and rich, and an institution free from religious and political domination. The university emphasized education in agriculture and engineering and was led by Cornell's own choice of president, Andrew D. White, who provided brilliant leadership from the opening day in 1868.

A university always needs money, especially a new institution. Land grants were assigned to various states by Congress on July 2, 1862, for educational purposes as part of the Morrill Act. The land scrip was distributed among the various states, and because there was so much of it, sales averaged about thirty cents per acre. This brought in minor income and Cornell felt that premature sale of the land scrip was unwarranted. He proceeded to purchase in 1866 over seven hundred thousand acres, pay the taxes and all other costs, and turn in any profits to the state treasury for the benefit of Cornell University. In this manner the university ultimately benefited to the extent of $2.5 million. Such financial transactions were often made even though they represented temporary financial hardships for the donor.

Cornell became totally absorbed in the building of Cornell University. Though he had a limited education, he could be counted upon to see what would bring enlightenment to young people. He had grown up as a Quaker and believed in the quality of life Quakers represented. He was stern and forbidding in countenance, practical and painstaking in his actions, but he always kept his attention directed toward the fulfillment of his goal, the creation of a great university. Andrew White knew him intimately and best described him: "Cornell was one of the simplest, noblest, truest and most self-sacrificing men I have ever known. Not a selfish thought ever tainted his efforts ... all the years I knew him he went about doing good."

HWS

References: Andrew Carnegie, Andrew D. White et al., *Centennial Anniversary of the Birth of Ezra Cornell* (Ithaca, N.Y.: Cornell University Press, 1907);

Andrew Dickson White, *My Reminiscences of Ezra Cornell* (Ithaca, N.Y.: Cornell University Press, 1890); Morris Bishop, *A History of Cornell University* (Ithaca, N.Y.: Cornell University Press, 1962).

Crazy Horse

(ca. 1849—September 5, 1877)

Biographical accounts of great American Indians are often deficient in facts and confused in chronology. Even though the names of earlier leaders like Pontiac and Tecumseh have entered tradition, it is difficult to verify many specific facts about their lives. To a certain extent the same situation exists for chieftains among the plains Indians of the nineteenth century. Thus there is no certainty about the birthdate of Crazy Horse, the remarkable Oglala Sioux who led his Cheyenne followers in more than one successful battle against troops of the United States army. Details of his youth are obscure too, but the fact if not the manner of his death at about the age of thirty at the Red Cloud agency in Nebraska is well documented. Once again confined to the reservation he hated, he was suspected of conspiracy. Believing that he was about to be imprisoned, he lunged with a knife at his captors. Possibly by his own weapon or probably by a soldier's bayonet, he was mortally wounded in the abdomen. But about one aspect of Crazy Horse's life there never has been any doubt. He was widely known among men both Indian and white for his courage, ability, and leadership.

Crazy Horse's Indian name was Tashunca-uitco, a name given the baby when a wild pony cavorted through the village at the time of his birth. In early manhood he gradually became known as a leader of Southern Sioux and Northern Cheyennes who fled from reservations and participated in forays against the Crows or isolated parties of whites. After he married a Cheyenne woman he was closely affiliated with that tribe, which eventually supplied most of his followers. He was active in the Fetterman massacre of 1866 and in the famous Wagon Box Fight of the following year. He ignored the War Department message ordering the Indian troops to return to their reservations on January 1, 1876. On March 17 his village of 105 lodges was surprised by Colonel J. J. Reynolds with a force of 450 men who destroyed it and captured the pony herd. After the army troops had withdrawn Crazy Horse followed them and regained some of the animals.

On June 17, 1876 Crazy Horse with about twelve hundred Oglalas and Cheyennes was attacked by General George Crook with an army thirteen hundred strong. Crook withdrew from further hostilities after sustaining serious losses. Crazy Horse and his followers moved to join the Sioux medicine man Sitting Bull in the valley of the Little Big Horn. In the battle that ensued on June 25 Reno and his troops were defeated and Custer and his Seventh Cavalry annihilated. Although Indians seldom formed a disciplined force and almost never acknowledged a supreme commander, Gall was probably the most influential in bringing about the Custer debacle; at least he led one group of the hostiles and Crazy

Horse another. When a group of Indians moved toward the agencies Crook followed, and Captain Anson Mills's attack at Slim Buttes in what is now South Dakota broke up American Horse's village. For a time Crazy Horse, despite losses and lack of supplies, held out, but finally he agreed to seek peace. On May 6, 1877 he and his band surrendered to the United States Army at the Red Cloud agency in Nebraska. He would not live much longer.

Crazy Horse has been described as a lithe, sinewy man standing about five feet eight inches. He had a facial scar. Generally called the greatest war chief of the Sioux and Cheyenne tribes, he symbolizes the resolute spirit of the plains Indians and their determination to fight as long as they could against the encroachment and superior military power of the white invaders. Crazy Horse also figures in literature. His death is the climactic event in the heroic couplet poem by John G. Neihardt called "The Song of the Indian Wars," and Mari Sandoz has written his biography. As Neihardt wrote, when the corpse was taken to the burial ground, "The last great Sioux rode silently away."

In 1982 the United States Post Office issued several stamps in a series called Great Americans commemorating, among others, Ralph Bunche and Igor Stravinsky. Included on the thirteen-cent stamp was Crazy Horse, one of the few American Indians so honored.

JTF

References: William J. Ghent, *DAB*, IV, 1930, pp. 530-31; Mari Sandoz, *Crazy Horse, the Strange Man of the Oglalas: A Biography* (Lincoln: University of Nebraska Press, 1972).

Hugh Roy Cullen

(July 3, 1881 — July 4, 1957)

After the discovery of oil at Titusville, Pennsylvania, in 1859, its value as a fuel was slow to be recognized. Not until the gasoline motor was developed did petroleum find its proper place in the economy of man. In the last half of the nineteenth century petroleum was used for light and grease, replacing whale oil and coal oil.

The discovery of Spindletop oil well in Texas in 1901 began the true age of petroleum. Though petroleum was now needed in large quantities, the science of oil discovery had not yet matured. Geologists were slowly becoming aware that accumulation of oil often occurred in salt domes and folded rocks called anticlines, but exploration laboratories were neither common nor large until the 1920s.

Without a scientific approach to oil discovery prior to the 1920s, drillers known as "wildcatters" came on the scene. They were a diverse group, ranging from the wholly reliable to the con artist. All were ambitious to make an oil strike; all followed the drilling activity of others hoping to get acreage near a discovery well. Some spoke a pseudoscientific jargon that duped the investor and some made money by selling more interest in the well than the well cost. Since there was a lot of undiscovered oil, it was natural that a small percentage of wells drilled in the early period would strike oil. Luck was involved; success often had nothing to do with scientific knowledge. If you drilled enough wells, a certain small number of them would be successful. The science of geology did not begin to play an important part until the 1920s, after the development of geophysical methods added to the knowledge of the subsurface.

Hugh Roy Cullen was one of the early wildcatters of the highest integrity. The road from poor farm boy to one of the world's richest men was built on a foundation of honesty and hard work in the true Horatio Alger tradition. Though he amassed a fortune that was measured in hundreds of millions of dollars, he gave most of it away while he was still living in a spirit of compassion for his fellow man. He had made his money in Texas; Texas should receive it back in the form of aid to youth and health care for all. He was a believer in honesty in politics as well as business. He was an ardent supporter of human rights and fought for the union of labor with business.

Cullen was born on a farm in Denton County, Texas. His grandfather, Ezekiel Cullen, was a well-known Texas pioneer who served in the Texas legislature and founded the Texas public school system. He was a strong advocate of education for all and six years before Texas was admitted to the Union he said: "Intelligence is the only true aristocracy in a Government like ours; and the improved and educated mind has and will ever triumph over the ignorant and uneducated mind." His mother, Louise Beck Cullen, was a strong woman who instilled into her children the importance of honesty and integrity. She helped with their education by reading stories from the works of famous authors such as Sir Walter Scott and Charles Dickens. Cullen's father, Cicero, separated from Roy's mother when Roy was only two years old. The mother moved to San Antonio and was supported by income from the Beck estate and in part from Cicero. Life was not easy for the family and young Roy at the age of twelve quit school for a job in a candy store at three dollars a week. At this time Cullen was on intimate terms with poverty.

Cullen was an avid reader and student of maps and charts. He continued to educate himself and by age eighteen was involved in the cotton trading business. This work took him to the dry, flat and dreary plains of western Oklahoma where he established himself as a successful trader in cotton, buying for a cotton firm.

After his marriage to Lillie Cranz on December 29, 1903, he returned to Oklahoma and set himself up as an independent cotton trader. He soon developed credit of a quarter million dollars, but the cotton business did not earn much profit. After a few years in Oklahoma and Arkansas the Cullen family ended up in Houston in 1911. He became interested in real estate and, in addition, acquired a seat on the Houston Cotton Exchange. Cullen became an advocate of enterprises for the betterment of the Houston community, including a bond issue for the Ship Canal which would permit ocean vessels to serve the city.

Cullen must have been aware of the impact of the great Spindletop oil well on the economy of Houston and Texas. In 1917 a friend in Houston invited him to go to West Texas and lease land for oil drilling. Cullen had no experience in this area but he was successful in acquiring large tracts of land during a three-year period. Unfortunately, the wells drilled were all dry and Cullen returned to Houston determined to try again. He had learned an important lesson, namely, that oil in west Texas was trapped mostly in folded rocks called anticlines and that information currently was inadequate to find this type of structure. He would, therefore, exert his new efforts on the southeast coast of Texas in the salt-dome province. New geophysical tools, the torsion balance and the gravity meter, could be successfully applied to salt domes. He was determined to follow the salt dome trend, both on new domes and old domes in which the production was declining. Most of these domes had been found by gravity methods. Later, Cullen would adapt to those geophysical methods using seismic reflections. Cullen was a self-taught student of petroleum geology, and his so-called "luck" was based upon sound scientific deductions and boldness of action.

Under the name of The Texas Petroleum Company Cullen made his first discovery at Pierce Junction. By 1930 he had added discoveries in the Blue Ridge and Rabb's Ridge fields. Interest held by him and his partner was sold for $20 million. A new company was formed, the Quintana Petroleum Company in 1932. Cullen was now the sole owner of his operations. Two years later he made the great discovery of every wildcatter's dream, the billion dollar oil field known as Tom O'Connor. Gusher after gusher was drilled in this field and Cullen became one of the world's richest men.

The Great Depression of the 1930s was in full sway. Cullen had supported Hoover and feared the effect of Roosevelt's program upon business and the free enterprise system. He became an active participant in Texas and national politics, opposing policies which, in his judgment, imposed governmental controls upon business. He gave financial support to many Republican candidates in different states. He believed that the social revolution which had its beginnings in America in the 1930s would lead to a deterioration of the quality of life as government established political controls and spent money over and beyond income.

Cullen's son, Roy Gustave, was killed in 1936 when a derrick collapsed on him. This tragic event resulted in the beginning of one of Cullen's greatest philanthropic enterprises, the support of Houston University. He gave $260 thousand to build the Roy Gustave Cullen Memorial building. This was followed by gifts exceeding $30 million. His donations had only one qualification: "The University of Houston must always be a college for working men and women and their sons and daughters."

The Cullen Foundation was created in 1947 by placing in it thousands of acres of oil producing land. It was among the largest foundations in America. Cullen granted large sums of money during his lifetime. Financial support given by Cullen personally and by the foundation had an impact on Texas society. The Houston College for Negroes, Texas Medical Center, Baylor School of Medicine, Gonzales Warm Springs Hospital for Infantile Paralysis, Houston Art Museum, Houston Symphony Orchestra and many other organizations have benefited from Cullen's wealth. He has become one of the greatest philanthropists in history; the good he did has had an impact long after his death.

Cullen was honored during his life by many awards. The University of Pittsburgh conferred upon him the degree of Doctor of Science in 1936. Baylor granted him an LL.D. degree in 1945 and the University of Houston an LL.D. in 1947. He received numerous awards and honors from various societies, but he was probably proudest of his membership in the Musician's Protective Association of the American Federation of Labor.

Cullen was devoted to his family and to America. He wanted to preserve a strong America and led an active political life. In addition, he found pleasure in giving away a great fortune for the public good.

HWS

References: Ed Kilman and Theon Wright, *Hugh Roy Cullen* (New York: Prentice-Hall, 1954); "Hugh Roy Cullen," *Current Biography*, pp. 145-47 (New York: H. W. Wilson, 1955).

Richard Henry Dana

(August 1, 1815 — January 6, 1882)

A member of a distinguished New England family, Richard Henry Dana was a graduate of Harvard and a successful maritime lawyer. He was equipped by training and temperament to serve the United States government in some diplomatic or elective post but like Henry Adams he hoped in vain for the summons. Instead as a young man he interrupted his college career for two years to sail aboard a merchant vessel to California and wrote a memorable book about his experiences. *Two Years before the Mast* appeared in 1840 and remains to this date a significant addition to the literature of the sea.

Dana was born in 1815, the grandson of the first American minister to Russia and at one time the chief justice of the Massachusetts Supreme Court. His father, Richard Henry Dana, Sr., was also a lawyer and a minor literary figure who had been a founder of the *North American Review* and whose poetry and prose were published in two volumes in 1833. Dana entered Harvard in 1831 but withdrew after two years of attendance because weak eyesight impeded his studies. He hoped that a sea voyage would strengthen his health. On August 14, 1834, he joined the crew of the brig *Pilgrim* as a common sailor and left Boston harbor for a two-year cruise which took him to California via Cape Horn. He did not see his native town again until the ship *Alert* brought him back September 19, 1836. Despite a spartan diet, cramped quarters, many hours of hard physical labor, and storms at sea which almost caused a small merchant vessel to founder, Dana returned in excellent health. He was able to complete his college career at Harvard and to prepare for a legal career.

Dana also taught, serving as an instructor in elocution at Harvard under Edward T. Channing in 1839-1840 and as a lecturer at the Harvard Law School from 1866 to 1868.

The year following the appearance of his first book, Dana published *The Seaman's Friend* and established a reputation as a supporter of sailors's rights. He joined the Free Soil Party and eventually was affiliated with the Republicans. Ill health again limited his activities, but in 1859 he was able to again visit California aboard a steamship and to see from a different point of view many of the places and persons which had intrigued him years before. Lincoln appointed him United States district attorney for Massachusetts, but Dana resigned his office after the assassination of the president. Private law practice in Boston occupied him until 1878, when he journeyed to England hoping to study international law. He died in Rome on January 6, 1882, and was buried in the Protestant cemetery there.

Two Years before the Mast is structurally a journal, specific in such matters as latitude and longitude, detailed in its descriptions of the duties and labors of the crew, vivid in its accounts of weather on the high seas, and replete with details of seamanship and the handling of spars and ropes. Although Dana came on board as a neophyte he sought no favors and shirked no duties. His social position in Boston counted for little during the double rounding of Cape Horn in execrable weather, and his superior education brought him personal solace but no temptation to soldier (a word he often used). Since the book is not fiction, although some of the dialogue seems invented, there is no dramatic hero and the treatment is both chronological and episodic.

The owners of the *Pilgrim* and the *Alert* were Yankee businessmen who underwrote the voyage for profit. Ships leaving Boston were loaded with trade goods meant to appeal to the small and sparse settlements along the California coast. In return the ships would bring back mostly products of the cattle industry, which in Mexican California was virtually the only way of life. When the *Alert* left for home it carried forty thousand hides and thirty thousand horns, plus barrels of otter and beaver skins. The voyage from San Diego to Boston required 135 days and because of its cargo the vessel sank low in the water and was a slow sailor. Dana gives a full account of how the merchandise was handled, how the hides were cured before being packed in the hold. But he also describes the small ports along the coast, activities ashore including a wedding fandango, horseback rides to various missions, the difficulties of loading and unloading where there were virtually no docking facilities, problems of communicating with the Spanish-speaking shore dwellers. Nor is Dana reticent about the uglier aspects of marine life in the 1830s. No reader of *Two Years before the Mast* will forget the portrait of the tyrannical captain who personally inflicted a flogging on two seamen for a minor infraction and who had difficulty in controlling his temper.

Dana wrote honestly and vigorously. His purpose was to report from personal experience the daily life aboard a small merchant vessel on a long and often hazardous cruise. Weather and wind were often changeable on the vast Pacific, and especially in the neighborhood of Cape Horn the vessels which were Dana's temporary home could float almost motionless in a calm or be driven by a raging hurricane with the deck awash and the sails fluttering or ripping. It should be remembered too that Dana's account is one of the earliest narratives of life on a small merchant ship by a participant. It precedes by ten years Herman Melville's novel about a different kind of Pacific voyage aboard a United States man-of-war, *White Jacket*, 1850.

JTF

References: Edwin F. Edgett, *DAB*, V, 1930, pp. 60-61; Charles Francis Adams, *Richard Henry Dana: A Biography* (Boston: Houghton Mifflin, 1890; revised edition 1891); Robert L. Gale, *Richard Henry Dana, Jr.* (New York: Twayne, 1969).

Richard Harding Davis

(April 18, 1864 — April 11, 1916)

During the course of his thirty-year journalistic career, Richard Harding Davis became the symbol of an adventurous, swashbuckling war correspondent. He convinced generations of college youths that the journalist's life was the most picturesque and exciting of all careers, full of glamor and romance. Along with Rudyard Kipling, he influenced such contemporaries as Frank Norris, Jack London, John Reed, and Stephen Crane, while his legend was inherited by Vincent Sheean and Ernest Hemingway.

Davis' family background was hardly indicative of a future filled with travel in exotic lands, reports on warring nations, and wild adventures. From early childhood, his surroundings were literary. His father was editor of the Philadelphia *Public Ledger* and his mother was one of the prominent women novelists of her generation. In his home he was surrounded by considerable luxury and educated in expensive private schools. One commentator noted that Davis "was probably the only newspaper man in America who would not look out of place in a dress suit."

Davis' newspaper career began in 1886, when he was twenty-two. It was destined to make him the most widely known reporter of his generation. For a brief time, he was employed by the Philadelphia *Record* and then the *Press*, for which he reported the Johnstown flood disaster. His first foreign assignment was for the *Telegraph*, which sent him to England with the Philadelphia cricket team. The next move was to join the staff of the New York *Sun*. His stories and special articles for that paper and *Scribner's Magazine* attracted wide attention. They probably brought him to the attention of *Harper's Weekly*, for which he became managing editor in 1890. In that capacity, he made a tour of the West, recounted in his book *The West from a Car Window*. While out West Davis fraternized with Mexican murderers, Texas Rangers, old prospectors, and women who smoked and drank in public. Later he went on an extensive tour of the Mediterranean, resulting in another book, *Rulers of the Mediterranean*, and spent time in England, Paris, and the Canal Zone region.

In the spring of 1896, the *New York Journal* sent Davis to Russia to cover the coronation of Czar Nicholas II. The following year, the *Journal* asked him to go to Cuba to report on the insurrection. He sent back some unusually dramatic stories, including several about the execution of Cuban revolutionaries. Davis' stories were biased, because he was sympathetic to the Cubans. In fact, he was always for the underdog, but he never deliberately distorted the facts.

The next war Davis covered was in the spring of 1897, when he was sent by the London *Times* to report on the battles between Greece and Turkey. He and a *Journal* correspondent were the only reporters present at the Turkish attack on Velestinos, one of the important engagements near the close of the war. The reporters narrowly escaped with their lives when caught in a precarious position in a Greek trench.

The Graeco-Turkish War soon ended in victory for the Turks, but then Davis, as a reporter for the *New York Herald*, began to cover the Spanish-American War, which had just begun. He sailed aboard the flagship *New York*, when the American squadron went out to bombard the Spanish shore batteries at

Matanzas. The naval action was soon over, and by June 1898, the U.S. Army was ready to land in Cuba.

Davis decided to attach himself to the Rough Riders, an odd mixture of college athletes, cowboys, and New York society men, who had been recruited by Theodore Roosevelt and who were under his command as a lieutenant colonel. Even though they were not as well trained as regular army troops, Davis thought that he would see more action and excitement with the Rough Riders.

After marching all morning through the steaming Cuban jungle, a thundering fusillade came from a hillside just ahead and American soldiers began falling all around Davis. He helped to drag the injured to cover, and then grabbed a rifle from a fallen soldier and joined the attack on the snipers. Roosevelt shouted for a charge and the Rough Riders followed him up the hill. A few minutes later the Spaniards were in flight and the skirmish was over. Roosevelt thanked Davis personally for his help and offered him a commission in the Rough Riders, which he refused.

Even more deadly was the assault by the Rough Riders on San Juan Hill. The hill was topped by a Spanish blockhouse protected by barbed wire and trenches, machine gun emplacements and artillery pits, all manned by Spanish sharpshooters. The American forces moved slowly against the entrenched enemy, but enough of them reached the crest to rush the Spaniards and put them to flight. A few days later, Santiago surrendered and the Spanish-American War was over.

By 1900, two years afterward, Davis was ready for more military action and glory. He went to British South Africa to cover the Boer War, first with the British army and then with the Boer commandos, intrepid bush fighters and raiders. While with the Boer army, Davis visited a schoolhouse in Pretoria which had been converted into a prison camp for British soldiers. Among the prisoners was a correspondent for the London *Morning Post*, young Winston Churchill.

A few years later, in 1904, Davis went to Tokyo to cover the Russo-Japanese War, but permission by the Japanese to go to the front was so long delayed, he saw little of the fighting. Also somewhat tame from Davis' viewpoint was a trip to Mexico in 1914 to cover the outbreak there, though Davis was arrested by Mexican soldiers and came close to facing a firing squad before being released.

Then came the first World War. Davis was not permitted to travel with the British army and therefore proceeded independently to Brussels, where he witnessed the German army marching through. Davis' dispatches on the highly efficient and ruthless German army on the march were smuggled to England and were hailed as one of the classics of war reporting.

David, however, wanted to cover battles, not marches. He hired a taxi and followed the German army. When the taxi could go no farther, he went along with the army on foot. After two days he was arrested and taken to division headquarters for a thorough interrogation. The German officer in charge accused him of being an English spy from the British army. Davis replied angrily that he was an American and a newspaperman. He showed the New York label on his hat as proof. Finally, he was allowed to return to Brussels. From there he proceeded by way of Holland to Paris.

At this time, everything written by war correspondents was severely censored by the Germans, British, and French. Davis was unwilling to have all his communiqués rewritten by the censors. He managed to get out a few stories, such as the recapture by the French and British of the city of Soissons from the

Germans and the destruction by German bombardment of the little cathedral city of Rheims.

As a matter of policy, Davis tried to avoid showing too much sympathy for either side in the war. It was plain, however, that he hoped Germany would be beaten and he thought that America should help to bring that about. He did not live to see the end of the story, for Davis died at his home in Mt. Kisco, New York, in 1916. The United States entered the war a year later.

Davis was a prolific writer. He published eleven collections of short stories, of which *Gallegher and Other Stories* (1891) and *Van Bibber and Others* (1892) are most notable. *Soldiers of Fortune* (1897) is typical of his novels, about an adventurous American engineer in South America. He wrote twenty-five plays and seven nonfiction books based on his experiences.

In the opinion of a leading literary critic, Van Wyck Brooks, Davis' "writings were commonplace enough, efficient, surely, but undistinguished," as compared for instance with Stephen Crane's writings. Brooks agreed that Davis' Latin American stories had special color and feeling as he responded to "the land of guitars and gorgeous silent nights." As a correspondent Davis was quick to see the picturesque and a genius in selecting features having news value. In all his journalistic work he tended to be sensational and dramatic.

RBD

References: Fairfax D. Downey, *Richard Harding Davis* (New York: Scribner, 1933); Gerald Langford, *The Richard Harding Davis Years* (New York: Holt, 1961).

George Dewey

(December 26, 1837 — January 16, 1917)

The Spanish-American War was a brief conflict in the summer of 1898, but represented the emergence of the United States as a world power. The basic cause of the war was the liberation of Cuba. American newspapers printed exaggerated accounts of Spanish misrule and when the battleship *Maine* was blown up on January 25, 1898, the American public was outraged. "Remember the *Maine*" became a rallying slogan and war was declared on April 25. Commodore George Dewey operated against Spain in the Pacific Zone; the Atlantic Squadron and the Army operated in the Caribbean. Lieutenant Colonel Theodore Roosevelt added to his public image as a fighter with the Rough Rider Regiment. On December 10, Spain signed a peace treaty ceding Guam, Puerto Rico, and the Philippines to the United States, and granted Cuba independence.

The Dewey family lived at Montpelier, Vermont, and their ancestors had been New Englanders since 1634. George Dewey's mother, Mary Perrin Dewey, died when he was five years old. His father, Dr. Julius Yemans Dewey, dedicated himself to raising his three sons. George credited his father with molding his life. At the age of sixteen he was appointed midshipman at the United States Naval

Academy. His academic development was slow but after two years at sea he ranked third in his class and was granted his commission in 1860.

Dewey's early naval career coincided with the beginning of the Civil War. After a year of visiting ports in the Mediterranean area he returned to the United States and was commissioned a second lieutenant in 1861. Dewey was fortunate when he was assigned as executive officer of the *Mississippi*, an armed ship in Farragut's fleet. Farragut was preparing to capture New Orleans, and twenty-five year old Dewey's attachment to the *Mississippi* was an ideal position to observe and participate in naval warfare under the tutelage of a master. In later years, when he approached the Manila Bay battle, he asked himself, "What would Farragut do?"

In the battle of New Orleans the *Mississippi* was in the first division as the squadron passed Fort Jackson and Fort Philip. Dewey, given the task of directing the ship in the narrow river channel, succeeded in keeping his ship from running aground. Later Dewey was made executive officer of Farragut's flagship *Monongahela* while he operated in the New Orleans area. To be associated with the first admiral was a fortunate experience and indicated the esteem in which young Dewey was held by the navy.

Dewey's early training was completed by 1867 when he was assigned to his first shore duty at the Naval Academy. He had experienced battle and had spent nine years in sea service by age thirty. He had been commended for his coolness and ability under battle conditions. It was no surprise when he was given command of the *Narragansett* and assigned to a survey of the Gulf of California. Dewey considered the location fortunate because he felt that if war with Spain developed he would be sent to the Philippines.

The California tour of duty was followed by a series of assignments which took him to Boston, Washington and the Mediterranean. His work brought him into contact with many political leaders of the time, both in America and Europe. He was promoted to captain in 1884 and five years later was made chief of the Navy Department's Bureau of Equipment. This was a critical position because cruisers were being built and battleships planned. By 1895 there was a new navy, far more powerful than any previous United States naval force. It consisted of battleships, cruisers and torpedo-boats. Dewey, as president of the Board of Inspection and Survey, had an opportunity to pass on construction of the ships. He determined whether such ships as the *Indiana, Iowa, Massachusetts, Maine,* and *Texas* met specifications.

Relations with Spain continued to deteriorate during the 1890s. Dewey, as commander of the Asiatic Fleet after November 1897, wanted to be prepared for any eventuality. His primary concern applied to supplies, especially ammunition. The ships had very little stored supplies, and only by unusual persistence was he able to get the necessary stores delivered.

Commodore Dewey took over command of the fleet at Nagasaki in January 1898. The port was available because Admiral Perry had opened Japan in 1854. Dewey wanted to be closer to Manila in case of war and moved first to Hong Kong and then Mirs Bay, buying supplies from the Chinese. Two days after the cruiser *Baltimore* delivered ammunition, Dewey received a cablegram that war had been declared on April 26. He set his fleet on a six hundred mile course to Manila and a date with fate.

Dewey approached Boca Grande, the entrance to Manila Bay, at midnight. He had been informed that the waters had been mined and he knew that the

Spanish land batteries had some guns of larger caliber than his ships carried. He had no way of repairing a damaged ship because the nearest navy yard was thousands of miles away. Dewey, in his flagship *Olympia*, led the *Boston*, *Concord*, *Petrel*, and *Raleigh* safely through the mine field. Shots from the shore batteries missed their targets and the squadron continued toward the Spanish ships anchored at Cavite. As dawn broke the *Olympia* began firing, followed by the whole squadron. Dewey turned westward in order to use his ship's guns broadside, and at the appropriate distance reversed direction in order to bring the opposite batteries into play. He repeated the maneuver twice to the west and once to the east. The Spanish fire, from ships and shore batteries, at a distance of about one to three miles, proved ineffective. Dewey withdrew after a two-hour battle, thinking that he had done little damage to the Spanish squadron. However, shortly after withdrawal, the *Castilla* and *Reina Cristina* either caught fire or blew up. Shortly after eleven a.m. Dewey renewed his attack and before the day was over had destroyed the Spanish fleet.

Dewey's victory at Manila was accomplished with no loss of ships and only eight wounded men. It was a remarkable achievement and made the United States a major power in the Pacific. The impact of Dewey's victory at Manila Bay has carried over into modern life, as indicated by our continued activities in the Philippines and the Asiatic sector.

Dewey's life after the Battle of Manila Bay was relatively uneventful. He spent one year in the East and upon his return was enthusiastically received by the public. Congress honored him with the rank of Admiral of the Navy and the public gave him a home in Washington. There was talk about Dewey becoming a candidate for president. Though he issued a statement indicating his willingness to serve, his name was not presented at the political conventions. He spent his remaining years as president of the General Board of the Navy Department.

Dewey's first wife, Susan Goodwin, died in 1872, five years after their marriage, leaving one son. He married his second wife, Mrs. Mildred Hazen, on November 9, 1899. Dewey had enjoyed good health until shortly before his death in Washington.

HWS

References: Carroll S. Alden, *DAB*, V, 1930, pp. 268-72; Ronald Spector, *Admiral of the New Empire: The Life and Career of George Dewey* (Baton Rouge: Louisiana State University Press, 1974).

Melvil Dewey

(December 10, 1851 — December 26, 1931)

The founder of library science and of education for librarianship in America, Melvil Dewey, was a truly dynamic, complex, and versatile character. His major achievements included the creation of the Dewey Decimal Classification, used in libraries around the world, the founding of the American Library Association, the establishment of the first school for the preparation of professional librarians, and inauguration of the *Library Journal*, the first periodical devoted to library affairs. Further, Dewey took the lead in advocating school library services, became the leading state librarian in America, one of the most prominent academic librarians of his time, and an active library entrepreneur.

If those achievements were not sufficient, Dewey was a central figure in a number of other social movements, such as the American Metric Bureau, the Spelling Reform Association, and the Lake Placid Club.

Dewey's interest in libraries began early. He entered Amherst College in 1870, graduating in 1874. During his junior year he was employed in the college library, and served as acting librarian for a short time after graduation. Thus was launched his notable career in librarianship. From the outset, Dewey was appalled by the lack of efficiency in library management. At the time, libraries normally arranged their collections by a fixed location scheme; a book's location was fixed on a specific shelf in a specific section or range of shelves. This meant that works on the same subject were not shelved together, and any building expansion required extensive shifting and renumbering on books and in catalogs — an expensive process.

To clarify his own ideas about more efficient operation of libraries, Dewey planned visits to more than fifty libraries in New York and New England. On the basis of his observations, he conceived the idea of relative location and a system of classification, the principal features of which should be that it would be simple to use, universally applicable, and would not be constantly changed. The first fruit of his inspiration was publication in 1876 of Dewey's *A Classification and Subject Index for Cataloguing and Arranging the Books and Pamphlets of a Library*. He presented the scheme to the Amherst Library Committee and received permission to use it in the Amherst library.

Thus was born the Dewey Decimal Classification, one of Dewey's major contributions to library science. The system assigns an appropriate identifying number to every book, thereby making it easier to arrange and to find books on the library shelves. The system is devised to bring all books on the same subject together and related subjects nearby. It divides all books into ten main classes with an infinite number of subgroups. Since its original publication, the Dewey Decimal Classification has gone through numerous editions, has been constantly expanded to recognize new fields and changing subjects, and is used worldwide.

In 1876, Dewey went to Boston. There he took an active part in the preparations for the conference of librarians to be held in Philadelphia, in October. The meeting led to the founding of the American Library Association. Dewey served as secretary of the conference and remained as secretary until 1890. He was elected to two terms as ALA president, 1890-1893, and served for three terms as treasurer. In effect, Dewey was the motivating force for beginning the American Library Association, and he dominated the organization for thirty years.

In the same year as the birth of the American Library Association, 1876, Dewey began editorship of the *Library Journal*, which he believed was a second essential step in establishing librarianship as a profession. The aim of the new periodical was to "cover the entire field of library and bibliographical interests." Later, in 1886, Dewey established another journal, *Library Notes*, designed to reach small libraries with information on recent developments of concern to them.

Moving next into a field which Dewey recognized was of great practical importance to libraries, for two years, 1877-1878, he used his office to test library supplies and equipment. In 1882 Dewey set up the Library Bureau and he remained as head of the firm for twenty-five years. He was always ready to adopt new materials and new methods, as shown by his adoption of the typewriter, the telephone, and other mechanical improvements. One biographer, John P. Comaromi, noted that Dewey "would have equally easily adopted the computer if he were working now."

Dewey always preferred the company of women to men, and his working relationships with women generally ran far more smoothly than with men. In 1878, he married Annie Godfrey, then librarian of Wellesley College, who remained his companion and adviser for the next half century.

Columbia University (then Columbia College) gave Dewey the opportunity to test his library theories, show his administrative ability and to establish the first professional field for librarians. The Columbia trustees were looking for a library leader who would bring fresh ideas, provide central direction and control of the college's scattered collections, and improve the library's service functions. Prior to his appointment, Dewey appeared before a trustees' committee on the library and presented his views on how the library should be organized and managed and his proposal for a library school. The trustees were impressed and with strong backing from President Frederick Barnard, Dewey was appointed librarian-in-chief for three years at a salary of thirty-five hundred dollars a year. It was destined to be a stormy period in Dewey's career.

Dewey attacked Columbia's library problems with his usual inexhaustible energy and enthusiasm. Completion of a new building provided a chance for more efficient library administration. Collections from a number of separate libraries were brought together under central control; all were sorted, weeded, classified, and cataloged. Serious deficiencies in the library's holdings were corrected by new acquisitions, with the cooperation of the faculty. The Dewey Decimal Classification, of course, was used. A key element, one of Dewey's key objectives, was to make the Columbia library of maximum usefulness to faculty, students, and the community. To that end, he publicized long hours of opening, including vacation periods, holidays, and evenings, and invited use by towns-people. The library became a center for meetings of such groups as the New York Library Club (formed by Dewey), the National Sunday School Library Union, and the Children's Library Association.

Dewey raised a storm at Columbia in 1887, when he started a School of Library Economy; seventeen of the first twenty students to matriculate in the first class were women, contrary to the University's regulations. The following year, 1888, the trustees voted to suspend Dewey from his duties in the library. The ostensible reason was a questionnaire in which applicants for admission to the library school were asked to state their height, weight, color of hair and eyes, and to send a photograph—all of which the trustees thought objectionable. A few weeks later, Dewey resigned.

Almost immediately, he found a new field for his efforts. The Regents of the University of the State of New York offered him the position of director of the state library. Dewey plunged into action at once and over the next several years brought the library to greatly increased usefulness. He developed the collections, and demonstrated the possibilities of the home education department, the extension division, traveling libraries, and the library school. The school he had started at Columbia—the first in the United States—moved to Albany with Dewey and soon gained a reputation for being the leading institution in its field. The Association of State Librarians and the New York Library Association were organized, with Dewey playing a leading role. Throughout the approximately seventeen years in Albany, he worked with incredible energy. Special collections and services were developed for medicine, the blind, women and children, and the library's operations and services expanded in almost every conceivable direction. Dewey's prime object was to extend the library's role in the schools, colleges, cities, and states.

Unfortunately, Dewey's somewhat abrasive personality created a number of powerful enemies. Although charges of financial irregularities were made against him, investigations cleared him of these charges. In 1904, however, Andrew S. Draper, former president of the University of Illinois, a man apparently as power-hungry as Dewey, and probably jealous of Dewey, was appointed to head the New York State Education Department. Draper did not admire Dewey, believed that Dewey had overestimated the importance of libraries, and wanted to strengthen the position of schools at the expense of libraries. Dewey's position under Draper gradually became untenable and in 1906 he resigned as New York State librarian. This was the effective end of his career as a librarian, at the age of fifty-four.

The remaining years of Dewey's life were spent in developing the Lake Placid Club in the Adirondacks, which had been incorporated in 1896 as a membership social club. The organization's rate of growth under the direction of Dewey and his wife was phenomenal. It became a multimillion dollar enterprise, with thousands of members. An equally prosperous branch was the Lake Placid Club in Florida, where the Deweys spent their winters. Controversy followed Dewey in the Lake Placid Club, too. Anti-Semitism was charged in the choice of guests invited to visit and use the club.

A distinguished public librarian, Frank P. Hill, a contemporary of Dewey's described Melvil Dewey as "the most influential and effective librarian who ever dwelt among us." The sum of his accomplishments would seem fully to justify such a superlative rating.

RBD

References: Grosvenor Dawe, *Melvil Dewey: Seer, Inspirer, Doer, 1851-1931* (Lake Placid Club, N.Y.: Melvil Dewey Biografy, 1932); Fremont Rider, *Melvil Dewey* (Chicago: American Library Association, 1944); Sarah K. Vann, *Melvil Dewey: His Enduring Presence in Librarianship* (Littleton, Colo.: Libraries Unlimited, 1978).

Emily Dickinson

(December 10, 1830—May 15, 1886)

Although unknown as a literary figure during her lifetime, Emily Dickinson's posthumous fame is so great that she has been generally accepted as a major American poet. Only a handful of her almost eighteen hundred poems were printed during her lifetime. But in recent years enough of her verse and many poetic fragments have been retrieved from various manuscripts to make up the three volumes of the definitive collection edited by Thomas H. Johnson in 1955. Probably no prominent writer has ever led a less eventful or more secluded life than Miss Dickinson. Indeed, several biographers have had difficulty in developing their narratives and frequently have had to rely upon conjecture rather than fact. Although psychoanalysis has sometimes proved helpful, as in the case of Walt Whitman or Edgar Allan Poe, in all three cases enigmas remain.

Born in 1830, in Amherst, Massachusetts, Emily Dickinson was the daughter of Edward Dickinson, a prominent lawyer and the treasurer of Amherst College. She attended Amherst Academy and spent one year at the Mount Holyoke Female Seminary. As a young girl she was witty, she enjoyed music and droll events, and she joined a Shakespeare club. She lived her whole life in the parental home with her sister Lavinia. Her brother Austin, who also served as treasurer of Amherst, resided nearby. She traveled little, briefly to Boston, Philadelphia, and Washington, and had few close friends. As she matured she grew to dislike social formalities more and more. In later years she had literary correspondence with the poet and critic, Thomas Wentworth Higginson, and she valued the friendship of the novelist Helen Hunt Jackson with whom she exchanged letters. She never married and biographers have had no luck in establishing a close romantic relationship with any man, although she certainly appreciated the religious and spiritual guidance of the Reverend Charles Wadsworth of Philadelphia. But Wadsworth's departure for San Francisco in 1862 is curiously coincidental with Miss Dickinson's withdrawal from participation in village society.

Emily Dickinson was a shy person, small in stature like a wren she said, eyes whose color resembled the sherry left in the wineglass by the guest. If one can judge by the contents of her verse, she had little interest in the economic and political world around her and certainly never kept a daily journal like Emerson, although she admired the journalist. But she read current periodicals like the *Atlantic Monthly* and the *Springfield Republican* (whose editor Samuel Bowles she knew), she knew the work of Keats, Carlyle, and Elizabeth Barrett, and among American writers she had sampled Poe and Hawthorne. Moreover, it was characteristic of her to let her mind and speculation project inwardly rather than externally. It is no accident that in a 1930 edition her poems are arranged under four rubrics: Life, Love, Nature, and Time and Eternity.

If the poet declared her dislike of social conformity by withdrawing from society, she manifested the same rebellious originality by scorning literary conventions. She wrote no long poems and few that exceed a dozen lines. She eschewed narrative verse unless one describes a walk in the garden during which she encountered bees, a butterfly, or a snake as an adventure. Generally she avoided labels, so that most of her poems have no titles. Her poetry is lyric poetry, often deceptively light and almost jocund but generally carrying a burden of thought or a startling paradox that was foreign to the poets of the romantic age.

Dickinson seldom used pentameters. She preferred shorter lines so that tetrameters and trimeters sufficed. She could and did use rhyme but she was never confined by it. Her rhymes are occasionally approximate and she often substituted assonance. Alliteration appears and surprising inversion of word order. In contrast to the prolixity of Whitman or the careful melody of Longfellow she resorted to abruptness, sudden pauses, what Stanley Williams once called "her frugal verse economy." Sometimes the result is unfortunate. Careless readers can miss her meaning or object to cryptic utterances which even a second perusal cannot clarify. But the Dickinson lyrics are concise, irregular, surprising in their sudden twists of thought or phrasing, and often witty.

Bound to her garden by choice, the poet found a small perspective marvelously revealing. The mayflower is "pink, small, and punctual." The daffodil "unties her yellow bonnet." A clover is aristocracy to a bee. The cricket is "a pathetic pendulum" that keeps "esoteric time." The bluebird "shouts for joy to nobody but his seraphic self." The oriole is the Jesuit of the orchards who "cheats as he enchants." But Nature, beautiful as it can be as a whole, sometimes loses its diadem. And the snake, inadvertently met on a garden path, causes the interloper to feel "zero at the bone."

Sometimes the Dickinson vision goes beyond the garden enclave. A coming storm approaches with a wind like a bugle. In one of the most famous lyrics, "The Railroad Train," the train arrives at its own stable door "punctual as a star." When she whimsically calls herself a nobody, she contrasts herself with a frog who is constantly telling his name to an admiring bog.

Probably most memorable of all the short lyrics are those touching on religion and immortality. The poet claims that she never saw a moor or the sea yet without even making a visit to heaven she knew where it existed. In the cemetery the one who died for truth and the one who died for beauty lie side by side in the tombs and talk until the moss covers up their names. Miss Dickinson thought stoically about life and fearlessly about death. The following gnostic lines reveal her convictions.

> A death-blow is a life-blow to some
> Who, till they died, did not alive become;
> Who, had they lived, had died, but when
> They died, vitality begun.

Emily Dickinson died in Amherst in 1886. Her sister Lavinia found many of the manuscripts tied up in fascicles with pink and blue ribbons in a bureau drawer. She was convinced that they should be published and got in touch with Thomas Wentworth Higginson, who had acted as a kind of literary advisor to the poet. He once declared that "the main quality of these poems is that of extraordinary grasp and insight, uttered with an uneven vigor sometimes exasperating, seemingly wayward, but unreally unsought and inevitable." The first volume, edited by Higginson and Mabel Loomis Todd, was published by the Boston firm of Roberts Brothers in 1890. A second collection appeared the following year. Both were commercially successful and ensured an immediate audience for what the poet called her letter to the world. In 1894 Mrs. Todd edited *Letters of Emily Dickinson* in two volumes. Later collections of her verse benefited from more careful editing and the incorporation of revisions which the poet herself had preserved. In 1937 Martha Dickinson Bianchi, the niece of Emily Dickinson, and Afred L. Hampson published *The Poems of Emily Dickinson*, which served well until Johnson's definitive edition eighteen years later.

JTF

References: George F. Whicher, *DAB*, V, 1930, pp. 297-98; George F. Whicher, *This Was a Poet: A Critical Biography of Emily Dickinson* (New York: Scribner, 1938); Thomas H. Johnson, *Emily Dickinson: An Interpretation* (Cambridge, Mass.: Harvard, 1955); Richard B. Sewell, *Life of Emily Dickinson*, 2 vols. (New York: Farrar, Straus & Giroux, 1974).

Walter Elias Disney

(December 5, 1901 — December 15, 1966)

One of the recurrent traditions in American life is the possibility of rising from obscurity and poverty to honor and wealth by a combination of intelligence, industry, determination, and to some extent good fortune. Horatio Alger developed this idea into a formula, the rags-to-riches theme, which became basic in his popular series of books for boys. Many examples of such success, involving inventors, businessmen, and even scientists, occurred in the nineteenth century when an expanding economy and a multiplying population created almost endless opportunities. But the tycoons of the twentieth century, involved in merchandising, petroleum, and the automobile industry, demonstrate that the possibility of rapidly obtaining both power and money in the United States still exists.

Walt Disney is certainly proof that the tradition is ongoing. He had an impoverished boyhood and an inadequate education. His work as a commercial artist was not highly remunerative and his first business project ended in bankruptcy. But he was only twenty-two when he and an older brother Roy formed a company to make cartoon films, and from that time on his career prospered. At the end of his life he was deeply involved in motion pictures, television, records, merchandise for children, and probably most conspicuous of all, amusement parks. Needless to say all these enterprises were vastly profitable.

Disney was born in Chicago, the son of a somewhat nomadic carpenter and farmer. In 1906 the family moved to a forty-eight acre farm near Marceline, Missouri, where the boy got a taste of rural life. Four years later the Disneys moved to Kansas City where young Walt delivered newspapers and was briefly a candy butcher on a Santa Fe railroad train. When the family returned to Chicago Disney went to McKinley High School and attended night classes in art at the Chicago Academy of Fine Arts. He was too young to join the army when World War I broke out, but by fudging a bit on his age he was able to enroll in the Red Cross Ambulance Corps. He spent some months in France, practicing his skill in drawing in his spare time. Back in Kansas City he got a job as an apprentice in a commercial art school and then for three years, 1920 to 1922, worked for the

Kansas City Film Ad Company at minimal wages. In 1923 Disney moved to California where he and Roy Disney were partners in a business venture despite difficulties in scraping up enough capital; henceforth Roy would be the business head of the partnership.

An early project called *Alice in Cartoonland* which ran in a series from 1923 to 1926 brought him $1,500 apiece from an eastern distributor named Charles Mintz. Next came a series featuring a rabbit and *Oswald the Rabbit* was born, bringing Disney $2,250 a reel. Eventually these cartoons were released through Universal Pictures. Then Disney conceived a mouse as his protagonist. He had always been interested in mice and actually had a collection of field mice as pets during his Kansas City days. Both Mickey Mouse and Minnie Mouse made their cartoon debut in 1928 in *Plane Crazy*, reappeared in *Gallopin' Gaucho*, and figured in *Steamboat Willie*, Disney's first sound film in which he used his own voice for Mickey. Thus was created one of the amazing characters in cinematic history. When the *New York Times* printed an obituary of Disney many years later it used as a headline, "Founded an Empire on a Mouse."

Disney's menagerie was quickly expanded. Mickey Mouse had all kinds of adventures in varied roles but shortly from the studio emerged Donald Duck, his inamorata Daisy Duck, the bloodhound Pluto, the comic chipmunks Chip and Dale, and even more. In time came the Silly Symphony cartoon series such as *Skeleton Dance*, 1929; *Flowers and Trees*, 1932; and, in color, *Three Little Pigs*, 1933.

Disney's first great critical and financial success was the full length animated film, *Snow White and the Seven Dwarfs*, 1937. It was followed by *Pinocchio*, 1940; *Dumbo*, 1941; and *Bambi*, 1942. The last of these, which made the little deer world famous, was not immediately profitable since box office receipts did not initially balance the original cost. Even less successful was the more ambitious *Fantasia* of 1940 with a sound track by the Philadelphia Orchestra which played music by Bach, Beethoven, and Tchaikovsky.

During World War II Disney worked for the government and his animated cartoons became a propaganda medium. In 1947 he combined cartoon characters with live actors in *Song of the South*.

Throughout the decade of the 1950s Disney was enormously productive; his work ranged from children's stories and film versions of familiar books to documentary films of natural creatures and habitats. *Cinderella* appeared in 1950, *Alice in Wonderland* in 1951, and *Peter Pan* in 1953. He also converted into films *Treasure Island*, in 1950, *Robin Hood* in 1952, and *20,000 Leagues Under the Sea* in 1954. His pioneer documentary film was *Sea Island*, produced in 1948. This was followed by several others, notably *The Living Desert* in 1953 and *The Vanishing Prairie* the next year.

The television show "Disneyland" opened in 1954 and "Davy Crockett" the year following. "Zorro" came in 1957. The 1964 film *Mary Poppins* reputedly grossed $50 million.

Nearly everything that Walt Disney pioneered, created, owned, franchised, or leased made money. But nothing that he ever was associated with proved more profitable or spread his name more widely than the amusement park. The first one named Disneyland opened in Anaheim, California, in 1955; its clone, Disney World, was completed in 1971 after the death of the promoter. Not only have hundreds of thousands of people visited them and enjoyed their spectacles, their rides, and their general atmosphere, they have become as celebrated an American curiosity as the Grand Canyon or the Empire State Building. To many Europeans or Asiatics it is more important to visit Disneyland than to journey to Washington.

Although Disney's name is commonly linked with an entertainment designed for children, his amusement park has been equally attractive to adults and youngsters. Indeed though he was sometimes referred to as Uncle Walt, he was not especially fond of children. Disney has been described as a tall, somber man who seldom smiled. He was infatuated with technology and an expert in applying or adapting it. By expanding the use of color, photography, and sound effects he brought about profound changes in film technique. During his lifetime he received twenty-nine academy awards and in 1956 won the French honor of "Officier de l'Academie." Disney was not inclined to pontificate about the state of the arts and said little about politics. It is perhaps enough to say that he revolutionized the world of the cinema. But the English political cartoonist David Low went much further: "It [his work] makes Disney, not as a draftsman but as an artist who uses his brains, the most significant figure in graphic art since Leonardo."

JTF

References: Richard Schickel, in *Encyclopedia of American Biography*, pp. 280-82 (New York: Harper & Row, 1974); Richard Schickel, *The Disney Version* (New York: Simon & Schuster, 1968); Christopher Finch, *The Art of Walt Disney, from Mickey Mouse to the Magic Kingdom* (New York: Abrams, 1973).

John Roderigo Dos Passos
(January 14, 1896 — September 28, 1970)

One of the important American men of letters of the twentieth century, John Dos Passos began to write during his Harvard days and continued to be productive almost to the time of his death. Some forty books came from his typewriter, including verse, drama, essays, tracts, history, and to the largest extent, fiction. But he was also a persistent traveler. From his days as an ambulance driver in World War I (like his friends in France and Italy—e. e. cummings, Robert Hillyer, John Howard Lawson, Ernest Hemingway) to his closing years as a country squire in Virginia, he spent time in the capitals and on the beaches of Europe as well as in Cape Cod, Washington, and New York. His early conversion to socialism and his dislike of a predatory, capitalistic society, both engendered in part by the cynicism of wartime, produced some of his best fiction written from the proletarian point of view. But he eventually mellowed and his natural addiction to history led him to focus his attention on the rise of Jeffersonian democracy. He finally cast off the radicalism of his youth completely and assumed the role of a conservative elder chronicler.

Dos Passos was born in a Chicago hotel room, the illegitimate son of a New York corporation lawyer of Portuguese descent, John Randolph Dos Passos, and a widow, Lucy Addison Sprigg Madison. The father was already married and continued to lived with his legal wife until she died in 1910. He then married Mrs. Madison. The boy was actually known as John R. Madison until 1912 when he took his father's surname as his own. One result of this bizarre situation was that the mother and son lived a rather lonely and nomadic life, much of the time abroad. What was awkward and almost impossible in the United States became convenient in Europe. Business trips brought John Dos Passos Senior across the Atlantic frequently where the three could live and travel as they pleased. Brussels and London provided a residence for mother and son, and young John attended school in London from 1901 to 1906. In the fall of 1906 Mrs. Madison brought the boy to Washington where there were relatives; a Dos Passos-owned farm on the Virginia side of the Potomac River also provided excellent vacation opportunities. But in 1907 John began a different kind of education which was not always pleasant. For four years he was enrolled in the Choate School at Wallingford, Connecticut, a distinguished preparatory school which was not always kind to students with erratic backgrounds. Nearsightedness and an obvious lack of athletic ability did not ingratiate him with the student body, but he was a voracious reader and he graduated near the head of his class. In June, 1911, he passed the entrance examination for Harvard. His father subsidized a trip abroad for him and a tutor, and after six months of travel in England, France, Italy, Egypt, and Greece he returned to the United States and entered Harvard in the fall of 1912.

Four years later he graduated cum laude, following years of hard study, desultory but wide ranging reading, exposure to painting and drama in Boston and New York, and serious efforts to write. He contributed editorials, criticism, stories, and verse to the *Harvard Monthly*. When an anthology entitled *Eight Harvard Poets*, partly underwritten by his father, was published in 1917 it included verse by cummings, Hillyer, and Dos Passos. In 1915 his devoted mother, Lucy Madison Dos Passos, died. Two years later his father also died, leaving Dos Passos without close family ties and deprived of an inheritance which he had to some extent expected. The news came to him when he was in Madrid, where he had gone following college to study architecture and to learn something about Spanish life and character at first hand. His new situation in life and the war clouds then gathering over Europe prompted an important decision. He determined to join the Norton-Harjes ambulance unit in France.

Although his service was brief he saw something of war and much of life behind the lines and of soldiers on leave in Paris. When the unit was disbanded he transferred to a Red Cross group in Italy and remained abroad until his enlistment expired. Back in America in August of 1918, he was more than ready to record some of his experiences and observations on the printed page. France, Italy, and Spain would appear frequently in the books which quickly followed.

In 1920 Dos Passos used his own life as an ambulance driver in his first novel, *One Man's Initiation ... 1917*; this was reprinted twenty-five years later as *First Encounter*. More significant was *Three Soldiers*, a 433-page novel published in 1921. Although set in wartime it had little to do with actual combat. Instead the author focused on three soldiers who differed in race and temperament but who each in his own way strove to get along in a world of cynicism and corruption. The Italian-American from San Francisco, Fuselli, wished only an advance in rank; the Indiana farm boy Chrisfield became a corporal but hated the brutality and regimentation of the army and killed his sergeant with a hand grenade; the Harvard music student Andrews fled to Paris on leave and was calmly composing a symphony when he was picked up for desertion.

Two inconsequential books appeared in 1922, a volume of verse entitled *A Pushcart at the Curb* and a collection of essays on Spanish art and culture called *Rosinante to the Road Again*. But in 1925 Dos Passos published *Manhattan Transfer*, a brilliantly original novel which had a lasting effect on later fiction. The book is thronged with characters but there is no central figure. We meet a farm boy who cannot find a job and commits suicide, a bootlegger, an unscrupulous lawyer, a politician, a radical unionist, a Wall Street broker who becomes a beggar, an actress who rises in her profession but finds no happiness in success, and Jimmie Herf, a newspaper reporter who at the end of the story still seeks a job and stability. Herf might have been the protagonist but his story is told in broken bits of narrative. The main character in the book is really the city of New York, as the novel proceeds irregularly with no transitions and little coherence. Dos Passos provides fascinating vignettes of the uglier sides of metropolitan life, some brilliantly evocative and most leading nowhere. His naturalistic panorama of street and restaurant and theatrical life is rich in urban sounds and colors. The book also anticipates some of his later stylistic experiments, chiefly his practice of running adjectives together and compounding words, sometimes effective, sometimes aggravating.

The fictional work which became Dos Passos's masterpiece is the novel which appeared as a trilogy in 1938 as *U.S.A.*, but had seriatim publication earlier. *The 42nd Parallel* was published in 1930 and is also rich in characters but they are more fully developed and intermesh better. Included are Mac, an I.W.W. journalist who wanders around the country, J. Ward Moorehouse, an advertising man and promoter, Eleanor Stoddard, an interior decorator, and Charley Anderson, a poor North Dakota boy who becomes a socialist and after various stages of disillusionment enlists in a French ambulance unit. But Dos Passos's purpose here is to create an intimate feeling for a period and he chooses various devices to achieve it. One is what he calls "Newsreel," a potpourri of headlines, popular songs, advertisements, slogans, and newspaper excerpts which are flung at the reader without much selection or emphasis. Another method is the "Camera Eye," which is full of impressionistic, stream-of-consciousness passages expressing the author's scorn for the materialism, corruption, and frustration of contemporary American life. A third interruption of the basic narrative is the insertion of brief, ironic biographies of actual celebrities in the United States of the period carefully selected from areas such as politics, invention, labor, and capitalism. His summaries of the lives of J. P. Morgan, Theodore Roosevelt, Carnegie, Debs, Woodrow Wilson, and Edison are probably the best writing Dos Passos ever did.

These methods are continued and some of the earlier fictional characters reappear in the later volumes of the trilogy. In *1919*, published in 1932, we meet Moorehouse and Eleanor Stoddard again, but the dramatis personae also include Richard Savage, another Harvard graduate who serves in the French ambulance corps, and Ben Compton, a bright Brooklyn Jew who drifts into socialism and is finally jailed for pacifist agitation. The third volume, *The Big Money*, 1936, reintroduces Charley Anderson, now a war hero and airplane promoter. Richard Savage also reappears, and Mary French, daughter of a doctor and herself a Vassar student, lives with Ben Compton and plunges into labor work. All three volumes attest to Dos Passos's interest in writing proletarian fiction and in condemning those aspects of American life which can be blamed on greedy capitalism.

Prior to the publication of his first fictional trilogy, Dos Passos had become briefly aligned with the political left. His interest in Communism and labor unrest led him to investigate conditions at first hand. In 1928 he traveled to Russia and spent time in both Leningrad and Moscow. He became concerned about the Sacco-Vanzetti case and joined a protest march in Boston just before the execution took place. With Theodore Dreiser he visited the coal sections of Harlan County, Kentucky, interviewed the striking miners, and heard Aunt Molly Jackson sing protest ballads. But there were growing indications that he disapproved of Communist tactics. This tendency toward conservatism was apparent in a personal reference in the *New Republic* where he proclaimed himself "a middle-class liberal, whether I like it or not." Also in 1929 he married Katherine (Katy) Smith, who knew Hemingway and his first two wives.

He also continued to write. The volume *Three Plays*, published in 1934, contained *The Garbage Man* and *Airways, Inc.*, which had previously been printed. Journalistic reports of his travels were collected in such books as *Journeys Between Wars*, 1938. And in 1939 came *Adventures of a Young Man*, the first volume of a second fictional trilogy which was completed as *District of Columbia* in 1952.

The protagonist of this novel is Glenn Spotswood, a young, idealistic Communist who tires of the party's program and is betrayed by its members. The second volume, *Number One*, published in 1943, deals with Glenn's brother Tyler who is the secretary to a southern politician and demagogue not unlike Huey Long. Tyler is victimized by alcoholism and campaign excesses and also becomes disillusioned with the rascalities of his patron. In the third volume, *The Grand Design*, 1949, one of the chief figures is a radio commentator, Herbert Spotswood, father of the two boys in the earlier books. Washington, not New York, is the urban background, and the author's intention seems to be to show the shortcomings of the New Deal even though he accepted its initial aims. Dos Passos does not repeat here his earlier stylistic devices but frequently employs a kind of prose poem for his editorial messages. A passage at the end of the trilogy is reminiscent of Carl Sandburg:

> Our
> century of
>   power to ruin has wrought no answering power
> to build,
>   to establish, to plant securely on foundations ...
>   To
> achieve
>   greatness a people must have a design before them
>   too great for accomplishment.

Before the end of his career Dos Passos published five more novels, the best of which is *Midcentury*, 1961, a celebration of American individualism. Curiously enough he relied again on documentary sections, inserted prose poems, and included fourteen biographical sketches of figures as diverse as General Douglas MacArthur and labor leader John L. Lewis. But Dos Passos's early interest in American history absorbed much of his writing time and he produced books about Thomas Jefferson and the constitutional fathers (for example, *The Men Who Made the Nation*, 1957).

The great tragedy of Dos Passos's life came in 1941 when the car he was driving on a road just off Cape Cod crashed into a parked truck. His wife Katy was instantly killed and he himself suffered the loss of his right eye. Eight years later he remarried. His second wife was Elizabeth Holdridge, a *Reader's Digest* staff member. His closing years were financially comfortable, he was given the Antonio Feltrinella prize for fiction in Rome (which brought him about thirty-two thousand dollars), and he was again enjoying some of the recognition he had received earlier.

Dos Passos has been described as a country squire living on his Virginia farm, appreciating both bourbon and cigars, retaining his liking for jazz and his sense of humor. Although he engaged in considerable journalistic controversy he disliked making speeches, but he would read from his work in a gravelly voice. His almost complete transformation into a political conservative may be suggested by his late support for Senator Barry Goldwater and for Senator Harry Bird in Virginia. He died in Baltimore in 1970.

JTF

References: A. S. Knowles, Jr., in *American Novelists 1910-1945*, IX, 217-36 (Detroit: Gale Research, 1981); Townsend Ludington, ed., *The Fourteenth Chronicle: Letters and Diaries of John Dos Passos* (Boston: Gambit, 1973); Townsend Ludington, *John Dos Passos: A Twentieth Century Odyssey* (New York: Dutton, 1980; John Rohrkemper, *John Dos Passos: A Reference Guide* (Boston: Hall, 1980); Virginia Spencer Carr, *Dos Passos* (New York: Doubleday, 1984).

James Buchanan Duke

(December 23, 1856—October 10, 1925)

Washington Duke was released from a federal prison at the close of the Civil War. Though he had been opposed to slavery and secession he had served in the Confederate army. After the war he returned with his family to his farm near Durham, North Carolina. The family was penniless, and they found only one thing on the farm of any value, a quantity of leaf tobacco in a log barn. Washington and the children, including son James, pulverized the leaf with flails, packaged it and labeled the bags "Pro Bono Publico." They journeyed through southern North Carolina with a covered wagon selling at farms, villages and cross-road stores. This was the beginning of the great tobacco empire built by James Duke, and eight years later they were processing and selling 125 thousand pounds per year.

The custom of smoking tobacco developed about nine thousand years ago by Indians in the Western Hemisphere. The habit was first observed by Europeans when Columbus visited the Caribbean in 1492. Though the Spaniards had a monopoly on European trade until about 1575 other countries entered the market, and by the early 1600s tobacco was used worldwide. Many countries took up the culture of tobacco, especially the planters of Virginia. Tobacco growing became one of the major money crops of colonial America. At one time or another many governments banned the use of tobacco and included punishment, even the death penalty, as a deterrent. Prohibition had little effect, and the popularity of smoking increased in most sections of the world. It was only natural that some enterprising American would recognize the commercial opportunities of processing the plant for the consumer.

James Duke's youth had been spent on his father's tobacco farm, and he had participated in the log barn manufacture of the finished product by primitive methods. His schooling was limited to an academy in Durham, a boarding school in Guilford County, and six months in the Eastman School of Business at Poughkeepsie, New York. His real education was in his father's tobacco business. In 1878 Washington Duke took his two sons into the business, operating as W. Duke and Sons Company. The business prospered under the guidance of James, but competition was growing with many small firms in the business. Durham slowly became the tobacco capital of the world, but competition for the Duke Company was serious. Bull Durham had become a famous trade name, and James felt that he could not compete and looked for new opportunities. He decided to go into the cigarette business, even though cigarette smoking was not popular at the time. Cigarettes had been used in Turkey and Russia for generations but had met with only minor success in America. Nevertheless, James began manufacturing cigarettes in Durham in 1881. Each cigarette had to be rolled by hand and an experienced "roller" could make about two thousand per day. The cost of operation was high and this limited sales.

Duke heard that a young Virginia inventor, James Bonsack, had perfected a cigarette-making machine. The machine consisted of a system of rollers which shaped the tobacco, sent it through tubes and ultimately cut it into the proper lengths. James made a contract with Bonsack for two machines and by April 30, 1884, both were successfully operating. W. Duke and Sons Company was now in possession of the finest cigarette machine known. They could produce millions of cigarettes per day and needed only a market. They reduced manufacturing costs from eighty to thirty cents per thousand and could meet any competition. But there was a problem. Where was the market? James decided to send an agent to Europe to develop trade and open a branch factory in New York. These decisions, coupled with bold advertising, established the Duke firm as the leading American manufacturer. One billion cigarettes were produced in the United States in 1885, and by 1889 Duke was selling more than one-half of all sold in this country.

The introduction of machinery, improved packaging and advertising resulted in lower prices and increased competition. Four other large companies felt the impact of Duke's new procedures and were forced to adopt his methods. The "tobacco war" raged in full fury. The inevitable merger of rival companies resulted in the creation of the American Tobacco Company in 1890 with James Duke as president. Duke began to penetrate all the marketing areas of the tobacco industry. By 1900 his trust had 92.7 percent of the national production of cigarettes, 80.2 percent of snuff, 62 percent of plug tobacco and 59.2 percent of smoking tobacco. The trust had become the dominant company in the manufacture of all kinds of tobacco products except cigars.

The American Tobacco Company had always enjoyed a thriving foreign trade. To improve operations in England Duke bought Ogden Ltd. of Liverpool in 1901, causing alarm among English manufacturers. A year later an agreement was arranged which permitted the Imperial Tobacco Company to retain all rights in England and the American Tobacco Company and its affiliates to retain all rights in the United States. A third company was formed, the British-American Tobacco Company, with Duke as president, which held control of all the open markets of the world. Duke had forged what represented a worldwide monopoly with two-thirds of the profits belonging to the Duke interests.

The factory in China produced 500 million cigarettes per month. Profits increased like a tidal wave. American Tobacco Company earned $13,291,460 in 1902 and Continental's earnings were even larger. Duke now controlled at least 150 factories worth more than one-half billion dolalrs. His companies, with an insatiable appetite, had absorbed an estimated 250 separate businesses in the process of becoming a giant. Duke was in a position to dictate the price of both the supply and the finished product; a monopoly had been achieved. By 1904 there was a severe revolt among tobacco growers over the price paid for the raw material. One producer claimed that 450 pounds of tobacco brought only $14.65. Dissension flared into open violence in many areas, but a more onimous threat was just over the horizon.

With the appearance of Theodore Roosevelt as president the great industrial monopolies of the day were challenged as combinations in restraint of trade. The Supreme Court upheld the dissolution of the Northern Securities Company in 1904. After five years of litigation, the American Tobacco Company was dissolved in 1911. Duke reorganized the various components into competitive units. After reorganization Duke became interested in other endeavors. He lavished attention on his twenty-two hundred acre farm, the Somerville Estate, and made investments in other industries. He attained outstanding positions in the southern cotton industry, real estate, railroads, aluminum and power generation.

After World War I Duke began to develop hydroelectric power in the Piedmont area of North and South Carolina under the name of Southern Power, later to become Duke Power Company. In addition, he made huge investments in hydroelectric development in Northern Quebec, Canada, an area where few customers existed. His Canadian interests were merged into the Aluminum Company of America. Duke acquired at this time a major investment in the aluminum industry. At his death he held 26,369 shares of Aluminum Limited, 102,476 preferred shares of Aluminum Company of America and 61,637 common shares.

Duke established in 1924 the Duke Endowment fund with an initial gift of $40 million. Beneficiaries included Duke University, Davidson College, Furman University, John C. Smith University, hospitals, orphanages, Methodist ministers and Methodist churches. Through his efforts North Carolina had recovered from the Civil War and became a busy and progressive state. He had developed water power to turn the state's cotton spindles, tobacco factories to utilize the agricultural production, and money to improve its educational system. He had become the major industrial figure in the South.

Duke married Lillian Fletcher McCredy in 1904. They had been long time friends but the stormy marriage lasted only a few months and was dissolved by divorce in 1906. A year later he married Mrs. Nanaline Holt Inman, a widow from Georgia. One daughter, Doris Duke, was left a major fortune.

HWS

References: John Wilber Jenkins, *James B. Duke, Master Builder* (New York: Doran, 1927); John K. Winkler, *Tobacco Tycoon* (New York: Random House, 1942).

Finley Peter Dunne
(July 10, 1867 — April 24, 1936)

Readers of editorials in American newspapers in the early part of the twentieth century became quite familiar with witty and often tart remarks on social and political life which were attributed to a pundit named Mr. Dooley. The gentleman is still cited today although his identity is less widely known. He never had more than a fictional existence, since he was the brain child of Finley Peter Dunne, a Chicago newspaperman. Dunne came to prominence in the 1890s when Eugene Field and George Ade were avidly read columnists and Chicago newspapers vied for their services. Columnists for the *Tribune*, *News*, *Post*, and *Herald* were encouraged to write clever topical comment and to satirize local celebrities. Styles naturally differed but could range from literary to dialectal. Dunne was unique in conceiving an Irish-American bartender who was not always literate and who used a recognizable brogue but who became notable for his bluntness, political awareness, and humor. In time Mr. Dooley became almost as well known as Babbitt and Willy Loman in a later age.

Dunne was born in Chicago, July 10, 1867. His parents had emigrated from Ireland and his father before he reached Chicago had been trained as a ship's carpenter. In his new location he was engaged in the retail lumber business. The Dunnes were numerous and religious and immediately at home in the neighborhood of Adams and Desplaines streets near St. Patrick's Church. As the boy grew up he absorbed many of the traits of the American-Irish and used them effectively in the Dooley sketches. But the family was also bookish and he was early introduced to novelists such as Dickens, Scott, and especially Thackeray. Young Peter Dunne attended Scammon Public School and then became the only one of the boys in the family to go to high school, an advantage which he owed partly to the insistence of his older sister Amelia who subsequently became a teacher and principal. He did not distinguish himself at West Division High and after his mother's early death and his father's business reverses his formal education was ended. He graduated in the spring of 1884, the last in a class of over fifty pupils.

His first job with the Chicago *Telegram*, that of an office boy, was hardly auspicious. But Dunne was amiable, made friends easily, and already knew a good deal about street life in the city. He soon had a chance to show his natural talent for writing and attracted the attention of the managing editor of the evening *News*. Other promotions followed as he shifted from one paper to another. At twenty-one he was city editor of the Chicago *Times*. In 1890 he moved to the *Tribune* and the *Herald*, meanwhile demonstrating his ability as reporter and editorial writer. At the *Evening Post* in 1892 he worked for a paper with some literary pretensions that permitted him to write unsigned dialect sketches which eventually stimulated the Dooley essays. But after several years with the Chicago *Journal* he decided that he wished to be closer to the publishing center of the country and in 1900 he moved to New York, where he was briefly associated with both the *American Magazine* and *Collier's Weekly*.

Dunne's humor and sharp social and political criticism had by this time drawn national attention. Publishers were willing to collect the dialect sketches in book form and his writings were now being syndicated. In 1898 the Boston firm of Small, Maynard & Company published his first book, *Mr. Dooley in Peace and War*, which was an immediate success. It was followed the next year by *Mr. Dooley in the Hearts of His Countrymen*. According to Elmer Ellis, more than seven hundred of Dunne's dialect sketches appeared in print and there were seven book collections before the last one, *Mr. Dooley on Making a Will and Other Necessary Evils*, in 1919. In that same year, however, Dunne retired from editorial work and wrote little of consequence thereafter. He died April 24, 1936, the victim of throat cancer. Newspaper obituaries of the time hailed Dunne as the greatest American humorist since Mark Twain.

Although Dunne was a prolific writer, in one sense he never wrote a book. None of his volumes have a basic continuity or any narrative interest. Rather, they are collections of essays or sketches reprinted from various newspapers and generally topical. Because they were intended for the daily press they are consistently short and concise. Dunne used a convenient framework for his pieces. They are simply observations from the voluble, feisty bartender who presides over an Archey Road (Archer Avenue) saloon in Chicago. There are a few other characters, notably the great listener Hennessy to whom Dooley addresses his remarks and whose occasional words interrupt the possibly tedious monologues. Hennessy is the ideal audience, generally quiet, nonargumentative, and ignorant. Dooley is an articulate, uneducated, Irish Catholic who speaks in a brogue which Dunne renders expertly. Dooley proves to be a rather trenchant observer of what goes on in the local ward, the city of Chicago, and sometimes even the nation.

Dooley is full of prejudices, a blue-collar stalwart who disapproves of high society, the packinghouse gentry, political corruption, social pretensions, the Republican party, and almost every ethnic strain save his own. But he is not awed by political or ecclesiastical power. Two of his best monologues deal with Cousin George (Admiral George Dewey, whose name, says Mr. Dooley, is spelled almost like his own) and Tiddy Rosenfelt (whose military egoism in the Spanish-American War resulted in a book which Mr. Dooley thinks should have been called Alone in Cubia). Interestingly, in later years Dunne and Theodore Roosevelt became intimate friends. Dooley's net ensnares a lot of game, big and little, which he deflates expertly. There was a kind of model for Martin Dooley in an actual public house keeper called McNeary. But Dunne altered and amplified the figure and best of all utilized the Irish ethos and speech which he had grown up with. Dunne did not write conventional fiction but he succeeded in blending reality with a touch of humor.

JTF

References: Louis Filler, *DAB*, XXII, Supplement 2, 1958, pp. 158-60; Elmer Ellis, *Mr. Dooley's America: A Life of Finley Peter Dunne* (New York: Knopf, 1941); Louis Filler, ed., *The World of Mr. Dooley* (New York: Collier Books, 1962).

Pierre Samuel du Pont

(January 15, 1870—April 5, 1954)

The life of Pierre du Pont involves the history of two of the greatest industrial concerns on earth, General Motors and E. I. du Pont de Nemours and Company. To build one great organization is a noble accomplishment, but to be responsible for two is unique in business history. The two companies were very different types of enterprises. General Motors manufactured automobiles to be sold directly to the consumer, whereas du Pont was a chemical company selling primarily to the processor. Pierre took over the management of the du Pont company when it was about one hundred years old and built it into a giant chemical organization; he took over General Motors when it was only seven years old and transformed it into the world's largest manufacturing company at a critical time in its early stages of development. The tasks in the two cases were quite different. At du Pont he changed a family firm, in spite of internal opposition, into a giant corporation with publicly held stock. To accomplish this he had to develop new management processes, overcome family opposition, negotiate with foreign cartels, compete with numerous American concerns, select qualified personnel, and integrate the company vertically to assure a supply of raw materials. In addition he had to be prepared to supply the nation's needs for explosives in time of war. The problem at General Motors involved bringing order out of financial and operational chaos. The company faced a financial crisis and had to compete with the Ford Motor Company.

The du Pont family had its roots in Paris, France. Pierre Samuel du Pont de Nemours, the great-great-grandfather of Pierre du Pont, took his family to America in 1799 to escape the French Revolution. He brought with him his youngest son Elèuthere Irénée who was twenty-eight at the time. Irénée had been introduced into the methods of manufacturing powder in the laboratory of Lavoisier, who held the position of chief of the royal powder works. Upon arrival in America du Pont de Nemours, a former participant in the economic school of physiocrats, organized a company to develop land in the James River valley of Virginia. Upon advice of Jefferson the investment was delayed. Young Irénée discovered that the powder made in America was of poor quality and high priced. With his experience in Lavoisier's laboratory he believed he could make better powder at a lower price. He returned to France in 1801 to buy machinery and borrowed about two-thirds of the capital needed from his father. Upon returning to America he bought land on the Brandywine River near Wilmington, Delaware.

Irénée built a mill on the river, moved his family into a log house, and produced his first powder in the spring of 1804. President Jefferson assured him government orders, and the little powder plant was off to a successful start. Its first year sales amounted to $10,000; the revenues in 1982 were listed at $33,331,000,000. The man responsible for the greatest increase was Irénée's great-grandson Pierre Samuel du Pont.

The du Pont family was closely knit. Pierre's grandfather, Alfred Victor, had been head of the firm, followed by his uncle Henry. His father, Lammot, was a working partner of Henry, second in command. Pierre had the advantage of a good education. After schooling in Philadelphia, he entered the Massachusetts Institute of Technology, graduating in 1890. In September of the same year he started work for the family firm in Wilmington, but found that the experience over the next nine years was frustrating because the directors of the company were entrenched in doing business in the old manner. He did not have the authority to make changes in operations. This unhappiness led him to resign in 1899 and accept a position with the Johnson Company at Lorain, Ohio, to supervise its liquidation. After successfully completing the task at Lorain, he bought, repaired and reorganized the street railway system in Dallas, Texas, selling it at a profit in 1902.

Pierre was called back to Wilmington when his cousin, Eugene, president of du Pont, died on January 28, leaving the company without a leader. After reorganization Pierre became the treasurer and Thomas Coleman du Pont the new president. They immediately began to remodel the company under the new name of E. I. du Pont de Nemours Powder Company. One of their first steps was the acquisition of other companies so that by June 1904, they controlled 60 percent to 80 percent of all powder manufactured in America. They were now ready to concentrate their efforts on eliminating high cost operations and streamlining internal procedures. This resulted in the creation of three departments: smokeless powder, black powder and dynamite. Also, it brought about vertical integration since the company gained control of source material and shipping and developing research laboratories.

Pierre, in order to improve accounting procedures in the new giant, hired John J. Raskob to aid in handling the financial structure. Raskob was to remain a valuable financial advisor for many years. However, as a supporter of Alfred E. Smith, Raskob became chairman of the Democratic National Committee in 1928. This caused Alfred P. Sloan of General Motors to request Raskob's resignation as chairman of the motor company's finance committee.

The program of government regulation of trusts, initiated by Theodore Roosevelt, finally reached Pierre's company. He was deeply disturbed and found it difficult to understand why a well-run corporation which charged reasonable prices was not in the public interest. Nevertheless, he lost the suit and set up Hercules and Atlas Powder companies in 1911 to satisfy government demands.

A family crisis developed in February 1915, when Pierre purchased the proffered stock of Thomas Coleman du Pont. This gave Pierre control of the company, and the sale was objected to by his cousin Alfred. A bitter family feud developed that was not resolved until four years later by a court decision in favor of Pierre. In the meantime World War I was raging in Europe. To supply the powder needed to fill the orders of the Allies it was necessary to greatly expand manufacturing capacity. This required huge new capital investment, which was a dangerous thing because there would be little need in the postwar period. Pierre, unlike other companies which failed, paid special attention to the contracts with the Allies and ended the war period with a profit. At the beginning of the war du Pont's capacity for the manufacture of smokeless powder was about forty-two thousand tons annually but it increased almost five-fold by 1918. Pierre was in full control of the company as World War I developed, and all changes are to be credited to him. The Armistice not only ended the war but it also terminated Pierre's direction of the company. He resigned the presidency on May 1, 1919, in favor of his brother Irénée. It was his intention to build his gardens at Longwood estate, but within a year and a half he would be called upon to reorganize General Motors Corporation.

Pierre became chairman of General Motors in 1915 but, because he was fully involved with the du Pont Company, did not devote much time to the business. However, in 1917 he invested $25 million of du Pont's money in General Motors. In the postwar recession General Motors was faced with serious financial troubles and its founder, William C. Durant, retired from the presidency in 1920 in favor of Pierre. Du Pont, with the aid of Alfred P. Sloan, completely reorganized the company. The chief innovation was to produce a car for each price class, thus covering the entire automobile market. This strategy, plus the installation of fiscal controls which had proved so successful at the du Pont Company, revitalized General Motors to such an extent that it was soon selling more automobiles than Henry Ford. After three years of service Pierre turned the presidency over to Sloan, but remained on the Board until 1929.

Upon returning to his gardens at Longwood he became involved in the educational problems of the state of Delaware. Even before World War I he had made gifts to Delaware College and Massachusetts Institute of Technology. He gave over one and a half million dollars to Delaware College which aided it in becoming the University of Delaware. He worked through the Service Citizens Committee to reform the Delaware school system and in the process gave $3.8 million for new school buildings. By 1935 he had contributed more than $6 million to public education; a large share of these funds had gone to the construction of buildings for black children.

His work with the Association Against the Prohibition Amendment brought him in on the side of Franklin D. Roosevelt in the campaign with Herbert Hoover. Pierre was happy that Roosevelt repealed the Prohibition Amendment but was extremely unhappy with his failure to balance the budget and returned to the folds of the Republican party. He served on Hoover's Committee for Relief, the Delaware Employment Relief Committee, Roosevelt's Advisory Board of the National Recovery Administration, and the National Labor Board. He also helped found the American Liberty League.

Du Pont took over the management of two companies, General Motors and E. I. du Pont de Nemours, and built them into the largest enterprises of their kind, an automobile producer and a chemical company. It is impossible to measure the impact of his achievement upon society. After his death his companies remain living memorials to his ability as an administrator.

HWS

References: Alfred D. Chandler, Jr., and Stephen Salsbury, *Pierre S. du Pont and the Making of the Modern Corporation* (New York: Harper & Row, 1971); Norman B. Wilkinson, *E. I. du Pont, Botamiste* (Charlottesville: University Press of Virginia, 1972).

James Buchanan Eads

(May 23, 1820—March 8, 1887)

The Mississippi River and its tributaries drain a large portion of the United States. The system extends to the Rocky Mountain front on the west and the Appalachian Mountains on the east. The river water is turbid from the sediment which is constantly added to it. The silt is carried in suspension and the sand is carried forward erratically until finally reaching the delta in the Gulf of Mexico. The sandbars and mud flats form shipping hazards that have wrecked many riverboats, especially in the nineteenth century when the rivers were main arteries of transportation. No one understood the rivers. The snags and shifting sandbars were unpredictable to riverboat pilots, especially at the mouth of the Mississippi.

James Buchanan Eads became an outstanding civil engineer who solved some of the navigational problems of the Mississippi and in the process made a fortune and gained fame. Eads was born in Lawrenceville, Indiana, four years after Indiana was admitted to statehood. His father, Thomas, had been unsuccessful in business ventures in Cincinnati and Louisville and in the summer of 1833 sent his wife Ann and three children by steamboat to St. Louis. James Eads got his first view of the Mississippi but tragedy awaited them at the St. Louis dock where their boat caught fire and the family barely escaped. Because they found themselves destitute in a strange city everyone in the Eads family had to work. James, thirteen, began by selling apples on the street but soon found employment in a dry goods store. His formal education had ceased, but fortunately his employer had a small library and Eads began to educate himself. His primary interest was to learn about the physical laws that govern nature and man's capacity to control them. Lacking a formal education beyond grammar school Eads substituted talent, ambition and labor.

Eads spent five years in the dry goods store where he ran errands and waited on customers. It was March 1839, when he left the store and walked up the gangplank of the *Knickerbocker* steamboat to report as a second clerk. During the first season the *Knickerbocker* hit a snag near Cairo and sank. This experience caused Eads to consider the possibility of salvaging the freight from sunken riverboats. Three years later, at age twenty-two, he had completed the design for a diving bell boat equipped with derricks and pumps. While his two partners were building the bell-boat, a barge with one hundred tons of lead sank near Keokuk. Eads undertook the job of recovering the lead using a barge with a makeshift diving bell. He obtained a forty-gallon whiskey barrel and modified it by attaching it to a block and tackle and using lead weights to make it sink. With this improvised bell Eads recovered the one hundred tons of lead as the first salvage job of many over the next twelve years.

Eads discovered sunken riverboats by a daring method; he walked on the river bottom under his diving bell. His boat was anchored with long lines that permitted it to swing from side to side in a five hundred foot arc. After Eads made the first trip on the bottom the boat was moved twenty feet down stream, and he walked back to the other shore. In this manner, he searched for the *Neptune* five miles south of Cairo for sixty days before he found it. In the process of walking on the river bottom he became thoroughly acquainted with the process of river erosion and deposition. There were so many sunken riverboats that Eads increased his fleet to ten bell-boats and worked all of the tributaries to the Mississippi. After twelve years of labor Eads retired at the age of thirty-seven with a fortune of more than one-half million dollars.

Eads enjoyed about four years of home life in St. Louis before Abraham Lincoln was elected president. Eads believed in the preservation of the Union and recognized the importance of the Mississippi River in the coming struggle. He argued that control of the river was an essential part of any strategic plan for victory. His own state, Missouri, was a border state which was proslavery but antisecession. Eads argued that the only way the Mississippi could be saved was with a fleet of ironclad gunboats. The Confederacy was building strong forts on the southern portion of the Mississippi but the Union had not placed a single gun on the Upper Mississippi or its tributaries. Eads urged Edward Bates, Lincoln's attorney general, to build an armed river fleet. After considerable delay Eads's proposal to build seven gunboats in sixty-five days was accepted on August 7, 1861. Within two weeks he had four thousand men working in shops and mills in several states. The *St. Louis* was delivered on October 12. Later, Eads wrote Lincoln, "The *St. Louis* was the first ironclad built in America. She was the first armored vessel against which the fire of a hostile battery was directed on this continent." Eads's ironclads led Grant's attack on Forts Henry, Donelson and Vicksburg.

By 1864 Eads had completed the construction of four big monitors. Admiral Farragut was preparing to attack Mobile Bay and asked that the monitors join his fleet. On August 4 the *Chickasaw* and *Winnebago* steamed into Mobile Bay and played an important part in Farragut's victory. By the end of the war Eads had constructed fourteen ironclads, four mortar boats and seven tinclads. His innovations attracted the attention of foreign countries, and his advice was sought by many navies. Eads realized that his work was only a step in naval development. He thought that improvements "in the future will be reached by submerging the entire vessel" and that battleships of the future would be equipped with "immovable turrets."

The population of St. Louis had grown from ten thousand, when Eads first arrived in 1833, to one hundred thousand in 1867. A bridge spanning the Mississippi was needed for the growing city. Eads formed a St. Louis bridge company and over much opposition, some of it dishonorable, began a bridge in August of 1867. The plans called for three spans consisting of units 502, 520, and 502 feet in length. The spans were 200 feet wider than any then known. Many said such a bridge could not be built. Eads asked, "Must we admit that because a thing never has been done, it never can be?" He went to Europe to discuss his plans and so impressed engineers in London that he was proposed for membership in the Royal Society of Arts.

Eads was prepared to build a bridge across the Mississippi because he knew more about the habits of the river than anyone else. The piers had to be set on bedrock more than a hundred feet below the river. Giant caissons had to be sunk through sand and mud to withstand the pounding of ice floes in the winter. Eads used compressed air in the caissons during digging operations, but some of the men developed the bends (caisson disease). Although he established medical services and followed the procedure of slow decompression several men died.

Eads demanded superior quality in all of the steel used in the bridge. Steel makers were astounded with the terms "elastic limit" and "modulus of elasticity." Andrew Carnegie stormed, "Nothing that would and does please engineers is good enough for [Eads]." Eads tested all materials and if they did not meet specifications they were returned. Many engineering aspects of the bridge were unique and even during construction opposition continued to mount. In 1873 Secretary of War Belknap joined the Chief of the Army Engineers in condemning the bridge. Eads obtained a hearing with President Grant. After questioning Belknap an irate president ruled that work on the bridge must continue.

The first arch was closed in September 1873 and the bridge opened on July 4, 1874, seven years after the first pier was commenced. It was a great engineering achievement, the forerunner of the Brooklyn bridge and other bridges spanning the Mississippi. Its extensive use of steel and tubular cord members set the pattern for new bridges in all parts of the world. During the process of construction the engineering innovations attracted so much favorable attention that the National Academy of Science elected Eads a member and the University of Missouri awarded him an LL.D. degree. The jubilant crowd at the dedication ceremonies used as one motto, "The Mississippi discovered by Marquette 1673; spanned by Captain Eads 1874."

Distributaries at the mouth of the Mississippi spread sand and silt in the form of a vast delta. For more than a hundred years ships trying to reach New Orleans found the passes clogged with shifting sediment. Dredging attempts gave only temporary relief. Ships were often prevented from coming in and many were marooned in New Orleans. Every method used to clear the channels had failed. To solve the problem a canal was proposed by engineers. Eads was opposed to an artificial canal because, he argued, the river could be made to cut its own canal faster and cheaper than man could build one. Eads proposed to develop a jetty channel 28 feet deep and 350 feet wide at his own expense. He would maintain it for ten years at a cost of $10 million. The government would make its first payment of $1 million when a depth of twenty feet was secured and $1 million for each additional two feet. The remainder was to be paid only if the jetty held its depth. After a long struggle against opponents of the jetty bill, including Chief Humphreys of the Army Engineers, Congress authorized Eads to proceed.

Eads began work on the jetty in May 1875. He was confident of success because he knew that the amount of sediment carried by a river is in direct proportion to its velocity. If a channel is restricted and velocity increased a river will dig its own channel deeper. At the end of eleven months work the depth of the channel had increased to sixteen feet and he invited the *Grand Republic*, then the finest riverboat on the Mississippi, to bring investors and guests to traverse the channel to the open Gulf. Serious opposition continued to come from Chief Humphreys but by October, 1876, the channel was twenty feet deep and the river had removed over 3 million cubic yards of silt. By 1877 the South Pass channel was so deep that 587 ocean vessels had gone through without difficulty. The work was completed in July 1879 with the channel obtaining a depth of thirty feet. The cost to the government was $5,250,000, a fraction of the cost of an artificial canal. Eads was hailed for his engineering accomplishments.

Eads's last venture, never realized, was the construction of a ship-carrying railway across Mexico that would link the Atlantic with the Pacific. Eads carried on a vigorous campaign in opposition to Ferdinand de Lesseps who wanted to build a canal across Panama. Though Eads lost the battle for the railway he continued to grow in the esteem of his countrymen. New Orleans staged a two-day Golden Jubilee in his honor in 1929. He had been mentioned as a candidate for the presidency in the 1870s and was elected to the American Hall of Fame in

1920. A boy with a grammar school education had become an honored civil and hydraulic engineer in his successful attempts to tame the Mississippi River. He was still struggling on behalf of the ship-carrying railway when, in 1887, doctors ordered him to rest. He took a vacation in the Bahamas where he died in March.

HWS

References: Lewis How, *James B. Eads* (Chicago: Houghton Mifflin, 1900); Florence Dorsey, *Road to the Sea and the Mississippi River* (New York and Toronto: Rinehart, 1947).

Thomas Eakins

(July 25, 1844 — June 25, 1916)

Although he remained obscure for much of his life, Thomas Eakins has generally been recognized as the greatest painter produced by the United States. He spent many years as a teacher, lecturer, and painter in Philadelphia and slowly achieved recognition for his rugged portraiture and his brilliant studies of the human body. Yet in 1916 only three major American museums owned examples of his painting. An exhibition of his work sponsored by the National Gallery of Art in Washington in 1961 did much to revive interest in Eakins, especially when the show was moved to Philadelphia and supplemented by material from the Philadelphia Museum of Art. Some three hundred items, including paintings, sculptures, and photographs, were put on display at that time.

Eakins was born in Philadelphia in 1844, the son of Benjamin Eakins. The father, of Irish descent, was a methodical, deliberate worker who was a writing master and engrosser of manuscripts. Eakins studied at the Pennsylvania Academy of the Fine Arts, but in 1866 at the age of twenty-two decided to journey to Paris for advanced training. At the École des Beaux-Arts he studied painting and sculpture under mentors like J. L. Gérôme and remained for three years. When he suffered from ill health he went to Spain for a few months and while there was greatly impressed by the work of such painters as Goya, Herrera, and Velasquez.

Back in Philadelphia in 1870 Eakins resumed work at the Pennsylvania Academy of the Fine Arts where he eventually became the principal instructor as well as the dean of the faculty. He also studied anatomy at the Jefferson Medical College (which became the owner of his finest painting, the *Clinic of Dr. Gross* in 1875). He was a careful student of the human figure, in action as well as in repose, and his treatment, whether of a surgical operation, an autopsy, a boat race, or a boxing match was meticulous. But the plain, undramatic, stark realism of his portraits often repelled viewers. Moreover, he was an intense, somewhat solitary artist who refused to sacrifice his principles to opportunism. In 1886, when the trustees of the Pennsylvania Academy objected to his practice of using nude models, he resigned his position. He also felt that, despite his own foreign training, young American artists should stay at home and study the people and environment of their own country. His advice sounded almost chauvinistic:

If America is to produce great painters and if young art students wish to assume a place in the history of the art of their country, their first desire should be to remain in America, to peer deeper into the heart of American life.

Among Eakins's students at Philadelphia were three young men who became in 1910 part of the group known as The Eight: Robert Henri, John Sloan, and William Glackens.

Eakins painted an extraordinary number of portraits, ranging from sportsmen (he himself enjoyed hunting and fishing), chess players, and oarsmen to collectors or dealers of art, professional men, and celebrities. He painted a number of Catholic churchmen, partly because he liked the colors of their vestments. He painted businessmen, musicians, Civil War veterans. As F. O. Matthiessen observed, "before he was through he had made a record of American types that has not been surpassed by any of our novelists." For many years he was a friend of Walt Whitman and visited the poet occasionally at Camden. Eakins's 1887 portrait of Whitman, now in the Pennsylvania Academy, is notable for the flowing locks of hair, the florid, benevolent face, and the loose fitting clothes of the poet. The unselfconscious nudity of the boys in Eakins's *The Swimming Hole* has suggested to viewers the frank imagery of Whitman's "Song of Myself."

Other notable portraits are *The Concert Singer* (owned by the Philadelphia Museum of Art), showing a young performer with her mouth open and her rose-pink satin gown contrasted with a gray-green wall behind; and *Mrs. Edith Mahon* (in the Smith College Museum), a rather sad face, shadowed and relaxed. In the 1878 *The Chess Players* (owned by the Metropolitan Museum) Eakins pictured three old men in a dim parlor, their personalities suggested economically and their rumpled clothes and knotted hands revealing his close observation. The artist's care in constructing an action painting is exemplified by his decision to make clay models of the horses he intended to use in *Fairman Rogers Four-In-Hand* and of the diving boy in *The Swimming Hole* before he ventured to create the work.

The famous *Clinic of Dr. Gross* derived from his observation of surgical procedure at the Jefferson Medical College and is in every sense a remarkable achievement. The enormous painting measures ninety-six by seventy-eight inches. The background is dusky and shows the audience, presumably students and interns, in rapt attention. The actual surgeons are not in laboratory gowns but wear coats and ties, and the doctor himself is illuminated by a shaft of light which reveals his nimbus of graying hair as he seems about to lecture on the operation proceeding to his left. Eakins's reputation at the time may be suggested by the fact that his great painting was shown at the Centennial of 1876 among the medical displays.

Eakins was a modest and reticent man who spoke slowly and bluntly. He commanded several languages and his devotion to his art was total. In his painting he did not comment on his subjects but painted them as he saw them, using clear, cool light but avoiding any glamor. During his lifetime he paid little attention to current art fads and seemed unconcerned about his contemporaries. Winslow Homer was the only living artist who won his attention and then largely because he felt that Homer shared his own attitude toward painting. Eakins continued doggedly to do the work which he felt inspired to accomplish. He married Susan H. Macdowell in 1881 and had no family. He died in Philadelphia in 1916.

JTF

References: William Howe Downes, *DAB*, V, 1930, pp. 590-92; Lloyd Goodrich, *Thomas Eakins*, 2 vols. (Cambridge, Mass.: Harvard University Press, 1983); Elizabeth Johns, *Thomas Eakins: The Heroism of Modern Life* (Princeton, N.J.: Princeton University Press, 1984).

George Eastman
(July 12, 1854—March 14, 1932)

The daguerreotype silver-plated sheet of copper developed by Louis Daguerre in 1837 for photographic reproductions started a new industry. By September 1839, the process had reached America and daguerreotype galleries, as well as travelling photographers, became commonplace. The mechanics of photography was so complex that a great amount of equipment was required. When Mathew Brady photographed the Civil War, it was necessary for him to carry his equipment in a specially designed wagon containing facilities for developing plates. To take a picture the camera had to be placed on a tripod and live subject matter posed. Photography was not available to the general population.

After the invention of the daguerreotype many attempts were made to improve the process. The first major change took place in 1851 when collodion was used to make glass negatives. The wet plate process was quickly adopted, because paper prints could be made in any quantity desired. It had some major handicaps; the photographer had to sensitize the plate just prior to exposure, and he had to have a darkroom available for development. Nevertheless, some of the most famous pictures of history were produced by this process. Tintypes (ferrotypes) were modifications of the glass plate method. The collodion emulsion was coated on thin iron sheets. Tintypes became popular forms of photographic art. The wet place process was displaced by the dry plate. The great advantage was that the photographer could buy plates and carry them with him. Also, he could delay development of the exposed plate to some future time. The gelatin-covered dry plate was many times more sensitive than the collodion coated plates. By 1880 it was the common process used in photography.

The next step in photographic technology was the development of flexible dry film to be used in a hand carried camera. These inventions would permit any person to become a photographer; the age of the snapshot artist began when George Eastman invented film and the Kodak camera. Along with the telephone and electric lights, photographic film and the camera would add to the changing ways of society in the late 1800s. Eastman built an industrial empire that made him one of America's wealthy men and an outstanding philanthropist.

Eastman's father, George Washington Eastman, moved his family from Waterville, New York, to Rochester when George was six years old. His father died two years later and the mother, Maria Kilbourn, found it necessary to take in boarders to maintain the family. Under these circumstances George's education was limited to seven years in a public school, at which time he accepted a job at three dollars per week with an insurance agent. Though he was only fourteen years old he was so frugal that he showed a balance of thirty-nine dollars at the end of the first year. Six years later his fortunes improved when he was offered a job in a bank as a junior bookkeeper, and by 1877 he had saved thirty-six hundred dollars. Poverty no longer knocked on the family door. He was now affluent enough to buy $94.36 worth of picture-making equipment and launch a lifelong career in photography.

Photography in 1877 was a tedious and laborious affair. The wet-coated glass plates had to be exposed while still wet and developed before they dried. This meant that when Eastman took pictures outdoors he had to carry camera, tripod, plate-holder, plates, chemicals, a dark-tent, and containers for water. Taking a picture was not only a form of art, it involved considerable physical labor. Eastman became an avid student of photography and read an article in the *British Journal of Photography* concerning coating a glass plate with an emulsion that dried. This would do away with the wet plate process and avoid the necessity of carrying so much paraphernalia in the field. Eastman saw an opportunity to develop a commercial enterprise. By mid-1879 he had composed a successful emulsion and had constructed a mechanical device for coating the plates. He received his first patent in England on July 22, 1879. A year later he was marketing dry plates and was recognized internationally for his invention.

In the early stages of his business he visualized the need for mass production by machinery in order to reduce prices. Low prices would increase demand in both foreign and domestic markets. He believed that mass production coupled with advertising would yield economic rewards. These principles became his guidelines for the conduct of business. He incorporated the Eastman Dry Plate & Film Company of Rochester on October 1, 1884, with his friend Henry A. Armstrong as president. This firm replaced the earlier Eastman Dry Plate Company, because Eastman had developed a new method of recording images on film. In the first half of 1884 he had experimented with the coating of a transparent film and after many attempts succeeded in creating a film upon which he could produce a picture. He applied for a patent on March 4, 1884, and the modern photographic industry was born. While Eastman was in his laboratory creating a new form of art, Bell was able to listen to his new telephone and Edison listened to squeaky voices on the new talking machine or turned on the magic electric light. Five years later Edison used the new film in a motion picture machine.

To make the film useful a new system of holding it had to be designed. A roll-holder was developed that held twenty-four exposures. Eastman soon realized that a camera was needed to hold his film. There were unlimited opportunities to market a specially designed camera loaded with film that could be carried in the hand. By May 1888, Eastman built a box-type camera, 6¾ inches long by 3¾ inches deep and wide. The price of the camera loaded with film was twenty-five dollars. He needed a name for the new creation and settled on "Kodak," because the name was short and easily pronounced. Photography had progressed from Daguerre in 1837 through the tin type stage to Eastman's flexible dry film. The industry of moving pictures soon followed.

Eastman was dissatisfied with the quality of the film and hired the chemist, Henry N. Reichenbach, to study the problem. Reichenbach's employment as a research chemist was one of the early efforts of corporations to hire chemists on a full-time research basis. By 1889 he had improved a flexible, nitro-cellulose, transparent film to such an extent that a patent was obtained by Reichenbach and Eastman, the company reserving all rights.

The decade of the 1890s saw the rapid development of Eastman's business. His goal was to create a product for the man on the street. Constant improvement of both camera and film met with acceptance by the public and permitted the company to constantly expand; it was capitalized in 1889 at $1 million, two years later at $5 million and five years later at $8 million. Improvement of the product was accompanied with a lowering of price. A boy could buy a camera for five dollars, load it in daylight, and carry it in his pocket. Eastman built a new plant in Rochester known as Kodak Park and expanded his factory at Harrow, England. In the meantime Edison was creating a successful motion-picture camera and Eastman had to be ready to furnish a satisfactory film for the new industry just over the horizon. In 1896 he produced the first strip of positive motion-picture film. The capability of producing hundreds of thousands of feet of film was soon realized, and Edison's camera and Eastman's film combined to establish the new cinema art form. Since Eastman had an early interest in color photography, he encouraged research in the company that resulted in Kodachrome. The company also developed X-ray plates and plates for astronomical photography.

Success did not come without numerous legal battles. Eastman had a policy of purchasing patent rights for his own protection, but this did not prevent lawsuits. Numerous competitors appeared and by 1911 at least eight manufacturers of cameras, four of film, and at least twenty of paper were active. Eastman attempted to buy out as many as possible and entered into exclusive contracts with the distributors of photographic supplies. His control of about 75 percent of the American market raised the charge of monopoly, and he was brought to court during the Woodrow Wilson administration. Settlement was reached when Eastman divested some of the subsidiary companies and altered certain company policies.

Eastman showed an early interest in the welfare of his employees. He gave his first wage bonus in 1899, established a benefit fund in 1911, and gave numerous wage dividends. The number of employees reached fifteen thousand by 1920, and Eastman arranged to improve their welfare by establishing medical facilities and improving safety devices. His final effort toward good employee relations was the sale of ten thousand shares of stock to longtime workers at par and the establishment of a welfare fund with the proceeds.

Eastman had anticipated World War I, and it was no surprise to him when America entered the conflict. He turned over his plant and expert research men to aid in war work and refused to accept abnormal profits, voluntarily returning a large sum of money to the government which he considered excess payments. Though he was normally adverse to committee work, he accepted the chairmanship of the local Red Cross drive for funds. In May 1918, the local papers announced gifts totalling $4,815,502 to the War Chest. Eastman had contributed $600,000 of the total. The War Department cited his company for meritorious service.

Eastman had progressed from poor boy to inventor to industrial giant acquiring the riches of fame and success. It was now time to consider the disposal of his wealth, the final step in the life of many rich men. He had made his first gifts of two hundred thousand dollars in 1899 to Rochester Mechanics Institute and sixty-five thousand dollars to the University of Rochester. In order to avoid the notoriety which often accompanies philanthropic gifts he commenced in 1912 making gifts under the name of "Mr. Smith." In this manner he gave away $11 million in the next seven years, including large gifts to the Massachusetts Institute of Technology and the Hampton and Tuskegee Institutes. When he gave a block of his company stock, his identity as "Mr. Smith" was disclosed. He established several dental dispensaries, including one in Rochester and one in Rome with the permission of Benito Mussolini. He contributed $1 million to the Rome clinic. The Eastman School of Music and the School of Medicine and Dentistry were established at the University of Rochester. He gave away about one-half of his fortune while living, and upon his death the remainder of his estate was given to the institutions he had previously aided, totalling over $75 million.

Though the industrial nabobs of his day were often criticized for greed and avarice, most of them were highly responsible citizens. Eastman, with his creative ability, produced jobs for more than fifteen thousand people at one time and contributed to the industrial might of America. In fact, through photography, Eastman added to the pleasure of countless people in the world by making available a cheap method of picture taking with both black and white and color film. In 1932 he apparently felt that he had completed his tasks on this earth and took his life.

HWS

References: Carl W. Ackerman, *George Eastman* (Boston and New York: Houghton Mifflin, 1930); K. T. Compton, "George Eastman," *Science*, 75, April 15, 1932.

Edward Kennedy (Duke) Ellington

(April 29, 1899 — May 24, 1974)

The world of music was enriched during the 1920 to 1940 era by such outstanding composers and lyricists as Handy, Porter, Hammerstein, Kern and Rodgers. The name of Edward Ellington, the Duke, must be added to this renowned list. He became celebrated as a pianist, orchestra leader and composer. Though he was not the father of jazz he was among the first to arrange jazz for large orchestras and is considered as one of its greatest composers. Though his life spanned the age of jazz, he considered himself a composer of Negro folk music. He wrote many popular songs and was one of the most prolific composers who ever lived. Ellington copyrighted about 950 songs in a fifty year period, an average of nineteen per year. In 1929 he copyrighted twenty-two songs, forty-three in 1939, thirty-nine in 1959 and fifty-two in 1967. The number of composed and unrecorded songs is unknown, but may reach a few thousand.

Ellington had a complex personality. He was a serious artist, yet a romantic. He could use poetic language fit for a queen, or he could hold his own with those from the ghetto. He composed jazz music that could be played in a Las Vegas casino or sacred concert music for the churches of the world. Though he had ability as a painter, writer, producer and organizer, his forte was music. Though he was constantly on the move all of his spare time was given to music. He never had a permanent home base, an office, or a place to call his own. He composed wherever he might be at any given time, in a hotel room or railroad car, in a bus or airplane, or on the back of a menu in a restaurant.

Ellington, as an orchestra leader, led a frenetic life without roots in any town. He was constantly performing — from a one-night stand in a night-club to a performance before a queen. Tirelessly, for fifty years, he led his band, held his players together, and wrote hundreds of compositions. Few musicians have equalled the quantity of Ellington's production. His admirers came from all walks of life. Paul Whiteman, "King of Jazz," Igor Stravinsky and Leopold Stokowski from the field of classical music paid tribute to his genius.

Ellington was born in Washington, D.C., the son of a butler and blueprint maker for the navy. His mother, Darcy, played the piano and his father, James, had some interest in opera. Though Ellington took piano lessons at the age of six, his formal musical education was minor. As a teenager he was very interested in graphic arts, but after graduating from high school chose music as a career. His marriage to Edna Thompson in 1918 proved unhappy. His son Mercer was born in 1919 and after a few years of marriage he and Edna were separated, but not divorced.

By 1923 Ellington was leading a small band in New York and writing songs for Tin Pan Alley. The songs included "Blind Man's Buff" and "Pretty Soft for You." His small band played for four years at the Kentucky Club before his big break came when he opened at the Cotton Club in Harlem on December 4, 1927. Ellington modified Paul Whiteman's soft-jazz and turned it into "jungle" music with "growls" and "wah-wahs." At this stage Ellington gave his musicians freedom to experiment and he listened to the new tones. Later, he composed music to fit the capabilities of his players. In this manner, a mutual relationship developed between the band and its leader. As the decade of the twenties approached its end Bing Crosby was crooning soft melodies, Al Jolson was singing "Sonny Boy," flappers were doing the Charleston, and college students were dancing cheek to cheek. Jazz was the popular form of music and Ellington was starting to dig deep into the roots of African tribal rhythms for new musical expressions.

The five year period from 1929 to 1934 was a banner era for Ellington. In 1929 he appeared in Ziegfeld's revue *Show Girl*, a short movie *Black and Tan Fantasy*, and continued playing at the Cotton Club. The following year he secured his first Hollywood contract and appeared in *Check and Double Check* with Amos 'n' Andy. Compositions began to flow from his pen, some on short notice. "Creole Rhapsody" was written one evening in Chicago in 1931 and performed the next day. "Solitude," "Mood Indigo" and "Sophisticated Lady" were composed in this period and became favorites of the dancing public. He began his first European tour in 1933 and upon returning began American tours.

By 1939 Ellington had created his own orchestra, and although he was an accomplished pianist the orchestra became his trademark. He took it on numerous tours of Europe, including Russia in 1971. The orchestra played a Royal Command Performance before Queen Elizabeth at the London Palladium. He went to Ethiopia and Zambia on behalf of the State Department. In 1963 the orchestra toured the Middle East and Far East where it was greeted with great warmth. This was a remarkable trip for an American orchestra and was a triumph in public relations. Among his American achievements were the famous Carnegie Hall concerts.

Ellington became one of the most honored musicians in American history. He received honorary degrees from fifteen universities and eight medals, including the President's Gold Medal from President Lyndon B. Johnson and the Presidential Medal of Freedom from President Richard M. Nixon. Forty different professional societies gave him various awards. Forty states and municipalities found ways of recognizing him with proclamations and keys. Magazines and a host of other organizations awarded him trophies, plaques and other honors. Hundreds of recordings of Ellington's musical compositions have been made and are still being produced.

Ellington died in New York in 1974. He was a talented black American who was admired throughout the world. His music was primitive yet new, untamed yet religious, violent yet mellow, and had an international appeal. He was the unchallenged master of the jazz band.

HWS

References: Edward Kennedy Ellington, *Music Is My Mistress* (New York: Doubleday, 1973); Derek Jewell, *Duke* (New York: Norton, 1977); Peter Gammord, *Duke Ellington: His Life and Music* (London: Dent, 1958).

Douglas Fairbanks

(May 23, 1883 — December 12, 1939)

In the early days of the motion picture there was no sound track to accompany the events on the screen. It has been pointed out that audiences did not have to rely entirely on visual perspective since even the smallest neighborhood theater generally had a pianist to perform loudly during tense or dramatic sequences. But spoken dialogue did not exist. *The Jazz Singer* featuring Al Jolson in 1927 was the first movie to be accompanied by a sound track. D. W. Griffith's memorable productions, like *The Birth of a Nation*, were silent films and his innovative uses of the camera preceded the synchronization of eye and ear effects. Moreover, the first group of Hollywood stars like Charlie Chaplin, Buster Keaton, and William S. Hart rarely maintained their celebrity when cinema actors were obliged to speak as well as act in films. For various reasons, not excluding vocal limitations, most of them chose not to appear in movies after the 1920s. A good example despite his rather long apprenticeship on the stage is Douglas Fairbanks.

Fairbanks was born in Denver in 1883, the son of H. Charles Ulman and Ella Adelaide Ulman. The father was a Jewish lawyer in New York and later a mining operator in the West; the mother came from a Catholic family in Massachusetts and had been married previously. After a divorce the mother reverted to the name of her first husband (John Fairbanks) and at seventeen Douglas legally adopted her surname. The boy was educated at Denver, attended the Jarvis Military Academy, East Denver High School, and later the Colorado School of Mines. He also took dramatic lessons and had the good fortune to meet Frederick Warde, an English actor, stock company proprietor, and lecturer on Shakespeare, who encouraged him. When Warde offered him an engagement, he and his mother chose to return to the east.

Fairbank's debut occurred in 1900 when he played the part of a lackey in a piece called *The Duke's Jester* in Richmond, Virginia. He then left the stage for a time and became a clerk in a Wall Street brokerage office. Also, like Sinclair Lewis at a similar time in life, he worked his way aboard a cattle boat for a brief trip to Europe. An early interest in gymnastic training aided his physical fitness in later life and made possible some of his acrobatic acting in his well-known films.

In 1902 Fairbanks joined Minnie Dupree's company playing *The Rose of Plymouth Town*. His rather florid style of acting caught the eye of the producer William A. Brady, who signed him to a contract beginning in 1904 and lasting for five to seven years. For two years he played the juvenile lead in a play called *A Gentleman from Mississippi* which was performed on the road and in New York City. This was followed by a stint in vaudeville, but in 1911 he became a star in pieces entitled *Officer 666* and *He Comes Up Smiling*. He married Ann Beth Sully in 1907 and this union produced his only child, Douglas Elton Fairbanks, born in 1909. In time the son also became a well-known actor.

About 1915 Fairbanks moved to Hollywood and signed with the Triangle Corporation at a salary of two thousand dollars a week. For the next twenty years he was closely identified with the California film industry and between 1915 and 1921 he made thirty pictures, including *He Comes Up Smiling*, 1918; *Knickerbocker Buckaroo*, 1919; and *The Mollycoddle*, 1920. Usually he played the role of a smooth-shaven, unassuming, likeable young American. His hearty athleticism, buoyant and healthy personality, and flashing grin won him admirers throughout the world.

Fairbanks joined with Charlie Chaplin, D. W. Griffith, and Mary Pickford to form the United Artists Corporation in 1919, and the next year, following the death of his first wife, he married Miss Pickford, widely known as America's Sweetheart. As it turned out they appeared together in only one film, *The Taming of the Shrew* in 1929.

Despite theatrical activities Fairbanks found time to write three booklets of an inspirational kind. With titles such as *Laugh and Live*, *Assuming Responsibilities*, and *Making Life Worth While*, they were published in 1917 and 1918.

The films that Fairbanks starred in during the 1920s showed the actor in a different role from his earlier pictures. Now he cultivated a big mustache, often wore a sword, and generally played a swashbuckling, highly active character. Moreover, he frequently wrote part of the script himself and strongly influenced the tone, style, and pace of the story. He identified with characters like Zoro, Robin Hood, and Sinbad and these became the roles that audiences familiar with Fairbanks found most appealing. They demanded flamboyance and athletic ability, traits which were almost indigenous with him, and needed little intellectual subtlety.

He made seven pictures of this type in the years 1921 to 1927: *The Mark of Zoro* in 1920, *The Three Musketeers* in 1921, and *Robin Hood* in 1922; and four more annually 1924 to 1927, *The Thief of Bagdad, Don Q, Son of Zoro, The*

Black Pirate, and *The Gaucho*. Collectively they were the climax of a busy and profitable career.

After a divorce from Mary Pickford in 1935, Fairbanks married for a third time. His wife was an English woman, Lady Sylvia Ashley, whom he wed in 1936. Much of his remaining life was spent in England and on the continent. He died at Santa Monica, California, in 1939. In May 1984 the United States Postal Service issued a twenty-cent postage stamp commemorating Fairbanks in the Performing Arts Series.

JTF

References: Arthur Knight, *DAB*, Supplement 2, 1958, pp. 172-73; Ralph Hancock and Letitia Fairbanks, *Douglas Fairbanks: The Fourth Musketeer* (New York: Holt, 1953); John C. Tibbetts, *His Majesty the American: The Cinema of Douglas Fairbanks, Sr.* (South Brunswick, N.J.: Barnes, 1977).

Fannie Farmer

(March 23, 1857 — January 15, 1915)

The origin and development of one of the most famous cookbooks can perhaps be best understood and appreciated by reviewing the author's background. Fannie Farmer was born in 1857, the daughter of a printer and ex-newspaperman. When seventeen years of age, she was stricken with a mysterious "paralysis" which crippled her for life. The misfortune forced the cancellation of her plans to attend college. Eventually, Fannie recovered her health sufficiently to assist her mother in housekeeping. During that period, she developed such an interest in cooking that her family urged her to enter the Boston Cooking School. After her graduation from that institution in 1889, she was asked to remain as assistant to the director. Two years later she became the head of the school. It was while in the latter position that Fannie Farmer, age thirty-eight, wrote her cookbook. Originally, the book was privately printed, and its sale was limited to Miss Farmer's pupils. Publication in 1896 soon made its author so famous and wealthy that she proceeded to organize a school of her own, Miss Farmer's School of Cookery, which has flourished to the present day.

The Boston Cooking-School Cook Book appeared at a time highly propitious for its success. The amateur or professional cook could choose between such pamphlets as *Fifteen-cent Dinners for Families of Six*, with their very imprecise directions, or enormous tomes by professional chefs of Paris or Delmonico's, whose instructions presupposed huge kitchens, richly stocked pantries, and large staffs. In contrast, Fannie Farmer's book was simple, comprehensive, and aimed at an average-sized family of six, with not more than one servant.

That Boston should be the birthplace of a work which was to become the standard guide for the setting of American tables was in itself an anomaly. The Puritans had once preached hellfire to those who took pleasure in eating. Shortly before the book came out, one of the Concord sages, Bronson Alcott, had been proclaiming the virtues of high thinking and plain living—mostly on apples and vegetables. Fannie Farmer was undeterred by such austere traditions.

The original edition of *The Boston Cooking-School Cook Book*, along with recipes and menus, gave elaborate instructions for building fires with such fuels as kerosene, gas, wood, charcoal, coal, coke, and alcohol. In harmony with the custom of preparing bounteous meals which prevailed in the 1890s, the menus recommended would shock modern calorie counters. Breakfast might be topped off with a generous wedge of apple pie or a piece of strawberry shortcake. A full-course dinner consisted of ten to a dozen courses, including for example clams or oysters, soup, rissoles or bouchées, fish, venison, beef or mutton, a meat entrée or light fish, one vegetable, cheese or punch, game with salad, cold dessert with fancy cakes, bonbons, crackers and cheese, and café noir.

Presented for the first time in Fannie Farmer's *Cook Book* was a complete soup-to-nuts collection of formulas so easy to follow that anyone could go into the kitchen and learn to cook by them. Though more emphasis was placed on eating for health than for enjoyment, the recipes obviously were aimed also at achieving delicious flavors.

When first published, *The Boston Cooking-School Cook Book* contained many recipes calling for wine and brandy. Such recipes were removed when prohibition went into effect, but they have been restored in recent editions. During her lifetime, Fannie Farmer was continually devising new recipes, thoroughly testing each one before putting it in her book.

In the Boston Cooking School the courses were designed for the training of teachers, but in Miss Farmer's own school the courses were planned for the training of housewives. The director's main interest was in practice not theory. Her school specialized in invalid cookery, supplied lecturers on that subject to training classes for nurses, and Miss Farmer herself gave a course on invalid cookery one year at the Harvard Medical School. A book in which she took particular pride, *Food and Cookery for the Sick and Convalescent*, never attained the popularity of her original masterpiece.

In her School of Cookery, Miss Farmer taught twice a week, dramatizing her lectures as she limped briskly about the demonstration platform. The classes were largely attended, usually by about two hundred students, and were reported at length in the Boston *Transcript*. In addition, Miss Farmer was much in demand for addresses to women's clubs, and for ten years, assisted by her sister, she conducted a popular page on cookery in the *Woman's Home Companion*.

The most important principle introduced into cooking by Fannie Farmer was uniform, accurate measurements. The cookbooks of her day contained only the vaguest of rules: "add flour to thicken," or "a pinch of lard," or "butter size of an egg" (pullet's or ostrich's?), or "scant cupful," or "rounded teaspooon," or "heaping spoonful." After Fannie Farmer, "the Mother of Level Measurements," it would never be necessary for housewives to wonder about the size of the egg or how heaping a tablespoon should be. Her tablespoons were never heaping, scant, or generous, but always level. Cups and teaspoons were level, too. The cup or spoon was to be dipped into the flour or sugar, a knife used to cut off the top, and what was left fitted exactly into the utensil used for measuring, the surface even with the top of the cup or the edges of the spoon. And so Fannie Farmer's system of level measurements, as elementary as the decimal system, changed cooking from a guessing game to a near science.

It is not surprising that *The Boston Cooking-School Cook Book* has been the target of criticism by epicureans, gourmets, and gourmands, with their widely individual notions about what constitutes good food. Culinary savants, with a background in foreign cuisines, especially French, are practically unanimous in turning up their noses at "Fannie."

One critic who savored the best in food and drink was H. L. Mencken, who reviewed the *Cook Book* in typical Menckenesque language. Mencken first commends the book for its "clarity, comprehensiveness and common sense," and recognizes that it is planned to serve ordinary housekeepers in kitchens with limited equipment, not "professional chefs with hordes of potato-peelers, beef-steak-beaters and fish-flayers to help them." The "weaknesses of the work," as seen by Mencken, "lie in two directions. First, it is written by a woman and addressed to women, and hence a certain tea-table preciosity gets into some of its recipes. What male with a normal respect for his pylorus, even in America, would actually eat a rasher of celery fritters? Or one of cherry fritters? Or one of sponge fritters? Clam fritters, yes, and apple and banana fritters perhaps, but who could imagine peach, apricot, pear or orange fritters?"

Mencken continues:

> The other defect of the book apparently flows out of the fact that it was hatched in Boston, where lower middle class British notions of cookery still prevail. Thus it deals very badly with the great dishes of more cultured regions. The recipe for terrapin à la Maryland, with its use of flour, cream and eggs, would make a true Marylander howl and so would the recipe for fried soft crabs ... an obscenity almost beyond belief.

Nevertheless, though Mencken holds that the Farmer opus is "too feminine" and "a shade too Yankee," it is "a very worthy work" and if followed closely would improve American cookery—"not a great deal perhaps, but still some."

Miss Farmer did not discuss such new-fangled subjects as calories and vitamins, but that she was aware of scientific research in the field is shown by a brief preface to the first edition. Recent editions of the *Cook Book* recognize only gas and electricity as fuels for cooking, and a variety of information is offered on vitamins, calories, and menu planning. Life for the cook and chef has been immensely simplified by refrigerators, deep freezes, electric blenders, and pressure cookers—all unavailable in 1896.

RBD

References: Obituary Sketches in *Woman's Home Companion*, December 1915, and *Journal of Home Economics*, May 1915.

David Glasgow Farragut

(July 5, 1801 — August 14, 1870)

Few, if any, men in history started their professional naval career as early in life as David Farragut. He was appointed midshipman at the age of nine and was placed in command of a prize ship at age twelve. This remarkable beginning in the United States Navy was due to his sponsor Commander David Porter. The Farragut family had befriended Porter's father during his last illness and Porter showed his deep appreciation by adopting David. David's mother, Elizabeth, died when he was seven. His father, George, born in Minorca, served in both the army and navy on the side of the Americans during the Revolution. President Jefferson gave him the command of a gunboat in 1807 with headquarters in New Orleans. He was an adventurer with the sea as his home.

The Farragut family moved from Campbell's Station near Knoxville, Tennessee, where David was born, to New Orleans in 1807. Commander Porter was in charge of the New Orleans naval station and decided to steer the Farragut child into a career in the navy. Porter, as guardian, was instrumental in getting David's first appointment as midshipman in 1810. The appointment was obtained under the name of James Glasgow, which was changed four years later to David Glasgow.

Farragut's baptism in naval warfare came during the War of 1812 when Porter was in command of the frigate *Essex*. Farragut acted as Porter's aide. The *Essex* made a cruise in the Pacific Ocean during the war and captured the *Alexander Barclay*. Farragut, now twelve years old, was made master of the prize by Porter and ordered to take the ship to Valparaiso. It was an ill-fated assignment because the *Essex* lost a bloody battle to the *Phoebe* and *Cherub* in Valparaiso harbor and Farragut became a prisoner of the English navy on March 28, 1814. After his release he spent most of his teenage years on board various ships stationed in the Mediterranean zone.

Farragut's formal education was very limited. His schools had been the decks of ships and his teachers had been sailors and the ships' commanders. Nevertheless, he proved himself to be an avid student and made every effort to learn by reading, observing and following the example of his commanders. When serving as an aide in the Mediterranean he had an opportunity to accompany Charles Folsom, naval schoolmaster and American Consul to Tunis. Here, Farragut pursued a course of studies under Folsom's direction for nine months. He learned to speak Arabic, French, Italian and Spanish. By systematically applying himself to the study of literature and mathematics he taught himself in those fields. He pursued an education whenever possible and when home-based attended lectures at Yale and the Smithsonian Institute.

Farragut passed an examination in 1821, making him eligible for the rank of a lieutenant. He then began a tour of duty in the Gulf of Mexico where he served on the ship *Grey Hound* under the command of his brother William. Shortly thereafter, he was given his first command of the naval vessel *Ferret*. By 1825 he had attained the rank of lieutenant and served on the *Brandywine*. The next thirty years were a relatively quiet time for the navy. Farragut spent the period at his home in Norfolk, Virginia, on occasional duty. Though he was not a favorite of the Navy Department he served on the *Vandalia* in 1829-1830, the *Natchez* in

1833, and the *Erie* in 1838, all in the capacity of a lieutenant. He received the rank of commander in 1841 and was assigned to the sloop *Decatur*.

The Mexican War presented the first opportunity for naval officers to distinguish themselves since the War of 1812. Farragut believed that the castle San Juan Ulloa could be captured by the navy and he requested assignment in 1845 that would permit him to participate in the attack. His appointment was delayed until February 1847, but before he could reach his objective as commander of the sloop *Saratoga* the castle had surrendered to the army of General Winfield Scott. Farragut was keenly disappointed and, after an argument with his superior, was ordered home.

The 1850s were quiet years for American naval officers. Farragut was not among the most favored elite. He spent about two years on ordnance duty at Norfolk and Washington, and in 1854 was ordered to the West Coast to build a navy yard at Mare Island. He spent four years at this task and then returned to take command of the *Brooklyn*. The *Brooklyn* conveyed the American minister to Mexico and called at several Mexican ports. Farragut spent the winter of 1860-61 at his Norfolk home as a respected, but not renowned, sixty-year-old naval officer. The Civil War was just over the horizon and Farragut's destiny with fame had arrived.

Farragut was living in Virginia when that state seceded from the Union on April 17, 1861. The next day he moved his family north to the village of Hastings-on-the-Hudson. Like Robert E. Lee, he was of southern origin, but unlike Lee he chose to support the Union. The government considered the capture of New Orleans as a primary goal in opening the Mississippi River. The city was protected by Fort Jackson on the west side of the river and Fort St. Philip on the east side. A heavily armed flotilla of Confederate ships patrolled above the forts. The capture of New Orleans represented a major undertaking. Farragut, along with other candidates, was considered to command the naval expedition. After a favorable report from Commander David D. Porter, Farragut was appointed on January 9, 1862 to command the West Gulf Blockading Squadron in the Gulf of Mexico. His orders also directed him to "reduce the defenses which guard ... New Orleans ... and take possession of" that city.

Farragut, on the flagship *Hartford*, collected seventeen vessels and a mortar flotilla for support during February and March of 1862. They rendezvoused on the east side of the Mississippi delta and on April 18 made their first attack on Fort Jackson by mortar fire. The mortars were not very effective, and after several days Farragut reached the conclusion that it was better to attempt to bypass the forts and attack the Confederate vessels than it was to try to reduce the forts. This decision was contrary to advice and fraught with danger from mortar fire and fire-rafts. Shortly before dawn on the twenty-fourth, Farragut's fleet of seventeen ships advanced in three sections. Fire from the forts was heavy but fourteen of the ships succeeded, the *Hartford* barely escaping a fire-raft. Farragut proceeded to attack the Confederate vessels, destroying or capturing them to gain a complete victory. When New Orleans surrendered on the twenty-sixth, the Union gained control of an important Confederate military and communication center. Farragut's victory had been attained with skill mixed with caution and boldness. It made him the outstanding officer in the navy and the President and Congress tendered their thanks. On July 16, he was the first naval officer to be commissioned a rear-admiral.

After New Orleans fell, Farragut was required, by government orders, to open the Mississippi northward. He proceeded to Vicksburg but recognized that that city could not be captured by naval attack because of the size of the Confederate fort. After a brief engagement he withdrew to the Gulf for further operations. All coastal cities west of the Mississippi soon came under his control. Only Mobile on the east remained in Confederate hands. However, 1863 was not so successful. Galveston and Sabine Pass were recaptured, the *Hatteras* was sunk, and Farragut's orders to guard the Mississippi held him in the New Orleans area.

Farragut's primary goal, after New Orleans, was Mobile. He had desired to attack Mobile in 1863 but was held at the New Orleans base. After assembling a fleet of fourteen ships and four ironclads in early 1864, he was prepared to attack. The defense of Mobile Bay consisted of Fort Morgan on the east, Fort Gaines on the west and mines, known as torpedoes, in the main channel. In the early morning of August 5 Farragut advanced. The *Tecumseh* was sunk when it hit a mine and the other ships hesitated. At this critical moment a cry was heard, "Torpedoes ahead" and Farragut gave his memorable command, "Damn the torpedoes." The fleet passed Fort Morgan, met the Confederates and dispersed them. Two days later Fort Gaines surrendered, followed by the surrender of Fort Morgan on August 23, 1864.

With the Mobile victory Farragut reached the acme of his career. In appreciation Congress passed a new bill creating the position of vice-admiral and Farragut was named to it on December 23. Two years later, on July 26, 1866, he was named to the newly created rank of admiral, fifty-seven years after joining the navy.

Farragut spent the last six years of his life as one of the most honored and respected naval men in American history. He had overcome the lack of a formal childhood education by applying himself to studying at every opportunity. He had survived the early death of his mother and the absence of a nomadic father. He had cared tenderly for his first wife, Susan Marchant, during her sixteen years of illness prior to her death in 1840. He had one son by his second wife, Virginia Loyall. Farragut knew what it meant to struggle for survival, and when the critical moments came at New Orleans and Mobile he was prepared to win; defeat never entered his mind.

Farragut has been celebrated in verse by poets and statues have been erected in Madison Square, New York, Farragut Square, Washington, and Marine Park, Boston. He died in Portsmouth, New Hampshire, but was later buried in Woodlawn Cemetery, Westchester County, New York. The procession in New York included President Grant, ten thousand soldiers and many officers from the army and navy. Though born in the South he played a major role in preserving the Union.

HWS

References: Charles O. Paullin, *DAB*, VI, 1931, pp. 286-91; A. T. Mahan, *Admiral Farragut* (New York: Appleton, 1892); Edwin Palmer Hoyt, *Damn the Torpedos! The Story of America's First Admiral: David Glasgow Farragut* (New York: Abelard-Schuman, 1970).

Marshall Field I

(August 18, 1834 — January 16, 1906)

The post-Civil War era of new America was a fantastic period of industriali-
zation. The war had settled the questions of slavery and secession and at the same
time gave impetus to building a new society. No one took time to ask where it was
all leading; the surge was forward. Bell was fooling around with a wire because he
thought he could send a voice through it, Edison was inventing, Rockefeller was
pumping oil, Carnegie was smelting steel, Morgan was financing, Harriman was
constructing railroads, and a host of other entrepreneurs were building the
foundations of the first great industrial nation. It is of interest to note the
birthdays of some of the founders of American industry: Morgan (1837), Hill
(1838), Rockefeller (1839), Carnegie (1835), Westinghouse (1846), Edison (1847),
Bell (1847), and Harriman (1848). Among these ambitious men was a merchant,
Marshall Field, born in 1834, who built his fortune selling dry goods to the
public.

The popular American success story was based upon the poor newspaper boy
who saved his nickels and became a captain of industry. The wonderful thing
about the story is that it was often true. Horatio Alger immortalized the
shoeshine boy, but he could have used Edison or a host of other real characters
with equal justice. Marshall Field fit the mold. He progressed from farm boy in
Massachusetts to Chicago's first citizen and built one of the world's great fortunes
in merchandizing, banking, real estate and railroads. He lived at a time when it
made no difference whether you were a penniless recent arrival from Europe or a
Virginia aristocrat. America was the land of opportunity. In fact, it seemed that
the penniless shoeshine boy had the advantage because he apparently had the
motivation and government put few, if any, restrictions on him, including taxes.

The first Field, Zechariah, arrived in 1629 and settled in Connecticut. Later,
the Field family settled on a farm near Conway, Massachusetts, where Marshall
lived as a youth with his three brothers and two sisters. His schooling stopped at
age seventeen and he began a business career in a dry goods store in Pittsfield. As
a young man he was thrifty, ambitious, and virtuous. His experiences on a New
England farm had developed a sense of responsibility to himself and his
associates. Frugality was a way of life; a penny saved was a penny earned. If you
saved your pennies they could be invested and grow into dollars. Field had
confidence in his own ability and as a young man of twenty-one took his saved
pennies and "went West" to Chicago. In 1856 Chicago and Field were about the
same age, but there was a great difference between the two. The city was uncouth
and untutored, boisterous and impulsive, filled with speculators and temptations
and uncertain of where it was going. On the other hand, Field was a New
Englander from the farm, quiet, industrious, persevering and a man who believed
in work rather than play.

Field obtained work in the dry goods house of Cooley, Wadsworth and
Company at a salary of about eight dollars a week. Since he was not tempted to
participate in Chicago's night life, he was able to save about two hundred dollars
the first year. This meant sleeping in the store and spending about fifty cents per
day for food. Seven years later he felt prosperous enough to marry Nannie
Douglas Scott of Ironton, Ohio, on January 3, 1863. After Cooley retired from

the firm, a new organization was called Farwell, Field, and Company (Wadsworth had dropped out earlier) but lasted for only a short time. In 1864 Field and Levi Leiter joined to form a new company in association with Potter Palmer to operate a wholesale and retail store on Lake Street. This arrangement lasted about three years when Palmer retired and Field, Leiter and Company, with associates, became the operating organization in 1869. The associates included Field's two brothers, Joseph and Henry. The store, under Field's management, was a great success, grossing millions annually.

Field's unusual success in merchandizing was based upon certain policies which he followed. He catered to women because they were the shoppers. His slogan was "Give the Lady What She Wants" and if she is dissatisfied let her exchange the unwanted article. Mark the price of each item clearly and honestly identify the goods. Buy and sell for cash, use window displays, and advertise. By using such methods he undersold his competitors and built a merchandizing empire.

The Civil War had a pronounced effect on Field's operations. During the war Chicago was somewhat isolated by closing of the Mississippi River to trade. Nevertheless, the city was bustling and had become in Carl Sandburg's phrase, "Hog Butcher of the World." It served the great farm belt of the Midwest and was, in part, resistant to the economic vagaries of other parts of the country. The scandals of Wall Street, the inefficient administration of Grant in Washington, and the boom and bust activities of postwar speculators left Field untouched. He continued to operate on a cash basis, secure in a strong economic base. He stood tall in Chicago business as honest and shrewd, and he and Nannie became the foremost leaders of Chicago society.

When Mrs. O'Leary's cow kicked over the lamp that started the Great Fire in 1871, State Street and Field, Leiter and Company were not spared. However, the disaster caused only a minor ripple in the operations. They carried insurance and had cash in the bank. They immediately posted a sign to pay all employees and two days later were selling to customers in another location. The year after the fire they had a surplus exceeding $2.5 million. A second fire destroyed their business on State Street in 1877, but Field survived, and bought the newly constructed building from Singer. Field had occupied seven different merchandizing locations in the previous ten-year period, but was now settled permanently in the famous State Street location.

In 1881 Leiter resigned and Field found himself the sole proprietor of the business. One of his new associates was Harry Selfridge, a young man from Jackson, Michigan, who later founded the famous London store bearing his name. The 1881 net income was $2.5 million. Field was the preeminent merchant in America. Marshall Field II was thirteen years old, heir apparent to the throne, and a daughter Ethel was nine. Things seemed right with the world as they existed in Chicago. But trouble was on the horizon in the form of social unrest. On the one hand, there was social Darwinism in which one class argued that "survival of the fittest" applied to business as well as nature. In contrast, labor was asking questions and organizing protest movements. The economic rebellion of the working man was slowly gaining momentum. As the wealth of individuals grew, the public removed them from the pedestal of honor and glory which they had occupied. Field was one who felt the sting of changing attitudes. The great railroad strike of July 17, 1877 reached Chicago and Field aided the side of law enforcement. A strike at the McCormick reaper plant in 1885 brought out the

National Guard, which was referred to as "Marshall Field's Boys." These events were merely a prelude to the Haymarket Riot on May 4, 1886 in which one policeman was killed, seventy wounded and six anarchists killed and seventy-two wounded. Eight of the rioters were sentenced to be hanged. At a meeting of civic leaders Field introduced the lawyer who announced that the request for commutation of sentence was denied. The sentence was carried out on four of the rioters, including the leader. The public supported the decision.

Field's philanthropy was extensive but he evaluated each request carefully to determine its merit. He supported the Art Institute of Chicago after 1878 and donated Millet's *Harvest Moon* to its collection, but refused to support a public library. When the new University of Chicago was attempting to establish itself in 1889 under Dr. William Rainey Harper's direction and Rockefeller's initial grant, Field donated land and money totaling about $360 thousand. He supported the founding of the Chicago Symphony in 1891 with a small grant. Field's major gift was a result of the World's Columbian Exposition in 1893. He was an enthusiastic supporter of the fair and had purchased the largest block of stock. The Field Museum of Natural History, now the Chicago Natural History Museum, was opened in the Art Palace of the fair. Field had contributed $1 million to get it started and later added $8 million.

The last years of Field's life were somewhat sad, though on occasion very constructive. He won a battle with Charles Schwab over the expansion of U.S. Steel, which resulted in the great steel development at Gary, Indiana. Some Democrats urged him to be a candidate in 1904 for the presidency, or even the vice-presidency. He declined both. His wife, Nannie, died in February 1896 after a life partially spent in Europe. He remarried in September 1905 but his new happiness was shattered a few weeks later when Marshall Field II was accidently shot and died in Chicago. Marshall I died two months later leaving a fortune of $120 million.

HWS

References: Stephen Becker, *Marshall Field III* (New York: Simon & Schuster, 1964); John Tebbel, *The Marshall Fields, A Study in Wealth* (New York: Dutton, 1947).

John Fiske

(March 30, 1842 — July 4, 1901)

In the late nineteenth century no American writer did more to interpret folklore and mythology or to clarify the Darwinian theory of evolution than John Fiske. He could be compared to Thomas Henry Huxley in England for his popularization of scientific theories, although Fiske lacked Huxley's brilliant expository style. Fiske was not an original thinker, but he wrote voluminously on philosophical and historical subjects. James Truslow Adams once called him perhaps the most popular lecturer on history that America has ever seen.

Fiske, born at Hartford, Connecticut, March 30, 1842, was originally named Edmund Fisk Green but changed his name to John Fisk in 1855 and added the final vowel a few years later. He was the only child of a father who had New Jersey Quaker roots, and even as a juvenile he was extraordinarily precocious. It is said that by the age of eight he had read some two hundred volumes representing such fields as chemistry, mathematics, and grammar, and by the time he was twenty he had developed a reading knowledge of the common European languages in addition to Latin, Greek, and Anglo-Saxon. Fiske attended the Betts Academy in Stamford, Connecticut, from 1855 to 1857 and then after some tutoring entered Harvard as a sophomore in 1860. By chance he encountered the writings of Herbert Spencer and became almost immediately a disciple of the English philosopher. Despite his brilliance he had some difficulty with the conventional curriculum of the day but in 1862 he published two articles in the *North American Review* and the next year was awarded his B.A. In 1864 he married Abby Brooks and in 1865, without professional legal study, passed the bar examination and acquired a law degree.

Fiske originally planned to practice law in Boston and did open a law office, but he had few clients and soon determined to make his living as a professional writer. A wealthy mother and a family subsidy assured him support and he chose to live in Cambridge for the rest of his life. In 1869 he was invited to lecture at Harvard on "The Positive Philosophy." He also lectured in Boston to a popular audience. From 1872 to 1879 he served as assistant librarian at Harvard for a salary of two thousand dollars a year. After he resigned this position he devoted the rest of his life to a career of lecturing and writing. He was a familiar figure on the lecture circuit in the United States and he also pleased audiences in London. From 1884 on he served as professor of American history at Washington University in St. Louis, but he retained his Cambridge residence.

In his first book, *Myths and Myth-Makers*, published in 1872, Fiske attempted to chronicle and define universal mythology and revealed his wide background. He expressed his point of view in a sentence in chapter 1: "The religious myths of antiquity and the fireside of ancient and modern times have their common root in the mental habits of primeval humanity." To Fiske a myth was an explanation by the uncivilized mind of a natural phenomenon. He illustrated this belief by citing material from India, the Scandinavian countries, Ireland, and elsewhere. Legends, on the other hand, were associated with localities and personalities. Among the subjects that held the author's attention were solar mythology, rhabdomancy (the use of divining rods), transformations, monsters, and heroes.

Other volumes suggest his concern with the advanced scientific thought of his day. He published a two-volume work entitled *Outlines of Cosmic Philosophy* in 1874 and *Excursions of an Evolutionist* in 1884. Indeed, he became the leading American exponent of the doctrine of evolution. But in the last decades of his life American history supplanted other interests and he concerned himself with the colonial period, the Revolution, and the Civil War. Typical volumes are *The American Revolution*, 1891; *The Discovery of America*, 1892; and *The Mississippi Valley in the Civil War*, 1900. Fiske's reputation as a historian has waned since his death. It is generally agreed that he did no original research and contented himself with using secondary material. But Fiske wrote lucidly and competently and for a time he enjoyed a large popular audience. Unlike the work of narrative historians like Parkman and Prescott who also worked extensively in archives and manuscript repositories, his books have not been kept in print. Fiske died July 4, 1901.

JTF

References: James Truslow Adams, *DAB*, VI, 1931, pp. 420-23; Thomas Sergeant Perry, *John Fiske* (Boston: Small Maynard, 1906); John Spencer Clark, *The Life and Letters of John Fiske*, 2 vols. (Boston: Houghton Mifflin, 1917); Milton Berman, *John Fiske: The Evolution of a Popularizer* (Cambridge, Mass.: Harvard University Press, 1961).

Abraham Flexner

(November 13, 1866 — September 21, 1959)

The educational historian Michael R. Harris found five true "counterrevolutionists" in American higher education: Irving Babbitt, Albert Jay Nock, Abraham Flexner, Robert M. Hutchins, and Alexander Meiklejohn. Probably none of these exerted more long-range influence on higher education in America than did Flexner.

Flexner is another character who belongs in the saga of great American success stories. His parents were Jewish immigrants who had built a successful wholesale hat business in Louisville, Kentucky, then been reduced to poverty by the 1873 panic. Abraham entered Johns Hopkins University in 1884, aided by a loan from an older brother, and received a B.A. degree in 1886. The Hopkins system of education, based on the German university system, made a permanent impression on him.

Flexner's educational career began with four years of high school teaching in Louisville, followed by organization of a private tutoring system to prepare students for college through brief, intensive work. In 1905, he left Louisville for graduate study in psychology at Harvard. After receiving a master's degree, he followed up his interest in German universities by entering the University of Berlin to study comparative education. One result was publication of Flexner's *The American College*, in which he urged more attention to intellectual matters in colleges and less to extracurricular activities.

The book proved to be a decisive factor in Flexner's career. It came to the notice of Henry Pritchett, President of the Carnegie Foundation for the Advancement of Teaching. The foundation was about to begin a major study of medical education in the United States and Canada, and Pritchett asked Flexner to undertake a survey of American medical schools. The proposal came as a complete surprise to Flexner, whose training was in the classics. He suggested that Pritchett must have him confused with his brother, Simon Flexner, the brilliant director of the Rockefeller Medical Institute. Pritchett assured him that there was no mistake — it was a job for an educator not a medical practitioner.

Flexner's landmark survey of medical education in the United States and Canada began on December 1, 1908. In preparation for the undertaking, Flexner read everything that he could find on the history of medical education in Europe and America. The most important and stimulating volume, he noted, was a German work, Billroth's *The Medical Sciences in the German Universities*. His second step was a visit to Chicago, where he interviewed officials of the American Medical Association and read the "creditable and painstaking," but "extremely diplomatic" reports in the AMA files on the country's medical schools. Finally, Flexner went to Baltimore to talk with distinguished members of the Medical Department of Johns Hopkins University, to try to find out what a medical school ought to be like. Only the Hopkins school then had standards comparable to the best European centers for medical education.

With the preliminary period of careful study and preparation behind him, Flexner proceeded on a swift tour of the 155 medical schools in the United States and Canada. He had no fixed pattern and used no questionnaire in his investigation. In each instance, however, he visited every one of the 155 schools and talked with medical school faculty members and their students. Flexner soon came to realize that five criteria were most useful in judging the quality and value of a medical school: entrance requirements, size and training of faculty, financial support, adequacy of laboratories, and relation between medical schools and hospitals.

The conditions uncovered by Flexner were shocking and he pulled no punches in applying such words as "disgraceful" and "shameful." The city of Chicago with its fourteen medical schools was described as "the plague spot of the country." It was found that entrance requirements were enforced in only ten of the medical schools in the United States. Libraries were inadequate or nonexistent in 140 of the schools, and laboratory courses for the first and second years were deplorably equipped and poorly conducted in 139 of the schools. The methods of instruction were mainly didactic, i.e., lectures, rather than laboratory experiments and observation. For the past twenty-five years there had been an enormous overproduction of uneducated and poorly trained medical practitioners, in complete disregard of the public welfare. Physicians in the United States were four or five times as numerous in proportion to population as in older countries like Germany. The mass production of ill-trained physicians was due to the existence of a large number of commercial schools, whose blatant advertising attracted unprepared youth to go from store clerks and factory workers into the study of medicine. Cutthroat competition for students was unbounded.

The proprietary or commercial schools investigated by Flexner were profitable businesses, paying large dividends to their owners and stockholders. Not only were laboratories lacking, but many medical schools provided no hospital facilities whatever. For the sake of respectability, a number of schools had allied themselves with universities, but the universities failed to make themselves responsible for the standards of the schools or for their support. Nearly one half of the medical schools had incomes below ten thousand dollars a year.

The existence of many of the unnecessary and inadequate medical schools was defended by the argument that a poor medical school was justified in the interest of the poor boy, because he could not afford to go to a more expensive school. Flexner's retort was that the poor boy had no right to go into such a life-or-death profession as medicine, if he was unwilling or unable to obtain suitable preparation. Furthermore, the argument was generally insincere, being put forward to save the poor medical school rather than from any genuine desire to help the poor boy.

Another major conclusion reached by Flexner was that a hospital under complete educational control is as necessary to a medical school as a laboratory of chemistry or pathology. For that reason, Flexner urged hospital trustees to open hospital wards to teaching and the universities to appoint to their staffs teachers who were devoted to clinical science.

At the end of his nearly two years of firsthand study, Flexner's report was issued by the Carnegie Foundation under the title *Medical Education in the United States and Canada*. It began with a historical and general review, demonstrating that most of the several hundred medical schools established during the previous period of nearly a century had been essentially private money-making ventures.

On the basis of his overview, Flexner concluded that fewer and better doctors were needed. He was particularly outspoken in his condemnation of the commercial exploitation of medical education. He reported that "the advertising methods of the commercially successful schools are amazing. Not infrequently advertising costs more than laboratories. The school catalogues abound in exaggeration, misstatement, and half-truths. The deans of these institutions occasionally know more about modern advertising than about modern medical teaching."

Flexner's mission, as he conceived it, was by no means limited to destructive criticism of existing medical education. He was anxious to find remedies, to point toward the road for reconstruction. The first essential, Flexner believed, was to reduce the number of medical schools and to improve their product. Several principles should govern such a reorganization and reconstitution: (1) a medical school should be a department of a university, preferably located in a large city, in order to procure clinical material; (2) even in small communities superior medical schools can be developed, if high scientific ideals are maintained, the university control is real, and strong financial support is provided; (3) there should be only one school to a single community, to avoid needless expense, to eliminate competition for students, to recruit one strong faculty, and to assure adequate hospital facilities; (4) since students tend to study medicine in their own state, the schools should be well distributed geographically.

State boards of examiners accepted the report and the press spread its findings among the general public. Medical schools which had been operated mainly for profit went out of business. A number of schools pooled their resources to survive and independent schools sought university connections. Seven schools in Louisville, Kentucky, became one. Fifteen in Chicago were shortly consolidated into three. Writing in 1924, fifteen years after his original investigation, Flexner reported that the number of schools had been cut in half, weak schools had been almost wholly eliminated, matriculation requirements had been tightened, everywhere equipment and facilities had been improved, and laboratory subjects were being taught by full-time, specially trained teachers.

Following completion of his study, Flexner was asked by the Rockefeller Foundation: What amount of money spent on what project would result in the greatest initial reform in medical education? The most needed reform, responded Flexner, was to pay clinical professors full salaries to free them from the necessity of outside practice. On his recommendation, the Rockefeller Foundation gave Johns Hopkins $1.5 million to endow professorial chairs in medicine, surgery, obstetrics, and pediatrics. Subsequently, Flexner influenced Rockefeller to grant $50 million to the General Education Board for medical research. Matching funds multiplied the original a dozen times, adding some $600 million to the endowment of American medical schools. George Eastman was persuaded to donate $5 million for the Rochester Medical School, the beginning of that institution's distinguished reputation.

Flexner, who was in his early forties when he finished his survey of American medical education, lived to the ripe age of ninety-two. His highly productive career in later years was marked by a study of medical education in Europe; an inquiry, for the Rockefeller Foundation, into prostitution in Europe, inspired by a grand jury investigation of prostitution, white slavery, and corrupt police organization that had rocked New York; service with the General Education Board to improve education in the South; the writing of another highly influential book, *Universities: American, English, German*; and the creation and directorship of the Institute for Advanced Study at Princeton. At Princeton, he brought together a small number of brilliant scholars, among them Albert Einstein, and gave them complete freedom to pursue conceptual research.

RBD

Reference: Michael R. Harris, *Five Counterrevolutionaries in Higher Education* (Corvallis: Oregon State University Press, 1970).

Felix Frankfurter

(November 15, 1882 — February 22, 1965)

There are striking similarities between the careers of Felix Frankfurter and his long-time friend and associate Louis Brandeis. Both were sons of Jewish immigrants from Europe, both graduated from the Harvard Law School, and their terms as justices of the U.S. Supreme Court overlapped.

The Frankfurter family emigrated from Vienna in 1894, when Felix was twelve years of age. Enrolled in a New York City public school, young Felix early demonstrated exceptional proficiency in speaking and writing. His education was further advanced by much time spent in the Cooper Union reading rooms and neighboring libraries and attending lectures and debates. He received an A.B. degree from the City College of New York in 1902.

After a year serving as a clerk in the tenement house department of the New York City government, Frankfurter was admitted to the Harvard Law School in 1903. Because of his small stature—about five feet five inches—he had a slight feeling of inferiority, but that was forgotten when he led his class at the end of his first year. While at Harvard, he formed a number of important friendships among men who later helped to shape his career.

Following graduation from Harvard in 1906, Frankfurter was associated for a short time with a New York law firm and then went on to join the U.S. Attorney's office, where he served under Henry L. Stimson. It was at this point that Frankfurter began a lifelong immersion in federal law and public affairs. As Stimson's assistant, his work was chiefly concerned with antitrust and criminal law and the legal problems of immigrants. A change came when Stimson was appointed secretary of war by William Howard Taft. Stimson in turn appointed Frankfurter legal officer of the Bureau of Indian Affairs, with jurisdiction over American territorial possessions.

For about a year after Woodrow Wilson became president, Frankfurter remained in the War Department. While in Washington, he was a member of a circle of literary and political commentators that included Francis Hackett, Herbert Croly, and Walter Lippmann. He also became a devoted friend of two men who were to exert a decisive influence on his professional life: Oliver Wendell Holmes and Louis D. Brandeis.

The next major step in Frankfurter's career came in 1914, when he was invited to return to Harvard as professor of administrative law. For the next twenty-five years, except for a leave during and after World War I, he was a member of the Harvard law faculty. In that capacity, he introduced new approaches to legal studies, bringing his characteristic zest to teaching. His teaching subjects were mainly concerned with administrative law, federal courts, and public utilities.

An important assignment during World War I was in the judge advocate's department of the army, where Frankfurter served as secretary and counsel to the President's Mediation Commission, dealing with labor stoppages in war industries. A famous case he investigated on President Wilson's instructions was the Mooney-Billings affair in San Francisco, where radical labor unions had been convicted for planting a bomb that killed many people during a Preparedness Day parade in 1916. Frankfurter found serious irregularities in the trial procedures. Mooney's death sentence was commuted and some years later Mooney and Billings were pardoned. As chairman of the interdepartmental War Labor Policies Board in 1918, one of Frankfurter's colleagues was Franklin D. Roosevelt, assistant secretary of the navy.

Of a similar nature was Frankfurter's work, by appointment, to defend aliens arrested and held for deportation, cases growing out of postwar hysteria. Nearly all those held were finally released. These activities, along with being an original member of the American Civil Liberties Union, led to a general conception of Frankfurter as a radical in political and social causes. Actually, he was motivated by a desire to protect those he considered victims of miscarriages of justice.

During the years at Harvard, Frankfurter's association with Brandeis became extremely close. When the latter was appointed to the Supreme Court in 1916, Frankfurter took charge of two of Brandeis' cases pending before the court. He won both cases, the first on the validity of maximum hours of labor legislation, originating in Oregon, and the second upholding minimum-wage laws for women.

Though his interest in Zionism was less intense than Brandeis', Frankfurter often acted as spokesman in Zionist affairs, after Brandeis became a Supreme Court justice and was less free to act or speak. In part, Frankfurter's ambivalence toward the Zionist movement derived from his dislike of nationalism, while his criticism of Britain's handling of the Palestine problem was tempered by his great admiration of that country and its traditions.

Frankfurter found himself in full sympathy with the New Deal and he offered encouragement and advice to President Roosevelt in every way possible, especially during a period when he was a resident guest at the White House. His counsel was called upon in proposals for the reconstruction and reform of securities regulation, labor legislation, and unemployment insurance. Frankfurter and his associates drafted legislation covering securities, stock exchanges, and public utility holding companies.

When the Supreme Court declared unconstitutional much New Deal legislation—the National Industrial Recovery Act, the Agricultural Adjustment Act, the Bituminous Coal Act, the Railroad Retirement Act, the Frazier-Lemke Farm Bankruptcy Act, and state minimum wage laws—Roosevelt introduced his "court-packing" proposal to enlarge the court's membership. Brandeis opposed the plan and Frankfurter remained silent, except to try to persuade Roosevelt that a better strategy would be to publicize the court's bad record in reviewing social legislation.

Justice Cardozo's death in 1938 created a vacancy in the Supreme Court. Roosevelt nominated Frankfurter for the opening; the nomination was reported favorably without dissent by the Senate Judiciary Committee, and Frankfurter took his seat on January 30, 1939.

When Frankfurter entered the Supreme Court, that body was becoming increasingly concerned with civil rights and civil liberties. In his view, the Constitution and its Bill of Rights provided full protection for basic rights and fair legal procedures. He worked closely with Chief Justice Earl Warren in obtaining a unanimous decision in the 1954 case outlawing racial segregation in public schools. Frankfurter also condemned the Attorney General's practice of designating organized groups as Communist. Other causes on which he was outspoken and aimed to shape legal procedures were excluding confessions extracted during excessively long preliminary detention, enforcing the requirements of a search warrant upon federal officers, and promoting academic freedom, particularly the immunity of the college classroom from governmental intrusion.

At the time of his appointment by Roosevelt, Frankfurter was considered a liberal. As a judge, however, he often took a middle-of-the-road and not infrequently a conservative position. For example, he wrote the Supreme Court opinion sustaining the compulsory flag salute in public schools, over the objection of Jehovah's Witnesses that it was a profanation, and then wrote a dissent when a majority of the Court later overruled that decision. A few years later, he joined in the decision upholding the Smith Act, which declared it illegal to organize a party that taught or advocated violent overthrow of the government, though he doubted the wisdom or effectiveness of such a law. Also coming down on the conservative side was his dissent from the Court's decision in 1962 holding that grossly unequal voting districts in a state violated the equal protection guarantee of the Fourteenth Amendment. Frankfurter maintained that the Court was entering a "political thicket" in this case.

Unlike John Marshall, Oliver Wendell Holmes, and Louis Brandeis, Felix Frankfurter did not make any great original contributions to legal thought. On the other hand, he was for many years a highly influential and significant figure in law and government. His tremendous intellectual and physical energy, his deep concern for people, his love of American institutions and traditions, and his breadth of learning left a profound impression on his time.

RBD

References: Liva Baker, *Felix Frankfurter* (New York: Coward-McCann, 1969); Wallace Mendelson, *Felix Frankfurter* (New York: Reynal, 1964); Helen S. Thomas, *Felix Frankfurter* (Baltimore, Md.: Johns Hopkins University Press, 1960).

Daniel Chester French

(April 20, 1850—October 7, 1931)

One of America's greatest sculptors although largely self-taught, Daniel Chester French lived a long, productive life, earned abundant honors at home and abroad, and left as his own memorial a number of monuments which won wide public acclaim. His achievements included architectural sculpture, bronze doors, commissioned busts, and enormous equestrian statues.

Born in Exeter, New Hampshire, in 1850, French was the son of Henry French, a scientific farmer and lawyer. The father tried agricultural experiments and was for a short time president of the Massachusetts Agricultural College. Later he lived in Concord, practiced his profession in Boston, and was briefly the assistant secretary of the treasury in Washington. Young Daniel enjoyed farm life but early showed his artistic interests by modeling turnips into comic figures and forming owls out of clay. The family abetted his youthful sculpturing but there was no art school in Boston for him to attend. Later he spent one year at the Massachusetts Institute of Technology. But probably more important to him were brief instruction from William Morris Hunt about the use of light and shade, a month in the New York studio of the sculptor J. Q. A. Ward, and lectures on art anatomy from William Rimmer in Boston.

French's own career began in the early 1870s when the people of Concord wanted a memorial to commemorate the first battle of the Revolution. French decided to construct a model of a Minuteman. He worked hard at the task and procured an authentic musket, a plow, and buttons for the young farmer's costume. The model which he submitted to a public meeting presided over by Ralph Waldo Emerson was immediately accepted. The statue was completed in the sculptor's Boston studio and in 1875 it was unveiled at Concord before an audience of ten thousand people including President U. S. Grant. Emerson pulled the cords. Ironically the artist was not present at the presentation. In October 1874 he had accepted the invitation of Preston Powers, son of the sculptor Hiram Powers, to join the family in Florence, and he remained abroad for two years.

The Italian experience was particularly fruitful. He worked in the studio of another American, Thomas Ball, and he naturally benefited from studying the museums and statuary of the city. He also completed a statue of Endymion which was cut in marble at Florence.

On French's return to the United States in August 1876, he received commissions from various projects. In 1877 he did a Peace and War group for the United States Custom House in St. Louis and two years later three statues representing Law, Prosperity, and Power for the Philadelphia Custom House. He created busts of Bronson Alcott and Ralph Waldo Emerson, both of whom he had known in Concord. When Emerson saw the finished statue he remarked, "That's the face I shave." His figure of John Harvard was done at the request of Harvard University in 1884. Two years later a statue of General Lewis Cass, commissioned by the state of Michigan, was placed in the Statuary Hall of the national capital. French also won admiration for his group sculpture *Gallaudet and His First Deaf-Mute Pupil.*

In 1886 French returned to Europe, visiting London where he met two expatriate Americans, John S. Sargent and Henry James, as well as the poet Robert Browning, and spending a short time in Italy seeing old friends. But he also worked in a Paris studio during a long cold winter.

Back in the United States he did a bust of John Adams for the Senate Gallery and statues entitled *Herodotus* and *History* for the Library of Congress. In 1893 he was chosen to contribute to the World Columbian Exposition in Chicago and responded with an allegorical statue called *The Republic*, a golden female figure standing sixty-five feet from toes to laurel-crowned head and grasping a spear and a liberty cap in one hand and a globe in the other. The face revealed no smile but suggested dignity and vitality. After the exposition the statue remained in Chicago. Later the gilded-bronze figure was reduced to twenty-four feet.

Around the turn of the century French was busy with various projects. He contributed six figures representing Bounty, Wisdom, Prudence, Courage, Truth, and Integrity to the loggia of the Minnesota state capitol which his friend Cass Gilbert had designed and which was completed in St. Paul in 1900. In the same year his statue of Governor John S. Pillsbury was unveiled on the campus of the University of Minnesota. In addition, French created three bronze doors for the Boston Public Library, architectural sculpture for the New York Custom House, a standing Lincoln for the Nebraska state capitol, and the fountain at Dupont Circle in Washington. There were also three large equestrian monuments, one of General Grant for Philadelphia, one of General Joseph Hooker for Boston, and one of Washington which the Washington Memorial Association contributed to France for the Place d'Iena. For this last sculpture French and his associate Edward C. Potter, who created the horse, received a fee of thirty thousand dollars. Eventually French also provided portrait busts of various American writers for the Hall of Fame at New York University. Poe, Hawthorne, and Emerson were so honored.

The sculptor's masterpiece is indubitably the famous seated Lincoln in the Lincoln Memorial in Washington. In 1900 the National Commission of Fine Arts was formed to plan a suitable memorial to commemorate the martyred president. French was chosen a member of the commission and eventually was named as the sculptor. The project took shape in the course of time: a small clay sketch, a nineteen-foot plaster cast, then finally the finished figure, overall with its pedestal thirty feet high and cut from Georgia marble. French captured magnificently the gaunt form of his subject and emphasized the powerful hands while he did not neglect small details like the ridges and folds of the president's clothing. The impact of the sculpture was subsequently increased by powerful floodlights in the roof. Lorado Taft may have been thinking of the Lincoln Memorial and the crowds that thronged to see it when he remarked that no other American sculptor ever won so appreciative a response from the general public.

In 1893 French was awarded a gold medal in Paris for his statue *The Angel of Death*. This was the earliest of many honors. He was a trustee of the Metropolitan Museum. He was president of the Architectural League and was given its medal of honor. He served on federal commissions. He was offered honorary degrees by various universities and colleges, most of which he rejected because his declining health made his physical presence at commencement imprudent. But he remained a director of the Corporation of Yaddo and a trustee of the American Academy in Rome until his death in 1931.

In 1888 French married his cousin, Mary French, and forty years later she published a volume about their relationship, *Memories of a Sculptor's Wife*. His daughter Margaret French Cresson also became his biographer in 1947.

JTF

References: Charles Moore, *DAB*, Supplement 1, XXI, 1944, pp. 320-23; Adeline Adams, *Daniel Chester French, Sculptor* (Boston: Houghton Mifflin, 1932); Margaret French Cresson, *Journey into Fame: The Life of Daniel Chester French* (Cambridge, Mass.: Harvard University Press, 1947).

Sarah Margaret Fuller
(May 23, 1810—July 19, 1850)

Although she wrote an important early book in which she expressed the feminist point of view and enjoyed temporary fame as a literary critic in New York City, Margaret Fuller is better known as a personality than as a writer. Certainly she lived on the fringe of transcendentalism, she was an associate of Emerson and Thoreau and Hawthorne, and she was the leading conversationalist in a group of intellectual women who convened in Boston. She developed from a precocious girl to a young woman familiar with philosophical trends and classical literature; she was familiar with the chief English poets of her day and she could read Goethe, whom she greatly admired, in German and Petrarch in Italian. She even figured in contemporary literature since she was probably the prototype of Zenobia in Hawthorne's *The Blithedale Romance* and was surely the model for the lady bluestocking whom Lowell satirized in "A Fable for Critics."

Margaret Fuller was born in Cambridgeport, Massachusetts, in 1810, the daughter of Timothy Fuller. The father, a Harvard-trained lawyer who later served as a Massachusetts state senator and as a representative in Congress, supervised the girl's education and insisted on a rigorous course of study which brought about her ill health in subsequent years. She was introduced to Latin at the age of six, read Ovid two years later, and shortly learned to know Shakespeare, Cervantes, and Moliere. Her proximity to Cambridge and Concord enabled her to meet such men as Frederic Hedge, William E. Channing, and Emerson, and she was generally accepted as an equal in a masculine group. For five years, from 1839 to 1844, she was the leader of a group of twenty-five women who met periodically at the home of Elizabeth Peabody in Boston to discuss literature and philosophy. Out of this experience came her book, unique at the time, *Woman in the Nineteenth Century*, 1845, which dealt with the economic, political, and sexual aspects of feminism. Earlier, in 1840 and 1841, she had been chosen to edit *The Dial*, a magazine acknowledged to be the literary organ of the

Transcendental Club which published verse and essays by Thoreau, Emerson, Alcott, and Ripley. As editor Fuller was eager to print original and diversified material but paid little attention to any basic theme. When Emerson replaced her in the final two years of publication, 1842-1844, *The Dial* achieved greater unity. The magazine never had more than three hundred subscribers but in its short existence enjoyed a remarkable influence.

A trip to Chicago via the Great Lakes prompted Fuller to write her interpretation of western life and she published *Summer on the Lakes* in 1843. This work plus some magazine articles caught the attention of Horace Greeley, editor of the *New York Tribune*, who invited her to join the staff of his paper and to reside in his house. For several years her discussions of contemporary writers found wide approval. She was scornful of Longfellow and quite aware of Cooper's faults but she praised Poe and Hawthorne as the best American writers of the day. Among English authors she could discuss Byron and Shelley and she admired Coleridge and especially Wordsworth. In 1846 these essays were collected in the volume called *Papers on Literature and Art*. In the same year the *Tribune* commissioned Fuller to journey to Europe and to become its foreign correspondent. Her letters from abroad appeared on the front page of the newspaper.

During her stay in England she met Wordsworth, Carlyle, and Harriet Martineau, and by chance the Italian patriot Giuseppe Mazzini, whose cause she soon espoused. A short interval in Paris enabled her to meet George Sand and Chopin. But she soon made her way to Italy and settled briefly in Rome. She had intended to write a book on the Roman revolution but her incomplete manuscript was lost later. In Rome Fuller met a young Italian marquis, Angelo Ossoli, whom she soon married. One child was born to the couple. When the Italian insurrection seemed doomed to fail, the Ossolis fled to Florence and shortly thereafter made their way to the coast in order to sail for the United States. As their ship approached Fire Island near New York City it was wrecked in a violent storm and all three Ossolis perished.

In 1852 Emerson, Channing, and J. F. Clarke combined to edit *The Memoirs of Margaret Fuller Ossoli* in two volumes. Fuller's letters to the *Tribune* were posthumously published in two volumes: *At Home and Abroad*, 1856, and *Life Without and Life Within*, 1859.

During much of her life Margaret Fuller suffered from ill health but worked hard as a journalist and critic. She was a dynamic personality and expressed her views on feminism and the role of women with vigor and assurance. She was also positive if not always graceful in her literary judgments. She once defined poetry as "the sublime and beautiful expressed in measured language." And she divided critics into three groups: the subjective (we would say impressionistic today), the apprehensive, and the comprehensive. Emerson who knew her well described her in a journal entry of 1851 as "a fine, generous, inspiring, vinous, eloquent talker, who did not outlive her influence." And Van Wyck Brooks almost ninety years later claimed that she was "an energetic, perceptive soul, not a great writer, but certainly a great woman writing." It must be said today that Margaret Fuller is remembered but little read.

JTF

References: Katharine Anthony, *DAB*, VII, 1931, pp. 63-66; Katharine Anthony, *Margaret Fuller: A Psychological Biography* (New York: Harcourt, Brace,

Howe, 1920); Mason Wade, *Margaret Fuller: Whetstone of Genius* (New York: Viking, 1940); Warner Berthoff, in *Notable American Women 1607-1950*, Vol. I, pp. 678-82 (Cambridge, Mass.: Belknap Press of Harvard, 1971).

James Gibbons
(July 23, 1834—March 24, 1921)

The second American to be named a cardinal of the Roman Catholic Church and probably the most distinguished clergyman of the Catholic Church in the United States, James Gibbons served for forty-four years as the head of the archdiocese of Baltimore. He early revealed his capacity for leadership and became prominent in both ecclesiastical and civic affairs. He knew every American president from Andrew Johnson to Warren G. Harding and was a close friend of presidents Cleveland, Taft, and Theodore Roosevelt. In 1911 he received unprecedented honors for an American churchman on the occasion of his jubilee as cardinal. His book, *The Faith of Our Fathers*, 1877, intended as a popular exposition of Catholic faith for the laity, sold some two million copies during his lifetime.

Gibbons was born in Baltimore, the city in which he spent most of his professional life, in 1834. He was the son of Irish immigrants from County Mayo who left Ireland not long before his birth. The Gibbons family returned to Ireland in 1837 and lived for ten years on a farm at Ballinrobe in Connaught. But after the father's death the widowed mother brought the family back to the United States and settled in New Orleans where the boy worked in the grocery business and later attended St. Charles College. At twenty-one he entered St. Mary's Seminary in Baltimore and was ordained to the priesthood in 1861.

During his initial years as a local pastor he showed unusual ability and was soon appointed chaplain at Fort McHenry where he ministered to both Union and Confederate soldiers. At the end of the Civil War Gibbons was named secretary to Archbishop Martin Spalding of Baltimore and in 1866 he drew attention at the Second Plenary Council. Rising rapidly in the church, he was nominated Prefect-Apostolic for North Carolina at the age of thirty-four. Although he found few supporters for his faith he had an attractive personality and made a good impression. A biographer, Allen Sinclair Will, remarked that since Catholic churches were uncommon Gibbons often had to borrow a Protestant meetinghouse. "The Bishop, standing in a Methodist pulpit, read from a Protestant Bible and the only part of the service which was distinctively of his own faith was the sermon."

In 1868 he was named titular bishop of Adramyttum and was the youngest of twelve hundred Catholic bishops convening in Rome for the Vatican Council of 1870. Although he played no prominent role in the proceedings he observed carefully, and after noting basic differences in church and state relationships in Europe and the United States he concluded that American procedures were simpler and preferable. By this time he had made his mark as an administrator and shown his ability to work with people of different creeds. In 1872 he was named bishop of Richmond and in May of 1877 he was appointed archbishop-coadjutor of Baltimore with right of succession. In the same year Archbishop Bayley died and Gibbons became head of the Baltimore archdiocese, a position which he would retain for forty-four years. In 1884 he organized the Third Plenary Council of Baltimore, over which he presided as Apostolic Delegate. One result of this event was the establishment of the Catholic University of America at Washington; Gibbons served as head of the board of trustees until his death.

In 1886 Pope Leo XIII named Gibbons to the cardinalate and for a quarter of a century he was the only American cardinal. As Theodore Maynard observed, he was for many people the unique embodiment of Americanism and Catholicism. He became well known for his support of the labor movement and persuaded the pope not to condemn the Knights of Labor. He also believed that immigrant groups should be allowed to blend with the native population rather than encouraged to preserve their original differences. Throughout his life he was admired for his promotion of religious toleration and he worked diligently to promote the compatibility of Catholicism and American democracy.

Gibbons was notable for his tact and humility. He was also more accessible than most churchmen of high rank and well known to his Baltimore parishioners. Although not marked as an intellectual, he read widely in history and biography. In addition to his best selling volume, *The Faith of Our Fathers*, Gibbons published several other books: *Our Christian Heritage* in 1889, a collection of topical sermons and discourses in 1908, and his *Retrospect of Fifty Years* in 1916. His death in 1921, in the words of Theodore Maynard, marked the end of an era for the American Catholic Church.

JTF

References: Allen Sinclair Will, *DAB*, VII, 1931, pp. 238-42; Allen Sinclair Will, *Life of Cardinal Gibbons, Archbishop of Baltimore* (New York: Dutton, 1922); Theodore Maynard, *The Story of American Catholicism* (New York: Macmillan, 1941); John Tracy Ellis, *The Life of James Cardinal Gibbons, Archbishop of Baltimore, 1834-1921* (Milwaukee, Wis.: Bruce, 1942).

Josiah Willard Gibbs

(February 11, 1839 — April 28, 1903)

Josiah Willard Gibbs is ranked by historians of science as probably the greatest of American scientists, and by world standards some would place him beside Newton and Maxwell, on the grounds that he did for thermodynamics and physical chemistry what they did for mechanics and electromagnetics.

Gibbs's name means little or nothing, however, to the man on the street, and a majority of scientists recall only that he discovered a principle of great importance called the "phase rule" and expressed it in terms which hardly any of his contemporaries could understand.

Why, in view of his lofty rank in the world of science, has Gibbs remained a relatively obscure and little-known figure? Primarily the difficulty lies in his method of expression: an application of mathematical principles to a solution of fundamental problems of chemistry and physics. Reading Gibbs with any understanding requires mathematical facility of a high order. One is reminded of Sir Isaac Newton's "glacial remoteness' of style.

Yet, Gibbs, who spent his entire active career as professor of mathematical physics at Yale University (1871-1903), is universally credited with creating the systems on which much of the modern industrial and scientific world rests.

The epoch-making work that assured Gibbs a permanent niche in the hall of fame is entitled *On the Equilibrium of Heterogeneous Substances*, published in three installments (1876-1878) in the *Transactions* of the Connecticut Academy of Arts and Sciences.

The nineteenth century was the age of steam. It was natural, therefore, that Gibbs should have directed his attention to thermodynamics, the branch of science dealing with the laws of one of the forms of energy—heat. The field of thermodynamics, however, was simply a springboard or point of departure for Gibbs, who went on to work out a series of universal laws governing the conditions or "phases," as he called them, of heterogeneous matter—any matter, anywhere. In his paper, Gibbs was concerned essentially with the famous "second law of thermodynamics," which, highly simplified, states that heat must always pass from hot to cold. "Heat cannot of itself, without the performance of work by some external agency, pass from a cold to a warmer body." This is the scientific reason why it is impossible to invent a "perpetual motion" machine. The "second law" has been defined as meaning simply that hot bodies cool off, that water must be raised if it is to fall, that clocks must be wound up after they have run down, that the universe is doomed to chaos.

Gibbs followed the principles laid down by Rudolph Clausius, German mathematical physicist: "The energy of the world is constant. The entropy of the world tends toward a maximum." The term "entropy," invented by Clausius, stands for a measurable quantity; when no heat reaches it, this quantity remains constant, but when heat enters or leaves the body the quantity increases or diminishes. Gibbs undertook to demonstrate mathematically the relations existing among temperature, volume, pressure, energy, and entropy.

Another complex term as interpreted by Gibbs is "equilibrium." In the pre-Newtonian era, equilibrium was thought of as a state of balance in which all things are motionless. Newton expanded the definition to include motion: for example, a planet moving in orbit. Gibbs further extended the definition, including in the concept of equilibrium the way in which matter changes its state and identity. For example, ice becomes water, water becomes steam, steam becomes oxygen and hydrogen. Hydrogen combines with nitrogen and becomes ammonia. In brief, every process in nature means change, and Gibbs discovered the laws determining such change. To establish the number of physical phases or states possible to a specific chemical system in equilibrium, Gibbs evolved his celebrated "phase rule" or law. The fundamental importance of the discovery may be illustrated by noting that the mathematical formulas of the phase rule made it possible to determine in advance the exact concentration of various substances that were to be used in making a required mixture. The formulas stated the temperatures and pressures best suited to produce a final mixture whose components would remain in equilibrium with each other and not separate out and destroy the mixture. Using the phase rule, an experimenter could also calculate the conditions necessary for making physical separations of one or more of the substances found in a complex mixture of salts or metals.

Though Gibbs devoted only four pages to the development of the phase rule, it has been estimated that other scientists have subsequently printed over eleven hundred pages describing applications of Gibbs' phase rule to mineralogy, petrology, physiology, metallurgy, and every other branch of science.

Gibbs's paper contains, as far as general principles are concerned, practically the whole of the science which is now called physical chemistry and which had scarcely been begun when the paper was written. The rules formulated by Gibbs have enormously facilitated and reduced the costs of a great variety of industrial processes — for example, in metallurgy, refrigeration, fuel and power engineering, and the manufacture of synthetic chemicals, ceramics, glass, and fertilizers. Today chemistry has become the basis of the world's greatest industries, and a substantial share of the progress in the field can be traced to Gibbs's remarkable discoveries.

Gibbs's work was recognized by honorary degrees from a number of universities, by award of the Rumford Medal by the American Academy, election as an honorary member of the Royal Society of London (which also awarded him its Copley Medal), membership in the National Academy of Sciences, and vice-presidency of the American Association for the Advancement of Science. He was also made a foreign honorary member or correspondent of a large number of European learned societies.

Gibbs's publication record is comparatively short. One of his biographers, however, noted that "A noteworthy general characteristic of his writing was the perfection of his English style, brief, precise, free from dogmatic statements, not given to ornamentation."

RBD

References: James G. Growther, *Famous American Men of Science* (New York: Norton, 1937); Muriel Hukeyser, *Willard Gibbs* (Garden City, N.Y.: Doubleday, 1942); Lynde P. Wheeler, *Josiah Willard Gibbs* (New Haven, Conn.: Yale University Press, 1951).

Cass Gilbert

(November 24, 1859 — May 17, 1934)

Although not distinguished for his originality or his innovations, Cass Gilbert enjoyed a long career as a successful architect who designed solid and often monumental buildings. Years of study in Rome confirmed his preference for traditional classical architecture. He had little interest in the modernistic revolt that became influential about the end of the nineteenth century and certainly disagreed strongly with the famous doctrine of Louis Sullivan that form follows function. Yet he was versatile and extremely competent. Even as a neophyte he was not greatly concerned with domestic projects but from his first important commission, designing the Minnesota state capitol in St. Paul, he was active in constructing federal, municipal, ecclesiastical, and library buildings. His work remains durable and impressive.

Gilbert was born in Zanesville, Ohio, where his family had settled in pioneer days. He was briefly a student at the Massachusetts Institute of Technology in 1878-1879 and then was for a time a surveyor. After extensive travel in England, France, and chiefly Italy he joined the New York architectural firm of McKim, Mead, and White in 1880, working as a draftsman. Sent to St. Paul by his employers to supervise a project, Gilbert chose to remain in the city and in 1882 formed a partnership with James Knox Taylor. Business was slack and Taylor soon left but Gilbert remained, sometimes painting watercolors as an avocation. In 1893 a Minnesota state commission was appointed to select a site and an architect for a new capitol building. Although Gilbert was young and obscure, he won the contract. The structure was begun in 1898 and completed in 1904. The capitol includes an arcaded loggia, Corinthian columns, and a central dome rising 220 feet which is a copy of Michelangelo's St. Peter's Church in Rome. There are various decorations within the building, including murals and six allegorical marble figures by Daniel Chester French. The Minnesota capitol influenced the structure of subsequent statehouses until the Nebraska building changed the pattern.

Gilbert was involved in another Minnesota project although he soon removed his headquarters to New York City. In 1909 the regents of the University of Minnesota offered a prize for the best design for an expanded campus. Gilbert again was chosen and planned a wide mall to be flanked eventually by buildings with a university auditorium at the head. The architect never designed any of the buildings but the substance of his plan was retained. He was given a fee of ten thousand dollars for his work.

In New York Gilbert opened his own office and proceeded without a partner. He had no trouble keeping busy. He won the prize for designing the United States Customs House and he also planned the Union League Club. In 1904 he conceived a plan for the Art Building for the Louisiana Purchase Exhibition, which subsequently became the City Art Museum, and somewhat later a plan for the St. Louis public library. From 1910 to 1918 he was a member of the National Commission of Fine Arts, and the prestige of this position eventually brought him the opportunity to work on a number of important Washington buildings. But one of the triumphs of his career was the Woolworth Building in New York City.

Tradition has it that Gilbert and Frank Woolworth were both on a liner bound for Europe when the architect convinced the businessman that he was the right man for the project. At any rate Gilbert was selected and what is usually called the best of the early skyscrapers was completed in 1913, sixty stories tall and 792 feet in height. For a time it was the tallest building in the world though it has since been dwarfed by the Empire State Building in New York and the Sears Tower in Chicago.

Other buildings designed by Gilbert include the New York Life Insurance Building, the Federal Courts Building, the West Virginia State Capitol, and libraries in New Haven and Detroit. In Washington he planned the United States Treasury Annex and the United States Chamber of Commerce. One of his greatest achievements is the Supreme Court Building finished in 1935, an enormous structure occupying a solid block and built to complement other federal edifices in the neighborhood. It has been praised for its solidity and mass but its acoustical qualities leave much to be desired. Gilbert at one time aspired to be involved in the erection of the Washington cathedral but this hope never materialized.

He also drew up plans for the construction of the George Washington Bridge across the Hudson River and some of his ideas were retained when it was finally built. But the heavy masonry towers enclosing steel piers and the monumental approaches were deemed too expensive and the original design was substantially modified.

Gilbert received many honors during his very productive career. He served as president of the Architectural League of New York and president of the National Academy of Design; he was also a founder of the Academy of Arts and Letters. Recognition came from abroad too. He was named a member of the French Legion of Honor and a foreign member of the Royal Academy of Arts. In January 1931 he was given the gold medal of the Society of Arts and Sciences.

Gilbert was a large man with a distinguished appearance though he became somewhat corpulent in later life. Critics who disliked his traditionalism and his preference for mass and bulk found him pompous and often too assertive of his own views. But he spoke fluently, was a good salesman for his projects, and had a flair for convincing prospective clients. Gilbert has a firm place in the history of American architecture. His buildings are his memorial. He died in Brockenhurst, England, and was buried in New York City.

JTF

Reference: Egerton Swartwout, *DAB*, XXI, Supplement 1, 1944, pp. 341-43.

Daniel Coit Gilman
(July 6, 1831 — October 13, 1908)

Two great pioneers in the field of American higher education, Daniel Coit Gilman of Johns Hopkins University and Andrew D. White of Cornell University, were close friends all through their lengthy careers, and frequently drew upon each other's counsel and advice.

Their friendship began in 1848 when they were fellow students at Yale College. After graduation from Yale in 1852, Gilman studied at Harvard College for several months. There, working under Arnold Gugot, he developed a life-long interest in geography. His association with White was resumed in 1855, when the two of them sailed for Europe as attachés of the American legation at St. Petersburg. Previously, in 1854-1855, Gilman had studied in Berlin. Following his return to America, he spent seventeen years at Yale as assistant librarian, professor of physical and political geography in the Sheffield Scientific School, and as secretary of the governing board of that institution.

During the period at Yale Gilman prepared a plan that was accepted for the Sheffield Scientific School's organization, and published his notes on European schools of science. As a member of the New Haven Board of Education, he became familiar with public school problems. In 1859, he announced the establishment of a high school in New Haven. He was one of the first to recognize the potentialities of the new Morrill Act, passed in 1862, for financing agricultural and mechanical colleges. As a result of his efforts, Sheffield was the first institution to make use of funds provided by the act.

Thus, with a strong background in general and scientific education, administrative and teaching experience, Gilman was ready for larger fields to conquer. In 1867, he was offered the presidency of the University of Wisconsin, the same year that Andrew D. White became president of Cornell. Feeling that he was not yet ready for such a position, Gilman declined and a short time later refused a similar offer from the University of California. Responding to a second call in 1872, however, he became president of the University of California. On his way to assume his new duties, Gilman stopped to visit President White at Cornell, stopped in Indiana to discuss with Governor Baker the plan for Purdue University, and in Urbana to study the University of Illinois organization. After arriving in San Francisco, he conferred with Louis Agassiz on the place of science in American education.

Gilman's three years in California were stormy. The University at Berkeley was only four years old when he assumed the presidency. Gilman was continually hampered in carrying out his policies by political interference. He wrote, "The University of California is nominally administered by the Regents; it is virtually administered by the legislature." Nevertheless, his extraordinary ability to judge people, to accomplish what he set out to do, and to overcome obstacles made a lasting impression on his Pacific Coast associates.

Meanwhile, things were brewing in Baltimore, where a new university was about to be created, under the terms of a will left by Johns Hopkins, businessman and philanthropist. The trustees of Johns Hopkins University were searching for a president. They sought the advice of President Eliot of Harvard, White at Cornell, and Angell of Michigan. Twenty-five years later, Angell said, "and now I have this remarkable statement to make to you: that without the least conference between us three, we all wrote letters, telling them that the one man was Daniel C. Gilman of California."

Gilman was inaugurated as the first president of Johns Hopkins University in 1875. Before leaving California, he had drawn up a budget, setting a high standard for professional salaries and making generous provision for the library and apparatus at Hopkins. His conception of the proper nature of a university was stated as follows: "Everywhere the real efficiency of a college is admitted to consist, not chiefly in buildings nor in sites, not in apparatus, but in the number and character of the teachers. We must discover and develop such men as have unusual ability."

The first twelve months of Gilman's presidency at Hopkins were devoted to a search for such individuals, persons who would enable him to succeed in his plans to create an institution of unique character. For this purpose, he drew upon the knowledge of educational leaders in America and Europe. On the basis of advice from notable scholars — Clerk Maxwell, Herbert Spencer, Lord Kelvin, and others — outstanding faculty members were recruited for mathematics, biology, chemistry, and Greek. From the start, primary emphasis was placed on graduate studies and research. Students attracted to Hopkins were already prepared for graduate work. Gilman insisted upon complete freedom of thinking and teaching. One of the first students, who later became famous as professor of philosophy at Harvard, Josiah Royce, wrote about the highly stimulating atmosphere surrounding the Baltimore institution. Gilman himself was undoubtedly the force who coordinated, guided, and shaped the university, as it grew in prestige and influence. Everything showed the stamp of his personality. No effort was made to attract students in large numbers; the watchwords were creative investigation and a spirit of discovery.

The next major step in Gilman's plans for development was the opening in 1889 of the Johns Hopkins Hospital, after twelve years of preparation. The control board for the hospital, which was separate from that for the university, proposed the immediate start of a medical school. Gilman insisted that when medical instruction began it should be under the administration of the university rather than the hospital. That principle was agreed upon but for financial reasons the school did not open until 1893, seventeen years later.

A special endowment, provided on condition that women be admitted, financed the medical school's establishment. The original faculty included such notable medical scholars as William H. Welch and William Osler. The school was open only to college graduates, an extraordinarily high standard, at a time when most medical schools had no university connection and required no more than high school graduation for admission. In view of the notable faculty assembled, the university connection, and the standards for admission, the Hopkins medical school should be rated as Gilman's second major contribution to American education, after Johns Hopkins University itself.

At age seventy, in 1902, Gilman decided to retire. To mark the occasion, a special convocation was held, at which Woodrow Wilson, himself a Hopkins alumnus, spoke. "If it be true," stated Wilson, "that Thomas Jefferson first laid the broad foundation for American universities in his plans for the University of Virginia, it is no less true that you [Gilman] be the first to create and organize in America a university in which the discovery and dissemination of new truth were conceded a rank superior to mere instruction, and in which the efficiency and value of research as an educational instrument were exemplified in the training of many investigators."

This was not the end of Gilman's educational career. In 1901, Andrew Carnegie proposed to grant a large endowment for the establishment of the Carnegie Institution of Washington and insisted that Gilman should be its president. The organization's main aim was to advance research, especially in the field of science. For three years, Gilman devoted all his energies to surveying American and European scientific activities and getting the institution off to a flying start.

Even beyond these demanding tasks, Gilman engaged in a variety of other activities. Because of his reputation as a leading geographer, as early as in 1896 President Cleveland appointed him a member of the U.S. Commission to determine the line between Venezuela and British Guiana. Among offices held by Gilman were the presidency of the American Social Science Association, trustee of John F. Slater Fund, the Peabody Education Fund, and the Russell Sage Foundation, member of the General Education Board, and president of the National Civil Service Reform League, from 1901 to 1907.

Gilman's influence upon American higher education was noteworthy in many respects, especially in the promotion of original and productive research. He appears to have been a singularly good judge of people and an exceptionally able administrator. For these and other reasons, Daniel Coit Gilman clearly ranks as one of America's great university presidents.

RBD

References: Franceso Cordasco, *Daniel Coit Gilman* (London: Brill, 1960); Abraham Flexner, *Daniel Coit Gilman* (New York: Harcourt, 1946); Fabian Franklin, *The Life of Daniel Coit Gilman* (New York: Dodd, 1910).

Stephen Girard

(May 20, 1750—December 26, 1831)

The United States had not yet recovered from the Revolutionary War when the country was faced with the War of 1812. The decades between the two wars were not favorable economic times, and it was unlikely that individuals could amass large fortunes. Yet, two Americans, John Jacob Astor and Stephen Girard, accomplished the feat even though foreign trade was controlled, for the most party, by European countries. Much of the continent was claimed by England, France and Spain and the resources of the land remained undeveloped. An industrial base had not been established to supplement an agricultural society. In this environment there was only one way to accumulate great wealth, trade on the high seas and investment of the proceeds. Astor accomplished it on a massive scale in New York real estate; Girard succeeded in Philadelphia on a lesser scale by investing in real estate and banking.

No one could have predicted Stephen Girard's success. He was physically small, poorly educated, blind in his right eye, introverted, socially handicapped, jealous, shy, shunned by others and a loner. On the other hand, he was disciplined, courageous, orderly, and he possessed an inner feeling of great compassion for the disadvantaged. This last trait was best expressed in his will when he left his fortune to disadvantaged boys, making him the first great American philanthropist to give a large fortune for public welfare.

Girard was born in Chartons, France, the son of a shipping merchant, Pierre Girard. The Girard family had been sea merchants as far back as 1642 and traded for generations among the Sugar Islands of the Caribbean. Their roots and life were deeply imbedded in Haiti. Pierre took his young son, Stephen, into the counting house in France where, in a stern and imperious manner, he taught him the mysteries of invoices and the joy of work. His childhood was unhappy, producing a young man of great sensitivity but with a quick temper and an aloofness from people. As a small boy he learned that industry was a prized virtue. The mocking and jeering from his peers caused him to become solitary and isolated from society. Inwardly, he craved friendship and desired the hospitality of friends, but outwardly he repelled others when approached. Because of conflicts with his father he was allowed at the age of fourteen to go to sea as a cabin boy on one of the family ships.

After several trips to the Caribbean, chiefly Santo Domingo, Girard was made second mate at age twenty-two and a few months later became captain of his own ship. He had prepared himself for navigation by hiring a tutor to teach him in nautical mathematics and astronomical calculations. He left Port-au-Prince in March 1773, and arrived at Bordeaux two months later, completing his first transatlantic voyage on his twenty-third birthday. Shortly thereafter he received his license as captain. In 1774 Girard returned to Port-au-Prince with goods to sell, but failed to liquidate them and was unable to pay his bills. He stayed in Haiti for a short time and studied the market, determining that trade in food was more profitable than in hard goods. He went to New York and entered the employ of Thomas Randall & Son, a shipping firm. He was never to return to France, swearing allegiance to the Commonwealth of Pennsylvania on October 27, 1778.

While with the Randall Company he purchased part ownership in some ships including *La Jeune Bébé*, named after Bébé Duplessis, a New Orleans belle who had rejected his courtship. The Revolutionary War interrupted his shipping trade, and for a time he acted as a merchandiser. Girard was in his twenty-seventh year and as yet had made no satisfactory romantic association. His few attempts had been repulsed until he met Mary Lum, a poor girl from the Northern Liberties suburbs of Philadelphia. After a very short courtship, they were married on June 6, 1777. This marriage brought temporary happiness but was doomed, because Mary soon became schizophrenic and had to be placed in a hospital where she died in 1815. This unhappy experience left Girard more lonely and withdrawn than ever before, but must have contributed to his compassion for the underprivileged. His housekeeper-paramour, Sally Bickham, brought some rays of happiness into an otherwise isolated existence.

Girard's shipping business prospered after the Revolution. He operated from quarters on North Water Street, Philadelphia, and traded primarily with the West Indies, but later added Europe and Asia to his expanding trade. Disappointed in personal human relations he turned his attention to commerce. During his life he owned eighteen vessels and used, on occasion, false identity papers to prevent capture by enemy ships. His trading was very successful and his wealth continued to grow. He began to invest in real estate, insurance and banking.

Girard believed in Hamilton's policy of having a strong central national bank and joined a committee in 1810 to petition Congress to renew the charter of the First United States Bank. Congress let the charter expire in 1811, but in the meantime Girard purchased 948 shares of the bank stock and was in a position of influence when the board of directors liquidated. Girard bought the old bank building and opened a new Bank of Stephen Girard in May 1812. He was convinced that a bank was necessary, especially since the nation was on the threshold of a new war. The public saw little change and assumed that Girard's bank was an affiliate of the United States Treasury. The bank prospered and at the outbreak of the War of 1812 assisted the government in avoiding a financial crisis by taking over the unsubscribed portion of a bond issue. Girard had become an important figure in national finance. As an aftermath of the war, the nation was in dire economic straits and A. J. Dallas, secretary of the treasury, decided to organize a Second United States Bank. Again, Girard came to the rescue and subscribed for all of the $3 million worth of bank stock. President Madison named him one of five directors, but he soon withdrew to attend to the affairs of his own bank.

Panic gripped Philadelphia between August and November 1793. Yellow fever had struck a serious blow, killing more than four thousand persons in about three months. Doctors knew nothing about its cause or its cure. Girard scorned the methods of treatment as ridiculous and considered the doctors no more than practitioners of magic. He publicly derided them and believed their pernicious methods of treatment were responsible for many deaths. He became dedicated to public service and gave of his time and money to the care of patients in the fever hospital at Bush Hill. Girard went to the hospital and took charge for a period of two months. He believed that the disease was filth-borne and that all that was needed was to clean the streets and docks of the accumulated garbage and waste. In fact, he knew no more about the cause than anyone else, but he did succeed in rendering a major service to the victims and to the city of Philadelphia. He was not afraid; cowardice and irresponsibility were not a part of his nature. If doctors failed, or if government could not solve problems of health, it became the duty of captains of commerce to take up the struggle. His public image of a morose miser changed. The public had never known that he gave assistance to many unfortunate individuals; his service in the yellow fever epidemic changed his relations with people.

In addition to real estate acquired in Philadelphia, Girard became owner of a vast tract of land in Ouachita County, Louisiana, when he settled the affairs of John Carrère, a Baltimore bankrupt. By additional purchases he ultimately owned more than 317 square miles of land. He used scientific methods of farming and introduced the highest quality of seed for growing cotton and the best blood lines of cattle. Only a year before his death he bought more than twenty-nine thousand acres of Pennsylvania land in Schuylkill and Columbia counties. It contained rich sources of timber and coal.

Girard's will was his greatest achievement. He left minor sums to various relatives and employees and remembered the Pennsylvania Hospital, the Deaf and Dumb Institute, an orphan asylum, the Philadelphia schools, the Society for the Relief of Poor and Distressed Masters of Ships, the city's Fuel Fund for the poor, and the Masonic Order. His Louisiana lands were divided between New Orleans and Philadelphia. The vast bulk of his estate, amounting to more than $6.6 million, went to public agencies, most of it being channeled into the school for orphan boys, later to be known as Girard College. The heirs filed suit to overthrow the will, but the Supreme Court upheld the terms of the will. Stephen Girard had become the first great American philanthropist to donate large sums of money to charity. Ridiculed and misunderstood in life he had grown from poor cabin boy to multimillionaire. Living in sadness and walking through life alone he found love and fame in death. His compassion for the unfortunate lives after him.

HWS

References: Harry Emerson Wildes, *Lonely Midas* (New York and Toronto: Farrar & Rinehart, 1934); J. B. McMaster, *Life and Times of Stephen Girard, Mariner and Merchant*, 2 vols. (Philadelphia and London: J. B. Lippincott, 1918).

Robert Hutchings Goddard

(October 5, 1882 — August 10, 1945)

Every time there is a major development in the progress of civilization we find someone had a new idea: Edison and the electric light, Morse and the transmission of messages over a wire, and Lawrence and the cyclotron. The Space Age, too, began with new ideas. Robert Goddard dreamed he could project a rocket beyond the confines of the atmosphere, even to the moon. As early as February 1909, he believed that he could propel a rocket with liquid hydrogen and a liquid oxygen oxidizer. Goddard was by no means the first to study rockets. The history of rocketry begins in ancient China with the development of fireworks. Reports of thunder-like explosions during warfare in 1232 A.D. suggest that some type of bomb had been invented. In 1248 Roger Bacon wrote the chemical formula for making black powder, a mixture of carbon, potassium nitrate and sulfur. After this, rockets were used occasionally in warfare as in Spain in 1249 and by the Venetians in 1380. In the late eighteenth century rocketry design was sufficiently advanced so that rockets were used extensively in India against the British. The success of rockets in India caused renewed interest in Europe. Size of rockets greatly increased and improvements in launching were attained. They played an important part in 1806 in the destruction of Boulogne and the burning of Copenhagen in 1807.

Rockets were used on several occasions by the British in America during the War of 1812. When they attempted to capture Baltimore, "The rockets' red glare" inspired Francis Scott Key to compose "The Star-Spangled Banner." The type of rocket used by the British at this time was commonly used throughout Europe. In the mid-1800s a major development took place when curved vanes were invented. The vanes caused the rocket to spin and stabilized the flight, but with the improvement of cannon with rifled bores the rocket became more or less obsolete in warfare during the last part of the nineteenth century. It was still used as a life-saving device for ships stranded near shore and for whaling vessels.

Robert Hutchings Goddard was born in a farmhouse near Worcester, Massachusetts, the son of Nahum and Fannie Goddard. Robert was frail and unable to keep up with his schoolwork, not graduating from Worcester's South Side High School until age twenty-one. In his spare time, while ill, he read scientific stories. In 1932 he wrote H. G. Wells, "In 1898, I read your *War of the Worlds* ... and I decided that ... 'high altitude research,' was the most fascinating problem in existence." After spending four years at Worcester Polytechnic Institute he entered Clark University for graduate studies in physics where he presented his dissertation in 1911. Following an additional year at Clark and a period of research at Princeton's Palmer Physical Laboratory, his health failed and he returned to Worcester in 1913 to recuperate. While recovering from tuberculosis, he organized his research data into patent applications. Two patents were granted, No. 1,102,653 on July 7, 1914 and No. 1,103,503 on July 14. The first patent covered the concept of a multistage rocket, so important in the lifting of spacecraft. In the patent he claimed "a primary rocket, comprising a combustion chamber and a firing tube, a secondary rocket mounted in said firing tube, and means of firing said secondary rocket." In the second patent he established the foundation of modern rocket design. In "the rocket casing I provide two tanks. These tanks contain materials which when ignited will produce an exceedingly rapid combustion ... for instance ... with gasoline and ... liquified nitrous oxide ... pumps are connected to the tanks ... so proportioned that the proper mixture of gasoline and nitrous oxide will be at all times fed to the combustion chamber ... the propelling force is therefore constant."

His health slowly improved, and by fall he returned to Clark University as a part-time teacher and researcher. One rocket tested in 1915 reached a height of 486 feet and a velocity of 8,000 feet per second. He wrote in his diary on August 8, "dreamed at 6:15 a.m. of going to the moon ... saw earth once during return — South America? Used combination crowbar and ladder, used tripod arrangement, to hold, in position." Goddard was working almost without funds for equipment, but his calculations were accurate and his dreams and enthusiasm were contagious. In the fall of 1916 he received a five-thousand-dollar grant from the Smithsonian Institution after submitting a request to build a rocket to study "A Method of Reaching Extreme Altitudes." He showed that if velocity could be adequately increased, escape from the earth's gravity was possible.

America's entry into World War I brought to a close his experiments at Clark. The Signal Corps granted him twenty thousand dollars through the Smithsonian Institution to continue his work on rockets at the Mount Wilson Solar Observatory. Nothing was developed quickly enough to use in the war, but in 1918 a demonstration before observers of the Signal Corps produced a rocket that could be fired by an individual soldier. One of the observers remarked, "the stuff you've got there is going to revolutionize warfare." Four days prior to Germany's surrender the army assured him of a grant to develop a six-inch rocket, but with the close of the war rocket development was forgotten. The principle involved would be found in the tank-killing bazooka during World War II.

In 1919 Goddard published his earlier paper on *A Method of Reaching Extreme Altitudes* in the Smithsonian Miscellaneous Collections, Volume 71. A few days after publication, newspapers reviewed it as an attempt to reach the moon. He became the moon-rocket man. The public thought he was ready to send a rocket to the moon, and when it became apparent that he hadn't built such a rocket, he was thought of as a Jules Verne. He commented that "Every vision is a joke until the first man accomplishes it." He explained to authorities at the Smithsonian that spacecraft could be used for landing a man on a planet and could photograph stellar bodies. He was especially interested in manned flight. "An operator is essential if investigations are made that would necessitate landing on, and departing from, planets."

Goddard's main problem in developing rockets was lack of adequate funding. The mathematical, physical and mechanical problems were, for the most part, solved. Goddard's unique accomplishment in 1926 of achieving the first liquid-fuel flight and repeating it in 1929 had convinced Charles Lindbergh of his ability. Lindbergh contacted Daniel Guggenheim and obtained for Goddard a one-hundred-thousand-dollar grant for a two-year program. This was a rare endowment for the time.

Goddard prepared to move to Roswell, New Mexico, and establish a base of operations. He took his wife, Esther Kisk, whom he had married in 1924, and an experienced crew. He built a launching tower on a ranch in Eden Valley in the desert, set up a machine shop, and spent the next ten years building a variety of rockets. Esther was his chief assistant. During the 1930s he experimented with perfecting flight stability and motors. Better stability was acquired with vanes and gyroscopes, and a 5.75 inch rocket motor was developed. The new rockets reached a height of two thousand feet in 1930, four thousand feet in March, 1935 and seventy-five hundred feet in May. By 1937 a height of nine thousand feet was attained. Lindbergh and the Guggenheims kept in close contact with developments in New Mexico and gave encouragement at all times.

While Goddard worked as an individual to perfect rocketry, organized research on the same subject was taking place in Germany and Russia. In December 1934, Germany fired a liquid-fuel rocket over the North Sea. Before World War II was over the German V-1 and V-2 rockets were in operation. The V-2 was almost identical to those Goddard had developed at Roswell except that alcohol was used as fuel. When he examined captured German V-2's in March 1945, he found them so similar to his own that he felt they had copied his designs. However, it was a case of parallel scientific development in different parts of the world.

When Goddard died he left as his sole survivor his wife, Esther. She had acted as secretary, keeping notes and records of the experiments. She even applied for several patents after his death. The extent of Goddard's research is indicated by the 214 patents granted. Though he was anticipated in certain theoretical matters by the Russian Konstantin Tsiolkovsky and the German Hermann Oberth, Goddard was the experimenter and creator and remains the pioneer of space flight. His patents were so all-inclusive that the American government settled with Mrs. Goddard and the Guggenheim Foundation an infringement claim for $1 million. He did not live to see his predictions come true when an American set foot on the moon or when Mars was photographed.

In 1957 the Goddard Power Plant was opened at Indian Head, Maryland. Two years later Congress ordered a gold medal "in recognition of [his] pioneering research in rocket propulsion." In 1960 he received the Langley Medal, the highest award for contributions in aerodynamics. The Goddard Space Flight Center was established to carry on the work of the National Aeronautics and Space Administration. Goddard's contributions will never fade away; like the Wright brothers' invention of the airplane, the missile and rocket will always be with us, sometimes for good, sometimes for evil.

HWS

References: Milton Lehman, *This High Man* (New York: Farrar, Straus, 1963); Esther C. Goddard and G. Edward Pendray, eds., *The Papers of Robert H. Goddard*, 1898-1945, 3 vols., (New York: McGraw-Hill, 1970).

Charles Goodyear

(December 29, 1800 — July 1, 1860)

From poor boy to rich man and finally philanthropist was the saga of many an inventor in the nineteenth century. Charles Goodyear did not fit the mold though he tried all his life to make his invention of vulcanized rubber pay dividends. He started as a poor boy and remained impecunious all his life, spending time in a debtors' jail and depending occasionally on friends to feed his family. He fitted the general pattern in that he was poor, had little formal education, and made a great invention that was a boon to the human race, but there the pattern was broken. Upon his death he left almost two hundred thousand dollars in debts.

Natural rubber, derived for the most part from the tree *Hevea brasiliensis*, had defied man's attempt to mold it to his needs for more than three centuries after it was discovered by Christopher Columbus on his second voyage to the New World. Columbus had seen Haitian Indians playing a game with a rubber ball, but the first important use made of rubber was by the Scottish chemist, Charles Macintosh, about 1820. He discovered that naphtha was an effective solvent of rubber. If he placed a solution of the two between two layers of cloth he could produce a garment without a sticky surface that was waterproof. Cloaks manufactured in this manner became known as "macintoshes." At about the same time an English inventor, Thomas Hancock, developed a method of producing elastic strips of rubber which he used in making shoes and clothing. The unsolved problem in the commercial use of natural rubber was its tendency to melt in hot weather and become brittle in cold weather. Many men had tried to solve the problem, but all had failed. The science of chemistry was not far enough advanced to aid in the solution. It would be another century before synthetic rubber was invented.

Charles Goodyear was an unlikely candidate to make the great breakthrough in shaping rubber to man's needs. He was born in New Haven, Connecticut, the son of Amasa and Cynthia Goodyear. Charles received a public school education, and after spending four years as an apprentice with a hardware firm in Philadelphia, he returned to New Haven as a partner in his father's business manufacturing tools for farmers. Five years with his father and four more in Philadelphia found him penniless; A. Goodyear & Sons were bankrupt in 1830. Charles had noted various products made from rubber and had observed the liquid gum oozing across the floor of warehouses. After a visit to New York in 1834, where he conferred with rubber companies, he decided to experiment with the substance that had baffled all manufacturers in their efforts to remove or control its undesirable qualities. Upon his return to Philadelphia he was arrested and placed in jail as a debtor. To pass the time he started his first experiments on rubber under these inauspicious circumstances. Following release from jail his kitchen became his laboratory and his fingers the source of power.

The years following 1834 were especially hard for Goodyear. He depended on the largess of friends and the sale of linen spun by his wife for survival. He was the eternal optimist and continued to experiment, producing an "acid gas" process which he patented in 1837. He claimed that the process produced a superior quality of rubber, reducing or destroying its adhesive tendency. He found new financial support and began to manufacture various items including clothing, but the process proved to be commercially unsuccessful and Goodyear was again without funds. He went to Roxbury, Massachusetts, where he borrowed abandoned rubber equipment and continued the manufacture of rubber goods. In this manner, he was able to support his family for a short period of time, but experimentation had to continue because the rubber products were inferior.

Goodyear had received an order from the government for 150 bags manufactured under the "acid gas" process. He thought this was the turning point in his career, but when he hung the bags up they soon collapsed; the acid gas process had failed. Again, he was reduced to poverty. He was ridiculed and derided for his obsession with rubber, but his enthusiasm and ardor for changing the substance into usable products never waned. Finally, in January 1839, the great discovery came about somewhat accidentally. He visited a rubber factory at Woburn, Massachusetts, and was discussing with some friends the quality of the rubber that had failed in the mailbag case. He said that "He was surprised to find that the specimen, being carelessly brought in contact with a hot stove, charred like leather." Of all the witnesses, only Goodyear was impressed. He proceeded to carry out a series of experiments over the next few months until he had perfected the process of vulcanization. After a series of tests, changing the chemical mixes and heating temperatures, Goodyear produced a rubber that remained elastic. Furthermore, it remained stable in both hot and cold weather. But his friends as well as the community had heard the cry of success followed by failure too many times to pay heed to his new claims.

A time of continued experimentation and hardship occurred from 1839 to mid-1844. Goodyear borrowed furnace privileges for heating his rubber. His family subsisted on the charity of neighbors. He pawned his family relics, his children's school books and his household belongings. He was so poor that no one trusted him, but he was willing to beg rather than give up his cherished discovery of the vulcanizing process. Finally he applied for a patent in 1843, and it (No. 3,633) was granted on June 15, 1844. The patent was reissued in 1849 and 1860 and granted in France on April 16, 1844, but denied in England.

As soon as the patents appeared a host of claim jumpers demanded their rights. As with most inventions, there are those who claim they thought of it first but fail to show evidence. His most serious and provocative opponent was a Mr. Horace H. Day who petitioned Congress in 1850 to deny an extension of Goodyear's patent. Congress denied the petition but the Day-Goodyear controversy was not settled. In the Great India Rubber Case Goodyear was defended by none other than Daniel Webster, then secretary of state, at Trenton, New Jersey in 1852. This is comparable to Secretary George Shultz defending in court the patent rights of General Motors in 1983. Webster's fee was twenty-five thousand dollars — more money than Goodyear made from licenses of his patent rights.

To advertise rubber, Goodyear organized exhibits at an international exhibit in London in 1851 and at the Exposition Universelle in Paris in 1855. For the two exhibits he had borrowed more than eighty thousand dollars. Louis Napoleon awarded him the Cross of the Legion of Honor and the Grand Medal of Honor. Unfortunately, Goodyear had raised money for the exhibits by endorsing notes to French companies under license to use his patent. When he was unable to fulfill their demand for payment, he was arrested by the French gendarmerie and placed in Clichy, the debtors' prison of Paris. After a few days he was released and found Napoleon friendly and impressed with the rubber exhibit.

While he was in Europe his wife died, and he married Fanny Wardell of London in 1854. Never a strong man, Goodyear's health began to fail in 1860 and after returning from Europe, he died in a New York hotel. Prior to his death the rubber industry expanded worldwide. Hundreds of different useful objects were being manufactured; his patents had claimed almost five hundred different products. Thousands of men found work in the industry in America and as many as sixty thousand may have been employed in Europe. Of all the uses Goodyear dreamed for rubber, he overlooked the automobile tire, because it would be almost forty years after his death until Henry Ford and others created the need. Poverty and an inventive mind stayed with him forever; fame in his day and fortune escaped him completely.

HWS

References: Ralph F. Wolf, *India Rubber Man* (Caldwell, Idaho: Caxton Printers, 1939); Albert C. Regli, *Rubber's Goodyear* (New York: Julian Messner, 1941).

William Crawford Gorgas
(October 3, 1854 — July 3, 1920)

The scourge of yellow fever menaced the West Indies, Central America, and American coastal regions for centuries. Any traveler in Panama, Cuba, Barbados, or Equador risked his life from the dread disease. Moreover, yellow fever was not confined to tropical regions. In 1793, some four thousand inhabitants of Philadelphia—one-tenth of the population died during an epidemic. Yellow fever had broken out in Portland, Maine, Portsmouth, New Hampshire, Boston, Providence, and New Haven. Sporadic epidemics occurred periodically in New York City, and farther south in Baltimore, Charleston, and Savannah.

No one knew what caused the disease. Climate was blamed by many, since it occurred mainly in the tropics. As early as 1881, Dr. Carlos J. Finlay of Havana, Cuba, read a paper at a medical meeting in Washington, D.C., theorizing that a black mosquito with long wings and white silver markings, the *Stegomyia* mosquito, was the carrying agent, but skeptics ridiculed the notion. Even if true, there was no effective way to get rid of billions of mosquitos, which were found everywhere.

Two heroes emerged in the long, drawn-out fight to eliminate the yellow fever pestilence: Walter Reed, American army surgeon, who by controlled experiments proved that yellow fever is transmitted by the mosquito known as *Aëdes aegypti* and also demonstrated the method of transmission; and William Crawford Gorgas, who used this knowledge to eradicate the disease by destroying the carriers.

William Gorgas was the son of a Confederate general. He was eager for a military career, but when he was unable to obtain an appointment to West Point, decided to join the army medical corps. In 1879, at age twenty-four, he received his doctor of medicine degree at Bellevue Medical College in New York. The following year, as a member of the U.S. Army Medical Corps, he was assigned to typical frontier posts in Texas, North Dakota, and Florida. An early tour of duty was at Fort Brown, Texas, near Brownsville, across the Rio Grande from Matamoras. When Gorgas arrived, he found the camp and all the surrounding countryside being devastated by yellow fever. More than twenty-three hundred cases were identified and towns were under rigid quarantine. Soon, Gorgas himself and the girl he was later to marry, were stricken by the disease and slowly convalesced.

As the years passed, Gorgas' interest in yellow fever grew. When the disease began its devastation of Fort Barrancas, Florida, he was ordered to that post. With the outbreak of the Spanish-American War, he joined the troops being sent to Siboney, Cuba. As U.S. soldiers arrived in Cuba they offered fresh blood to the virus and yellow fever increased alarmingly. It threatened to decimate the victorious United States Army.

About this time, an Army Yellow Fever Committee arrived in Havana, headed by Walter Reed, who began a series of experiments to determine the cause of yellow fever. When these experiments had progressed far enough to indicate that a certain mosquito is the carrier of yellow fever, Gorgas announced that he proposed to rid Havana of mosquitoes. The task appeared impossible. When Gorgas was appointed sanitary officer of Havana, he found a filthy city. Not only yellow fever, but typhus, typhoid, dysentery, and other filth diseases were rampant. Flies, mosquitoes, roaches, and lice were everywhere. Buzzards provided most of the city's sanitation. The narrow, crooked, dirty streets of Havana had not been cleaned since the days of settlement.

Gorgas' first major step in the cleanup of Havana was to eliminate filth, segregate the sick, and to enforce strict quarantine. Ignoring criticism and ridicule, Gorgas sent sanitary agents throughout Havana, forcing people to clean streets and houses. He ordered that standing water and water containers should be treated with films of oil so that larvae of mosquitoes could not live.

The sanitary forces were discouraged, however, after the highly efficient cleanup when yellow fever again began to sweep through the city. With the end of the war, tens of thousands of Spanish immigrants arrived in Havana. The "Yellowjack" epidemic of 1900 was one of the worst in Cuban history.

Gorgas began a diligent study of the *Aëdes aegypti* mosquito. He noted that this mosquito is expert in the ways of man. It usually stings on the underside of the wrist where the skin is tender. The female must be nourished with blood before she can produce eggs; preferably she deposits these in clear water in man-made receptacles, usually avoiding mud puddles or filth.

With the full support of General Leonard Wood, newly appointed military governor of Cuba and himself a physician, Gorgas began the final stage of the great anti-yellow fever war, in March 1901. The death rate steadily declined and during the following four years Havana had no deaths from the disease.

Next, Gorgas was directed to proceed to Panama, notorious as the "White Man's Grave." The French had attempted to build a canal across the isthmus and had failed, largely because of the appalling death rate from tropical diseases among the workmen. The French lost twenty thousand men before giving up the project as hopeless. When the United States took over from the French and began to construct the canal, Gorgas was appointed chief sanitary officer with the Canal Commission. Because of bureaucratic interference, his efforts at first were almost futile. The commission even went to the length of recommending to Washington that Gorgas and his entire staff be fired—a move vetoed by President Theodore Roosevelt. An epidemic of yellow fever caused a panic among the workers and wholesale desertion of the isthmus. Washington authorities finally realized that control of tropical disease was absolutely essential to success of the canal enterprise, and gave orders that Gorgas be allowed to proceed.

Gorgas introduced in Panama the same measures that had been so effective in Cuba. The isthmus was cleaned up and kept clean, modern sanitary laws were applied to the supply of drinking water and to the disposal of sewage, and finally a successful campaign was carried on against mosquitoes. Yellow fever quickly disappeared and the incidence of malaria, a more difficult disease to control, was gradually reduced. By 1914, the death rate in Panama was lower than in the United States.

In 1913, Gorgas was invited by the Transvaal Chamber of Mines to visit South Africa and to make recommendations for the control of pneumonia among the Negro mine workers. While there, he was notified that he had been appointed Surgeon General of the United States Army with the rank of major general. The recently organized International Health Board enlisted him as an adviser and asked him to tour Brazil, Ecuador, Venezuela, Peru, Colombia, Central America, and Mexico to procure exact information about where yellow fever still persisted. As a world-renowned authority upon Yellowjack, he was received with open arms throughout Latin America.

During World War I, Gorgas served as head of the medical service of the army until after the armistice, at which time the army had about twelve thousand medical officers in active service.

In the course of a visit to London in 1920, Gorgas suffered a paralytic stroke, and died about a month later. While hospitalized, he was visited by King George V, who conferred upon him the insignia of the Knight Commander of the Most Distinguished Order of St. Michael and St. George.

Many other honors came to Gorgas, including the presidency of the American Medical Association and numerous honorary degrees. A permanent memorial is the Gorgas Memorial Institute of Tropical and Preventive Medicine, established in Panama in 1921.

As the man who made possible the construction of the Panama Canal, Gorgas' name will always be linked with that great work. His outstanding achievement in Havana is somewhat overshadowed by this later and greater success. Today, yellow fever has been driven almost out of existence and travelers visit freely in places once considered pestholes.

RBD

References: Marie C. Gorgas, *William Crawford Gorgas* (Garden City, N.Y.: Doubleday, 1924); Thomas W. Martin, *Doctor William Crawford Gorgas of Alabama* (New York: Newcomen Society, 1947); Willard H. Wright, *Forty Years of Tropical Medical Research* (Washington, D.C.: Reese Press, 1970).

Asa Gray

(November 8, 1810 — January 30, 1888)

Physicians played an important part in the development of science in America prior to the 1880s. It was not uncommon for a man trained in medicine to divert his interest to natural history. It was an age of generalization rather than specialization. As America expanded westward under Manifest Destiny, new schools on all levels were created. The sciences slowly developed, first in a general way by students of natural history and later by the emergence of specific discipline such as botany, geology, and zoology. Specialization within these subjects would arise at a still later date. The naturalist found before him a new continent, its fauna, flora and rocks unknown entities. Some naturalists were educated in Europe such as Samuel Lathrop Mitchell who studied geology under Dr. John Walker in Edinburgh, and returned in the 1790s to the New York area to report on the origin of some rock strata. Others, such as Louis Agassiz, were native Europeans who emigrated to America and contributed to the study of natural history.

Asa Gray was a native New Yorker educated in medicine in the College of the Physicians and Surgeons of the Western District of the State of New York at Fairfield. The medical school had been granted a charter in 1812 only two years after Asa's birth to Moses and Roxana Gray. The curriculum included mineralogy and botany. After exposure to botany, Gray became dedicated to its study even though he continued his medical courses, serving as a medical apprentice in 1828 and receiving the doctor of medicine degree in 1831. He had served his apprenticeship under Dr. John F. Trowbridge, who charged twenty-five cents for a house call and prescribed a miscellany of pills, plasters and emetics but, fortunately, not much blood-letting.

Gray's interest in medicine waned rapidly and in 1832 he accepted a teaching position at the Utica Gymnasium. His duties included the teaching of geology, mineralogy, botany, chemistry and zoology, the typical assignment for a student of natural history. The best part of the job was that he had time to collect plants; he had turned his back on medicine and hereafter would devote his energies to botany. He had studied Brewster's *Edinburgh Encyclopedia* and Eaton's *Manual of Botany*, thus becoming acquainted with Linnaeus's artificial system of classification of plants. In 1832 he met Dr. John Torrey, then the leading American botanist, in New York. This was a fortunate association because Gray became Torrey's aide and worked with him on the *Flora of North America*. He lived for a time in the Torrey home where he was greatly influenced by Mrs. Torrey. She was a cultured woman educated in the classics, capable of reading Latin and Greek. Her kindness to Gray improved his manners and social contacts.

Gray became an important collaborator with Torrey and in time was included as joint author for the work on *Flora of North America* (vol. 1, 1838-1840; vol. 2, 1841-1843). This was a major accomplishment in the life of a young botanist who, as yet, had no continuous gainful employment. His lack of any kind of appointment in the mid-1830s was discouraging, but rather than forsake a scientific career he decided to write a botany textbook. The most popular text of the day was one by Amos Eaton which followed the Linnaean system of classification. Gray was using a natural system and knew that it would displace the artificial system of Eaton. Gray published *Elements of Botany* (1836) at age twenty-six and thus established himself as one of the foremost botanists of the day. His work on *Flora* and the text attracted enough attention to get him invited to participate in an expedition to the South Seas in 1836. This seemed to be a glorious opportunity for a young scientist, but after two years of waiting for the expedition to be organized Gray resigned.

In March of 1838 Gray applied for a professorship at the newly organized University of Michigan. Unfortunately it was still a paper university, but his appointment as the first permanent paid professor in the university carried another honor, namely, "Professor of Botany in the University of Michigan." It was unusual in American education in 1838 for professors to carry a title in a specific science. Gray accepted the appointment and in November sailed for Europe on behalf of the university to purchase books of science for a proposed new library. The year spent in Europe was of great importance. He met the leading botanists of the day and established a working relationship that continued throughout his life. He made a casual acquaintance with a young man known as Charles Darwin, a relationship that would become significant in a few years. Gray never had an opportunity to assume his duties at Michigan; the state fell upon hard economic times but accepted the collection of books which he bought in Europe.

When Gray returned to America in 1841 he was again unemployed. There were few jobs for American scientists, but Gray did not have long to wait. On April 30, 1842 he was appointed Fisher Professor of Natural History at Harvard at a salary of one thousand dollars a year. The unique thing about the position was that he could have "time, to prosecute the important work, in which ... [he was] engaged." His duties would be confined "to instruction and lecturing in Botany and to superintendence of the Botanic Garden." Gray's appointment to Harvard was really a turning point in botanical research in America, if not in all sciences. It set a pattern for the future development of scientific research.

Gray's life at Harvard was happy and productive. He wasted no time in informing botanists of the world that he intended to make the Botanical Gardens serve "the promotion of botanical science." He initiated a program of field collecting and international exchange of plants. In addition, he began a series of lectures at the Lowell Institute at a thousand dollars for twelve lectures in 1844. By doubling his income he was, for the first time in his life, financially solvent. He continued the Lowell lectures in 1845 and 1846 and felt affluent enough to marry Jane Lathrop Loring of Boston in 1848. Though his research diminished his professional activities expanded. His *Botanical Textbook* became the standard text. His activities made him America's leading botanist and one of the world's outstanding scientists.

When Louis Agassiz arrived at Harvard in 1846, he brought with him concepts concerning the development of life which were deeply rooted in religion. He believed that each species was specially created by a divine being who had an overall plan. Gray, on the other hand, though religious, did not consider the Bible as a scientific text. He did not confuse the facts of science, as he determined them from a study of plants, with his emotional concepts. Though he was friendly with Agassiz he did not agree with his ideas of the origin of species. Gray's position was consolidated in 1857 when Darwin wrote him a letter in which he described the evolution of life and the development of species by natural selection. This letter and a copy of *Origin of Species* transformed Gray into one of Darwin's most vocal supporters in America, publishing two lectures in 1880 on *Natural Science and Religion*. Gray believed that species were closely related genetically and varied by adaptation to the environment. He cited the close relationship between certain plants in America and East Asia and called upon geological information to explain their occurrence in such diverse regions. James D. Dana, one of the most capable geologists of the day, aided in explaining the geographical dispersal of modern plants. Gray and Agassiz came into direct conflict in lectures and published papers, Agassiz continuing to espouse the divine origin of species until his death and Gray gaining stature with his defense of Darwinism.

During an active life of more than fifty years Gray wrote more than 350 papers, books and monographs. His monograph on the botany of North America as compared with that in Japan brought him scientific recognition. It covered the history of plant life from the Cretaceous period to the present, linking the fossil plants and modern forms in the temperate belt. Gray was at his best in describing the flora of North America. Most of his work dealt with this subject. His *Manual of the Botany of the Northern United States* (1848) was used more than any other reference book on the subject.

Gray had defended religion as well as evolution; he was aware that the two did not really conflict. He discarded the concepts of spontaneous generation and divine creation for genetic control of species origin. He had found in the 1830s a whole continent in front of him covered with plants that, for the most part, were undescribed. He was confronted with a colossal task but in pursuing it became one of the foremost botanists of all time. Gray liked to travel and in his last years crossed the continent with F. V. Hayden, geologist, as leader and Sir William Hooker, president of the Royal Society of London, as companion. His last major trip was made in 1887 when he toured Europe. Cambridge awarded him an honorary Doctor of Science degree, Edinburgh granted an LL.D., and Oxford bestowed a D.C.I. He crossed the Atlantic for the last time in October 1887 and continued to decline in health, dying the following year.

HWS

References: George Harvey Genzmen, *DAB*, VII, 1931, pp. 511-14; A. Hunter Dupree, *Asa Gray* (New York: Atheneum, 1968); A. Hunter Dupree, *Dictionary of Scientific Biography*, 10, 1972, pp. 511-14.

William Green

(March 3, 1870—November 21, 1952)

William Green inherited a long background of coal mining and trade unionism. His father Hugh, a Welsh miner, emigrated to the Ohio coalfields with his family. There he participated in the Knights of Labor, predecessor of the American Federation of Labor, and then in the Progressive Miners' Union. Family poverty forced William to leave school after the eighth grade and to enter the mines at age sixteen. Naturally he joined the union, later a local of the United Mine Workers of America.

William worked in the mines at Coshocton, Ohio, for some twenty-two years, but at the same time he was moving steadily up toward union leadership. At age eighteen he was elected secretary of his local union and subsequently served as treasurer, president, subdistrict president, and by 1906, at age thirty-six, president of the Ohio district. Labor historians are agreed that Green was not a brilliant leader nor did he possess any special charm of personality. Instead, his rise in the labor movement came from his persevering nature, honesty, and efficient service. Outside labor organizations, he was elected to two terms in the Ohio Senate, during the second of which he became Democratic floor leader. As a legislator, a major achievement was authorship of the Ohio Workmen's Compensation Law (1911), which became a model bill for other states.

Green's first venture on the national scene came with his appointment as statistician of the United Mine Workers of America, followed by his election as UMWA secretary-treasurer. The latter position placed him in line for the AFL presidency, made vacant by the death of Samuel Gompers in 1924. The support of John L. Lewis and the UMWA were key factors in Green's gaining that office, despite the fact, as AFL historian Philip Taft pointed out, "his prior record reveals no activity or reputation of a character that would have brought him to the fore for consideration of the office."

The Great Depression of the thirties created problems, of course, for the labor unions, which were forced to turn to the federal government for aid. Green reversed Gompers' long standing policy by favoring unemployment insurance, declaring "that the labor movement would not be harmed by giving workers more insurance protection than the unions could afford and by placing the responsibility for this protection upon society."

Green was a staunch Democrat and backer of Roosevelt's New Deal. As AFL president, he was labor's principal lobbyist and spokesman. He was, for example, actively involved in shaping the National Industrial Recovery Act in 1933, the National Labor Relations Act in 1935, and social security and relief legislation. Phrases relating to hours and wages were influenced by him to protect the unions.

The prolonged controversy over the issue of industrial versus craft union organization erupted in the 1930s. The predominant type of organization, the craft union, was being bitterly criticized because it had given little attention to the problems of the unskilled workers. A largely unsuccessful organizing drive in the auto industry was undertaken by Green in 1926. He saw that the newly organized mass-production workers could not be effectively divided up among a variety of unions, and he attempted to meet the problem by setting up federal unions — a failure because the craft unions insisted on taking over all workers in their trades.

The fight brought on a major confrontation in the AFL. The leader of the labor progressives, John L. Lewis, demanded a vigorous campaign to organize workers on an industrial union basis. When the 1935 AFL convention rejected this demand, Lewis proceeded to set up the Congress of Industrial Organizations. Thus a rival labor movement was created, Green's long association with Lewis ended, and the UMWA was expelled by the AFL. Green apparently felt that he had to remain loyal to the craft union principle, even though he was basically sympathetic to the industrial unionists. The split between the AFL and CIO troubled Green for the remainder of his career.

For the most part, the AFL under Green adhered to Samuel Gompers' non-partisan policies, refusing to endorse any presidential candidate. After passage of what Green called "a slave labor" law, the Taft-Hartley Act of 1947, the AFL set up Labor's League for Political Education. In 1952, the federation broke precedent by supporting Adlai Stevenson.

On other fronts, Green and the AFL were militantly anti-Communist and opposed recognition of the Soviet Union in 1933. Green was a member of the governing board of the International Labor Organization, 1935-1937. In 1944 the federation used its Free Trade Union Committee to aid in rebuilding non-Communist labor movements in war-torn Europe. Further participation in the international labor movement occurred when Green went to London in 1949 to join in setting up the International Confederation of Free Trade Unions.

At the time of his death, the AFL was moving toward political activism, internal reform, and toward unity with the CIO, the last of which was not achieved until 1955, three years after Green's death in 1952.

RBD

Reference: Max D. Danish, *William Green* (New York: Inter-Allied Publications, 1952).

David Lewelyn Wark Griffith
(January 22, 1875 — July 23, 1948)

Although he was able to satisfy his interest in the theater at an early age and had considerable experience as a member of stock companies, David Wark Griffith was never a star performer. It was only after he began to work with motion pictures and ventured to Hollywood that he found his true metier and made his invaluable contribution to the art of the cinema. As Robert Sklar, one of his biographers, has said, "D. W. Griffith was the first important creative artist in the motion pictures."

Griffith was born in Oldham County, Kentucky, in 1875, one of seven children. His parents had moved to Kentucky from Virginia and Maryland. The father served as colonel of the Kentucky cavalry and in the Kentucky legislature. He was also a plantation owner but met hard times and died when the son was young. The mother later ran a boardinghouse in Louisville. Griffith was educated in country schools and in Louisville but also had early work experience in a dry goods store and a bookstore. At one time he had an interest in writing and actually published a story in *Cosmpolitan Magazine* and some verse. In 1891 he was employed briefly by the *Louisville Courier-Journal*. But his deep voice and somewhat flamboyant manner propelled him toward the stage and about 1895 he joined an amateur acting group that performed in the smaller communities of Kentucky and Indiana. He wrote one play that actually reached the boards and tried to suggest ideas for films to various motion picture studios. In 1908 he was engaged by the Biograph Company as a director on trial and soon became the principal director, a position he retained until 1913. In this period he produced almost five hundred one and two reel films.

In this work with films Griffith was able to experiment, moving the camera closer to the actors, using separate shots, and trying to get away from some of the conventions of the stage. Although in his own days as an actor he had been more exuberant, when he directed others he strove for restraint in action and gestures and relied on small movements and subtle expressions. He may not have been the first to employ fade-ins and fade-outs, flashbacks, parallel montage for suspense, and night photography but he was quick to develop such methods. He was also insistent on the primacy of the director rather than the camera man. From the beginning of his production years he became known for his ability to judge and teach cinema actors and actresses, and the performers that he coached included such later stars as Mary Pickford, the Gish sisters Lillian and Dorothy, Mae Marsh, Blanche Sweet, and Henry B. Walthall. One of his earliest films was called *The Adventures of Dollie* in 1908. After leaving the Biograph Company he worked for Reliance-Majestic and began to produce longer films, five to seven reels in length. He hoped to earn enough money at this time to create a film based on the Civil War.

In 1914 his ambition was realized when he directed *The Birth of a Nation*, released the next year and destined to be one of the landmarks of the American motion picture industry. Its twelve reels made it the longest and most expensive picture produced up to that time. Based on a novel by Thomas Dixon called *The Clansman*, the story traced the rise of the Ku Klux Klan in South Carolina until the overthrow of carpetbag rule. The overwrought ending showed hooded clansmen ready to rescue a white girl apparently menaced by a black man. Griffith's film became famous as a spectacle and notorious as a kind of plea for white racial solidarity. Middle-class white audiences applauded it, Negroes resented it.

The next year Griffith released another long and spectacular film, called *Intolerance*, which was somewhat less popular but equally influential. It included four historical epochs and places; the modern United States, sixteenth century Paris, Palestine in the age of Christ, and ancient Babylon. The Babylon segment was notable for its control of crowd movement and its spectacular setting and color. Both *The Birth of a Nation* and *Intolerance* were extremely profitable, the first film earning $48 million during the director's lifetime.

In 1917 Griffith signed with Adolph Zukor and produced pictures for the Artcraft Corporation. Two years later he joined Charles Chaplin, Mary Pickford, and Douglas Fairbanks to form the United Artists firm. But about the same time he built a studio in Mamaroneck, New York, to make films for other studios. Between 1917 and 1924 he produced some eighteen films, many of which proved quite profitable. Included among them were *Hearts of the World* (1918), *Broken Blossoms* (1919), and *Orphans of the Storm* (1921), in all of which the Gish sisters appeared. He also made a film version of Lottie Blair Parker's successful melodrama, *Way Down East*, which in 1898 had a Broadway run of 361 performances. Other Griffith pictures of this period were *True Heart Susie*, in 1919, and *Isn't Life Wonderful?* a socially realistic story which was filmed in 1924 in Germany. After 1925 Griffith relinquished his independence and signed again with Zukor, now chairman of Paramount Pictures. He made three movies for this studio. His first sound film came in 1930 and portrayed the life of Abraham Lincoln with Walter Huston playing the role of the president. His last film was entitled *The Struggle* in 1931 and its temperance orientation did not help its box office appeal.

The last seventeen years of Griffith's life were marred by a debilitating struggle with debt and alcoholism. He had little connection with the motion picture world and small chance of returning to studio employment. Moreover, he objected to the administrators and tinkerers who had entrenched themselves in the cinema business, and to some extent the advent of the talking pictures had left him behind. Certainly his fame was secure. Griffith pictures had been shown throughout the world and had become enormously influential. Wherever movies were planned, screened, or displayed his name was known. Probably no one had ever matched his contribution to the growth of mass culture. But there was no cure for his final despondency.

Griffith's first marriage, to Linda Johnson in 1906, ended in divorce thirty years later. There were no children. He married again in 1936 and this marriage also ended in divorce, eleven years later. He died in Hollywood and was buried at Centerfield, Oldham County, Kentucky. Details of his personal life were chronicled by his first wife and by Lillian Gish and Anita Loos.

JTF

References: Robert Sklar, *DAB*, Supplement 4, 1974, pp. 348-51; Robert M. Henderson, *David Wark Griffith: His Life and Work* (New York: Oxford, 1972); Richard Schickel, *D. W. Griffith: An American Life* (New York: Simon & Schuster, 1984).

Oscar Hammerstein II

(July 12, 1895 — August 23, 1960)

Every successful musical play is a cooperative effort of talented people. The librettist, lyricist, composer and producer all work as a team to create a performance pleasing to the public. There is an amalgamation of stage talent with the work of writers, musicians and producers. Oscar Hammerstein II became an important link in the development of the American musical play. As a librettist and lyricist, he worked with Jerome Kern to create *Show Boat* in 1927, thus departing from the traditional format of musical theater. Prior to *Show Boat* Hammerstein had been content to follow the norm of chorus girl lines as a part of lavish and spectacular shows of the *Follies* type. The 1927 play focused on American social scenes with native dialogue and local humor, all set in familiar environments.

Hammerstein's grandfather, Oscar Hammerstein I, started the family's interest in musical theater in New York City. He built the Olympia and Victoria theaters in New York and used the profits to build and operate the Philadelphia and Manhattan opera houses. His competition with the Metropolitan caused that company to offer him $1.25 million in 1920 to get out of the opera business. Hammerstein's father, William, successfully operated the Victoria and his Uncle Arthur managed the operas.

Oscar's mother died in 1910 and his father in 1914. Though he was deeply affected by the death of his parents he continued his education, entering Columbia University in 1912. In the fall of 1914 Hammerstein joined the Columbia University Players and a year later made his debut in the theater with a part in *On Your Way*. He met Lorenz Hart and Richard Rodgers in the players group, the latter eventually becoming a part of the famous team of Rodgers and Hammerstein.

Although Hammerstein's father had exacted a promise from him that he would not enter the theater as a profession, he prevailed upon his Uncle Arthur to take him as an assistant stage manager in 1917 because he wanted a career as a

Broadway playwright. His work with the hit musical *You're In Love* was so outstanding that his uncle made him stage manager. He felt that the theater was in the family blood, and now that he had a job in his chosen field he married Myra Finn. With the death of Oscar I in 1919 he no longer worked in the shadow of his grandfather and began to carve out a niche in the musical theater for himself.

Post-World War I America was ready to accept the lavish productions of the 20s. The stage spectacle with its jazz rhythm was an escape for pleasure-seeking, war-weary Americans. Hammerstein followed the pattern at this time and provided the story and lyrics for his first musical comedy *Always You*, which opened in January 1920. It had good songs but lacked an interesting plot. He learned at this time that playgoers wanted good plots as well as good music. He put into practice what he learned and in his next musical *Tickle Me* he collaborated with Frank Mandel and Otto Harbach to produce a hit.

After some failures Hammerstein began breaking away from the hackneyed, stereotyped musical comedy and tried a new approach in *Mary Jane McKane* in late 1923. *Wildflower*, in the same year, was a success, but *Rose Marie* in 1924 was a great hit, running on Broadway for more than a year and ultimately grossing at least $21 million. It was followed by Kern's *Sunny* in 1925 and Romberg's *The Desert Song* in 1926, both great successes. Innovations carried out in the early 20s prepared Hammerstein and Kern to make the final break and create *Show Boat* in 1927, a landmark in American musical plays.

On a trip to London in 1927 to direct a production of *The Desert Song* he met Dorothy Blanchard, an actress from Melbourne, Australia. Myra and Oscar's marriage was not wholly compatible and after their divorce he married Dorothy. Their son, James, became a director and producer.

Hammerstein signed a contract in 1929 with Warner Brothers-First National Pictures to write four operettas for Hollywood. However, the Great Depression soon reached the filmmaking industry and producers lost interest in musicals. The flood of musical films in 1929 and 1930 gave way to serious films which were closer to the public mood. Oscar returned to New York, but the decade of the 30s was not very successful for him. He was unable to produce or write a successful musical during this period. He put the failures behind him and started the most successful period of his life when he agreed in 1942, after completing the libretto to *Carmen Jones*, to work with Richard Rodgers.

Rodgers and Hammerstein started work on *Oklahoma* which opened in 1943 and became one of the all-time American favorites. *Oklahoma* opened a two-decade period of musical theater unparalleled in stage entertainment. It was followed by *Carousel* in 1945, *South Pacific* in 1947, and the *King and I* in 1951. *Oklahoma* was the second milestone in the development of the musical play, after *Show Boat*. It had a run of 2,243 performances in New York and received a special Pulitzer prize in 1944. When we add to these the musicals *Me and Juliet* in 1953, *Flower Drum Song* in 1958, *Sound of Music* in 1959, the score for the film *State Fair* in 1945, and the television production of *Cinderella* in 1959, we recognize the genius of both the lyricist and composer.

Hammerstein's success as a lyricist was based on his ability to use simple words to portray the character of real people. His descriptive phrases were part of everyday language and when set to Rodgers' music appealed to all people. He had made the lights on Broadway brighter during his life and shortly after his death

Mayor Robert Wagner of New York declared a temporary blackout in the theater district in his honor.

HWS

References: Hugh Fordin, *Getting to Know Him* (New York: Random House, 1977); Stanley Green, *The Rodgers and Hammerstein Story* (New York: Holt, 1963).

William Rainey Harper
(July 24, 1856 — January 10, 1906)

Large endowments given by wealthy benefactors, such as Johns Hopkins provided for Johns Hopkins University, Leland Stanford for Stanford University, Ezra Cornell for Cornell University, and John D. Rockefeller for the University of Chicago, made possible the creation of some of America's greatest private universities. But without the inspired leaders under whom these universities began, it is unlikely they would have achieved the eminence they subsequently attained.

A prime example is William Rainey Harper, first president of the University of Chicago, who from 1892 until his death in 1906 made a permanent impression on this famous center of learning.

As a youth, Harper was remarkably precocious. At age fourteen, he graduated from Muskingum College in Ohio, with a bachelor of arts degree, and a Ph.D. degree from Yale College at age eighteen, on the basis of a dissertation entitled "A Comparative Study of the Prepositions in Latin, Greek, Sanskrit, and Gothic."

Throughout his career, Harper had a consuming interest in the study of languages, especially Hebrew. His salutatory oration at Muskingum was delivered in Hebrew. In 1876, at age twenty, on the faculty of Denison University in Ohio, he continued his private studies in the Semitic languages and gained a reputation as an inspiring teacher. Three years later, an opportunity to teach Semitic languages came, when he joined the faculty of the Baptist Theological Seminary at Morgan Park in Chicago. Outside the classroom, his immense energy and initiative were used to develop correspondence courses in Hebrew, to prepare a series of textbooks and vocabularies for the study of Hebrew, to publish two journals (*Biblical World* and the *American Journal of Semitic Languages and Literatures*), and to organize a summer course in Semitic languages and Biblical studies.

Two years later, in 1881, Harper was called back to Yale, where for the next five years he took an active part in the work at Chautauqua, teaching courses in summers, and at Yale established a national reputation as teacher, lecturer, organizer, and editor. Yale recognized him with an appointment to a professorship in Semitic languages, in 1886, and serving at the same time as Woolsey professor of Biblical literature.

The final major step in Harper's rapid rise came in 1891, when at age thirty-five he became president of the newly established University of Chicago, apparently the first choice of philanthropist John D. Rockefeller. Prior to accepting the appointment, however, Harper made clear to the trustees his conception of a university, to avoid any later misunderstanding. First of all, there must be complete freedom of teaching and research for everyone associated with the institution, and second, a cardinal point in view of Chicago's subsequent history, the new institution was not to be an ordinary American college but a great university, exercising leadership in education and research. Further plans outlined by Harper, and accepted by the trustees, included university extension, a university press, an academic year divided into four quarters (one a summer quarter), faculty control of athletics, a limited number of courses to be taken by students at one time to allow more concentration, and an emphasis on graduate study and research. Perhaps none of these was original, even at the time, but the stress which Harper placed on them and his other views on education were widely influential. He expounded on them in numerous addresses at universities and before educational organizations around the nation.

With his usual indefatigable energy, Harper went about the task of bringing a great university into existence. Within a few years, a brilliant faculty had been assembled, attracted by higher than average salaries, Harper's personality, and his ambitious plans for the future of the university. In Berlin, Harper bought a collection of more than two hundred thousand books and pamphlets, providing a working library for various departments. It was highly appropriate, therefore, for the University of Chicago later to name its central library the William Rainey Harper Library. Shortly, the university was offering degrees at all levels.

Despite these constant demands on his time and strength as he continued to establish the University, Harper was unwilling to forego other activities. Literally, it may be said that he worked himself to death. He taught full time and was also chairman of the department of Semitic languages, for a time he remained president of Chautauqua in New York, and he held the editorship of several journals. For eight years he was superintendent of the Hyde Park Baptist Church Sunday School, and for several years was an active member of the Chicago Board of Education. He also attended educational conferences and planned and supervised publication of many textbooks. Differences had to be resolved between the divinity school and other faculties who had been promised full academic freedom. Budget problems needed to be dealt with as expenditures were always threatening to exceed income. There were demands for the establishment of professional schools in a variety of disciplines before existing departments had become soundly established.

For ten years before his death, Harper handled such problems, campaigning for an increased endowment, watching the continuous growth of the university and the erection of an impressive group of buildings. During the decennial year alone, 1901, cornerstones were laid for five new buildings. Highlights for the period were the establishment of the Ogden Graduate School of Science, the transfer to Chicago of Clark University's faculty of science (including Michelson, Donaldson and Loeb), construction of the Hull Biological Quadrangle, and the Haskell Museum, building an observatory for the Yerkes telescope at Williams Bay, Lake Geneva, establishment of the College of Commerce and Politics in 1897, of the School of Education in 1901, and of the Law School in 1902. To mark the Centennial, twenty-eight volumes were published, for which Harper claimed that "No series of scientific publications so comprehensive in its scope and of so great a magnitude has ever been issued at any one time by any learned society or institution."

Harper's iron constitution began to rebel against overwork. As far back as 1889, he had obtained some rest by a voyage to Europe to attend the Oriental Congress in Stockholm. He made a second trip to Europe in 1897, following an illness. He began to give up some of his responsibilities, such as membership on the Chicago Board of Education and the principalship of Chautauqua. An operation for appendicitis in 1904, from which he never fully recovered, and the discovery of a cancerous condition proved too much and Harper died on January 10, 1906.

William Rainey Harper aspired to scholarly research and productivity for himself, but found little time for them. Every member of his faculty was expected to be more than a mere classroom teacher—research, popularization of knowledge, or administrative and committee work—though it was left to the individual to decide how his or her time should be spent. Harper was highly successful in raising funds for the university and for other purposes; he maintained, however, that he never asked for money, but only presented opportunities. Furthermore, any attempt by donors to influence policies or to interfere with academic freedom was summarily rejected. As an executive, Harper was said to have been a dominating but not a domineering personality, and on many occasions showed a willingness to compromise when convinced of the wisdom of following other courses.

Harper's biographer Paul Shorey commented that "The University of Chicago is his monument ... the University still in large measure embodies his spirit, and may not too fancifully be thought to exhibit his qualities and what his censors regard as his defects. It has the self-confidence, the energy, the breadth, the tolerance, the hope, the enthusiasm for creative work, the determination to be a pace-maker, and the desire to prove all things."

RBD

References: Thomas W. Goodspeed, *William Rainey Harper* (Chicago: University of Chicago Press, 1928); Richard J. Starr, *Harper's University* (Chicago: University of Chicago Press, 1966).

Edward Henry Harriman

(February 20, 1848—September 9, 1909)

Certain mechanical developments have had a major impact on society. The creation of a railroad system profoundly influenced communication, travel and transport freight. The widespread use of railroads resulted in a revolution, the first in rapid transportation, comparable to what occurred later when the automobile and airplane were developed. The railroad was capable of moving rapidly across country, whatever the weather conditions, carrying a great load of people and freight at a reasonable cost. The railroad's superiority in transportation made the canal and stagecoach immediately outdated. It was especially important in opening up the American West by carrying emigrants from the East Coast to the interior of the country. The speed of the railroad was a welcome respite from the slow and ponderous movement of the Conestoga wagon that carried so many pioneers westward.

From 1825 to 1850 the American railroad developed slowly, reaching a maximum mileage of about nine thousand miles, but took a giant step in the 1850s with the construction of an additional twenty-one thousand miles. The Civil War interrupted the progress, but seventy thousand miles of new track were built in the 1880s. Railroad construction was carried out by private enterprise, but in some cases subsidized by land grants from the federal government. The grants consisted of alternate square miles, the government retaining the intervening sections. More than 131 million acres of undeveloped land were acquired by the railroads in this manner. This was a major factor in opening up the Great Plains region as well as the westernmost states. Between the Civil War and 1920 railroads enjoyed almost a monopoly in transportation, increasing mileage in excess of 250,000 miles. Much of the mileage was created by roads west of the Mississippi River, including the Northern Pacific, the Great Northern, the Union Pacific and the Southern Pacific.

The cost of railroad development had reached $2.5 billion in 1870 but expanded to $18 billion by 1917, with more than 1.7 million employees. Capital investment was the key to success. Into this picture stepped the financiers J. P. Morgan and his ally, James J. Hill. Morgan had become the dominant force in post-1873 American railroading. His influence was felt in most Eastern railroads, and with investments in the Northern Pacific and Great Northern he had a major voice in railroads that spanned the continent. Edward Harriman appeared on the scene as a novice in 1881. His influence was to become major in the next thirty years, and even the great Morgan would have to listen as he became a reorganizer and builder of railway systems.

Harriman was born in Hempstead, Long Island, but grew up in Jersey City. His formal education was limited to public school and a short term at Trinity School. At age fourteen he announced to his father that he was going to work and soon acquired a job as messenger clerk on Wall Street at five dollars per week. He soon became a "pad-shover," a clerk who kept records of offers to buy and sell securities. At age twenty-one he had educated himself enough in the intricacies of the stock market to warrant borrowing three thousand dollars from an uncle and purchasing a seat on the New York Stock Exchange.

While working as a broker Harriman became interested in underprivileged boys and as a result formed the Thompkin's Square Boys' Club in 1876. This was probably the first club of its kind. It was successful and Harriman maintained an interest in its welfare, contributing almost all of $185,000 for a building in 1901. He made many annual gifts to support the club's budget.

Harriman's interest in railroads may be traced, in part, to his marriage in 1879 to Mary Averell, daughter of the president of the Ogdensburg & Lake Champlain Railroad Company. The company operated a small railroad that was in financial trouble. Harriman thought it could be improved and might form an important link to the New York Central. With this in mind he, with friends, bought the railroad in 1881 and renamed it the Sodus Bay & Southern. He sold it to the Pennsylvania two years later at a profit and his career in railroading from this time was to dominate the remainder of his life.

The Illinois Central Railroad was completed in 1857 through the heartland of America, with its southern terminus at Cairo, Illinois. After the panic of 1873 the Illinois Central acquired additional roads that allowed it to reach New Orleans. It was a successful road carrying farm produce from the rich farmland area to the city markets. Harriman was impressed with its future and became a director in 1883. Four years later he was vice-president and his friend, Stuyvesant Fish, was president. He helped rebuild the railway as well as becoming its chief financial advisor. Harriman knew his way around Wall Street and his experience on the Illinois Central gave him a detailed working knowledge of railroading. He was bold and aggressive in financial matters and applied his talents to improving the services of the Illinois Central, thus keeping the company in a sound financial position. In the first ten years of his tenure he added fifteen hundred miles of new track, bought 274 new locomotives, and more than doubled earnings.

The Union Pacific went into bankruptcy after the panic of 1893. Congress had created the Union and the Central Pacific in 1862 as a means of connecting California with the states east of the Mississippi. At the time of formation the Union had received in excess of $27 million in government bonds and more than 11 million acres of land. Though the railway expanded in size it was deeply in debt and went into bankruptcy in the panic of 1893. Various reorganization attempts, including one by J. P. Morgan, failed. Three years later Harriman joined the forces of Kuhn, Loeb & Company as a director and member of the executive committee that succeeded in reorganizing the railroad. Within a short time Harriman was made chairman of the executive committee and remained in charge for the rest of his life. At the time he assumed command of the Union Pacific the railroad had an indebtedness of $81 million and was in poor physical condition. Harriman rebuilt the Union by upgrading the physical plant, repossessing the Oregon Short Line, and taking control of the Oregon Railroad & Navigation Company. By the time he was made president in 1903 the railroad was in superior condition and its finances in good health. He was in a position to take advantage of the post-panic recovery period. The success of his program is best illustrated by comparing the net surplus before dividends of more than $9 million in 1898 with the sum of $41 million in 1909.

To efficiently handle the great volume of traffic to San Francisco, Harriman realized that control of the Central Pacific, a connection between Ogden and San Francisco, was necessary. This section was under the control of the Southern Pacific, a railroad created by Collis P. Huntington. When Huntington died in August 1900, the 475,000 shares of stock in his estate became available. Harriman convinced the Union Pacific board of directors to issue $100 million of convertible bonds. With money derived from the sale of the bonds Harriman bought Huntington's stock and enough additional to equal 46 percent of Union's stock. This gave him control of a transportation empire, including shipping lines in both the Atlantic and Pacific. The scope of improvements made to the Southern Pacific may be judged from the total of $241,944,000 spent on improvements and extensions to bring it up to standards that would permit it to serve its customers and thereby grow. In spite of the enormous improvement in services and quality of the railroad, Harriman's control attracted the attention of the Interstate Commerce Commission. The Commission regarded Harriman's control as an evil, even though it was a tremendous asset to the public and promoted the development of the West.

Harriman needed an entry from the west to Chicago and his attention turned to the Chicago, Burlington & Quincy, but James J. Hill won control. As a result Harriman began buying stock in the Northern Pacific which had a one-half interest in the Burlington. A conflict developed between Hill and Harriman that was finally settled by the creation of the Northern Securities Company in 1901, a company organized to hold the stock of the Northern Pacific and Great Northern companies. Three years later the Supreme Court ordered Northern Securities to divest itself of the railroad stock. President Roosevelt had won one of his trust-busting cases.

Though Harriman lost control of the Northern Pacific, he sold his stock in a rising market at a $50 million profit and began to invest in other railroads. He seemed to have an inner desire to be involved in the entire field of railroading. His holdings and activities were so vast that the Interstate Commerce Commission started an investigation in 1906. At the hearings Harriman did not endear himself to the public. He expressed his intent to make further investments in other railroads, and only the federal government could stop additional acquisitions. He became, in the eyes of the public, the archetype of the evil businessman: stern and forbidding, involved with political bribery, corporate monopoly, and unfair practices. Whether his acts had improved transportation for the public welfare, or whether combinations of companies resulted in improved services and lower prices were not the questions. He had incurred the disapproval of the public and brought the wrath of government down on his head. His drive toward a goal, his persistency of purpose, his self-confidence, and his recognized genius as an administrator all stood for nothing when the public considered his accumulated power over interstate transportation as unacceptable.

In contrast to his cold approach to business there was another side to Harriman. It was expressed in his support of the boys' club, his work in helping control the flooding by the Colorado River of Imperial Valley, and his 1899 scientific expedition to Alaska (*Harriman Alaskan Series*, 14 vols., 1902-1914). The rigors of an active life brought death at age sixty-two. He should be remembered more for his constructive contributions to fulfilling the transportation needs of millions of Americans than for his ruthless methods in acquiring control of transportation systems. Though he was king of railroad builders he was also servant.

HWS

References: George Keenan, *E. H. Harriman: A Biography*, 2 vols. (Boston and New York: Houghton Mifflin, 1922); H. J. Eckenrode, *E. H. Harriman: The Little Giant of Wall Street* (New York: Greenberg, 1933).

Lafcadio Hearn

(June 27, 1850 — September 26, 1904)

Few writers of English in the last hundred years have had a greater command of a voluptuous, romantic style than Lafcadio Hearn and few have handled legends, ghostlore, folklore, and colorful atmosphere so deftly. Whether he wrote about New Orleans, Martinique, or Japan he wove together the exotic, the mystical, and the fanciful in intricate patterns. His life spanned three continents and various cultures, and although history and politics were not his metier he was considered for a time a leading interpreter of oriental beliefs and ideas for the Western world. He is still remembered in Japan today, if not under his own name under the name of Koisumi Yakumo which he assumed when he became a citizen of his adopted country. Many of the twelve books he wrote while living in Nippon are still available, and for a long time reminiscences of Hearn flowed across the Pacific as students remembered what he said in classrooms or reconstructed his lectures from notes.

Patrick Lafcadio Hearn (much later simply Lafcadio Hearn) was born in 1850 on the Greek island of Leucadia, the son of Charles Bush Hearn and Rosa Cassimati. The mother was a beautiful Greek girl who was unfortunately illiterate; the father, scion of an Anglo-Irish military family, was surgeon major in the British army. After their marriage according to Greek Orthodox rites the parents lived briefly at Fort Santa Maura in Leucadia, but when the father was posted for duty in Grenada he arranged for his wife and their infant son to go to Dublin where there were Hearn relatives. Lafcadio's boyhood was not a happy one. Finances were not ample. The father was away much of the time and later served in the Crimea and India. The mother was reluctantly accepted by her inlaws and was soon homesick enough to return to her Greek island. The boy was brought up by a greataunt, Mrs. Brenane, who eventually became indigent. Lafcadio had desultory schooling in Dublin and was briefly enrolled in a kind of seminary in France where he learned the French language. For a short time he attended a Catholic college near Durham, St. Cuthbert's, where a rigid curriculum stressed languages (especially Latin and Greek) and religion seemed always dominant. Since Lafcadio was a Protestant and somewhat of a dissident in matters of faith he did not fare well with his priestly instructors. Moreover, he was not particularly athletic and while participating in a juvenile game he suffered a blow which destroyed the sight of his left eye. In 1867 he left St. Cuthbert's and stayed briefly in London at the home of an acquaintance. This was the end of his formal education. Two years later, his father now dead and his family in depleted finances, he made his way to the United States, bound for Cincinnati where he expected to find friends.

At nineteen Hearn was ill equipped to earn a living; he was half blind, was trained for no trade, and had little work experience. In Cincinnati he did menial jobs and slept where he could, but he met a printer who befriended him and taught him typesetting, and eventually he found work with a local publisher and became a space writer for the *Cincinnati Enquirer*. He early demonstrated his reportorial skill and his writing ability, and he was allowed to write caustic and humorous accounts of spiritualism, missions, and temperance activities and to review books. Past reading in such authors as Hugo, Gautier, and Flaubert affected his choice of subjects and his style. He also observed Negro life on the Cincinnati levee and wrote vividly about it although he made no attempt to use dialect in the manner of Joel Chandler Harris. On the other hand, his liaison with a mulatto woman produced criticism. When the *Cincinnati Commercial*, which now employed him, offered to send him to New Orleans on assignment he was quite willing to go.

E. L. Tinker remarked that Hearn did not make an impressive appearance. Standing only five feet three inches, with delicate hands, and abnormal eyes, "he suggested a small, shy, studious, ship-wrecked sailor." But the *New Orleans Item* employed him and encouraged his vignettes of creole life. The posthumous collection called *Fantastics*, 1914, included many of the sketches which he had contributed to various newspapers. In 1882 he published his first book, *One of Cleopatra's Nights*, a translation of six stories by Gautier. This was followed in 1884 by *Stray Leaves from Strange Literature*, a thin book revealing his eclectic reading, and in 1885 by *Gombo Zhêbes*, a gathering of Negro patois proverbs from Louisiana and the West Indies. *Chita*, a brilliant account of a tidal wave which engulfed Last Island, furthered his reputation in 1889. And the next year, the result of a lengthy residence in Martinique, his *Two Years in the French West Indies* combined memorable description with his interest in voodooism, legendry, and folklore. By this time Hearn had been accepted by such magazines as the *Century* and *Harper's*, and when the editors of the latter suggested that he visit Japan on assignment he quickly agreed.

From 1890 to his death he never left Japan. Although he failed to master the language he became Japanese in other ways, but still earned his living by teaching English. Basil Hall Chamberlain, an English scholar in Japanese philology, sponsored him, procured a job for him at the provincial town of Matsue, and eventually arranged for his appointment as a lecturer at Tokyo University, where he served from 1894 to 1903. In 1891 he married the daughter of a somewhat impoverished Samurai family, Setsuke Koizumi; the union produced three sons and one daughter, all of whom helped their father in gathering material for his writing.

Hearn's Japanese books are not well constructed. He did not write formal treatises and he had trouble concocting plots; frequently he would incorporate folk tales or episodes within essays. He was not interested in the beginning of modern industrialism in Japan or anywhere else. One would need to look elsewhere for chronicles of the daimios or feudal battles. He often preferred to deal with Japanese supernaturalism, with vestiges of ancestor worship which he found endemic in Japanese culture, and with minutiae such as birds, flowers, and insects. But few westerners have written with such sensitivity and understanding of Japanese spiritual life and practice, of Japanese folk traditions and beliefs, and of the Japanese character. Hearn knew only nineteenth century Japan but Japanese writers themselves confirm the fact that he knew it well.

Glimpses of Unfamiliar Japan in 1894 was the first of a series of books about his adopted country. *Out of the East*, the next year, *Kokoro* (1896), and *Kwaidan* (1904), all reveal his success in capturing the moods of the people and their attitudes toward the supernatural. *In Ghostly Japan* (1899), and several collections of *Japanese Fairy Tales* further illustrate the inclination of his mind and the kind of material which fascinated him. *Japan: An Attempt at Interpretation*, published in the year of Hearn's death, is perhaps his most serious collection of mature views about the mind and the soul of the people among whom he lived for fourteen years. Hearn was impressionistic rather than analytical, but his poetic use of language and his sympathy for exotic places and people won him a large audience.

JTF

References: Edward L. Tinker, *DAB*, VIII, 1932, pp. 484-87; Elizabeth Bisland, *The Life and Letters of Lafcadio Hearn*, 2 vols. (Boston and New York: Houghton Mifflin, 1906); Elizabeth Stevenson, *Lafcadio Hearn* (New York: Macmillan, 1961); O. W. Frost, *Young Hearn* (Tokyo: Hokuseido, 1958).

Hinton Rowan Helper

(December 27, 1829 — March 8, 1909)

A battle of the books erupted a decade before the firing on Fort Sumter. It began with Harriet Beecher Stowe's *Uncle Tom's Cabin*, followed by Frederick Law Olmsted's several books on Southern plantation life, describing his extensive travels.

The same theme, more explosively presented, was used by Hinton Rowan Helper a few years later in his book *The Impending Crisis of the South: How to Meet It*. Basing his work on statistics from the 1850 census, Helper produced what he believed to be irrefutable proof that Southern backwardness, especially the depressed state of the poor whites, was due to one factor alone—slavery. Using numerous statistical tables, Helper showed that the slave states of the South had long since lost their early preeminence and fallen behind the North in their progress because of a system which depleted the soil and depended on inefficient, unwilling workers who could never compete with free labor.

A distinguished Civil War scholar, Earl Schenck Miers, commented, "Although a single book cannot bear the responsibility for beginning the American Civil War, no list of the decisive causes of that tragic conflict would be complete unless it included the publication of *The Impending Crisis of the South: How to Meet It* by Hinton Rowan Helper."

Helper was born on a small farm near Mocksville, North Carolina, in 1829, the son of an illiterate farmer who died early, leaving eleven children and four slaves, and an impoverished household struggling for economic survival. Hinton's limited education was obtained at a local academy, following which he clerked in a bookstore at Salisbury for three years, spent a short period in New York City, and then set off by clipper ship for the gold fields of California. During three years of hand-to-mouth existence there, he failed to strike it rich, and in 1854 he returned to Salisbury, bitter and frustrated.

As a boy and young man, Helper had often reflected on the evil effects of slavery. His travels in the North and the West had convinced him that the average man in other regions was far better off from an economic standpoint than his Southern counterpart. The situation could be explained in only one way, Helper thought—it was a direct consequence of the institution of slavery. *The Impending Crisis* was the result of his conclusion.

Helper's almost rabid hatred of the Southern slaveholding oligarchy permeated his book. He had no interest whatever in the moral aspects of slavery. The Negro he regarded as subhuman, incapable of being civilized. His sole concern was to eliminate slave competition and the monopoly held by the large planters, thereby benefiting Anglo-Saxon American workers and farmers. While there were more than 5 million white people in the South, less than half a million owned slaves, and there were only forty-six thousand planters in the South.

For two and a half years Helper traveled about the country gathering information and writing. Abundant statistics to support his case were found in the recently published De Bow's census of 1850, which revealed that the Northern rate of material progress far exceeded that of the Cotton Kingdom. James D. B. De Bow, superintendent of the census, ironically, was a native of Charleston, South Carolina, and a confirmed apologist for slavery.

Helper had great difficulty finding a publisher. No Southern firm would touch the book and neither would established Northern publishers, for fear of offending their Southern customers. Finally, a book agent, A. B. Burdick, accepted the manuscript, after being guaranteed against loss, and the book appeared in June 1857.

Helper marshalled the facts, as he saw them, by presenting detailed statistical comparisons between the free and the slave states. Despite advantages in soil, climate, rivers, harbors, minerals, forests, and other natural resources, the South had steadily lost ground. The lack of industrial development in the South had left the region dependent upon the North for almost every commodity.

Helper's primary concern, constantly reiterated throughout *The Impending Crisis*, is the effect of slavery on the poor whites and other nonslaveholders of the South. In fact, the book is dedicated to "The Non-Slaveholding Whites of the South." Though this element in the population outnumbered the slaveowners five to one, it had virtually no political power.

A more subtle, but direct effect of slavery was its blight on Southern literature, to which Helper devotes his last chapter. In comparison to the North, he concludes, "the South has no literature." Using his statistical method applied to publishing, Helper shows a great disproportion between Northern and Southern literacy. Nine-tenths of existing published houses were in the nonslave states. The quality of material published in the South was equally low.

The Impending Crisis met with an extremely hostile reception in the South, as could have been anticipated. Slaveholders considered it a "deadly attack" upon their "peculiar institution," especially resented because the author was a Southerner. Helper was vilified as a "poor traitor to his native sod and native skies," "one of the most miserable renegades and mendacious miscreants the world has ever seen" and his book as "incendiary, insurrectionary, and hostile to the peace and domestic tranquility of the country." Southern legislatures passed laws forbidding its possession or sale. Three men in Arkansas were hanged for owning copies. Mobs in North Carolina drove several ministers out of the state for defending the book, and there was a public book burning in one town. In other slave states men were mobbed and beaten for having Helper's book in their homes. Soon the author became "the best known and worst hated man in America."

Some thirteen thousand copies of *The Impending Crisis* were sold during its first year, after which sales languished. Then, two years later, Horace Greeley set about making the book the campaign document for the Republican party in the coming election. Suddenly the book became a center of dissension. After a bitter debate in the House of Representatives, lasting more than two months, the Republican candidate for speaker lost because he endorsed the book, without reading it. An abbreviated version, *Compendium of the Impending Crisis of the South*, was issued for campaign purposes. The number of copies of the original work and of the *Compendium* sold or given away has been estimated at a million or more.

Unfortunately for Helper, he was unable to reach his intended audience: the 5 or 6 million nonslaveholding whites in the South. In part because of widespread illiteracy and in part because of severe restrictions on its circulation, few read his book or received his message. Only in the North was it freely available. The historian James Ford Rhodes stated the case: "The reasoning, supported as it was by a mass of figures, could not be gainsaid. Had the poor white been able to read and comprehend such an argument, slavery would have been doomed to destruction, for certainly seven out of ten voters in the slave States were nonslaveholding whites. It was this consideration that made Southern congressmen so furious, for to retain their power they must continue to hoodwink their poorer neighbors."

Quoting again an editor and historian: Earl Schenck Miers describes Hinton Rowan Helper as an "unhappy victim of circumstance, compulsive genius, irreconcilable bigot, child of an age caught up in a not-too-well-understood struggle with human aspiration," and concedes that he was not an attractive figure. "And yet for one moment in American history," Miers points out, "because he represented the meeting of mind and emotion at the instant the nation was ready to receive both, he became a person of devastating importance. And all because he wrote this book."

Helper's later career was anticlimactic. President Lincoln appointed him consul in Buenos Aires, where he married an Argentine wife. After returning to the United States, he wrote three books on the Negro question, expressing his extreme dislike of the race. Most of his own fortune was wasted in a project to construct a railroad from Hudson Bay to the Strait of Magellan. One critic called him "a man of keen intellect, with a touch of genius, akin to madness." As one scheme after another failed, Helper became despondent and bitter, finally committing suicide in 1909 in a cheap rooming house on Pennsylvania Avenue in Washington.

RBD

Reference: Hugh T. Lefler, *Hinton Rowan Helper* (Charlottesville, Va.: Historical Publishing Co., 1935).

Patrick Henry

(May 29, 1736 — June 6, 1799)

Perhaps the stormiest character in the Virginia dynasty which dominated American affairs before, during, and after the Revolutionary era was Patrick Henry. He was in the thick of virtually every controversy.

Henry's early enterprises were failures. On two occasions, he tried to operate country stores and quickly became hopelessly in debt. At age twenty-four, with a wife and three or four children and ruin staring him in the face, he found his true calling: the practice of law.

As a lawyer, Henry won immediate success. During his first three years, he appeared in 1,185 suits, won most of them, and his name became known throughout his area of the colony. Most celebrated among his early cases, one that made him the idol of Virginia, was a lawsuit known as the "Parsons' Cause." The case was concerned with the king's repeal of Virginia legislation on clergymen's salaries. Henry denounced the interference of the king in a stirring speech appealing to the jealousies and hatreds of a community already losing its loyalty to the established church and resentful of the crown's encroachments upon the rights of Virginia's freemen.

Henry became a member of the Virginia House of Burgesses in 1765. Soon thereafter he rose to prominence by preparing and presenting a series of resolutions against the Stamp Act and asserting the virtual independence of the colonial legislatures, at least as far as the British Parliament was concerned. A fiery speech by Henry in support of his resolutions concluded: "Caesar had his Brutus— Charles the First, his Cromwell—and George the Third—may profit by their example. If this be treason, make the most of it."

The Virginia Resolutions, of which Henry was author, amounted in essence to a declaration of resistance to the Stamp Act and an assertion of the right of the colonies to legislate for themselves independently of the control of the British Parliament. Approval of the resolutions by the Virginia legislature gave a powerful impetus to the movement which culminated in the American Revolution.

In the decade 1765-1775, Henry was a radical spokesman for all actions opposing the British government. He was a guiding spirit in the Virginia Committee of Correspondence, similar to a committee for the same purpose formed in Massachusetts. Henry was also appointed a member of a delegation of seven sent to represent Virginia at the First Continental Congress, meeting at Philadelphia in September 1774, and also in the Second Continental Congress in 1775.

On May 20, 1775, the Virginia members of the party favoring revolution met in Richmond to decide what actions that colony should take. Three resolutions were offered by Henry, who regarded war as inevitable. One resolution provided for arming the Virginia militia. It was on this occasion that Henry delivered his most famous declaration: "Is life so dear or peace so sweet as to be purchased at the price of chains and slavery? Forbid it, Almighty God! I know not what course others may take, but as for me, give me liberty or give me death!!" Under the spell of Henry's eloquence, the convention authorized the arming and training of companies of infantry, cavalry, and artillery. As a member of the Second Continental Congress, Henry had a part in the legislation under which a continental army was organized and George Washington was made general in chief.

Henry was placed in command of the Virginia forces, but because of differences with the Committee of Public Safety, he resigned the post after a short time. During the 1776 Virginia convention he favored delaying a declaration of independence until the colonies had arranged a union with France and Spain. At the same convention, Henry served on a committee which drafted

Virginia's first constitution and was elected governor of the state. He was reelected governor in 1777 and 1778. One of his important actions as governor was to send George Rogers Clark to the Northwest Territory to capture the British forts.

Thomas Jefferson succeeded Henry as governor of Virginia. Early in his career, Jefferson had been Henry's political lieutenant and close friend. A break came when Henry was critical of Jefferson's conduct of the governor's office. A feud between them never healed.

Until 1786, Henry was a leading advocate of a strong central government. When chosen as a member of the 1787 constitutional convention in Philadelphia, however, he declined to serve and led the opposition to Virginia's ratification of the new constitution. His criticisms were based on the fear that its provisions were dangerous to the liberties of the country and infringed on states' rights. When the constitution was ratified despite his opposition, Henry announced his support for it. Furthermore, his earlier objections to the original document produced fruitful results. They helped to bring about the prompt passage of the first ten amendments—the Bill of Rights.

During his last years, Henry declined a number of opportunities for government service at the national level. In 1794 he refused a seat in the U.S. Senate. George Washington offered an appointment as secretary of state in his cabinet and soon thereafter the chief justiceship of the U.S. Supreme Court. Henry could also have been envoy to France or had another term as governor of Virginia. All were passed over, in part because of ill health and in part because of his dislike of certain trends in government.

RBD

References: Joseph Axelrad, *Patrick Henry* (New York: Random House, 1947); Richard R. Beeman, *Patrick Henry* (New York: McGraw, 1974); Robert D. Meade, *Patrick Henry*, 2 vols. (Philadelphia: Lippincott, 1957-1969); George F. Willison, *Patrick Henry and His World* (Garden City, N.Y.: Doubleday, 1969).

Victor Herbert

(February 1, 1859—May 26, 1924)

Victor Herbert was to the Gay Nineties and the first two decades of the twentieth century what Kern, Romberg, Gershwin, Hammerstein, Rodgers and others were to the post-1920 period of musical comedy. From the date of his first operetta, *Prince Ananios* in 1894, to his death in 1924 he was recognized as America's foremost composer of light opera. He was influenced by his European background in musical education and never developed music with a distinctly American character. Herbert was never able to produce the type of lyrics found in Gilbert and Sullivan or the American style of Rodgers and Hammerstein, because he acted as his own lyricist. Nevertheless, the charming rhythms in his operettas were usually successful with the public and he became one of the best known musicians of his day.

Herbert was talented in many musical disciplines. Though he is remembered for his melodious operettas such as *Naughty Marietta* in 1910, he composed two serious operas, *Natoma* in 1911 and *Madeleine* in 1913. In addition to at least fifty operettas his list of compositions and arrangements exceeds five hundred in number. He was a cello virtuoso, a conductor of symphonies, a bandleader, and a chamber music artist. He excelled in all these pursuits, bringing joy to millions of people. Though his shows have died his melodies still live.

Herbert was born in Dublin, Ireland, the grandson of Samuel Lover. Samuel was an artist of many talents. In addition to painting, poetry and acting he was a songwriter and novelist. If Herbert inherited any talent it was from his grandfather. His father died when he was about two years old and his mother, Fanny, married a German physician, Dr. Carl Schmidt, and moved to Stuttgart, Germany, in 1867. Herbert was pursuing a premedical course when he decided to withdraw at the age of fifteen and specialize in the cello. He had already learned to play the flute, piccolo, and piano. His teacher was the great cellist Bernhard Cossmann. Under Cossmann he developed musically and technically until he became a cello virtuoso in his own right. He performed as a soloist in Germany, France and Italy and became cellist with the Eduard Strauss waltz band in Vienna. During this period he started composing for the cello and orchestra.

When Therese Foster, a twenty-four year old dramatic soprano, came to Stuttgart Herbert fell in love with her. When Frank Damrosch offered her a place in the Metropolitan Opera of New York, she refused to accept unless Herbert also was invited. In this manner the young Irishman from Germany found himself in the fall of 1886 sitting in the orchestra pit to play the cello while he listened to his wife sing the part of the Queen of Sheba. Four days later she would take the part of Aida.

Therese soon left the opera stage for the more mundane chore of a housewife. Herbert involved himself in the world of music by playing cello in the Thomas and Seidl orchestras. In 1893 he was appointed band master of the Twenty-second Regiment Band of the New York National Guard. He stayed with the band for a short time and in the same year was asked to compose his first operetta, *Prince Ananios*, which opened in New York in November 1894. Its success led him to compose *The Wizard of the Nile* the following year and Herbert found his niche in the musical world as a composer of operettas. He served for a six-year term as conductor of the Pittsburgh Symphony Orchestra, conducting his first concert on November 3, 1898. The enthusiastic audience included Andrew Carnegie and Charles M. Schwab.

Herbert's success at Pittsburgh aroused bitter comment from the *Musical Courier*, a trade journal. The *Courier* carried on a scurrilous attack on Herbert and accused him of plagiarism. It became so offensive that Herbert filed suit against the magazine. The trial started on October 22, 1902 and Herbert was vindicated and a monetary fine assessed against the *Courier*. Walter Damrosch had been Herbert's chief witness.

After Herbert left Pittsburgh in 1904 he returned to New York and established the Victor Herbert Orchestra giving concerts on Sunday evening. Unlike Sousa's Band it did not go on tour. Herbert acted as guest conductor of the New York Philharmonic Society and, at the same time, concerned himself with the stage.

By the beginning of the twentieth century he had become the outstanding composer of light opera. With *Babes in Toyland* in 1903 Herbert scored one of his great triumphs. This was followed by a series of successes, *It Happened in Nordland* in 1904, *Miss Dolly Dollar*, *Wonderland* and *Mlle. Modiste*, all in 1905. *Mlle. Modiste* with its melodic music had a run of 202 performances in New York before giving way to another Herbert smash hit, *The Red Mill* in 1906. A long list of successes followed: *The Rose of Algeria* and *Little Nemo* in 1908, *Naughty Marietta* in 1910, *The Mad Dutchess* in 1913 and *Eileen* in 1912.

Most of Herbert's operettas were successful. By 1913 he was one of the best loved and most widely known Americans. His fame did not rest solely on the operetta. He composed numerous pieces for the orchestra, including a *Suite of Serenades* for Paul Whiteman and interpolated songs for the Ziegfeld Follies. He began making phonograph records for the Edison Company in 1909, but switched to the Victor Talking Machine Company in 1911. A few million records were sold.

In February, 1914, Herbert with eight associates formed the American Society of Composers, Authors and Publishers (ASCAP). He served as one of the directors until his death in New York in 1924. His fellow artists have erected two monuments in his honor in New York.

Herbert is loved and revered for his music. He was an accomplished composer, performer, conductor, lyrist and teacher. He taught the American public to enjoy good music. The strains of "Kiss Me Again," "Ah, Sweet Mystery of Life," "Gypsy Love Song," "Italian Street Song," and "Thine Alone" are melodies which have had a long time popularity.

HWS

References: Joseph Kaye, *Victor Herbert* (New York: Watt, 1931); Edward H. Waters, *Victor Herbert: A Life in Music* (New York: Macmillan, 1955).

Oliver Wendell Holmes
(August 29, 1809—October 7, 1894)

The father-son combination of Oliver Wendell Holmes, senior and junior, has been equaled in American history only by John and John Quincy Adams. Unlike the two Adamses, however, Holmes and his son followed strikingly different careers. The father was a poet, an essayist, teacher, and physician, while the son won long-lasting fame as a justice of the U.S. Supreme Court (see *Memorable Americans 1750-1950* (Littleton, Colo.: Libraries Unlimited, 1983), pp. 154-56.

By strange coincidence, the year 1809 witnessed the births of more extraordinary world leaders than perhaps any other single year in history. Each was destined to gain preeminence in his chosen field. Two of them, Charles Darwin and Abraham Lincoln, were born on the same day and nearly in the same hour. Other remarkable individuals who first saw the light of day in this year included William Gladstone, Alfred Tennyson, Edgar Allan Poe, Elizabeth Barrett Browning, Felix Mendelssohn, and Oliver Wendell Holmes.

The older Oliver Wendell Holmes was a prominent figure in the New England literary renaissance, along with such memorable names as Emerson, Longfellow, Hawthorne, Thoreau, Whittier, and Lowell.

Holmes was a native of Cambridge, Massachusetts, and the son of the Reverend Abiel Holmes, pastor of the First Church in Cambridge, a strict Calvinist, whose highly orthodox theology was ultimately rejected by the son.

Holmes's *Autocrat of the Breakfast Table* (1858) established his literary reputation as an essayist, poet, and wit. It is a collection of informal discussions and dialogues with interspersed verse which appeared first in *The Atlantic Monthly*. Incidentally, this journal was named by Holmes. Among the best-known poems in the collection are "The Chambered Nautilus," in which the growth of a mollusk's shell is compared to the growth of a human soul. Another poem in the collection is "The Deacon's Masterpiece; or, the Wonderful 'One-Hoss Shay.' " Later, Holmes wrote *Elsie Venner* (1861) and two other novels in which he stressed the effects of heredity and environment on character development. Other literary efforts included biographies of Emerson and the historian John Lothrop Motley, and a travel book, *One Hundred Days in Europe*.

Critics are in general agreement that Holmes's literary reputation was over-inflated in the nineteenth century, and there has since been a steady drop. Howard Mumford Jones commented, "The decline of many New England reputations has gone hand-in-hand with the decline of New England as a major shaping force in American culture, and in this decline Holmes undoubtedly participates."

In a nonliterary sphere, notably medicine, Holmes's reputation will probably always shine brilliantly. After graduation from Harvard in 1829, he became a student at Lane Law School in Cambridge. But any idea of entering the legal profession was quickly abandoned. Instead, he decided on a medical career. After two years of study in a private medical school in Boston, with the addition of courses in the Harvard Medical School, in the spring of 1833 Holmes sailed for Europe. For more than two years he continued his studies in Paris hospitals under the instruction of great teachers, in what was then regarded as the medical center of the world.

Holmes returned to Boston from Paris in December 1835, received an M.D. degree from Harvard and began the practice of medicine. He never built up an extensive clientele, nor attempted to. His mark on the profession was made as a writer on medical subjects and as a teacher of anatomy, first at Dartmouth College and later at Harvard. Aside from his classroom duties, he took an active part in forming the American Medical Association.

As a teacher of anatomy, Holmes needed human cadavers for dissection. He received permission from the city of Boston to use the bodies of certain persons buried at public expense. The most spectacular corpse obtained at the Harvard School during Holmes's term as dean was that of Dr. George Parkman, who was murdered by professor of chemistry John Webster in 1849, when Parkman came to collect a debt Webster owed him.

Holmes's contributions to medical literature began early. He won a Boylston Prize for a medical essay at Harvard in 1836 and two more in 1837. He wrote two papers on homeopathy, which he attacked with trenchant wit. He also published a valuable paper on the malarial fevers of New England.

Most celebrated and most influential of Holmes's writings in the field of medicine was an article on puerperal or child-bed fever.

The notable researches of Louis Pasteur on fermentation and applied bacteriology, of Joseph Lister on aseptic surgery, and Robert Koch's demonstrations that specific bacteria cause specific diseases all came after the middle of the century. Until then, few medical men suspected that lack of sanitation might be responsible for widespread infection and innumerable deaths. Surgical instruments were cleaned only casually; silk threads used for stitches were carried in the surgeon's lapel or pocket; when his hands were otherwise busy, the surgeon held the operating knife in his teeth; his coat, covered with stains and blood, was seldom if ever washed; and the surgeon did not trouble to wash his hands when going from one type of disease to another or from an autopsy to a living patient. Microorganisms naturally flourished and multiplied.

Particularly perilous was childbirth in the hospitals — so hazardous indeed that it came near ruining the new science of obstetrics. When men doctors began to replace midwives, using forceps and making frequent examinations during labor, there was an immediate and rapid increase in "child-bed fever." The cases ordinarily began with a chill on the fourth day after the birth, fever rose, the abdomen became distended, and death nearly always followed. Autopsies revealed peritonitis and the formation of pus throughout the body.

Child-bed fever had long been known in the medical profession, but its causes remained a dark mystery. An English surgeon, Charles White, devoted the first chapter of his *Treatise on the Management of Pregnant and Lying-in Women* (1773) to "The Causes and Symptoms of the Puerperal or Child-bed Fever." The devastating plague was common throughout Europe. Dr. Logan Clendening cites a report of Paris' largest hospital, which lost more than half of the women in its maternity cases, and in Vienna in 1846 the First Clinic of the University lost from child-bed fever over 11 percent of the 4,010 patients it delivered.

A number of years earlier, alert observers among the doctors had begun to speculate on the reasons for the deadly infections. Alexander Gordon of Aberdeen published in 1795 *A Treatise on the Epidemic Puerperal Fever*, in which he states, "By observation, I plainly perceived the channel by which it was propagated, and I arrived at that certainty in the matter, that I could venture to foretell that women would be affected with the disease upon hearing by what midwife they were to be delivered, or by what nurse they were to be attended, during their lying-in; and almost in every instance, my prediction was verified." Dr. Gordon confessed, "It is a disagreeable declaration for me to mention, that I, myself, was the means of carrying the infection to a great number of women." Many of the leading doctors, medical school teachers, and nurses of the period, on the other hand, ridiculed the notion that they might be guilty of transmitting the deadly illness.

Child-bed fever was no less a curse in America than abroad. In the Boston area, puerperal fever became prevalent in the spring of 1842. At meetings of the Boston Society for Medical Improvement, of which Dr. Oliver Wendell Holmes, professor of anatomy at Harvard University, was a member, various physicians reported and discussed cases coming to their attention. Some fourteen or fifteen cases had occurred in Salem, and the disease was frequently seen on Cape Cod. There had been fifteen fatal cases of puerperal fever in Boston and vicinity within a period of about a month. New York was also suffering from an epidemic.

A shocking new turn of events came later in the year when several men contracted child-bed fever. A Dr. Whitney of Newton and two students, all of whom had lesions on their hands, did a postmortem examination on a woman dying of puerperal fever. The three became desperately ill, showing the usual symptoms of the disease, and a few days later died. A similar case was reported from Lynn, where a Dr. Barker made an examination of a patient who had died of puerperal fever. It was reported that "he had at the time several open sores on each hand, and pricked himself while sewing up the body." The following day he was ill and six days later was dead—doubtless not helped by the excessive bleeding which had been prescribed by the attending physician.

The cases thus reported to the Boston Society for Medical Improvement led to "animated discussion," and a question rose as to the contagion of puerperal fever and the possibility of physicians communicating it from one patient to another.

The suggestion that the disease was probably communicable struck a spark with Dr. Holmes and three weeks later, on February 13, 1843, he had a paper, revolutionary in its impact, ready to read to his fellow members. The title was "The Contagiousness of Puerperal Fever." By vote of the membership, the essay was published the following April in *The New England Quarterly Journal of Medicine and Surgery*. In writing his utterly convincing argument against needless deaths in childbirth, Holmes's superb literary powers and his knowledge of medicine were combined in the most telling fashion.

Essentially, "The Contagiousness of Puerperal Fever" presents a long array of facts in support of the contention that the disease was contagious, was usually transmitted by the doctor or the nurse, and was due to a specific infection. Holmes opens with a declaration that every well-informed member of the medical profession realizes puerperal fever is sometimes passed on from one person to another. Anyone who thinks otherwise has not examined the evidence. "No negative facts, no opposing opinions," he writes, "be they what they may, or whose they may, can form any answer to the series of cases now within the reach of all who choose to explore the records of medical science."

To those who asserted that the case for contagion was not proved because not all exposed patients contracted child-bed fever, Holmes retorted, "Children that walk in calico before open fires are not always burned to death; the instances to the contrary may be worth recording; but by no means if they are to be used as arguments against woolen frocks and high fenders."

Illustrating the misinformation being disseminated by medical authorities, Holmes cites Dewees' standard *Treatise on the Diseases of Females*, which states unequivocally, "In this country, under no circumstances that puerperal fever has appeared hitherto, does it afford the slightest ground for the belief that it is contagious." On the contrary, Dr. Holmes was fully persuaded that "the disease known as Puerperal Fever is so far contagious as to be frequently carried from patient to patient by physicians and nurses."

Holmes concedes that little of a positive nature was known about how infection occurs, why some patients were susceptible and others escaped, how the disease was spread, or why epidemics waxed and waned. The clinching argument, in his view, was "that if it can be shown that great numbers of lives have been and are sacrificed to ignorance or blindness on this point, no other error of which physicians or nurses may be occasionally suspected will be alleged in palliation of this; but that whenever and wherever they can be shown to carry disease and death instead of health and safety, the common instincts of humanity will silence every attempt to explain away their responsibility."

Further reference was made to the 1795 treatise by Dr. Gordon of Aberdeen, who had observed that the only women who contracted puerperal fever were those who had been attended by a physician or nurse who had previously been in contact with patients suffering from the disease. According to Dr. Gordon, "the infection was as readily communicated as that of the small-pox or measles, and operated more speedily than any other infection with which I am acquainted."

Other citations to the professional literature on the subject, British and American, were offered by Dr. Holmes — all arriving at the same conclusion, that a direct relationship existed between the incidence of the disease and the doctor's or nurse's previous contacts with afflicted patients or postmortems. A Dr. Blundell, quoted by Holmes, was so discouraged "that in my own family I had rather that those I esteemed the most should be delivered, unaided, in a stable, by the manger-side, than that they should receive the best help, in the fairest apartment, but exposed to the vapors of this pitiless disease."

Based on numerous firsthand accounts, it is, said Holmes, "the plain conclusion that the physician and the disease entered, hand in hand, into the chamber of the unsuspecting patient."

After reviewing a "long catalogue of melancholy histories" of individual doctors and nurses responsible for multiple cases of puerperal fever, Holmes philosophizes on how much kinder nature unaided "deals with the parturient female, when she is not immersed in the virulent atmosphere of an impure lying-in hospital, or poisoned in her chamber by the unsuspected breath of contagion." Under other circumstances, the percentage of deaths from childbirth was extremely low.

Given the general atmosphere prevailing in the maternity hospitals of Holmes's time, there were long odds against a patient when she entered the doors. "Within the walls of lying-in hospitals," Holmes wrote, "there is often generated a miasm, palpable as the chlorine used to destroy it, tenacious so as in some cases almost to defy extirpation, deadly in some institutions as the plague ... the loss of life occasioned by these institutions completely defeats the objects of their founders."

Near the conclusion of his paper, Holmes rises to a high point of eloquence in pleading his case:

> It is as a lesson rather than as a reproach that I call up the memory of these irreparable errors and wrongs. No tongue can tell the heart-breaking calamities they have caused; they have closed the eyes just opened upon a new world of life and happiness; they have bowed the strength of manhood into the dust; they have cast the helplessness of infancy into the stranger's arms, or bequeathed it with less cruelty the death of its dying parent. There is no tone deep enough for record, and no voice loud enough for warning. The woman about to become a mother, or with her new-born infant upon her bosom, should be the object of trembling care and sympathy wherever she bears her tender burden, or stretches her aching limbs. The very outcast of the street has pity upon her sister in degradation when the seal of promised maternity is impressed upon her. The remorseless vengeance of the law brought down upon its victims by a machinery as sure as destiny,

is arrested in its fall at a word which reveals her transient claims for mercy. The solemn prayer of the liturgy singles out her sorrows from the multiplied trials of life, to plead for her in the hour of peril. God forbid that any member of the profession to which she trusts her life, doubly precious at that eventful period, should regard it negligently, unadvisedly, or selfishly.

Eight conclusions were drawn by Holmes from his research and studies, all based upon practical experience and common sense. Among them were these: A physician engaged in the practice of obstetrics should not participate actively in the postmortem examination of cases of puerperal fever; if a physician is present at such autopsies, he should bathe thoroughly, change all his clothing, and allow twenty-four hours to pass before treating a patient; similar precautions should be taken in dealing with cases of erysipelas; a physician in whose practice a single case of puerperal fever has occurred "is bound to consider the next female he attends in labor" to prevent carrying the infection to her; if a physician has two cases of puerperal fever occurring within a short space of time, "he would do wisely to relinquish his obstetrical practice for at least one month," and try to rid himself of any contamination he may be carrying; if three closely connected cases occur in the practice of one individual, it "is prima facie evidence that he is the vehicle of contagion"; the physician should also take every precaution against nurses or other assistants transmitting the disease.

Holmes's eighth and last recommendation is so cogently expressed that it deserves to be quoted in full: "Whatever indulgence may be granted to those who have heretofore been the ignorant causes of so much misery, the time has come when the existence of a private pestilence in the sphere of a single physician should be looked upon, not as a misfortune, but as a crime; and in the knowledge of such occurrences the duties of the practitioner to his profession should give way to his paramount obligations to society."

Predictably, the conservatives and traditionalists reacted violently and adversely to the Holmes thesis. Such a forthright, forceful statement challenging fixed ideas was certain to arouse the antagonism of those whose teachings had been for years diametrically opposed to the concept of the contagiousness of puerperal fever. At the time, Philadelphia was the American center for the teaching of obstetrics, and two of the biggest guns in that city were wheeled out to demolish the upstart Holmes. Charles D. Meigs, professor of obstetrics at the Jefferson Medical College, and Hugh Lenox Hodge, professor of obstetrics and of the diseases of women and children at the University of Pennsylvania, attacked Holmes vituperatively. Meigs pointed to the many cases of women during an epidemic of child-bed fever who did not contract the disease. "I prefer to attribute them (puerperal fever attacks) to accident, or Providence," he disclaimed, "of which I can form a conception, rather than to a contagion of which I cannot form any clear idea, at least as to this particular malady." In 1852 Hodge published an essay on the noncontagious character of puerperal fever, in which he asserted: "The result of the whole discussion will, I trust, serve, not to exalt your views of the value and dignity of our profession, but to divest your minds of the over-powering dread that you can ever become, especially to woman, under the extremely interesting circumstances of gestation and parturition, the minister of evil; that you can ever convey, in any possible manner, a horrible virus, so destructive in its effects, and so mysterious in its operations as that attributed to puerperal fever."

Undaunted, Holmes returned to the fray. In 1855 he reprinted his original essay unchanged in pamphlet form, in order to give it wider circulation, but retitled *Puerperal Fever as a Private Pestilence*, preceding it with a lengthy introduction, bringing his facts up to date. The introduction is prefaced with a quotation from the 1852 edition of Copland's *Medical Dictionary*, designed to put Drs. Hodge, Meigs, and their kind to shame:

> Boards of health, if such exist, or, without them, the medical institutions of a country, should have the power of coercing, or of inflicting some kind of punishment on those who recklessly go from cases of puerperal fevers to parturient or puerperal females, without using due precaution; and who, having been shown the risk, criminally encounter it, and convey pestilence and death to the persons they are employed to aid in the most interesting and suffering period of female existence.

Point by point, Holmes replied to his critics, exposing the fallacies of their arguments. Referring to the strong and personal language used by Meigs, he says: "I take no offense and attempt no retort; no man makes a quarrel with me over the counterpane that covers a mother with her new-born infant at her breast." Holmes was especially concerned that medical students might be led astray by the statements of the two distinguished professors, which seemed to him to condone, if not actually encourage, professional homicide. One famous paragraph of the introduction, directed at students, suggests, "They naturally have faith in their instructors, turning to them for truth, and taking what they may choose to give them; babes in knowledge, not yet able to tell the breast from the bottle, pumping away for the truth at all that offers, were it nothing better than a professor's shriveled forefinger."

Holmes concludes with a strong appeal to the reasonable men: "The teachings of the two professors in the great schools of Philadelphia are sure to be listened to, not only by their immediate pupils, but by the profession at large. I am too much in earnest for either humility or vanity, but I do entreat those who hold the keys of life and death to listen to me also for this once. I ask no personal favor; but I beg to be heard in behalf of the women whose lives are at stake, until some stronger voice shall plead for them."

Dr. Holmes was being heard. The circulation of the *New England Quarterly Journal of Medicine and Surgery* was necessarily limited, but twelve years later, by the time the second edition of Holmes's work appeared, he could report, "I have abundant evidence that it has made many practitioners more cautious in their relations with puerperal females." His arguments had been prepared with such care that before long they became accepted facts among enlightened members of the medical profession. His essay undoubtedly saved many a mother from untimely death, or as a commentator for the Grolier Club's catalog of *One Hundred Influential American Books* phrased it, "No American publication in the nineteenth century saved more lives than this unassuming pamphlet, founded solely on the evidence of observed cases."

In his *The Professor at the Breakfast Table*, published some years later, Holmes indulged in reminiscences: "When, by the permission of Providence, I held up to the professional public the damnable facts connected with the conveyance of poison from one young mother's chamber to another's, — for doing which humble office I desire to be thankful that I have lived, though nothing else good should ever come of my life, — I had to bear the sneers of those whose position I had assailed, and, as I believe, have at last demolished, so that nothing but the ghosts of dead women stir among the ruins."

"At the time it was delivered," states the medical historian Dr. Henry R. Viets, "this paper was the most important contribution made in America to the advancement of medicine." The assertion may be questioned, if originality is the criterion, for William Beaumont's researches on the physiology of digestion were far more pioneering in character. As a matter of fact, Holmes laid no claim to great originality. Toward the end of a long life, he wrote that "others had cried out with all their might against the terrible evil, before I did, and I gave them full credit for it. But I think I shrieked my warning louder and longer than any of them, and I am pleased to remember that I took my ground on the existing evidence before the little army of microbes was marched up to support my position."

The story would not be complete without reference to a young Hungarian physician, Ignaz Philipp Semmelweis, a graduate of the University of Vienna's medical department. When Semmelweis became an assistant in the obstetrical clinic at Vienna, in 1848, he required students to wash their hands in chlorine water before entering the clinic. Later a solution of chloride of lime was used. Immediately there occurred a dramatic decrease in the previously high mortality rate from puerperal fever until it had almost vanished. Thereafter, Semmelweis continuously preached the doctrine that the obstetrician must come to his patients aseptically clean. Like Holmes, he was attacked viciously by the diehards, driven from one hospital to another, and eventually died insane. To Semmelweis, nevertheless, belongs the major credit for our first knowledge of the means to eliminate the horrible pestilence of puerperal fever.

RBD

References: Mark De Wolfe Howe, *Holmes of the Breakfast Table* (New York: Oxford, 1939); Robert S. Feuerlicht, *Oliver Wendell Holmes* (New York: American R.D.M., 1965); John T. Morse, *Life and Letters of Oliver Wendell Holmes*, 2 vols. (Boston: Houghton, 1896); Miriam R. Oliver, *Oliver Wendell Holmes* (New York: Twayne, 1962).

Winslow Homer

(February 24, 1836 — September 29, 1910)

One of America's most outstanding painters, Winslow Homer had two unusual distinctions: since he was not trained abroad he was quite indifferent to Europe (of which he knew little), and he became one of the finest painters of the sea. He began his professional career as an illustrator, contributed sketches to magazines, eventually began to produce oil paintings, and finally created a number of watercolors which museums are proud to possess. Long a resident of the Maine coast, he made frequent visits to Bermuda, Florida, and the Bahamas; consequently his seascapes represent both northern and tropical waters. In all cases they reveal his love of the sea and his ability to record its color, its turbulence, its power, and its terror.

Homer was born in Boston in 1836. He was apprenticed to Bufford, a Boston lithographer, in 1855 and two years later set up his own studio. In 1858 he moved to New York. He early began to contribute drawings to *Harper's Weekly*, which commissioned him to do illustrations at Lincoln's inaugural in 1861. At the beginning of the Civil War he was attached to General George McClellan's army and went to the front to sketch soldiers and battle scenes. After his return to New York he produced pictures of war subjects which were exhibited at the National Academy of Design in 1863. The well-known *Prisoners at the Front* illustrates his command of detail and his ability to do genre scenes. His experiences in Virginia also introduced him to Negro life and he frequently treated such subjects in his art. He became widely recognized for his contributions to various magazines throughout the 1870s.

Homer spent the year 1881-1882 in England, much of the time at Tynemouth on the east coast. A year earlier he had lived on Ten Pound Island in Gloucester Harbor where he watched American youngsters playing on the beaches. His English sojourn not only introduced him to the wives of English fishermen staring at the gray skies and the grayer ocean but also impressed him with the awesomeness and fascination of the sea. He returned to the United States ready to change the course of his life. He would give up his work as an illustrator, successful as he had been; he would also devote his remaining years to painting and he would paint primarily the ocean, in all its moods and in various places. For more than a quarter of a century Homer made his home at Prout's Neck, Scarboro, Maine. He ventured south in the winter to study currents and colors in the Caribbean or the Gulf Stream just as he took occasional jaunts toward Canada to observe deer hunters or lumberjacks. But Maine remained his headquarters. To ensure his ability to work without undue interference from the elements he had constructed a portable hut with a plate glass window. The hut was placed on runners so that it could easily be moved from place to place. With this contrivance he could observe surf, motion, wind, and especially lights on the rocks from many angles.

Homer liked to portray rough men in action, coastguardsmen, fishermen, hunters, woodsmen, soldiers, Negro laborers, or sometimes men confronting nature. The familiar *Eight Bells* (now in the Addison Gallery) depicts two oilskin-clad figures, their hats pulled down over their ears, as they study the dying tempest. They look into the storm and their bearded faces are almost invisible. Homer's characters are shown doing their jobs, sometimes heroically but always calmly; there is neither exaggeration nor sensationalism. Color dominates the famous *Gulf Stream* (owned by the Metropolitan). The blue sea contrasts sharply with the black torso of the Negro as he lies dazed on the deck of his helpless boat; pale sharks are half-visible in the foreground, and a sinister water spout beyond. At the Columbian Exposition of 1893 in Chicago Homer was represented by fourteen paintings, including *Eight Bells* and *The Fog Warning*. The artist was awarded a medal and a diploma for his contribution.

Not all of Homer's work, of course, dealt with the ocean. He was certainly aware of rural New England and at home in the Adirondacks. The charming but lively *Snap the Whip* shows youngsters in front of a schoolhouse playing a juvenile game, the barefooted lads wearing caps and pants held up by suspenders. *Waiting for a Bite* depicts three boys astride a fallen log on the edge of a pond; they hold fishing rods from which lines descend into the lily pads. The viewer is immediately conscious of the water, grass, and trees. *The Bridle Path* shows a young woman riding a white horse in the mountains, a kind of paradigm of slow motion. *Campfire* (owned by the Chicago Art Institute) pictures a gray-bearded hunter resting on a rock, his rifle across his knees, the blueish smoke of the small fire gradually rising. *The Fallen Deer* (in the Boston Museum of Fine Arts) shows a young animal lying on the edge of the water, its head already partly submerged, its leg probably broken.

One of Homer's spectacular wilderness scenes, *The Fox Hunt*, is also his largest canvas, measuring thirty-eight by sixty-eight inches. The season is winter and a red-brown fox wallows in the heavy snow. A flock of crows have converged on the animal and the two foremost birds seem ready to make a plunge. No human being is in sight; this is a drama of bird versus beast. As Lloyd Goodrich observed, the painting is a "superb piece of selective naturalism."

But Homer's greatest work is his marine painting, especially his watercolors. Years of experience in different scenes and seasons, a fascination with the moods of the ocean, an appreciation of the sea's beauty and fury (sometimes the same thing), and always a remarkable ability to use color combined to make his marine scenes unsurpassed.

Homer never married. He died in 1910 and his ashes were interred in Mount Auburn Cemetery, Cambridge. In 1958-1959 the National Gallery of Art held an exhibition of Homer's work which was later presented at the Metropolitan Museum.

JTF

References: William Howe Downes, *DAB*, IX, 1932, pp. 186-91; William Howe Downes, *The Life and Works of Winslow Homer* (Boston and New York: Houghton Mifflin, 1911); Lloyd Goodrich, *Winslow Homer* (New York: Whitney Museum, 1944); *Winslow Homer: A Retrospective Exhibition* (Washington: National Gallery of Art, 1958).

Herbert Clark Hoover

(August 10, 1874 — October 20, 1964)

Herbert Hoover is another prototype of the American rags to riches saga. His father, a village blacksmith, died when Herbert was age six and his mother four years later. Thereafter, the orphaned lad worked on a farm and as an office boy for an Oregon land company, managed by an uncle. Early on, he determined to become a mining engineer. His sketchy education in a Quaker academy had not prepared him for college, but after home study and two attempts he was admitted to Leland Stanford University and graduated in 1895 with a degree in engineering. The expenses of his college years were paid by starting delivery routes for San Francisco newspapers, operating a laundry service, managing athletic events, and, during the summers, working for the U.S. Geological Survey.

Hoover gained practical experience immediately after graduation by working as a day laborer in California mines. About two years later, he went to London to join a mining firm which sent him to Australia as a mine "scout." There he found one of Australia's richest gold mines and developed new technologies for the economical mining of gold.

Another foreign assignment came in 1899, when Hoover was sent to China as chief engineer for the Chinese Engineering and Mining Company. Lou Henry, a Stanford classmate, whom he married just before leaving the United States, accompanied him. In China, the Hoovers found themselves in the midst of the Boxer Rebellion of 1900. After the rebellion ended, Hoover returned to London, where he was rewarded with a partnership in his firm.

During the following fourteen years, Hoover's mining interests became worldwide. His geological expertise—knowledge of drifts and leads, rock formations, and metallurgy—was instrumental in finding silver, lead, and zinc in Burma, zinc in Australia, and copper and petroleum in Russia. By age forty, Hoover had become a consulting engineer of international renown and had amassed a large personal fortune.

An unusual project, undertaken by Hoover and his wife, in 1912, was a translation into English of a Latin work Agricola's *De Re Metallica*, originally published in 1556. George Sarton, historian of science, commented that "Mr. Hoover is no doubt the only chief of state who ever translated one of the great scientific classics."

The coming of World War I channeled Hoover's time and energies into new fields. He was asked to supervise the exodus of some two hundred thousand Americans caught in Europe at the war's outset. The success of that undertaking made him a logical choice to head the Commission for Relief in Belgium; from 1915 to 1919 he directed the feeding of 10 million people in Belgium and northern France. The enterprise was not without controversy, for it was charged that much of the food was diverted to feed the Germans.

After the American declaration of war in 1917, Hoover returned to Washington to become U.S. Food Administrator and a member of President Wilson's War Council. Under Hoover's guidance, the United States had accumulated a great food surplus, in anticipation of postwar needs. Following the Armistice, Hoover was in charge of distributing 20 million tons of food to about 300 million people, running a fleet of overseas ships, directing the railways and coal mines of central Europe, reopening ports, canals, and other communications closed by war. During the Russian famine in 1921-1923, Hoover, then secretary of commerce, helped to save millions of lives by shipments of food to the Soviet Union. Ironically, it has been suggested that despite his intense dislike of Communism, this action may have saved the Bolshevik Revolution. In any case, Hoover received effusive thanks from the Russian government, the recognition of which he strongly opposed.

On the basis of the international reputation Hoover achieved, he appeared to be the logical candidate for the Republican nomination for president in 1920, but instead Warren G. Harding was chosen, and Hoover reluctantly accepted the post of secretary of commerce. Previously, this cabinet position had been regarded as of minor importance, but under Hoover the Bureau of Mines and Patents, the

All-American High Commission, and the Radio Division were taken over, and he worked closely with chambers of commerce, boards of trade, and trade associations, especially in standardization of manufactured articles.

During his early career, Hoover exhibited liberal tendencies. In his textbook, *Principles of Mining* (1909), he endorsed collective bargaining, the eight-hour day, and the importance of safety in mines. As vice chairman of the Second Industrial Conference in 1919, he urged a federal employment service, a home loan bank, and a fairer distribution of profits between capital and labor. He also endorsed a minimum wage law, equal pay for men and women, prevention of child labor, a forty-eight-hour week, better housing, and insurance plans. He also backed the Norris-La Guardia Anti-Injunction Act of March 1932. He was a vigorous supporter of the League of Nations, and later supported ratification of the United Nations Charter.

The year 1928 finally brought to Hoover the Republican nomination for president and he overwhelmingly defeated the Democratic candidate, Alfred E. Smith. Among the bitter issues were Smith's Roman Catholicism and opposition to prohibition, and Hoover's accusation of socialistic tendencies against his opponent.

It was the worst of times, however, for a White House occupant. Within a few months of Hoover's inauguration, the stock market crashed and the Great Depression struck. Even prior to that catastrophe, the "Hoover honeymoon" with a Congress overwhelmingly Republican in both branches had ended. Criticisms were focused on the Federal Farm Board which had revised agricultural tariffs upward, the Hawley-Smoot tariff bill, opposed by nearly every leading economist in the country, and a growing army of unemployed. The worst problem was the American banking system; by 1932, thousands of banks had failed.

National sentiment turned against Hoover in the spring of 1932 when unemployed veterans and their families flocked to Washington to lobby for early payment of a bonus due in 1935. They lived in abandoned buildings and shantytowns, like those springing up in many cities. In a clash with federal troops under General Douglas MacArthur, the veterans were dispersed with tanks and tear gas. Hoover had seen the march as an attempt at mob rule, but the harsh response badly damaged his reputation as a great humanitarian.

As the national emergency went on and the economic situation of much of the population became desperate, Hoover's attitude began to change. A program of public works was initiated for the construction of highways, river and harbor improvements, and Hoover Dam at Boulder Canyon. Federal loans were made to the states to be used for local relief programs; the Reconstruction Finance Corporation was established to loan money to business, especially banks, to prevent their failure; and the President's Organization on Unemployment Relief was created. Meanwhile, Hoover tried strenuously to assure the country that "prosperity was just around the corner," and the worst was over. He still had profound faith in private enterprise. In one of his most widely quoted speeches, he warned about the results of free trade; "the grass will grow in the streets of a hundred cities, a thousand towns, the weeds will overrun the fields of millions of farms, churches and schoolhouses will decay."

Hoover was renominated for a second term by the Republicans in the 1932 election. As the campaign progressed, the economy continued to deteriorate. Hoover lost to Franklin D. Roosevelt by 22,810,000 to 15,759,000 popular votes and 472 to 59 electoral votes. *Time* magazine remarked that "Only tough old John Quincy Adams had gone out of the Presidency so thoroughly unpopular."

In his postpresidential years, Hoover generally favored American isolationism, opposed American intervention in World War II until Pearl Harbor, and was against U.S. participation in Korea and Vietnam. At the request of President Truman, he served as advisor in post-World War II relief, to coordinate world food supplies for thirty-eight countries. Another major activity was to serve, first under Truman and later under President Dwight D. Eisenhower, as head of the Hoover Commission to reorganize and streamline the federal government.

Hoover's greatest monuments are probably the Hoover Institution and Library on War, Revolution, and Peace at Stanford University, and the Herbert Hoover Library, housing presidential papers and mementos, at West Branch, Iowa. Hoover died in New York City in 1964, at the age of ninety.

RBD

References: Eugene Lyons, *Herbert Hoover, a Biography* (Garden City, N.Y.: Doubleday, 1964); C. O. Peare, *The Herbert Hoover Story* (New York: Crowell, 1965); Alfred Sternberg, *Herbert Hoover* (New York: Putnam, 1967).

Johns Hopkins

(May 19, 1795—December 24, 1873)

In 1800 a group of Quakers lived in Anne Arundel County, Maryland. Among them was Samuel Hopkins, whose ancestors had settled there as early as 1657. Samuel was a devout Quaker and was active in the West River Meetings of Friends. He operated a large plantation, "Whitehall," where he raised five hundred acres of tobacco with slave labor. His large family was accustomed to the good life on the plantation. Horseback riding and fox-hunting were the chief pastimes of the day. Samuel's second child, Johns, was born into this environment and had the advantage of good schooling and a happy life until he was twelve years old.

In the first few years of the nineteenth century the Quakers became disturbed over the moral issue of slavery. The common subject at the meeting house was the question of freeing the slaves. It was a perplexing question that had become a matter of principle with the Quakers. To free the slaves meant financial ruin, hardship and decay of Whitehall. It meant drastic changes in family life, including an interruption in education for the children. After long and conscientious consideration the momentous step was finally taken in 1807; the ablebodied slaves were freed and the Samuel Hopkins family would never again be the same.

Johns' formal education ceased, and the twelve-year-old boy became a plantation worker. Five years later he was taken by his uncle, Gerard Hopkins, as an aide in the Baltimore wholesale grocery business. Johns Hopkins was being educated in the school of necessity and his Quaker background of thrift, industry and self-denial came to the forefront. Baltimore was an important shipping center. Many ships from the Caribbean and South America called at the city docks. It was a great tobacco shipping port and was an ideal location for wholesale traders. At age nineteen Johns was left in charge of the business while his uncle was in Ohio. At this time the British fleet, after burning the capitol in Washington, made its way up the Chesapeake. Three days prior to the bombardment of Fort McHenry, when Francis Scott Key was inspired to write the "Star-Spangled Banner," Gerard Hopkins returned in time to relieve Johns of his responsibilities.

Johns Hopkins and his uncle Gerard developed differences of opinion as to the conduct of their business. At age twenty-four Johns set up his own business with the aid of a ten thousand dollar loan from his uncle. The business prospered and after about one year he established, with three brothers, a new firm known as Hopkins Brothers. Again, his relatives invested in the business, adding twenty thousand dollars to the original investment. Hopkins was not adverse to accepting whiskey in exchange for groceries, reselling it under the trade name "Hopkins Best." He distributed goods by means of the Conestoga Wagon as far westward as Ohio, but this mode of transportation was slow. When the Baltimore & Ohio Railroad was built, Hopkins recognized at once its potential for transporting freight and passengers at low cost. He became a director of the railroad in 1847 and chairman of the finance committee in 1855. This railroad assured Baltimore a share of the western market, and as a wholesale merchant it was a great asset to Hopkins. He acquired more than fifteen thousand shares of stock and protected the financial structure of the road during times of economic stress by lending it as much as nine hundred thousand dollars.

His interest in Baltimore business led him into investments in real estate and banking. In addition to being president of the Merchants' Bank he was director of the First National, The Mechanics, Central, The National Union, The Citizens and Farmers, and the Farmers' and Planters'. He was very receptive to any loan which was for the benefit of the city of Baltimore and helped underwrite a five hundred thousand dollar loan to the city during the Civil War. It was during his period of financial growth that he witnessed the terrible effects of smallpox, cholera and yellow fever upon the populace. He noted the total ignorance of the medical profession concerning the cause of cholera and yellow fever, and observed that the treatment, blood-letting, may have killed many patients. He resolved to create a modern hospital with research facilities as well as a university for both general and advanced studies.

Planning for the future he established two corporations in 1867, one for the Johns Hopkins University and a second for the Johns Hopkins Hospital. He provided for their creation in his will by leaving about $7 million to be divided equally among them. In addition he included gifts to the Baltimore Manual Labor School for Indigent Boys, the Maryland Institute for the Promotion of the Mechanic Arts, the Home of the Friendless, and the Baltimore Orphan Society. The University was inaugurated February 22, 1876, with an address by the renowned English scientist, Thomas Henry Huxley. Hopkins was an abolitionist and was careful to provide for services to black people. In 1927-1928 the hospital admitted 582 white patients and 529 black patients. Both the university and hospital have become famous institutions in serving educational and medical needs.

Hopkins loved the Maryland countryside around Baltimore and built a country place on Hartford Road which he called "Clifton." He gave close attention to improving Clifton and built an Italian villa surrounded by beautiful gardens. His Scottish gardener kept the grounds planted with trees and flowering shrubs. He intended that the Clifton estate be used as the site of the Johns Hopkins University and that a great avenue would lead from it to the hospital. In his will he stipulated that the boards of trustees of the two new institutions be in part overlapping. He also directed that the trustees could use only the income from the trust to construct buildings. This restriction prevented the trustees from building the university at a point as far away as Clifton and postponed the opening of the Johns Hopkins Hospital until 1889. To get the university under way classrooms were established in the downtown section of the city and at an early time Clifton was used as an athletic field. In 1901 the city purchased Clifton as a city park for $1 million, and the University relocated at "Homewood."

Hopkins never married because during the seven-year period he lived with uncle Gerard's family he fell in love with his cousin Elizabeth. What started out as a youthful attachment between two young cousins living in the same house grew into devotion and they planned to be married. However, the prejudice against the marriage of first cousins was especially strong among the Quakers. Elizabeth's father adamantly refused to permit the marriage. Elizabeth finally agreed with her parents but begged Johns to remain friendly toward her. Their unusual friendship lasted; for all their lives neither Johns Hopkins nor Elizabeth Hopkins ever married. This may be one of the reasons he turned his full attention to business and philanthropy.

HWS

References: Broadus Mitchell, *DAB*, IX, 1932, pp. 213-14; Helen Hopkins Thom, *Johns Hopkins: A Silhouette* (Baltimore: The Johns Hopkins Press; London: Humphrey Milford, Oxford University Press, 1929).

Samuel Houston

(March 2, 1793 — July 26, 1863)

The most colorful and dynamic figure in early Texas history was Sam Houston, whose career as a soldier and statesman included terms as governor of Tennessee, commanding general of the Texas army, first president of the Republic of Texas, first U.S. Senator from Texas, and governor of Texas.

Houston was a native Virginian, the son of Major Sam Houston, a veteran of the Revolution. After the father's death, the mother moved to Tennessee with her six sons and three daughters. Sam's adventurous spirit led him to live with the Cherokee Indians for three years. There he learned the Indian language and customs, and came to deeply sympathize with the Indian character. Later, in 1817, President Andrew Jackson appointed him as sub-agent among the Cherokees.

Houston had a commanding presence. He was a large man physically, possessing all the qualities to appeal to a frontier community, an unexcelled stump speaker, and with boundless energy. In 1818, he spent several months in the study and practice of law. After his first year of practice, his personal popularity brought about his election as district attorney for the Nashville district. The next step up the political ladder was election to Congress in 1823 and reelection in 1825. At the end of his second term, Houston was elected governor of Tennessee, at the age of thirty-four. While still in the governor's office, he married the daughter of a prominent Tennessee family, but for reasons never revealed, they separated within three months and the marriage was annulled.

The experience appears to have been traumatic for Houston, who proceeded to resign as governor and to leave for the Indian country. He used his influence to prevent a war between the Cherokees and the Pawnees. Late in 1829 he set up a trading post near Fort Gibson in Oklahoma territory. He was formally adopted by the Cherokees and took an Indian wife. Houston made frequent trips to Washington on behalf of Indian rights. On one such occasion, he administered a beating to an Ohio representative, William R. Stanbery, who had accused him of fraudulent attempts to obtain a contract for Indian rations.

Houston's first involvement with Texas affairs occurred in 1832 when he traveled there to arrange a peace treaty between the Cherokees, among whom he was living, and the dangerous Comanches, who had headquarters near San Antonio. He attended the convention in 1833 that sent Stephen Austin to Mexico to petition for statehood for Texas. The 1833 census listed Houston at Nacogdoches, Texas, though he did not definitely establish himself there until 1835.

As an armed conflict with Mexico approached, there was general confidence in Houston's leadership and he was chosen as commander of the Texas army, first of the local volunteers and then of the provisional government's regular army. His first move, in 1836, was to meet with the Indians in north Texas to arrange a treaty which would keep them quiet during the forthcoming struggle. The formal declaration of independence followed shortly and then came news of the fall of the Alamo. Meantime, Houston was actively recruiting and training his men. He avoided confronting Santa Anna, the Mexican commander, until April 20, 1836, when the outnumbered force under Houston surprised the overconfident Mexicans in their camp and completely defeated them. During the battle, which lasted about fifteen minutes, the whole Mexican force, numbering about thirteen hundred, was killed or captured. Santa Anna was among the prisoners and signed an order for the retreat of his other forces. Houston was shot through the ankle.

At the end of hostilities, Houston went to New Orleans to get surgical attention. Soon after his return, in September 1836, he was elected first president of the Republic of Texas. Despite bitter opposition, he sent Santa Anna safely back to Mexico. A few months later, the new republic was recognized by the United States. Houston served a second term as president from 1841 to 1845. In the interim between his two terms, he represented one of the Texas districts in the U.S. House of Representatives.

After prolonged negotiations, in 1845 Texas was formally annexed to the United States. Houston was elected one of its first U.S. Senators, was reelected in 1853, and remained in the Senate until 1859. As a senator, he was always an ardent champion of Indian rights, and a strong supporter of the Union. He was opposed to the Kansas-Nebraska Act (which would have permitted slavery in the new territories and have repealed the Missouri Compromise).

Houston became increasingly alienated from his Southern colleagues and other adherents over the issues of slavery and the preservation of the Union.

Thomas Hart Benton was the only Southerner who voted with him on the organization of Oregon under the antislavery provisions of the Northwest Ordinance of 1787. Two years before the end of Houston's term in the Senate, the Texas legislature, to show its displeasure, elected his successor. Nevertheless, he was still a potent force in Texas politics. As he was leaving the Senate, in 1859, he was elected governor of Texas on a platform which called for a new Indian policy to make the frontiers safe and for the preservation of the Union. In his final speech before the Senate, he declared: "I make no distinction between southern rights and northern rights. Our rights are common to the whole union. I would not see wrong inflicted on the North, or on the South, but I am for the Union, without any ifs in the case, and my motto is, it shall be preserved."

A series of events, however, turned the Texans increasingly toward secession. Houston's speeches, pointing out the certainty of war and the danger of defeat, were ignored. The legislature ordered a popular vote on the question of secession. When the people by a large margin accepted secession, Houston refused to take an oath of allegiance to the new Confederate government. Instead, he regarded Texas as again an independent republic. He was deposed as governor on March 18, 1861. Houston remained adamantly opposed to secession to the end and regarded it as a serious mistake. His death came in the middle of the Civil War.

One commentator characterized Houston "as the one commanding figure in the history of the Republic of Texas." His real greatness was not recognized until the heat and passion of the Civil War era had died down.

RBD

References: L. B. Friend, *Sam Houston* (Austin: University of Texas Press, 1954); Marquis R. James, *The Raven: A Biography of Sam Houston* (Dunwoody, Ga.: Berg, 1968); M. K. Wisehart, *Sam Houston, American Giant* (Washington, D.C.: Luce, 1962).

William Dean Howells
(March 1, 1837 — May 10, 1920)

For the last twenty-five years of his life William Dean Howells was unquestionably the best known and most influential literary man in the United States. For ten years he had edited the most prestigious American literary magazine, the *Atlantic Monthly*, and after moving to New York City he had contributed the "Editor's Study" to *Harper's* for another six years. Beginning as a poet and journalist in a number of small Ohio towns, he became enormously prolific in various literary forms. His work included some thirty-five novels, five volumes of tales, two utopian fictions, thirty-one short plays, eleven books of travel, and three autobiographies, not to mention numerous reviews and critical essays. Howells did much to introduce to American readers such European novelists as Tolstoy, Turgenev, and Zola but also encouraged younger American writers like Frank Norris, Stephen Crane, and Hamlin Garland. Recognition from the critic often deemed the dean of American literati was tantamount to the attainment of a secure position. And yet the man who was awarded honorary degrees by several universities and who refused literary professorships never went to high school or college. Howells was basically self-taught.

Howells was born in Martin's Ferry, Ohio, the son of a small town newspaperman William Cooper Howells. The Howells family was originally Welsh and affiliated with the Quakers. William Cooper Howells had been brought to this country as an infant in 1808 and in early maturity had tried business and became converted to Swedenborgianism. During his son's childhood the family lived briefly in a succession of Ohio towns, Hamilton, Dayton, Ashtabula, plus a communal settlement near Xenia, where the father had an interest in the local newspapers. Money was never plentiful but the family managed to survive on an income of less than twelve hundred dollars a year. Before William Dean Howells was ten years old he was put to work setting type. Two years later when Dayton was the family home his schooling was permanently over. Howells could say with Mark Twain, his close friend in later years and his neighbor in Hartford, that the printing office was his school.

But he was not deprived of the usual childish activities, and his charming autobiographical account of life in Hamilton, A Boy's Town, published in 1890, is full of details about swimming, hunting, fishing, and playing games during the years when he did attend elementary school. Moreover, there were books in the home and other books could be borrowed. The father would read poetry aloud and the boy early became familiar with Goldsmith, Scott, Irving, even Cervantes and Homer in Pope's translation. It was not long before Howells tried to teach himself other languages, Spanish and German for example, and in early maturity one of his favorite authors was the German poet Heine. When Howells in 1861 sailed to Italy to begin his four years of service as the American consul in Venice, he found his language ability not only a convenience but a necessity.

One advantage of his early experience in a newspaper office was his chance to write as well as to set type. He early began to contribute news items, book notices, and eventually poems and editorials to various periodicals, for example, the Ashtabula Sentinel, the Columbus Ohio State Journal, the National Era. At this time his ambition was to become a poet. The year 1860 was a significant year for the young writer. James Russell Lowell accepted and printed five poems submitted to the Atlantic Monthly by Howells, and he and a young friend, John James Piatt, jointly published a small volume, Poems of Two Friends. In the same year Howells was also the author of a short biography of Abraham Lincoln, then involved in his first campaign for the presidency.

Up to this time Howells had traveled little but with some funds in hand he resolved to visit New England and to meet some of the authors personally whom he knew only through their work. Long afterward he gave a full account of his experience in Literary Friends and Acquaintance, 1900. He visited Quebec and Montreal first, then journeyed to Boston and Concord. Lowell, with whom he had corresponded, proved to be a delightful host, Oliver Wendell Holmes was witty and friendly, Emerson was polite and reserved, and Hawthorne was enigmatic and taciturn, but not unapproachable. To the young journalist from Ohio these men were literary giants and he was flattered to be admitted to their company. Six years after this trip and following his sojourn in Venice, Howells was named assistant editor under James T. Fields of the Atlantic Monthly and began his residence in Boston.

Since the Civil War was fought during Howells's stay in Italy, his consular duties were not especially arduous and he took advantage of his opportunities to study a foreign people. He was not deeply interested in history or politics, but Italian art and architecture as well as the customs of the people fascinated him. Eventually he published not only such books as *Venetian Life* in 1866 and *Italian Journeys* the year following but also several international novels involving American characters abroad, the best of which is *Indian Summer*, 1886.

During his Boston years Howells turned his attention more and more to fiction. His early novels were generally romantic, dealt with New England scenes, and often utilized his own experiences in his adopted region. Examples are *Their Wedding Journey* (1872), *The Undiscovered Country* (1880), and *Dr. Breen's Practice*. The last of these depicts a woman doctor but the chief interest is whom she will marry. The novels share a direct and fluent style, substantial narrative interest, and recognizable characterization. In the next twenty years Howells developed a more realistic approach to his subject matter and his major novels show a much closer affinity to the growing naturalism of succeeding generations of writers. It is true that he invited criticism with his statement that our novelists ought "to concern themselves with the more smiling aspects of life, which are the more American," but the later protagonists of his own fiction possess greater reality because he chose to depict them honestly as he saw them.

A Modern Instance, which Howells published in 1882 and which is his only study of married life, deals with Marcia and Bartley Hubbard. Marcia falls passionately in love with Bartley, a self-indulgent and unscrupulous journalist who is neither professionally successful nor morally admirable. Again Howells uses adeptly his personal knowledge of Boston boardinghouses and newspaper life.

Three years later *The Rise of Silas Lapham*, generally regarded as his best novel, appeared. This is the first significant picture of the businessman in American fiction. Lapham is a poor farm boy who made a fortune in the paint business and then tried to transpose himself and his family to the social and economic atmosphere of Boston. As a symbol of his ambition he builds a house on the water side of Beacon Street. The nouveaux riches Laphams are contrasted deftly with the socially secure but less affluent Coreys, and Silas himself is shown ill at ease and drunk at a dinner party but able at the end to withstand financial reverses and to return to a small New England town with dignity and honesty. Silas is no Babbitt but some of his gaucheries are presented frankly and realistically.

New York City is the scene of another superior Howells novel, *A Hazard of New Fortunes*, 1890. This is one of the author's most crowded canvases since it depicts metropolitan journalism, the poor of the lower East Side, socialistic activities, and a streetcar strike. A central character is Basil March, who like Howells has left Boston to edit a New York magazine, but there are also a voluble German socialist named Lindau and a greedy Ohio capitalist Dryfoos, who profited enormously from the discovery of natural gas on his farm. These are certainly not the smiling aspects of life which Howells proposed for themes to American novelists, but they do suggest that he was moving more and more toward the middle of the stream of realism which would soon engulf native writing.

Only a few of the later novels merit critical attention today. Howells tried his hand twice at utopian fiction, in *A Traveler from Altruria* (1894), and *Through* the *Eye of the Needle* (1907); both books are concerned with satire on social conditions through the characters of Mr. Homos, a visitor from another country, and the American woman who marries him. *The Landlord at Lion's Head* (1897), contains Jeff Durgin, a New England innkeeper's son who is basically selfish but has both bravado and charm. *The Son of Royal Langbrith* (1904), tells the story of a man whose misdeeds are never fully revealed so that his son can never be disillusioned. In his last novel Howells returned to the Ohio of his youth to narrate the life of a religious impostor, one Joseph Dylks. *The Leatherwood God* (1916), is Howells's only excursion into historical fiction and testifies to his awareness of emotional faith in a primitive society.

Howells's consummate mastery of ordinary dialogue and his ability to depict realistic characters led him many times to try his hand at dramatic writing. He wrote a few full-length plays without success, but he completed over two dozen one-act plays, many of which were witty and clever in both characterization and setting. For Howells chose a sleeping car, an elevator, and a dining room as his venue and managed to make ordinary people interesting on the stage. Unfortunately for him and his public, most of these one-act plays never had professional production and to some extent remained closet drama. But readers of *The Unexpected Guests*, *The Sleeping Car*, and *The Garroters*, farces or social comedy, were delighted with Howells's achievements. He even used the same characters more than once. And Arthur Hobson Quinn, one of the authoritative historians of American drama, remarked that Mrs. Agnes Roberts was one of the best of the author's dramatis personae, who without being a caricature was a perfect fountain of humor and a "living woman whom we have all known and heard, thinking aloud in private and public."

Oscar W. Firkins, whose *Dictionary of American Biography* article is one of the best short estimates of Howells's work, remarked that Howells as a self-educated man never mastered any literature, not even English, but whenever he ventured into criticism he deserved to be heard. He was analytical, sympathetic, and tolerant, and especially toward the end of his life he was aware of the profound changes that were occurring in the tone and form of literature. His own work showed substantive changes as he welcomed new voices. If he could find merit worth recognizing in Stephen Crane and Frank Norris, he could also encourage younger playwrights like James A. Herne, Augustus Thomas, and Clyde Fitch, all of whom expressed their obligations to him. His long relationship with Mark Twain was affectionately expressed in *My Mark Twain*, published in 1910 the year that his intimate friend died. Incidentally Twain later returned the compliment in a handwritten remark made to his own biographer when he wrote that Howells was "the first critic of the day."

Howells received an honorary degree from Yale in 1901, another from Oxford in 1904, and still another from Columbia in 1905. In 1908 he was elected the first president of the American Academy of Arts and Letters and he held this office until his death. He died in New York City in 1920, the year that Sinclair Lewis's *Main Street* was published. He might well have disapproved of the staccato style but he would have appreciated the realistic observation and language since these were qualities he had been working toward for a long time.

In 1928 Mildred Howells, the author's daughter, edited *Life in Letters of William Dean Howells*. In 1941 the Indiana University Press began to issue what was planned to be a forty-one-volume edition of the complete works of William Dean Howells.

JTF

References: Oscar W. Firkins, *DAB*, IX, 1932, pp. 306-11; Oscar W. Firkins, *William Dean Howells: A Study* (Cambridge, Mass.: Harvard University Press, 1924); Edwin H. Cady, *The Road to Realism: The Early Years, 1837-1885, of William Dean Howells* and *The Mature Years: 1885-1920, of William Dean Howells* (Syracuse, N.Y.: Syracuse University Press, 1956, 1958).

Charles Ives

(October 20, 1874 — May 19, 1954)

Europe, especially Germany and Austria, represented the focal point of operatic and symphonic music for Americans in the nineteenth century. Developing America relied on European composers for the importation of culture. Foreign musicians were lionized in New York and Boston. If an American musician wanted to study composition he went to a foreign conservatory, preferably Germany. Americans were considered incapable of developing their own form or style of music. Because of this Edward MacDowell had matured as a composer and pianist in Germany in the late 1800s. When he returned to America he imported the European techniques and became the first American to be accepted as an outstanding composer of serious music.

Charles Ives was an American composer of the late nineteenth and early twentieth centuries, who did not fit the European mold. He completed his study of music at Yale between 1894 and 1898 under the tutelage of Horatio Parker and became the most individualistic American composer of the early twentieth century.

Ralph Waldo Emerson, referring to literature, said in 1837 that "We have listened too long to the courtly muses of Europe." Science, literature and art had been under the influence of European culture for a long time. Music was one of the last to discover its own American resources. Ives decried the Germanic influence and sought to express himself as an individual American in his own way. In order to be free and independent he established an agency with the Mutual Life Insurance Company of New York in 1909 after several years experience with the company.

The firm was known as Ives & Myrick and quickly became successful. Though Ives was shy and far from the type of flamboyant insurance salesman, he was the idea man in the firm which sold $49 million worth of insurance in 1929. He always believed that his business was good for his music composition and that his music was good for his business. Ives became a wealthy businessman but was forced to take early retirement on January 1, 1930 because of declining health. During his life few people, including his family, thought of him as a composer of music; he was considered a successful businessman. His decision to go into business was basic to his success as a composer of music because it gave him economic independence and he did not have to act as a struggling musician catering to the whims of the public.

Charles Ives was the son of George Ives, a Danbury, Connecticut band master and music teacher. His father started him in music lessons at age five and had a major influence in developing his musical appreciation. By age twelve he played the organ for the local church and by age fifteen he understood harmony and counterpoint well enough to compose a piece for the local town band. Though Ives was trained by his father in Bach and traditional classical music, he was encouraged to have an open mind as to the meaning of sound. Charles's father was once asked how he could bear to listen to "old John Bell bellow off key." The father answered that "Old John is a superb musician ... Don't pay too much attention to the sounds, If you do, you may miss the music." This anecdote is pertinent in explaining the musical education of Ives and the type of music he composed. Though Ives acted and thought independently he was not completely free from the influences of society even in a democracy. Ives was a middle-class, educated, American businessman with family responsibilities. There were few national musical traditions to follow, but the pressures from his environment influenced his compositions. He said, "You cannot set an art off in the corner and hope for it to have vitality, reality and substance ... [art] comes directly out of the experience of life and thinking about life and living life." Ives had grown up in an American musical culture in which the vernacular dominated the cultivated. This did not disturb him; on the contrary, he adopted both and experimented with new modes that set the pattern for future generations.

During Ives's early life, the years when he actively composed, he was artistically isolated from society. His works were not played; he was unknown within his own fraternity. Not until the 1930s did young musicians discover Ives to be a composer of original American music; some went so far as to hail him as the father of American music, though others considered this claim an exaggeration. Real discovery came after World War II when his works won widespread recognition. The dichotomy of his life, businessman and composer, did not prevent him from breaking away from his middle-class background to explore new paths in musical composition. His music differed from any prior to his day. He searched for vitality; a church hymn, a Beethoven sonata, a Negro spiritual, or a small-town band parading down Main Street were all equally inspiring. He used polytonality and extreme dissonance to produce effective sounds. Jazz and off-beat rhythms, as well as melodic skips, were commonly employed to produce what were later thought of as modern effects.

Ives had a heart attack in 1918 and this may have been the reason that he decided to publish some of his works at his own expense. He published "Essays before a Sonata" in 1920 and "Concord Sonata" in 1921. These publications were followed in 1922 with a book of songs called *114 Songs*. The volume was accepted by a few as one of the most important books of its kind, but was ignored or treated as a joke by others. The *Musical Courier* and *Musical America* treated the new publications with scorn.

Ives showed great diversity in his compositions. *114 Songs* contained lyrics and poems, war and religious songs, folk tunes, cowboy songs and ballads, and varied from simple to complex songs filled with dissonances. "Two Little Flowers," composed in 1921, was a simple song in contrast with the longer and more complicated "General William Booth Enters into Heaven" which had been written as early as 1914 and was based in part on a poem by Vachel Lindsay. *114 Songs* includes about one-half of the total number of songs composed by Ives.

Ives had played the organ in church as a youth and religion was one of the strong traits in his compositions. He composed forty or more sacred choruses for the church. Most of the better known choral works were composed between 1898 and 1902. They include "Psalm 67," "Psalm 24," and "Psalm 90." Some, such as "Psalm 67," were written for choirs with mixed voices in which the men sang in one key and the women in a different key.

Ives wrote many instrumental works including piano pieces and a great number of chamber ensembles. The ensembles ranged from compositions for two pianos, such as "Three Pieces" in 1923 and 1924, to combinations involving several instruments such as "From the Steeples" in 1901. In some of the ensembles dissonant and harmonious sounds coexist. He composed many works for chamber orchestra, including string quartets, piano sonatas, piano-violin sonatas and pieces for other instruments. He was a diverse and prolific composer.

The First Symphony was written between 1896 and 1898 in four movements. The Second, composed between 1897 and 1902 in five movements, reflects the nineteenth century bandstand on Main Street in America rather than the conventional European music of the day. Ives described it as "suggesting a Steve Foster tune ... [with] barn dance ... jigs, gallops and reels" in the background. It takes a large orchestra thirty-five minutes to perform. The Third Symphony was composed between 1901 and 1904 and was designed for a small orchestra. Ives composed his Fourth Symphony between 1909 and 1916. It is considered to be one of the most important musical contributions in American musical history. It was one of Ives's most complex compositions and had to wait for its first full performance in 1965. It requires a large orchestra with special arrangements for strings, harps and percussion instruments.

In the two-year period of 1909 and 1910, Ives composed the "Second Pianoforte Sonata" with the subtitle of "Concord, Mass., 1840-1860." The first edition of the "Concord Sonata" was published at Ives's expense in 1919. The four movements are titled, "Emerson," "Hawthorne," "The Alcotts," and "Thoreau." At this time Ives was unknown among his contemporaries. In the dedication of "Concord" he wrote that the "essays were written by the composer for those who can't stand his music — and the music for those who can't stand his essays." In the sonata Ives depicts Emerson's "Transcendental Journey," Hawthorne's world including the circus parade and "Scarecrow," the Alcotts' Orchard House and Concord village, and the flute singing over Thoreau's Walden Pond.

Charles Ives was virtually unknown during his active years of composing. After discovery, Ives was acclaimed as a pioneer musician of great talent. He was an independent artist in music who did not depend upon the popularity of his compositions for income and did not seek publicity. He lived his life in isolation from his musical contemporaries but not from the environment which molded him. Typical of his late recognition was the refusal by Yale to offer him an honorary degree in 1953. The degree was offered in 1954, but as Mrs. Ives said, it was "too late," he had died in the New York City Roosevelt Hospital in May 1954.

HWS

References: Frank R. Rossiter, *Charles Ives and His America* (New York: Liveright, 1975); Gilbert Chase, *America's Music* (New York, Toronto, and London: McGraw-Hill, 1955); H. Wiley Hitchcock, *Music in the United States: A Historical Introduction* (Englewood Cliffs, N.J.: Prentice-Hall, 1969).

John Jay

(December 12, 1745 — May 17, 1829)

Except for the presidency, which he never attained, John Jay held the most important offices that his country could bestow during the colonial and early statehood periods. Born with a silver spoon in his mouth, Jay was the son of a wealthy New York merchant, a graduate of King's College (now Columbia University), and married into the William Livingston family, one of the most influential in the New York colony. After his admission to the bar in 1768, Jay settled down to a busy and profitable legal career — an idyllic life shortly to be interrupted by the Revolution. Thenceforth, his activities were entirely devoted to public service.

In the beginning, Jay was reluctant to support the independence movement, perhaps sharing the fear of the conservative colonial merchants that independence might be followed by mob rule and democracy. Within a short time, however, he became one of the most ardent supporters of the patriot cause. His first assignment was to serve as a member of the New York committee of correspondence, following which he was sent as a delegate to both the First and Second Continental Congresses meeting in Philadelphia. As a member of the provincial congress, Jay helped to ratify the Declaration of Independence. During the years 1778 and 1779, he served as president of the Continental Congress. Also active in state affairs, Jay was chairman of a special committee that drafted the state constitution of New York in 1777, and was first chief justice of the state from 1777 to 1779.

Jay's exceptional talents as a writer were demonstrated on a number of occasions. He drafted the *Address to the People of Great Britain*, issued by Congress in 1774, the *Address to the Canadians* in 1775, and other important state papers. With Alexander Hamilton and James Madison he was one of the authors of the famous *Federalist* papers which exerted a powerful influence in obtaining ratification of the federal Constitution of 1787.

Jay's reputation as a diplomat, one of the ablest of the American foreign representatives during the Revolutionary period, began in 1779, when he was sent to represent the Continental Congress in Spain. His mission had two objectives: to obtain Spanish recognition of American independence and financial aid. The first was a failure, because Spain feared to imperil its own colonial interests by directly aiding the revolt of Britain's former colonies. A small grant of funds was approved. The Spanish would go no further than to continue their policy of secret assistance in munitions and money to keep the American rebellion going.

At the conclusion of his Spanish mission, Jay proceeded on to Paris to join John Adams and Benjamin Franklin as peace commissioners. He helped to negotiate the Treaty of Paris (1783), ending the Revolution. Prior to Jay's arrival, Franklin had proposed the cession of Canada, but this possibility was rejected after the British negotiating position was strengthened by victory over the Spanish at Gibraltar.

Back in America, Jay found that Congress had drafted him in 1784 as secretary of foreign affairs, in effect the first secretary of state. He remained in that office until Thomas Jefferson assumed the post of secretary of state in 1790. Jay's principal problems as secretary of foreign affairs were settling a dispute with the British, who had kept their garrisons in the Northwest Territory, contrary to terms of the peace treaty, and negotiating with the Spanish over Mississippi River navigation. Jay felt that his position as secretary was weak under the Articles of Confederation, because of which he strongly advocated adoption of the Constitution, providing for more centralization of governmental powers.

When Washington assumed the presidency, Jay was nominated chief justice of the United States. During the following five years, basic court procedures were adopted, but it appears that Jay did not enjoy the office, for he wrote that the Supreme Court was lacking in "energy, weight, and dignity." The most famous case to come before the Jay court was *Chisholm vs. Georgia* in which the question was whether a state can be sued by a citizen in another state. Jay decided against Georgia, a case which led to adoption of the Eleventh Amendment to the Constitution, prohibiting any suit being brought in the federal courts against any state by a citizen of another state or by a foreign citizen.

While still serving as chief justice, Jay negotiated a treaty between the United States and Great Britain, in 1794, which adjusted some of the differences between the two nations. The "Jay Treaty," as it was called, was violently attacked in the United States, on the ground that it made too many concessions to the British, but it was ratified by the Senate. Historians believe that the terms of the treaty were not ideal, though perhaps the best possible. It prevented war with Britain and brought prosperity to American merchants.

When he returned from England in 1795, Jay was nominated and elected governor of New York. No great political issues arose during his term as governor. Noteworthy was the act which he signed to abolish slavery in New York. After six years in the gubernatorial chair, Jay retired to his estate at Bedford, New York, where he spent the remaining twenty-eight years of his life. A certain degree of cynicism is detectable in these comments written in the course of his retirement: "The post, once a week, brings me our newspapers, which furnish a history of the times. By the history, as well as by that of former times, we are taught the vanity of expecting, that from the perfectability of human nature and the lights of philosophy the multitude will become virtuous or wise, or their demagogues candid and honest."

RBD

References: Herbert A. Johnson, *John Jay* (Albany, N.Y.: Office of State History, 1970); Frank Monaghan, *John Jay* (Indianapolis, Ind.: Bobbs-Merrill, 1935); George Pellew, *John Jay* (Boston: Houghton, 1909).

John Paul Jones

(July 6, 1747 — July 18, 1792)

No American naval officer has been the subject of as much romance as John Paul Jones. His feats of daring have become legendary. His life has been the subject of many famous writers including Alexander Dumas, Herman Melville, J. Fenimore Cooper, Rudyard Kipling, Winston Churchill, William Thackeray, and Benjamin Disraeli; even Franklin D. Roosevelt prepared an introduction to a proposed biography. He has been glorified and idolized, censured and criticized, and extravagantly praised, as well as lied about. Fact and fiction have been woven into novels and ballads. One thing is certain; his deeds left an impression on his contemporaries as indicated by a Scottish ballad almost two hundred years old:

> You have heard o' Paul Jones,
>
> Have you not, have you not?
>
> And you've heard o' Paul Jones
>
> Have you not?

John Paul (Jones was added later) was born in Scotland at Arbigland. His father, John Paul, was a poor gardener and was unable to provide educational opportunities for his children. From obscurity this poor lad rose by his own efforts to become a distinguished American naval officer who was accepted in the Court of Versailles as well as the Court of Catherine II, Empress of Russia. As a sailor he was tough and rough, daring and always looking for a fight. As a man he deported himself as a fastidious gentleman, suave and courteous, but without pretensions. "Here comes Paul Jones" was said with either fear of his fighting ship or in awe of his renown.

At the age of thirteen, John made his way by packet sloop to the port of Whitehaven where he signed to serve as a ship's boy on the brig *Friendship* for seven years. The *Friendship* made its first call at Barbados where she picked up freight and transported it to Hampton, Virginia, and thence to Fredericksburg, where John met his brother William who had become a tailor. The *Friendship* plied between Scotland and America for several years. The Captain sold the brig in 1764, and the new owner released John Paul from his apprenticeship. John entered the slave trade and by age nineteen was chief mate of the slaver *Two Friends*. He became disenchanted with the foul business of slave trading and in 1768 became master of the ship *John*. John Paul was only twenty-one when he found himself master of a merchant ship involved in the West Indies trade. He had earned the responsibility thrust upon him through hard work and ambition. His second voyage in the *John* resulted in a tragedy that almost destroyed his career. The ship's carpenter, Mungo Maxwell, was flogged with the cat-o'-nine-tails. When the *John* docked at Tobago in May 1770, Mungo filed charges against Paul. Unfortunately, Mungo shipped home in another vessel and died at sea with a fever. Mungo's father filed charges of murder against Paul, but Paul was able to procure affidavits proving his innocence. Paul's troubles were only beginning. He obtained command of the *Betsy* and on the second trip to Tobago in 1773 his crew mutinied. In the fight that followed the man known as the "Ringleader" was killed when he attacked Paul. John Paul's friends persuaded him to flee Tobago for his personal safety because the Ringleader was a local man and the courts couldn't be trusted. He made his way to America incognito and next appeared in 1774 in Fredericksburg, Virginia, with the name of John Paul Jones.

The Thirteen Colonies were in turmoil. Jones was unemployed and longed to return to the sea. The new Congress had created a Continental Navy and on December 7, 1775, "John Paul Jones Esq." was commissioned first lieutenant. The navy consisted of a few merchant ships, and a lieutenant's salary was twenty dollars a month. The Naval Committee fitted out four vessels with guns. They were, according to size, the *Alfred*, *Columbus*, *Andrew Doria* and *Cabot*. Jones was assigned to the *Alfred*. Seven smaller merchant vessels were purchased and converted by 1776. The first naval expedition was the invasion and capture of New Providence in the Bahamas. Jones had little opportunity to show his skill until he was placed in charge of the *Providence* on May 10, 1776, and by August obtained a captain's commission from Congress.

The Marine Committee ordered Captain Jones to take the *Providence* "on a cruize against our enemies ... in about the Latitude of Bermuda" This was his first independent command and he quickly established himself as America's foremost naval commander, capturing sixteen prizes on his first assignment. In October 1776, he was placed in command of the *Alfred* and embarked on a raiding foray in the Cape Cod-Cape Breton area. He was successful in capturing several prizes, but lost the ship *John* to the British frigate H.M.S. *Milford*.

New ships were being built but Jones, never popular with other naval officers, found it difficult to get a suitable command. He had been infuriated when he was ranked eighteenth in the list of captains. Nevertheless, on June 14, 1777, Congress appointed him to the command of the *Ranger*. The appointment was made on the same day that Congress "Resolved, That the Flag of the thirteen United States be thirteen stripes, alternate red and white; that the union be thirteen stars, white in a blue field." The *Ranger* carried eighteen nine-pound guns and a crew of 150. The Marine Committee ordered him to report to Paris, France, where he would be given command of the newly built *L'Indien*. Upon arrival in France he was deeply disappointed when the *L'Indien* was given to the French.

The American Commissioners in Paris ordered Jones on January 16, 1778, to "proceed with her (*Ranger*) in the manner you shall judge best for distressing the Enemies of the United States, by sea or otherwise." The execution of these orders began in April when Jones headed for the Irish Sea and fame. His first major assault was on the port Whitehaven where minor damage was inflicted on the fort and shipping facilities. The following day he invaded St. Mary's Isle and the home of the Earl of Selkirk with the intention of taking hostages in order to force proper treatment of American prisoners. The Earl was away, but his silver plate was taken. Later, Jones wrote to the Countess expressing regret for her loss (the plate was ultimately returned) and stated, "I am not in Arms as an American ... I profess myself a Citizen of the World." After capturing the British man-of-war *Drake*, Jones returned to Brest, France, after twenty-eight days of raiding and fighting in British waters. He had walked into the lion's den and came out a winner. The British were outraged and considered Jones a pirate; the French and Americans deemed him a hero.

With the help of Benjamin Franklin, Jones acquired the command of a French built ship *Le Duras* in February 1799. Jones renamed *Le Duras* the

Bonhomme Richard in honor of his friend Franklin. Late in the summer Jones was ready with the *Bonhomme,* five naval vessels and two privateers to go to sea with his first fleet. He sailed around Ireland and Scotland, capturing seventeen ships in route and reached a point off Flamborough Head on September 23. Here, he came in contact with a fleet of forty-one sail, convoyed by the frigate *Serapis* (forty-four guns) and the sloop of war *Countess of Scarborough* (twenty guns). Jones had only three ships for the battle, the *Bonhomme, Pallas* and *Alliance.* The *Pallas* confined her attention to the *Countess,* the *Bonhomme* attacked the *Serapis,* and the *Alliance,* with a disgruntled captain, watched the events. It is possible that the *Alliance* directed some fire at the *Bonhomme.* Jones maneuvered the *Bonhomme* along side the *Serapis* and lashed the two ships together. The sea battle that followed, with guns firing directly into the hulls, was a desperate fight for survival. At one stage of the battle, Captain Pearson of the *Serapis* called out, "Has your ship struck?" It was at this point that Jones gave his immortal reply, "I have not yet begun to fight." The *Bonhomme* was so badly damaged that the pumps were in constant operation to prevent sinking. The *Serapis* tried to break away, but the *Bonhomme* clung to her in desperation. At last the *Serapis,* after about three and one-half hours of furious fighting, was forced to surrender. The *Countess* was bested by *Pallas* and Jones ended up with 504 prisoners of the Royal Navy, all captured in British waters. Success was due, according to Admiral Mahan, to "the immovable courage of Paul Jones." The *Bonhomme* sank, but Jones reached Texel, Holland, with his squadron on October 3. The French government finally took possession of the prizes and prisoners.

Paris lionized Jones as a hero, and he was happy to play his part. The Queen presented him with fob-chain and seal, and the King gave him a gold-hilted sword. Also, the King sent to Philadelphia the cross of the Institution of Military Merit to be conferred upon him with permission of Congress. The Masonic Lodge ordered a bust to be executed by Houdon. Jones did not return to America until February 18, 1781, three years and three months after he had left in the *Ranger.* He was awarded l'Ordre du Mérite Militaire at Philadelphia shortly after his return. This award carried the title Chevalier.

Jones was assigned to the command of the largest ship in the line of the United States, the *America.* Unfortunately, it was still under construction and when completed the government gave it to France, depriving Jones of the opportunity of exercising his command. The loss of the *America* was a keen disappointment to Jones. During the next few years he was involved with collecting payment for services rendered and in obtaining satisfactory settlement for prizes taken by his ships in European waters.

In December 1787, Empress Catherine of Russia made Jones a rear admiral in the Imperial Russian Navy to fight Turkey in the Black Sea. He was called Kontradmiral Pavel Ivanovich Jones. Though the appointment gratified his desire for a title, he soon discovered that he would receive little honor from the Russians for his services. The Russian experience ended on a sad note. His only reward was a secondary medal, the cross of the Order of St. Anne. In July of 1789, he kissed the hand of the Empress at a public audience and was given a curt bon voyage. Two months later he left Russia, never to see it again, and never again to command a ship. He spent his last two years in Paris with friends in comfortable circumstances. His health slowly declined and when he died in 1792 he was buried in the Protestant Cemetery in Paris.

Jones was buried in a leaden coffin, because his friends hoped that his remains might someday be transferred to America. Efforts were made in 1845 and 1851 to return Jones's remains, but both attempts failed. With the aid of the American ambassador, General Horace Porter, they were conveyed to Annapolis in 1905. A year later, President Theodore Roosevelt gave one of the addresses at commemorative exercises held in the Naval Academy. John Paul Jones finally came home to rest permanently in one of America's most elaborate tombs. His most important contribution was his memorable comment, "I have not yet begun to fight."

HWS

References: Samuel Eliot Morison, *John Paul Jones: A Sailor's Biography* (Boston and Toronto: Little, Brown, 1959); Valentine Thomson, *Knight of the Seas: The Adventurous Life of John Paul Jones* (New York: Liveright, 1939); John S. C. Abbott, *Life of John Paul Jones* (New York: Dodd, Mead, 1916).

Scott Joplin
(November 24, 1868 — April 11, 1917)

One of the interesting episodes in the history of American popular music was the rise and vogue of ragtime from the last years of the nineteenth century to about the end of World War I. Although the first published ragtime composition was the work of a white bandmaster, William H. Krell, whose "Mississippi Rag" was published in 1897, ragtime is generally associated with a group of Negro pianists who flourished early in the twentieth century. The most conspicuous of these musicians was Scott Joplin, Texas-born and widely known as a performer, teacher, and composer.

Joplin came from Texarkana, Texas, one of six children in a musical but impoverished family. The father, Giles Joplin, was born a slave but learned to fiddle and played dance music at his master's parties. The mother, Florence Givens Joplin, was a Kentucky black born free who sang and could play the banjo. All but one of the children could sing or play some instrument. The father contrived the purchase of an old square grand piano and the boy at an early age taught himself to play it. Tradition has it that he was given instruction by a German music teacher but this mentor has never been identified. It is likely, however, that since the boy's ability was soon known outside the family circle he was encouraged by others and eventually picked up some knowledge of musical theory. His mother worked as a domestic and often took her son with her to homes possessing a parlor piano which he was allowed to play while she did her chores.

Facts about Joplin's adolescent years are few. But he reached St. Louis in 1885 and remained there until 1893, supporting himself by playing at churches and bordellos. An itinerant Negro musician at this time had difficulty performing outside the honky-tonk atmosphere. Joplin got some training at the George R. Smith College for Negroes at Sedalia, Missouri, where he was admitted to courses in harmony and composition. He also served as accompanist for the Texas Medley Quartette, which included two of his brothers, and in 1885 he played at "Honest" John Turpin's Silver Dollar saloon in St. Louis. In 1893 he went to the Chicago World's Fair and competed with other specialists in "jig piano" pieces, an early name for ragtime. Back in Sedalia the next year he was an employee of the Maple Leaf Club and for a time he played the cornet with the Queen City Concert Band, a Negro group which performed ragtime. In 1896 he reorganized and expanded his male quartet and toured in vaudeville.

Joplin's first music publication was oddly enough not ragtime. He was the author of two banal songs, "Please Say You Will" and "A Picture of Her Face," published in Syracuse, and of several piano pieces printed in Temple, Texas. In 1899 Carl Hoffman published in Kansas City Joplin's *Original Rags*, composed two years earlier. In the same year an event occurred which changed the course of the composer's life. His famous "Maple Leaf Rag" had been rejected by two music publishers before it was brought out by John Stark of Sedalia. A million copies of the sheet music were eventually sold, royalties flowed in, and Joplin earned the sobriquet of the King of Ragtime. For the first time in his life he had a comfortable income and could escape performing in the saloons and brothels which had been his destiny for some years. By nature he was a serious and quiet man who hoped to elevate popular music into an art. As Vera Brodsky Lawrence put it, "Joplin found his native language in ragtime; as a gifted creative artist, he fashioned from its essentially commonplace elements an appealing music of high and enduring quality."

In 1900 Joplin married a widow, Belle Hayden, and the couple established a home in St. Louis. During the next five years he turned his attention to both composition and teaching. He produced nineteen piano pieces including marches, waltzes, and rags, all melodic and carefully constructed. But he never realized his ambition to create something grander. "The Ragtime Dance," a kind of choreographic song, was produced in Sedalia and John Stark reluctantly published a voice and piano version of it in 1902 but it was not a commercial success. A ragtime opera entitled *A Guest of Honor* was performed in St. Louis in 1903 by a group called Scott Joplin's Ragtime Opera Company and was apparently performed in various towns in Nebraska, Iowa, Illinois, Kentucky, and Missouri, but it never was printed. The score has disappeared.

Joplin's first marriage did not last and his movements from 1905 to 1907 are uncertain. After separating from his wife he moved to New York, where he resumed performing. He also did some touring but he spent much of his time on the composition of his opera, *Treemonisha*. When his wife's death left him free to remarry he wedded Lottie Stokes in 1909. The marriage was successful until professional frustration and physical deterioration brought a tragic end to Joplin's life. He published various piano pieces and in 1911 completed *Treemonisha*, but he found no financial backing for the opera. Sponsors were reluctant to subsidize such a work by a black composer of ragtime. Finally in 1915 Joplin arranged a production in Harlem without scenery or an orchestra; he himself played the piano accompaniment. The performance attracted little attention and his disappointment was crucial. he became moody, temperamental, not always lucid, and he suffered from syphilis. His wife committed him to the Manhattan State Hospital in the fall of 1916 and he died the following spring.

The great irony of Joplin's life is that the fame which once eluded him seemed suddenly restored in the 1970s. His piano rags were played in public by orchestras. Although not generally acclaimed, *Tremonisha* had a world premiere in Atlanta in 1972. Later in the same year it was produced at Wolf Trap Farm near Washington and again by the Houston Grand Opera Company in May 1975. A New York production directed by Gunther Schuller took place September 25, 1975. Much wider recognition of Joplin's rags came when the motion picture producer George Ray Hill made a film called *The Sting*. Five of Joplin's pieces were used for background music and the one that the composer had originally entitled "The Entertainer" was rebaptized "The Sting." It became celebrated throughout the country. Hill's picture won an award for the best film of the year in 1974; both the score and the title song were given Oscars; the sound track sold more than two million records and tapes.

Joplin was not an important writer of songs but some of his thirty-three ragtime pieces have become popular classics. Nonesuch Records issued two records including sixteen Piano Rags, played by Joshua Rifkin and provided with excellent liner notes by the musician. No documented biography of Joplin has yet appeared. In 1971 Vera Brodsky Lawrence edited *The Collected Works of Scott Joplin*. On May 3, 1976 the composer was honored with a special posthumous Pulitzer Prize for his achievements.

Joplin's better known ragtime pieces include "Gladiolus Rag," "Pine Apple Rag," "Elite Syncopations," "Solace," and "Euphonic Sound." Ragtime, unlike jazz, left little opportunity for improvisation. But the composer had one message for performers of his music: "Notice: Do not play this piece fast. It is never right to play 'Ragtime' fast."

JTF

References: Vera Brodsky Lawrence, in *Dictionary of American Negro Biography*, eds. Raymond W. Logan and Michael R. Winston, pp. 369-71 (New York and London: Norton, 1982); Joshua Rifkin, liner notes to Nonesuch Records, H-71248 and H-71264.

Chief Joseph

(ca. 1840 — September 21, 1904)

A native American who has been called the greatest Indian strategist, Chief Joseph won admiration and praise from his followers, his opponents, and even those to whom he had to surrender in 1877. The famous retreat in which he led his band of warriors, women, and children over one thousand miles through parts of Yellowstone Park, Montana, and Idaho to within thirty miles of his goal, the Canadian border, remains a unique event in American Indian history. Long after peace was restored he was invited to Washington by President Theodore Roosevelt and in 1903 met again his former adversary, General Nelson A. Miles.

Joseph was probably born in the Wallowa Valley of Oregon in 1840. His father, also named Joseph, was a chief of the Nez Percé Indians and after his death in 1873 his son succeeded him. The Nez Percé group to which both men belonged refused to recognize the validity of a treaty with the United States government signed in 1863 because they felt it was fraudulently obtained from signatories not qualified to act. The treaty, which was intended to confine the Nez Percé Indians to the Lapwai reservation in Idaho, was not enforced until 1876. In the meanwhile squatters had intruded on the land supposedly ceded by the Indians and there had been incidents in which some twenty whites had been killed. General O. O. Howard, commanding federal troops, strove to negotiate but was unsuccessful. At this point Chief Joseph gathered his band, which included fewer than two hundred warriors, and started his march toward Canada, where he hoped to find sanctuary.

The Indians had several skirmishes with the troops and actually won a battle at Big Hole, Montana, on August 9, 1877. Joseph skillfully led his small group of fugitives but was pursued by the soldiers and blocked by a detachment commanded by General Miles ahead of him. For five days the Indians held out despite a siege but Joseph felt that further resistance would be futile. His band had been reduced to 431 persons with only 87 warriors and almost half of them wounded. The survivors were moved to Fort Leavenworth in Kansas in July 1878, and many of them died there. Joseph and some 150 of his followers went to the Colville reservation in the state of Washington where the chief eventually died.

Joseph was an erect, handsome man who stood six feet tall. He was somber and seldom smiled. In his later years he did what he could to educate the tribal children, to foster industry, and to discourage drunkenness and the passion for gambling. At the time of his surrender to federal troops he made a short speech which has often been quoted. He said in part: "Hear me, my chiefs! I am tired; my heart is sick and sad. From where the sun now stands I will fight no more forever."

Needless to say Chief Joseph was faithful to his vow until his death.

JTF

References: W. J. Ghent, *DAB*, X, 1933, pp. 218-19; Cyrus T. Brady, *Northwestern Fights and Fighters* (New York: McClure, Phillips, 1907).

Henry John Kaiser

(May 9, 1882—August 24, 1967)

The saga of Henry Kaiser is the story of the poor boy who created Kaiser Industries, a $1.7 billion organization. His far-reaching empire of factories and mines touched the nation and the lives of all Americans in times of peace and war. He was a builder of highways, bridges, levees, dams, prefabricated ships, hotels, cement plants, magnesium and aluminum plants, and automobiles. His factories created steel and chemicals and were distributed over nineteen states and several foreign countries. Two of his most famous products were Kaiser-Frazer cars and Liberty ships, the latter produced on short notice for World War II. Prior to 1942 Kaiser had constructed projects exceeding $380 million in value. The biggest of these were Boulder and Grand Coulee dams. The construction of one great dam might be considered a great achievement, but Kaiser built four and furnished most of the material for a fifth. Building one ship would be considered a noteworthy enterprise, but Kaiser built more than one thousand in a short period of time.

Kaiser believed intensely in the free enterprise system. "There is no limit to human ingenuity" if not repressed by government. He believed fervently that "production" was the key to maintaining the progress of civilization. Production meant jobs, work, growth and the solution to society's problems. He considered production as America's "fifth freedom," and during World War II he proposed that plans be made for the revitalization of industry for peacetime purposes. One of his suggestions was that the automobile industry announce new models and accept war bonds as down payments. No problem was insolvable if the individual was "given the opportunity to risk and to venture; to lose as well as to gain ... and most of all to escape the compulsions of excessive government." To Kaiser the purpose of living was to work, and he practiced his philosophy by putting in sixteen to twenty hour days. To keep in touch with his widely dispersed industrial operations he traveled extensively and spent up to $250,000 per year on long distance phone calls.

Labor relations never represented a serious problem to Kaiser. He believed that most labor problems were the fault of management. His method was simple; go to labor headquarters and sign a fair contract before the work began. If fair wages were paid, the job would be efficiently done. Though Kaiser drove his men hard, he drove himself harder. Every job was handled on a three-shift basis, seven days a week. He spent his time rushing from one project to another, but his most important work was "thinking big."

Kaiser was born near Canajoharie, New York, the son of a mechanic in a shoe factory. His formal schooling stopped when he took a job in a clothing store at age thirteen at $1.50 per week to help support the family. After a period of running a photographic service he went to Spokane, Washington, in 1906 and became a salesman for a hardware company where he earned enough to afford marriage to Bessie Hannah Fosburgh. At age thirty he made the change that was basic to his future by becoming manager for a street paving company. The Northwest was booming with new towns, and new roads and bridges were needed. In 1913 Kaiser set up his own construction firm and gradually enlarged his services until he was able to build concrete highways. By innovation and improving procedures he was able to acquire contracts for highway construction in Idaho, California, Washington and British Columbia. He moved his company to Oakland, California in 1921 and six years later got his first big construction job, a $20 million contract to build two hundred miles of concrete highway in Cuba. From this experience he learned how to handle huge contracts on a cooperative basis. After the Cuban experience he turned to the construction of river levees on the Mississippi and pipelines in the Southwest.

When the government decided to build Boulder Dam, dedicated in 1936, (renamed Hoover Dam in 1947), Kaiser organized Six Companies and acted as its chairman. Hoover Dam, in Black Canyon on the Colorado River, impounds water that forms Lake Mead and is used for flood control, power and agricultural purposes. With five thousand workers he completed the dam ahead of schedule because he designed new equipment to handle large volumes of material and built Boulder City to house the workers. In 1934 he became president of Columbia Construction Company to build Bonneville Dam forty-two miles east of Portland, Oregon. It was the first government dam built on the Columbia River and was dedicated September 28, 1937. It includes a passageway for salmon to move up and down the river. The Grand Coulee Dam, a 355 feet high structure, was completed in 1942. It is the largest of a series of dams on the Columbia River. Parker Dam (1938) was built below Hoover Dam to aid in the control of floods on the Colorado River. Its special fame lies in the fact that though it extends only 85 feet above the river bed, its base extends 235 feet below the floor of the river. Kaiser lost out in the bidding for the Shasta Dam but supplied most of the material for its construction.

Kaiser operated large sand and gravel plants, the basic source material for construction. The business was run under the name of Henry J. Kaiser Company. This operation, in conjunction with the great cement plant at Permanente, made him the dominant figure supplying building material on the West Coast. When Kaiser lost the contract to build the Shasta Dam, he signed a contract to deliver the 5.8 million barrels of needed cement though he had never produced cement. He started construction of the Permanente plant in August 1939, and was in production in December. It supplied Shasta Dam and became an important asset during the war while the navy operated in the Pacific zone on the islands of Hawaii, Wake and Guam. Also, it was the foundation of Kaiser's shipbuilding successes.

Kaiser received in December of 1940 a contract from the British government for thirty merchant ships. He had never built a ship but informed his associates, Clay P. Bedford and John Reilly, that his five thousand construction workers and engineering staff were ready to start work. By pooling resources into the Todd-California Shipbuilding Corporation (1941) they built a shipyard on San Francisco Bay in three months and completed the first ten thousand-ton freighter 197 days later. In a nearby shipyard they began to construct Liberty ships for the U.S. Maritime Commission. This was only the beginning of his shipbuilding endeavor. He added yards at St. Johns on the Columbia River and one at Vancouver, Washington. His companies also had an interest in shipbuilding at Seattle, Houston, Tacoma, Los Angeles and Bath, Maine. The total number of troop and cargo carriers projected up to February 1942, was in excess of sixteen hundred, more than one thousand of which were prefabricated Liberty ships. They had revolutionized the process of shipbuilding.

Part of the secret of rapid construction was that Kaiser built ships upside down so that it was easier for welders to work. Another major factor was the dispersal of men over a wide area which allowed them more elbowroom. At the Todd-Cal. yard 9,640 men worked three shifts and another 9,700 worked at Richmond. At the peak of construction Kaiser had 80,000 men working on San Francisco Bay and at the Columbia River yards. They built ships in sections, and when the sections were completed, they were hoisted by large cranes, turned right side up, placed in proper position and welded together to form the finished ship. Kaiser's success in shipbuilding was one of the most spectacular achievements of World War II.

Supplying ships to carry troops and freight was not the only war effort contribution. In 1941 he built a magnesium plant to triple the nation's output of that important lightweight metal. At the same time he was constructing a new lock on the Panama Canal and a naval air base at Corpus Christi, Texas, as well as laying plans for the erection of a steel mill at Fontana. The mill was completed in 1942 and produced more than 1 million tons of ingot to supply his other factories during the war. By 1959 it had been expanded to the point that Kaiser Steel became the largest producer in the West.

World War II was hardly over when Kaiser and Joseph W. Frazer turned Willow Run, the Ford aviation plant, into an automobile manufacturing center. They produced their first car in 1946 and two years later were the fourth largest American motor company. In 1953 the business became unprofitable, and car manufacturing was discontinued. The compact car "Henry J." was ahead of its time; only the "Jeep" survived.

Kaiser and Sears Roebuck & Company jointly produced (1947) household ware for kitchens and bathrooms as well as some components for missiles and airplanes. At San Marcos Island, Mexico, Kaiser built a large gypsum plant for the production of building materials using gypsum as a base. In 1949 he started the Kaiser Aluminum & Chemical Company which had gross sales in 1982 of $2,912,000,000.

Kaiser initiated numerous real estate ventures including the Kaiser Center in Oakland (1957), Hawaiian Village (1954), and a resort city on Oahu Island. The total houses, hotels, factories, hospitals, roads, dams, ships, docks, levees, pipelines, and automobiles built by Kaiser cannot be determined but probably reaches a number far exceeding that ever produced by any other man.

During his lifetime Kaiser did not forget his civic duties. He was involved in many civic groups, both welfare and educational. The Kaiser Foundation offers a prepaid health plan to bring medical services within reach of those with a low to average income. For his services to mankind Kaiser was awarded several honorary degrees and medals including the French Legion of Honor. His epitaph should read "builder extraordinary" in peace and war.

HWS

References: Frank J. Taylor, "Ships on Short Order," *Reader's Digest*, vol. 40, 1942, pp. 34-36; *Current Biography*, 1961, pp. 231-33; Allan H. Cullen, *Rivers in Harness: The Story of Dams* (Philadelphia and New York: Chilton Books, 1962).

Helen Adams Keller

(June 27, 1880 — June 1968)

Through most of human history both mentally and physically handicapped people have had a difficult time finding acceptance in society. In most primitive societies they were unable to survive. Even in the nineteenth century most were disregarded and often mistreated or misunderstood. The achievement of Helen Keller near the beginning of the twentieth century was a major turning point in society's attitude toward the handicapped in general and the deaf and dumb in particular.

Prior to 1831, when Samuel Gridley Howe opened the first school for the blind in America in Boston, most people thought that it was impossible to train the deaf and dumb. Howe changed this attitude by teaching the blind to read by using embossed letters, later known as the Howe Type. His success attracted wide attention and he was given the mansion of the Perkins family, which became the Perkins Institution for the Blind. Helen Keller was not the first to reap the benefit of Howe's methods, but through her courage and indomitable spirit she became a world leader for the handicapped. She overcame the affliction of blindness and deafness to such an extent that she graduated from Radcliffe College *cum laude*, wrote her own life story, gave public lectures and appeared on the stage. During her life she was considered one of the most remarkable women of her century.

Helen Keller was a normal child at birth. She was the daughter of Captain Arthur and Kate Keller of Tuscumbia, Alabama. The first year and a half of Helen's life was typical of a child raised on a southern plantation. The Keller family owned land and enjoyed a high standing in the community but lacked ready cash. Helen, in her first year of life, had learned a few words and had the pleasure of seeing the flowers and trees and hearing the mockingbirds sing. In February 1882 she became ill and the doctor questioned whether she would survive. Though she recovered, her eyesight and hearing were completely destroyed. The family attempted to cope with their handicapped daughter without expert advice for the next four years, but the result was an unruly child.

Captain Keller took his six-year-old daughter to Baltimore for medical attention, but the report was discouraging. He was advised to see Dr. Alexander Graham Bell, inventor of the telephone and former teacher of the deaf. Bell recommended that the father contact the Perkins Institution. The director of Perkins found a young twenty-year-old woman who was willing to come to Tuscumbia and act as a teacher. Helen describes her arrival as "The most important day I remember in all my life is the one on which my teacher, Anne Mansfield Sullivan, came to me." Anne arrived on March 3, 1887, three months before Helen's seventh birthday. The child was tense and anxious, wondering who was arriving; the teacher faced the dark unknown with hope, tenderness and determination. Without the teacher there could be no future for the child to grow mentally; teacher and child soon became an inseparable pair.

Miss Sullivan was born in April 1866, the daughter of Thomas Sullivan, an Irish immigrant who was an illiterate, ill-tempered alcoholic, unable to provide for his family. Anne had a miserable childhood. At age ten she was delivered to the Tewksbury, Massachusetts, poorhouse and was listed on the records as blind. She survived the evils of Tewksbury until she was transferred to the Perkins Institution on October 7, 1880. Here, her rebellious nature often got her into trouble, and she found it difficult to adjust to the discipline of schooling at Perkins. However, through the slow process of education and maturity she overcame the shame and humiliation of the Tewksbury almshouse episode. Operations restored her eyesight and permitted normal reading and progress. As she approached the age of twenty, love and understanding began to take the place of hatred and her eight classmates designated her valedictorian of the graduating class. After graduation an uncertain future faced Anne. In her valedictorian address she said "Today we are standing face to face with the great problem of life." She didn't realize the extent of her problem, but within a year a letter came from Captain Keller inviting her to take over the education of his daughter. The pay would be twenty-five dollars per month, board and room and the status of a family member.

Anne brought a doll from Perkins with her and the day after arrival in Tuscumbia she handed it to Helen and at the same time spelled "d-o-l-l" with her fingers in Helen's hand. The child was intrigued with the symbolism and in the next few weeks learned many new words without realizing their true meaning. Not until water was poured over one hand while Anne spelled "w-a-t-e-r" in the other did she come to the realization that everything had a name. This was the turning point in her educational process. She was such an avid student and so hungry for knowledge that by age ten she knew the alphabet and could read and write. She experienced the pleasures of communing with nature when "Teacher" took her through the meadows in springtime and let her feel the differences between the various plants and smell the fragrance of different flowers.

Helen made the first of her many trips to the Perkins Institute in May 1888. By 1890 she had heard of the successful story of a Norwegian girl, Ragnhild Kaata, who had been taught to speak. She was determined to learn how to talk and entered Miss Sarah Fuller's Horace Mann School for the Deaf in Boston on March 26, 1890. After one hour she had learned six elements of speech, "M,P,A,S,T,I" and had begun to conquer the difficult field of vocalization. With the constant aid of Miss Sullivan, and the willingness to practice day and night, Helen not only mastered the English language but learned to speak French and German. Part of her training in foreign languages was obtained at the Wright-Humason School for the Deaf in New York between 1894 and 1896. Her enunciation of German and French was superior to her English.

One of the early clues to Helen's mental capacity was her ability to write. Three and one-half months after Anne Sullivan started teaching her she wrote her first letter on June 17, 1887. When eight years old she was composing excellent letters that included sentences in French and Greek. At age twelve she contributed to the *Youth's Companion* and was writing as well or better than most seniors in high school. When she was sixteen she entered Cambridge School for Young Ladies to prepare for Radcliffe College. Miss Sullivan was always at her side, even in the classroom, to interpret the instruction. A misunderstanding caused her to withdraw in 1898 and she was taught by a tutor in preparation for the entrance examinations. The courses consisted of algebra, geometry, Greek and Latin. Helen took the entrance examinations in late June 1899 and enrolled in the fall of 1900, receiving her B.A. degree in June 1904. Though deaf and dumb she had accomplished what seemed to be impossible; she had successfully competed with those who could see and hear and had attained excellence in English literature and was adept in foreign languages and history.

Helen and Anne moved to a small farm near Wrentham, Massachusetts, after graduation from Radcliffe. Keller began to concern herself with the problems of the blind. She published several articles in the *Ladies' Home Journal* in 1907 concerning blindness of the newborn, a subject that had been previously shunned for public discussion because it was related to venereal diseases. *The Story of My Life* first appeared as a serial in the *Journal* in 1902 and was later published in book form.

Miss Sullivan's marriage to John A. Macy in 1905 did not disrupt her relationship with Helen. He acted as manager and shared in the income of the various ventures. By 1913 Helen was able to speak well enough to appear before the public. Thus, in 1914 she went on her first lecture tour. After they sold the Massachusetts home in 1918 they moved to Forest Hills, New York, but their economic base was inadequate. They agreed to make a film of Helen's life story and in May signed a contract calling for ten thousand dollars on signing and an equal sum upon completion plus royalties. The film *Deliverance* was completed and opened in 1919 at the Lyric Theater to highly favorable reviews but was not a financial success. With the failure of the Hollywood venture Helen decided to try vaudeville. From 1922 to 1924 the two women followed the Orpheum Circuit and after that settled for lectures and writing. Their income was supplemented for a time by a five thousand dollar annuity from Andrew Carnegie.

Helen had a natural interest in furthering the cause of the deaf and blind. Since her college days at Radcliffe she supported enterprises to aid the handicapped. She started the Helen Keller Endowment Fund for the American Foundation for the Blind in 1932 with a goal of raising $2 million. Her efforts and private world were temporarily shattered in October 1936 when Anne died. At first, there seemed to be no future, but her secretary, Polly Thomson from Scotland, took over as companion. Polly was not a real substitute for Anne, and a void remained in Helen's life.

Polly and Helen travelled first to Scotland and later to other parts of the world. Wherever Helen appeared she was received as an honored guest by political leaders and other notable people. Her travels included Europe, New Zealand, Japan, South Africa, the Near East, India and Latin America. She became a friend of most of the famous people of the world. Among them were political leaders, Hollywood people, educators, industrialists, and a host of literary people. They included Theodore Roosevelt, Franklin and Eleanor Roosevelt, Katharine Cornell and Mary Pickford, Henry Ford, and Mark Twain. Twain idolized her and in a letter wrote, "You are a wonderful creature, the most wonderful in the world—you and your other half together—Miss Sullivan, I mean, for it took the pair of you to make a complete whole ... her brilliancy, penetration, originality, wisdom, character, and the fine literary competencies of her pen—they are all there."

Helen became a Socialist in 1909 and supported the suffragist movement, as well as other causes which she deemed in the best interest of the underprivileged. John Macy, an active Socialist, may have had some influence on her political thinking. Her first interest was aid to the deaf and blind, but she soon enlarged her scope to include the economic and political fields. She was an ardent socialist because she thought the principles of socialism showed the way to a better life for the underprivileged. She actively supported the campaigns of Eugene V. Debs and Robert La Follette for the presidency, but after 1924 did not make a political endorsement until 1944 when she supported Roosevelt.

An indefatigable worker, Helen spent the latter part of her life working and enjoying life. She participated in sports, especially horseback riding and bicycling. She enjoyed music, especially symphonies, which she heard through vibrations. She continued to write, lecture and raise money for special projects. In her *Journal*, published in 1938, she dedicated herself to service for the unfortunate in order to justify "her teacher's faith in her."

In recognition of her unusual contributions King Alexander of Yugoslavia awarded her the St. Sava Order in 1931. Temple University honored her with the Doctor of Humane Letters in 1931, and the following year the University of Glasgow granted her the Doctor of Law degree. Harvard gave her an honorary degree in 1955. Though she was recognized during her life as one of the world's outstanding women her greatest contribution was the sense of attainment and hope she left for all handicapped people. When a deaf, blind and mute child grows into an intellectual adult who writes, reads, lectures, and enjoys life there is hope for all. She summarized her own philosophy of life when she wrote, "It seems to me that there is in each of us a capacity to comprehend the impressions and emotions which have been experienced by mankind from the beginning."

HWS

References: Helen Adams Keller, *The Story of My Life* (New York: Grosset & Dunlap, 1904); Helen Keller, *Midstream: My Later Life* (Westport, Conn.: Greenwood, 1929); Helen Keller, *Journal* (Garden City, N.Y.: Doubleday, 1938); Joseph P. Lash, *Helen and Teacher* (New York: Delacorte Press/Seymour Lawrence, 1980).

Jerome David Kern

(January 27, 1885—November 11, 1945)

Many of the most notable leaders of the twentieth century musical theater attended the funeral of Jerome Kern. They included Oscar Hammerstein II, Irving Berlin, Richard Rodgers, Mary Martin and Sigmund Romberg. All came to pay tribute to the man who had composed some of the most melodious tunes ever produced for the stage and motion pictures. Some of his melodies continue to be popular generation after generation. Who can forget the rhythms from the 1927 musical play *Show Boat*, " 'Ol' Man River," "Why Do I Love You?" and "Can't Help Lovin' Dat Man"?

The lyric theater had a long history of development prior to Kern's appearance. One of the early great successes was *The Black Crook* in 1860, followed later by Gilbert and Sullivan's *H.M.S. Pinafore*. By 1895 young Kern was introduced to the theater by his parents, a time when the musical play was in transition. The American theater still followed the path laid out by Gilbert and Sullivan, but American composers, led by Victor Herbert, were breaking new ground with musicals like *The Wizard of the Nile*. It was a good time to be a youth with an interest in music.

Jerome was born in New York City, the son of Henry and Fannie Kern. His father was a successful businessman and his mother started his piano lessons when he was five years old. The middle-class Kern family moved to Newark, New Jersey, when Jerome was ten. After high school Kern studied piano and harmony at the New York College of Music. One of his earliest known compositions was an "Overture, Medley" for the Newark Yacht Club's presentation of *Uncle Tom's Cabin* in January 1902. The following year Kern went to Germany for study and returned by way of London. He was greatly impressed with London and the liveliness found at Daly's and the Gaiety Theater. Upon returning to New York he was hired at seven dollars a week to become a song plugger. Nineteen-year-old Kern was an excellent pianist and soon acted as rehearsal pianist on Broadway. His new compositions were good enough to be interpolated into Broadway musicals needing additional songs. His first success was furnishing songs for *Mr. Wix of Wickham* in 1904. Though the songs, including "Rub a Dub," were not memorable they were important in establishing Kern on Broadway.

Kern's progress from 1904 to 1912 was slow, but when the Shubert Brothers asked him in 1912 to prepare a complete score for a musical the pace of his life picked up. *The Red Petticoat* opened November 13, 1912 and late program changes included the statement, "Music by Jerome D. Kern." His first big success came with his song "They Didn't Believe Me" in *The Girl from Utah* which opened in the Knickerbocker Theater on August 24, 1914. "They Didn't Believe Me" was a turning point in Kern's career as well as a landmark song in popular musical comedy. Kern had four other songs in *The Girl from Utah* which were popular melodies with dancers of one-steps, two-steps, and fox-trots. *Ninety in the Shade* arrived in New York in January 1915 and, though it failed, it established Kern's style. This musical become his trademark and made him the leader in developing a new and exciting American theater. World War I interrupted the continuity of European musical creativity and the impetus shifted to New York. During the war Kern composed musicals which were presented in the small New York Princess Theater. Among them were *Nobody Home* which opened April 20, 1915, and *Very Good Eddie* which opened in December.

Kern's technique of using realistic situations in modern settings matured into an American style. It was soon emulated by other composers. *Oh, Boy*, which opened at the Princess in February 1917, included the hit song "Till the Clouds Roll By." It was a great success with 463 performances in New York and a company that toured the country until 1922.

Kern's first association with Florenz Ziegfeld appears to have been in 1911 when one of his songs was used in the *Follies*. Kern contributed to other *Follies* but his greatest joint production with Ziegfeld was *Show Boat* in 1927. Critics glorified Ziegfeld's part in the production and, at first, underestimated the contributions of Kern and Oscar Hammerstein II. Kern had conceived the idea of making a new musical when he read Edna Ferber's *Show Boat*. With Oscar Hammerstein's help Ziegfeld was convinced that Ferber's story had a great title and he agreed to produce it. *Show Boat* became a well known American musical with several songs that enjoyed a wide popularity. It enjoyed 575 performances in New York, but its run could not survive the collapse of the stock market in 1929 and the onset of the Great Depression. The appearance of sound films also had an unfavorable effect upon the musical play. During the depression years Kern participated in several musical productions. They included *The Cat and the Fiddle*, in 1931, *Music in the Air* in 1932 with its exquisite collection of melodies, and *Roberta* in 1933 with its hit song "Smoke Gets in Your Eyes."

Metro Goldwyn Mayer commissioned Kern in January 1935 to compose songs for Hollywood. He moved to the West Coast where in June he signed with RKO and worked almost solely for the film industry. He composed melodies for such films as *Swing Time* in 1936 and *Cover Girl* in 1944.

Kern was a charter member of ASCAP, the American Society of Composers, Authors and Publishers. He made a fortune from his musical talent and at an early date began to collect rare books. He amassed a great collection of English literature of the eighteenth to the twentieth century, specializing in Dickens, Shelley, Thackeray and others of the period. He sold the collection in January 1929 for $1,729,462.

Kern married Eva Leale, an English lady from the village Walton-on-Thames, on October 25, 1910. Eva was supportive of Kern's career and was with him when he made a trip to New York from Hollywood in November 1945. After three days in New York he collapsed on the street with a cerebral hemorrhage.

One of Kern's chief contributions to theater music was the Americanization of the operetta. He brought American speech, scenes and characters into the musical play.

HWS

References: Gerald Bordman, *Jerome Kern: His Life and Music* (New York and Oxford: Oxford University Press, 1980); Michael Freedland, *Jerome Kern* (New York: Stein and Day, 1978).

Alfred Charles Kinsey
(June 23, 1894—August 25, 1956)

Prior to the investigations conducted by Alfred Kinsey and his associates at Indiana University's Institute for Sex Research, human sexual behavior was the least explored area of biology, psychology, and sociology. As Dr. Kinsey points out in a historical introduction to his pioneer work, *Sexual Behavior in the Human Male* (1948), "Scientifically more has been known about the sexual behavior of some of the farm and laboratory animals." The subject was largely taboo because of religious, legal, and social restrictions. A breakdown of Victorian conventions and interdictions in the twentieth century, however, led to an increasing demand for objective data among physicians, psychiatrists, and persons concerned with such matters as sexual adjustments in marriage, the sexual guidance of children, and sex education. The prevailing situation was described by Alan Gregg of the Rockefeller Foundation's Medical Sciences division, in a preface to the Kinsey work:

Certainly no aspect of human biology in our current civilization stands in more need of scientific knowledge and courageous humility than that of sex. The history of medicine proves that in so far as man seeks to know himself and face his whole nature, he has become free from bewildered fear, despondent shame, or arrant hypocrisy. As long as sex is dealt with in the current confusion of ignorance and sophistication, denial and indulgence, suppression and stimulation, punishment and exploitation, secrecy and display, it will be associated with a duplicity and indecency that lead neither to intellectual honesty nor human dignity.

Years of strict scientific discipline had prepared Dr. Kinsey for his task. A biologist who had spent decades of research on a minute field of specialization, Dr. Kinsey's previous publications had borne such esoteric titles as *The Gall Wasp Genus Cynips*, *The Gall Wasp Genus Neuroterus*, *The Origin of Higher Categories in Cynips*, and *Edible Wild Plants of Eastern North America*. (A report on a single species of gall wasp was based on 150,000 individual specimens.) His concern with studies of human sexual behavior began late and appears to have been inspired originally by inability to answer students' questions on the subject. Current research was practically nonexistent, and available publications had so little solid basis that they were almost worthless.

Ten years passed between the start of Dr. Kinsey's work in his new field of inquiry and the appearance of the first report, *Sexual Behavior in the Human Male*. During that period he was joined by Wardell B. Pomeroy, a clinical psychologist, and Clyde E. Martin, a specialist in statistical procedures, both of whom aided in perfecting the methodology for the investigation and participated in the thousands of interviews which form the foundation for the book. Various psychologists and scientists from other disciplines also took part in the project as full-time staff members or consultants. Financial support came from Indiana University and the Rockefeller Foundation's Division of Medical Sciences.

Throughout his researches, Kinsey had one objective: to study all aspects of human sexual behavior without "preconception of what is rare or what is common, what is moral or socially significant, or what is normal and what is abnormal." At the outset, Dr. Kinsey announced his intention strictly to avoid social or moral interpretations of facts discovered, though some critics question whether he was fully successful in that aim.

As the first in a projected series of reports, *Sexual Behavior in the Human Male* places specific limitations on its scope: the data are confined to information collected from 5,300 white American males (omitting Europeans and Negroes), chiefly from the northeastern quarter of the United States. Social groups represented include inmates of penal institutions and the underworld in general, laborers, clerks, farmers, business executives, lawyers, physicians, high school students, college students and professors, and clergymen. The population is subdivided by race-cultural group, marital status, age, age at adolescence, educational level, occupational class (ten categories), occupational class of parents, rural-urban background, religion, degree of religious adherence, and geographic origin.

One reviewer commented that "Kinsey has studied the sex behavior of the American male as though the American male, too, were a gall wasp." His book is described by Kinsey himself as "a taxonomic study of the frequencies of sources and sexual outlets among American males." Data were obtained in intimate personal interviews in which each individual was asked between three hundred and five hundred questions. The interviews lasted from one to six hours, and elaborate care was exercised to make them valid, painless, and confidential.

Courage was required to gather data for the study and later to publish the findings. The mere news that the investigation was in progress aroused violent opposition in some quarters. Kinsey notes in his introduction that he and his associates were

> repeatedly warned of the dangers involved in the undertaking and were threatened with specific trouble ... there were attempts by the medical association in one city to bring suit on the ground that we were practicing medicine without a license, police interference in two or three cities, investigation by a sheriff in one rural area, and attempts to persuade the University's administration to stop the study or to prevent the publication of the results, or to dismiss the senior author from his university connection, or to establish a censorship over all publications emanating from the study.

In one city the president of the school board, a physician, dismissed a teacher because he had assisted in getting histories outside of the school. A hotel manager refused to allow interviews under his roof. But for every individual or group that opposed the study, hundreds cooperated, ranging from Harvard and Columbia Universities to the Kansas state police and the Salvation Army's Home for Unwed Mothers.

Why should a report of a scientific investigation prepared by an Indiana University zoologist arouse so much antagonism and cause so many attempts at suppression even before publication? The primary reason, of course, was the fact that it dealt with a taboo subject. Another factor undoubtedly was the fear of what the inquiry might disclose. Those who had reason to be nervous about the findings were justified, for when the book came off the press its revelations upset numerous popularly held opinions, prejudices, and superstitions.

Among the most important findings of the Kinsey report, in summary, are that the sex impulse exists in every individual, of whatever age, beginning in infancy; in nearly every person it is extremely powerful; and it has numerous forms of expression. Further, there is a vast difference between the moral pretensions of the community and actual behavior, that is between what we do and what the conventions say that we should do. There is a wide range in the sexual activity of individuals, sexual activity begins much earlier and continues longer than is commonly believed, and the period of highest activity in the male comes much earlier than is generally supposed.

Sexual Behavior in the Human Male includes findings about masturbation, petting, intercourse, prostitution, and homosexuality. The book is filled with facts obtained from the survey such as these: 88 percent of single men between sixteen and twenty practiced masturbation; 99 percent of American boys began having a sexual life at adolescence; 37 percent of young married males and 22 percent of men aged sixty had extramarital relations; 27 percent of the youngest unmarried group had had some form of homosexual experience, and that figure increased to 39 percent among unmarried males over thirty-six years old; 70 percent of preadolescent boys reported sex play with other children between the ages of five and fourteen; 75 percent of boys who went no further than high school had premarital heterosexual experiences, in contrast to those who went to college, of whom 42 percent had indulged in teenage premarital sex relations.

Kinsey's research seems to verify Sigmund Freud's theories of infantile sexuality. Kinsey's data show that sexual activity in the male is present from birth to death. The popular belief in "sex conservation" as a reason for continence is refuted by Kinsey, who finds that boys who attained early puberty and began sex activity earlier had the highest rate of sex activity and continued such activity longer. The facts clearly made nonsense of the oft-repeated warning that early indulgence will weaken the sexual powers in later life; the exact opposite appears to be true. Prior to Kinsey, it had not been recognized that maximum sexual activity occurs in the teens. According to his study boys between sixteen and seventeen have more frequent sexual arousals than at any other period in their lives. By fifteen years of age, 95 percent of males were found to be regularly active. This is a fact of challenging significance in the light of the increasing lag between biological maturity and economic security and marriage. During the years when a boy's sexual drive is at its highest, no socially approved outlet is provided. The boy seeks his outlet in various forms, all of which are banned by society and give rise to much anxiety and conflict in the individual. Concerning the physical and psychological harm caused thereby, Kinsey remarks:

> Whether there should be sex instruction, and what sort of instruction it should be, are problems that lie outside the scope of an objective scientific study; but it is obvious that the development of any curriculum that faces the fact will be a much more complex undertaking than has been realized by those who think of the adolescent boy as a beginner, relatively inactive, and quite capable of ignoring his sexual development.

With advancing age, Kinsey's data show, there is a slow and steady decline in sexual activity, but no evidence was found of sudden male climacteric. Responses to Kinsey's interviews indicated that even at seventy years of age only 30 percent were impotent.

Another unexpected finding of the Kinsey study was that sexual behavior was influenced in many significant and complex ways by social level, as measured by educational attainment, grade school, high school, or college graduation. Social levels are not supposed to exist in a democratic society, but realistically there is an "upper class" and a "lower class," and "most people do not in actuality move freely with those who belong to other levels." There were wide and consistent differences discovered in the sphere of sexual behavior between educational and occupational classes. Single males with only grade school education were found to practice only half as much masturbation as did the college group, and tended to be more ashamed of it, while their frequency of intercourse was, in the lower-age levels, almost three times as high. Lower-level groups were also inclined to frown on nudity, petting, oral eroticism, and unconventional poses in intercourse—all practices which the upper-level population indulged in frequently. Among the lower economic and sociological groups, intercourse with prostitutes was six times more frequent than in the upper.

Grade school graduates showed considerable extramarital intercourse during the first years of marriage, but with time became increasingly faithful to their wives, whereas the college population began marriage with high fidelity and in time became increasingly promiscuous. Dr. Kinsey comments, "Some persons may interpret the data to mean the lower level starts out by trying promiscuity and as a result of that trial, finally decides that strict monogamy is a better policy; but it would be equally correct to say that the upper level starts out by trying monogamy and ultimately decides that variety is worth having." Another commentator suggests that the changing pattern may simply be a matter of opportunity. Upper-class males are surrounded by a surplus of unmarried, divorced, and widowed women and also have more money and freedom to arrange liaisons with such women, while the lower-level male has fewer women available and less means to maintain his personal attractiveness.

The incidence of homosexuality among males was found to be considerably higher than was realized prior to the Kinsey investigation, which indicated that "at least thirty-seven percent of the male population has some homosexual experience between the beginning of adolescence and old age." Actually, the high percentage may be misleading, as the author notes, for it applies to men who have had any kind of homosexual experience in their lives; in some instances this may have been a single experience. Nevertheless, the figures show that 10 percent of men surveyed between the ages of sixteen and sixty-five were homosexuals for at least three years, and 4 percent were entirely homosexual throughout their lives.

The legal implications of the Kinsey report are obvious. Numerous commentators have suggested that important changes in our laws and social customs are desirable to close the wide gap that still exists between what we preach and what we practice. The dimensions of the problem Kinsey revealed were startling: 85 percent of the total male population had premarital intercourse, 37 percent had had homosexual experience, 59 percent had experienced oral-genital contacts (a criminal offense in a number of states), 30 to 45 percent had extramarital intercourse, nearly 70 percent had had relations with prostitutes, and 17 percent of farm boys had intercourse with animals—altogether a total of 95 percent of the entire male population had been involved in illicit activities. As Dr. Kinsey remarks, the periodic call for a "clean-up of the sex offenders in a community is, in fine, a proposal that five percent of the population should support the other 95 percent in penal institutions," if strict legal penalties were enforced.

The psychological effects of the Kinsey findings were also significant. Millions of people, Kinsey points out, carry around with them feelings of guilt, believing that they belong to a small minority that has transgressed moral law. Some individuals are so conscience-smitten that they break down under the burden and end up in psychiatrists' offices or hospitals. Such people still regret their actions, but their feelings of remorse might be less acute knowing that they belong to 90 percent instead of 1 percent of the population.

A barrage of criticism greeted the Kinsey report on its appearance. It was argued, for example, that people will not answer questions of this nature honestly; either they will conceal important facts or lie about their sexual prowess. Kinsey and his fellow interviewers took great precautions to avoid such pitfalls. Other critics observed that the study's emphasis was too exclusively on the physical and mechanistic aspects of sexual activity, largely ignoring the influence of affection, tenderness, and human sentiment in sex behavior. The word "love" is scarcely mentioned. Similar in character is a point stressed by Lionel Trilling in a lengthy critique appearing in the *Partisan Review*, that is, Kinsey's equating of *much* sexuality with *good* sexuality; Trilling maintains that there is almost no relationship between sexual frequency and sexual satisfaction. On the contrary, an unusually high frequency may be a symptom of deep sexual disturbance.

Kinsey's sample of 5,300 males has been criticized, also, as unrepresentative of the total population: too high proportions of college students, professional psychologists and psychiatrists, and male prostitutes; too small a percentage of men over thirty and of residents of rural areas; and too limited a geographic distribution.

A hostile comment on *Sexual Behavior in the Human Male*, heard not infrequently, is that it only proved what everyone already knew. The statement is misleading, for it is quite evident that the Kinsey report contains material that surprised everyone when it was revealed. Previous impressions and suspicions were confirmed or disproved with a mass of detailed facts useful to parents, teachers, psychiatrists, ministers, jurists, and legislators. The broad findings of the study presented a picture of a people endowed with sexual drives of various intensities, whose sexual activities began early in life and were often conditioned and modified by society. For a large proportion of the population sexual activity was not limited to the institution of marriage, and there was a higher degree of homosexuality than was previously realized. Finally, it seemed clear from the study that strong and insistent sexual drives are a basic biological element in everyday life.

Complementing the original Kinsey report, *Sexual Behavior in the Human Female* was published in 1953, followed by a series of more specialized studies. The path blazed by Kinsey was taken later by scores of other writers, popular and scientific. Probably most original and constructive, because it was based on extensive laboratory research, was William H. Masters and Virginia E. Johnson's *Human Sexual Response* (1966), the work of a gynecologist and of a psychologist on the staff of the Reproductive Biology Research Foundation of St. Louis, supported by the Washington University School of Medicine.

RBD

References: Cornelia V. Christenson, *Kinsey: A Biography* (Bloomington: Indiana University Press, 1971); Wardell B. Pomeroy, *Dr. Kinsey and the Institute for Sex Research* (New York: Harper & Row, 1972).

Robert Marion LaFollette

(June 14, 1855 — June 18, 1925)

Robert M. LaFollette, whose political career extended over a period of about forty-five years, was a congenital nonconformist. Though ostensibly labeled as a Republican most of his life, he was in almost constant revolt against the conservative elements who dominated his party. The many successes he achieved were a result of his own dynamic personality, and owed little to party affiliation or support.

LaFollette maintained an old American tradition by being born in a log cabin. His grandfather had lived on a Kentucky farm adjacent to that of Abraham Lincoln's father. Robert graduated from the University of Wisconsin in 1870. After a period of legal study, he was admitted to the bar in 1880 and began practice in Madison. His wife, Belle Case, also became an attorney and worked closely with her husband in law and politics.

LaFollette's first venture into politics came in 1880 when he was elected, and two years later reelected, district attorney of Dane County. He was the only Republican elected on the county ticket. Without the backing or endorsement of older leaders in his party, he won the Republican nomination for Congress in 1884, was elected and continued to serve in the U.S. House of Representatives until 1891. LaFollette was a casualty, however, of the landslide against the Republican party in the 1890 election, and he returned to the practice of law in Madison.

Ten years passed before LaFollette regained political office. During that time, he had been formulating certain definite views on reforms that he felt were needed in the political process. The principal features of the program conceived by him were a system of direct primary nominations; equalizing taxation of corporate and other property; regulation of railroads and other corporations;

and the setting up of expert commissions for the regulation of railroads and other public interests.

In 1901 LaFollette was elected and inaugurated governor of Wisconsin, providing him with an opportunity to promote his reform ideals. Unfortunately, the legislature was dominated by "stalwart" Republicans, who blocked him at every turn. By attacking corrupt and greedy politicians who opposed his policies, LaFollette caused a deep split in his party. Nevertheless, he carried his campaign to the farmers and common people in numerous speeches revealing the unfair system of taxation and the need for public control of railroad rates.

Despite the schism, the Republicans carried Wisconsin in 1904 and LaFollette had the support of a friendly legislature in 1905. He himself was elected to the U.S. Senate, but delayed resigning as governor until the successful completion of his legislative agenda. The reforms he initiated in Wisconsin, such as the direct primary, equalization of taxes, income taxes, railroad control, and regulatory commissions, were emulated nationwide.

Meanwhile, the Republican hierarchy refused to recognize his leadership on the state or national level. He was entered as a candidate for the presidency at the 1908 Republican National Convention, but owing mainly to Theodore Roosevelt's backing, the nomination went to William Howard Taft. Similarly, in 1912, LaFollette was proposed as the Progressive candidate, but the nomination went to Roosevelt instead.

As a senator, LaFollette became a leader of the progressive element. He advocated a tax on corporations, an income tax, direct election of senators, full publicity on campaign expenditures, and women's suffrage. He supported the early reforms of the Woodrow Wilson administration, but took a strong stand against the policies he thought would involve the country in World War I. In the Senate he filibustered at length against passage of legislation to arm merchant ships, later spoke and voted against the declaration of war, and during the war opposed the draft and the espionage bill, though he gave support to most wartime legislation. Because of the large German element in Wisconsin's population, he was inclined to be anti-British and pro-German. His resultant unpopularity led to an attempt to have him expelled from the Senate, and he was censured by the Wisconsin legislature. At the end of the war, LaFollette voted against ratifying the League of Nations Covenant and membership of the United States in the World Court. Regardless of such sometimes unpopular stands, he maintained a strong hold on his constituents who continued to return him to his seat in the Senate.

The years of the Harding administration were trying for LaFollette. He was author of the resolution authorizing a senatorial investigation of the Teapot Dome and other naval oil leases.

In 1924 LaFollette was the presidential candidate of the Progressive party on a platform calling for public ownership of railroads and water power, a government marketing corporation, and a ban on the use of injunctions in labor disputes. He carried on an active campaign against Coolidge and Davis and received about 5 million votes in the November election, about one-sixth of the total popular vote.

It was LaFollette's last campaign. His health had been precarious for some time and he died in Washington the following summer.

The magic of the LaFollette name remained powerful in Wisconsin. His son, Robert Marion LaFollette, Jr., succeeded his father in the Senate, 1925-1946, and another son, Philip Fox LaFollette, was governor of Wisconsin, 1931-1933 and 1935-1939.

RBD

References: Edward N. Doan, *The LaFollettes and the Wisconsin Idea* (New York: Rinehart, 1947); Robert S. Maxwell, *LaFollette* (Englewood Cliffs, N.J.: Prentice-Hall, 1969).

Samuel Pierpont Langley
(August 22, 1834—February 27, 1906)

Man has dreamed of flying like a bird for centuries. From the fifteenth century, when Leonardo da Vinci made sketches of a flying machine, to the last half of the nineteenth century little progress occurred. The first aerial flight of any kind was made by balloon in France on November 21, 1783. This aroused great interest in flight but man was not yet ready to apply scientific principles to the problem of heavier-than-air transportation. However, an adequate source of power was finally available when Edwin L. Drake discovered oil in 1859 and the gasoline combustion engine was invented. Several men experimented in the last half of the nineteenth century with gliding and flying machines, but none succeeded in flying heavier-than-air bodies. The scientific application of principles of aerodynamics would be required before successful flight occurred. Samuel Langley, self-educated scientist, became convinced that flight was possible and began the study of the theory of flight in 1886. He placed the study of aerodynamics on a scientific basis.

Langley was born in Roxbury, Massachusetts, the son of Mary and Samuel Langley, a wholesale merchant. The training of a scientist usually involves a long educational experience including postgraduate work in a university. Langley overcame the lack of education beyond the high school level by his own efforts. As a youngster, Langley showed an abiding interest in astronomy and built a telescope for celestial observations. After graduation from high school in 1851 he worked as an engineer and architect in Boston until 1864. His interest in astronomy led him to visit the observatories and centers of learning in Europe. Upon his return he received an appointment as an assistant professor of mathematics at the United States Naval Academy in 1866. A year later he was placed in charge of the Allegheny Observatory at Western University of Pennsylvania, now the University of Pittsburgh. In addition, he was professor of physics and astronomy and retained this position for the next twenty years. In 1887 he became secretary of the Smithsonian Institution and served in that capacity until his death. He became a member of the National Academy of Sciences and was elected to membership in several foreign scientific societies. Also, he served as president of the American Association for the Advancement of Science.

One of Langley's most important contributions pertained to aerodynamics, the theory of flight. He began the study at Western University by constructing a whirling arm that attained speeds up to seventy miles per hour. With this device he measured the differences in air resistance on differently shaped bodies. He continued his experimentation after he went to the Smithsonian in 1887. As early as 1891 he believed that mechanical flight was possible with the power derived from existing engines. But, flight could not occur until an adequate power source was available. Langley was confident that he could build the proper frame if he could find an engine that was light in weight and could deliver enough power. He was unable to find such an engine in either Europe or America, and after exhausting all possibilities hired Charles M. Manly in 1899 to design a new lightweight engine. Langley had tried a number of launchings between 1894 and 1896 from a catapult on a barge on the Potomac River. Most of them failed but on May 6, 1896 Aerodrome Number 5 flew 3,200 feet on its first flight. In November a modified model, Number 6, flew 4,200 feet. These successes attracted the attention of the army and a fifty-thousand-dollar research grant from the Bureau of Ordance was awarded Langley for the construction of a larger machine in December of 1898. It was now possible to visualize a machine transporting a human being in the air and this device would have military consequences.

By 1901 Manly had developed an engine that weighed 187 pounds and developed fifty horsepower. In the meantime, a small, gasoline engine developing three horsepower flew one thousand feet on a model sized Aerodrome on August 8, 1903. The full-size model with a larger engine was ready for testing and on October 7 was launched. It was a total failure, falling into the Potomac River. Another attempt was made, with Manly again at the controls, on December 8 and again failure. Langley was severely criticized by the press for squandering public money on such harebrained schemes as trying to carry a man through space in a flying machine. Nine days after the second failure Orville Wright made the famous flight at Kitty Hawk, North Carolina, and Langley's work became a part of aviation history.

Regardless of the criticism, Langley brought aerodynamic research into the realm of scientific investigation. Though airplane development followed the pattern set by the Wrights, Langley's methods and beliefs were important factors in the history of flight. Langley believed that a faulty launching mechanism was the cause of failure. With the cutoff of government funding Langley ceased his investigations and died two years later.

Langley published technical articles including "Experiments in Aerodynamics" in 1891 and "The Internal Work of the Wind" in 1893. His most important contributions toward the Age of Flight were his scientific investigations and his unswerving belief that flight was possible.

Before concerning himself with aerodynamics Langley had carried out research in physics and astronomy. He recognized the need for an instrument to measure the amount of heat radiation received from the sun and invented the bolometer between 1879 and 1881. With the bolometer he could pursue three lines of study: 1) the selective absorption of the earth's atmosphere, 2) the selective absorption of the sun's atmosphere, and 3) a study of the solar constant. His studies on Mount Whitney in 1881 resulted in important new discoveries concerning the sun and the radiation received by the earth.

Langley's studies with the bolometer included an investigation of long wavelengths and measurements of spectra to five microns. He published "Researches on Solar Heat and Its Absorption by the Earth's Atmosphere" in 1884, but much of his work is to be found in *Langley Memoir on Flight* in 1911. Langley's name is appropriately commemorated in Langley Flying Field and associated laboratory. He founded the Smithsonian Astrophysical Observatory in 1890 and was instrumental in the creation of what became the National Gallery of Art as well as the National Zoological Park. He is remembered first for his scientific approach to the problem of heavier-than-air flight.

HWS

References: C. D. Walcott, "Biographical Memoir of Samuel Pierpont Langley," *Biographical Memoirs*, National Academy of Science, 7, Washington, D.C.: 1917, pp. 247-68; Cyrus Adler, "Samuel Pierpont Langley," *Bulletin of the Philosophical Society of Washington*, 15, 1907, pp. 1-26; Don F. Moyer, *Dictionary of Scientific Biography*, pp. 19-21 (New York: Scribner, 1973).

Ernest Orlando Lawrence

(August 8, 1901 — August 27, 1958)

Beginning with the discovery of fire, man has long struggled to harness the forces of nature for his own benefit. In the early stages of civilization each step toward progress was far apart and required many millennia to accomplish. As time went on the intervals between new discoveries became shorter and shorter until the latter part of the nineteenth century when a number of significant discoveries were made, culminating in atomic energy in the 1940s. Science has developed through accumulating information, each investigator contributing some small bit until the final solution is attained. But one of the striking facts of human history is that only a few great minds have led the way to progress. Only one human being in many millions has the ability to make a contribution that significantly advances civilization. Ernest Lawrence was such a man.

Lawrence received the Nobel Prize for physics in 1939 for inventing the cyclotron, an atom-smashing instrument that is one of the most useful of all tools in research. His work on the structure of the atom and his contributions to medicine and chemistry have identified him as possessing one of the great minds of history. During World War II he was a key figure in charge of the successful program for separating uranium-235 for the atomic bomb in the Manhattan Project. The Lawrence Livermore Laboratory at Livermore, California, and the Lawrence Berkeley Laboratory at Berkeley were named in his honor. Lawrence's cyclotron produced technetium, the first new element created by man, and another new element lawrencium (atomic number 103) was named to honor him.

Lawrence was born in Canton, South Dakota, into a family of teachers. His grandfather, father and mother all had been professionals in the field of education. His father, Carl Gustav Lawrence, of Norwegian ancestry, was a graduate of the University of Wisconsin and had held positions in education in South Dakota, including the presidency of a teacher's college. Lawrence's early family life was in a cultured environment supportive of education. He developed a strong sense of loyalty to his country and the work ethic of his South Dakota environment.

After attending St. Olaf College for a year, he transferred to the University of South Dakota, graduating in 1922 with high honors. He enrolled in the graduate program at the University of Minnesota under the direction of W. F. G. Swann, earning his master's degree on a research project involving the rotation of an ellipsoid in a magnetic field. The following year Swann went to the University of Chicago and in 1924 transferred to Yale. In each change Lawrence followed Swann, earning his Ph.D. at Yale in 1925 on a study of the photoelectric effect in potassium vapor. Both his master's and Ph.D. research projects were published in the *Philosophical Magazine*. At Chicago Lawrence met A. A. Michelson and Arthur Compton, two of the great investigators of the day.

From the beginning of his education Lawrence had always impressed his teachers with his originality. Thus, he was always encouraged to pursue excellence in research. After receiving his doctoral degree Lawrence remained at Yale as a fellow of the National Research Council for two years and one year as an assistant professor. He quickly gained a reputation as a superb researcher in the field of photoelectricity. In 1928 he accepted a position at the University of California at Berkeley. This appointment was part of a program that led to the establishment on the Berkeley campus of one of the all-time great departments of physics. It included not only Lawrence, but also J. R. Oppenheimer, R. B. Brode and Samuel Allison. Some of these men would lead the way to the new age of atomic energy.

While at Yale Lawrence met Mary Kimberly Blumer, daughter of the retired dean of the Yale Medical School. Her family belonged to the social elite of the community and Lawrence's frankness and open demeanor, so natural to the Midwest, took Molly some time to accept. By 1932 Lawrence had convinced her to marry him and come to his new home in Berkeley.

Lawrence's enthusiasm for research and labor quickly rubbed off on students at Berkeley. Curtis Haupt and Niels Edlefsen began research on photo-ionization. In early 1929 Lawrence was reading an article in *Archiv für Electrotechnik* by Rolf Wideröe describing the acceleration of potassium ions in a linear plane, a suggestion which had been made by the Swedish researcher G. Ising. Lawrence became immediately excited about the possibility of using a circular scheme for acceleration by introducing charged particles at the center and then forcing them into a circular path with a magnetic field. This concept resulted in the cyclotron, which made high acceleration possible. Progress from the first small cyclotron to larger and larger ones was only a matter of time; a 60-inch unit was in usage in 1939 and a 184-inch unit was completed by the end of the war. The cyclotron was a turning point in research in physics. One of the early applications of new knowledge was to the field of medicine, especially cancer research. Lawrence's brother John, a medical doctor, teamed up with him to supervise medical research. The Sloan-Lawrence X-ray machine in the San Francisco Hospital was used successfully to treat their mother in 1937.

Invention of the cyclotron made Lawrence famous immediately. He was invited to many other universities for lectures and asked by both industry and educational institutions for advice on building large cyclotrons. Cornell University, Michigan and Illinois were involved in construction. In addition foreign countries and institutions were interested; Paris, Copenhagen, Stockholm, Birmingham, Calcutta and Russia became involved and sought

Lawrence's advice. Job opportunities at other universities were available, but he declined to accept any. Honorary degrees were given from many universities, the first being the University of South Dakota, all leading to the Nobel Prize in 1939.

The Great Depression was an eventful period for Lawrence and the science of physics. World War II brought into focus the possibility of an atomic bomb, and all of the accomplishments of the 1930s were brought to bear upon the development of a nuclear weapon. One of the major problems was to discover a method of separating uranium 235 from uranium 238. Lawrence exerted all his energies between 1941 and 1945 toward this project. He used an electromagnetic process that became the prototype for similar models at Oak Ridge, Tennessee, and succeeded in producing uranium 235, which was used in the first bombs dropped on Japan. The electromagnetic technique was displaced by the gaseous diffusion process. The discovery of the fissionable properties of plutonium and the production of plutonium 239 owed much to Lawrence's scientific ability.

In July 1931, Lawrence succeeded in producing ions of 1 million volts with an accelerator only eleven inches in diameter. It was a momentous event in the history of science; he had developed a method of splitting atoms. The question now was how to build bigger and better cyclotrons. From the 11-inch model to the 27-inch, 37-inch, 60-inch and the 184-inch would take time and money. Lawrence was always dreaming of the next step while a given unit was under construction. When the cyclotron with a two thousand ton magnet was being constructed he was already planning one with a five thousand ton magnet; when a 1 million volt unit succeeded he was thinking in terms of creating a larger unit that would produce a 100 million. He wrote, "until we cross the frontier of a hundred million volts, we will not know what riches lie ahead, but that there are great riches there can be no doubt ... (we) may be able to tap the unlimited store of energy in the atom."

By 1941 research had progressed to such a point that President Roosevelt inquired as to the cost and feasibility of an "A-bomb." Lawrence took the positive approach, whereas most stressed the uncertainties. He wrote, "to my mind ... there is a substantial prospect that the chain reaction will be achieved ... and that military application of transcendental importance may follow." He made the first proposal for the creation of a bomb and a plan for carrying the project forward. The whole research program on the atom progressed to a point that Lawrence, on July 16, 1945, from an observation station near the Trinity test sight in New Mexico, nervously awaited the countdown when the first atomic explosion took place. The results exceeded all expectations; the destruction of Hiroshima and Nagasaki would soon follow. World War II would soon be over and though it might, in time, be forgotten, the power of the atom would be remembered forever. The cyclotron and Lawrence had left a permanent impact upon mankind.

Lawrence was proud to be an American and supported the war effort with all his energy and mental ability. But he could not imagine scientists in foreign countries supporting dictatorships. Though he was only one among many working on the perfection of the A-bomb, his contributions were critical. He supported the development of a thermonuclear bomb, whereas Oppenheimer opposed it. He was unable to agree with Oppenheimer's desire to unionize scientists and opposed even the suggestion. He believed in freedom of research as well as freedom of the individual. Freedom of research in his laboratories resulted in a host of Nobel Prize winners, including Alvarez, Chamberlain, McMillan, Seaborg and Segrè.

Lawrence was involved in many conferences dealing with atomic energy, for example, one on the peaceful uses of atomic energy, Atoms for Peace, the Geneva Conference of Experts to Study the Possibility of Detecting Violations of a Possible Agreement on Suspension of Nuclear Tests, and the Stanford University Nuclear Conference. He was elected to membership in most of the prestigious scientific societies and received numerous awards, both foreign and American. He was awarded, among others, the Medal of Merit (1946), the Fermi Award (1957), Comstock Prize of the National Academy of Sciences (1937), and Hughes Medal of the British Royal Society (1937). At least thirteen universities granted him honorary degrees. The Lawrence Berkeley Laboratory and the Lawrence Hall of Science commemorate his name. The trans-uranium element 103 was discovered at Berkeley and named *lawrencium*.

It was while attending the conference in Geneva that Lawrence became critically ill and was flown back to Palo Alto for surgery in August of 1958. He did not recover and the world lost one of its greatest intellects at an early age. He had changed the world in his laboratory in the 1930s as Edison had changed it in the late 1880s.

HWS

References: Roger H. Stuewer, *DAB*, Supplement 6, 1956-1960, pp. 369-72; Herbert Childs, *An American Genius* (New York: Dutton, 1968).

Charles Augustus Lindbergh, Jr.
(February 4, 1902 — August 26, 1974)

Charles A. Lindbergh was the most adored American hero of the twentieth century. Sports heroes, such as "Babe" Ruth, were admired by a special section of society and their fame was fleeting; movie actors were temporary heroes, worshipped by a fickle clientele; politicians were admired by some but hated by others, and the fame of military leaders was seldom accompanied by love. Lindbergh was universally admired. He was different. The world followed him on the front pages of the newspapers. He was the daring young man who alone conquered space, the "Lone-Eagle" who soared across the Atlantic without help from government or corporation. His was the indomitable spirit of the individual which overcame all odds. Every man of the 1920s could identify with him. When he referred to his airplane, *The Spirit of St. Louis*, he always used the word "we." The public identified with "we" to include all men.

Lindbergh's elevation to demigod was unique. After his time, corporation or government-organized groups conducted enterprises through team effort. The astronauts were admired for their feats but never received the individual devotion and acclaim accorded Lindbergh. Many men have performed feats of bravery before and since but their fame was temporary and often local. Many individuals have been explorers and adventurers, but the public did not elevate them to the mystical status accorded Lindbergh. He may well have been the last great hero, almost deified because of the solo nature of his accomplishment at a time when the world wanted a hero.

Lindbergh fitted all the requirements of a hero. He epitomized the individual who dared to venture forth to conquer the evil forces, whether they be dragons, armies, or the forces of nature. He challenged the unknown while his fellow man watched in the safety of his home and applauded Lindbergh's feats. He conquered the supernatural area of space where the evil forces of wind, ice, and loneliness challenge all men. He conceived the plan, went forth into the unknown, won the battle, and thereby bestowed his gifts of courage upon all when he returned. His fame attracted so much attention that Lindbergh went to great efforts to protect his privacy. But even his hatred of the press and publicity did not detract from the adoration extended to him; in fact, it seemed to increase the aura of mystery that surrounded his every movement. In time the invasion of his privacy would drive him temporarily from his country and indirectly cause a great family tragedy. The public wanted more from its hero than any man could give.

Lindbergh was born in Detroit, Michigan, but soon thereafter was brought to a farm near Little Falls, Minnesota. His father was a lawyer and was elected to Congress in 1906, serving from 1907-1917. He was later defeated for the Senate as well as the governorship of Minnesota. Lindbergh Jr. reflected his father's isolationist sentiments during World War II.

During his youth Lindbergh was interested in mechanical things such as automobiles, motorcycles and machinery. He completed his formal education after two years of study at the University of Wisconsin and in 1922 entered the Nebraska Aircraft Corporation flying school at Lincoln, Nebraska. After a few months of instruction he participated in stunt flying, barnstorming and parachute jumping. Flying was now a way of life and he required more experience. He became a flying cadet at Brooks Field, Texas, earning his first commission as second lieutenant in 1925. A year later he was flying the airmail route between Chicago and St. Louis. He reported that during one of these airmail trips he conceived the plan of a trans-Atlantic flight. The motivation was a twenty-five thousand dollar prize offered by Raymond B. Orteig to the first person to complete a nonstop flight between Paris and New York.

Lindbergh's year in the Air Service Reserve had made him a professional flier. He had worked hard to make himself an excellent pilot. The air service had given him discipline and prepared him to approach all flying problems in a methodical manner. When he first considered the flight from New York to Paris, it was only natural that he would weigh the pros and cons of success. Success would depend upon several factors, but the most important was the load of gasoline a plane could carry. Lindbergh decided to sacrifice everything possible to permit additional fuel. These included safety devices, hot lunches, cabin appointments, and multiple radios. But the most startling idea in Lindbergh's mind was the possibility of using only one motor and one pilot. A solo flight appealed to his imagination. This would reduce the load and allow for added fuel. Also, he liked the idea of being alone. But could one man stay awake for forty hours and fly a plane? He believed it could be done. He tersely listed the possibilities, "1. Successful completion, winning $25,000..., 2. Complete failure." There were no alternatives. With these decisions in mind he approached financial backers in St. Louis and sold them on the idea of advertising the city as an aviation center. He purchased a Ryan monoplane with a single air-cooled nine-cylinder engine and named it *The Spirit of St. Louis.* He left the San Diego, California factory on May 10, 1927, and flew to New York via St. Louis, arriving on May 12. It took him twenty-one hours and twenty minutes, a new transcontinental record.

The race to be the first to span the Atlantic was hectic in 1927. Commander Noel Davis and copilot Stanton Wooster in the *American Legion* crashed and died on April 10. Admiral Richard Byrd with his pilot Floyd Bennett crashed in the plane *America* on April 16, both suffering injuries. Charles Nungesser and Francois Coli left Paris for New York on May 8 in the *White Bird* and were lost at sea. Clarence Chamberlain was standing by to take off in the *Columbia.* While these tragic affairs were taking place, Lindbergh was preparing *The Spirit of St. Louis* for departure. All other planned and previously attempted flights had been manned by crews of two or more. Lindbergh's plan to fly alone captured the attention of the public; was he foolish or brave? Could a "Lone Eagle" conquer the Atlantic? At 7:52 in the morning of May 20 *The Spirit of St. Louis* slowly and laboriously rose from the runway at Roosevelt Field, Long Island, just clearing telephone wires, as he started for Paris.

The 3,610 mile journey to Paris was accomplished in thirty-three hours, twenty-nine minutes and thirty seconds. A turning point in human transportation had been reached. International communication and travel henceforth would become commonplace. Access to all parts of the world was soon to become available to most people within a few hours travel time. Lindbergh described his achievement in the book *We* and later in another book *The Spirit of St. Louis.* His accomplishment was hailed by many people, and governments honored him with receptions and awards. America awarded him the Distinguished Flying Cross, France conferred upon him the decoration chevalier of the Legion of Honor, Belgium gave him the Order of Leopold, and Great Britain honored him with the Royal Air Cross. Many other awards included the Congressional Medal of Honor and the Langley Medal. After returning to the United States from Paris he took *The Spirit of St. Louis* on a tour of seventy-five American cities. At all places he supported the development of commercial aviation.

In 1927 he was invited by President Plutarco Calles to visit Mexico. Here, he met Anne Morrow, the daughter of Ambassador Dwight W. Morrow, and married her on May 29, 1929. Anne attained distinction as a popular writer. Her work shows a sensitivity to the problems of being a woman. She often uses objects of nature as symbols to create images to convey her thoughts, both in essay and poetic form. *Gifts from the Sea* (1955) concerns the married woman's search for identity. *The Unicorn and Other Poems* (1956), *Dearly Beloved* (1962) and the five volumes of letters and diaries show her to be a sensitive person determined to establish her identity, even though she was the wife of America's most famous hero. Three years later, tragedy struck when their first son, Charles A. Lindbergh III, was kidnapped. Bruno Richard Hauptmann was found guilty of the crime and executed in April 1936.

Lindbergh had always been a person jealous of his privacy. He was unostentatious and the invasion of his life by the media was a traumatic experience. The more he tried to live a normal life and avoid the press, the more mysterious he appeared to the public. The kidnapping of his son and the publicity during the subsequent Hauptmann trial became unbearable. He took his family first to England and then to France where he collaborated with Dr. Alexis Carrel in scientific experiments, later published in the book *Culture of Organs* in 1938.

While in Europe Lindbergh studied the air power of France, England, Russia and Germany. Hermann Goering invited him to inspect the German air fleet and hung upon his chest the Silver Cross, the six-pointed silver star. Lindbergh's report on the strength of the German air force was in general ridiculed. This was the beginning of his opposition to World War II, and upon his return to America in 1939 he joined the America First Committee and publicly opposed America's entry into the war. This aroused the wrath of President Roosevelt and resulted in Lindbergh resigning his commission as colonel in the reserve. His radio talks and published comments aroused mixed feelings. He was accused by some as being in sympathy with nazism; by others he was acclaimed as a loyal American hero. He understood, better than most, the strength of German air power and the weakness of the French and English.

When America entered the war, his services were refused by the War Department. Henry Ford engaged him as a consultant at Willow Run. Later he worked for the United Aircraft Company improving the Corsair, a navy fighter. After Pearl Harbor, Lindbergh went to the Pacific theater and flew more than fifty missions. Subsequently he worked with a United States navy commission which studied the development of German air power, especially jet engines, missiles and rockets. He always believed that the war in Europe could have been prevented and that we should have remained on the sidelines "while Nazi Germany and Communist Russia fought out their totalitarian ideas."

In the postwar years Lindbergh contributed, often without pay, to the improvement of aircraft. He flew to many bases and pioneered many new air lanes. His isolationist position as to World War II reduced his image from national hero and demigod to that of a normal mortal man. One of the positive effects of this change was that his privacy was no longer invaded; the last great hero could live his life in peace.

In addition to honors conferred upon him by governments he received academic degrees from New York, Northwestern, Princeton, and the University of Wisconsin. President Dwight D. Eisenhower appointed him brigadier general in the Air Force Reserve in 1954. Honored, feted, loved and adored by millions, yet troubled and misunderstood during the war, Lindbergh continued to contribute to the development of aviation until his death at his home at Maui, Hawaii.

HWS

References: Kenneth S. Davis, *The Hero* (New York: Doubleday, 1959); Walter S. Ross, *The Last Hero* (New York: Harper & Row, 1964).

Jack London

(January 12, 1876—November 22, 1916)

One of the most widely read American writers of the twentieth century, Jack London tried many occupations in his strenuous early life, endured poverty and ill health, and was an ordinary seaman on the Pacific Ocean and a miner in the Klondike before he established himself as a successful professional author. His tales of maritime brutality and savagery in the Yukon territory during the gold rush won him instant popularity while his conversion to socialism and his partial acceptance of Marxism created a demand for translations of his books in Russia and China. He was also extremely prolific and in a period of sixteen years produced over forty volumes, mostly fiction but also including essays and autobiography.

London was born in San Francisco, presumably the illegitimate son of an itinerant astrologer. He was brought up in the family of John London, a nomadic pioneer who lived on the Oakland waterfront. He finished grammar school in Oakland but had only desultory education, supplemented by voracious reading. Thereafter his education consisted of a few months in high school, about a year at the University of California in Berkeley. Family poverty required him to work at what jobs he could find: a newspaper boy, a pin setter in a bowling alley, the driver of an ice wagon, a cannery worker. Life on the waterfront fascinated him and he early developed a longing to go to sea. He owned a skiff in the harbor as a youth, became an oyster pirate briefly, served as a fish patrol deputy, tried the life of a hobo, and in 1893 joined the crew of the *Sophie Sutherland*, a sealer bound for operations off the coast of Siberia. Back in California he continued his extensive reading and began to try his hand at writing. Vigorous cramming enabled him to pass the college entrance examinations, but he dropped out of school when he heard of the discovery of gold in Alaska and joined the Klondike rush in 1897. He survived one winter but contracted scurvy and the next year he returned to California.

The acceptance by the *Overland Monthly*, a regional periodical published in San Francisco, of the story entitled "To the Man on the Trail," in 1898, inaugurated London's writing career. The same magazine accepted eight stories in 1899, and in January 1900 the *Atlantic Monthly* published "An Odyssey of the North." London's first collection of stories, *The Son of the Wolf*, was issued by Houghton Mifflin also in 1900. In the next four years London averaged about twenty-four periodical contributions annually: short stories, serials, essays, articles, and verse. Most of the fiction dealt with his experiences in the Klondike. His most famous book, *The Call of the Wild*, published in 1903, has been widely reprinted.

In 1900 London married Elizabeth Maddern, a marriage which ended in divorce in 1905. London went to England in 1902 and lived for some time in the city's East End. His observations of the life in the slums and his sympathy with the residents brought about his book *The People of the Abyss* in 1903. After his divorce he married Charmian Kittredge, who became his travel companion and eventually his biographer. She accompanied him on a cruise aboard the forty-five foot yacht called the *Snark*, which he intended to sail around the world, but the journey ended after the couple reached Australia where London became ill. Adventures on the cruise produced the book *The Cruise of the Snark* (1911).

The popularity of his writing brought London affluence and recognition. He made lecture tours, went on other sailing voyages, and became a war correspondent to report the Russo-Japanese War for the *San Francisco Examiner*. He eventually bought a patriarchal estate in California where he spent the remainder of his short life. He committed suicide in 1916.

London frequently used his own life as a pattern for his fiction. Thus *Martin Eden* (1909) deals with a writer who struggles for recognition, achieves it, but is disillusioned with the empty ideals of the social class to which he had aspired. *John Barleycorn* (1913) becomes a temperance tract and reflects the struggle which its author once had with the temptations of drink.

His most durable works are solidly built on his observation of primitive and sometimes brutal life in the Klondike or on the open sea. *The Call of the Wild*, which has been praised as the best dog story ever written, deals with canine retrogression to savagery. Buck, originally a domestic dog, is taken to Alaska, becomes a sledge dog, and when the master to whom he has become devoted is murdered, reverts to being the leader of a wolf pack. On the other hand, in *White Fang*, 1906, the dog hero has lupine blood and is goaded into savagery but is eventually domesticated by his mining engineer owner and is removed to California. Yukon stories which do not focus on animals include *Burning Daylight* (1910) and *Smoke Bellew* (1912), both of them concerned with human adventures in the Alaskan wilderness. London's most powerful novel with an ocean setting is *The Sea Wolf*, 1904, a story much indebted to the author's own early adventures. But the ruthless captain, Wolf Larsen, is contrasted almost too obviously with the hypercivilized Van Weyden, and the episode of the man and the woman finding refuge on a deserted island seems too contrived.

Several of London's many short stories have been widely anthologized and won an immediate audience because of the author's firsthand knowledge of background and activities about which his readers knew nothing. This situation explains the impact of tales like "To the Man on Trail," as well as "An Odyssey of the North," a powerful account of an Indian's revenge. Best known probably is "To Build a Fire," which appeared in the collection entitled *Lost Face*, 1910. Readers cannot quickly forget this tale about a newcomer to the arctic who faces almost immediate death from the cold if he is unable to start a fire. When the last match fails there is no hope.

A writer who produced almost fifty books in sixteen years cannot always have been at his best, and London despite his sureness of touch in describing scenes and characters that he knew intimately was often guilty of haste and clumsiness. Moreover, when he left the Yukon behind him he chose themes and regions which his readers found more familiar and therefore less interesting. Nevertheless, his vigorous narratives sustain readership, and although there is no collected edition of London's works, individual titles have been often reprinted. In late years critical writing about London has increased and a number of special studies have appeared. London's debts to Rudyard Kipling, Charles Dickens, and even Herman Melville have been explored.

JTF

References: T. K. Whipple, *DAB*, XI, 1933, pp. 370-71; Charmian (Kittredge) London, *The Book of Jack London*, 2 vols. (New York: Century, 1921); Irving

Stone, *Sailor on Horseback: The Biography of Jack London* (Boston: Houghton Mifflin, 1938); Franklin Walker, *Jack London and the Klondike* (San Marino, Calif.: Huntington Library, 1966); Charles N. Watson, Jr., *The Novels of Jack London: A Reappraisal* (Madison: University of Wisconsin Press, 1983).

Stephen Harriman Long

(December 30, 1784—December 30, 1864)

When President Thomas Jefferson authorized the Lewis and Clark expedition, he set a precedent of government-supported, organized exploration of the West. During the first two decades of the 1800s America concluded treaties with France, Great Britain and Spain that added vast territories to the young nation. The United States now extended from the Atlantic to the Pacific, the northern boundary dispute had been resolved, and Florida had been added to the realm. Pioneers were flooding into new states and territories east of the Mississippi and a few, like Daniel Boone, found Kentucky too crowded as early as 1799 and migrated to Missouri. The Indians were being pushed out of Ohio, Indiana, Illinois, and Wisconsin and their villages were being replaced by cities such as Cincinnati. The primeval forest and the broad prairies were overrun by the expanding population moving rapidly westward.

American political leadership recognized the need for information concerning lands west of the Mississippi. Maps were needed which would aid in determining the best routes of travel. Information concerning soils was necessary for the new farmer and knowledge of the botany, geology and zoology was mostly lacking. Where were the streams, the water supplies, the forests and prairies and the minerals? These were vital questions that needed answers for the welfare of an expanding nation. Also, certain military and political goals were involved in exploring the West. Information was needed concerning the Indians, their number and distribution, as well as their attitudes toward the people who were rapidly overwhelming them. But above all it was necessary to establish American presence and counter any foreign influence in the newly acquired lands.

It fell to the lot of Stephen Long, a young professional engineer, to lead government-organized expeditions to explore the West between 1816 and 1823. Historians have both criticized and lauded Long's three journeys. Criticisms have been leveled at what by some have been seen as poor planning and leadership as well as failure to reach the source of the Red River and Long's description of the Great Plains as "The Great American Desert." However, as explorers the Long parties collected much scientific data that became a permanent part of American scientific knowledge. In addition, the expeditions were politically successful, establishing the American presence in new territories and enabling the army to determine the most desirable sites for defense. The area from the Canadian boundary in Minnesota to the front range of Colorado south to the Texas Panhandle and east to Arkansas was covered during the three expeditions. At that time the American pioneer was avidly interested in any information about the West. The geographic gazetteers were popular sources of information. Long opened up unknown areas for settlement and trade and helped to secure the new frontier.

Long was born in Hopkinton, New Hampshire, the son of Moses and Lucy Long. He was one of thirteen children and his father, a barrel maker, could afford no family luxuries. His educational process was slow, but he managed to be accepted to Dartmouth College at the age of twenty-one. He was a superior student and was elected to Phi Beta Kappa in 1808. After graduation he was involved in teaching in public schools in New Hampshire and Germantown, Pennsylvania. Stephen was an excellent mathematician and became interested in surveying. This work attracted the attention of the Army Corps of Engineers and on February 16, 1815, he was offered a commission as second lieutenant. He accepted and thus began a lifelong career as a professional engineer.

With the conclusion of the War of 1812 the army was cutting its personnel, but at precisely this time Long accepted his commission and was assigned as a teacher of mathematics at West Point. At the time, acquisition of an engineering education was difficult; American students still relied upon European universities for technical education. Long was essentially a self-taught mathematician except for elementary studies. Within a year he transferred to the Topographical Engineers, a division of the Army Corps of Engineers. The Army Engineers were involved at an early date giving attention to civilian needs such as making rivers navigable.

Long was designated leader of three expeditions, 1) the 1816-1817 investigation of the Mississippi Valley frontier forts, 2) the 1819-1820 trip to Colorado and the Southwest, and 3) the northern journey up the Mississippi to the 49th parallel and east along the Great Lakes. The first of these expeditions was authorized by the secretary of war, William Crawford. The second and third journeys were authorized by John C. Calhoun during the Monroe administration.

Long had been in service with the engineers for only a year when he was ordered to report in 1816 to Prairie du Chien. He was to plan a new fort and then investigate the topography of the Mississippi Valley southward to St. Louis. However, he reported to the military post of Belle Fontaine near St. Louis, and from there was assigned the task of investigating the valley of the Illinois River between St. Louis and Chicago. He rejected Fort Clark, situated on Lake Peoria, as ill-suited for defense but noted the connection of the Illinois River through its tributaries to Lake Michigan and recommended connecting them with a canal. While at Fort Clark he noted the presence of timber, coal and brick. A second trip took him through central Illinois and northern Indiana and back to Washington where he reported on his findings in the Illinois country. The following year (1817) he returned to Belle Fontaine from which base he explored the northern portion of the Mississippi as far north as St. Anthony Falls. He examined the condition of the forts on the upper Mississippi and upon return to Belle Fontaine was ordered to go down the Mississippi to the Arkansas River and proceed up that river to choose a fort site, later to be named Fort Smith. This concluded his investigation of the Mississippi Valley area. The frontier was moving westward, and new forts were needed to protect the expanding population. The Mississippi River was no longer a political or physical barrier. British fur traders and nomadic Indians were still active in the plains region. Long began to urge the investigation of the Missouri, Platte and Arkansas rivers. He proposed that the Missouri be explored by using a shallow-draft boat. John

Calhoun agreed because it was his policy to protect the frontier, control the Indians, and expand the fur trade.

The second expedition (1819-1820) began with the construction of the *Western Engineer*, the watercraft which he hoped would carry his crew up the Missouri. It was reported to draw only two and one-half feet of water and was powered by sails and paddle wheels placed in the stern. Long spent the winter months collecting a crew including scientists. He enlisted the services of Thomas Say, one of the best known zoologists of the time. Say had published the first volume of *American Entomology* (1817) and was one of the notable men who made their home at New Harmony, Indiana. Other scientists included William Baldwin, doctor and botanist, and Augustus E. Jessup, mineralogist. When the *Western Engineer* left Pittsburgh in May 1819, it carried a qualified crew for the purpose of exploring the Missouri and its principal tributaries, as well as the Red and Arkansas Rivers. After a slow trip to St. Louis, Long left on June 21 for the Missouri. Progress against the current of the Missouri was difficult: floating logs, sandbars, the silt-laden muddy water and lack of engine power combined to frustrate all concerned. The *Western Engineer* progressed up the Platte River to a point near Council Bluffs where winter quarters were established. Baldwin died and Jessup left the group. A new crew was organized for continuation of the expedition in 1820. The new group proceeded up the Platte and crossed into northeastern Colorado, gaining their first sight of the Rocky Mountains on June 30. What they first saw is now known as Long's Peak. They moved slowly southward until they reached Pike's Peak where a three-day halt was called while four members of the party made the first ascent of the mountain. Long named it James Peak on his map in honor of the leader of the party, but the name was never accepted. Their journey continued down the Arkansas River with part of the party crossing to the Red River in the Texas Panhandle and rejoining at Fort Smith on September 13.

Long's group had experienced many hardships: lack of food, illness, lack of adequate sleeping facilities, desertions of three soldiers, poor equipment, and the unsatisfactory operation of the *Western Engineer*. Long has been criticized for these shortcomings. Even his failure to reach the source of the Red River has been cited as incompetence. However, all expeditions into unknown territory are subject to hardships. His men, other than the three deserters, expressed their desire to accompany him on other exploration journeys. Critics were primarily armchair writers who were not familiar with the problems of travel into the unknown. In retrospect the trip was a scientific and geographic success. It served its purpose in making the American presence known to the Indians and in its scientific accomplishments, especially in the fields of botany, geology, geography and zoology.

Long's last expedition was conducted in 1823 and extended up the Mississippi River to its source and as far north as Lake of the Woods and Fort Alexander in Canada. The return route was along Lake Superior through Lake Huron to Lake Erie and concluded at Rochester, New York. The Convention of 1818 had established the northern boundary as a line along the 49th parallel and north to the Lake of the Woods. As Long's western expedition had been considered a success, he was chosen to explore the area along the new international boundary.

After completing his exploration ventures Long remained with the Corps of Engineers until his retirement in 1863. He was active in the development of the railroad era as a consulting engineer. He served the Baltimore & Ohio Railroad Company, the Atlantic & Great Western, and a number of other companies in selecting routes and in engineering matters. He contributed to bridge construction, obtaining a patent (1836) on bridge bracing.

Long died in Alton, Illinois, and was survived by his wife, Martha Hodgkins. His life had spanned the era of time between the War of 1812 and the Civil War. He had played an important part in one of America's most important periods of expansion, the winning of the West.

HWS

References: Richard G. Wood, *Stephen Harriman Long, 1784-1864* (Glendale, Calif.: Arthur H. Clark Company, 1966); Roger L. Nichols and Patrick L. Halley, *Stephen Long and American Exploration* (Newark: University of Delaware Press, 1980).

Samuel Sidney McClure
(February 17, 1857—March 21, 1949)

One of America's most colorful and controversial journalists, Samuel Sidney McClure, was a native of Ireland. His father was killed in a shipyard accident, after which the mother and four sons immigrated to Indiana. Samuel was then nine years of age. The family battled poverty on a farm near Valparaiso. At his mother's urging, Samuel attended a new high school in Valparaiso, worked for his keep, and then enrolled in Knox College's preparatory department.

As a student at Knox, Samuel began to show journalistic talent, served as editor of the *Knox Student*, began to issue an intercollegiate news bulletin, and formed the Western College Associated Press, with himself as president. Following graduation, he moved to Boston and was employed by a bicycle manufacturer. A new magazine, *The Wheelman*, catering to the increasingly popular bicycle craze, was launched and edited by McClure.

The next steps in McClure's publishing career occurred when he left the bicycle firm and moved to New York to join the DeVinne printing company, and then the Century Company's dictionary office. As a result of disagreements with the management, McClure lost the Century job. Undaunted, he proceeded to develop one of the first literary syndicates. The plan, which was already used in England, was to circulate a flow of novels, stories, and other literary material by well-known authors to subscribing newspapers.

By 1887, the syndicate was well established. McClure took a number of trips abroad to enter into contracts with noted foreign authors. He succeeded in obtaining signed agreements with Stevenson, Kipling, Doyle, Meredith, Edmund Gosse, Hardy, H. Rider Haggard, Ruskin, Swinburne, Zola, Harte, Henry James, Whitman, Julia Ward Howe, Stephen Crane, Hamlin Garland, Joel Chandler Harris, O. Henry, Jack London, Gertrude Atherton, Booth Tarkington, and many others. McClure's biographer, Peter Lyon, concluded that the effect of the literary syndicate was to change the character of journalism and of

American fiction by getting fiction into the largest newspapers and stimulating creative writing.

McClure's next major enterprise, *McClure's Magazine*, started in 1893, blazed new trails. Its price, of fifteen cents a copy, undercut the *Century* and other magazines of its class. The future was precarious, however, until *McClure's* published Ida M. Tarbell's biography of Napoleon, which proved to be extremely popular. Even more successful was Tarbell's series on Abraham Lincoln. All through the 1890s, the magazine offered new works by famous authors who had been circulated by the syndicate. By 1900, the magazine had four hundred thousand subscribers.

An even more spectacular hit was made by a series of muckraking articles, starting with the January 1903 number. The first major exposé of the corruption existing behind the facade of representative government in American cities was the work of Lincoln Steffens, who had been tagged by Theodore Roosevelt, along with Ida Tarbell, Ray Stannard Baker, and others, as a "muckraker." Actually, other writers had preceded them as muckrakers, notably Mark Sullivan on Pennsylvania's morals, Finley Peter Dunne (speaking through "Mr. Dooley") on trusts and government, Ernest Poole on slum conditions, Frank Norris on railroads and stock exchanges, and David Graham Phillips on social and ethical problems.

In any case, the January 1903 issue of *McClure's* presented contributions by three of the principal muckrakers: Lincoln Steffens' sensational article "The Shame of Minneapolis," an installment of Ida Tarbell's history of the Standard Oil Company, and Ray Stannard Baker's "The Right to Work." Having discovered this rich vein, McClure continued to mine it. Issue after issue of the magazine exposed scandals, and other periodicals followed its lead. Over the next several years the reading public learned about corruption in local, state, and national governments, industrial management, race relations, railroads, insurance, patent medicines, liquor and white slave traffic, slum housing, food and drugs, child labor, stock and money markets, poverty, unemployment, the judicial system, and the press.

Disagreements between McClure and some of his writers caused him to lose several of his stars — Tarbell, Phillips, Baker, and Steffens — to the new *American Magazine*. The popularity of *McClure's* declined, and it was eventually bought by Hearst's International Publications.

Other undertakings by McClure included the establishment in 1899, with John H. Phillips of the publishing house of McClure, Phillips and Company, later sold to Doubleday, Page and Company. McClure retired in 1914, but returned a year later to edit the New York *Evening Mail* for a short time.

McClure joined the idealists on Henry Ford's 1915 Peace Ship, but soon left the group. After the First World War, he became an admirer of Mussolini and was enthusiastic about some of fascism's accomplishments, such as making trains run on time. He appears to have ended up in poverty, with friends and relatives paying his bills. At age ninety-three, he died of a heart attack while living in a New York hotel, and was buried in Galesburg, Illinois, the site of his alma mater, Knox College.

RBD

Reference: Peter Lyon, *Success Story: The Life and Times of S. S. McClure* (Deland, Fla.: Everett/Edwards, 1967).

Edward MacDowell

(December 18, 1861 — January 23, 1908)

There were not many American composers of serious music in the nineteenth century. Among them was Edward MacDowell, a musician who stood head and shoulder above all others. Some critics have called him America's greatest composer. Most list him among the best this country has produced in any era. His music was a reflection of nature. He interpreted the moods of the environment, the rain and the wind, the fields and the mountains and the seas and rivers. MacDowell was a musical genius in tune with the world around him. He has been compared with Grieg, and his piano sonatas have been compared favorably with Beethoven's music.

MacDowell was born in New York City, the son of Thomas and Frances MacDowell. His Scotch-Irish parents recognized his musical talents at an early age and gave him every advantage to develop his natural musical ability. He started piano lessons at age eight and was recognized by his teachers as musically gifted. His mother took him to Paris when he was fifteen to study with Marmontel at the Paris Conservatoire. After two years at the Conservatoire he felt the need of a new challenge to the learning process. He went to Germany, first to the Stuttgart Conservatory and then to the Frankfurt Conservatory where he studied composition under Joachim Raff and piano with Karl Heymann. Raff recognized the talents of his pupil and through his encouragement MacDowell became a composer.

By age nineteen MacDowell had developed into a confident trained musician. He began giving private piano lessons to German students but, what was more important, under Raff's prodding, he began to compose. After composing the "First Modern Suite," the "Second Modern Suite," and a piano concerto, Raff introduced him to Liszt. With Liszt's recommendation the "First Modern Suite" was played by MacDowell in 1882 at the concert of the Allgemeiner Musikverein. The "Suite" and concerto were published in Germany. He was the first American to receive a favorable reception in European musical circles.

On a short trip to America in 1884 MacDowell married Marian Nevins, a former pupil. They returned to Germany where MacDowell started composing his second concerto. After a short stay at Frankfurt they moved to Wiesbaden. During this period he composed "Hamlet and Ophelia" in 1885, "Lancelot and Elaine" (1888), "Lamia" (1889), the "Saracens and the Lovely Alda" (1891), and completed the second concerto. These compositions consolidated his position in Europe as one of the leading composers of his day.

Raff's death, followed by Liszt's in 1886, probably influenced MacDowell to return to America as a permanent resident in 1888. He and Marian moved to Boston where, for the next eight years, he performed as a concert pianist, teacher and composer. In order to get his music before the public it was necessary for him to play his own compositions. He became accepted as an outstanding composer of serious music and his studio was crowded with students. In spite of his shyness he became a well-known figure in Boston and expanded his acquaintances through concert tours. In this manner he became known as "MacDowell the composer."

MacDowell was, by far, the best-known American composer of serious music in the nineteenth century. He had achieved recognition in Europe and was widely known in his own country. Though he was influenced by the European romantic school he was a postromanticist expressing his individuality. He always opposed the development of an American form of music based on Indian and Negro folklore, yet some of his own compositions are based on his American experience. He was essentially a poet reflecting his own environment in his music. He makes use of Indian themes in his second suite "Indian" by using melodies from the Iroquois and Iowa tribes.

However, MacDowell did not create a new trend in music. He looked backward and represents the closing phase of an old era. Nevertheless, his works were so highly regarded that the Boston Symphony played them as soon as they were completed. He composed all of his works between 1880 and 1902. They include sixteen compositions for the piano, two orchestral suites, two concertos, four sonatas, sixty-two songs for voice, and four symphonic poems. His Scottish background was expressed in Celtic themes but many were in the tradition of Liszt and Wagner where rich harmony was required. MacDowell considered himself a tone-poet whereby he explored landscapes and seascapes, medieval romances, childhood memories, and legends. The best of his orchestral works is the "Indian Suite," Opus 48. It consists of five movements, 1) "Legend," 2) "Love Song," 3) "In War Time," 4) "Dirge," and 5) "Festival." MacDowell considered the "Dirge" as his most beautiful orchestral music. It was based upon a mournful chant of a Kiowa Indian woman lamenting the death of a son. It is somewhat ironic that MacDowell did not believe in establishing an American form of music based upon ancient ethnic cultures yet based some of his most beautiful compositions on Indian chants. Most of MacDowell's compositions were short musical reveries. He believed that the mission of a musician was the same as that of the poet. He remarked that music "is a language ... a kind of soul language" and he attempted to express in music the emotions and visions created by the successful poet. Shakespeare inspired his "Hamlet and Ophelia," but he composed most of his own poems to accompany his music.

His reputation was such that when Columbia University offered him the Robert Center Chair of Music in 1896, he was referred to as "the greatest musical genius America has produced." MacDowell accepted the offer, hoping that he could create an integrated department of music combining all the fine arts. Unfortunately, as time would tell, it was an unhappy relationship. Though the university obtained the services of America's premiere composer and MacDowell attained security and additional prestige, friction ultimately developed. MacDowell was a temperamental artist and did not possess the talents necessary for university administration. After a few years of teaching harmony and composition he proposed the creation of a major university music department. Nicholas Murray Butler, president of the university, had his own ideas of how to build a great university. Butler's concepts did not coincide with MacDowell's and the latter was unable to adjust to the failure of his own plans. In January 1904, MacDowell, tense and nervous, told President Butler that he was resigning. Butler announced that the resignation was a result of MacDowell's desire to have more time for composing. MacDowell answered that he was leaving because he saw no chance to create a new department. This set off a public controversy between Butler and MacDowell.

MacDowell became moody and was unable to regain his mental stability. He brooded over the affair until he lost all comprehension, and after a three-year period died in the Westminister Hotel in New York. Marian MacDowell devoted the remaining forty-eight years of her life to building support for the MacDowell Colony at Peterboro, New Hampshire. The colony was a meeting place where artists and composers could work in quiet and profit from the contacts with each other. It was here that MacDowell had composed his "Fireside Tales" (1902), "New England Idyls" (1902), and "Sea Pieces" (1898). The years 1889 to 1902 had been MacDowell's golden years of composition. His career began with his first composition in Germany under the encouragement of Raff and Liszt and continued through his early years at Columbia. His mental depression, starting in 1904 and resulting in his death at age forty-seven, cut short the career of America's first great composer of serious music.

HWS

References: John Tasker Howard, *Our American Music* (New York: Crowell; 3rd ed. 1954); Gilbert Chase, *America's Music, from the Pilgrims to the Present* (New York, Toronto and London: McGraw-Hill, 1955).

Edgar Lee Masters
(August 23, 1868 — March 7, 1950)

No American poet of the twentieth century was more prolific or more versatile than Edgar Lee Masters. And no American poet of the period produced a single book of verse which had wider readership, greater celebrity, or more numerous editions than the *Spoon River Anthology*. During his lifetime Masters published some fifty books, including numerous volumes of verse, verse drama, four biographies (one of which dealt with Abraham Lincoln), a remarkably candid autobiography, miscellaneous volumes dealing with history and travel, legal or business tomes, and seven novels. The *Spoon River Anthology*, which appeared in 1915 after many of the individual poems had been published in a St. Louis magazine, stimulated critical discussion for at least a decade and attracted more attention than any American book of verse since Whitman's *Leaves of Grass*. But Masters never repeated his first great success and although in later years he produced commendable verse and prose his reputation gradually waned. He was never a rigorous self-critic, and when toward the end of his life depleted finances drove him to write it would have been more prudent for him to remain silent.

Masters is usually associated with Illinois but though he did spend much of his early life in the Lincoln country and in Chicago, he was actually born in Garnett, Kansas, August 23, 1868. His father, Hardin Masters, was a lawyer and a liberal Democrat in a conservative Republican area. His mother, born Emma Dexter, was the daughter of an itinerant Methodist minister; she had musical and bookish tastes and disliked her husband's advocacy of saloons. Shortly after the son's birth the family moved to Illinois and Masters spent his boyhood in the

Sangamon River valley, notably in such towns as Petersburg and Lewistown. He also visited frequently the farm of his paternal grandparents and when it came time to include portraits of local figures in his poetry he used them as models. One of his best known characterizations is Lucinda Matlock, the name he gave to his idealized grandmother in the *Spoon River Anthology*.

After the usual public school education, which was considerably amplified by experiences with the local newspapers and by extensive reading in classical literature, Masters enrolled at Knox College in Galesburg. He remained only one year, devoting much time to German and Greek and in deference to his father's wishes preparing to study law. In 1892 he finished his formal education and moved to Chicago where various menial jobs supported him until he became familiar with the city and could establish himself in a profession. He worked for a time as a collector for the Edison Company and of necessity familiarized himself with taverns, bars, and roominghouses. He also met Chicago newspapermen like Ernest McGaffey and Opie Read and often contributed verse under a pseudonym to the local dailies. By 1893 he had learned enough law to join another legal neophyte in practice, and for the next quarter of a century Masters was a Chicago attorney. He became quite adept in cross-examination and soon won a reputation for supporting the rights of labor and the underdog. Toward the end of his Chicago residence he was a partner of Clarence Darrow.

Despite some success as a lawyer Masters never abandoned his desire to write and in the next dozen years he published ten volumes of verse and plays, some of which he subsidized himself. He also made the acquaintance of Harriet Monroe, who in 1912 had begun to edit *Poetry*, a magazine of verse. But the year 1914 was crucial. Using the pseudonym of Webster Ford he began to contribute verse portraits to the *St. Louis Mirror*, edited by William Marion Reedy. Reedy not only welcomed these often satiric epitaphs but identified their author in the issue of November 20. Masters had chosen not to acknowledge his authorship out of fear that the publicity might jeopardize his law practice. When the Spoon River sketches were collected in a book and published by the Macmillan Company in 1915 he made his decision to give up the law for literature. Subsequently he left Chicago for permanent residence in New York and for many years his home was the Hotel Chelsea on West Twenty-third Street.

Nine years after the appearance of the *Spoon River Anthology* he published a sequel, the *New Spoon River*, in which he retained the original format but added figures to represent some occupations which had not existed in an earlier time. But in the interval Masters was certainly not idle. Three books of miscellaneous lyrics and short poems appeared in rapid succession, *Songs and Satires* and *The Great Valley*, both in 1916, and *Toward the Gulf*, two years later. His first novel, *Mitch Miller*, a kind of rough imitation of Mark Twain, was published in 1920 and his *Domesday Book* in the same year. The latter work is a long narrative poem in blank verse focusing on the discovery of the body of a girl Elenor Murray on the shore of the Illinois River. In a series of descriptive and analytical portraits of the persons who had known the girl Masters reveals slowly her life and character. Critics found the poetry pedestrian and verbose but conceded that the story had a dramatic impact. Between 1920 and 1924 four other novels appeared, the most ambitious of which, a historical tale entitled *Children of the Market Place*, enabled Masters to present one of his favorite heroes, Stephen A. Douglas, in a favorable light.

The verse which Masters published after 1925, the year of *Selected Poems*, added little to his reputation. But several of his later prose works commanded attention. The biography of Lincoln was justly criticized as partisan and biased against its subject and the account of Mark Twain added little to our knowledge of the novelist. But Masters's study *Vachel Lindsay: A Poet in America* (1935) remains an important evaluation of a fellow Illinois poet, even though their approaches to verse were strikingly different. In 1936 Masters published his autobiography, *Across Spoon River*, an informative chronicle of his introduction to writing with salient views of Chicago writers he had known. The picture of his marriage is less satisfactory since Masters was often evasive, failed to identify the various women with whom he had affairs, and was obviously unwilling to conform socially. At the end of his authorial life Masters collected descriptive and nostalgic lyrics about the Illinois country in two minor volumes and also contributed a book on the Sangamon River to the Rivers of America series. The Sangamon is hardly an important stream, but it was useful as a central theme for Masters's recollections of people and places that remained vivid to him after many years.

Masters's fame today is linked irrevocably with the *Spoon River Anthology*, a book which appealed to an enormous audience, was translated into many other languages, and stimulated several imitations. Basically it presents the denizens of a village cemetery, 244 in all, who speak their own epitaphs with uninhibited candor. These self-portraits are generally honest but often satiric or cynical. The Spoon River of their existence was not a happy place and the poems reveal the resentment, frustration, and disillusion of many of the residents. Masters arranged the portraits in groups with the failures and the weaklings, in many ways the most interesting characters, coming first, to be followed by the idealists and leaders. He derived many of the names and some of the figures from the Spoon and Sangamon river valleys of Illinois but usually transposed the patronymics and filled out the portraits imaginatively. Thus Hannah Armstrong, William H. Herndon, and Anne Rutledge retain their own names whereas some recognizable characters of the period have been rebaptized. Oddly enough, there is no sketch of Lincoln.

Prior to 1915 Masters generally used conventional verse forms without great distinction. The Spoon River sketches are couched in free verse, irregular in length and form, with occasional alliteration and even some rhyme. Masters was never a euphonious poet and certainly much of his later verse sounds harsh and careless to the ear. The brevity and concision of the portraits, however, won immediate approval from readers, who also relished the startling comparisons and the occasional epigrams. The poet's tendency to philosophize, very apparent in later work, seldom intrudes in the *Spoon River Anthology*. The forthright sketches of people like Lucinda Matlock, Fiddler Jones, Daisy Fraser, Margaret Fuller Slack, and the Village Atheist are the gems of Masters's work. It should be added that Masters rarely described the faces of his dramatis personae since he was more interested in their deeds and aspirations than in their appearance. Thus when an artist came to depict the Spoon River people on canvas he could use his imagination freely. No one has done this better than Boardman Robinson in the illustrations for the volume published by the Limited Editions Club of New York in 1942.

JTF

References: Christine Gibbons Mason, *DAB*, Supplement 4, 1974, pp. 554-56; Edgar Lee Masters, *Across Spoon River* (New York: Farrar & Rinehart, 1936); John T. Flanagan, *Edgar Lee Masters: The Spoon River Poet and His Critics* (Metuchen, N.J.: Scarecrow Press, 1974).

John Muir

(April 21, 1838—December 24, 1914)

Some men are more in tune with nature than others. Some drive past the mountain peak covered with glaciers and never see it; others notice the beauty of moss hiding within a crack in the rock and marvel at the wonders of creation. Some are repelled by the vastness of the earth and the universe; others are drawn to it as if by magic. Ralph Waldo Emerson remarked that "Every rational creature has in Nature a dowry and estate. It is his if he will." Emerson's words deeply influenced John Muir, who became nature's disciple in the late 1800s. Asa Gray, Agassiz, Audubon and many others found the North American continent a haven for the study of new things in nature. Muir joined them and went to live with nature. He spoke for the mountains, the glaciers, the redwoods, the deer and the bear because they could not speak for themselves. He fought for their survival and protection in the media and legislative halls of government. His elegant pen described their beauty as well as their plight when faced with advancing hordes of humans. He found joy in being alone with a tree, a rock, a mountain, or a flower. He was the complete naturalist with the added ability to express himself in vivid prose and plead the case of nature. He believed that man was the alien, exploiting nature as a predator. He conceived his mission in life to be nature's spokesman and turned his face toward the wilderness rather than toward his fellow man. He went to the mountain top for inspiration but returned to lead a crusade for the protection of the environment because he believed that "Each for all and all for each" included all living things. To John Muir, more than any other single person, we are indebted for the preservation of many of America's most scenic wonders. Today, millions of Americans enjoy the heritage which he left us.

Daniel Muir, a Scottish farmer, emigrated with his family to the wilderness near Portage, Wisconsin, in 1849, a year after Wisconsin became a state. His third child, John, received some education in an elementary school in Scotland as well as certain required reading at home. Daniel was somewhat of a martinet and enforced his rules by corporal punishment. After arriving in Wisconsin he required his son to perform the tasks of a man in clearing the forests and doing all of the chores required on a pioneer farm from cradling grain to rail-splitting. He was forbidden to read in the evening but could arise as early as he wanted and read prior to the day's work. John was so anxious to acquire knowledge that he bought all available books and read them in the early morning. In order to be awakened at an early hour he devised a clock from wood and attached it to his bed in such a manner that the bed, balanced on a crossbar, tilted at a given time and propelled young John on his feet. With the aid of this ingenious device he managed to educate himself adequately to be admitted to the University of

Wisconsin in 1860. Prior to entering the university he received only two months of formal elementary education in a Wisconsin log schoolhouse between 1849 and 1860.

John's father belonged to the old school of traditionalists who based their every act upon a strict interpretation of the Bible. He went so far as to assume that the Creator did not want man to eat meat. When this interfered with the family's diet and health, John, who was better read in Scriptures than his father, pointed out certain passages which contradicted Daniel's beliefs. John had many occasions to instruct his stern father in a more liberal and accurate understanding of the meaning of biblical passages. His childhood and teenage life was not easy and serene. While on the farm he began to invent various items out of wood, including a variety of clocks. Some were exhibited at the Wisconsin State Fair in Madison in 1860 and attracted much attention. But the most important aspect of the trip to Madison was Muir's visit to the University of Wisconsin. This led to three years of study and the acquaintance of Dr. and Mrs. Ezra Slocum Carr. Dr. Carr taught geology and chemistry and Mrs. Carr became a devoted disciple of Muir, giving him encouragement for the remainder of his life.

When John left the university after three years, without a degree, he spent some time walking in the Lake Superior district and into the Canadian wilderness. By 1865 he had decided to try becoming an inventor and made his way to Indianapolis, where he was involved with designing machinery for the manufacture of broom handles. An injury to his eye two years later caused him to abandon this line of work. His first great adventure was about to begin, a walking trip from Jeffersonville, Indiana, through Kentucky and Tennessee to Savannah, Georgia. Muir kept a journal of this trip, *A Thousand Mile Walk to the Gulf*, published in 1916. By 1868 he had found his way to San Francisco and soon discovered Yosemite Valley which he explored for the next six years. On all exploration trips Muir kept copious notes including drawings. These journals formed the basis of his later writings.

While exploring the Yosemite area he observed that some of the rocks were grooved with striae and he interpreted these as glacial in origin. The deep "U-shaped" valley, the waterfalls and smooth rock surfaces of Half-Dome as well as the hanging valleys, confirmed his suspicions. He was the first to correctly attribute the origin of the physical features of Yosemite to glaciation, even though the state geologist, Professor Josiah D. Whitney, maintained that glaciation had had no effect on Yosemite Valley. He maintained the fanciful idea that the bottom of the valley had dropped down and had only bitter words for John Muir, "the sheep-herder ... an ignoramus." Later in 1870, Professor Joseph LeConte, professor of geology at the University of California, visited Muir and confirmed his observations. Louis Agassiz arrived in San Francisco in August of 1872 but was too ill to visit Muir. He received a letter from Muir and commented that Muir knew, "all about ... glacial action." Ralph Waldo Emerson visited in 1871 and accompanied Muir to Yosemite. They became warm friends. Other famous men who called upon Muir included John Tyndall, the British scientist; Professor Asa Gray, botanist from Harvard; and John Torrey, botanist. But the most important visitor was Theodore Roosevelt in 1903.

Muir's marriage to Louie Strentzel in April 1880 was a strong and happy relationship. His roaming the forests as nature's "tramp" required understanding if a marriage was to survive. Louie indicated that she understood when she wrote shortly before their marriage, "sometimes I think I comprehend the delight and precious value of your work to your own soul."

Muir had been writing about preservation of the natural habitat for years. He had published articles in *Century Magazine, Scribner's Monthly, Harper's Weekly* and *Atlantic Monthly.* With national circulation his name had become synonymous with conservation. Muir, with the urging of Robert Underwood Johnson, an editor of *Century Magazine,* founded the Sierra Club in 1892. He considered the Sierra Club one of his great achievements and used it to promote the preservation of natural environments for the public good. After thoroughly studying Yosemite Valley and recognizing its glacial history, he went to Alaska where he described many glaciers, including the one now known as Muir Glacier. His interests were not confined to glaciers. He had a special interest in the sequoias and pines. In order to understand these trees he travelled to Africa, Australia and South America to explore similar great forested areas.

In 1889, with the help of Robert Johnson, he started a campaign to establish Yosemite National Park. Muir published popular articles on the natural beauty of the area and solidified public opinion in favor of the park. Congress passed the Yosemite National Park bill in October 1890, and a new era in government protection of the natural environment began. Muir had argued that the beauty of nature should be passed on to future generations. He was now the leader of conservation in America; it was not by chance that Roosevelt sought his company in 1903. The Muir-Roosevelt conference in Yosemite resulted over the next six years in the establishment of 148 million acres of new forest reserves, an increase of sixteen national monuments and a doubling of national parks. The conservation movement was at its height and Muir led the way by influencing popular opinion and reaching national political figures.

Muir had earned a living by writing, lecturing and manual labor. He found time to write for magazines and published several books including *The Mountains of California* (1894), *Our National Parks* (1901), and *The Yosemite* (1912). He received honorary degrees from California, Harvard, Wisconsin and Yale, and was a member of the American Association for the Advancement of Science.

Muir's saddest failure was his struggle to prevent the construction of the Hetch-Hetchy Valley dam. He spent the last six years of his life in a losing struggle to preserve the pristine character of Yosemite National Park. He saw Hetch-Hetchy as the entering wedge that would allow the destruction of the parks bit by bit. He had fought hard, enlisting the aid of the Sierra Club, which called the Project "the Hetch-Hetchy steal." Chief Forester Gifford Pinchot opposed Muir by supporting the construction of the reservoir and in a letter of May 28, 1906, said, "I will stand ready to render any assistance which lies in my power." Some thought that Muir's struggle over Hetch-Hetchy so weakened him physically that it contributed to his death.

This gentle man lived the life envisioned by many Americans. He had become "a giant Sequoia," a part of the American landscape, a tall and sturdy image for posterity.

HWS

References: William Frederic Badè, *The Life and Letters of John Muir* (Boston and New York: Houghton Mifflin, 1924); Linnie Marsh Wolf, *Son of the Wilderness* (Madison: University of Wisconsin Press, 1945).

Philip Murray

(May 25, 1886—November 9, 1952)

Like two other outstanding American labor leaders, William Green and John L. Lewis, Philip Murray belonged to a coal mining family from Britain— Green and Lewis of Welsh and Murray of Irish and Scottish descent.

At the age of ten, Philip joined his father as a coal miner at New Glasgow, Scotland. When Philip was sixteen, the family emigrated to the United States. He and his father found work in the coal fields near Pittsburgh, Pennsylvania. Philip became a naturalized American citizen in 1911, at age twenty-five.

Young Murray became active in labor union affairs in 1904, when he was elected president of a United Mine Workers local during a strike. From that point on he had a steady rise. In 1912, he was elected a member of the United Mine Workers' international executive board; four years later, in 1916, he became president of District 5; and in 1920 John L. Lewis, UMW president, appointed him vice-president of the union.

Murray and Lewis were closely associated for twenty-two years, a period during which, even though he was Lewis' subordinate, Murray began to demonstrate exceptional talent for leadership. He had acquired a thorough knowledge of the coal industry and the economy in general, making him a highly effective negotiator in dealing with the mine operators. Murray became Lewis' righthand man during the twenties, when the UMW was contending with competition from unorganized southern districts.

The coming of the Great Depression and the New Deal in the 1930s provided the UMW with an opportunity to reorganize the union and to achieve a great increase in its membership. A favorable atmosphere was created by the National Industrial Recovery Act, followed by the Wagner-Connery Act giving workers the right to organize and to bargain collectively.

The campaign to bring large numbers of previously unorganized workers into industrial unions immediately precipitated a crisis in the American Federation of Labor—were they to be allowed to form industrial unions of their own or be divided among the craft unions? Both Lewis and Murray fought for the principle of industrial unions, but when their arguments were rejected by the craft unions at the 1935 AFL convention, eight industrial unions, led by the UMW, withdrew to form a rival federation, the Committee for Industrial Organization, CIO, under Lewis' presidency.

Murray became chairman of the Steel Workers' Organizing Committee in 1936 and began plans to unionize United States Steel. The chairman of U.S. Steel's board of directors, Myron C. Taylor, signed a contract agreeing to union demands and recognizing the workers' right to organize. Similar agreements were accepted by the Carnegie-Illinois Steel Corporation and Inland Steel. The other companies, known collectively as "Little Steel," refused to sign the union contract. Murray recommended a strike, which culminated in a bloody confrontation. In the Memorial Day 1937 "massacre" in South Chicago, ten workers striking against Republic Steel were killed by police and many others were injured. The issue was not settled until 1941, when the steel companies were found in violation of the Wagner-Connery Act and were forced by the courts and the National Labor Relations Board to sign union contracts.

The famous break between John L. Lewis and Franklin D. Roosevelt's New Deal administration occurred in the late thirties. Murray, who was concurrently chairman of the Steel Workers' Organizing Committee and vice-chairman of the UMW, did not share Lewis' hostility to Roosevelt, but remained discreetly silent. Lewis opposed a third term for Roosevelt in 1940, and announced that he would resign as CIO president if Roosevelt were reelected. He made good his threat, after which, with the support of Lewis and Sidney Hillman, president of the Amalgamated Clothing Workers, Murray was elected CIO president at the 1942 convention.

Lewis apparently resented Murray's insubordination and used his influence to have him removed as vice-president of the United Mine Workers. The break between the two strong-minded men was made permanent when Lewis pulled the UMW out of the CIO. About the same time, the SWOC became the United Steelworkers of America, with Murray as president. He remained in that position until his death, in 1952, ten years later.

During World War II, Murray strongly supported governmental policies. He agreed, for example, that wage increases should be based on rises in the cost of living. As a member of the Combined War Labor Board, he favored wartime price and rent controls and taxes on excess profits.

Related to his leadership of the labor movement, Murray was a member of the National Association for the Advancement of Colored People, actively supported the rights of minorities, and insured that blacks would receive all the privileges of membership in unions to which they belonged. A Committee to Abolish Racial Discrimination was established by the CIO. On another front, Murray organized the CIO's Political Action Committee (an early PAC) to enable workers to exert their power in governmental matters.

Perhaps reflecting his own foreign origin, Murray was convinced that the CIO should be represented in international labor bodies. Under his urging, the British Trades Union Congress called a number of conferences, leading in 1945 to the formation of the World Federation of Trade Unions. The AFL refused to join that organization, but the national federations of other democratic countries and the Soviet Union became members. Later communist-dominated unions were expelled from the international body.

According to Philip Taft, labor historian, Philip Murray was not power hungry, readily delegated authority, and was "a man of great personal worth and quiet strength." He showed genius in holding the CIO together after 1940.

RBD

References: Vincent D. Sweeney, *The United Steel Workers of America* (Pittsburgh? 1946?); Juanita D. Tate, *Philip Murray as a Labor Leader* (Ann Arbor, Mich.: University Microfilms, 1967).

Reinhold Niebuhr

(June 21, 1892 — June 1, 1971)

Reinhold Niebuhr was an outstanding American theologian, teacher and author of the twentieth century. He had an impact on religion as it defined society and the individuals in it. He concerned himself with the dynamics of the community from a Christian perspective. He reported on responsibilities of the individual as well as the broader responsibility of those in power to both the community and the individual.

Niebuhr was born in Wright City, Missouri, to a religious family; his father was pastor of an Evangelical church. He studied at Elmhurst College and Eden Theological Seminary and graduated from Yale Divinity School in 1914. He became pastor of Bethel Evangelical Church in 1915 in Detroit, Michigan, remaining until 1928. Between 1928 and 1960 he served as professor of philosophy of religion at Union Theological Seminary, New York. During this period he expressed himself on a number of issues related to the structure of society and wrote many articles and books dealing with religious philosophy. He edited the journal *Christianity and Society* and published his first important book *Moral Man and Immoral Society* in 1932. His Gifford Lectures in 1938-1939 at the University of Edinburgh were published as *The Nature and Destiny of Man.*

In the broadest sense Niebuhr was concerned with "agape," the love of all men, the loyal concern of one who gives freely to another. He helped organize the Fellowship of Socialist Christians in 1930. The Fellowship sought to develop a cooperative society on socialist principles. Though the depression years in America strained the capitalistic system, by 1940 Niebuhr recognized the failure of Russian communism. His observations led him to believe that Marxism's illusion of utopianism led to tyranny. He reacted to the pressures of world and political events and his ideas matured with the changing environment. His goal was social justice and in his early thinking democracy was unable to change and supply the needs of the people. Later, he became a convert to Franklin Roosevelt's programs, believing that democracy, after all, could make social gains. At the same time, he looked upon fascist dictatorships as an evil that might emerge if social gains were not forthcoming. He completely rejected Stalinism and communism. Niebuhr was often challenged by European theologians about whether his "interests were theological rather than practical ... [I] thought the point well taken because the distinction did not interest me."

He searched for an ethic that ensured justice in government, in economics, and between individuals and communities. As a social critic he attempted to retain the values enunciated by Martin Luther. Niebuhr has been referred to as a liberal, pacifist, conservative, socialist and pragmatist. Certainly, he was a liberal in his desire to improve the status of man, but he did not trust "the abstract schemes which liberals were inclined to advance," or the "dogmas of the idealist." Niebuhr was once deemed a pacifist and was for a time chairman of the Fellowship of Reconciliation. However, he changed his viewpoint and after 1932 became a sharp critic of pacifism. Niebuhr progressed through various stages of thinking and was willing to cast aside outmoded ideas. His early positions on socialism and pacifism were changed to a pragmatic viewpoint, leaving him to argue for a practical approach to the solution of problems. He became the champion and interpreter of pragmatism, discarding as unworkable the romantic illusions of the socialist. Social issues could not be measured and treated as scientists test substances in a laboratory. There were no absolutes in the social structure, all were variables. He considered Winston Churchill a great statesman, and in the sense that Churchill was a conservative or pragmatist, so was Niebuhr. He believed that social questions must be solved according to the necessities of a given situation. Niebuhr found his answers in history and wrote many books and articles with history as a background. Among them are *The Irony of American History* (1952), *The Self and the Drama of History* (1955), and *Beyond Tragedy: Essays on the Christian Interpretation of History* (1961).

Niebuhr believed that the liberal culture of a modern democracy under-valued the contributions such a society made to the liberal's freedom. Such liberal shortcomings are a threat to democracy because they ignore the necessity of keeping power over society limited. Marxism acquired complete power because it assumes man is tame and bows willingly to authority. Therefore, collectivism overlooks man's historical search for individual freedom. Some of Niebuhr's major books deal with man's relationship to government. Among them are *Christianity and Power Politics* (1945) and *The Structure of Nations and Empires* (1959).

Economic philosophy during much of the twentieth century has been a war between Marxist creeds on the one hand and free enterprise successes on the other. Niebuhr, in his *Goals of Economic Life* (1953), maintained that the economic life of a community is best served when society relies "on the self-interest of men ... [without] restrictive political controls." He recognized that uncontrolled free trade may result in economic and political inequities, and that some restraints are therefore needed to maintain justice and freedom. Individuals and groups must exercise responsibility.

Niebuhr was aware that ownership of property represents power to resist the state and to defend oneself. Excessive ownership of property may produce excessive power; the ultimate abuse of power is represented by the communist state which owns all property. Fair distribution is the key to social justice and order.

Niebuhr considered democracy a necessary form of government, repre-senting the culmination of man's political freedom. This was the foundation of his strong anticommunist position. He wrote often about communism, but summarized his thoughts in an essay, "Why Is Communism So Evil?" He gives four basic answers: 1) power is in the hands of a few, 2) the utopian concept misleads the masses, 3) communism, as a substitute for religion, revolutionizes the state of human society for the proletarian class, and 4) dogmatic Marxism is deemed scientific. Niebuhr recognized that the socialization of property merely transferred economic and political power from the people to an oligarchy composed of a few individuals. The utopian concept of communism holds out the hope of a final solution to man's problems and, therefore, attracts the liberal in search of an ideal goal. Finally, science's search for truth is the antithesis of communistic dogmatism.

Niebuhr recognized the need for not only an open, but also a responsible society. He found it best represented in the democratic system of government. He believed that "Man's capacity for justice makes democracy possible; but man's inclination to injustice makes democracy necessary." In this statement Niebuhr shows a profound understanding of human nature and man's search, through time, for freedom from tyranny. When he discusses politics or human nature, he does it in the context of theological thought.

Niebuhr embraced the socialist creed early in his career because of what he considered to be the unfair labor practice of the Ford Motor Company. He did not visualize the rising power of the labor union which corrected the imbalance of power between management and labor. Neither did he anticipate the development of excessive power and scandals in union leadership.

He believed that Christian faith and political theology were closely linked. Our belief in religious freedom permits us to be less critical of Christians with faiths differing from our own than of Christians with different political or economic viewpoints. Niebuhr, in his search for a just society, observed the forces at work around him and noted that the economic system of the United States is capable of modifying itself so that the people can have "a decent life for all without the destruction of free enterprise." Religion is a part of the larger social structure and the triad of love, power and justice is of concern to all theologians.

Niebuhr was one of the most thoughtful social critics of the twentieth century. He commented in depth on almost every aspect of the social scene in terms of Christian ethics. He expressed the Christian viewpoint which seemed to him to come nearest a solution to specific social problems. He thought no political doctrine providing a final solution was in sight and said so, but as one of the great philosophers of religion his impact on society through the church will be long lasting. Reinhold Niebuhr did more in his generation than any other religious philosopher to extol the virtues of demographic pragmatism as measured by Christian ideals.

Niebuhr gave serious consideration to the question of racial conflict and tensions, especially black-white relations in America. He believed it to be the most serious social problem in the world, "man's primary collective sin." After examining the question of "group pride" in depth he concluded that there is "no absolute solution for this problem." He examined the question from the viewpoint of Christian ethics and majesty of law rather than genetics.

HWS

References: Hans Hoffman, *The Theology of Reinhold Niebuhr* (New York: Scribner, 1956); Charles W. Kegley and Robert Bretoll, eds., *Reinhold Niebuhr, His Religious, Social, and Political Thought* (New York: Macmillan, 1956); Gordon Harland, *The Thought of Reinhold Niebuhr* (New York: Oxford University, 1960); Roger C. Hutchinson, "Reinhold Niebuhr and 'Contextural Connections,' " *This World* 6 (1983): 102-14.

Chester William Nimitz

(February 24, 1885 — February 20, 1966)

As fleet admiral, in command of Pacific operations during World War II, Chester Nimitz was at the head of one of the greatest military organizations ever assembled. It was Nimitz who planned the step by step progress that led from the Pearl Harbor disaster to the recapture of the Philippines and the capitulation of Japan. Nimitz had watched the growth of Hitler's military power and predicted in the mid-1930s a major war with Japan and Germany.

Nimitz was born in Fredericksburg, Texas, and received a congressional appointment to the United States Naval Academy at age fifteen. After graduation in 1905, he served with the Asiatic Fleet and in the Philippines. He became a submarine commander and an expert in submarine warfare. During World War I he served in the Submarine Force of the Atlantic Fleet. Between the two major wars he was involved with the creation of the Naval Reserve Officer's Training Corps and acted as assistant chief of the Bureau of Navigation, appointed chief in 1939.

The responsibilities of the bureau involved the procurement and training of personnel for the navy. A congressional act in 1934 permitted an expansion of naval forces that grew to a two-ocean navy. This required the training of a great number of civilians. Nimitz, as the officer responsible for the program, had numerous occasions to confer with President Franklin Roosevelt. Roosevelt admired Nimitz and in 1941 offered him the post of commander in chief of the U.S. Fleet. Nimitz considered himself to be junior to too many other career officers and declined. Admiral Husband Kimmel accepted the appointment and was assigned to the Pacific Fleet, based at Pearl Harbor. A few months later on December 7, 1941, the Japanese attacked Pearl Harbor, and the American Pacific Fleet was mostly destroyed. Nine days later Secretary Frank Knox told Nimitz that he was to be the new Admiral of the fleet and to proceed to Hawaii. He left San Diego Christmas Eve and started a new chapter in his life and a new phase in history.

Nimitz's superior was Admiral Ernest Joseph King, Commander in Chief of the U.S. Fleet. Nimitz was commander of the Pacific Fleet and the Pacific Ocean areas. He methodically rebuilt the strength of the U.S. Navy and Marine Corps forces, as well as the confidence of the personnel. He refused to attack until his forces were strong enough to succeed. In 1942 he initiated the plan of attacking enemy-fortified islands. This resulted in task forces striking the Marshalls and Gilberts and Wake Island. The island raids were successful, but Nimitz, in general, bided his time before initiating a major offensive. The Coral Sea confrontation in April resulted in the loss of the carrier *Lexington*, but the real test came during the first week of June in the great Battle of Midway. Nimitz had deployed his forces to protect the three thousand defenders on the island. After severe fighting Admiral Nagumoto's Japanese fleet was repelled. It had lost four carriers, one cruiser sunk and another wrecked, a battleship, an oiler, 322 aircraft, and twenty-five hundred men were killed. The American victory was not without its costs: one carrier and one destroyer sunk, 147 aircraft lost and 307 men killed. But the course of the war in the Pacific had been reversed. It was welcome news for all Americans, especially after the fall of Corregidor in the Philippines only a month earlier.

Both antagonists lost ships and men in the Pacific war, but the American power continued to increase by replacements and additions, whereas the Japanese forces declined. Nimitz was now able to go on the offensive and supported General MacArthur's "island-hopping" back to the Philippines. One of the major encounters was the battle for Guadalcanal. After several confrontations and heavy losses the island was occupied. By late January 1943, eastern New Guinea also fell. Guadalcanal was used as a supporting base for forward movement in the Solomon Islands. Nimitz opened a new offensive in the central Pacific in 1943. The direction of movement would be westward through the Gilbert and Marshall islands to Kwajalein and Eniwetok. Saipan, in the Marianas, was reached by June 1944. The battles in the Philippine Sea in June 1944, and Leyte Gulf in October 1944, further reduced the strength of the Japanese Navy.

In 1945, Nimitz had advanced to Iwo Jima and Okinawa, and was close enough to raid Japan. With Nimitz's help the Philippines had been reoccupied by MacArthur. After the surrender of Germany on May 8, 1945, Nimitz was convinced that Japan would also surrender in the near future. Japan was expressing an interest in peace through the Soviet government in July. Nimitz had been informed about the atom bomb but hoped it wouldn't be used. He thought the bomb was indecent, but the Japanese procrastinated over surrender terms and on August 6, the B-29, *Enola Gay*, left Tinien for Hiroshima and a place in history.

On September 2, Nimitz signed the document of Japanese surrender on board the *Missouri*. He had successfully come to the end of a long hard trail. His organizational abilities, his choice of men and his habit of making his own decisions had won the final victory in a war that relied largely on the Navy. He had wielded power over the nation's large Pacific fleet in a quiet manner, without ostentation or undue posturing.

Nimitz did not retire after the war. He became Chief of Naval Operations, served on the United Nations commission that mediated the 1949 dispute between India and Pakistan over Kashmir, and served as regent of the University of California between 1947 and 1955. His wife, Catherine Freeman Nimitz, guarded and tenderly took care of him in his days of final illness. He died in California and, after his body lay in state in the Treasure Island Naval Station chapel, was buried in a grave in the Golden Gate National Cemetery at San Bruno, marked by a simple headstone with his fleet admiral's five stars.

HWS

References: Samuel Eliot Morison, *History of United States Naval Operations in World War II*, 15 vols., 1947-1962 (Boston: Atlantic, Little, Brown); E. B. Potter, *Nimitz* (Annapolis, Md.: Naval Institute, 1976).

George William Norris

(July 11, 1861 — September 4, 1944)

Few members of Congress leave a permanent impress on that body, on government at large, or on the nation's affairs. George W. Norris of Nebraska was one of those rare exceptions.

Like many self-made men in American history and politics, Norris came up the hard way. He was born on a farm in Sandusky County, Ohio, the eleventh of twelve children. The family had emigrated by wagon from upstate New York to Ohio in 1846. Both parents were nearly illiterate. The father died when George was only three. Despite these handicaps, George was ambitious for an education. After attending the local district school, he entered Baldwin-Wallace College and later Valparaiso University. From the latter institution he received a bachelor of laws degree in 1883. As a student, he excelled in rhetoric and debate—valuable talents for a future legislative career.

Two years spent teaching school in Ohio and Washington state were followed by Norris' move to Nebraska in 1885, and his opening of a law office. From 1895 to 1902, he served as judge of the fourteenth Nebraska district. In addition, he engaged in milling and mortgage-loan businesses and acted as local attorney for the Burlington and Missouri Railroad.

An economic depression in Nebraska in the 1890s persuaded Norris to seek public office for a living. His first run for Congress came in 1902, when he won the Republican nomination in his district and then went on to defeat the Democratic incumbent by a narrow margin. He was to remain in the House from 1903 to 1913. During that period, Norris demonstrated his liberal leanings by supporting legislation in Nebraska to curb the railroads and brewers and to make government more efficient and representative. He also joined House insurgents who were trying to curb the dictatorial powers of Speaker Joseph Cannon. In 1910, Norris introduced a resolution providing for an elected Rules Committee, on which the Speaker would be ineligible to serve. The resolution, of great importance for achieving progressive social and economic legislation, was adopted.

A further break from party conformity occurred in 1912, when Norris endorsed Robert M. LaFollette for the presidential nomination and then threw his support to Theodore Roosevelt. In the senatorial campaign the same year, he defeated the incumbent Senator Norris Brown in the primary and won the seat in the regular election that followed—the only major Republican victor in a Democratic landslide in Nebraska. From 1913 until 1943, Norris served in the Senate without a break, a total of thirty years.

In the Senate, Norris maintained his reputation for independence. He supported many of the Wilson administration's key programs, such as the Federal Reserve and antimonopoly bills, and he was one of only three Republican senators to vote for Louis Brandeis' nomination for the Supreme Court. He was extremely critical, however, of Wilson's Mexican policy and was one of only six senators who voted against the American declaration of war in April 1917. With the coming of hostilities, Norris backed the war effort without reservation. He was one of the small group of "irreconcilables" who voted against approval of the Versailles Treaty because of his belief that it contained serious inequities and faults.

The Republican party was dominant in the 1920s, with three presidents—Harding, Coolidge, and Hoover—in succession. Norris disagreed, however, with his party on various issues, because of which he and a few like-minded colleagues were labeled "sons of the wild jackass." He successfully opposed a number of nominations for high office, and disagreed with certain foreign policies. For example, he favored recognition of the Soviet Union, was against sending U.S. Marines to Nicaragua, and was in sympathy with the aims of the Mexican revolution. On the domestic front, Norris supported farm relief and the rights of labor, believed in more efficient use of natural resources, and advocated the direct election of presidents.

Important legislation introduced by or cosponsored by Norris included a plan for government purchase and sale abroad of farm surpluses, and the Norris-La Guardia Anti-Injunction Act to curb the use of injunctions in labor disputes. He was the father of the Twentieth ("Lame Duck") Amendment to the Constitution, to inaugurate presidents in January instead of March, changing a custom dating back to horse-and-buggy days.

Perhaps most revolutionary and most long-range in influence was Norris' advocacy of public production, transmission, and distribution of hydroelectric power. His bill for government ownership and development of Muscle Shoals in Alabama was passed by Congress, but vetoed by both Coolidge and Hoover. With the advent of the New Deal, Norris was the chief author of the act creating the Tennessee Valley Authority (TVA) in 1933. His sponsorship of that huge project was recognized when the first TVA dam built was named Norris Dam. A smaller project of the same nature was constructed in Nebraska, with Norris' support.

With the passage of time, Norris' ties to the Republican Party continued to loosen. He refused to support Herbert Hoover's candidacy, and endorsed Alfred E. Smith instead. Later, in 1932, he came out for Franklin D. Roosevelt's election and in fact openly backed all four of FDR's presidential races. He was a staunch supporter of most New Deal legislation. By 1936, Norris had become a political independent, and won a fifth Senate term with endorsements by FDR and the Democratic party in Nebraska. In 1942, however, the Republicans retaliated, expelled him from the party, and Norris' bid for a sixth term was defeated by the Republican nominee.

Though he had opposed American entry into World War I, Norris concluded that totalitarian aggression during World War II had to be stopped and he voted for a declaration of war after the Japanese attack on Pearl Harbor. During that stressful period, his liberal leanings were shown by his criticism of the treatment of aliens and other suspect persons and by his efforts to enact legislation to repeal poll taxes in national elections.

Norris' major achievements as a political leader were the Anti-Injunction Law, the "Lame Duck" Amendment, TVA, the Rural Electrification Act, and persuading Nebraska to adopt a unicameral (one house) legislature. He came to be regarded as one of the outstanding legislators in American political history and the greatest independent. His remarkable career is chronicled in an autobiography *A Fighting Liberal* (1945), published the year after his death.

RBD

References: Richard Lowitt, *George W. Norris* (Syracuse, N.Y.: Syracuse University Press, 1963); Richard Lowitt, *George W. Norris* (Urbana: University of Illinois Press, 1971); Richard L. Neuberger, *Integrity: The Life of George W. Norris* (New York: Vanguard, 1937); Norman L. Zucker, *George W. Norris* (Urbana: University of Illinois Press, 1966).

Adolph Simon Ochs

(March 12, 1858—April 8, 1935)

By common consent, the *New York Times* is accepted as America's only truly national newspaper, the newspaper of record, a kind of daily encyclopedia, indispensable to future historians. As expressed by a leading critic, Oswald Garrison Villard, the *Times* has "established itself as the foremost daily of the world ... it outshines the London *Times*, which no longer thunders."

How the *New York Times* achieved this unique status is in large part one man's story, the life of Adolph Ochs.

Adolph's parents were German Jewish refugees, who had settled in Knoxville, Tennessee. The son's journalistic career began at age eleven as an office boy on the *Knoxville Chronicle*. As printer's devil on the *Chronicle* he learned the newspaper business from the ground up in all its branches—news, business, and mechanical. Two years later he became a practical printer on the *Louisville Courier-Journal*. At age nineteen he moved to Chattanooga to take a job on a new paper, which soon failed. Its rival, the *Chattanooga Times* was also about to go bankrupt. With $250 of borrowed money, Adolph bought a controlling interest in the *Times*, assumed its debts, and in 1878 began his career as a newspaper publisher, before he was old enough to vote.

The *Chattanooga Times* under Ochs's guidance set a pattern later applied to the *New York Times*—in his words, "clean, dignified, and trustworthy." Gradually, as Chattanooga grew, Ochs succeeded in raising his paper to a position of prosperity and prestige. His reputation was further enhanced by chairmanship (1891-1894) of the Southern Associated Press and later affiliation with the old (Western) Associated Press, from which developed the nationwide organization of that name.

Early in 1896 came Ochs's opportunity to achieve fame and fortune on a much larger scale. He was informed that the *New York Times* could be bought. The *Times*, established in 1851, once prosperous and powerful, had been running down for years. Its circulation had dropped to nine thousand, it was losing a thousand dollars a day, and it was facing bankruptcy. After a thorough investigation, Ochs concluded that the paper could be saved. Using seventy-five thousand dollars, which he mostly borrowed, a reorganization was arranged whereby Ochs would become publisher of the *Times*, with full control and a majority stockholder, if he could make the paper pay for three consecutive years.

The competition Ochs faced in New York was rich and powerful. It was the heyday of yellow journalism. Pulitzer's *World* and Hearst's *Journal* (later the *New York American*) had built up enormous circulations by setting a sales price of one cent, while the *Times* and other papers were selling for three cents. Ochs refused to indulge in the typographical pyrotechnics, comic strips, and emphasis on crime and sex featured by Pulitzer and Hearst. The war with Spain almost finished the *Times*, for it could not afford to employ the special correspondents needed to report the news.

At this stage, as the *Times* was almost ready to go on the rocks, some of its executives proposed to reach a "quality public" by raising the price to five cents. Ochs was convinced however, that many people bought the *World* and the *Journal* because they were cheap and would buy the *Times* instead if they could get it at the same price. It was a stroke of genius. Within a year the *Times*'s circulation had trebled and the paper was making money. From there on, the record of Ochs's career is one of steadily increasing influence and prosperity.

Most basic to the *Times*'s reputation and future greatness were the policies firmly established by Ochs. He believed that a large segment of the reading public is composed of intelligent, thoughtful people. His main object, therefore, was to give all the news, especially "all the news that is fit to print," and to reject coarse, vulgar, and inane features, muckraking, and any kind of crusade. As Benjamin Stolberg, writing on the history of the American press, stated, "The *Times* has no leg shows, side shows, or circuses. It employs no middle-aged, rundown newspaper men to grind out advice to the lovelorn. It peddles no funny sheets, Krazy Kats, Nize Babies, or humor by Andy Gump, Mutt and Jeff, and FPA." As Ochs himself expressed it, "The *Times* is the sort of newspaper which no one needs to be ashamed to be seen reading."

An important policy set by Ochs was to exclude advertising considered fraudulent or improper, and to refuse to let powerful and wealthy advertisers influence the *Times*'s editorial and news policies, regardless of the loss of revenue. These high standards eventually raised the standards of both news and advertising in the news world as a whole.

To its usual news columns the *Times*, under Ochs's direction, added three innovations: a book review supplement, treating newly published books as news; a Sunday magazine section, devoted mainly to news of an informative nature; and a weekly financial review, presenting a detailed survey of worldwide economic, financial, and commercial trends. Also innovative were the ways in which the *Times* extended the scope of the news, as the paper set out to print happenings in every area of possible interest to its readers. There was emphasis on pure and applied science. Beginning with World War I, the *Times* began publishing in full the speeches of the leaders of all European governments, the "white papers" of the British and German governments, and other diplomatic records. In that way, the *Times* became over the years an invaluable source of original documentary records pertaining to current history.

Editorials in the *Times* have the reputation of being innocuous and somewhat colorless, carefully avoiding firm stands. Ochs may have planned it that way, because of his respect for things as they were; he was temperamentally convinced that there was merit on most sides of most questions and taking a firm editorial position was often unwise. One commentator, Silas Bent, in his book *Strange Bedfellows*, suggested that Ochs's early experience in a small town where his readers were also his friends had taught him to get out "a paper that hurt nobody's feelings." Ochs himself never wrote editorials, though he presided over the daily editorial council and directed general editorial policy. His editorial writers often disagreed with him and he gave them considerable freedom in stating their views in the paper. His editors-in-chief Charles R. Miller and Rollo Ogden were usually in harmony with him. In any case, Ochs always felt that editorial opinion should be kept subordinate to the news. The Ochs concept of news was greatly strengthened after 1904 by C. V. Van Anda, a genius as a managing editor, who was interested in everything and made a major contribution to the paper's success.

There has been no lack of critics of Ochs and the *Times*, ranging from the moderate differences expressed by Silas Bent, Benjamin Stolberg, and Elmer Davis to the extreme views of Upton Sinclair in *The Brass Check* and *Crimes of the Times*. The liberal opinions are well summarized by Oswald Garrison Villard in a chapter of his *The Disappearing Daily*. After praising the dispatches of Walter Duranty from Russia, Herbert L. Matthews from Ethiopia, Italy, Spain, and India, Anne O'Hare McCormick for her distinguished foreign correspondence, Hanson W. Baldwin's military and naval commentaries, Arthur Krock's Washington reporting, and others, Villard maintains that the *Times* was biased and unfair in its reporting on the Soviet Union, the Spanish revolution, and in its handling of matters relating to the Jews. "Standing up for the privileged was part of Ochs' philosophy," according to Villard, "a great secret of his business success — that and his unending devotion to the god of things as they are."

Nevertheless, Villard concedes, "Ochs was a remarkable newspaper manager, the most successful in the whole history of American journalism. As such he created our foremost daily, which will never lose its commanding position if its directors but realize their responsibilities and their duties to this country and all of its people, and rise to them." Unquestionably the political and economic opinions of the *Times* have remained conservative, as they were under Ochs. But the *Times*'s concept of news has deeply impressed the newspaper world, providing the American people with the most comprehensive information in their history. It raised the standards of American journalism and broadened the outlook of the American people. Thus, whatever his weaknesses, the *Times* remains a monument to Adolph Ochs's memory.

Some of his coreligionists never forgave him his opposition to Zionism; he believed in Judaism as a religion, not as a separatist racial culture. But it was no perfunctory faith expressed merely in benefactions; it colored his whole life. In later years he was happiest at his summer home on Lake George, surrounded by his family and a circle of old friends; but he died, as perhaps he would have wished, on a visit to Chattanooga.

RBD

[He left no writings except occasional speeches, reprinted from the newspapers in pamphlet form; and a voluminous correspondence, as yet unedited, which has not been used in this memoir. His own view of his achievement was published in *The New York Times* on his twenty-fifth anniversary as publisher, August 18, 1921, and in Elmer Davis, *History of The New York Times* (1921), pp. viii-xxii. Part II of the *History*, where it treats issues and policies relevant to his critical years in New York, includes his own recollection, often in his own words. The obituary in *The Times*, April 9, 1935, incorporates reminiscences of many associates of both his earlier and later life. Virtually everything else so far published about him is commentary and appraisal, not source material.]

Reference: Gerald W. Johnson, *An Honorable Titan: A Biographical Study of Adolph S. Ochs* (New York: Harper, 1946).

Alice Freeman Palmer

(February 21, 1855 — December 6, 1902)

When Alice Freeman was a young girl in the mid-nineteenth century, women did not ordinarily attend college. There were a few women's colleges, such as Mt. Holyoke, blazing a trail, and other institutions led by Oberlin in 1833, were beginning to open their doors to women. Nevertheless, higher education for women was at an experimental stage. The National Education Association, founded when Alice Freeman was two years old, did not admit women to membership at that time.

Alice's parents objected to her going to college, for several reasons: it was contrary to general custom, financial resources were limited, and it was more important for Alice's brother to receive a college education. None of these arguments changed Alice's determination to earn a college degree. She promised her parents that if they would help with her expenses at the University of Michigan, she would later assist her brother and younger sisters to gain an education — a promise that she kept. The parents were finally convinced and gave their consent.

Alice Freeman was a precocious child. She taught herself to read at the age of three, and began attending the village school at Colesville, New York, at age four. Her father, a country doctor, moved his family to the nearby village of Windsor in 1865 and Alice entered Windsor Academy, a preparatory and finishing school for boys and girls, at age ten. The "preparatory" feature was apparently not sufficiently thorough, for Alice failed the University of Michigan's entrance examination. Her personality had so impressed President Angell, however, that he asked the examiners to allow Alice to enter on trial, and she remained. Time out was taken to serve as head of the high school at Ottawa, Illinois, for twenty weeks, and after her graduation from Michigan to teach in a seminary at Lake Geneva, Wisconsin, and in the Saginaw, Michigan, high school.

Meanwhile, Alice refused two offers from Wellesley College, one to teach mathematics and the other to teach Greek. A third offer, to head Wellesley's department of history, was accepted. Alice was then age twenty-four. From there on her career was inextricably connected with Wellesley College. She had been on the faculty only two years when the president resigned. At age twenty-six, Alice Freeman was appointed vice-president and acting president. In 1882, Alice became president and began to demonstrate her administrative ability and talent for organization.

Alice Freeman remained as president of Wellesley for only six years, but during that period she established the Academic Council, composed of heads of departments, formed standing committees of the faculty, made entrance examinations stricter, standardized and simplified courses of study, reequipped the gymnasium, strengthened the faculty personnel, and made connections with a number of leading preparatory schools in different parts of the country. When Alice Freeman assumed Wellesley's presidency, she found a poorly organized college with inadequate funds and a faculty underprepared and underpaid. During her term of office, Wellesley became nationally known, with professional prestige, better financial support, and a stronger faculty. The institution was changed from a glorified boarding school to a genuine college. In the general field of education, she made the motion, at a meeting in Boston in 1882 of women from eight different colleges, to organize the Association of Collegiate Alumnae, aimed at promoting the educational interests of women. Alice Freeman served two terms as president of this organization, which subsequently became the American Association of University Women. In 1884, she was one of three American delegates at the International Conference on Education in London.

In 1887, Alice Freeman married George Herbert Palmer, a distinguished member of Harvard's philosophy department, at which time she resigned her presidency of Wellesley. Her connection with the college, however, continued. She was elected a trustee, and remained on the board the rest of her life. In 1889, Governor Ames appointed her a member of the Massachusetts Board of Education, and in 1891 she served on the board of managers for the Massachusetts exhibit at the World's Columbian Exposition in Chicago. Another Chicago connection, undertaken by appointment of President William Rainey Harper, was to serve as dean of women at the University of Chicago from 1892 to 1895. The duties of that office included supervision of the housing and food of women students, their conduct, and their study programs. During the same period, Mrs. Palmer took a leading part in promoting the changes whereby Radcliffe College became formally attached to Harvard University. Other activities which filled her busy life included the International Institute for Girls in Spain, Bradford Academy, the Women's Education Association, the American Board of Commissioners for Foreign Missions, and the Women's Home Missionary Association.

In December 1902, while on a European holiday with her husband, Alice Freeman Palmer died in Paris of a heart attack after surgery, at age forty-seven. During her lifetime, she received many honors and posthumously was elected to the Hall of Fame at New York University. A tribute to her by William Dewitt Hyde, before the National Council of Education, in 1903 reads: "Alice Freeman Palmer has left us the ideal of the educated woman; scholarship without a particle of pedantry; optimism with no blinking of unpleasant facts; efficiency unsevered from winsomeness; power unspoiled by pride."

RBD

Reference: George H. Palmer, *The Life of Alice Freeman Palmer* (Boston: Houghton, 1909).

George Smith Patton, Jr.

(November 11, 1885 — December 21, 1945)

George Patton, Jr., was one of the most flamboyant and paradoxical of military leaders. In the mind of the public he was a dashing swashbuckler with six-shooters on his hip, a John Wayne in real life, who boldly led his men into danger and came out a winner. His actions inspired confidence in his men. On the one hand, his profanity and toughness inspired his men to follow his example; on the other hand, his arrogance and braggadocio created enemies. His idiosyncrasies were overlooked in the wake of his success.

Patton's skill as a military strategist was recognized by all. His concept of rapid deployment and quick thrusts with tanks ruthlessly destroyed Hitler's German army. His success was based on mobility, encirclement and pursuit. To belong to Patton's army became a symbol of pride even though he was known as "Old Blood and Guts." Some soldiers commented, "Our blood, your guts," but followed his leadership. Patton's image was consciously promoted. He had a desire to succeed and to be recognized. His temper often flared and he drove his men in a violent, aggressive manner in his desire to win the game of war. In the process he became the outstanding personality on the battlefields of World War II.

In spite of his posture as a tough, profane commander, there was another side to Patton. He hated the slaughter and waste of war. He had a wide range of interests that covered the arts and history, as well as poetry. Though he expected loyalty from his subordinates he had a capacity for compassion and sensitivity for the soldier in the ranks.

The Patton family was proud of its heritage and felt that they were born to the right of leadership. George was born in San Gabriel, California, the son of George Smith Patton and Ruth (Wilson) Patton. His grandfather, with the same name, was a graduate of Virginia Military Institute and was killed in the Civil War while acting as a Confederate colonel. His father also graduated from V.M.I. in 1877, and after teaching French there for one year returned to California to practice law. Because of Patton's family history he acquired an interest in military affairs early in life. In 1903 he enrolled in the Virginia Military Institute, following the steps of his grandfather and father, but after one year entered the United States Military Academy at West Point. He was not a superior student, but was recognized as an outstanding athlete and student leader. He was commissioned a second lieutenant in 1909, graduating just above the middle of his class.

A year after graduation Patton married Beatrice Ayer, a Boston heiress. She was ambitious for her husband's success and played an important role in creating the Patton legend. She believed in his destiny and encouraged him in all of his endeavors, as well as collecting and cataloguing his papers. She was an ardent horsewoman and sailor and supported her husband's athletic activities. He participated in the 1912 Stockholm Olympics, placing fifth in the military pentathlon.

Patton's first assignment was with the Fifteenth Cavalry at Fort Sheridan, Illinois. After further training at Fort Riley he was assigned as an aide to General John J. Pershing in the 1916 punitive expedition into Mexico. He attracted enough attention to be promoted to captain and Pershing took him to France in 1917 where he was detailed to the newly organized United States Army Tank Corps. He led his unit, including 144 American tanks and 33 French tanks, in the St. Mihiel offensive in mid-September 1918, and was wounded on September 26, in the great battle known as the Meuse-Argonne offensive. He was unable to participate in further action, but was awarded the Distinguished Service Cross and the Distinguished Service Medal for his contributions to tank warfare. In addition he was promoted to colonel.

Patton spent the twenty-two year period between the two world wars on various assignments. They included Fort Myer, Cavalry School at Fort Riley, Command and General Staff College and the Army War College. He published numerous articles on military matters and, in general, prepared himself for leadership in World War II. During the Great Depression he aided General Douglas MacArthur in removing the Bonus Army veterans from their encampment in Washington.

After the German army quickly conquered France and Poland the United States began to rearm. Patton was given command of the Second Armored Division in 1940. By January 1942 he was commanding general of the I Armored Corps and in November led the land forces that entered Morocco, near Casablanca. His knowledge of amphibious operations was a factor in the successful invasion.

After the Germans won a victory at Kasserine Pass, Tunisia, Patton was given command of the II Corps. He retrained and reorganized his forces and reversed the losses. Shortly thereafter, he was promoted to the rank of lieutenant general and placed in charge of forces preparing to invade Sicily. On July 11, 1943, Patton led the United States Seventh Army on a blitzkrieg operation that ended in success thirty-eight days later.

The Sicilian victory embroiled him in an affair that nearly cost him his career. He believed that fear and cowardice should be punished in order to maintain the morale of an army. Otherwise, discipline would fail and the army would deteriorate. When he saw two soldiers exhibiting what he considered cowardice he slapped them. He considered the action to be in the best interest of the shell-shocked patients, but the public outcry was so great that he made an apology. The incident was never forgotten, but Eisenhower, recognizing his military genius, retained him as a leader.

The invasion of Europe, the last great offensive in which Patton would participate, started on D-Day, June 6, 1944. He led the Third Army into France and spread westward into Brittany, southward to the Loire and eastward toward the Seine. By rapid deployment in the Normandy area he encircled the German Fifth Panzer and Seventh armies. He moved eastward toward Metz in late August and thoroughly demonstrated the value of rapidly moving tanks in cooperation with other ground forces and aircraft. His tactical maneuvers forced the Germans to retreat, but his supplies of gasoline could not keep up with the tanks and the German army stabilized its position.

The Battle of the Bulge started on December 16, and Patton's response to it was to turn his forces against the southern flank. The action stopped the German offensive. By March of 1945 the Third Army had crossed the Rhine and Patton headed his tanks across Germany. He progressed to Budejovice, Czechoslovakia and Linz, Austria as the war closed. Political decisions brought the Allied forces to a halt along the Elbe and Enns rivers.

Patton was opposed to the political decision that divided Europe with the Russians. He was outspoken in his belief that the division of Europe represented a major Communist expansion. He encouraged a continuation of the war, if necessary, to drive the Russians back to their own boundary because he didn't want half of Europe under Communist domination. For expressing his opinions, which were counter to prevailing American political policy, he was relieved of his command of the Third Army and assigned to the more or less inactive Fifteenth Army.

Patton was injured in an automobile accident and placed in an army hospital in Heidelberg. He died several days later. He had said that he expected to die on a field of battle. The battle that he helped win was over, but death came unexpectedly in peace. He rests in the Military Cemetery at Hamm, Luxembourg.

Patton remains a controversial figure, admired for his military exploits and leadership by all, but criticized for his egotistical posture by some.

HWS

References: Fred Ayer, Jr., *Before the Colors Fade* (Boston: Houghton Mifflin, 1964); Martin Blumenson, *The Patton Papers* (Boston: Houghton Mifflin, 1972); Ladislas Farago, *The Last Days of Patton* (New York: McGraw-Hill, 1981).

Charles Willson Peale

(April 15, 1741 — February 22, 1827)

It would be difficult to find a more talented and active American in the colonial and federal period than Charles Willson Peale. He was by turns a fervent patriot, a military officer, a state legislator, a museum promoter, and always an artist. Although born in Maryland he was blessed with Yankee ingenuity and showed skill and dexterity in working with metals and glass. Apprenticed as a youth to a saddler he developed ability as a silversmith, watch or lock repairer, and upholsterer; he also showed his inventive streak by devising a velocipede, a new kind of eyeglass, and an early polygraph in which his collaborator was Thomas Jefferson. Most of all he was a portrait painter, a pupil of Benjamin West in London briefly, and subsequently a painter of political and economic dignitaries as well as military officers. In 1772 he painted the first known portrait of George Washington and followed this up with six other portraits of Washington from life as well as many replicas. Nor did the Peale artistic streak end with his death. He married three times and fathered many children, four of his sons eventually becoming painters in their own right. They were appropriately baptized Raphaelle, Rembrandt, Rubens, and Titian.

Peale was born in St. Paul's parish, Queen Anne County, Maryland, the first of five children of Charles Peale of Rutlandshire, England. The father was a schoolteacher. At the age of thirteen the son was indentured to a saddler and learned various crafts before he was relieved of his indenture in 1762. The same year he married Rachel Brewer. Peale planned to continue his work as an artisan and bought the necessary materials on credit, but when he could not pay his debts he changed his course. He became interested in painting, bought a manual of instruction, and benefited from the teaching of a Swedish artist named John Hesselius. In 1765 his brother-in-law offered him passage on a ship to New England, which he gladly accepted, and at Boston he had the good fortune to meet John S. Copley who encouraged him. When Peale returned to Annapolis, having already painted some portraits, he was given money raised by a group of gentlemen which permitted him to travel to England for further training. He took with him a letter to West, who welcomed him and provided useful instruction. Peale also supplemented his funds by modelling (he even posed for West), miniature painting, and mezzotint engraving. Back in the United States he continued doing portraits in Maryland and adjacent regions but in 1776 moved his family to Philadelphia. Before this time Peale had become associated with patriotic movements. In Pennsylvania he enlisted in the city militia and eventually joined the army, his first assignment being to recruit volunteers. He was named a captain in the Fourth Battalion or Regiment of Foot and saw service at the battles of Princeton and Trenton. But when the British evacuated Philadelphia he ended his active service. In 1779 he was elected a Philadelphia representative to the General Assembly of Pennsylvania. Throughout these years he found time to paint miniatures of his fellow officers, which he later proceeded to convert to replicas in head size. In this way he created his own war record.

Hearing of the discovery of mastodon bones near Newburgh on the Hudson in New York state in 1801, Peale ventured to the spot, organized a crew of workers, and removed the relics to Philadelphia. This find persuaded him to begin a museum, which in the years that followed was enormously augmented to include Indian relics, mineralogical and zoological specimens, and portraits by himself and his son Rembrandt. Peale's Museum, which later was incorporated as the Philadelphia Museum, was opened in 1786, was accepted for the hall of the American Philosophical Society in 1794, and in 1802 was given free space in the famous Independence Hall. The collection is said to have numbered one hundred thousand objects. At the age of eighty-three Peale painted himself standing at the entrance to his museum and lifting a curtain so that the viewer could get a glimpse of the marvels within. The artist is clad in black and the curtain is dark, but the head is marvelously modelled and impressive. This is one of Peale's best achievements.

He also had a role in the creation of an art school. His first attempts were futile but in 1805 he was chiefly responsible for the formation of the Philadelphia Academy of the Fine Arts. Peale began to limit his activities in the 1790s and in 1810 retired to his country home called "Belfield." But although he no longer attempted the large canvases of his youth and avoided family pictures, he continued to do portraits to ensure the influx of funds. During his long lifetime he painted a galaxy of celebrities including Hamilton, Jefferson, Franklin, Martha Washington, John Hancock, John Adams, and John Paul Jones. In addition he produced a number of pictures of representative colonial figures. Indeed as Horace Wells Sellers has remarked, Peale did for Pennsylvania, Maryland, and Virginia what John S. Copley did for Massachusetts. But as a painter Peale's greatest fame was achieved by his portraits of George Washington.

The 1772 portrait, a three-quarters length, showed Washington wearing the uniform of a colonel of Virginia militia. Later Peale did a miniature on ivory, several bust portraits with his subject in a continental uniform, a full-length in 1779, and a bust portrait showing Washington as president at Philadelphia in 1795. Gilbert Stuart's portraits of Washington are of course more celebrated and more familiar, but Peale had greater personal knowledge of his subject and did creditable work. Oliver Larkin expressed the difference in their work astutely. "A Washington by Peale is posed none too gracefully with a hand on a cannon and one long leg stiffly crossed over the other, his homely features recorded by a man who shared with him the dark days of 1776." Where Stuart tried for glamor, Peale depended on verisimilitude.

Some other works by Peale merit comment. His portrait of his second wife's uncle, John De Peyster, now at the New York Historical Society, is notable for its delineation of an older face revealing both dignity and benignity while the artist's care is shown in his treatment of the clothing. The *Staircase Group* now at the Philadelphia Museum of Art depicts two of Peale's sons climbing steps; the boys's faces are bright and the treatment of the garments of the boy in the foreground is again meticulous. Another canvas by Peale, *Exhuming the Mastodon*, is an unusual genre work showing the digging crew using an enormous bucket wheel to drain the swamp in which the fossil remains of the animal were found. The crowded canvas, which the artist later admitted was too small for its subject, includes some fifty figures counting both workers and spectators, and Peale himself appears holding some kind of sketch of what he hoped to have when the reconstruction process was complete.

Charles Willson Peale was not the first rate painter that Copley and possibly Stuart were, but he was an important figure in the development of domestic portraiture and his contributions to American art were both multiple and memorable.

JTF

References: Horace Wells Sellers, *DAB*, XIV, 1934, pp. 344-47; Oliver W. Larkin, *Art and Life in America* (New York: Rinehart, 1949); Charles Coleman Sellers, *Charles Willson Peale* (New York: Scribner, 1969). Yale University Press published in 1984 the first volume of *The Selected Papers of Charles Willson Peale and His Family*, edited by Lillian B. Miller; eight volumes are projected.

Matthew Calbraith Perry

(April 10, 1794 — March 4, 1858)

Most military leaders gain fame by winning battles during warfare. Matthew Perry was an exception. He won renown during peace by negotiating a treaty with Japan in 1854. The treaty opened Japan to Western civilization and ended a long history of Japanese isolation. It had a permanent effect on Japan and changed that nation, in time, from a feudal oriental society to a modern industrial nation.

Matthew Perry was born in South Kingston, Rhode Island, the fourth child of Christopher and Sarah Perry. The Perry family had developed a deep attachment for service in the United States Navy. The father was a captain during the War of Independence, serving in both the army and navy. Matthew's eldest brother Oliver was in the Battle of Lake Erie in the War of 1812; his brother Raymond commanded a vessel in 1826; his brother James was a midshipman and served with Oliver at Lake Erie and won renown on September 10, 1813 when he led his nine vessels into battle on Lake Erie. After victory he sent a laconic dispatch to General Harrison that read, "We have met the enemy and they are ours." His youngest brother Nathaniel was a purser in the navy and two sisters married naval men.

Perry entered the navy as a midshipman at age fifteen on January 16, 1809. His first service was on the schooner *Revenge*, commanded by his brother Oliver. Matthew was too young to play a major part in the War of 1812. He became a lieutenant in 1813 and served in several capacities before being promoted to captain in 1837. His most important contributions during this early period were his part in developing the naval apprentice system and his command of the

Fulton II, the first naval war vessel powered by steam. He was impressed with the potential of steam power and planned the construction of the first two naval frigates, the *Missouri* and the *Mississippi*.

During the War of 1812 the Barbary Coast pirates, under the leadership of the Dey of Algiers, captured and enslaved the crews of American merchant ships. Perry accompanied an American squadron in 1815 that put an end to the depredation of the pirate princes. Perry learned the technique of tough diplomacy and used the same methods when he went to Japan in 1853-1854.

There was a movement in America as early as 1773 to repatriate black slaves to Africa. Perry was interested in the humanitarian aspects of the project and volunteered to assist. He was appointed first lieutenant of the U.S.S. *Cyane* on August 3, 1819 to escort one of the first groups of free Negroes to Africa. His mission involved four orders: 1) to escort the merchant ship *Elizabeth* carrying freed slaves to Africa, 2) to search for slave ships, 3) to return any captured slaves to Africa, and 4) to give support to the new Liberian colony. The first load did not leave New York until January 3, 1820. The *Cyane* performed its duties and returned to the Brooklyn Navy Yard. Perry made a second trip to Africa as commander of the schooner *Shark*. He played an important part in the initial establishment of Liberia and in choosing the site of Monrovia. As commander of the *Shark* the sailors nicknamed him "Old Bruin," because of his habit of roaring his orders to his seamen. Later, in 1843-1845, Perry was given command of the African Squadron for the purpose of protecting American commerce and suppressing the slave trade. He returned just as war clouds began to gather over Mexico.

At the beginning of the Mexican War Perry was vice commodore with the Gulf Squadron, an unofficial name. Mexico did not offer the navy many opportunities for major battles. The primary duty of the squadron was to serve as blockaders. This was dull duty enlivened only when Perry captured Frontera and the town of Tobasco. On March 20, 1847, the U.S.S. *Mississippi* arrived with orders for Perry to take over Commodore David Conner's command. Two days later Vera Cruz was under siege by Perry's guns. The attack ended in a few days with General Winfield Scott's troops in command of the city. This proved to be Perry's only war experience.

Perry's single great achievement was his success in negotiating a treaty with Japan in 1854. The United States government was anxious to conclude a treaty because it was particularly concerned about refueling ships in the whaling industry, repatriation of American castaway seamen, and trade. Perry began his expedition on November 24, 1852 and arrived in Hong Kong the following April. After a call at the Shanghai port he proceeded to Naha, Okinawa, where he demonstrated as much patience and obstinacy as the Okinawans in gaining a conference with the regent. After a trip to the Bonin Islands, Perry returned to Naha for another successful conference and then headed for his historic trip to Japan.

At 5:00 P.M. on July 8, 1853 Perry's squadron, including the *Susquehanna*, *Mississippi*, *Saratoga* and *Plymouth*, anchored near the entrance to Edo Bay, now Tokyo Wan. There was general alarm on the shore where thousands of defenders gathered to repel the "invasion." After several days of confrontation, during which excellent discipline on both sides prevented open warfare, Perry landed and delivered his letter from President Fillmore on July 14. Perry had sent 250 heavily armed men ahead of him, and his march to the conference was one of pomp and circumstances. The band played "Hail! Columbia," the marines presented arms, and two black Americans escorted the Commodore. He promised to return in the spring.

Perry returned to Edo Bay in February 1854, and anchored his squadron near present Yokohama. The first treaty between the United States and Japan was concluded, with all due ceremony, on March 31, 1854, and was proclaimed by both countries in June of 1855. The treaty provided for "permanent and universal peace." Shimoda and Hakodate were designated as ports for American ships to obtain "articles their necessities may require." Shipwrecked American sailors were to be guaranteed safety and any privileges granted other countries were to be granted to the United States. The door to Japan had been opened and peaceful relations were maintained until World War II. After the war, the goodwill of both nations was rebuilt by President Truman, Emperor Hirohito and General Douglas MacArthur acting together to weld a new friendship. Perry returned in 1854 and died four years later in New York.

HWS

References: Samuel Eliot Morrison, *"Old Bruin," Commodore Matthew C. Perry* (Boston and Toronto: Atlantic Monthly Press, 1967); *Narrative of the Expedition of an American Squadron to the China Seas and Japan ... 1852, 1853, and 1854, under the Command of Commodore M. C. Perry* (Washington, D.C.: U.S. Government Printing Office, 1856).

Gifford Pinchot
(August 11, 1865—October 4, 1946)

The numerous organizations presently devoted to the conservation of natural resources had notable predecessors. The names of Theodore Roosevelt, Gifford Pinchot, and John Muir stand out.

Pinchot fully deserves to be known as the father of professional forestry in America. As early as his student days at Yale University in the 1880s, he had decided on a career in forestry. This decision had been influenced by his father, a wealthy New York merchant, who believed strongly in the importance of natural resources to a nation's welfare. At the time, however, no American university offered formal instruction in forestry. Gifford, therefore, enrolled for related courses in botany, meteorology, and other sciences. After graduation, he went to France, where he and his family had spent much time during his youth, and entered the French National Forestry School at Nancy for a year's study. Pinchot took advantage of the opportunity, also, to become acquainted with forests under government management in France, Switzerland, and Germany. The United States government had made no such provision for the care and protection of its vast forest resources. Upon his return home, Pinchot soon became an influential advocate of public forestry.

Among Pinchot's early assignments were supervision of George W. Vanderbilt's forests at Biltmore, North Carolina, extensive travel throughout the country to become acquainted with the nation's forest resources, and surveys of New Jersey's forest lands. His approach was utilitarian: regulated commercial use of forests, selective cutting, provision for future growth, and proper fire prevention.

Pinchot was appointed to the National Academy of Sciences' National Forest Commission in 1896, charged with making recommendations on the Western States' national forest reserves. The study resulted in passage of the Forest Management Act, forming a legal basis for the commercial use of the reserves. A short time later, in 1898, Pinchot was appointed chief of the Forestry Division of the U.S. Department of Agriculture. With strong support from President Theodore Roosevelt, Congress was persuaded to transfer the General Land Office of the Interior Department to his division, then renamed the Forest Service. Under Pinchot's administration, as stated by him, the policy was "to make the forest produce the largest amount of whatever crop or service will be most useful and keep on producing it for generation after generation of men and trees."

Under Pinchot, the Forest Service established precedents for federal regulation of natural resources and he was instrumental in developing the conservation policies of the Roosevelt administration. In addition, he branched out to have a hand in related activities, such as serving as a member of the Committee on the Organization of Government Scientific Work, the Committee on Department Methods (to increase government efficiency), the Inland Waterways Commission, a White House Conference on the Conservation of Natural Resources, and a National Conservation Commission.

All the dedication to the preservation of natural resources changed when Theodore Roosevelt's presidency ended and William Howard Taft entered the White House. Taft's Secretary of the Interior was a James Watt-type character, Richard A. Ballinger, who began changing conservation policies on all fronts. The fight between Ballinger and Pinchot caused bitter divisions in the Taft administration. Ballinger was accused of supporting fraudulent claims to Alaskan coal lands. Taft supported his secretary of the interior, however, and Pinchot was dismissed from government service. The controversy did much to cause the split between Taft and Roosevelt.

Pinchot next turned to a political career. He campaigned against Taft's reelection, helped found the National Progressive Republican League, and later the Progressive Party, which nominated Roosevelt in 1912. His campaign for a Senate nomination in 1920 failed, but in 1922 he was elected governor of Pennsylvania. Pennsylvania law barred him from succeeding himself as governor, though after an interval of four years, in 1930, he ran for governor again and was elected for a second term.

Pinchot's most important achievements during his first term as governor were government reorganization, better administration of the state's finances, and tighter regulation of public utilities. The second term was dominated by economic problems caused by the Great Depression. A major accomplishment during this period was the construction of thousands of miles of rural roads, taking Pennsylvania farmers out of the mud.

Pinchot's concern with conservation remained throughout his career. He founded the National Conservation Association in 1909 and remained its head until 1923. His influence was used to obtain passage of the Weeks Act in 1911, providing for expanding forest reserves by purchase, and the Waterpower Act of

1920 for federal regulation of the power industry. In the field of forestry itself, Pinchot served on the Yale School of Forestry faculty, and he was the founder and president of the Society of American Foresters. American participation in World War II won his wholehearted support, and he endorsed Franklin D. Roosevelt's campaign in 1940. In 1942, he showed the navy how to extract drinking water from the juices of fresh fish, an important survival technique for men in lifeboats.

RBD

References: Martin L. Fausold, *Gifford Pinchot* (Syracuse, N.Y.: Syracuse University Press, 1961); N. M. McGeory, *Gifford Pinchot* (Princeton, N.J.: Princeton University Press, 1960); Harold T. Pinkett, *Gifford Pinchot* (Urbana: University of Illinois Press, 1970).

Edgar Allan Poe

(January 19, 1809—October 7, 1849)

No major American literary figure has ever excited more controversy than Edgar Allan Poe in his brief life of forty years. Despite extensive biographical research, a clear, detailed account of his youth has not appeared, and the marriage to his thirteen-year-old first cousin Virginia Clemm still seems eccentric. The circumstances of his death in Baltimore remain obscure. He was a poet, a short story writer, a literary critic, and a highly competent magazine editor until personal irresponsibility and a compulsive addiction to alcohol deprived him of editorial positions. He published some fifty poems and about seventy short stories, many of which are known to readers of the English language throughout the world. He was a bold and forthright critic who accused Longfellow of plagiarism and gave short shrift to literary mediocrity. But his own conception of poetry, which has given pleasure to a multitude of readers, has been challenged and even maligned. After all Emerson termed him "the jingle man" and Lowell in a famous line declared "Three fifths of him genius and two fifths sheer fudge." On the other hand, his basic literary contentions, his opposition to didacticism and his emphasis on a single effect for example, have affected many critics after his time. In France he was praised and translated by Baudelaire, and in England and America he influenced, among others, Stevenson and Conan Doyle and Ambrose Bierce. Despite differences of opinion there is general agreement that Poe was one of the great innovators in American literature and one of the most original writers of the nineteenth century.

Poe was born in Boston in 1809, the son of itinerant actors. He was orphaned two years after his birth and was taken into the home of but never legally adopted by John Allan, a merchant of Richmond, Virginia. Here the boy, who eventually took the name of his benefactor as his middle name, remained until 1815, when the Allan family moved to London and stayed there for five years. Young Poe attended a boarding school in London and also the Manor House School at Stoke Newington. Some years later he used reminiscences and physical details of his English instruction in the psychological story "William Wilson." After the family returned to Richmond, John Allan, whom an inheritance had made quite wealthy, subsidized a year at the University of Virginia for Poe but was never generous in his allowances. When Poe resorted to gambling and contracted debts, friction developed between him and his foster father, and he quit school after a violent quarrel and made his way to Boston. There in 1827 he published his first book anonymously and at his own expense, *Tamerlane and Other Poems*; it was virtually stillborn. In the same year using a pseudonym and falsifying his age he enlisted in the United States Army and was sent to Sullivan's Island, South Carolina, which eventually served as the locale for his famous tale, "The Gold Bug."

After the death of Mrs. Allan there was a temporary reconciliation between her husband and Poe. He was released from the army in 1829 and was given a cadetship at West Point. In the meanwhile he had arranged for the publication of a second volume of poems, *Al Aaraaf*. But Allan's remarriage convinced Poe that he would be disinherited and he contrived by minor violations of discipline to gain his dismissal from the school in 1831. In the same year he stopped in New York and saw the publication of another collection of his verse, *Poems by Edgar A. Poe*. The volume included early versions of two of his best known lyrics, "Israfel" and "To Helen." From 1831 to 1835 he made his home in Baltimore, residing with his aunt, Mrs. Maria Clemm. He also began to contribute stories to magazines. One of them, "Ms. Found in a Bottle," won a contest for short fiction and attracted the attention of John P. Kennedy, who got Poe an editorial position in 1835 on the newly established *Southern Literary Messenger* published in Richmond. At the end of the year Poe became editor of the magazine with a salary of fifteen dollars a week and retained the position until excessive drinking brought his discharge in 1837. During his tenure he had contributed verse, stories, and slashing reviews, and he had also raised the circulation from five hundred to more than thirty-five hundred. In 1836 he had married Virginia Clemm. The next year Poe moved with his wife and mother-in-law to New York.

The next several years were marked by restlessness and frequent changes of position and residence. Under the circumstances amazing productivity followed. In Philadelphia he became co-editor of *Burton's Gentleman's Magazine*, 1839-1840, to which he also contributed one of his most remarkable stories, "The Fall of the House of Usher." In 1840 he also published his first collection of short fiction, *Tales of the Grotesque and Arabesque*, which included both "Ligeia" and "Berenice." The culminating point of his literary career came in 1840 and 1841. He was named literary editor of *Graham's Magazine* and increased its circulation from five thousand to thirty-seven thousand. The magazine published such stories as "The Murders in the Rue Morgue" and "The Masque of the Red Death" as well as his memorable critical essay, "The Philosophy of Composition." It was about this time that Poe had high hopes of publishing his own magazine but adequate financing was never available. Also he came to know Rufus W. Griswold, an anthologist and critic who succeeded Poe as editor and who bitterly attacked him after his death.

Another move took Poe back to New York, where he and his family lived and suffered in the famous cottage in Fordham with a negligible income. He was briefly a literary critic for the *New York Mirror*, became editor and part owner of the *Broadway Journal* in 1845, and was associated with *Godey's Lady's Book* in

1846. The last periodical printed Poe's series called "The Literati" in which he poured scorn upon most of the thirty-eight New York authors whom he chose to notice. The animosities aroused by these sketches did not help his finances. But he was also able to collect previously published prose and verse in book form. *Tales* in 1845 included both "The Black Cat" and "The Purloined Letter," and *The Raven and Other Poems* appeared in 1846. "The Raven," undoubtedly Poe's most famous single poem, originally had been published by the *New York Mirror* on January 29, 1845.

In the remaining two years Poe's health disintegrated badly. Virginia Poe died of tuberculosis in 1847 and Poe himself suffered a severe illness. Alcoholism became more of a problem, and he also may have been addicted to laudanum. He lectured on the origins of the universe and published a prose tract called *Eureka* in 1848, but his attempts to find personal solace were disastrous. An infatuation with a Rhode Island poet, Mrs. Sarah Whitman, was temporary. He returned to Richmond and wrote "Annabel Lee," published posthumously, and he became engaged to Mrs. Shelton, a childhood sweetheart and now a widow. En route north to get his aunt to attend the wedding, he stopped off at Baltimore. There he was found in a delirious condition near a building formerly used as a polling place. He died within days and was buried in Baltimore beside his wife's grave.

Poe's theory of poetry and his limitations as a poet are explicitly stated in his essay "The Philosophy of Composition." In keeping with his conviction that poetry should be essentially musical, he defined it as "the rhythmical creation of beauty." Moreover, he argued that "Beauty is the sole legitimate province of the poem." The most poetical topic in the world, he claimed, was the death of a beautiful woman. The melancholy produced by such an event "is thus the most legitimate of all poetical tones." Convinced that moralistic art was a contradiction in terms, he firmly expressed his objection to didactic verse, and he also declared that since no great poetry could be consistently sustained there should be no long poems. Obviously Poe wrote no epics and no lengthy narratives. His insistence that verse should be musical led him to the extravagant echolalia and alliteration found in "The Bells," a poem in which sound transcends sense. And his account of the mechanical construction of "The Raven" for which he claimed that he wrote the end before the beginning is not always convincing.

In his edition of Poe's short stories Killis Campbell observed that a number of types could be discerned. Least important were stories that were chiefly anecdotes, burlesques, satires, and hoaxes. But the author also created psychological studies, allegories, and perhaps most memorable of all stories of ratiocination. Preeminent here of course are "The Purloined Letter," "The Murders in the Rue Morgue," and "The Gold Bug." Because of his belief in unity of effect Poe naturally eschewed the novel. His fantastic tale of adventure in the Antarctic seas, *The Narrative of Arthur Gordon Pym*, is his longest work. Campbell also pointed out that Poe's characters lacked any local habitation; he depicted idealized heroines and heroes who were seldom presented against realistic settings. In his taste for the gruesome and the macabre he was actually following one of the fashions of his age. But his imagination made it possible for him to fill his tales with striking if bizarre details. Furthermore, he was a master of suspense and mood, and especially in his short stories he used his doctrine of single effect with telling results. Poe did not invent the detective story but his mastery of the form had an inestimable effect on his successors.

JTF

References: Hervey Allen, *DAB*, XV, 1935, pp. 19-28; Joseph W. Krutch, *Edgar Allan Poe: A Study in Genius* (New York: Knopf, 1926); Hervey Allen, *Israfel: The Life and Times of Edgar Allan Poe* (New York: Doran, 1926); Arthur Hobson Quinn, *Edgar Allan Poe: A Critical Biography* (New York: Appleton-Century, 1941); F. O. Matthiessen, in *Literary History of the United States*, ed. R. E. Spiller, et al. (New York: Macmillan, 1953).

James Knox Polk

(November 2, 1795 — June 15, 1849)

James K. Polk, eleventh president of the United States, deserves the title "The Great Expansionist." During his four-year term in the White House, a total of 1,205,381 square miles was added to the United States. Included were the entire west coast — California, Oregon, and Washington — and a large share of the southern border, Texas and New Mexico. As a result of the Mexican War of 1846-1848, during Polk's administration, the present states of California, Nevada, and Utah and parts of Arizona, New Mexico, Colorado, and Wyoming came into permanent U.S. possession.

Polk was a native of North Carolina, the eldest of ten children. The family migrated to Tennessee when James was eleven years of age, but he returned several years later to enter the University of North Carolina, from which he graduated with first honors in mathematics and classics in 1818.

From early youth, James had a keen interest in politics. Following his return to Tennessee, he began the study of law and in 1820 was admitted to the bar. According to a contemporary source, "his thorough academical preparation, his accurate knowledge of the law, his readiness and resources in debate, his unswerving application to business, secured him, at once, full employment, and in less than a year he was already a leading practitioner." At age thirty, Polk entered Congress from Tennessee. His close friendship with and loyalty to President Andrew Jackson were soon rewarded. Polk became the recognized leader of the administration forces in the House of Representatives. For example, Jackson chose him as his spokesman in the prolonged battle to close the Bank of the United States.

During Jackson's second term controversies arose that affected Polk's political future. As a friend and admirer of Jackson, Polk opposed the policies of John Quincy Adams and his secretary Henry Clay. After considerable infighting, Polk was elected and served two sessions as speaker of the House. Partisan politics made the office a difficult one, and the speaker was the object of constant heckling and abuse. His enemies accused him of being the abject slave of the administration. An effort was even made to force him to fight a duel. In his farewell address Polk stated, "It has been my duty to decide more questions of parliamentary law and order, many of them of a complex and difficult character, than had been decided by all my predecessors from the formation of this Government."

Though he would have preferred to remain in Congress, Polk was drafted by the Democrats to run for governor of Tennessee, as the one person who could "redeem" the state from the Whigs. He was elected to serve for the 1939-1941 term, but was defeated for reelection in 1841 and 1843.

On the national level, the dominant party, the Whigs, was getting ready to nominate Henry Clay for the presidency in the 1844 election. It was expected that Van Buren, with Jackson's backing, would be the Democratic nominee. Annexation of Texas was the chief political issue. Both Clay and Van Buren announced their opposition to annexation, while Polk strongly endorsed the proposed action. Jackson declared that Van Buren had committed political suicide and threw his support to Polk for the nomination. At the convention in Baltimore which followed, Polk was nominated on the ninth ballot, in competition with Van Buren, Lewis Cass, James Buchanan, and John C. Calhoun. He went on to defeat Clay in the election.

In attesting to Polk's fitness for the office, Jackson wrote, "his capacity for business is great — and to extraordinary powers of labor, both mental and physical, he unites that tact and judgment which are requisite to the successful direction of such an office as that of Chief Magistrate of a free people."

Polk was just short of fifty years of age when inaugurated, the youngest man to reach the presidency until his time. Shortly after taking office, he announced that he would serve for only a single term, and "four great measures" were to be the goals of his administration: a reduction of the tariff, an independent treasury, settlement of the Oregon boundary question, and the acquisition of California. His plans met with powerful opposition in Congress, but before Polk left the White House in 1849, all four aims had been successfully achieved.

The Texas matter had been substantially resolved before Polk entered the presidency. His election had impelled Congress to vote for annexation in December 1845. In 1846 a tariff law was enacted that put import duties on a revenue basis and substituted *ad valorem* duties (based on the value of imported products) for specific duties. Despite dire predictions to the contrary, manufacturers flourished and government revenues increased after the new law went into effect. The independent treasury act of 1846 established a national monetary system that remained in effect until the Federal Reserve System was set up in 1913.

The Oregon problem involved a long-standing dispute with Great Britain over the ownership of the territory between California and Alaska. The Democratic platform had laid claim to the entire area. Polk's stand was more moderate: to divide the region at the 49th parallel. After considerable negotiation, the British accepted the proposed boundary line, except that all Vancouver Island should remain in British possession. A treaty to that effect was passed by the Senate and signed on June 15, 1846.

Polk's original intention had been to obtain California by purchase from Mexico. He was willing to assume certain debts owed to the United States and to pay $15 to $20 million for the cession of New Mexico and California. The Mexican government refused to receive an envoy sent to Mexico City with the offer. At that point news arrived of American troops being killed by the Mexican army on American soil. At the conclusion of the Mexican War that followed, in 1848, the United States acquired both New Mexico and California — 529,017 square miles of territory — in return for which Mexico was paid $15 million and had its debts forgiven.

Polk was the first president to change the fundamental character of the Monroe Doctrine. Monroe had opposed forcible interference in American affairs. Polk took a firm stand against any interference, even the acceptance of sovereignty over Yucatan by Spain or Great Britain, when voluntarily offered by the people of this region. Polk was the first to suggest that intervention by the United States might be used to support the doctrine.

Polk was an adamant opponent of "pork-barrel" legislation and applied his veto to specific measures. He had a supreme contempt for the spoils system and for the unscrupulous methods used by members of Congress to win offices for their adherents.

On March 4, 1849, Polk wrote in his diary: "I feel exceedingly relieved that I am now free of all public cares. I am sure I shall be a happier man in my retirement than I have been during the four years I have filled the highest office in the gift of my countrymen."

One of his biographers, Eugene I. McCormac, commented: "Seldom in American history has such an ambitious and so varied a program as that of Polk been consummated in the brief period of four years. It was a program conceived, mainly, by the President himself, and his dogged persistence procured the legislation necessary to put it in operation ... he was a sound statesman, an unusually capable executive, and an unwavering patriot." Polk undermined his health by arduous labor and died only three months after retirement.

RBD

References: John S. Jenkins, *The Life of James Knox Polk* (Auburn, Ala.: J. M. Allen, 1850); Milton Lomask, *This Slender Reed: A Life of James K. Polk* (New York: Farrar Straus, 1966); Charles A. McCoy, *Polk and the Presidency* (Austin: University of Texas Press, 1960); Eugene I. McCormac, *James K. Polk* (Princeton, N.J.: Princeton University Press, 1922); Charles G. Sellers, Jr., *James K. Polk* (Princeton, N.J.: Princeton University Press, 1967).

Cole Porter

(June 9, 1891—October 15, 1964)

Cole Porter, musical comedy composer and lyricist, creator of tuneful melodies and witty phrases, was one of America's most colorful theater personalities. He contributed to Hollywood as well as Broadway. Porter was one of the most productive composers in American history, writing his first composition for the piano at age ten. He wrote more than 850 songs during his career. He became wealthy as well as an international celebrity.

Porter's heritage had nothing in it which would have caused anyone to predict his possession of musical talent. His maternal great-grandfather, Albert Cole, had settled in Peru, Indiana, in 1834, long before the town was incorporated. Albert's son, James O., became a multimillionaire through investments first in California and later in the home town of Peru. His daughter, Kate, married Samuel Porter, a druggist, in April 1884. Kate's father continued to support, in part, the Porter family in the style of life in which his daughter had been reared. Kate's first two children died and after Cole's birth she became protective. She raised him to believe that he was part of an upper-class family. His French lessons and instruction in piano and dancing, as well as his dress, could hardly be considered characteristic of an Indiana village boy in the 1890s.

Kate was the dominant influence in Cole's musical education and encouraged studies in both violin and piano. The influence of his mother is indicated by his first childhood compositions, "Song of the Birds" in 1901 and "Bobolink Waltz" in 1902. The first was dedicated to his mother and the second was published by her. Neither was indicative of the talent that was to flower later. In addition to providing music lessons, she often took him to Chicago to attend opera and theater performances.

After his elementary education in Peru he was sent in 1905 to Worcester Academy in Worcester, Massachusetts, over the protest of his grandfather, who wanted him to go to a military school. Cole pursued a classical education at Worcester. He was greatly influenced by Professor Daniel W. Abercrombie who taught him that words and music must be in harmony. The Worcester experience was Cole's first break with the Peru family and he succeeded so well that he was chosen valedictorian of the class of 1909, and graduated with honors. Grandfather Cole relented and gave him a trip to Paris as a graduation present. Cole and the French people developed a long mutual love for each other. He returned to enroll at Yale where he did not distinguish himself as a scholar. Cole seems to have spent more time on social affairs than books but graduated with his class of 1913. During his student days at Yale he wrote several songs including "Bingo Eli Yale" and "Bridget" in 1910. Grandfather James O. Cole insisted that Cole enter Harvard law school in 1914, but the experience didn't suit him and he transferred the second year into the School of Arts and Sciences. In the meantime, he was writing numerous songs for Yale musicals.

When America passed the Selective Service Act of May 1917, Cole joined the Duryea Relief Party to distribute food supplies in France. His wartime activities are little known. There is no evidence that he served in a military capacity. At the close of the war he remained in France until early 1919, and after a few months in America he returned to Paris and married a wealthy American divorced socialite, Linda Lee Thomas. Linda helped him become a part of the international social set during the 1920s and worked for his professional success. In America, this period was known as the Roaring Twenties when the girls were called "flappers" and "gigolos" were common. Porter became a Parisian playboy, living an affluent life on Linda's wealth.

In spite of his glittering social life Porter studied music and composed new songs for *Kitchy-Koo*, with two editions in 1919 and 1923 and *Greenwich Village Follies* in 1924. The revue *Paris* in 1928 consolidated his position as an important musical personality.

With the death of his grandfather in 1923, Cole inherited a considerable fortune and lived more lavishly as a bon vivant than ever before. Continent-hopping became routine, but after 1930 he spent most of his time in New York and California. If the Great Depression of the 1930s was a time of austerity for the public it was a decade of affluence and success for Porter. After *Fifty Million Frenchmen* and *Wake Up and Dream* in 1929, Porter had many successes in the Naughty Thirties. Among them were *The Gay Divorcee* in 1932 with the lyric "Night and Day"; *Anything Goes* (1934) and "I Get a Kick Out of You," "You're the Top," and "Blow Gabriel, Blow"; *Jubilee* in 1935 with "Begin the Beguine," "Red Hot and Blue" (1936), *Leave It to Me* (1938) "My Heart Belongs to Daddy," and *DuBarry Was a Lady* in 1939. The original scores for the films *Born to Dance* and *Rosalie* in 1936 made the 1930s a banner decade.

Porter had a knack of choosing words and combining or misspelling them to create catchy sounds to fit his melodies when sung. Alliteration was a key factor in his creative process. The "Kling-Kling Bird on the Divi-Divi Tree," "Begin the Beguine" and "Rick Chick-A-Chick" are typical Porter combinations of vowels for musical effects. He mastered the poetic art of rhyme by modified spelling. Instead of saying "flatter her" he used *flatter'er* and rhymed it with "Cleopatra" by spelling the name *Cleopaterer*.

He continued to be creative after 1937 despite a serious accident when he fell from a horse and received multiple fractures of both legs. It was a personal disaster that brought him pain for the remainder of his life. After undergoing more than thirty operations over the next thirty-one years he finally suffered the removal of his right leg in April 1958. Though handicapped by the injury to his legs he continued to compose popular music and lyrics for both films and the stage. Among his successes in late life were *Panama Hattie* (1940), *You'll Never Get Rich* (film, 1941), *DuBarry Was a Lady* (film, 1945), *The Pirate* (film) and *Kiss Me Kate* in 1948, *Can Can* (1953) and *Les Girls* (film, 1957).

Linda died in May 1954, leaving to Cole an estate just short of $2 million. After the amputation of Porter's leg he lost his desire to be creative and his health continued to decline until his death in 1964. His earnings had skyrocketed to more than five hundred thousand dollars a year by 1963. Yale University was one of the beneficiaries of his $6 million estate. He was buried between his mother and Linda in the Mount Hope Cemetery, Peru, Indiana. After a long absence on Broadway, and in the glittering social sets of the world, the boy from an Indiana village came home to stay. He had proven the truth of Shakespeare's famous words, "All the world's a stage, And all the men and women merely players."

HWS

References: Charles Schwartz, *Cole Porter* (New York: Dial, 1977); David Ewen, *The Cole Porter Story* (New York: Holt, Rinehart, Winston, 1965); Robert Kimball, *The Complete Lyrics of Cole Porter* (New York: Knopf, 1983).

Emily Post

(October 3, 1873 — September 25, 1960)

Over a period of decades, the name of Emily Post became synonymous with good manners in America. Her *Etiquette: The Blue Book of Social Usage* first appeared in 1922, and thereafter went through twelve revisions and ninety-nine printings up to 1970, with sales amounting to more than a million copies.

Since colonial days Americans have been concerned with matters of social behavior. Breaches of right conduct — scandalmongering, cursing, lying, name-calling, flirting, and drinking to excess — might be punished by ducking, flogging, being placed in the stocks, or other unpleasant chastisement. George Washington, at the age of fifteen, composed his own rules, including such precepts as "Contradict not at every turn what others say"; when dining, "Put not another bit into your mouth until the former be swallowed"; "Cleanse not your teeth with the table cloth, napkin, fork or knife"; "Spit not in the fire"; "Kill no vermin as fleas, lice, ticks, etc. in the sight of others"; and "Reprehend not the imperfections of others for that belongs to parents, masters and superiors."

Considerable room for improvement remained in the young American republic after Washington's time. In her *Domestic Manners of the Americans*, based on a visit to this country in 1831, Mrs. Frances Trollope observed that a typical theater audience was like nothing that she had ever experienced back in England: "The noises were perpetual, and of the most unpleasant kind," she wrote. "Men came into the lower tier of boxes without their coats.... The spitting was incessant," and "the mixed smell of onions and whiskey" made her regret ever having come. Other travelers from abroad, notably Charles Dickens (in his *American Notes* and *Martin Chuzzlewit*), drew equally unflattering pictures of nineteenth-century American society and its behavior. And even as late as 1922 Emily Post had to remind her readers that in the theater it is "very inconsiderate to giggle or talk" or to drag your coat "across the heads of those sitting in front of you."

Made self-conscious and ill at ease by such comments from foreign and domestic critics, the Americans provided a ready market for a large homegrown literature of etiquette and improvement books, which began to flourish in the nineteenth and early twentieth centuries. The mass of such writings was pretty dreadful.

To fill the breach came Mrs. Post's *Etiquette: In Society, In Business, In Politics, and At Home*. The first edition, in a modest print of five thousand copies, immediately caught the public fancy, and in successive versions the work attained a position of commanding authority in its field. Generations of brides arranged their wedding plans by Mrs. Post's rules, thousands of teenage swains followed her advice about corsages, and countless American matrons placed the fish forks where Emily Post said they belonged.

Mrs. Post's qualifications for the job of regulating American social life were impeccable. Her family could be traced back to the seventeenth century, and she was ten times great-granddaughter of John and Priscilla Alden. Her father was a famous architect, and Emily grew up in New York, with summers in Bar Harbor or Tuxedo Park and frequent trips to Europe. A celebrated beauty, there were many candidates for her hand, from whom she chose a handsome banker, Edwin Main Post. Within a few years, unfortunately, both her father and husband lost their money, and the Posts' marriage went on the rocks, leaving Emily with two sons to support. At that point she turned to writing. Her first literary efforts consisted of five novels with high-society backgrounds.

Mrs. Post's venture into the etiquette field came about by chance. Not without considerable persuasion, Richard Duffy, a Funk and Wagnalls editor, convinced her that existing books on etiquette were of miserable quality and that she should undertake to write a better one. The rest is history. Within a year, Post's *Etiquette* was at the top of the nonfiction, best-seller list. "No social climber should be without one," suggested one critic.

Since she was writing about the kind of society she had known so intimately, Mrs. Post inevitably filled the first edition with advice concerning the right livery for footmen, the order of precedence at formal dinners, the duties of a kitchen-maid in a staff of twelve servants, and other problems of fashionable life. Edmund Wilson, in his *Classics and Commercials*, reports that he "fell under the book's spell and read it almost through," adding that "Mrs. Post is not merely the author of a comprehensive textbook on manners: she is a considerable imaginative writer, and her book has some of the excitement of a novel. It has also the snob-appeal which is evidently an important factor in the success of a Marquand or a Galsworthy." Wilson was reading the first edition.

The fictional atmosphere of *Etiquette* is enhanced by the creation of a cast of characters personifying various traits, who move in and out of the several editions. In a tradition that goes back to the medieval morality play *Everyman* and John Bunyan's *Pilgrim's Progress*, a group of abstract characters carries on the action for Mrs. Post. Undesirable and not to be emulated players include the Richan Vulgars, the Upstarts, Mr. and Mrs. Unsuitable, Mr. Parvenu, Mr. and Mrs. Gotta Crust, rich young people like the Lovejoys and the Gailys, newly rich such as Bobo and Lucy Gilding (she "smokes like a furnace and is miserable unless she can play bridge for high stakes"), "that odious Hector Newman," and, worst of all, "The Guest No One Invites Again."

Other memorable members of Mrs. Post's cast of characters are Mr. and Mrs. Kindheart, the Toploftys, the Oldnames, the Wellborns, the Eminents, the Notquites, the Spendeasy Westerns, Professor Bugge (the one intellectual admitted to the charmed circle), the Newlyweds, Mr. Stocksan Bonds, Miss Nobackground, the Greatlakes (representing the Midwest), the Littlehouses, and a clutch of eligible young bachelors or men-about-town: Frederick Bachelor, John Hunter Titherington Smith, and Clubwin Doe. The one artist we meet in the best society has a derisive name, Frederick Dauber.

Not until after publication of *Etiquette* did Mrs. Post discover the true nature of her mass audience, when letters began pouring in from all over the country. Desperate people wanted answers to simple questions: "Is it true that bread, before being eaten, must be broken into pieces exactly one inch in diameter?" "When passing your plate for a second helping, must you hold your knife and fork in your hand?" "Should a widow sign her letters Mrs. John Jones or Mrs. Mary Jones?" "How can I give a formal dinner for eight people and cook and serve it myself?" "How many butlers should a really elegant house have?" (From the wife of a postwar millionaire—the answer was one).

Responsive to obvious omissions in her book, Mrs. Post endeavored to clarify such matters in later editions. A chapter entitled "American Neighborhood Customs" was added dealing with showers, sewing circles, and other suburban activities, and a new character was born: Mrs. Three-in-One. Here was a wife who had no servant, but who managed to be an efficient cook, waitress, and charming hostess all at once. Nine pages of *Etiquette* came to be devoted to Mrs. Three-in-One, and only two and a half pages to butlers. A series of revisions kept *Etiquette* in tune with changing social mores.

Mrs. Post's fame and influence were spread further by a syndicated column that appeared in more than two hundred newspapers, with a circulation of some 6.5 million, and, starting in 1929, regular radio broadcasts.

The phenomenal success of Emily Post's *Etiquette* naturally encouraged the rise of competitors and emulators. In the early years, Lillian Eichler's *Book of Etiquette* was the chief rival, attracting sales comparable to Mrs. Post's. More recently, Amy Vanderbilt's *Complete Book of Social Etiquette*, first published in

1952, has had a great vogue. Some young moderns believe that Mrs. Vanderbilt is more in tune with the times because of her extended attention to such topics as servantless entertaining, gossip columnists, babysitters, buying an automobile, and divorce. Critics of strict etiquette and social conformity who question the need for guides on the subject are answered by Amy Vanderbilt in these words: "You can't be a social maverick today except on a Texas ranch. I don't advocate intellectual conformity, but rules of etiquette are for everybody's protection."

In an attempt to explain the popularity of Mrs. Post's *Etiquette*, Edmund Wilson asserts: "What you get in Emily Post, for all her concessions to the age's vulgarization, is a crude version of the social ideal to which the mass of Americans aspired after the Civil War: an ideal that was costly and glossy, smart, self-conscious and a little disgusting.... Today this ideal must be fading with the money that kept it up, but, such as it is, a great many people must still enjoy reading about it." A more recent commentator, Justin Kaplan, points out that the concept of the book has changed over the years from "a guide to forms and etiquette to a general encyclopedia of modern living which now gives practical and for the most part sensible advice on how to conduct yourself" in virtually any situation. In any event the remarkable staying powers of Emily Post and her *Etiquette* show little sign of weakening.

RBD

Reference: Edwin Post, *Truly Emily Post* (New York: Funk & Wagnalls, 1961).

Walter Philip Reuther

(September 1, 1907 — May 9, 1970)

Walter Reuther was for long one of the most dynamic and aggressive of American labor leaders. Participation in union affairs was an old tradition in his family. He was born in the heart of the coal and mining industries of West Virginia. His father was president of the Ohio Valley Trade and Labor Assembly, and his grandfather was for many years international organizer of the United Brewery Workers.

At the age of fifteen, Reuther went to work for the Wheeling Steel Corporation. There, symbolic of his future, he organized the workers in protest against Sunday and holiday work. Looking for larger fields to conquer, he moved on to Detroit in 1927 and was employed successively by the Briggs Manufacturing Company, Coleman Tool and Die plant, General Motors, and Ford Motor Company. As an expert Ford technician, he became a foreman over some forty men in the tool and die room. His future with Ford seemed assured, but in 1932 he was fired for union activity. During this period his interest in labor unions had grown. He organized and served as president of the Social Problems Club at Wayne University (where he was a night student), specialized in labor and industrial problems, and led students on the picket lines when strikes were in progress in Detroit.

Following termination of his job with Ford, Reuther and his brother Victor spent the next three years on a world tour, traveling in England, Russia, Central Asia, China, and Japan. They paid particular attention to the operation of auto plants and machine shops wherever they traveled, working wherever possible in shops and studying the labor movement. For a while, Walter held a job in a Russian auto factory.

By 1935, conditions seemed ripe for organizing U.S. auto workers and the brothers returned home. Walter's first move was to organize and to become president of the United Automobile Workers West Side Local, which in one year acquired thirty thousand members. In 1936 he was elected to the Executive Board of the International Union. He was active in the 1937 sit-down strikes and in major automobile industry strikes after that time.

Continuing his rise in the labor movement, Reuther became director of the United Automobile Workers' General Motors Department in 1939, vice-president of the UAW in 1942, and UAW president in 1946. In 1952 he was elected president of the CIO, and after the merger in 1955 of the CIO and the American Federation of Labor, which he helped to negotiate, a vice-president of that organization.

During World War II, Reuther supported labor's no-strike pledge. He won contracts with the Ford Motor Company and General Motors that called for a modified form of the guaranteed annual wage. He was a supporter of President Roosevelt in 1936 and again in 1940, and was a strong advocate of greater participation of labor in national defense matters.

With general acceptance of unionism by automobile corporations, Reuther worked on problems to make collective bargaining more efficient. In 1937, he reached an agreement with General Motors for the appointment of an impartial umpire to rule on disputes between labor and management. In general, Reuther took a middle-of-the road position. He was bitterly opposed to Communists in the ranks of labor, and fought to root out corruption in the unions. His contract demands and methods of negotiating for auto workers were widely copied by other unions. He was especially noted for his active interest in social welfare.

In physical appearance, Reuther was described as red-haired, pint-sized, and pale. He was athletically inclined and in college had won medals in swimming and basketball. Reuther died in a plane accident in 1970.

RBD

References: Eldorous L. Dayton, *Walter Reuther* (New York: Devin-Adair, 1958); Jean Gould, *Walter Reuther* (New York: Dodd, 1972); Irving Howe, *The UAW and Walter Reuther* (New York: Random, 1949); Robert L. Tyler, *Walter Reuther* (Grand Rapids, Mich.: W. B. Eerdmans, 1973).

Paul Revere

(January 1, 1735 — May 10, 1818)

Few passages of American poetry are as well known as Longfellow's tribute to Paul Revere, American Revolutionary War hero:

> Listen my children, and you shall hear
> Of the midnight ride of Paul Revere,
> On the eighteenth of April, in Seventy-Five;
> Hardly a man is now alive
> Who remembers that famous day and year.

Justin Winsor, American historian, declared that Longfellow "paid little attention to exactness of fact" in this commemorative verse, but it was undeniably stirring and easily remembered.

Paul Revere was named for his father, a French-born silversmith, and learned his father's craft. After service at Green Point, 1756, in the French and Indian War, the son became a leading silversmith in Boston, and also experimented with other crafts, such as copperplate engraving, dentistry, and cartooning.

Revere's intense interest in the American colonies' revolutionary movement began early. One of the manifestations was the production of political cartoons, which became highly effective propaganda for rebellion. During that period, he also satisfied a constant demand for seals, bookplates, certificates, and coats-of-arms, carved frames for Copley's portraits, and manufactured dental devices, which he advertised as both ornamental and "of real use in Speaking and Eating."

In 1773 Revere took direct action to protest Britain's unfair treatment of the colonies. As a member of the North End Caucus, probably the most influential of all the political clubs, in opposing the selling of tea by the East India Company, he helped to plan the Boston Tea Party and was one of the "Indians," wearing warpaint and feathers, who took part in that affair.

Revere was official courier for the Sons of Liberty, 1773-1774, and for the Massachusetts Provincial Assembly, 1774-1775. He rode to Philadelphia with the "Suffolk Resolves," made in defiance of the Intolerable Acts of September 9, 1774. On April 18, 1775, learning that the British regulars were about to march on Concord, he crossed the Charles River at night and rode from Charlestown to Medford and Lexington, giving warning to minutemen along the way. The patriots were thereby allowed time to move their military stores from Concord to avoid their capture. From Lexington, where he warned John Hancock and Samuel Adams that the British had sent out an expedition to capture them, he rode on to Concord with two other couriers, William Dawes and Samuel Prescott. It was this ride that was immortalized in Longfellow's poem. Actually, only Prescott reached Concord. Revere was stopped by British scouts and allowed to return to Lexington, sans horse. Back in Lexington, he rescued a trunkful of documents and papers, which Hancock had abandoned in his hasty flight.

Continuing his versatile career, Revere printed the first Continental money, 1775, using his own copperplates, designed the first official seal for the colonies and the Massachusetts State Seal, and directed a gunpowder mill at Canton, Massachusetts. With the rank of lieutenant colonel, he was in charge of Fort William (defending Boston harbor), 1778-1779, and served in the Penobscot Expedition in 1779.

After the war, Revere returned to gold and silversmithing, making pieces that are now collectors' items. He also cast bells and made cannons. His foundry manufactured bolts and copper fittings for the *Constitution* ("Old Ironsides"). He also invented a process for rolling sheet copper, used in Robert Fulton's steam ferryboat boilers. In 1795, as grand master of the Masonic order, Revere laid the cornerstone of the new state house in Boston. His copper business was continued and enlarged by his descendants and survived into the twentieth century. In his later years, Revere was deeply involved in numerous civic activities, especially in agitating for the ratification of the federal Constitution.

Paul Revere was the most distinguished of American silversmiths of his period and the most popular. He generally followed British styles. Two of his widely imitated pieces are the Revere Bowl, from a Chinese porcelain original, and the Revere Pitcher, after a Liverpool model. His bells were famous in his time; one of the best known was installed at King's Chapel, Boston.

Until his death at age eighty-three, Revere persisted in wearing the costumes of Revolutionary days.

RBD

References: Esther Forbes, *Paul Revere and the World He Lived In* (Boston: Houghton, 1942); Elbridge H. Goss, *The Life of Colonel Paul Revere* (Boston: Gregg, 1972); Belle Moses, *Paul Revere: The Torch Bearer of the Revolution* (New York: Appleton, 1916).

William Penn Adair (Will) Rogers

(November 4, 1879—August 15, 1935)

Will Rogers, the most popular American humorist and entertainer of his generation, was in the tradition of Civil War cracker-box humorists, such as Artemus Ward, the anecdotal genius of Abraham Lincoln, Mr. Dooley during the Spanish-American War era, and Mark Twain.

Rogers was born in Indian Territory (now Oklahoma) near the present town of Claremore. His father, a prosperous rancher and banker of mixed Irish and Cherokee blood, was high in the councils of the Cherokee Nation and served as a member of the constitutional convention when Oklahoma was admitted to the Union. Will's mother was a graduate of the Indian Female Seminary at Tahlequah. Will was proud of his Indian ancestry from both parents. One of his most quoted remarks, made to a Boston audience, was "My ancestors didn't come over on the *Mayflower*—they met the boat."

Will had a restless and adventurous youth, perhaps characteristic of a frontier upbringing. He owned the best horses on the range and became expert at roping calves, a talent that later became an essential feature of his skill as showman and humorist. His formal education was spotty—study at several boarding schools and attendance for a time at Kemper Military School at Boonville, Missouri. Despite his limited education, Will developed precision in speech and writing, though like earlier humorists he used misspellings and grammatical slips for humorous effect.

Possibly from boredom and looking for more lively activity, Will quit school in 1898 to become a cowboy in the Texas Panhandle. Four years later, in 1902, he sailed for Argentina as a ranch hand. Later the same year he went on to South Africa and began earning his living with a roping and horseback riding act in a road show. Will's wanderlust was further satisfied with trouping in Australia before he returned home in 1904. He came back in time to appear in the tanbark ring at the St. Louis Exposition.

Will's first appearance in a New York show occurred in 1905 as a member of the Colonel Zach Mulhall outfit. Shortly thereafter, while performing at a supper club at Keith's Union Square Theatre, the audience was amused at Rogers' southwestern drawl. From then on his informal jokes, while chewing gum and doing a rope act, became part of his performance. His first musical show, *The Hill Street Girl*, was staged in 1912, and Will was the star in the 1915 show *Hands Up*. Most popular of all the Rogers roles was played in the Ziegfeld Follies, in which he performed in the years 1916-1918, 1922, and 1924-1925. As described by one biographer, Dixon Wecter, Will had "a shock of coarse black hair, later iron-gray, unruly as a schoolboy's, frank blue eyes lifted suddenly in shrewd appraisal, face weather-beaten and crinkled by his contagious grin, and clothes that looked as if he had taken a long nap in them." In short, Will played his natural self, with no pretensions.

As time went on, Rogers became increasingly involved as a humorous commentator on politics and public affairs in general. Calvin Coolidge was a close friend, and as Coolidge's "ambassador of good will," and correspondent for the *Saturday Evening Post*, Rogers toured Europe in 1926, writing *Letters of a Self-Made Diplomat to His President*. Other humorous works included *The Illiterate Digest* (1924), *There's Not a Bathing Suit in Russia* (1927), and *Ether and Me* (1929). The circle of his readers expanded immensely after 1926, when he began to write a daily telegram, syndicated to about 350 newspapers and read by an estimated 40 million people.

Rogers once remarked, "I do not belong to any organized party—I am a Democrat," and on another occasion he stated that he belonged to the Democratic party because "it is funnier to be a Democrat." His standard line was "Well, all I know is what I read in the papers." Herbert Hoover and Al Smith were among his intimate friends. By nature, he was a conservative and all politicians and parties were targets for his gentle barbs.

After about 1925, Rogers was in great demand as lecturer and radio speaker. He also became a favorite motion picture actor, with such successes as *They Had to See Paris, State Fair, A Connecticut Yankee, David Harum, Judge Priest*, and *Steamboat Round the Bend*. His box office appeal is attested to by his annual income of six hundred thousand dollars in the mid-thirties from pictures, radio, lecturing and writing—a phenomenal sum in the Great Depression, making him the highest paid entertainer of his time. His reputation with the public was further enhanced by his generosity in giving to charity.

Will Rogers was an early enthusiast for air travel. He flew around South America in 1931 and in the Far East the following year. In 1935, he planned a flight north to the Orient with his fellow Oklahoman Wiley Post. Near Point Barrow, Alaska, on August 15, their single-engine plane developed trouble. They crashed in shallow water and both men were killed. Rogers' home, now a museum, is part of Will Rogers State Historic Park in Pacific Palisades, California.

RBD

References: E. Paul Alworth, *Will Rogers* (New York: Twayne, 1974); Donald Day, *Will Rogers: A Biography* (New York: McKay, 1969); Richard M. Ketchum, *Will Rogers: His Life and Times* (New York: McGraw, 1972); Betty Rogers, *Will Rogers* (Indianapolis, Ind.: Bobbs-Merrill, 1942).

Elihu Root

(February 15, 1843 — February 7, 1937)

Elihu Root was one of the most successful corporation lawyers in American legal history. He was even more noted as a statesman and advocate of international peace.

After graduating from Hamilton College in 1864, Root decided to enter the legal profession. He enrolled in the New York University Law School, received his degree in 1867, and was admitted to the bar. His rise was rapid and in the course of his legal career, he became the acknowledged leader of the American bar. Root's practice was primarily concerned with cases relating to banks, railroads, wills, and estates, and to New York City's municipal government. Later, when he became prominent politically, his enemies damned him for being a "Wall Street lawyer."

In politics, Root remained a conservative Republican throughout his career, though, not infrequently, he was in opposition to leaders of his party. A close connection was formed early with Theodore Roosevelt, whom he supported for mayor of New York, as police commissioner, and later for New York State governor. In the governor's office, Roosevelt often drew upon Root's advice, especially in matters relating to trusts and franchise taxes.

In 1899, President McKinley appointed Root to his cabinet as secretary of war, at the same time making him responsible for governing the former Spanish colonies, taken over at the end of the Spanish-American War. Root's achievements in that position were outstanding in two areas. The war had revealed scandalous inefficiency in the War Department. Root proceeded to reorganize the regular army, to create a general staff, and to establish the Army War College, despite bitter opposition by an entrenched military bureaucracy. It was a stormy period, marked by the Boxer uprising in China, an insurrection in the Philippines, the withdrawal of U.S. troops from Cuba, and the establishment of a government for the Philippines. Another one of the conquered territories, Puerto Rico, where 90 percent of the population was illiterate, presented a simpler problem, because the island had not been ravaged by war. The elimination of tariffs opened mainland markets to the Puerto Ricans and aided the economy there.

In the case of Cuba, Root's selection of General Leonard Wood as military governor was a stroke of genius. Under his guidance, the program of sanitation, school-building, and other reforms proceeded rapidly, and by 1902 the Cubans were ready to govern themselves. The situation was different in the Philippines where two years of guerilla fighting had gone on before peace was established. A commission under William Howard Taft was sent out in 1900. Taft and Root, with Roosevelt's support, were as effective in solving the Philippine problems as Root and Wood had been in Cuba.

A later secretary of war, Newton D. Baker, commented that Root's work was "the outstanding contribution made by any Secretary of War from the beginning of history." For family and health reasons, Root resigned from the cabinet in 1903. He served as chairman of the 1904 Republican National Convention which nominated Roosevelt for the presidency. In 1905, Roosevelt called Root back to Washington as secretary of state.

As secretary of state, one of Root's major accomplishments was to improve relations with Latin American nations, which had reached a low ebb. Root made a tour of South America in 1906. He established friendly contacts with leading Latin-American diplomats and cooperated with Mexico in mediating Central American disputes. Likewise, Root worked for friendly relations with Japan, arranging an agreement to control Japanese emigration to the United States and, with Roosevelt's support, opposed exclusion laws. Further to strengthen international peace, arbitration treaties were concluded with numerous nations.

Root resigned from the State Department shortly before the end of the Roosevelt administration and was elected in 1909 as U.S. senator from New York. The office was uncongenial to him, however, and he declined to be a candidate for reelection when his term ended. Meanwhile, he was chief counsel for the United States in settling a long-standing controversy with Britain over the North Atlantic Coast fisheries. President Taft appointed him as a member of the Permanent Court of Arbitration. In the same year, Root was elected president of the Carnegie Endowment for International Peace.

As the recognized leader of the peace movement in the United States and as a tribute to his contribution to peace in the Western Hemisphere, his work for arbitration, and for setting up an enlightened colonial system, Root received the Nobel Peace Prize in 1912.

During his senatorial term, Root was caught in the rift between Roosevelt and Taft, which split the Republican party in 1912. He presided over the Republican National Convention that nominated Taft, followed by the secession of the Bull Moose Party. Thus ended Root's long friendship with Theodore Roosevelt. Roosevelt never forgave him.

Root had little sympathy for Woodrow Wilson and his New Freedom. He opposed most of the important administration measures, except for taking a leading part in passage of the Federal Reserve System in 1913, but after the United States entered World War I in 1917 he preached and worked for support of the president. He was asked by Wilson to head a mission to Russia in 1917 to try to persuade that government to carry on the war. By then the Bolsheviks had gained control and the mission was a failure.

Root was in favor, with certain reservations, of the United States joining the League of Nations, believing that the interests of the United States would be best served as a member of that body. After American rejection of the league, he helped to establish the Permanent Court of International Justice.

In his later years, Root, who lived to age ninety-four, became an elder states-man of the Republican party. One biographer, David Brody, characterized him as "a preeminent example of American conservatism, a man of great rectitude, a public servant of high talents, but utterly lacking in popular appeal."

RBD

References: Philip C. Jessup, *Elihu Root* (New York: Dodd, 1938); Richard W. Leopold, *Elihu Root and the Conservative Tradition* (Boston: Little, Brown, 1954); James B. Scott, *Elihu Root's Services to International Law* (New York: Carnegie Endowment for International Peace, 1925).

Augustus Saint-Gaudens

(March 1, 1848 — August 3, 1907)

The man who is generally acclaimed to be the greatest American sculptor was born in Dublin to an Irish mother and a French father, was given a French name, and studied in Rome at a critical time of his life. But Augustus Saint-Gaudens was brought to New York City as an infant and spent the major part of his life creating statues and monuments commemorating American subjects. His two Lincoln statues in Chicago, his equestrian monument to General Sherman in New York's Central Park, and his memorial to Mrs. Henry Adams in Rock Creek Cemetery in Washington exemplify the highest achievements of sculptural art in the United States.

Saint-Gaudens was the son of Bernard Saint-Gaudens, a shoemaker who lived originally near Toulouse in southern France. The father moved to Dublin, where he resided seven years, married Mary McGuinness, and transported his wife and their baby son to the United States in 1848. After some schooling in New York City Augustus was apprenticed at the age of thirteen to a stone cameo-cutter, and he worked at this trade and also as a shell cameo-cutter while studying at night at Cooper Union. He also attended the National Academy of Design where he had his first experience in drawing from the nude.

Convinced that his son had genuine artistic ability and an ambition to succeed, Bernard Saint-Gaudens paid for his passage to Europe and gave him one hundred dollars to attend the Paris Exhibition of 1867. Augustus was finally able to enroll at the Ecole des Beaux-Arts and to enter the atelier of an artist named Jouffroy at the same time that he found employment as a cameo-cutter in Paris. He remained there until the breakout of the Franco-Prussian War in 1870. At that time he decided to continue his artistic training in Rome.

In Italy he was interested in studying classical sculpture and began to copy traditional statues. But as Royal Cortissoz pointed out, Saint-Gaudens, when he attempted something original, did not produce one more Apollo or Venus but instead chose to model a Hiawatha. During his Roman days, which lasted to 1877, he early showed his high spirits, his persevering industry, and his skill at portraiture. An American friend subsidized the carving of Hiawatha in marble and also arranged for a commission to do a bust of William M. Evarts, later a secretary of the treasury and a senator from New York. In 1877 Saint-Gaudens married Augusta F. Homer of Roxbury, Massachusetts.

Back in the United States, Saint-Gaudens established a studio on Thirty-sixth Street in New York City which became an occasional meeting place for artistic and intellectual friends: the Episcopal clergyman Phillips Brooks, the painter John La Farge, the architects Henry H. Richardson and Stanford White. Another friend, Henry Adams, had already begun to talk with Saint-Gaudens about a possible memorial to his wife.

The sculptor was commissioned to do a statue of Admiral Farragut, which was unveiled in Madison Square in 1881. It was a masterpiece, in the words of Royal Cortissoz, "a living embodiment, a public monument with the stamp of creative art on it." Stanford White designed its pedestal. The Farragut was the first in a series of important American historical figures whom Saint-Gaudens sculptured: Lincoln and General John A. Logan in Chicago, Dr. James McCosh, Col. Robert Gould Shaw in Boston, Deacon Samuel Chapin in Springfield, Massachusetts (the statue commonly called for its symbolic nature the "Puritan"). The sculptor also did a statue of Robert Louis Stevenson for St. Giles Cathedral in Edinburgh, which he completed in his Paris studio in 1902.

There were other achievements. The Luxembourg National Museum acquired the *Amor Caritas* in 1887 and in 1892 the twenty-foot nude *Diana* was installed at the top of Madison Square Garden in New York City. Saint-Gaudens was not a fast worker but he worked hard and steadily. He once penned an axiom: "Conceive an idea. Then stick to it. Those who hang on are the only ones who amount to anything."

The sculptor's greatest monuments are undoubtedly the equestrian Sherman in New York and the Rock Creek Cemetery *Grief*. General Sherman had sat for a portrait bust in 1888, but after the monument was commissioned in 1892 it took the artist eleven years to complete his task. The result, however, was admirable; the bare-headed rider, the horse apparently in motion with flowing mane, and the symbolic figure in advance leading the way make an amazing unit. As Oliver Larkin expressed it, "Horse, rider, and companion unite to complete a rhythm which is almost musical."

Quite different is the Adams memorial, described as enigmatic, mysterious, solemn, yet simple, an inscrutable seated, hooded figure. Instead of the naturalism and specific details of the historical sculpture, this is intentionally brooding and reverent. John Hay, a friend of Henry Adams, wrote to the bereaved husband before he had seen the monument: "It is full of poetry and suggestion. Infinite wisdom; a past without beginning and a future without end; a repose, after limitless experience."

In 1885 Saint-Gaudens acquired a summer home at Cornish, New Hampshire, which he called Aspet and which became both headquarters and sanctuary. But this decision did not curb his activities until ill health set in. He taught at the Art Students' League from 1888 to 1897. He was a founder of the Society of American Artists, a member of the Royal Academy in London, and the winner of the Grand Prix at the Sorbonne in 1900. Harvard, Yale, and Princeton awarded him honorary degrees. Theodore Roosevelt, a friend of his, interested him in reforming the American coinage and he designed the twenty dollar gold piece. Saint-Gaudens was also known for his kindness to and encouragement of young artists. Frederick MacMonnies, for example, was once his student and he supported the choice of MacMonnies to design a large fountain for the Chicago World's Fair of 1893.

Henry Adams once accompanied the sculptor on a visit to Amiens Cathedral. Both the connoisseur of architecture and the experienced sculptor admired the great church but they looked at it differently. Where Adams discerned force, Saint-Gaudens found only a "channel of taste." Adams remarked in his autobiography that his companion was really a man of the fifteen hundreds: "Saint-Gaudens was a child of Benvenuto Cellini, smothered in an American cradle."

JTF

References: Royal Cortissoz, *DAB*, XVI, 1935, pp. 296-302; Homer Saint-Gaudens, *The Reminiscences of Augustus Saint-Gaudens*, 2 vols., edited and amplified by Homer Saint-Gaudens (New York: Century, 1913); Louise Hall Tharpe, *Saint-Gaudens and the Gilded Era* (Boston: Little, Brown, 1969).

Carl Sandburg

(January 6, 1878 — July 22, 1967)

It might be supposed that Carl Sandburg would have been the inevitable recipient of the Nobel Prize for literature. An American-born writer of Swedish descent, a versatile author who made his mark in both verse and prose, a creative figure who enjoyed a long literary career, and a familiar bard and speaker on the lecture circuit, he was awarded medals, honorary degrees, and three Pulitzer prizes. But the Nobel Prize eluded him. He had, of course, strong competition for the honor during his most productive years — Sinclair Lewis and Eugene O'Neill, and eventually Faulkner and Hemingway. He wrote little fiction and virtually no drama and most of the American honorees were novelists. Also he never had the European reputation that O'Neill and Hemingway, for example, achieved. But not even his fame as a foremost biographer of Abraham Lincoln brought him the required recognition. Nevertheless, Sandburg remains one of the outstanding American literary figures of the twentieth century.

Sandburg was born of Swedish immigrant parents in Galesburg, Illinois. His father, who could read but never learned to write, was employed in the blacksmith shop of the Chicago, Burlington & Quincy railroad. Carl, who at one time called himself Charles, was one of seven children, who grew up on the fringe of poverty but were inured to hard work. He himself, in his incomplete autobiography, *Always the Young Strangers*, published in 1952, is the best source for details about his childhood and youth. He attended the Galesburg schools and at the age of eleven acquired the first of a number of jobs, that of an office boy. Later he delivered newspapers, worked in a brickyard, peddled milk from a wagon, served as a porter in a barber shop, and harvested ice. These years were educational in several ways: they taught him the need to make a living, they developed a strongly proletarian point of view, and they gave him a folk vocabulary which influenced much of his later poetry.

In 1897, nearing manhood but with an adolescent's restlessness and craving for experience, Sandburg headed for the Kansas wheatfields, a boxcar his method of transportation. He got to Denver and Omaha, joined a railroad section gang, worked with a threshing crew, washed dishes. Back in Galesburg he became an apprentice to a house painter. But when the Spanish-American War broke out Sandburg enlisted with the Sixth Infantry of Illinois Volunteers and served for half a year in Puerto Rico. After his return home he decided that he needed more formal education and he enrolled at a hometown school, Lombard College (later Knox College) in Galesburg. He eked out his limited funds by being a fireman, a bell ringer, and a janitor. It was at Lombard that Sandburg first showed his ability as a writer, and one of his mentors, Philip Green Wright, not only encouraged him but aided him in the publication of his first book in 1904, *In Reckless Ecstasy*. Sandburg remained at Lombard until 1902 but did not graduate.

His next decision took him into the world of business and journalism. He served as organizer for the Social-Democratic party and was secretary to the mayor of Milwaukee from 1910 to 1912. In Chicago he was briefly the associate editor of the *System Magazine* in 1913 and also worked with an experimental tabloid called *Daybook*. In 1917 he joined the staff of the Chicago *Daily News*, a paper with which he was associated for the rest of his journalistic career. By this time he had become known as a poet. Although Sandburg had written verse since his college days, recognition came to him first when the Chicago magazine *Poetry*, edited by Harriet Monroe, published nine of his poems in the March 1914 issue. One was the celebrated "Chicago," which was awarded the Helen Haire Levinson prize of two hundred dollars. Two years later he published his first important book of verse, *Chicago Poems*, a collection of 146 brief lyrical impressions many of which were only a half page long. The book also included such longer pieces as "To a Contemporary Bunkshooter," "Skyscraper," and the title poem.

Three other collections of verse followed in quick succession: *Cornhuskers* (1918), but awarded a prize the next year; *Smoke and Steel* (1920), and *Slabs of the Sunburnt West* (1922). The four volumes illustrate the full gamut of his work and also illustrate his dependence on personal experience. For Sandburg was both an urban and a rural poet, fascinated by the smokestack industry of working America and by the hues and sounds of prairies and cornfields. Affected by the imagist movement, Sandburg was chiefly a lyric poet, with a memorable ability to capture a specific scene, a touch of beauty, a glimpse of human life. He generally chose to write free verse, often with long lines reminiscent of Whitman, with no regular rhythm and a sparing use of alliteration. But his poems often had a sinuous strength and a verbal candor which won audiences. T. K. Whipple once spoke of Sandburg's verse as "much power ill controlled." Poems like the well known "Fog," "Prairie," and "Nocturne in a Deserted Brickyard" lingered in the minds of readers who also admired "Killers" and "Smoke and Steel." Sandburg's *Complete Poems*, published in 1950, won him a second Pulitzer Prize.

In the meanwhile he had produced *The People, Yes*, in 1936, an extraordinary compilation which may well be Sandburg's most enduring book. This is a combination of original verse with proverbs, maxims, fragments of popular ballads, native legends, and the daily speech of the people. Its 107 numbered sections have neither coherence nor sequence but are alive, sometimes humorous, sometimes pithy and tart, and basically showing the poet's faith in the vitality and determination of the American people to survive. In the book's final section Sandburg reiterates his faith: "Man is a long time coming, Man will yet win."

In 1908 Sandburg married Lillian Steichen, the sister of the well-known photographer, and somewhat later he changed his residence to Harbert, Michigan; in the spring of 1946 he moved to Flat Rock, North Carolina. During the Michigan years he gave up daily journalism to devote himself to verse and collecting folk songs and ballads. Although imperfectly trained musically, he had a naturally rich voice and taught himself to play a guitar and a banjo. For years he recited or sang for audiences throughout the country. One result of this experience was his compilation *The American Songbag* (1927), which he described as a ragbag of 280 songs, ballads, and ditties with both words and music. The book included minstrel songs, blues, and songs about hoboes, lumberjacks, sailors, bandits, and railroad workers. It remains an important collection of native folk songs.

Probably the major interest of Sandburg's life was the biography of Abraham Lincoln. He had been born in the state in which Lincoln first achieved celebrity, his hometown had once been the locale of a Lincoln-Douglas debate, and he grew up familiar with the legends and lore that had become attached to Lincoln's name. He gradually immersed himself in the Lincoln story, collecting material, scouring magazines and newspapers, reviewing the biographical accounts, studying the economic and military aspects of the Civil War. In 1926 he published the first results of his work, *Abraham Lincoln: The Prairie Years*, in two volumes.

Thirteen years later he completed his project in four more volumes. *Abraham Lincoln: The War Years*. The six volumes were condensed into a single book in 1954. Sandburg was not a professional historian and probably dredged up no significant new facts but it would be impossible to impugn his devotion to his task. Readers have generally preferred the beginning part of the monumental biography because of Sandburg's command of the background, but his delineation of Lincoln in the presidential office, humane, sympathetic, sometimes uncertain, but always dedicated to the Union and his country has won consistent admiration.

Sandburg added other books to his literary achievement. More poems appeared in *Good Morning, America* (1928), which also included the thirty-eight definitions of poetry which he had published first in the *Atlantic Monthly* in 1923. His statement that "Poetry is a sliver of the moon lost in the belly of a golden frog" speaks well for his imaginative use of language but less persuasively for his sense of analysis. At the age of seventy in 1948 he published his only extensive piece of fiction, a long historical novel entitled *Remembrance Rock* which won him few plaudits. *The Sandburg Range* (1957), is a Sandburg anthology including excerpts from his novel, his autobiography, the Lincoln biography, his verse, and his children's stories, plus a scattering of new material. Another gathering of verse, *Honey and Salt*, was published in 1963, and in 1968 the year after his death Herbert Mitgang edited *The Letters of Carl Sandburg*, including 640 items.

JTF

References: Harry Golden, *Carl Sandburg* (Cleveland, Ohio: World, 1961); North Callahan, *Carl Sandburg: Lincoln of Our Literature* (New York: New York University, 1969); Richard Crowder, *Carl Sandburg* (New York: Twayne, 1964); Helga Sandburg, *A Great and Glorious Romance* (New York: Harcourt Brace Jovanovich, 1978) (written by Sandburg's youngest daughter).

George Santayana
(December 16, 1863 — September 28, 1952)

One of the prominent American men of letters of the twentieth century, George Santayana was born in Madrid and died in Rome. But he was brought to the United States as a child, he was educated in Boston, and he served as a distinguished member of the department of philosophy at Harvard University from 1889 to 1912. Although he retained Spanish citizenship throughout his life, he valued his long association with the United States and published most of his books here. In 1894 he began his long career as a writer with a volume of poetry called *Sonnets and Other Verses*. This was followed by other books of verse, literary and aesthetic analysis, and philosophy. The last subject became his major interest and is the focus of most of the titles which make up the fourteen volume edition of *The Works of George Santayana*, published in New York in 1936-1937. After resigning from Harvard he returned to Europe, residing briefly in Oxford and Paris but finally making his home at the Santo Stefano Rotondo convent in Rome. A family inheritance and increasing profit from his many publications enabled him to live as a free spirit and to devote his time to writing. He never married and had virtually no family life. His only novel, *The Last Puritan*, won wide acclaim and was the choice of the Book-of-the-Month Club in 1936. His literary work, no matter what the subject was, consistently won him praise for his elegant and graceful style. But he has also been ranked with William James and John Dewey among the leading American philosophers.

When Santayana's mother, who had children from an earlier marriage, chose to move to New England in order to benefit from family property there, she left the boy in the custody of his father in Spain. For a short time he lived in Avila. Then his father took him to Boston, where he was enrolled in the Brimmer School and later in the Boston Latin School. By this time the parents were separated and young Santayana continued his American education. At Harvard, from which he graduated in 1886, he had the good fortune to study under George Herbert Palmer, William James, and especially Josiah Royce, who eventually directed his doctoral dissertation. Santayana spent two years in postgraduate study in Germany and was awarded the degree of Ph.D. from Harvard in 1889, after which he was immediately appointed to the faculty. He enjoyed teaching and was a popular lecturer. In later years he lectured at Oxford and the Sorbonne. But as soon as his financial situation permitted it he relinquished any educational appointment and adopted the role of a private scholar.

Santayana followed his early book of poetry with *Lucifer: A Theological Tragedy*, a verse play which was published in 1899 and revised in 1924. His multivolume study, *The Life of Reason*, 1905-1906, dealt with reason as applied to common sense, society, religion, art, and science. It attracted considerable attention among philosophers and won the approval of William James. Santayana's next book, *Three Philosophical Poets: Lucretius, Dante, and Goethe*, 1910, combined his two chief intellectual interests, poetry and philosophy. His 1913 volume, *Winds of Doctrine*, expressed his views of contemporary opinion. Two volumes of what might be called *obiter dicta*, terse essays or observations of life on both sides of the Atlantic, deal with *Character and Opinion in the United States* (1920), and *Soliloquies in England and Later Soliloquies* (1922). The year 1923 saw the appearance of *Scepticism and Animal Faith*. Four years later Santayana published the first of four volumes dealing with his personal sense of ontology, the philosophical concept of reality. *The Realm of Essence* was followed by books concerned with matter, truth, and spirit, the last appearing in 1940. Although the work can appeal only to a limited audience it is, in the words of one of the historians of American philosophy, Herbert Schneider, "one of the masterpieces of philosophic construction, and will undoubtedly survive our times, since it is addressed to a reflective reader of any age or culture and seeks to express in a fresh idiom an enduring truth."

The three volumes of Santayana's autobiography, collectively called *Persons and Places*, completed in 1953, are respectively entitled *The Background of My Life* (1944), *The Middle Span* (1945), and *My Host the World*, published posthumously. Irwin Edman's *The Philosophy of Santayana: Selections*, originally issued in 1936, was amplified and revised in 1953. Daniel Cory edited *Letters of George Santayana* in 1955.

Readers who are not well grounded in philosophy may prefer his single novel to his treatises on theory. *The Last Puritan* can be illuminating and delightful reading. The author himself came from a Roman Catholic background and a warm, sunny climate. Although never a partisan member of the church he was not insensitive to its pageantry and traditionalism. As a youth he was plunged into an often cold northern climate and an environment which preserved vestiges of theocracy and Unitarianism. The conflict which ensued in his own mind and experience is dramatized in the novel in two characters: Oliver Alden and Mario Van de Weyer. Oliver, heir to an effete, affluent New England family, is brought up by his mother and a governess. He is intellectual and moralistic, austere and ascetic, in other words the last Puritan. Mario, a friend and relative, is a hedonist brought up in England and on the continent, basically a dilettante. Oliver's love affair goes badly and he, dejected and morose, joins the army in World War I and is killed in France. The two characters are alive as well as symbolic of conflicting points of view. Temperaments and philosophies clash and sometimes the dialogue is heavy and likely to be enmeshed in abstruse or abstract subjects. But the style is firm and dignified, modulated with a wise humor, and reveals the author's mellow knowledge of life.

JTF

References: John K. Roth, *DAB*, Supplement 5, 1977, pp. 601-3; George Santayana, "A Brief History of My Opinions," in Irwin Edman, ed., *The Philosophy of Santayana*, pp. 1-21 (New York: Random House, 1936); Richard Butler, *The Life and World of George Santayana* (Chicago: Regnery, 1960); Willard Arnett, *George Santayana* (New York: Washington Square Press, 1968).

John Singer Sargent

(January 12, 1856 — April 15, 1925)

Many of the most prominent American painters in the eighteenth and nineteenth centuries went to England and France for training. John S. Copley, John Vanderlyn, Charles Willson Peale, and John Trumbull chose London and actually worked in the studio of Benjamin West (who was born in Pennsylvania but made his reputation abroad). A later group like Mary Cassatt, Thomas Eakins, and George Inness profited from study in the ateliers of Paris. But John Singer Sargent spent so much of his life across the Atlantic that it was sometimes difficult to classify him as an American. He was born in Florence and he died in London. He was twenty years old when he saw the United States for the first time. He travelled extensively in Spain, Italy, and Morocco, and in 1884 established his residence in England where he was notably successful. But in the last decades of the nineteenth century he temporarily made his headquarters in Boston and when he was offered a knighthood in England in 1907 he refused on the ground that he was and would remain an American citizen. Samuel Isham's tribute, in which he declared that Sargent was the first portrait painter since Reynolds and Gainsborough, is ironic but flattering.

Sargent was the son of American parents residing in Italy. His father was a doctor, Fitz-William Sargent, whom his mother persuaded to become an expatriate before the son's birth. She was interested in art and encouraged the boy at an early age. He attended the Academy in Florence and painted landscapes from nature as his family moved through Germany, Italy, and France. In 1874 Sargent began formal study at the Beaux-Arts in Paris and enrolled in the atelier of Carolus-Duran, the youngest student admitted. In a short time he developed some of the facility for which he became famous and excelled his master. A picture which he exhibited at the Paris Salon in 1878 won early recognition, which was considerably enhanced by the time he moved to London in 1884. Some of his portraits provoked criticism because they violated the academic conventions of his time. Parisian critics of his picture *Madame Gautreau* felt that the artist was malicious but Sargent himself contended that he had painted the costume as the subject chose. Early pictures like *El Jaleo* and *Girl with a Rose* displayed an innate vitality. He was also recognized for his competent draftsmanship, virtuosity in his brushwork, and his brilliant colors. Moreover, his sitters liked him because he flattered them.

In his London studio Sargent began to produce a series of pictures of children which were generally admired for their delicacy and beauty. His success in this field seems odd when one remembers that Sargent never married and grew up with no domestic experience. When the canvas *Carnation, Lily, Lily, Rose* was exhibited at the Royal Academy in 1887 it was highly successful. One of his triumphs of this kind is *The Daughters of Edward D. Boit*, now in the Boston Museum of Fine Arts. As Oliver Larkin wrote, "no painter of the time could so have managed the range between black stockings and starched white pinafores, the polish of high blue-and-white Chinese vases, the corner of a red screen."

In the 1890s Sargent made almost annual transatlantic trips to Boston and in the opening year of that decade painted his *Carmencita*, preferred by many as his masterpiece. Later portraits of Henry Marquand, William M. Chase, and the

Wyndham sisters are in the possession of the Metropolitan Museum. He also did portraits of various American actors such as Edwin Booth, Joseph Jefferson, and Lawrence Barrett, and became celebrated for his Wertheimer family pictures. An American cultural historian like Charles Beard could speak of the artist's work with enthusiasm: "There was a polished finesse and steel-like accuracy in the portraits of the lords, ladies, and rich bourgeois that sprang into phantom life under the brush of John Singer Sargent."

Portraiture was not the only kind of painting that Sargent engaged in although it brought him his greatest acclaim. The trustees of the Boston Public Library commissioned him to paint mural decorations for that building. Sargent began his work in 1891, completed the first part in 1894, and supervised its implacement the following year. The work was not finished until 1916. Sargent was later asked to decorate the rotunda of the Boston Art Museum.

He also in the course of his career painted many landscapes, especially of Venice and the Tyrol, and in the summer of 1916 he travelled to Glacier Park and the Canadian Rockies and sketched many of the scenes he encountered. One of his most admired American landscapes is the view of Lake O'Hara, now in the Fogg Art Museum at Harvard University.

Probably no painter ever worked harder than Sargent. He travelled a good deal but seldom let his travels interfere with his painting. He took no vacations although he used his numerous transatlantic crossings as rest periods. His work was featured in various exhibitions. One of the first was held at the St. Botolph Club in Boston in 1887. In 1897 he was made a Royal Academician and two years later the Copley Hall Sargent exhibition at Boston included 110 pictures. In 1918 at the end of World War I he went to the front and recorded his impressions on canvas for the Imperial War Museum in London. In 1924 another large Sargent show was held in New York but by this time his vogue had diminished somewhat and the modernists began to find fault with his work.

Samuel Isham has provided one of the best evaluations of Sargent's work. There were limitations. The painter was not at his best when engaged with murals and not all of his landscapes are of superior quality. But Isham notes especially the careful realism which extended to the artist's use of background and necessary properties, his depiction of inanimate things, and particularly the integrity of his rendering of character. Sargent seemed able to suggest pomposity or shyness, humor or stolidity, conventionality or eccentricity. And withal he provided smooth and flowing paint and brilliant and pure color. No wonder Henry James remarked about the painter that on the threshold of his career he had nothing more to learn.

JTF

References: William Howe Downes, *DAB*, XVI, 1935, pp. 363-67; William Howe Downes, *John S. Sargent: His Life and Work* (Boston: Little, Brown, 1925); Samuel Isham, *The History of American Painting* (New York: Macmillan, 1927).

William Henry Seward

(May 16, 1801 — October 10, 1872)

William H. Seward is probably best remembered today for the purchase of "Seward's Icebox" or "Seward's Folly" (Alaska) from Russia for $7.2 million in 1867.

Seward was an influential figure in American political life for nearly half a century. Shortly after graduating from Union College, New York, in 1820, he began to practice law. As a member of the Anti-Masonic party, he was elected to the New York state senate in 1830. His principal concerns, both as a legislator and later as governor of New York (1838-1842), were improvement of the state's transportation system, abolition of imprisonment for debt, judicial reform, and the establishment of public schools free from sectarian influences in New York City. Laws were passed during his term putting obstacles in the way of returning runaway slaves. Seward soon became recognized as the leader of the antislavery Whigs; in fact, he was one of the earliest political opponents of slavery. This stand won him the support of the growing abolitionist movement.

Seward refused to be a candidate for reelection as governor in 1843 and for seven years returned to private legal practice. His keen interest in politics continued, however, and he took part in every campaign. He was an ardent champion of Irish freedom, thereby gaining the support of Irish-American voters. His strong antislavery sentiment won election for him as a Whig to the U.S. Senate in 1848.

In the course of his first Senate speech, on March 11, 1850, Seward opposed compromise bills, especially Henry Clay's resolution, that would have allowed extension of slavery into new territory. His assertion that "there is a higher law than the Constitution," meaning that account should be taken of moral principles, was widely quoted. Further, Seward maintained that the fugitive slave law could not be enforced in the North; the slave trade should be abolished, slavery in the District of Columbia ought to be made illegal, and the territories should have no authority to organize themselves with or without slavery. In a speech at Rochester, New York, Seward made the famous statement that there was "an irrepressible conflict between opposing and enduring forces, and it means that the United States must and will, sooner or later, become either entirely a slave-holding nation or entirely a free-labor nation."

The year 1854 saw the effective demise of the Whigs and the rise of the new Republican party, with which Seward became affiliated. With the backing of the remnants of the Whigs and the Know-Nothing Party which had strongly emerged in the South and West, he gained reelection to the Senate.

From 1855 to 1860, Seward was the chief spokesman in Congress for the growing antislavery sentiment of the North. He was an economic conservative, but his extreme views on the slavery question led many people, even in the North, to regard him as a dangerous radical. Therefore, even though he was the acknowledged leader of his party, the Republicans, when they convened in Chicago in 1860, nominated Abraham Lincoln for president.

Seward campaigned hard for Lincoln's election and was rewarded by appointment as secretary of state in the Lincoln cabinet. When he took over this post, he assumed that he, not Lincoln, would be the dominant figure in the administration. Lincoln took full control, however, Seward gave him full support and rendered invaluable service to the nation.

A peril faced by the Northern side was the possibility of European intervention in the Civil War. The situation was met with great adroitness by Seward, who warned European powers of the dangerous consequences of intervention. He made skillful use of the slavery issue to counteract anti-Northern agitation in England and France. Lincoln's Emancipation Proclamation was effectively used by Charles Francis Adams, minister to Britain, and W. L. Dayton, minister to France.

Seward was also most skillful in his handling of the French intervention in Mexico and the scheme to establish Maximilian on a Mexican throne. After the Civil War was over, tactful diplomatic treatment of the project by Seward eventually led to a promise from the French that they would evacuate Mexico in a fixed period of time.

By inclination and temperament, Seward was an expansionist. In 1867 he negotiated with the Russians for the purchase of Alaska and secured the prompt ratification of the treaty by the Senate. He advocated the annexation of Hawaii— not actually voted by the U.S. Congress until 1898. Seward's proposals for annexing Cuba, Danish West Indies, and the Dominican Republic never materialized.

Seward suffered serious injury in a carriage accident in the spring of 1865. That was followed by a brutal attack upon him in his home at the time of Lincoln's assassination, by a fellow conspirator of John Wilkes Booth. Yet he carried on and was a central figure in the Johnson administration. As a member of Johnson's cabinet, he advocated an unpopular conciliatory policy towards the South, wrote some of Andrew Johnson's most important veto messages, and supported the president in many speeches. A biographer, Dexter Perkins, commented that Seward "looms up as one of the most attractive, as well as most important figures in a critical period of American history."

RBD

References: Frederic Bancroft, *The Life of William H. Seward* (New York: Harper, 1900); Thornton K. Lothrop, *William Henry Seward* (Boston: Houghton, 1899); Glyndon G. Van Deusen, *William Henry Seward* (New York: Oxford, 1967).

Upton Beall Sinclair
(September 20, 1878 — November 25, 1968)

The palm for achieving foremost rank among modern American propagandist novelists easily belongs to Upton Sinclair. He was one of the most prolific writers in the nation's literary history (author of ninety books) and is almost certainly the most widely read abroad of all American authors. According to a recent count, there are nearly eight hundred translations of his books in some fifty languages in forty countries.

Sinclair has been aptly compared to another great propagandist, Thomas Paine. Like Paine, he attacked with burning indignation and reckless courage every variety of social abuse and injustice. He was called "a pamphleteer for righteousness" and "the last of the muckrakers"—apt descriptions of Sinclair's stormy literary and political career.

Sinclair, who lived to age ninety, devoted a lifetime to crusades: smiting labor spies, the meat-packing industry, a corrupt press, Wall Street speculators, New York society, alcoholism, the murderers of Sacco and Vanzetti, Tom Mooney's persecution, bourgeois morality, coal mine conditions, popular evangelism, secondary and higher education, the oil industry, the evils of war. As one critic, Robert Cantwell, summed up the case: "Few American public figures, let alone American inspirational novelists, have written as many books, delivered so many lectures, covered so much territory, advocated so many causes or composed so many letters to the editor, got mixed up in so many scandals, been so insulted, ridiculed, spied on, tricked and left holding the bag—few in short, have jumped so nimbly from so many frying pans into so many fires, and none has ever managed to keep so sunny and buoyant while the flames were leaping around him."

Sinclair was an early convert to socialism, though he frequently failed to follow orthodox party lines. His propagandistic efforts carried a constant refrain: the theme of the capitalist as a heartless scoundrel and the workingman as an oppressed hero. In the midst of the depressed thirties, he narrowly missed an opportunity to put into practice his socialistic theories when, as Democratic nominee for governor of California, he conducted a spectacular campaign on the EPIC platform—"End Poverty in California." The bitter and determined opposition of the state's powerful business interests cost him the election.

Sinclair's leap from obscurity to fame was sudden. In his early twenties he had made up his mind to become a successful writer or to starve in the attempt. His ability as a writer was demonstrated early. During his years as a student in the City College of New York he began to earn an income from the sale of juvenile fiction and jokes and quips contributed to newspapers and other publications. While still a student, he was under contract to produce fiction at the rate of fifteen thousand words weekly. On one occasion he wrote a novel of sixty thousand words in less than a week. However, Sinclair's first five novels, published from 1901 to 1906, produced altogether less than a thousand dollars in royalties.

The turning point came with *The Jungle*, in 1906, the most popular and most influential of all Sinclair's numerous novels. This savage indictment of labor and sanitary conditions in the Chicago stockyards first appeared serially in *The Appeal to Reason*, a Socialist weekly, when the author was a mere twenty-seven.

The times were ripe for *The Jungle*. Still fresh in the public's memory was the "embalmed beef" scandal of the Spanish-American War. Also helping to set the stage for *The Jungle* was the whole school of muckrakers. Among the highlights of the genre were Lincoln Steffens' articles on municipal graft, Ray Stannard Baker on the railroads, Ida M. Tarbell's *The History of the Standard Oil Company*, Thomas W. Lawton on contemporary financiers, Charles Edward Russell on the beef trust, and Samuel Hopkins Adams' sensational series of articles on patent medicines and the press. As revealed by the muckrakers, wholesale corruption permeated the nation's life, and their charges were documented with stories of stolen franchises, payroll padding, fraudulent letting of contracts, alliances of police with vice, foul slum dwellings, poverty in the cities, worthless stock schemes, dishonest insurance companies, and thieving monopolies. Probably none of the previous muckraking exposés had the terrific impact on public consciousness of *The Jungle*, because it hit people where they were most sensitive—in the stomachs. The book immediately created a sensation at home and abroad. The country was swept by a storm of indignation as it began to realize that the canned goods and other meats it consumed were prepared among filth and degradation.

So impressed was Theodore Roosevelt with *The Jungle*'s revelations that he wired Sinclair to visit him in the White House at once to discuss the problem. With the president's approval, a bill providing for government inspection for all the processes of preparing meat passed Congress without a dissenting vote. Both the Pure Food and Drug Act and the Beef Inspection Act became laws of the land—less than six months from the appearance of *The Jungle* in book form.

Sinclair's prolific literary output continued unabated in the years ahead, often in the muckraking mode. In *The Profits of Religion* (1918), he accused organized religion of being a tool of capitalism. He attacked corruption in journalism in *The Brass Check* (1919) and in the oil industry in *Oil* (1927). In *The Goose Step* (1923) and *The Goslings* (1924) he criticized regimentation in American education. *King Coal* (1917) attempted to do to that industry what *The Jungle* had done to the meat packers.

Beginning with *World's End* (1940) Sinclair wrote a long series of historical novels centering on a hero Lanny Budd, expressing the author's political and social convictions. One novel in the series, *Dragon's Teeth*, dealing with the rise of nazism in Germany, was awarded the 1943 Pulitzer Prize. Other novels in the series, featuring the adventures of Lanny Budd, a blasé, cosmopolitan superman of goodwill as he wanders through Europe, America, and Asia, provide a kind of chronicle of world events in the first half of the twentieth century. They include *Between Two Worlds* (1941), *Wide Is the Gate* (1943), *Presidential Agent* (1944), *Dragon Harvest* (1945), *A World to Win* (1946), *Presidential Mission* (1947), *One Clear Call* (1948), *O Shepherd Speak!* (1949), and *The Return of Lanny Budd* (1953).

Sinclair was deeply interested in music, physical culture, and telepathy, though his writings were devoted primarily to social, educational, and industrial reform.

Though often a candidate, Sinclair never attained political office. Before moving to California in 1915, he had been nominated for Congress by the Socialist Party in New Jersey. Starting in 1920, he ran for Congress, for the U.S. Senate, and for governor of California (first as a Socialist and then as a Democrat). All were unsuccessful. He founded the California Civil Liberties Union.

From the outbreak of World War II until his death in 1968, Sinclair continued to write "exclusively in the cause of human welfare." By the contrast which he emphasized between wealth and poverty in the American scene, by his attacks on organized greed, his condemnation of man's inhumanity to man, Sinclair was a moving force in awakening the nation's conscience and bringing about drastic changes in the organization of society.

RBD

References: Leon Harris, *Upton Sinclair, American Rebel* (New York: Crowell, 1975); Jon A. Yoder, *Upton Sinclair* (New York: Unger, 1975).

Alfred Emanuel Smith

(December 30, 1873—October 4, 1944)

One of the ablest and most popular political leaders produced by New York state, Alfred Emanuel Smith, came up the hard way. At age fourteen, he was forced to drop out of school to help support his widowed mother and a sister. Al worked at a succession of odd jobs in New York City's East Side, including seven years at the Fulton fish market.

Smith's talent and attraction to the community's social life were shown early by his participation in amateur dramatic offerings and his gift for oratory. A first step toward a political career came when he formed a close friendship with Tom Foley, Democratic precinct leader and active in Tammany Hall. In 1903, Foley chose Smith as the Democratic nominee for state assemblyman. Nomination was equivalent to election.

In Albany, Smith began to learn assembly politics and state government from the inside. Robert Wagner, one of his mentors, was also his roommate for a time, a young lawyer, later New York state governor and U.S. Senator. Gradually, Smith's reputation grew as he became an eloquent spokesman in defense of home rule and the rights of the common people. Following a Democratic victory, Smith was selected by Charles F. Murphy, head of Tammany, as majority leader of the assembly and chairman of the ways and means committee. He became speaker of the assembly in 1913, an office second only to the governor in power.

Among the issues of principal concern to Smith as legislative leader were support for home rule for New York City, a state conservation department, and improvement in workmen's compensation. Of special significance in Smith's development as a reformer was a disastrous fire in 1911 in New York's garment industry, which killed a large number of working women and girls. Smith introduced a bill to establish a factory investigating commission. The commission launched a statewide series of surveys and on-the-spot investigations of factory conditions. The commission's work continued until 1915 and Smith sponsored much of the social legislation it recommended, such as sanitary, health, and fire laws, wage and hour regulations for women and children, and stronger workmen's compensation laws—perhaps Smith's major political achievements as a legislator.

Back in New York City, Smith was elected in 1915 to a two-year term as sheriff of the city, a position paying more than fifty thousand dollars a year, due to the system of fees then prevailing. Smith was also elected president of the board of alderman.

By 1918, Smith's statewide popularity had made him the favorite Democratic candidate for governor. He had the support of Tammany, of upstate politicians, and independent reform organizations. In an aggressive campaign, Smith urged a broad reorganization of the state government, and such social legislation as regulation of hours and wages for women and children. Despite the fact that 1918 was a Republican year, Smith won the governor's office by the narrow margin of fifteeen thousand votes. A Republican majority in the legislature required the governor to use all his political skills to enact his legislative program. Such key items on his agenda as wartime rent controls, tax incentives for the construction of low-cost housing, and price-fixing of milk by a state commission were rejected. It was a period of political reaction and Smith demonstrated his liberal convictions by vetoing several antisedition bills, which would have severely restricted the civil liberties of Socialists and other minority groups. He pardoned or granted executive clemency for several radicals sent to prison, but signed a bill virtually outlawing the Ku Klux Klan.

Smith lost his bid for a second term as governor in 1920. In the next three elections, however, he defeated Nathan L. Miller in 1922, Theodore Roosevelt, Jr. in 1924, and Ogden L. Mills in 1926. Thus Smith became the only governor in New York's history to serve four terms, though not consecutively. Often his party was a minority in the state legislature, but by using persuasion, compromise proposals, referenda, and radio appeals, he was successful in obtaining legislative approval for much of his program. Smith's most significant accomplishments during his several terms of government were administrative reorganization, eliminating overlapping taxing agencies, state support for low-cost housing projects, using the State Labor Department to enforce safety requirements, bond issues to develop an extensive park and recreation system, more state aid for education and ratification of the federal suffrage amendment.

By 1924, Smith had become New York's most important Democratic leader and was recognized nationally as having strong potentials for the Democrats' presidential nomination. He also had strong support in the states with the largest electoral votes. A memorable nominating speech by Franklin D. Roosevelt at the 1924 Democratic National Convention described Smith as a "Happy Warrior." His chief opponent for the nomination was William G. McAdoo, Woodrow Wilson's son-in-law. Unfortunately for Smith, the convention was badly split between the rural—dry-Protestant forces, centered in the South and West, which supported McAdoo, and the urban—wet-Catholic representatives backing Smith. After two weeks of conflict and 103 ballots, the deadlock ended with the nomination of John W. Davis, a compromise candidate who was subsequently defeated by Warren G. Harding. Key elements in the opposition to Smith were his religion, his stand against prohibition, and his condemnation of the Ku Klux Klan.

At the Houston convention in 1928, Smith was again nominated by Franklin D. Roosevelt, and on the first ballot, won the required two thirds of the delegates and the nomination. He had the solid support of the party's organization and carried on an aggressive campaign, including several extended speaking tours in the South and West. In the end, the forces of bigotry won, mainly on the religious issue. Smith was the first Roman Catholic to be nominated for the presidency by a major party. Opposition to Smith in the rural districts of closely contested states in the West and South defeated him in the election, won by Herbert Hoover by a popular margin of 15,000,000 to 21,400,000 votes. The campaign was undoubted influenced by the voters' fear of "demon rum," big city politics, and the Catholic Church. Scandalous literature and a whispering campaign against the candidate and his wife spread across the country.

The religious issue came to the fore again in 1960 when John F. Kennedy, another Catholic, was nominated by the Democrats, but by then the forces of reaction were not strong enough to deny Kennedy the presidency.

Disillusioned and unhappy, Smith withdrew from active politics after the 1928 election, and entered business as president of the Empire State Building Corporation. From being a leading liberal, he became increasingly conservative and was highly critical of Roosevelt's New Deal. Smith began, for example, to play an active role in the right-wing, anti-Roosevelt American Liberty League. He charged that Roosevelt's administration was socialistic and was concentrating too much power in the federal bureaucracy. His criticism of the Democratic ticket in the 1936 and 1940 elections was for the most part ineffectual. With the approach of World War II, Smith's break with Roosevelt was partially mended. He supported Roosevelt's 1939 Neutrality Act and the lend-lease program, and visited informally at the White House on two occasions.

Smith found satisfaction in his life as a private citizen. He was knighted by the pope, participated in many church charities, and became the best-known Catholic layman of his time. He also served as editor of a magazine, the *New Outlook*, and published his autobiography, *Up to Now* (1929).

RBD

References: Thomas H. Dickinson, *The Portrait of a Man as Governor* (New York: Macmillan, 1928); Frank Graham, *Al Smith, American* (New York: Putnam, 1945); Oscar Handlin, *Al Smith and His America* (Boston: Little, Brown, 1958); Matthew Josephson, *Al Smith: Hero of the Cities* (Boston: Houghton Mifflin, 1969).

Sophia Smith

(August 27, 1796 — June 12, 1870)

The founder of Smith College, at Northampton, Massachusetts, was a true eccentric. Sophia Smith's own education was elementary, though she appears to have read widely. For the most part, Sophia was a recluse, shy, and deaf, a stay-at-home, except for occasional trips to watering places and one visit to Washington.

Sophia was a descendant of Samuel Smith, who emigrated from England in 1634. The family was noted for thriftiness, the ability to make money and hold on to it. While Sophia's younger sister Harriet was alive, Harriet took over management of the household. After her death in 1859, Sophia shifted responsibility to an older brother, Austin. Austin Smith's saving ways and success in speculation enabled him to accumulate a fortune. Sophia inherited her brother's estate upon his sudden death in 1861.

Thus bereft of family, with no one left to whom she could shift responsibility for managing her affairs, Sophia turned to her young minister, John Morton Greene. Greene suggested that she keep a journal as a way of expressing herself. This record became the main source of Sophia's inner thoughts and limited activities. As noted by one of her biographers, "It reveals an anxious and suspicious spirit, battling with afflictions, bewailing her sins, praying for self-improvement and for greater perfection of character."

The establishment of Smith College, Sophia Smith's chief claim to fame, is actually to be credited to the young Congregational Church minister Greene, who for years remained Sophia's loyal friend and wise adviser. Various possibilities were considered for the use of her money, most of which did not interest her. In the end, Greene urged her to endow a woman's college. At Sophia's request, he prepared a "plan for a woman's college." A new will was drawn up providing for a college "with the design to furnish for my own sex means and facilities for education equal to those which are afforded now in our colleges for young men." It was specified that the college should be located in Northampton. By the time Smith College opened in 1875, the bequest amounted to about a half million dollars. During the last 110 years, Smith has become one of a half dozen most prestigious American women's colleges.

Sophia was as parsimonious as other members of her family. One extravagance was the building of a fashionable, but architecturally hideous mansard-roofed mansion in which she spent her last three years.

RBD

Reference: Elizabeth D. Hanscum, *Sophia Smith and the Beginning of Smith College* (Northampton, Mass.: Smith College, 1925).

Gertrude Stein
(February 3, 1874—July 27, 1946)

Writer, lecturer, art collector, mistress of a Paris salon frequented by artists and men of letters, Gertrude Stein was one of the most colorful personalities of the early twentieth century. A long time resident of France, she made her home at Twenty-seven rue de Fleurus in Paris a gathering place for American expatriates, British writers, and French painters. During World War I she was in and out of Paris, but when France was an occupied country in World War II she lived unmolested in a small provincial town. When Stein first went to Paris in 1903 she shared a house with her brother Leo, a painter and also an art collector, but later when Leo and Gertrude had an amicable estrangement he departed for Italy, and she remained in France. For many years she had as a companion and secretary Alice B. Toklas, whose name she gave to an autobiography which was certainly written by and mostly about herself.

The Steins were of German-Jewish origin. Daniel Stein and his brothers emigrated to the United States in 1841 and settled in Baltimore where they soon opened a clothing store. Some years later Daniel and his brother Solomon moved to Allegheny, on the Ohio River opposite Pittsburgh, where Gertrude was born in 1874. She and her brother Leo were the youngest of five surviving children born to Daniel and Amelia Stein and the closest in temperament and taste. The Stein family was restless and nomadic. They moved back to Europe briefly and spent some time in Gemünden and Vienna, Austria. In 1878 they were in Paris and Gertrude at the age of four saw for the first time the city which would be home for most of her later life. Back in the United States in 1879 the Steins went to Oakland and remained there until 1892. The California episode was one of the most peaceful and pleasant times of Stein's life. She enjoyed excursions with Leo and she found the world of books: Shakespeare, Wordsworth, Burns, Scott, Fielding, Carlyle, as well as Lecky's constitutional history and the *Congressional*

Record. Daniel Stein's sudden death in 1891 put a crimp in the family's finances but the oldest son Michael proved to be more of a financial genius than his father, and eventually Gertrude Stein became the recipient of an ample and dependable income.

When Leo went to Harvard, Gertrude followed him and was enrolled as a special student at Harvard Annex, later called Radcliffe College. Here she listened to George Santayana lecture on American philosophy and attended a seminar on psychology led by William James. Probably James's empiricism was the central intellectual influence on her life. Certainly his emphasis on the stream of consciousness affected much of her later writing. Gertrude was granted her A.B. degree magna cum laude in 1898. Although she was interested in both philosophy and psychology, she enrolled in the Johns Hopkins University Medical School and resided in Baltimore. But after four years she withdrew from the program without a degree.

By 1902 Leo Stein was in Italy studying art with Bernard Berenson. Brother and sister were reunited in London, which Gertrude Stein never really liked, and the next year they began their residence in Paris. Focusing their attention on painting, they began to acquire the canvases of Cezanne, Renoir, Gauguin, Derain, and Matisse. As an example of Stein's shrewdness in forming her collection one might cite the purchase of Matisse's *La Femme au Chapeau*, for five hundred francs. When the picture was sold after Gertrude's death it brought twenty thousand dollars. A particular artist friend of the Steins was Pablo Picasso, who did a portrait of Gertrude; she in reciprocity composed a word portrait of Picasso, the artist's first public appreciation.

Having tried both philosophy and psychology Stein eventually turned to writing and began by translating Flaubert into English. Then she turned to fiction and poetry. Her first book, *Three Lives: Stories of the Good Anna, Melanctha, and the Gentle Lena*, was published in 1909. This account of two servant girls and a Negro woman was not especially successful, but in retrospect it seems significant because of its fusion of naturalism with an emphasis on characterization rather than plot. It also revealed the fondness for flat statement and banal repetition which became a Stein trademark. Incidentally Alice B. Toklas began her association with Stein as secretary and amanuensis by reading the proofs of *Three Lives.*

Stein's next book, *Tender Buttons*, published in 1914, was a collection of poems or prose still lifes analogous to cubist paintings; it produced more scorn than recognition. The novel called *The Making of Americans* (1925) dealt fundamentally with three generations of her own family but by extension became the history of "everyone who ever was or is or will be living." Over nine hundred pages long, it is a tedious narrative in simple language which strives to present a kind of continuous present and constant beginning. One biographer of Stein, Donald Sutherland, compared it to the Pentagon building, both magnificent and appalling. Stein's only commercial success, *The Autobiography of Alice B. Toklas*, appeared in 1933 and was selected by the Literary Guild. This volume plus the production in 1934, of Stein's opera, *Four Saints in Three Acts*, with music by Virgil Thomson, gave the author the celebrity which she always coveted. Henceforth she became widely known as an author and lecturer. In October 1934, she came back to the United States for the first time in almost thirty years. She was greeted by reporters, by headlines, and by numerous audiences. As John

Malcolm Brinnin remarked, Americans could not take her seriously but being unable to ignore her they made her into a popular darling.

Stein's later work did not add much to her literary reputation. *Lectures in America* and *Narration: Four Lectures*, both published in 1935, made available some of her critical beliefs in book form. *Wars I Have Seen* (1944) obviously reflected personal experience largely in France, and *Brewsie and Willie* (1946) dealt with her memories of meeting American servicemen. She was pleased when soldiers on the troop trains would extend envelopes and notepads for her autograph. To her the infantry of the Second World War were less provincial than the doughboys of World War I and had learned, in their progress from adolescence to men, to dominate their language.

Gertrude Stein's significance as a literary figure has never been clearly established. Most of her books puzzled, irritated, or bored their readers because of her style. Her incoherence, her deliberate shifts in syntax, and probably most of all her repetitions alienated more readers than they attracted. Clifton Fadiman once dubbed her "the Mama of Dada." For other readers she was the author of a famous statement, "Rose is a rose is a rose is a rose." She was commonly charged with being unintelligible and wordy. Edmund Wilson declared that he had not read *The Making of Americans* all through and was doubtful that it could be done. On the other hand, she had a sense of humor, definite ability in characterization, and a certain freshness in her approach to language which influenced some contemporary writers.

Stein's relationships with Ezra Pound, T. S. Eliot, Sherwood Anderson, and particularly F. Scott Fitzgerald and Ernest Hemingway are well known. Anderson, already a published writer when first they met, felt that Stein was attempting to achieve a new feeling for words, a goal that he himself was approaching in a different way. When Hemingway first came to the Stein home he was the author only of poetry and some short stories. Stein urged him to begin over again and to concentrate. For awhile the two frequently met and discussed writing. Later there was an estrangement which proved to be permanent, Stein disliking Hemingway's addiction to sex and violence and calling him yellow, Hemingway ridiculing—in his printed work—Stein's repetitions and limitations.

Stein's later days were busy and crowded. She kept on writing, trying her hand again at opera. She was often interviewed and retained her salon but the visitors were different. Although she had always enjoyed good health, illness began to plague her and her intestinal disorders were diagnosed as cancer. Just before her death in 1946 she willed her manuscripts and important correspondence to Yale University. She was buried in the cemetery of Père-Lachaise in Paris.

JTF

References: Douglas Day, in *Notable American Women 1607-1950*, III (Cambridge, Mass.: Belknap Press of Harvard, 1971); Donald Sutherland, *Gertrude Stein: A Biography of Her Work* (New Haven, Conn.: Yale, 1951); Elizabeth Sprigge, *Gertrude Stein: Her Life and Work* (New York: Harper, 1957); John Malcolm Brinnin, *The Third Rose: Gertrude Stein and Her World* (Boston and Toronto: Little, Brown, 1959).

John Ernst Steinbeck

(February 17, 1902 — December 20, 1968)

A native Californian, whose major books dealt with the state of his birth, John Steinbeck became the sixth American writer to win the Nobel Prize for literature. Although in the course of a prolific career he tried his hand at drama, film scripts, and journalistic dispatches, he is most notable for his short stories and novels. *The Grapes of Wrath*, which was awarded a Pulitzer Prize, ranks as one of the best American novels of the century and brought national attention to the plight of the landless farm laborer.

Steinbeck was born in Salinas, the center of California's lettuce country and the scene of much labor discord. He had German and Irish ancestry, an inheritance which gave him a massive frame and a strong sense of humor. He attended Salinas schools but during his high school days had considerable work experience running cultivators, bucking grain bags, doing odd jobs around cattle, and helping in the laboratory of a Spreckles sugar refinery. Bunkhouse talk and bunkhouse life were almost indigenous to him and he put his knowledge of both to good use in his fiction. Three times he enrolled and then withdrew from Stanford University, which he finally left without a degree in 1925. But he learned something about history and English and made his first efforts to write. A freight boat took him to New York but en route he stopped at Panama briefly and acquired some of the local color which he would eventually use in his first novel, *Cup of Gold*. The book was published in 1929 and dealt with the life of the buccaneer Henry Morgan. In New York he worked for a time as a reporter and then carried bricks for the new Madison Square Garden building. Back in California he took a job as a seasonal watchman for a house on Lake Tahoe and spent much of his free time writing.

He published two more books after *The Cup of Gold*, neither of which was profitable. *The Pastures of Heaven* (1932) collected short stories dealing with a farm community in a California valley. *To a God Unknown* (1933) focuses on a California farmer who permits his pagan religion of fertility to become a mystical obsession and commits suicide on the altar where he had worshipped. The author's first popular success was *Tortilla Flat* (1935) a picaresque tale of romance and adventure set in Monterey and populated with "paisanos," a mixture of Spanish, Mexican, Indian, and diluted Caucasian bloods.

Tortilla Flat introduces characters who are amoral and naive but worldly-wise, who consume quantities of red wine, patronize promiscuous women, retain a superstitious affection for the church, and are content with their life until their patron dies and his house burns. Steinbeck returned to the Monterey locale later in *Cannery Row* (1944) and described similar figures who live by their wits and revolve around Doc, the lonely, sympathetic owner of a biological laboratory. Both books are written in a simple, spare style, and the author is alternately ironic and amusing as he chronicles the behavior and peccadilloes of his characters. Steinbeck once again used the Cannery Row scene in *Sweet Thursday*, 1954, reintroducing Doc, who served in World War II as a technical sergeant, and some of the hustlers and parasites who flutter around him.

In the late 1930s Steinbeck's interest in the plight of migratory workers led him to write more serious fiction. *In Dubious Battle*, published in 1936, deals with a strike of the fruit pickers who rebel against the virtual peonage in which they work. But Communist organizers arouse the orchard owners who mobilize the authorities and vigilantes. Violence ensues and the strike is broken, but one of the party leaders argues that the cause of labor will benefit if working stiffs will hold together. The book displeased reactionary readers although the Commonwealth Club of California awarded a gold medal to Steinbeck for producing the best novel of the year by a California writer.

In 1937 Steinbeck published *Of Mice and Men*, a short novel written deliberately in quasi-dramatic form and which he himself transformed into a successful Broadway play the following year. The scene again is a California ranch where two itinerant farm laborers are employed. Lennie is strong but mentally deficient, George is deft and talks hopefully of a farm that these two homeless men can someday own. But Lennie accidentally is a murderer and George kills him before the enraged ranchers can lynch him.

An excellent collection of short fiction, *The Long Valley*, appeared in 1938. In these stories Steinbeck's love of the land, his knowledge of the Salinas Valley, his awareness of nature, and his choice of simple, earthy people to write about served him well. Included are "The Chrysanthemums," "The White Quail," and "The Leader of the People" (with its affectionate portrait of the old grandfather who had led a small group on the westward trek but tires out his family by repeating old stories about hunting and Indians). The longest story in the volume is one of Steinbeck's best known tales, "The Red Pony," which was originally printed in 1937.

Steinbeck's most impressive book is unquestionably *The Grapes of Wrath*, the novel published in 1939 which was largely responsible for his winning of the Nobel Prize twenty-three years later. The Joad family, forced out of Oklahoma by drouth and a faltering economy, head west for California where they expect to find utopia. A dozen people plus Casy, a former preacher and rustic Socialist, travel in a dilapidated automobile and most of them despite little money and many hardships reach their promised land (the grandparents die en route). But in California they are victimized by sheriffs and labor contractors, they take refuge in a government camp, and they work in a black-listed orchard. Inevitably the migrant workers strike and Casy is killed by vigilantes. Tom Joad, an ex-convict who has already committed murder, revenges Casy's death and then flees. At the end of the novel the Joads having survived inadequate housing, illness, and a flood face starvation, the daughter gives birth to a stillborn child, and the future is bleaker than ever. But Ma Joad, who has been throughout the unifying and uncomplaining force, is not ready to quit. To her life is a stream which continues. "Woman looks at it like that. We ain't gonna die out. People is goin' on— changin' a little, maybe, but goin' right on.... Jus' try to live the day, jus' the day."

Steinbeck's theme in *The Grapes of Wrath* is of course the exploitation of the indigent, rootless worker. But the Joad family, their speech, their superstitions, at times their surprising knowhow, is treated naturalistically. The narrative flow of the book is interrupted and often complemented by insertions of descriptive or background material which remind a reader of John Dos Passos's use of headlines or news quotations. Thus Steinbeck pictures a turtle crossing a highway, a used car lot, a segment of the main migrant road Highway 66, and California opposition to the growth of Hoovervilles. In these expository chapters the author shows his strong reportorial ability. Coming at the end of the depression when many people had tragic memories of Dust Bowl conditions, the novel had a strong impact on the reading public. It still does.

Nothing that Steinbeck wrote in the years that followed had comparable merit and some critics felt that the award of the Nobel Prize was both dilatory and unjustified.

Steinbeck was both productive and versatile. He had been interested in marine biology since his school days. In 1941 he coauthored with his friend Edward F. Ricketts a journal of their travels and research in the Gulf of California which they called *Sea of Cortez*. The next year he went far afield to write *The Moon Is Down*, a novelette about Norwegian resistance to the German occupation. This story he also dramatized. In 1948 he published *The Pearl*, a short parable relating the story of a Mexican fisherman whose good fortune in finding a valuable pearl brings his family only trouble. *The Wayward Bus*, published in 1947, described a group of travelers stranded in a rural bus and through their problems reflecting some of the frustrations of life in contemporary America. Steinbeck's travels are the base of his comments on the Soviet Union in *A Russian Journal*, 1948.

His most ambitious work after *The Grapes of Wrath* was a long historical novel called *East of Eden*, which appeared in 1952. This deals with Adam Trask who in the 1890s brought his wife, a former prostitute, from the Connecticut Valley to Salinas. The wife bears twin sons, who are named Caleb and Aron (they were supposed to be baptized Cain and Abel), and the rest of the novel chronicles their lives. The characters are on a level superior to the Joad family and lack their interest while the allegorical implications seem rather heavy.

Despite his long and intimate connection with California, Steinbeck spent much of his later life in the East. He chose a seaside Long Island village, Sag Harbor, which may have reminded him of Pacific Grove near Monterey where he did much of his writing, for a refuge. But he also maintained an Upper East Side town house in New York City and obviously relished at times the restaurant and club life of the metropolis. This somewhat surprising change of venue explains in part the subject matter of his last important novel, *The Winter of Our Discontent*, 1961.

The protagonist of the story is Ethan Allen Hawley, supposedly a resident of New Baytown, Long Island. He comes of good bloodstock but has seen his fortune decline sharply until he is driven to running the neighborhood grocery store for its immigrant owner. Four men happen to combine to rehabilitate Hawley: his banker, a bank teller, the grocery store proprietor, and a former schoolmate and now a town drunk who happens to own a desirable piece of land. The book is oddly compact for a Steinbeck novel, with a rigid time scheme listed to the period between two weekends in 1960. Hawley's rehabilitation is satisfactory in itself if perhaps overly contrived.

One other Steinbeck volume, published in 1962, deserves mention. Although *Travels with Charley in Search of America* did not add much to the writer's reputation it pleased many readers. Steinbeck at fifty-eight wished the freedom of anonymity and the luxury of no set destination or route. So he bought a comfortable camper, equipped it modestly, named it Rocinante, and invited a blue poodle named Charley to accompany him. He traveled over ten thousand miles in thirty-four states and was recognized by no one. The book is casual and anecdotal.

Steinbeck's final place in American literature needs careful definition. Although the Nobel Prize certainly increased his readership, it could not prevent the decline of his reputation among critics. Yet *The Grapes of Wrath* remains an important novel, and many of the short stories as well as the books about Salinas and Monterey will always have their readers.

JTF

References: Warren French, *John Steinbeck* (Boston: Twayne, 1975); Peter Lisca, *The Wide World of John Steinbeck* (New Brunswick, N.J.: Rutgers University Press, 1938); Elaine Steinbeck and Robert Wallstein, eds., *Steinbeck: A Life in Letters* (New York: Penguin, 1976); Jackson J. Benson, *The True Adventures of John Steinbeck, Writer* (New York: Viking, 1984).

Wallace Stevens

(October 2, 1879—August 2, 1955)

One of the major American poets of the twentieth century, Wallace Stevens came to the publication of verse relatively late and in a sense kept his devotion to literature separate from his professional work. He was not widely known for much of his career nor was he a prolific poet. But once having achieved publication he produced a number of slender volumes. His *Collected Poems* appeared in 1954 on his seventy-fifth birthday, and in 1966 his daughter Holly Stevens edited *Letters of Wallace Stevens*, a volume which included almost a thousand items plus fragments of a journal.

Stevens was born in Reading, Pennsylvania, in 1879, the son of a lawyer. He expressed in his youth some desire to write but prompted by his father after his graduation from Harvard in 1900 he enrolled at the New York Law School and was admitted to the bar in 1904. For a time he practiced law in New York City. But in 1916 he became associated with the Hartford Accident and Indemnity Company, a firm which eventually named him a vice-president. Clients of the insurance company seldom knew that their agent was a competent and finally a much admired poet. Stevens traveled little during his life but enjoyed business and vacation trips to Florida, a scene which is often reflected in his verse. In one of his best known poems, "The Idea of Order at Key West," he wrote of the "dark voice of the sea," of "sunken coral water-walled," and of summer sounds "repeated in a summer without end."

Shortly before World War I Stevens began to contribute verse to the little magazines which proliferated at the time, and four of his poems appeared in the war number of *Poetry: A Magazine of Verse*, in 1914. But he did not collect his verse into a volume until 1923 when *Harmonium* appeared; it had a revised and enlarged edition in 1931. Somewhat later three volumes were published in consecutive years: *Ideas of Order* (1935), *Owl's Clover* (1936), and *The Man with the Blue Guitar* (1937). Subsequent collections were entitled *Parts of a World* (1942), *Transport to Summer* (1947), and *The Auroras of Autumn* (1952). In a special issue of the *Harvard Advocate* of December 1940, his work was featured and there were articles about the poet by a variety of writers such as Harry Levin, F. O. Matthiessen, and Robert Penn Warren. Stevens himself published a book of essays in 1951, *The Necessary Angel: Essays on Reality and the Imagination*, in which he expressed his theory of poetry. The "necessary angel" was his metaphor for the imagination.

Stevens received the Bollingen Prize for poetry in 1949 and the Pulitzer Prize for his *Collected Poems* in 1955. Individual poems have been frequently anthologized, notably "Peter Quince at the Clavier," "Sunday Morning," "Thirteen Ways of Looking at a Blackbird," and "The Comedian as the Letter C." Stevens was not a narrative poet; his verse is primarily lyrical with a strong philosophical undercurrent. He reveals some of the traits of the imagist group with whom he was contemporary and he occasionally used free verse, but he could also employ metre in original ways and his poetry is often musical. He did not scorn rhyme and frequently his rhymes are surprising; he showed his acute sense of langauge in his descriptions and his use of colors and sounds.

Stevens admired French literary style and often incorporated French into his verse and sometimes even his titles, as for example in the poems "Le Monocle de Mon Oncle" or "Anglais Mort à Florence." He also could write with wit and subtlety such as when he pictured the biblical Susanna disturbed by the elders while bathing.

> And then, the simpering Byzantines
> Fled, with a noise like tambourines.

The luxurious background of "Sunday Morning," which pictures a woman musing over a late Sunday breakfast, strikes a contrast between the beauties of the physical world and the grimness of traditional religion, but ends at evening when "casual flocks of pigeons make Ambiguous undulations as they sink, Downward to darkness."

Stevens is an elusive poet who is not always easy to understand. But his technical mastery and his diversity of form and thought justify his reputation today.

He was an admirer of the French symbolists and a poet who sometimes seemed to lose command of his thought through his obsession with the witty and the alliterative. As Alfred Kreymborg once observed, "If one cannot always understand his poems, there is always the orchestration." In recent years Stevens has attracted a good deal of critical attention and has been the subject of several specialized treatments.

Stevens tended to keep his creative life private so that few of his professional associates knew much about his writing. Physically, he was a big man, six feet three inches tall and weighing perhaps 250 pounds. He had a peculiar sense of humor which sometimes discomfited those who were subjected to it. He enjoyed dinners and restaurant conviviality but seldom welcomed guests to his home. At the end of his life when he was terminally ill with cancer he was baptized a Roman Catholic. He died in Hartford in 1955.

JTF

References: Samuel French Morse, *DAB*, Supplement 5, 1977, pp. 658-61; Daniel Fuchs, *The Comic Spirit of Wallace Stevens* (Durham, N.C.: Duke, 1963); Helen Vendler, *On Extended Wings: Wallace Stevens's Long Poems* (Cambridge, Mass.: Harvard University Press, 1969); Samuel French Morse, *Wallace Stevens: Life as Poetry* (New York: Pegasus, 1970).

Mark Sullivan

(September 10, 1874 — August 13, 1952)

A prominent American journalist notable for his political commentary, Mark Sullivan spent most of his career working for major eastern newspapers and compiled the six-volume history of American daily life, *Our Times: The United States, 1900-1925*, which was published between 1926 and 1935.

Sullivan was born in Avondale, Pennsylvania, the son of Irish emigrants. In his early years he lived on a fifty-two acre Pennsylvania farm. He attended West Chester Normal School from 1888 to 1892, then took a reporter's job with the West Chester *Morning Republican*. After he finished school he and John Miller bought a neighboring newspaper, the Phoenixville *Republican*, for which he worked as reporter, editor, and publisher for three years. By this time he realized that his education had been somewhat inadequate for a journalist whose vision exceeded the parochial and in 1896 he decided to enter Harvard, where some years later he was awarded a bachelor of laws degree. During his university years he also contributed to the Philadelphia *North American*.

His anonymous article entitled "The Ills of Pennsylvania," which appeared in the October 1901 *Atlantic Monthly*, dealt with political corruption and aligned him with the muckraking school then prominent. It also attracted the attention of Edward Bok, editor of the *Ladies' Home Journal*, who invited him to investigate the patent medicine industry for his magazine. After a stint at *McClure's Magazine* Sullivan joined the staff of *Collier's Weekly* where he remained from 1906 to 1919, serving as its editor from 1914 to 1917.

Sullivan's early political commentary reflected his staunch Republicanism to which he returned later in life. But he was a loyal admirer of Theodore Roosevelt and he followed the ex-president into the Progressive camp. He rejected the political doctrines of Robert LaFollette, however, became a mild supporter of both Harding and Coolidge, and was an intimate friend of Herbert Hoover. He strongly rejected the New Deal of Franklin Roosevelt.

Sullivan served from 1919 to 1923 as the Washington correspondent for the New York *Post* and later was associated with the New York *Herald* and its successor the *Herald-Tribune*. Besides his authorship of *Our Times* he wrote an autobiography, *The Education of an American*, 1938, which surveyed his educational years, his work as a muckraking journalist, and his militant support of the early Progressive party.

Our Times has been called a classic piece of descriptive social history. In chapter 4 of his final volume he defined his modus operandi, actually a method which in later years was called oral history. He not only examined the biographies and autobiographies of the principal figures involved in his chronicle but he also studied the *Congressional Record* and relevant newspaper files. In addition he relied on correspondence, interviews, and the scrutiny of his manuscript by many of the subjects of his history. National politics and especially presidential campaigns are the focus of *Our Times*, but Sullivan included a great deal more: for example, the index to volume 6 gives the names of some hundred actors and actresses, over two hundred authors, and long lists of plays and popular songs. The chapters entitled 1919 to 1925 conclude with lists of the books and plays of the year. Illustrations also add to the appeal of the work, about two hundred photographs of the people involved, cartoons, even sample headlines. The details are sometimes overwhelming and the order of events is chronological rather than dramatic. But it would be difficult to find a livelier survey of what Sullivan himself called contemporary history.

JTF

References: David M. Kennedy, *DAB*, Supplement 5, 1977, pp. 666-68; Mark Sullivan, *The Education of an American* (New York: Doubleday, Doran, 1938); Mark Sullivan, *Our Times: The United States, 1900-1925*, 6 vols. (New York: Scribner, 1926-1935).

William Graham Sumner
(October 30, 1840 — April 12, 1910)

William G. Sumner, who occupies top rank among American social scientists, was a person of amazing versatility. He could be aptly described as an outstanding educator, economist, and publicist, as well as a pioneer sociologist. He came near meeting the Renaissance ideal of a universal man, familiar with all the social sciences, well informed on such subjects as anatomy, biology, and mathematics, and having a sound working knowledge of at least a dozen languages.

Sumner entered Yale in 1859 and there achieved a brilliant scholastic record. From early youth it had been his ambition to enter the ministry. His preparation for that profession was furthered by periods of study at Geneva, Göttingen, and Oxford. After returning to the United States he served as tutor at Yale from 1866 to 1869. At the same time he was pursuing his clerical duties for the Protestant Episcopal Church. He was ordained a priest in 1869.

Sumner was an able and successful preacher, but as time passed he became increasingly interested in public affairs, particularly economic and social issues. Accordingly, in 1872 he accepted an offer from Yale to fill the newly created chair of political and social science. The remainder of his life was spent at that institution, though his activities and influence extended far beyond its borders. Locally, from 1873 to 1876, he was a member of New Haven's board of alderman, and for twenty-eight years, 1882-1910, served on the Connecticut State Board of Education, in which capacity he made important contributions toward the improvement of the common school system.

Sumner was a prolific author and in constant demand as a speaker. In his numerous books and articles and public speeches, he was a vigorous supporter of free trade, a sound currency, big business, and laissez-faire economics. Teaching was considered by Sumner to be his most important business, however, and he was rated as one of the most effective teachers of his generation. Yale students crowded into his classes, convinced that their education was incomplete without his courses. Everyday affairs served as the text of his lectures, and in these he stated his conception of economic and social facts and principles. As described by one biographer, Harris Elwood Starr, Sumner was "Honest and fearless, despising gush and sentimentality, indifferent to tradition, he struck hard blows, never glossed over anything, and never spared anybody's feelings." He was an outspoken proponent of academic freedom, as was shown, for example, when President Noah Porter objected to his use of Herbert Spencer's *The Study of Sociology* as a textbook. In his time, Yale was an inherently conservative institution; Sumner worked to broaden the curriculum, to place less emphasis on the classics, and to introduce more scientific studies into the academic department.

Outside the classroom, Sumner's writings and speeches attacked economic and social evils on a broad front, treating practically every social question of the day. All through his career he advocated a sound monetary system, opposed free silver and bimetallism, fought protectionism, was against government interference with industry and business, and condemned socialism. He was especially concerned about the "Forgotten Man," a term he coined to describe the self-supporting, self-respecting person who has to bear the cost of political bungling and social quackery.

With the passage of time, Sumner's interests expanded into viewing society as a whole. He turned away from an early concentration on economics and more toward anthropology and sociology, in order to study all the institutions of society, beginning with the simplest, primitive forms. Out of his researches, extending over a period of years, developed two classics on the science of society: *Folkways* (1907), an analysis of custom; and *Science of Society* (1927), the latter a four-volume work not completed and published until some years after Sumner's death, by his successor at Yale, Albert G. Keller. Both works remain required reading for students of sociology.

RBD

References: Albert G. Sumner, *Reminiscences of William Graham Sumner* (New Haven, Conn.: Yale University Press, 1933); Harris E. Starr, *William Graham Sumner* (New York: Holt, 1925).

Roger Brooke Taney

(March 17, 1777—October 12, 1864)

Roger Taney [pronounced tawny] along with John Marshall came to be regarded as one of the ablest chief justices in the history of the U.S. Supreme Court. He was also probably the most controversial of anyone who has ever filled the office.

Taney's judicial career and bitterly debated decisions were doubtless shaped and influenced by his beginning. He belonged to Maryland's landed gentry, generations of wealthy planters. As a youth, Roger absorbed the culture and accepted the values of his class. After graduating from Dickinson College in 1795, he prepared for a career in law and politics by reading law in a judge's office. Roger was admitted to practice in 1799.

Taney's first political experience came at age twenty-two, when he was elected to the Maryland state legislature, for the 1799-1800 term. When he failed to be reelected, along with many other Federalist party candidates, he settled in Fredericksburg in 1801, where he lived until 1823, becoming a leading citizen and establishing a successful law practice.

Taney's reentry into active politics came in 1816, when he was elected to the state senate for a five-year term. His chief attention there was directed at two issues: fighting to maintain a sound currency, and enacting laws to protect the rights of Negroes in the state, both slaves and freedmen.

In 1823, Taney moved to Baltimore, where he recognized greater opportunities, and soon emerged as one of the most eminent members of the bar. By that time, the Federalist party had virtually disappeared and Taney threw his support to Andrew Jackson. He had been appointed attorney general of Maryland in 1827, and the following year became chairman of the state central committee of the Jackson party.

It appears that Taney had no desire for an appointment to a federal office at this time, since that would have meant giving up a lucrative private legal practice. But after Andrew Jackson was elected president in 1828, he found that he needed Taney to help carry out his policies. In 1831, Jackson drew on Taney's legal ability and banking experience by appointing him attorney general and acting secretary of war.

The key issue at the time was whether to recharter the Bank of the United States. Taney advised Jackson to veto the charter that had been passed by Congress and he helped Jackson to write the veto message. The bank had become a hot political question, and Jackson and Taney were convinced that its officers had been guilty of ruthless and unethical practices. Jackson had already decided to withdraw government deposits, about one-fifth of the bank's assets. William J. Duane, secretary of the treasury, was unwilling to execute the administrative order, and Jackson dismissed him. While Congress was in recess, Taney was appointed in Duane's place and proceeded with the withdrawal of funds. The action precipitated a major battle when Congress returned and Taney's nomination to be secretary of the treasury was rejected. He returned to private practice. Jackson was frustrated again in 1835 when he nominated Taney an associate justice of the Supreme Court and the Senate took no action on the nomination. By 1836, however, a Democratic majority in the Senate confirmed Jackson's nomination of Taney as chief justice of the Supreme Court. Thus began the most noteworthy phase of Taney's career.

One of the first major judicial decisions for which the court under Taney is remembered concerned corporation rights. During John Marshall's tenure as chief justice, restraints had been placed on the states' legislative activities, and contract rights, including those provided under corporation charters, were carefully guarded. Taney held that the rights granted by charter should not be so broadly interpreted that corporations were free to expand their activities unrestricted. As Taney expressed it, "While the rights of private property are sacredly guarded, we must not forget that the community also have rights, and that the happiness and well being of every citizen depends on their faithful preservation." This decision reflected Taney's firsthand knowledge of the predatory actions of some corporations, especially the Bank of the United States. The doctrine stated by the Taney court became a fundamental tenet of American constitutional law. The basic view was that unregulated private aggregations of wealth and power did not always work for the good of the country and required restraints.

Taney was inclined to grant wide scope to states' rights. He believed that the states were sovereign within their respective spheres, but were not free to act in matters clearly the province of the federal government, such as admiralty laws regulating inland waters or the management of federally owned lands within their borders. On many occasions, Taney did not hesitate to assert the power of the Supreme Court. A number of times during the Civil War, he came close to defying the military and civil officers of the federal government.

Events leading up to the Civil War, and especially issues relating to slavery, involved the Supreme Court in bitter and prolonged controversy. Taney's southern agrarian heritage was shown in his judicial decisions. He himself had cooperated in projects for colonizing free Negroes in Africa, had freed his own slaves, and had bought other slaves to give them a chance to work out their freedom. He was convinced, however, that whites and blacks could not satisfactorily live together in large numbers as equals, and slavery was the best solution as long as Negroes remained in the United States. Further, Taney believed that the South should be free to work out problems with slavery, rather than Northern abolitionists unfamiliar with the complexities of the matter.

The crucial case was a decision of the Supreme Court in 1857 regarding the status of slavery in the territories. Officially, it was known as the *Scott v. Sandford* case. The facts were these: Dred Scott, a Negro slave belonging to Dr. John Emerson, an army surgeon, had been taken from the slave state of Missouri to the free state of Illinois and from there into Wisconsin Territory, where slavery was prohibited by the Missouri Compromise of 1820. In 1838 Emerson returned with Scott to Missouri. After Emerson's death, abolitionists persuaded Scott to sue for his freedom, on the basis that having lived in a free state and territory he should no longer be in bondage. A lower court ruled in Scott's favor, but the Missouri Supreme Court reversed the decision. Meanwhile, Scott was sold to J. F. A. Sandford of New York with the understanding that he would be freed after his case was carried to the federal courts. It reached the Supreme Court in 1856.

The decision announced by Taney and his colleagues made three points: first, Scott remained a slave under Missouri law; second, Negroes of slave descent were "inferior" and could not sue in federal courts; and, finally, the Missouri Compromise, which had prohibited slavery in certain territories, was unconstitutional.

The Dred Scott decision has been called a political bombshell. The Democratic party was split between the North and South wings and it infuriated the new Republican party, one of whose main aims was to prevent slavery from spreading into the territories. The decision became an important issue in later elections and has commonly been regarded as one of the major causes of the Civil War. Charles Sumner prophesied that Taney's name should be "hooted down the page of history."

As the Civil War approached, Taney was sympathetic to the South. He opposed the North's conduct of the war and believed that force should not have been used to prevent the South from leaving the Union. In the famous *Merryman* case, he made a strong defense of the rights of civilians in wartime — a case which exposed Taney to further attacks. He belonged to a minority on the court who doubted the legality of some of Lincoln's acts taken under presidential "war powers."

Taney was a devout Roman Catholic, though he was broadly tolerant. He deeply resented the Know-Nothing Movement's attacks upon his faith, but never entered into any public controversy on the matter.

Charles Evans Hughes, some years later, declared that Roger Brooke Taney "was a great Chief Justice." With the passage of time, as one of his biographers, Carl B. Swisher, commented, "resentment against him has died down, and his character and his motives have come more and more to be understood."

RBD

References: Walker Lewis, *Without Fear or Favor: A Biography of Chief Justice Roger Brooke Taney* (Boston: Houghton, 1965); Benjamin W. Palmer, *Marshall and Taney* (New York: Russell & Russell, 1939); Charles W. Smith, *Roger B. Taney, Jacksonian Jurist* (Chapel Hill: University of North Carolina Press, 1936).

(Newton) Booth Tarkington
(July 29, 1869 — May 19, 1946)

One of the most successful popular writers of the first half of the twentieth century, Booth Tarkington was both prolific and versatile. In a productive writing career of over forty-five years he wrote more than forty volumes of fiction plus a number of plays and several collections of essays. He first tried his hand at historical romance at a time when such stories were in vogue. Later he published sentimental and humorous studies of adolescence and at the peak of his career produced mildly realistic novels about midwestern life which pleased a large audience. Tarkington's reputation has waned since his death and a revival of interest in his work seems unlikely. But the Penrod stories have retained readership and in at least one novel, *Alice Adams* (1921), he revealed not only narrative competence but a willingness to deal with serious themes.

Tarkington was born in Indianapolis in 1869, the city which remained his home for most of his life. His father, John Tarkington, a Civil War veteran, was an Indianapolis lawyer who later became a judge. The family lived on Meridian Street in the state capital and enjoyed moderate affluence. An uncle, Newton Booth, was later a governor and senator in California and left his nephew a modest inheritance, which helped him when his finances were lean. The boy attended local schools and was sent to Phillips Exeter Academy in 1887 and 1888 for his final high school instruction. While resident there he showed some talent in both writing and drawing.

The family planned a Princeton education for Tarkington but he did not go there directly. After brief intervals at a business college and an art school, he enrolled at Purdue University in 1890. His experiences at Purdue included an early friendship with John T. McCutcheon and George Ade, alumni who returned periodically for weekend visits. Their influence on his writing was important as was his long friendship with the Indiana poet, James Whitcomb Riley. Tarkington transferred to Princeton in 1891 and entered the junior class at the age of twenty-one. His undergraduate record was hardly distinguished but he was a social success. He served as editor for student publications, acted in theatrical productions, and he not only joined the prestigious Princeton Glee Club but became the admired bass soloist of that organization. The college tradition has it that he was frequently called on to sing "Danny Deever." Following graduation Tarkington seemed to lack a goal beyond his determination to succeed as a writer. For five years he lived in the paternal home, devoting himself to reading and composition; at this time his uncle's bequest was providential. As his biographer James Woodress points out, Tarkington worked slowly but consistently to perfect his technique and his mature work benefited immensely from this apprenticeship.

In 1899 Tarkington published his first novel, *The Gentleman from Indiana*, the story of a rural Hoosier newspaper editor who fights corruption. The implausible heroine runs the newspaper during his illness and helps to nominate him for Congress. From the beginning Tarkington's novels with an Indiana setting revealed his knowledge of the background but also his penchant for a happy and sentimental ending. He also briefly tried his hand at historical romance. *Monsieur Beaucaire*, a long short story published in *McClure's Magazine* before it appeared as a book in 1900, was set in eighteenth century England and won immediate popularity. It also became a successful stage play. In the next dozen years Tarkington published a book almost every year, including *The Two Vanrevels* (1902), a story of Indiana during the Mexican War, and *The Conquest of Canaan* (1905), about a small-town maverick who comes back home as a returned prodigal to ultimate success. These earlier books about Indiana dealt with middle-class life and were moderately successful. In 1914, however, Tarkington published *Penrod*, the story of a boy who naturally suggested Tom Sawyer but was acceptable in his own right. Penrod, a lively, mischievous, adventurous eleven-year-old who was gifted with a strong imagination, also had a fear of being laughed at. Two sequels followed the original novel and in 1931 they were collected as *Penrod: His Complete Story*. Because of the humor and sympathy of these books they still find readers. In *Seventeen* (1916), Tarkington treated the adolescent Willie Baxter, whose misadventures in puppy love also amused a large audience.

Tarkington's best work appeared in *Alice Adams* (1921) and in three novels which were combined in *Growth* (1927). The three novels form a trilogy about a nameless city which is clearly Indianapolis and which chronicle its growth from a country town to an industrial metropolis with many of the usual problems. In the initial book, *The Turmoil* (1915), James Sheridan is a self-made capitalist dedicated to money-making and business; he and his family represent the vulgarity and greed of the nouveau riche. It is ironic that the youngest son, dreamy and unsympathetic to his father's goals, eventually succeeds in a business career and marries a young woman from a more cultured family. Tarkington describes effectively the feverish pace of life as the city grows in size and power. *The Magnificent Ambersons* (1918) is a chronicle of three generations. Major Amberson's original fortune is not insurance against real estate fluctuations and he refuses to build apartment houses. Nor does he benefit from the appearance of horseless carriages on the streets of the town. His grandson George Minafer is pictured as arrogant and decadent. Tarkington emphasized the physical changes in the large midland city and ridiculed the pretense and flamboyance of social life in the decaying upper class: fashionable dinners, servants, elegant houses, fantastic statuary. The novel also illustrates Tarkington's real ability to write social satire if he wished to do so. The last book, in the trilogy, *The Midlander* (1923), contrasts a New York girl with a midwest man at a somewhat later time but lacks the characterizations of its predecessors.

Alice Adams is perhaps Tarkington's best attempt to write realistic fiction. The heroine is attractive and intelligent but without a secure social position. Her family is gauche and unable to help her; Alice's attempts to win a proper suitor are futile. Finally she decides to live her own life and enters a business college for professional training. The book, oddly enough for a Tarkington novel, does not end happily but it leaves Alice determined to succeed in her own way. Both *Alice Adams* and *The Magnificent Ambersons* were awarded Pulitzer prizes.

In 1916 Tarkington bought property at Kennebunkport, in Maine, and spent his summers in that state while retaining his Indianapolis home. One of his neighbors, the novelist Kenneth Roberts, became a close friend. Tarkington used the Maine setting for a number of books but they did not substantially add to his reputation. The social satire that he proved he could write in his books about the midland city is missing in the later novels. Tarkington was never basically concerned with plot and his fiction is often structurally weak; characterization and dialogue interested him more. His gifts here led him to write for the theater, and several of his plays were popular successes although without conspicuous literary merit. Some of his novels were dramatized and in many cases he collaborated with Harry Leon Wilson. One of his most adroit dramas although conceived with a farcical plot is *Clarence*, produced in 1919.

In his later years Tarkington suffered severely from eye trouble. He submitted to cataract operations and was virtually blind for almost three years, but he continued to produce books during this time and resorted to dictation when necessary. He died May 19, 1946, in Indianapolis.

JTF

References: Scott Donaldson, *DAB*, Supplement 4, 1974, pp. 815-17; Fred B. Millett, *Contemporary American Authors* (New York: Harcourt, Brace, 1940); James Woodress, *Booth Tarkington, Gentleman from Indiana* (Philadelphia: Lippincott, 1955).

Tecumseh

(ca. March 1768 — October 5, 1813)

Most American Indians who won celebrity on the frontier between the settlements and the hostile areas were war chiefs. Roman Nose, Red Cloud, and Geronimo, for example, were primarily military strategists who became famous for their bravery and feats on the battlefield. Tecumseh, on the other hand, although known as a young man and in maturity for his prowess in warfare, was chiefly a kind of aboriginal statesman who envisaged a grand Indian confederation which would bind together the tribes of the Old Northwest, parts of the

Mississippi Valley, and even perhaps the South. The battle of Tippecanoe in 1811 marked the collapse of his plan.

Tecumseh was probably born near Oldtown in Greene County, Ohio, in 1768. His father, a chief of the Shawnee Indians, was killed at the battle of Point Pleasant in 1774. He and his brother, Tenskwatawa, known as The Prophet, lived for a time in a Delaware village and from 1805 to 1808 at what is now Greenville, Ohio. Forced out by encroaching white settlement, Tecumseh moved to the Indian country in northwest Indiana and settled on the Wabash River near the mouth of the Tippecanoe River at a location later known as Prophet's Town. In 1795 the United States government had negotiated a treaty with various Indians providing for the cession of vast tracts of land on the assumption that the Indians had title to the land concerned. Tecumseh felt strongly that the area occupied by the Indians was owned by the tribes in common and that individual tribes had no right to cede or sell it to the government. He endeavored to prevent further land cessions and also to encourage agriculture among the Indians, to persuade them to live on their earnings, and to avoid rum. He traveled extensively throughout the Ohio Valley and even further south, where he influenced the Creeks, in the hope of promoting tribal unity. Even his military antagonist, General William Henry Harrison, bore witness to Tecumseh's ability and to his skill in imposing discipline on his followers.

Increasing white rapacity for land produced a critical situation and Tecumseh, inveterately opposed to the federal government, sought help from the British in Canada. He was in fact supplied with arms, ammunition, and even clothing. He cautioned his brother not to invoke a battle since the Indians were short in food supplies and war between the British and the Americans seemed imminent. But Tecumseh was away when General Harrison's army moved against the hostiles. The Indians led by The Prophet improvidently attacked Harrison's troops at dawn but were repulsed, and after the soldiers razed the Indian village they retreated. Tippecanoe is generally called a drawn battle today. Yet when Tecumseh shortly returned to the scene he found his plan in shambles and the Indian power broken.

At the outbreak of the War of 1812 Tecumseh joined the British army and was appointed a brigadier general. He supported the attack on Detroit by Sir Isaac Brock and fought in the battles of the River Raisin and Fort Meigs. When Perry's victory over a British fleet in the battle of Lake Erie signaled the collapse of British power, Tecumseh realized that Detroit would probably be abandoned and he became disillusioned. He covered the British retreat of Sir Henry Proctor's outnumbered army and led a force of approximately one thousand Indians facing Harrison's advancing troops. He died at the battle of the Thames fought near Chatham, Ontario, in 1813.

Tecumseh was known as a man who would keep his word. He did not believe in torturing prisoners and he was generally admired for his mercy and humanity. In American history he will be remembered as the native leader whose ambition to lead a pan-Indian movement came closest to success.

JTF

References: Katherine Elizabeth Crane, *DAB*, XVIII, 1936, pp. 358-60; Glenn Tucker, *Tecumseh: Vision of Glory* (Indianapolis, Ind.: Bobbs-Merrill, 1956; reprinted 1973).

John Trumbull

(June 6, 1756—November 10, 1843)

Two men in colonial America had identical names but were only distantly related and achieved considerable recognition in completely unrelated fields. The first John Trumbull (1750-1831) was a man of letters, a member of the group known as the Connecticut Wits, and a widely read satirical poet in his day. The second John Trumbull (1756-1843), the subject of this sketch, was the son of a colonial governor of Connecticut, an officer in the Revolutionary Army, occasionally a businessman in both Europe and America, and a painter who excelled in portraiture and in historical documentation. He spent much of his time abroad, in England and France, served on the federal commission which negotiated John Jay's treaty with England, and left on canvas recognizable visages of many of the dignitaries of the Revolutionary period. Trumbull has been called by a biographer the creator of "the most important visual record of the heroic period of American history."

Trumbull was born in Lebanon, Connecticut, the son of the governor of the state. He had a cranial injury at birth and some time later suffered a serious eye injury but survived both afflictions and became a child prodigy. He early showed an affinity for languages and by the age of six, according to family tradition, could read Greek. He also revealed at an early age a talent for drawing. The boy attended an excellent local school run by Nathaniel Tisdale. His father suffered financial setbacks about this time but Trumbull had the benefit of tutors and finally was able to go to Cambridge and was admitted to the Harvard junior class in 1772. He graduated from Harvard the next year and returned to Lebanon, where he temporarily replaced Tisdale as the master of the local school. With the Revolutionary War imminent Trumbull learned the use of musket and drill and in April 1775, joined the army, being appointed immediately the adjutant of the first Connecticut regiment. His skill in drawing enabled him to sketch the British defenses around Boston and when the plan reached General George Washington he appointed Trumbull a second aide-de-camp. The young soldier also attracted the attention of General Horatio Gates, who named him deputy adjutant general with the rank of colonel, and he accompanied Gates to Crown Point and Ticonderoga. Unfortunately there was a delay in the official commission, which exasperated Trumbull. Manifesting the impetuosity and extreme sensitivity which often distinguished him in later life he resigned his appointment, and in 1777 at the age of twenty-one he left the army to resume his profession as an artist in Boston. In March of 1780 Trumbull sailed for Europe where he soon made the acquaintance of Benjamin West and began to paint in West's studio. The British government, however, probably acting in reprisal for the execution of Major Andre, imprisoned him as a spy and Trumbull spent some months in jail before he was released by royal order and allowed to travel back to New England. After the restoration of peace between the two countries Trumbull returned to London in 1783 and resumed work in West's studio in addition to engaging in some commercial activity. By this time he had done considerable work as a portrait painter. But he had also conceived a much more ambitious project.

Certainly influenced by the success of West's famous painting, *The Death of General Wolfe*, Trumbull decided to paint a number of dramatic scenes reflecting the American Revolution. Before 1786 he had completed his paintings *Death of General Montgomery* and *Battle of Bunker Hill*. He also had begun work on probably his most famous single picture, the *Declaration of Independence*, with its multitude of characters. Of the forty-eight figures in the painting, thirty-six were done from life, the rest from portraits by other artists or from memory. The completed work took eight years. But Trumbull had other subjects in mind and they eventually materialized as the *Surrender of Lord Cornwallis*, the *Surrender of General Burgoyne*, and the *Resignation by General Washington of His Commission to Congress*. Between 1787 and 1789 Trumbull spent much time in Paris where he was the guest of Thomas Jefferson while he worked on the heads of French officers for his military pictures.

Trumbull's original historical pictures were quite small and many of them are the property of Yale University. The artist sought competent engravers in Stuttgart, Copenhagen, and London so that prints could be made and distributed to subscribers to his project. In later years when both his health and his finances deteriorated it was essential to find some kind of subsidy. In 1817 he finally got an award from Congress to provide four historical canvases for the Rotunda of the national capitol in Washington. He was paid thirty-two thousand dollars for his work and the four pictures, specifically the *Declaration*, the *Burgoyne*, the *Cornwallis*, and the *Resignation of Washington*, were installed in 1824. But Trumbull was approaching the end of his creative life at the time and the task of enlarging the original studies to six times their dimensions could not be completed without some sacrifice of their artistry. They did not meet with general approbation although their merits as historical documents cannot be impugned.

In 1817 Trumbull had been named president of the American Academy of Fine Arts, but this organization was soon overshadowed by the formation in 1826 of the National Academy of Design. He received a military pension in 1832. In the same year the artist negotiated a plan with Yale University which stipulated that he would donate to the school all of his unsold canvases in return for an annuity of one thousand dollars. Trumbull also wished to be buried beneath the gallery which was to hold his paintings. Thus the Trumbull Gallery became the first art museum in the country to be associated with an educational institution.

Before Trumbull had left Europe permanently he was involved in the American diplomatic service. From 1794 to 1797 he served as private secretary to John Jay and from 1796 to 1804 he was a member of the commission which negotiated Jay's Treaty with Great Britain. While in London at this time he married an English girl named Sarah Harvey; she died in 1824. Trumbull also wrote his own account of his life. The *Autobiography, Reminiscences and Letters of John Trumbull from 1756 to 1841* was published by the firm of Wiley and Putnam in New York and London in 1841 and was republished by Yale University Press in 1953 edited and fully annotated by Theodore Sizer.

During his lifetime Trumbull painted many portraits and apparently worked with great rapidity. He required only five sittings for a likeness and charged one hundred dollars a portrait. Among his subjects were many of the most prominent Revolutionary figures, including Alexander Hamilton, John Howard Payne, John Jay, Timothy Dwight, and in full length Governor George Clinton and George Washington. For economic reasons he painted many of the New York merchants and their wives and some domestic groups, such as the picture of John Vernet and his family. But Gilbert Stuart was the premiere American portrait painter of his time and John Singleton Copley had preceded him. Trumbull could equal neither.

Nevertheless, his importance as a documentary painter of dramatic events during Revolutionary times is indisputable. His large canvases of historic scenes are a national treasure and even his many miniatures of secondary figures in the federal period retain their value as records. The epitaph on his tomb beneath the Trumbull Gallery at Yale seems justified:

> Patriot and Artist
> To his Country he gave
> his Sword and his Pencil.

JTF

References: Theodore Sizer, *DAB*, XIX, 1936, pp. 11-15; Oliver W. Larkin, *Art and Life in America* (New York: Rinehart, 1949); John Trumbull, *The Autobiography of John Trumbull* (New Haven, Conn.: Yale University Press, 1953).

Harriet Tubman

(ca. 1821 — March 10, 1913)

Harriet Tubman, traditionally known as the "Moses of her people," was born a slave on the eastern shore of Maryland. The most arduous labor was demanded of her — she plowed, drove oxcarts, cut timber with her father, and drew heavy logs — from which she developed great physical strength, an important asset in her subsequent career, when she needed remarkable powers of endurance.

In 1844, her master forced Harriet to marry John Tubman, who soon deserted her. Later, she married a man named Nelson Davis. There is no record that she ever had any children.

Around age twenty-eight, Harriet determined to escape from slavery and persuaded her two brothers to accompany her. The brothers became frightened and turned back, while Harriet proceeded alone, traveling mainly at night until she reached freedom. In nineteen return trips to the land of slavery she escorted to Canada groups of men, women, and children, her aging father and mother and her brothers among them, more than three hundred persons in all. The escape route was the famous underground railroad. As the leader, Harriet walked, traveling with her frightened charges by night in all kinds of weather, crossing swamps, wading across rivers, throwing bloodhounds off the scent. She found her way in the darkness by feeling the moss on tree trunks and following the north star. During the day the fugitives were hidden in caves, graveyards, churches, barns, and the attics of friendly people along the way. The end of the line was Canada. Bounty hunters roamed the northern United States looking for runaway slaves to return to their owners.

In all her long and perilous journeys by way of the underground railroad, Harriet never lost a "passenger." She threatened with death any slave who thought of surrender or tried to turn back. A prize of forty thousand dollars was offered for her capture, but she was never caught. She never learned to read or write and according to one legend she was once found fast asleep under a poster offering the forty-thousand-dollar reward for her capture.

The scene of another legend was Troy, New York. A runaway slave was about to be judged a fugitive and sent back. Harriet was in the courtroom, disguised as a decrepit old woman in a sunbonnet. When the decision was announced, Harriet ran to the window, spreading confusion, and yelling "Give me liberty or give me death." She pulled off her hoopskirt, threw it over the head of the guard and rushed the slave to safety.

After the outbreak of the Civil War, Harriet was sent to join the Union army in South Carolina, working as a cook, laundress, and nurse. She also frequently acted as guide in scouting parties and raids, and served as a spy within the Confederate lines. One of the most important episodes in which Harriet took a leading part was Colonel Montgomerie's exploit on the Combahee River. Several gunboats were sent up the river in an attempt to collect the slaves living near the shores, and to take them to Beaufort within the Union lines. The slave drivers used their whips to try to force the refugees back to their quarters, but inspired by Harriet's singing a motley crowd of about eight hundred men, women, and children scrambled on board the gunboats and were transported to freedom.

After the war, Harriet attempted to establish schools for freedmen in North Carolina. At her home in Auburn, New York, she supported several children and penniless old people. In belated recognition of her Civil War activities Congress voted a monthly pension of twenty dollars for her support. The Harriet Tubman home for indigent aged Negroes continued to exist for a number of years after her death.

RBD

References: Sarah H. Bradford, *Harriet the Moses of Her People* (New York: Little, 1901); P. E. Hopkins, "Harriet Tubman," *Colored American Magazine*, January-February 1902; Lillie B. C. Wyman, "Harriet Tubman," *New England Magazine*, March 1898; Anne Fitzhugh Miller, "Harriet Tubman," *American Magazine*, August 1912.

Jonathan Baldwin Turner

(December 7, 1805 — January 10, 1899)

Writing on the origin of the Land Grant Act of 1862, Edmund J. James, who was president of Northwestern University and later the University of Illinois, maintained that "Jonathan B. Turner was the real father of the so-called Morrill Act of July 2, 1862, and he deserves the credit of having been the first to formulate clearly and definitely the plan of a national grant of land to each state in the Union for the promotion of education in agriculture and the mechanic arts, and of having inaugurated and continued to a successful issue the agitation that made possible the passage of the bill." Historians of education are in accord with James's assessment.

Under the federal act signed by President Lincoln in 1862 a grant was made to each state of the Union of thirty thousand acres of land for each senator and representative in Congress for the purpose of promoting "the liberal and practical education of the industrial classes in the several pursuits and professions in life." This action marked the beginning of a comprehensive policy of federal support for higher education which has continued in various forms to the present day.

A long and tortuous trail led to the achievement of the land-grant act. The name of Jonathan Turner is intimately involved with its history.

Turner was a native of Massachusetts, the son of a farmer. Encouraged by his brother Asa, he entered Yale. Early in the spring of his senior year, 1833, the president of Illinois College in Jacksonville wrote to President Day of Yale seeking an instructor in Latin and Greek. Day recommended Turner and as a result the latter became a member of the Illinois faculty, in May 1833. The following year Turner was appointed professor of rhetoric and belles-lettres.

It did not turn out to be a happy relationship. Turner's religious and political views were not in accord with those of the founders of the new college. He was an abolitionist, surrounded by people who were largely proslavery in sentiment. Moreover, Turner was a Congregationalist and a liberal in religious matters. The college was under Presbyterian control. Turner was successful as an instructor, but his vigorous condemnation of slavery alienated the Southern students in the college and slavery advocates in Jacksonville. He soon came to be looked upon as a dangerous radical and there were calls for his dismissal from the faculty. In 1847 Turner resigned his professorship because of ill health and disagreement with the college officials over slavery and denominational questions.

At this point, Turner began to devote himself primarily to his gardens and orchards, which he had begun soon after coming to the college, and to agricultural experiments. One of his interests was the Osage orange, which he made popular for farm hedges. He also invented several implements for planting and cultivating crops. The preservation of wild game and natural resources was another major concern.

Turner soon placed himself in the forefront of the movement for public education. He had begun to look into the state of common schools in Illinois as early as 1834, immediately after his arrival. He gained prominence by advocating tax-supported public schools in Illinois. The free-school law of 1855 was largely the result of his untiring efforts, and his influence was instrumental in the establishment of the first normal school in Illinois in 1857. Agricultural education was close to Turner's heart; at first he proposed that a professor of "the green earth" be added to the faculty of an existing college, who would make agricultural and horticultural experiments on a farm attached to the college. Later, in 1850, Turner became a strong advocate of a State University for the Industrial Classes. In May of that year, he was president of the State Teachers Institute (later the Illinois State Teachers' Association and now the Illinois Education Association) which held its annual session at Griggsville. Turner's address outlined a plan for a university that would provide for education of the industrial classes, including agriculture and all other industrial occupations. The scheme would extend to every state. The Griggsville speech was the opening shot in the campaign which led eventually to the establishment of a system of land-grant universities throughout the nation.

The following year, the same plan was presented at a convention of farmers meeting in Granville. The proposal was approved and several resolutions were adopted, including one which pledged the members of the convention to "take immediate steps for the establishment of a university in the state of Illinois." The Turner plan was printed and widely distributed.

Other conventions were scheduled. A key meeting in Springfield January 4, 1853, agreed on a petition to the Illinois legislature to ask Congress to appropriate lands to each state for the establishment of industrial universities. The petition was accepted by the legislature and transmitted to Congress — the first such proposal from any state. An Illinois Industrial League was organized in Chicago to carry on propaganda for industrial education. As principal director of the League, Turner gave time and effort to the movement for years.

Illinois congressmen, whose constituents were mainly concerned with agriculture, saw the great possibilities of the land-grant proposal. Richard Yates, a member of Congress, and a friend of Turner, agreed to sponsor the required legislation. The idea was beginning to gain support throughout the country. Messages were sent to the governors and legislatures of all the states asking for their cooperation. Unfortunately, Yates was not reelected and Senator Trumbull who was next asked to push the measure advised delay because of the troubled times.

In 1857 Justin S. Morrill, a representative from Vermont, entered Congress. Shortly thereafter, he introduced a bill providing that public lands be donated to the states and territories to provide colleges of agriculture and the mechanic arts, but the Committee on Public Lands was unfriendly. Reintroduced the following year, the bill got through the House but failed in the Senate. In 1859, it was again introduced and passed both houses, but was vetoed by President Buchanan on the grounds that it was an unconstitutional exercise of federal power.

In 1860, prior to the presidential nominations, Turner met with Abraham Lincoln and Stephen A. Douglas. Both promised that if nominated and elected they would sign the land-grant legislation. Morrill, by then a senator, introduced the bill in 1862; it passed Congress and was signed by Lincoln.

Shortly after passage of the Land-Grant Act, the small colleges of Illinois combined to obtain for themselves the grants of land specified therein. Chiefly through Turner's activities, the Illinois Legislature at its 1857 session decided to establish "a single new industrial university" (now the University of Illinois), to be located at Urbana in Champaign County. The new university was incorporated in February 1862. By 1870, a total of thirty-six states had taken advantage of their rights under the land-grant law.

Jonathan Turner lived on for another thirty-seven years, dying at the age of ninety-three. He was a deeply religious man, an ordained Congregational minister. His later years were devoted mainly to a study of the Bible and its teachings and to writing on religious subjects.

RBD

References: Mary Carriel, *The Life of Jonathan Baldwin Turner* (Urbana: University of Illinois Press, 1961); Judith Ann Hancock, *Jonathan Baldwin Turner* (Seattle: University of Washington Press, 1971).

Mary Edwards Walker

(November 26, 1832 — February 27, 1919)

The twentieth-century emancipated woman wearing fashionable, beautifully designed trousers had the trail blazed for her by a nineteenth-century physician and women's rights advocate, Mary Edwards Walker.

Mary's first deviation from accepted feminine behavior was her decision to study medicine. The inspiration for this ambition doubtless came from her father, a physician in Oswego, New York. Prejudices against women in any profession except teaching was strong in the 1840s and 1850s, and Mary Walker was confronted with the usual scandalized disapproval. Despite the obstacles, she persisted in her studies and in 1855 received her physician's certificate from the Syracuse Medical College. She began practice in Columbus, Ohio, and later Rome, New York. Demands for her services were few.

Prior to entering the medical profession, Mary Walker, at age sixteen, had taught school in New York City. There she began to take an active interest in "women's rights." One daring step was to discard skirts in favor of trousers, partially concealed by long flopping coats. With the coming of the Civil War, she served in the Union army for three years as a nurse, but in 1864 she was commissioned and assigned to duty as an assistant surgeon. At the same time, Mary continued her masculine attire, dressing like her brother officers — trousers with gold stripes, felt hat encircled with a gold cord, and an officer's greatcoat. Her jacket was fitted like a blouse and fitted loosely at the neck.

At the conclusion of the war, Mary Walker was employed briefly on a New York newspaper, one of the first women to do this type of work, and then set herself up as a practicing physician in Washington, D.C. Her regular dress was a frock coat and striped trousers by day, and full evening dress on the lecture platform and for evening social occasions. Her hair was worn in curls so that "everybody would know that I was a woman."

The conservative society of the time did not accept Mary Walker's persistence in wearing men's dress. Boys threw rotten eggs at her, she was the target of men's ribald humor, and other women disapproved of her. A popular humorist, Bill Nye, called her a "self-made man." She was arrested several times for "masquerading in men's clothes," which gave her an opportunity to display the permission said to have been given her by Congress to wear trousers. She also took pride in the bronze medal received from Congress for her war service.

During her Washington stay, other causes concerned Mary Walker, including the popular election of United States senators and similar reforms. The improvement of women's status, however, remained at the center of her interests. She founded a colony for women, called "Adamless Eden," in 1897. She was a believer in spiritualism, found time for several minor inventions, and to compose two books, written in what a critic called "a highly individualistic literary style." Mary Walker never married.

RBD

References: *DAB*, XIX, 1937, p. 352; *Literary Digest*, March 15, 1919; *New York Times*, February 23, 1919.

Henry Agard Wallace

(October 7, 1888 — November 18, 1965)

Agriculture as a philosophy and way of life was deeply ingrained in the Wallace family. Henry A. Wallace was born on a farm and his father and grandfather were agricultural leaders. The family-owned newspaper, *Wallace's Farmer*, one of the most influential and widely read journals in the Midwest, was edited in succession by each of them, and both Henry and his father served as U.S. secretaries of agriculture. All shared a common belief in the basic importance of an agricultural civilization.

Henry Wallace's contributions to agricultural science began early. One of his first achievements was to work out a statistical correlation to be used by hog farmers to determine a fair price level. His experiments with various strains of corn led to production of the first hybrid corn suitable for commercial use. On the basis of this discovery, he established a hybrid seed company, pioneering an important new industry.

A matter of deep concern for Wallace during the 1920s and 1930s was the hard times being suffered by midwestern farmers. One of the chief causes was overproduction. After World War I, European demands decreased and prices for farm products declined drastically. As a counter measure, Wallace advocated the McNary-Haugen bill, a kind of export "dumping" plan. When the bill was twice vetoed by President Coolidge, he switched his allegiance to the Democratic party and supported Al Smith's bid for the presidency. Wallace decided the farmers' critical economic situation could be alleviated by reducing agricultural surpluses through lowering tariffs, increasing world trade, and paying the farmers to restrict production.

Wallace's opportunity to put his ideas into practice came when he was appointed Franklin D. Roosevelt's secretary of agriculture, and was faced with the problems of the Great Depression and the virtual collapse of the agricultural economy. In 1933 Congress passed the Agricultural Adjustment Act, giving the secretary broad authority to meet the emergency. His first step was to push the voluntary domestic allotment plan, paying the farmers to decrease their production. Further to meet the desperate situation, he adopted drastic and controversial actions to bring about immediate cuts in surpluses held by cotton and hog farmers. In the summer of 1933, he authorized paying the farmers for plowing up 10 million acres of growing cotton and slaughtering 6 million pigs.

Such a radical solution was widely condemned by those who recognized there were worldwide shortages of food and clothing. Wallace defended his decision as an emergency and a one-time measure that would not need to be repeated. In addition to cutting production, he promoted efforts to find markets abroad for American farm products, especially reciprocal trade agreements, lower tariffs, and increased world commerce. Wallace also emphasized national and regional planning, soil conservation, erosion control, and distribution of surplus food products through school lunch and relief programs. He started the plan of crop insurance, set up laboratories to study nutrition, and tried to find industrial uses for agricultural products. Farm income doubled during his term of office and U.S. agriculture was better prepared to meet the enormous demands placed on it during World War II.

A queer trait in Wallace's character became evident during the Great Depression. Always religious, he believed that the depression, after a fashion, had been caused by failure to subordinate selfish interests to the general welfare, and a spiritual reformation was demanded. He became intrigued by various unorthodox doctrines and, according to one commentator, "displayed a prominent strain of mystical idealism."

In any event, Wallace's programs for relieving agricultural problems, such as support payments for crop control, soil conservation, food stamp distribution, assistance for tenant farmers, and government-operated warehouses for storing surpluses, were generally successful, did much to relieve the distress of American farmers during the depression, and established guidelines followed in succeeding years for dealing with agricultural questions.

Inevitably, however, Wallace's policies created enemies, and there was strong opposition to Roosevelt's choice of him for vice-president in the 1940 election. As vice-president, he was active in a variety of ways, including goodwill tours of Mexico and other Latin American nations, Soviet Asia, and China. He served as chairman of the Board of Economic Warfare, set up to coordinate economic defense programs. Wallace's idealistic statements about postwar policies made him a leader of liberal opinion in the United States, but at the same time aroused the antagonism of conservatives. They attacked his views as "globaloney," and claimed that he wanted to provide "a quart of milk to every Hottentot."

As the 1944 election approached, party regulars urged Roosevelt to drop Wallace and select another running mate. Lacking strong endorsement from Roosevelt, Wallace's chance for renomination was lost, and the Democratic National Convention chose Harry Truman for vice-president.

Nevertheless, Wallace campaigned for the Democratic ticket. After the election, Roosevelt named him secretary of commerce. In that position, his policies were designed to give more assistance to small business, promote international cooperation and world peace, provide full employment and higher standards of living in the United States. He was especially interested in finding ways to reduce tensions between the United States and the Soviet Union. After making a foreign policy speech sharply critical of the Truman administration policies, his resignation of secretary of commerce was called for.

No significant achievements marked Wallace's final years in the public eye. He served for a year as editor of the *New Republic*, and in 1948 was the presidential candidate of the ultraliberal Progressive party, but failed to carry a single state.

RBD

References: Dwight Macdonald, *Henry Wallace: The Man and the Myth* (New York: Vanguard, 1948); Edward L. Schapsmeier, *Henry A. Wallace of Iowa* (Ames: Iowa State University Press, 1968); James W. Wise, *Meet Henry Wallace* (New York: Boni, 1948).

Henry Watterson

(February 16, 1840 — December 22, 1921)

For decades, Henry Watterson was the prime representative of Southern journalism. As the leader of the press for that section of the country he exerted unusual authority and influence and there was no one to challenge his preeminence. Watterson typified the opinion of the South in the minds of most Northern editors, for which reason his views were widely sought and quoted.

Watterson's journalistic and editorial career began before the Civil War and lasted until after World War I. Thirteen presidents occupied the White House during his active newspaper years and he knew all of them more or less intimately, from Lincoln to Harding. Only Abraham Lincoln won his whole-hearted admiration. Most of the rest, Democrats and Republicans, he quarrelled with, for a variety of reasons.

Watterson entered the newspaper field at age eighteen, in 1858, by way of a brief time spent as a reporter for the *New York Times*, after which he held a reportorial assignment with the *Daily States* of Washington.

Then came the outbreak of the Civil War and though he was a strong Unionist opposed to secession, Watterson's sectional sympathies led him to become a secessionist and Confederate soldier. Apparently he saw little military action. Much of his time was spent working on a Southern propaganda newspaper in Nashville, Tennessee. After the fall of Nashville, he was appointed editor of a Chattanooga newspaper, which he named *The Rebel* and made the organ of the army.

With the war just over, Watterson held several short-term jobs: an editorial position with the Cincinnati *Evening Times*, and appointments in Nashville. His great opportunity came in 1867, when he was offered two jobs in Louisville, Kentucky — editorships of the *Louisville Daily Journal* and the *Courier*. He joined the *Journal*. After six months, the two papers merged and the *Courier-Journal* came into existence.

Henry Garrison Villard, the great liberal editor, suggested that "probably Henry Watterson will be best remembered in the years to come by what he did to bring North and South together." Immediately after joining the *Courier-Journal*, Watterson began a campaign for the restoration of Southern home rule. He had always been opposed to slavery and he agitated for the complete bestowal of civil and legal rights upon the Negroes simultaneously with the end of reconstruction rule. Even after emancipation, he realized that the nation could not exist half slave and half free.

Watterson backed the wrong horses in several presidential races. He supported Horace Greeley in 1872 and Governor Samuel J. Tilden of New York in 1876, both of whom came out on the losing end. Tilden was the ideal statesman in Watterson's view. Except for Lincoln, he was the editor's only public hero. During the Tilden-Hayes controversy growing out of the election, Watterson served in Congress for a short time and led the floor fight for Tilden. After the inauguration of Hayes, he never held public office or strongly supported any Democratic presidential nominee or president.

Ulysses S. Grant was an easy target for Watterson's diatribes. He was also highly critical of Grover Cleveland and bitterly opposed his third nomination.

William Jennings Bryan he considered a menace to the nation. Theodore Roosevelt, said Watterson, was not merely dangerous, he was insane. Roosevelt, he wrote, was "as sweet a gentleman as ever scuttled a ship or cut a throat." Roosevelt's aim, he believed, was to run for office again and again until he became King Roosevelt. In 1909, Watterson bet the *New York World* a dinner that Roosevelt would quarrel with his chosen successor, Taft, and won the bet easily. In 1912, Watterson supported Champ Clark or Oscar Underwood for the Democratic nomination, but endorsed Woodrow Wilson in 1916. He rejected the idea of the League of Nations after the First World War and broke with Wilson over that issue. The nomination of Bryan as secretary of state in Wilson's cabinet had been deplored in 1913, and Watterson assailed him as an impractical dreamer when Bryan resigned over the war issue. He had been damning the Germans since the outbreak of the war in 1914.

The Haldeman family, which shared ownership of the *Courier-Journal* with Watterson, gave him complete editorial freedom, realizing that he was the paper's greatest asset and had won national fame for their newspaper. It was no longer purely local or sectional.

During Watterson's lifetime, he was temporary chairman of several national conventions and wrote the resolutions passed by four of them. He was in wide demand as a lecturer and public speaker.

In 1918, at age seventy-eight, Watterson transferred control of the *Courier-Journal* to Judge Robert Worth Bingham, retaining the title of editor-emeritus for a short time. Two years earlier, he had written a two-volume autobiography, entitled *Marse Henry* which one critic described as "rambling, discursive, without form." Watterson had the distinction of having been a top editor during a period when journalism was highly personal and when editorial opinions sometimes had quick and dynamic effect.

RBD

References: *Who's Who in America*, 1920-1921; files of the *Courier-Journal* (Louisville), 1868-1921; Watterson's *The Compromises of Life* (1903), and *"Marse Henry": An Autobiography*, 2 vols. (1919); letters to the author from Watterson; long personal and professional association; obituary in *Courier-Journal*, December 23, 1921; *The Editorials of Henry Watterson* (1923), compiled by Arthur Krock; Royal Cortissoz, *The Life of Whitelaw Reid* (1929); R. S. Baker, *Woodrow Wilson: Life and Letters*, vol. III (1931); W. F. Johnson, *George Harvey* (1929); and *Courier-Journal*, March 2, 1919, Watterson supplement; Isaac F. Marcosson, *"Marse Henry," A Biography of Henry Watterson* (New York: Dodd, 1951); Joseph F. Wall, *Henry Watterson* (New York: Oxford, 1956).

Anthony Wayne

(January 1, 1745 — December 15, 1796)

When the Revolutionary War started in 1776 military leadership could not be supplied by trained officers from a professional military academy. The leadership had to come from citizens who were leaders in their own community. Anthony Wayne was such an individual. He attracted public attention first in 1774 as chairman of the Chester County, Pennsylvania, committee to draw up a set of resolutions to protest the unpopular acts of the British government. Leadership in his local area resulted in his appointment in 1775 as representative of his county in the provincial assembly, and his appointment as colonel in 1776.

Wayne, sometimes known as "Mad Anthony," was born in Waynesboro, Pennsylvania, the son of Isaac and Elizabeth Wayne. Isaac, with his father Anthony, had settled in Chester County about fifty years before the Revolution. The family had acquired a large tract of land and successfully operated a tannery. Not much is known about Wayne's early education. He may have had some log-cabin schooling before attending an academy in Philadelphia for a short time, but he did not distinguish himself as a student. His interest, even as a teenager, seemed to lie in make-believe Indian warfare. He was not devoid of intellectual ability because by age twenty he had mastered surveying and was sent to Nova Scotia to survey a large tract of land for settlement. When the project failed, through no fault of Wayne, he returned to take charge of his father's tannery and supervise the Wayne estate.

Eastern Pennsylvania played an active part in the pre-Revolutionary War unrest that permeated all sections of the thirteen colonies. Political unrest was brewing in Philadelphia, near Wayne's home. In every section of the country new leadership was arising out of the colonial population. Wayne was a brash young man as willing to fight for his viewpoint in an assembly as upon the battlefield. His bravery was recognized by all, but he was considered to be impetuous and therefore untrustworthy.

His first military assignment, in the spring of 1776, was under General William Thompson with the Pennsylvania brigade to reinforce the Canadian expedition. At Three Rivers Wayne faced the main British Army. His forces were outnumbered and he retreated to Fort Ticonderoga, which had been taken by Ethan Allen's Green River Boys on the Vermont frontier, where he was put in charge of that garrison. The Continental Congress had little money and was unable to organize transportation systems to supply its army, or even to assure medical attention to the wounded or ill. Wayne learned at Ticonderoga the importance of behind-the-line support, a problem that would plague the Continental Army throughout the war.

Wayne conducted himself so bravely at Ticonderoga that he was made a brigadier general in command of the Pennsylvania line in February 1777. He assisted Washington in the defense of Philadelphia and in September 1777, faced the British at the point of their strongest attack at the battle of Brandywine. When he was forced to retreat, Washington sent him to attack the rear of the British, but Cornwallis defeated him at the battle of Paoli on September 20. Though he fought a losing battle at Germantown on October 4, he distinguished himself as an inspiring leader. When Washington retired to Valley Forge Wayne spent the terrible winter at that station, training his men for the upcoming battles.

The British were active in the Hudson River area, and when Wayne was placed in command of a corps of light infantry he made a surprise attack on the Stony Point garrison on July 16, 1779. He captured the post, taking many prisoners and valuable supplies. But most important, he relieved pressure on the upper Hudson from British occupation. Congress showed its appreciation by ordering a medal struck in his honor. He moved his corps to the lower Hudson and harassed the British supply lines. He was in a strategic position to occupy West Point in September 1780 when Benedict Arnold tried to deliver that post to the enemy.

Lafayette was defending the lower James River area in Virginia in 1781. Wayne moved south to support Lafayette, and with eight hundred men attacked a contingent of Cornwallis' army of about five thousand. Wayne's misinformation concerning the size of the enemy force was quickly discovered, and on July 6, 1781, he led a surprise attack that deluded Cornwallis long enough for his corps to escape. Wayne's service did not end with the surrender of Cornwallis at Yorktown. He was sent to Georgia to confront hostile elements in the southern sector. The news of the Yorktown victory was slow to reach the Creek and Cherokee tribes. After defeating the Creeks in May of 1782, Wayne negotiated a treaty that became effective the following year.

Wayne retired from the army in 1783 as brevet major general and returned to civilian life. He failed to successfully operate an eight hundred acre rice plantation which Georgia had given him. He was a representative from Chester County to the State General Assembly in 1774-1785 and was, in general, opposed to liberal reform; yet, he was for men in government who would form just laws and be responsible to the people. As a conservative he voted for the ratification of the federal constitution. Because of his ownership of land in Georgia he was elected to Congress as a representative from that state and served one year starting in March 1791. He was deposed after his residence qualifications were questioned.

George Rogers Clark had temporarily put a halt to Indian raids from the Maumee River area when he led a force of Kentuckians against them in 1782. The Maumee tribes had been particularly troublesome to the Kentucky settlers and Clark's retaliation raid was effective in stopping incursions south of the Ohio, but it did not subdue the Shawnee or stop their attempts to prevent American settlement of the Ohio territory. Wayne, as major general, was put in command of the army by Washington in 1791. He trained a new organization first at Legionville, Pennsylvania, and then in the Northwest Territory at Fort Jefferson and Fort Washington. In the meantime peace negotiations that had been in progress with the Indians failed in August of 1793. The Indians had made a half-hearted attack on Fort Recovery in June and when British aid failed to materialize they gave up their aggressive action and became disorganized. Reassembling at Fallen Timbers, near present day Toledo, Ohio, the Maumee Indian tribes prepared to fight. Wayne decisively defeated them on August 20, 1794. The final surrender was accepted in August 1795. Though the victory at Fallen Timbers solved the Ohio Indian problem it did not resolve problems with the British. Wayne was assigned to the Detroit post after Fallen Timbers and died the following year at what is now Erie, Pennsylvania.

HWS

References: C. J. Stille, *Major-General Anthony Wayne* (Philadelphia: Lippincott, 1893); T. A. Boyd, *Mad Anthony Wayne* (New York: Scribner, 1929); S. W. Pennypacker, *Anthony Wayne* vol. 32, pp. 257-301 (Philadelphia: *Pennsylvania Magazine of History and Biography*, July 1908).

Edith Wharton

(January 24, 1862 — August 11, 1937)

Three important American woman novelists of the early twentieth century are often grouped together as writers influenced by the fiction of Henry James. Of the three—Willa Cather, Ellen Glasgow, and Edith Wharton—the last is perhaps the best example. Wharton not only admired the work of James but limited her characters and scenes very much as he did, dealt with the same themes, and is notable for the same precise use of language and almost equivalent felicities of style. Moreover, she was a personal friend of the novelist and often discussed problems of technique with him. In one other way they were similar too; both cared little for the United States beyond the west bank of the Hudson River.

Edith Newbold Jones was born in New York City in 1862, the descendant of well established colonial ancestors. She was also born to modest wealth. Her father, George Frederick Jones, was free to travel, and although the daughter lived in New York and Newport at first she was taken to foreign countries when she was quite young. Temporary residences in Paris, Florence, and the Black Forest introduced her to French, German, and Italian at an early age. Back at home she was taught by governesses and was given superior training in English, foreign languages, and poetry. Her natural inclination toward literature also brought her early familiarity with English and French classics, and she began to write verse and even fiction before she had entered adolescence. When she was seventeen the family became disturbed about her shyness and insularity from social life and temporarily she was launched into a swirl of luncheons, parties, and drives. Her father's ill health and early death again changed the routine. But she continued her participation in New York social life until her marriage to Edward Wharton, a Boston banker, in 1885. Foreign travel remained an important part of her life, including a yacht cruise on the Mediterranean in 1888, but eventually the young couple settled at Newport and a little later at Lenox, Massachusetts.

By this time Wharton had determined to write for publication and magazines began to accept her contributions. The *Atlantic Monthly* printed some of her verse, and her first short story, "Mrs. Manstey's View," appeared in *Scribner's Magazine* in July 1891. By 1899 she had enough stories in print to justify a collection, *The Greater Inclination*. Such success convinced her that the social life of New York and Newport, although it eventually provided material for her work, was less important than a literary career. Moreover, in her travels abroad she had met Thomas Hardy, John Singer Sargent, and George Meredith, while at home her friends included Howells and James. Although she never became a legal expatriate like James, she spent most of her time after 1907 in France, with trips to Italy, Spain, and northern Africa. During World War I she plunged into Red Cross work, organizing an American committee, raising funds, and becoming involved in the needs of hospitals. For her services during these critical times she was awarded the Cross of the Legion of Honor by France and made a chevalier of the Order of Leopold by Belgium. After the war she resided chiefly in a villa near St. Brice and at property near Hyères in Provence. Her marriage ended in divorce in 1913.

Edith Wharton was a prolific writer, largely of fiction, including eleven volumes of short stories, a dozen novelettes, and fourteen full-length novels. But she also wrote Italian travel sketches, a book entitled *The Writing of Fiction* in 1925, and a revealing autobiography in 1934 called *A Backward Glance.*

Her first full-length novel, a story of eighteenth century Italy called *The Valley of Decision*, appeared in 1902. It documented the author's knowledge of Italian life and culture but it was not characteristic of her mature work. In 1905 she published *The House of Mirth* which focused on Lily Bart, an adventuress who planned to win power and luxury through marriage. Using the New York background which she knew intimately, Mrs. Wharton also revealed her skill as a social satirist. A novelette entitled *Madame de Treymes* followed in 1907; set in Paris it dealt with conflicting French and American standards of honor and is reminiscent of Henry James's international novels. Four years later came one of Mrs. Wharton's best-known stories, *Ethan Frome.* This tragic tale of rural New England about a grim farmer, his invalid wife, and a young female cousin is dramatic and convincing. Because of a sledding accident the wife and the cousin reverse their roles, and the three people confront their misery together. Farm life was not one of Mrs. Wharton's usual themes but shrewd observation during vacations in New England allowed her to treat the subject memorably. *Ethan Frome* was converted into a successful play by Owen and Donald Davis in 1936.

The author's best work derived from the metropolitan society in which she herself once figured and the extensive foreign travel which she enjoyed during much of her life. *The Custom of the Country* , which she published in 1913, is the story of Undine Spragg, a selfish beauty who tried marriage three times and remained perpetually discontented. The protagonist came from an undesirable social class and lacked any sense of honor. In 1920 the novel called *The Age of Innocence* brought Mrs. Wharton a Pulitzer Prize. It is an excellent picture of fashionable New York in the 1870s, but it is satirical as well as documentary. The author emphasized here the stability of society as more important than the attainment of individual happiness. Arthur Hobson Quinn thought that the portrait of Ellen Olenska was not only one of Mrs. Wharton's finest achievements but gave the author unquestionable priority among the novelists of the period. In 1924 four novelettes under the collective title of *Old New York* appeared; the best is *The Old Maid.* Set in the decade of the 1850s, the story again deals with the sacrifice of love to social mores and is rich in characterization. *The Age of Innocence* was dramatized by Margaret Ayer Barnes and *The Old Maid* by Zoë Akins; both became stage successes.

The world in which Edith Wharton published her last novels was rapidly growing more promiscuous, as Edward Wagenknecht pointed out, and social order was disintegrating. Her dislike for such changes is noticeable in novels like *Twilight Sleep* (1927) and *Hudson River Bracketed* (1929), but her gift for feminine characterization is still apparent in *The Children* (1928), with its admirable creation of Judith Wheater, the young girl who assumes responsibility before it would normally come.

In the fictional portrait gallery that Wharton created, the men are consistently weaker than the women. This may have been due to her limited acquaintance with the masculine professional world and her dislike of an American aristocracy with limited culture but ample funds. Her male figures, like those of Henry James, are singularly lacking in any real occupation with the possible exception of the artists. On the other hand, she knew the women much better, the social climbers as well as the grandes dames, and she could picture them realistically, sometimes satirically, always with understanding and perhaps even a bit of affection.

Her technique, as befits an admirer of Henry James, was always impressive, even though she sometimes overused coincidence and occasionally failed to motivate sufficiently some of the actions of her characters. She handled the short story effectively and even wrote some ghost stories. Her style, in a period when literature grew increasingly flamboyant, was somewhat austere, but she always wrote precisely with a pleasant command of irony.

Edith Wharton died in 1937. She was buried in the Protestant Cemetery at Versailles in the grave next to that of her old friend and admirer, Walter Berry.

JTF

References: Leon Edel, *DAB*, Supplement 2, 1958, pp. 703-6; Percy Lubbock, *Portrait of Edith Wharton* (New York: Appleton-Century, 1947); Blake Nevius, *Edith Wharton: A Study of Her Fiction* (Berkeley: University of California Press, 1953); R. W. B. Lewis, *Edith Wharton: A Biography* (New York: Harper & Row, 1975).

Andrew Dickson White

(November 7, 1832 — November 4, 1918)

Among the late nineteenth and early twentieth-century American university presidents whose names stand out — such as Charles Eliot, Daniel Gilman, William Rainey Harper, and Nicholas Murray Butler — Andrew D. White of Cornell ranks high.

White's eighty-six-year career spanned the last two-thirds of the nineteenth century and ran well into the twentieth. A wealthy father enabled him to travel, indulge his cultural tastes, and gain a first-class education. His desire was to enter Yale College, but his orthodox Episcopal parents sent him to Geneva College (later Hobart) instead. When Andrew rebelled, the parents finally consented to allow him to join the class of 1853 at Yale. There he and Daniel Coit Gilman became fast friends. Together the two of them set out for study abroad. A semester in Paris was followed by a year as attachés to the American legation at St. Petersburg (1854-1855), a semester in Berlin, and a ramble through Italy. Back at Yale, White completed a master's degree, and then, at age twenty-five, was appointed professor of history at the University of Michigan.

White was an inspiring and imaginative teacher, unwilling to follow perfunctory textbook instruction. At this early stage, he was dreaming of a different American university, one that would combine the best features of European universities he had observed abroad. Unlike Yale, it would not be narrowly sectarian, nor would it be restricted by sex or color. The plan made proper provision for languages and mathematics, philosophy and history, law and medicine, and also for agriculture and engineering, with an emphasis on the natural sciences.

The opportunity for White to make his dreams a reality came in 1864, when his Syracuse neighbors elected him a state senator, and he assumed the chairmanship of the Senate committee on education. In that capacity, he went about codifying the state's school laws and establishing a system of normal schools.

As chairman of the education committee, White was also responsible for looking after New York's share of the landed endowment under the 1862 Morrill Act — a total of a million acres granted New York by the federal government. Equally important from the point of view of White's vision for a major university was his meeting with Ezra Cornell, also a state senator. Cornell had acquired a fortune through the electric telegraph. He was deeply interested in creating a new agricultural college through the use of the federal funds. White persuaded him that an even better plan was to add a large endowment by Cornell himself to the Morrill grant. Together they drew the charter for a new institution to be located at Ithaca, later to be named Cornell University by White. A broad program of instruction was outlined, including not only agriculture and mechanic arts but "such other branches of science and knowledge as the Trustees may deem useful and proper." There were to be no religious restrictions in appointments of officers and faculty nor in the control board.

Cornell's principal features, as planned by White, were the following: no separation of the sciences and the humanities, all to be taught by the same faculty; equal rank for modern languages and literatures and for history and political sciences; use of eminent scholars as "non-resident professors"; and treatment of students as mature adults, with their teachers as friends and companions.

Ezra Cornell insisted that White should become president of the new university. White accepted and began the process of finding a distinguished faculty. The formal opening occurred in 1868 with six hundred students enrolled. White reserved for himself the chair of history. The panic of 1873 and Ezra Cornell's death the following year caused serious financial problems for the university, but it escaped ruin.

In 1885, after twenty years in the presidency, in poor health, probably fatigued from struggling with financial and other administrative problems, but seeing his university off to a successful start, and wanting time for other interests, White resigned the office of president of Cornell. He was succeeded by his old student at Michigan, Charles Kendall Adams.

While still at Cornell, White had found time for a number of other activities, such as leading the fight for civil service reform and helping to found and serve as first president of the American Historical Association.

White's lengthy career in the diplomatic service had begun, as noted, at age twenty-two, as an attaché to the American legation in Russia. In 1871 he was appointed by President Grant to visit Santo Domingo, then being considered for annexation. In 1878, on leave from Cornell, President Hayes made him minister to Germany, where he formed close ties with German men of letters and assisted Americans studying abroad. In 1892, after his retirement from Cornell, President Harrison called him back into foreign service, as minister to Russia, where he spent two years, before resigning in 1894. The Russian court he deemed corrupt and unreliable in its dealings, but he found some satisfaction in becoming acquainted with such literary lights as Tolstoy. The next assignment came from President Cleveland, who named him to the commission charged with finding the division line between Venezuela and British Guiana. A member of the same commission was his old friend Daniel Coit Gilman. White was still in Washington when William McKinley made him ambassador to Germany. The most important event of those years, in his eyes, was his leadership of the U.S. delegation to the Hague Conference in 1899.

White had long been a zealous advocate of the abolition of war. At the Hague conference he succeeded in obtaining an agreement to establish an international court of arbitration and for the approval of international commissions of inquiry. His efforts were hampered by the opposition of the German Emperor and of Admiral Alfred T. Mahan, a member of the American delegation. In 1900 White urged Andrew Carnegie to finance the building of a Palace of Justice to house the International Tribunal at The Hague, a plan accepted by Carnegie, who also endowed a great library of international law there. A short time later, the famous philanthropist funded the creation of the Carnegie Institution of Washington, which opened in 1902, with Gilman as president and White as a trustee.

It was ironic that the Armistice, bringing World War I to an end, came exactly a week after White's death.

White was a prolific writer. A theme pervading his works was the conflict between science and religion. In part, he was inspired by fierce attacks on Cornell University as a "godless" school because it had no denominational ties. White defended this policy on the basis that both religion and science benefited from freedom of teaching and research. His response came first in the form of a lecture, then a magazine article, and in 1826 a pamphlet entitled *The Warfare of Science*. Long afterward, White continued to be preoccupied with the controversy. His definitive work on the subject appeared in 1896, in two volumes, entitled *A History of the Warfare of Science with Theology in Christendom*. Later came an important related work, *Seven Great Statesmen in the Warfare of Humanity with Unreason* (1910). A two-volume *Autobiography* was published in 1905.

White presented his rich historical library to Cornell and in his honor the "President White School of History and Political Science" was named by the university. White combined to an extraordinary degree the qualities of scholar and man of action. His chief recreation was reading, especially in the field of biography. He was devoted to the fine arts, to music, and enjoyed travel. Of all the departments established by him at Cornell, architecture was his favorite, and he never lost an opportunity to study architectural monuments around the world.

Looking back at Andrew Dickson White's career as a whole, it is clear that he devoted himself to three great causes: in his youth, campaigning against slavery; in his prime, freedom of teaching and research; and in his old age, a crusade against war and for international peace.

RBD

References: Walter P. Rogers, *Andrew D. White and the Modern University* (Ithaca, N.Y.: Cornell University Press, 1942); Ruth Bordin, *Andrew Dickson White, Teacher of History* (Ann Arbor: University of Michigan Press, 1958).

Walter Francis White

(July 1, 1893 — May 21, 1955)

The black race in America has produced a number of outstanding leaders in the long fight against racial discrimination and mistreatment, notably W. E. B. DuBois, Booker T. Washington, James Weldon Johnson, A. Philip Randolph, Roy Wilkins, Martin Luther King, Jr., and Walter White. The long-range impact of Walter White's activities — crusading, speaking, and writing — stands at the top among these valiant heroes of the struggle for racial equality.

White's parents were Georgians — the father, a letter carrier in Augusta, was one-fourth Negro, and the mother, a schoolteacher in Lagrange before her marriage, was one-sixteenth black. The family were devout Congregationalists. As a result of his racial make-up, Walter White was blond, fair-skinned, and blue-eyed. He did not choose, however, to pass for white.

In his book, *A Man Named White*, Walter White recounts his terrifying experience during an Atlanta race riot when a mob approached his parents' home. "In that instant," he wrote, "there opened up within me a great awareness. I knew then who I was. I was a Negro, a human being with an invisible pigmentation, which marked me as a person to be hunted, hanged, abused, discriminated against, kept in poverty and ignorance."

Because blacks were not admitted to public high schools in Georgia, White attended Atlanta University's preparatory school and went on to graduate from the college division.

Active involvement in racial problems began for White when the Atlanta Board of Education announced that the seventh grade in black schools would be dropped to provide financing for a new white high school. Walter White helped to organize a protest against the action, and then went on to take the lead in establishing a branch of the National Association for the Advancement of Colored People in Atlanta, of which he was elected secretary. The school protest was successful. Shortly thereafter, in 1918, at James Weldon Johnson's invitation, White became assistant secretary on the NAACP's national staff in New York.

As an official of the NAACP, White became an authority on lynchings. He investigated at firsthand numerous lynchings and race riots, often at great personal risk. His ability to pass for white was an asset, enabling him to move freely in southern towns and to talk to everyone. Efforts to obtain legislation making lynching a federal crime failed, but White wrote magazine articles and a book on the brutal practice, helping to turn national sentiment against it.

Walter White succeeded James Weldon Johnson in the NAACP as executive secretary in 1929. He continued to wage the campaign against and to win passage of antilynching legislation. Due in good measure to these efforts, lynchings became rare after 1937.

The NAACP under White's leadership began legal battles on other important fronts, especially white primaries and poll taxes, residential segregation, and educational segregation and discrimination. He became recognized as one of the ablest lobbyists for the black cause on Capitol Hill. He was also effective in convincing presidents to act. White and A. Philip Randolph, union leader, persuaded Franklin D. Roosevelt to issue an executive order in 1941 banning discrimination in defense industries and establishing the Fair Employment Practices Commission. On White's recommendation, Truman appointed the President's Committee on Civil Rights. That committee, in turn, prepared a report which formed the basis for the controversial plank on civil rights included in the 1948 Democratic platform.

During World War II, White became a correspondent for the *New York Post*. In that position he traveled in the European, North African and Pacific areas to investigate discrimination against black soldiers. An important result of his findings was President Truman's 1948 executive order desegregating the armed forces.

White's activities on behalf of racial justice were by no means confined to the United States. He recognized that the problems of colored peoples were international in character. He served as a delegate to the Second Pan-African Congress in 1921, as a member of the Advisory Council for the government of the Virgin Islands in 1934-1935, and as adviser to the U.S. delegation to the United Nations at its founding conference at San Francisco in 1945, and at the General Assembly meeting in Paris in 1948. He took a particular interest in India and the West Indies, and their racial problems, and traveled to many countries abroad to lecture on race relations. White's prolific writing in magazines and as a newspaper columnist further publicized the basic issues.

Walter White's indefatigable support for race rights made him a hero to countless blacks. His administration of the NAACP, however, involved him in bitter controversy, especially with W. E. B. DuBois, founder of the NAACP and editor of the influential journal *Crisis*. His biographer, Nancy J. Weiss, commented that White "could be tough, arrogant, ambitious, prone to vanity and egotism, and autocratic." These qualities caused friction in the NAACP staff. There was controversy also over White's divorce of his black wife and marriage to a white writer, food editor, and advertising executive. Nevertheless, White retained his post as NAACP executive secretary, though with restricted authority, until his death in 1955 in New York City.

RBD

Reference: Poppy Cannon, *A Gentle Knight: My Husband, Walter White* (New York: Rinehart, 1956).

Marcus Whitman

(September 4, 1802 — November 29, 1847)

The War of 1812 did not establish any boundary lines in the far Northwest. It was primarily a war that settled ownership of land east of the Mississippi and permitted frontiersmen to move into such states as Ohio, Indiana and Illinois. The strong voices of John Calhoun and Henry Clay supported Manifest Destiny. The old forts on the Mississippi, which had served so well, were no longer needed and by the 1820s Stephen Long was exploring the plains area between St. Louis, Colorado and the Red River. The Oregon Country in the 1830s was jointly occupied by the United States and Great Britain under the Convention of 1818. The territory covered a vast area in the northwest, including the present states of Washington, Oregon, Idaho and a small portion of western Montana. It was a primeval area made up of diverse physiographical provinces including mountains, lava plateaus, rain forests, deserts and great rivers.

Many small Indian tribes had established themselves as gleaners and hunters throughout the region. They were among the most primitive of American Indians, having no agriculture or domesticated animals other than the dog and horse. These tribes included the Cayuse and Nez Percé east of the Cascades. The maximum population at an early time may have been in the neighborhood of 125,000, averaging about 1,000 per tribe. By the time the early settlers from the Midwest arrived the number of Indians had been greatly reduced by measles and smallpox.

The Spanish and English had explored the coast as early as the sixteenth century. Americans in the ship *Columbia* arrived on May 11, 1792, leaving its name upon a great river. John Jacob Astor established *Astoria* as a fur-trading center in 1811 in competition with the Hudson Bay Company. Permanent settlement by Americans took place first in 1830. They were soon followed (1834) by Methodist missionaries who established a mission in the Willamette Valley.

A spiritual awakening that swept through the new nation in the beginning of the nineteenth century resulted in the formation of the American Board of Commissioners for Foreign Missions (1810). Several missions had been established among Indian tribes east of the Rockies prior to any attempt to carry the word of God to the "heathens" in Old Oregon. The board authorized Samuel Parker and Marcus Whitman to make a reconnaissance by going to the Green River Rendezvous near Daniel, Wyoming, in 1835 to determine the attitude of the Indians. In addition to the two thousand Indians in attendance, white fur traders and mountaineers were present. Among the white men was Jim Bridger, a famous mountaineer who had carried an Indian arrow in his back for three years. Whitman, a qualified doctor, removed the arrow by surgery. Also, he removed one from the back of an Indian, probably the first surgery performed by an American west of the Continental Divide. This was proof that Whitman was a great medicine man, and he won the friendship of all present. The Nez Percé and Flathead tribes expressed their approval for the creation of missions among their people. Whitman returned home and reported to the board.

Marcus Whitman was born in Rushville, New York. As a young man he studied medicine and was awarded a M.D. in 1832 from the College of Physicians and Surgeons of the Western District of New York. The romanticism of serving in a mission, especially on the far frontier, had greater appeal to Whitman than the more prosaic practice of medicine in New York. After his initial trip to the Green River Rendezvous he was convinced that he should spend his life in converting the red man to the ways of Christianity.

Narcissa Prentiss, a young lady from Angelica, New York, had also enlisted with the Board of Commissioners for service as a missionary. Marcus married her in February 1836, and prepared to start the trek to Oregon. They went via Pittsburgh and Cincinnati to St. Louis, taking along two Indian boys whom Marcus had brought back east in 1835. While in St. Louis the Whitmans visited a new cathedral during High Mass. There was a strong anti-Catholic feeling among Protestants at the time and Narcissa expressed it when she commented, "While sitting there and beholding this idolatry." One of the reasons for going to Oregon was to spread the concepts of Protestantism among the Indians prior to or in competition with other religious groups. The Whitmans and the Reverend Henry H. Spalding and wife Elizabeth left St. Louis under the protection of the American Fur Company, making their way along the Missouri and Platte Rivers to the Green River, Wyoming. From this point they traveled toward Oregon under the protection of the Hudson Bay Company.

At South Pass, Wyoming, on July 4, 1836, Narcissa and Mrs. Elizabeth Spalding were the first white women to cross the Continental Divide. What these two women did set the pattern for the emigration of women westward. The feat of the women crossing the Divide at South Pass caught the imagination of the public. Seven years later the first wagon train to Oregon passed the same point. Where two could go thousands would follow and the colonization of the Northwest by Americans was assured. Whitman recognized the importance of the feat, and a few years later wrote that if he did nothing more than to be "one of the first to take white women across the Mountains ... and establishing the first wagon road across the borders of the Columbia River, I am satisfied."

The Whitman caravan progressed from Rendezvous to Fort Hall to Fort Boise and finally reached Fort Walla Walla on the Columbia on September 1, 1836. It had been a long honeymoon trip for Narcissa. After Whitman made a trip down the river to Fort Vancouver for supplies, he returned to Walla Walla and established a mission at Waiilatpu, about twenty-five miles east of the fort. The Whitman Mission was among the Cayuses, and the Spalding Mission was among the Nez Percés at Lapwai, near modern Lewiston, Idaho. The Whitmans, as pioneers, had to construct a dwelling and prepare for the winter's food supply. In addition, they used every opportunity to learn the language of the Cayuse. It was impossible to evangelize a nomadic people unless their language could be understood. The Whitmans introduced agriculture at Waiilatpu and acquired hogs and sheep in 1837. Ten years later an inventory listed 290 head of cattle under Whitman's control.

The Spaldings and Whitmans formed the First Presbyterian Church in the Oregon Territory in 1838. It did not add much to the success of converting the Indians to Christianity. The record shows that the Church baptized only twenty-one natives in the next eleven years. The success of the mission cannot be judged by the number of conversions. There had been little trouble with the Indians prior to 1840. After that time dissensions slowly increased at most of the stations. The Indians were aware of the increasing number of whites settling in their territory. They considered the land theirs and wanted to move the whites off. The first family of emigrants passed Waiilatpu in the fall of 1840. The Indians tried to provoke Whitman into some rash act. The trials and tribulations imposed upon the missionaries resulted in dissension within their own organization. The complaints reached the board and after duly considering the matter it decided to close one of the missions. This order disturbed Whitman to such an extent that he decided to return East and present his case to the board and request an expansion of effort rather than a reduced program. This was the real cause of Whitman's return journey to the East. The trip had nothing to do with the "save Oregon" from the British theory advocated by some writers.

On October 3, 1842, Marcus left Narcissa at Waiilatpu and with his friend Asa Lovejoy left for Boston. They learned that Indians in Wyoming were on the warpath, and this forced a great southward detour that took them to Taos and then Fort Bent in southeastern Colorado. Marcus reached St. Louis in early March and Boston in early April, after having been on the trail for six months. The long trek was not a journey of exploration, but was a feat of bravery and perseverance under great hardships.

After Whitman called on Horace Greeley he proceeded to Boston and had a successful visit with the board, which rescinded its order to close the mission. Marcus started his return trip to Oregon by joining a group of emigrants in Missouri constituting the 1843 caravan. He gave advice to the emigrants and ultimately led them over a wagon trail from Fort Hall to the Columbia, the first large wagon train to accomplish this feat. The road to Oregon was opened at last. Marcus returned to Waiilatpu on September 28, only five days short of a full year from the time he left.

The Indians began to show hostility toward the Whitmans. The influx of white settlers was disturbing to them. Marcus was often threatened and by 1847 the situation had become dangerous. Recent emigrants brought measles with them and both Indian and white children called upon Dr. Whitman for his services. Unfortunately, the Indian children had no natural immunity and died, but the white children lived. The Indians concluded that Whitman was killing their children. They attacked on November 29, 1847 and massacred fourteen people, including Marcus and Narcissa. The massacre created a public outcry. Five Cayuse were apprehended, tried and found guilty, and sentenced to be hanged nine days later. Law and order had come to the Oregon country. Perhaps Marcus Whitman's ultimate contribution to the winning of the West is epitomized in a biblical quotation, "it is in dying that we are born to eternal life."

HWS

References: Nard Jones, *The Great Command* (Boston: Little, Brown, 1959); Clifford M. Drury, *Marcus and Narcissa Whitman and the Opening of Old Oregon*, 2 vols. (Glendale, Calif.: Arthur H. Clark Company, 1973).

Wendell Willkie

(February 18, 1892—October 8, 1944)

In a sense, Wendell Willkie was the spiritual founder of the United Nations. The dramatic story told by Willkie in his book *One World*, based on his world travels, gripped the popular imagination, rousing strong sentiment for international organization and cooperation following World War II.

Willkie came to the front through big business channels. He was a native of Indiana and a graduate of the Indiana University Law School. Incidentally, his mother was the first woman ever admitted to the Indiana bar. As a boy and college student, Wendell supported himself by harvesting grain, and acting as "barker" for a tent hotel during a South Dakota land boom. On the Indiana campus he became known as a radical, spreading socialistic ideas, advocating abolition of inherited wealth, and preaching against fraternities.

Any trace of radicalism vanished, however, with Willkie's entry into the world of business. After making a brilliant record as a lawyer in the legal department of the Firestone Company and the law firm of Mather and Newbitt, the president of the Commonwealth and Southern, a giant utility holding company, appointed him in 1929 as the corporation's attorney. Four years later, when the president retired, Willkie succeeded him. There, too, as a utility executive, Willkie made an outstanding record.

Then came Roosevelt's New Deal and the creation of the Tennessee Valley Authority. The TVA was bitterly fought by Willkie, who maintained that it was unfair competition with private industry. A spectacular feud ended when the TVA paid Willkie's company $78 million for its Tennessee properties. Meanwhile, Willkie, who had been a lifelong Democrat, switched to the Republican party because of his opposition to the New Deal.

Willkie's potentialities for the U.S. presidency were recognized early by prominent political leaders. A widely read news commentator, Raymond Clapper, declared that Willkie was the only man the Republicans could choose who had "a ghost of a chance" to win. On June 27, 1940, he was nominated by the Republican convention, on the sixth ballot.

Four months of strenuous campaigning by Willkie followed. Nevertheless, in the November 5 election he was defeated by Franklin Delano Roosevelt, running for a fourth term. Willkie's popular vote totaled nearly 23 million compared to FDR's 27 million.

Shortly after the election, Willkie became Roosevelt's unofficial emissary to the world. His travels by plane, undertaken at the height of hostilities in World War II, lasted forty-nine days and covered thirty-three thousand miles, in the fall of 1942. The route followed took him to North Africa, Turkey, Iran, the Soviet Union, China, and Siberia, and enabled him to hold conferences with the principal wartime leaders and many others.

Throughout his account of his travels, as recorded in his remarkable book *One World* (1943) Willkie reiterates three main points: First, the smallness of the world which we now inhabit; second, the speed of social, political, and economic change in the Eastern half of that world; third, the obligation that all Western people had to learn these facts and to act magnanimously in international affairs. The net impression of his flight, Willkie wrote, "was not of distance from other peoples, but of closeness to them.... The world has become small not only on the map, but also in the minds of men. All around the world there are some ideas which millions and millions of men hold in common, almost as much as if they lived in the same town." What these ideas are and their implications for mankind, Willkie elaborates in his book. In essence, *One World* is a stirring appeal for self-government among the peoples of the Far and Middle East, for the end of white imperialism everywhere, and for the immediate creation of international machinery to keep the peace.

Willkie's circumnavigation of the globe in a world immersed in war required great personal courage. His travels occurred before American troops had invaded Africa, when Hitler's armies dominated Central Europe, and Marshall Rommel held North Africa. The consensus among historians is that Willkie's flight performed a major service to the Allied cause, principally in favorable publicity, by showing that America and her Allies were united in their determination to defeat the Axis Powers.

Willkie was impressed with the industrial, agricultural, and cultural progress made under the influence of the Zionist movement in Palestine. The Jewish viewpoint came out in an interview which Willkie held with Henrietta Szold, founder of Hadassah, who maintained that the Jews must have a national homeland and there was no other appropriate place in the world where the persecuted Jews of Europe could come. Furthermore, there was no "necessary antagonism between the hopes of the Jews and the rights of the Arabs." Willkie concluded, however: "It is probably unrealistic to believe that such a complex question as the Arab-Jewish one, founded in ancient history and religion, and involved as it is with high international policy and politics, can be solved by good will and simple honesty."

Willkie's comments on colonialism and imperialism, as he saw them functioning in Africa and Asia, were highly critical. Some of the leaders with whom he conferred in Egypt and Jerusalem, for example, told him that "the natives don't want anything better than what they have," to which Willkie retorted, "That is the argument that has been used everywhere for centuries against the advancement of the underprivileged, by those whose condition makes them satisfied with the *status quo*." Colonial officials of the Middle East, Willkie found, were derived from "Rudyard Kipling untainted even with the liberalism of Cecil Rhodes."

The colonial people of the Near, Middle, and Far East, Willkie discovered, were demanding social, political, and economic equality with the advanced nations of Europe and America—stirrings over a vast region which have since brought about profound changes in areas formerly administered as colonial empires by Britain, France, Belgium, Holland, Japan, and other outside powers. The awakening forces, Willkie predicted with remarkable foresight, "if they are flouted or ignored, will continue to disturb the world." He concedes that "there is much historical and even present-day justification for the current 'protective' colonial system."

Willkie's criticisms of colonialism were favorably received by most Americans, but not generally by the British or by ruling groups in the colonies themselves. Winston Churchill was provoked into a belligerent rejoinder: "That there may be no mistake in any quarter, we intend to hold what we have. I have not become the King's First Minister to preside at the liquidation of the British Empire." On the other hand, the *Times* of London pointed out that the modern

British Empire had "become in a certain sense a self-liquidating concern, dissolving itself by an orderly process into a commonwealth of peoples united by a common ideal of partnership in freedom."

Willkie was in the Soviet Union only two weeks, during which he met with Stalin for two extended sessions, both off the record. Willkie's chief purpose in visiting Russia was to find an answer "to the actual problems posed for our generation of Americans by the simple fact that the Soviet Union, whether we like it or not, exists." He concluded that "Russia is an effective society. It works. It has survival value," and he found much to admire in the U.S.S.R., whose dynamic spirit he compared with the pioneer era of the American West. The most important consideration, in Willkie's estimation, was that "we must work with Russia after the war. At least it seems to me that there can be no continued peace unless we learn to do so."

On every possible occasion in *One World*, Willkie urges the importance of international organization to preserve future world peace. He was distressed to find in the Middle East, Russia, and China "everywhere a growing spirit of fervid nationalism, a disturbing thing to one who believes that the only hope of the world lies in the opposite trend." A fatal weakness of the Atlantic Charter in his view was that it "forecast the recreation of western Europe in its old divisions of small nations, each with its own individual political, economic, and military sovereignty" — a system that had greatly facilitated Hitler's conquest. The proper solution, in Willkie's opinion, was: "The re-creation of the small countries of Europe as political units, Yes; their re-creation as economic and military units, No, if we really hope to bring stabilization to western Europe, both for its own benefit and for the peace and economic security of the world." These comments foreshadowed the establishment after World War II of the North Atlantic Treaty Organization (NATO), the European Community (Common Market), and the European Free Trade Association.

For America, when the war ended, Willkie foresaw three choices: narrow nationalism, which "means the ultimate loss of our own liberty"; international imperialism, which "means the sacrifice of some other nation's liberty"; or the creation of a world with "equality of opportunity for every race and every nation."

As a first step toward the last goal, Willkie proposed to set up a common council of the United Nations. The United Nations had begun simply as a phrase, coined by President Roosevelt, to include all the nations at war with the Axis Powers. The phrase meant a united front in war, but with no commitments beyond. In *One World* and in numerous articles and speeches, Willkie urged that the United Nations make a firm commitment to establish a postwar world organization, "a new society of independent nations, free alike of the economic injustices of the West and the political malpractices of the East."

The United Nations organization, the concept of which Willkie had so actively promoted, began to become a reality in October 1943, when the American, British, and Russian foreign ministers, meeting in Moscow, drew up a statement pointing out "the necessity of establishing at the earliest practicable date a general international organization based on the principle of the sovereign equality of all peace-loving states ... large and small, for the maintenance of peace and security." The proposal was endorsed by the United States Senate with a declaration that "the United States, acting through its Constitutional processes, join with free and sovereign nations in the establishment and maintenance of international authority with power to prevent aggression and maintain the peace of the world." Willkie urged that beyond such general principles the United Nations should be armed with "the machinery needed to enforce its decisions," in order to avoid becoming a "mere debating society," as in fact it has gradually degenerated into being.

In an introduction to a 1966 edition of *One World*, Donald Bruce Johnson comments: "The international organization about which Willkie dreamed came into existence, but the unified world of free and democratic people that was the foundation of the dreams disintegrated gradually as the forces of nationalism were resurrected over the earth." In any event, Willkie contributed immensely to the creation of public opinion and to the bipartisan political support which made the United Nations possible.

The reception of *One World* was phenomenal. The book came off the press on April 4, 1943, and within four days had sold 170,000 copies. By the end of the year, an estimated 3 million copies were in print, translations were appearing in numerous foreign languages, and underground editions were circulating in Nazi-controlled territories. No accurate record exists of the final sales of the most important and influential book published in America during the war. In addition to various hardback and paperback editions issued at home and abroad, several magazines published it in digest form, and a condensed version was syndicated in 107 daily newspapers.

The dramatic story told in *One World* gripped the popular imagination, making firm the latent sentiment for world cooperation and international organization. Even the title influenced people's thinking and helped to destroy any remaining support for isolationism. Great appeal lay in Willkie's basic premise: People are people, and regardless of race, language, religion, and nationality, all human beings have certain desires and needs in common, among them a degree of material comfort, some participation in their own governance, and a measure of individual freedom. As Donald Bruce Johnson points out, Willkie's messages about liberty, domestic imperialism, and freedom of choice "ring as freshly and as necessarily as ever."

Willkie did not long survive his strenuous world tour and publication of *One World*. He died in October 1944, about six months before Franklin Roosevelt's death in April 1945.

RBD

References: Ellsworth Barnard, *Wendell Willkie* (Marquette: Northern Michigan University Press, 1966); Joseph Barnes, *Willkie* (New York: Simon and Schuster, 1952); Mary E. Dillon, *Wendell Willkie* (Philadelphia: Lippincott, 1952); William Severn, *Toward One World: The Life of Wendell Willkie* (New York: Washburn, 1967); Steve Neal, *Dark Horse: A Biography of Wendell Willkie* (Garden City, N.Y.: Lippincott, 1984).

Grant Wood

(February 13, 1891 — February 12, 1942)

The United States in the 1920s and 1930s experienced a surge of nationalistic fervor which found expression in music, architecture, literature, and painting. Characteristic of this period was the development of a strong regionalism, especially in the Midwest where such painters as John Steuart Curry of Kansas, Thomas Hart Benton of Missouri, and Grant Wood of Iowa became both prominent and influential. All three worked in various media, studied in Europe, were successful as muralists and landscapists, and produced canvases which often combined patriotism and satire. In subsequent years the reputations of all three men, conflicting with such trends as impressionism and abstractionism, which quickly moved westward from Europe, tended to deflate. But probably no American painting of the twentieth century achieved wider celebrity, or stimulated more imitation and more parody than Wood's *American Gothic*, submitted in a contest at the Art Institute of Chicago in 1930 and immediately bought by the museum for three hundred dollars. Wood's central figures, his sister Nan and his family dentist, became nationally recognizable although their identity was sometimes confused.

Wood was born on a farm near Anamosa, Iowa, February 13, 1891, one of four children. His father was a farmer of Quaker origins, his mother an elementary school teacher and organist at the local church. For the first ten years of his life he knew little of the outside world and grew up without exposure to radios, telephones, or automobiles. But after the unexpected death of his father in 1901 the family moved to Cedar Rapids, where the boy went to better public schools, substituted gardening for farming, and soon began to find odd jobs in order to help support the family. It took Wood many years before he realized the significance of Iowa farm life, undoubtedly transmuted by memory, as subject matter for painting. But eventually he transferred corn fields, harvesting, thresher crews, and barnyard chores to canvas and found figures from family life to people his paintings. One of his best later paintings, *Woman with Plants*, is an idealized portrait of his mother; he never quite got around to finishing a portrait of his father, against whose domestic tyranny he often rebelled.

Wood attended high school in Cedar Rapids, where he graduated in 1910, and spent the next two summers studying at the Minneapolis School of Design and learning a good deal from an instructor named Ernest Batchelder. Desultory schooling followed. He tried his hand at making jewelry and doing metal work in Cedar Rapids and Chicago. After a year in the army he taught art classes in a Cedar Rapids high school from 1919 to 1925. During a leave of absence from school work he made his first trip to France, enrolled in a painting class in Paris, traveled in the provinces and in Italy, and in general exposed himself to the current trends in sculpture and art. Back in the United States he decided to relinquish his teaching job and try free-lancing. He did occasional portraits, some of which were awarded prizes in general competition, he tried his hand at murals for various Iowa hotels, accepted commissions for particular projects, and contributed such paintings as *Daughters of Revolution* and *Midnight Ride of Paul Revere* to important exhibitions at New York and Pittsburgh. A trip to Munich in 1928, his final European experience, introduced him to many early masterpieces of genre painting and convinced him that Iowa landscapes were just as worthy of painterly attention as Flemish farms or festivals.

Throughout the 1930s Wood was increasingly busy as craftsman, teacher, and lecturer. He taught at the Stone City Colony and Art School in 1933 and 1934 and met John Steuart Curry there for the first time when Curry participated in the instruction. The next year he also met Thomas Hart Benton and Thomas Craven, the latter an art critic of note who praised Wood's work. In 1934 Wood was named the director of public works of the art project in Iowa, a position which required him to supervise artists in producing murals. The same year gave him an established position in the academic world since he was appointed an associate professor of fine arts at the University of Iowa. Wood was a competent teacher of lithography and mural painting but relatively untrained in art theory and inclined as he grew older to be somewhat unyielding in his methodology. His position at Iowa in the art department was not always secure, and his frequent absences to take lecture tours or make appointments elsewhere provoked criticism from some of his colleagues, although an understanding dean frequently supported him.

A bachelor much of his life, Wood married in 1935. His wife, Sarah Sherman Maxon, was five years older than Wood and already a grandmother. She had some ability as an actress and opera singer and had been kind to Wood's mother during her failing health. But it was not a happy marriage. Wood moved to Iowa City and settled in a Victorian house which he immediately set about restoring and refurnishing. His wife also introduced him to a more active social life, which proved to be expensive and hardly conducive to continuing his career as a painter. For financial reasons he accepted lecture invitations and requests to judge paintings in competitions. He also did book illustrations, a prime example being the nine paintings he did for the Limited Editions Club republication of Sinclair Lewis's novel *Main Street*. In 1939 Wood divorced his wife and apparently began a new and more productive career. He made a long lecture trip to California, he sold his picture *Parson Weems' Fable* to the writer John Marquand, he was awarded honorary degrees by Northwestern and Wesleyan universities, and he was promoted to a professorship of fine arts at the University of Iowa. But his health was rapidly deteriorating. He died of inoperable liver cancer on February 12, 1942 and was buried at Anamosa.

When Wood returned to Iowa from Europe, he was convinced that the Midwest should be his home and that the physical scene and his memory of rural life would provide him with ample subject matter. Thus the paintings which made him famous dealt with familiar objects and creatures: fruits, vegetables, corn shocks, trees (frequently made rather bulbous), outhouses, a rural school, a plough, animal prints in the snow, chickens, horses. And the human figures were husbandmen, farm wives, farm children, many of them documentary portraits of persons known to the painter. Wood had a sense of humor and many of his characters show his bent for satire, the *Daughters of Revolution* for example, and his interpretations of Sinclair Lewis's people in *Main Street, Sentimental, Yearner, Booster*, and *The Good Influence*. Surely the famous *American Gothic* with its tight lipped and sour looking woman and its dour, bald man holding an upright pitchfork, both profiled against a country church with a Gothic window, is a good example.

Grant Wood taught for years and delivered many lectures but published very little. A projected book, partly autobiographical and partly expository, tentatively named *Return from Bohemia* was never completed. Aided by Frank Luther Mott he did write an essay, entitled "Revolt against the City," which expressed quite sincerely and cogently his belief in regionalism.

A memorial exhibition of Wood's paintings was held in 1942. No other comprehensive showing of his work was mounted until 1983 when the exhibition "Grant Wood: The Regionalist Vision" opened at the Whitney Museum in New York and subsequently moved to Minneapolis, Chicago, and San Francisco. Art critics in general since the heyday of American regionalism have not been too friendly to Wood; they have accused him of provincialism, narrowness, and even unawareness of major trends in the international art world. But like Andrew Wyeth in more recent times he has consistently appealed to a large public audience.

JTF

References: Darrell Garwood, *Artist in Iowa: A Life of Grant Wood* (New York: Norton, 1944; reprinted 1971); James M. Dennis, *Grant Wood: A Study in American Art and Culture* (New York: Viking, 1975); Wanda M. Corn, *Grant Wood: The Regionalist Vision* (New Haven, Conn. and London: Yale University Press, 1983).

Appendix I

Memorable Americans by Birth Dates

1722
Samuel Adams

1735
John Adams
Paul Revere

1736
Patrick Henry

1738
John Singleton Copley

1741
Charles Willson Peale

1744
Abigail Adams

1745
John Jay
Anthony Wayne

1747
John Paul Jones

1750
Stephen Girard

1752
George Rogers Clark

1756
John Trumbull

1768
Tecumseh

1774
John Chapman

1777
Roger Brooke Taney

1784
Stephen Harriman Long

1785
William Beaumont

1788
Alexander Campbell

1793
Samuel Houston

1794
Matthew Calbraith Perry

1795
Johns Hopkins
James Knox Polk

1796
Sophia Smith

1800
George Bancroft
Charles Goodyear

1801
David Glasgow Farragut
William Henry Seward

1802
Marcus Whitman

1805
Jonathan Baldwin Turner

1807
   Jean Louis Rodolphe Agassiz
   Christopher (Kit) Carson
   Ezra Cornell

1809
   Oliver Wendell Holmes
   Edgar Allan Poe

1810
   Sarah Margaret Fuller
   Asa Gray

1814
   Samuel Colt

1815
   Richard Henry Dana

1820
   James Buchanan Eads

1821
   Harriet Tubman

1826
   Frederic Edwin Church

1829
   Hinton Rowan Helper

1830
   Emily Dickinson

1831
   Daniel Coit Gilman

1832
   Louisa May Alcott
   Mary Edwards Walker
   Andrew Dickson White

1833
   Edwin Thomas Booth

1834
   Marshall Field I
   James Gibbons
   Samuel Pierpont Langley

1836
   Greene Vardiman Black
   Winslow Homer

1837
   Stephen Grover Cleveland
   George Dewey
   William Dean Howells

1838
   John Muir

1839
   Josiah Willard Gibbs

1840
   Chief Joseph
   William Graham Sumner
   Henry Watterson

1842
   John Fiske

1843
   Elihu Root

1844
   Mary Cassatt
   Thomas Eakins

1846
   William Frederick Cody

1848
   Edward Henry Harriman
   Augustus Saint-Gaudens

1849
   Luther Burbank
   Crazy Horse

1850
   Edward Bellamy
   Daniel Chester French
   Lafcadio Hearn

1851
   Melvil Dewey

1853
David Belasco

1854
William Crawford Gorgas
George Eastman

1855
Alice Freeman Palmer
Robert Marion LaFollette

1856
Louis Dembitz Brandeis
James Buchanan Duke
William Rainey Harper
John Singer Sargent

1857
Fannie Farmer
Samuel Sidney McClure

1858
Franz Boas
Adolph Simon Ochs

1859
Carrie Chapman Catt
Cass Gilbert
Victor Herbert

1860
William Jennings Bryan

1861
Edward MacDowell
George William Norris

1862
Nicholas Murray Butler
Edith Wharton

1863
Edward William Bok
George Santayana

1864
Richard Harding Davis

1865
Gifford Pinchot

1866
Abraham Flexner

1867
Finley Peter Dunne

1868
Scott Joplin
Edgar Lee Masters

1869
(Newton) Booth Tarkington

1870
Benjamin Nathan Cardozo
Pierre Samuel du Pont
William Green

1873
Willa Sibert Cather
Emily Post
Alfred Emanuel Smith

1874
Herbert Clark Hoover
Charles Ives
Gertrude Stein
Mark Sullivan

1875
David Lewelyn Wark Griffith

1876
Jack London

1878
Carl Sandburg
Upton Beall Sinclair

1879
William Penn Adair (Will) Rogers
Wallace Stevens

1880
Helen Adams Keller

1881
Hugh Roy Cullen

1882
    John S. Barrymore
    Felix Frankfurter
    Robert Hutchings Goddard
    Henry John Kaiser

1883
    Douglas Fairbanks

1884
    Roy Chapman Andrews
    Charles Austin Beard

1885
    Jerome David Kern
    Chester William Nimitz
    George Smith Patton, Jr.

1886
    Van Wyck Brooks
    Philip Murray

1888
    Henry Agard Wallace

1889
    Thomas Hart Benton

1891
    Cole Porter
    Grant Wood

1892
    Pearl S. Buck
    Reinhold Niebuhr
    Wendell Willkie

1893
    Walter Francis White

1894
    Alfred Charles Kinsey

1895
    Oscar Hammerstein II

1896
    John Roderigo Dos Passos

1899
    Edward Kennedy (Duke) Ellington

1901
    Walter Elias Disney
    Ernest Orlando Lawrence

1902
    Charles Augustus Lindbergh, Jr.
    John Ernst Steinbeck

1907
    Walter Philip Reuther

Appendix II

Memorable Americans According to Their Principal Careers

Arts:
- Thomas Hart Benton
- Mary Cassatt
- Frederic Edwin Church
- John Singleton Copley
- Walter Elias Disney
- Thomas Eakins
- Daniel Chester French
- Cass Gilbert
- Winslow Homer
- Charles Willson Peale
- Paul Revere
- Augustus Saint-Gaudens
- John Singer Sargent
- John Trumbull
- Grant Wood

Business Leaders:
- Ezra Cornell
- Hugh Roy Cullen
- James Buchanan Duke
- Pierre Samuel du Pont
- Marshall Field I
- Stephen Girard
- Edward Henry Harriman
- Johns Hopkins
- Henry John Kaiser

Educators:
- Nicholas Murray Butler
- Melvil Dewey
- Daniel Coit Gilman
- William Rainey Harper
- Helen Adams Keller
- Alice Freeman Palmer
- Sophia Smith
- Jonathan Baldwin Turner
- Andrew Dickson White

Explorers:
- Roy Chapman Andrews
- Charles Augustus Lindbergh, Jr.
- Stephen Harriman Long
- John Muir

Folk Heroes:
- Christopher (Kit) Carson
- John Chapman
- William Frederick Cody

Historians:
- George Bancroft
- Charles Austin Beard
- John Fiske

Indians:
- Crazy Horse
- Chief Joseph
- Tecumseh

Inventors:
- Samuel Colt
- George Eastman
- Charles Goodyear

Journalists:
- Edward William Bok
- Richard Harding Davis
- Samuel Sidney McClure
- Adolph Simon Ochs
- Henry Watterson

Labor Leaders:
- William Green
- Philip Murray
- Walter Philip Reuther

Legal Lights:
    Louis Dembitz Brandeis
    Benjamin Nathan Cardozo
    Felix Frankfurter
    Roger Brooke Taney

Literary Figures:
    Louisa May Alcott
    Van Wyck Brooks
    Pearl S. Buck
    Willa Sibert Cather
    Richard Henry Dana
    Emily Dickinson
    John Roderigo Dos Passos
    Finley Peter Dunne
    Sarah Margaret Fuller
    Lafcadio Hearn
    William Dean Howells
    Jack London
    Edgar Lee Masters
    Edgar Allan Poe
    Carl Sandburg
    Gertrude Stein
    John Ernst Steinbeck
    Wallace Stevens
    (Newton) Booth Tarkington
    Edith Wharton

Medical Leaders:
    William Beaumont
    Greene Vardiman Black
    Abraham Flexner
    William Crawford Gorgas
    Oliver Wendell Holmes
    Alfred Charles Kinsey

Military Leaders:
    George Rogers Clark
    George Dewey
    David Glasgow Farragut
    John Paul Jones
    Chester William Nimitz
    George Smith Patton, Jr.
    Matthew Calbraith Perry
    Anthony Wayne

Musicians:
    Edward Kennedy (Duke) Ellington
    Oscar Hammerstein II
    Victor Herbert

Musicians (cont'd):
    Charles Ives
    Scott Joplin
    Jerome David Kern
    Edward MacDowell
    Cole Porter

Religious Leaders:
    Alexander Campbell
    James Gibbons
    Reinhold Niebuhr
    Marcus Whitman

Scientists:
    Jean Louis Rodolphe Agassiz
    Franz Boas
    Luther Burbank
    James Buchanan Eads
    Robert Hutchings Goddard
    Asa Gray
    Samuel Pierpont Langley
    Ernest Orlando Lawrence

Showmen:
    John S. Barrymore
    David Belasco
    Edwin Thomas Booth
    Douglas Fairbanks
    David Lewelyn Wark Griffith

Social Critics:
    Edward Bellamy
    Hinton Rowan Helper
    William Penn Adair (Will) Rogers
    George Santayana
    Upton Beall Sinclair
    Mark Sullivan
    William Graham Sumner
    Walter Francis White

Statesmen:
    John Adams
    Samuel Adams
    William Jennings Bryan
    Stephen Grover Cleveland
    Patrick Henry
    Herbert Clark Hoover
    Samuel Houston
    John Jay

Statesmen (cont'd):
Robert Marion LaFollette
George William Norris
Gifford Pinchot
James Knox Polk
Elihu Root
William Henry Seward
Alfred Emanuel Smith
Henry Agard Wallace
Wendell Willkie

Women Leaders:
Abigail Adams
Carrie Chapman Catt
Fannie Farmer
Emily Post
Harriet Tubman
Mary Edwards Walker

Index

Compiled by Clara D. Keller